CRIMINAL LAW

ASPEN SELECT SERIES

CRIMINAL LAW
CASES, STATUTES, AND PROBLEMS

Patrick Corbett
Distinguished Professor Emeritus
Western Michigan University, Cooley Law School

Ronald Bretz
Distinguished Professor Emeritus
Western Michigan University, Cooley Law School

Alan Gershel
Grievance Administrator
Michigan Attorney Grievance Commission

Wolters Kluwer

About Wolters Kluwer Law & Business

Wolters Kluwer Law & Business is a leading global provider of intelligent information and digital solutions for legal and business professionals in key specialty areas, and respected educational resources for professors and law students. Wolters Kluwer Law & Business connects legal and business professionals as well as those in the education market with timely, specialized authoritative content and information-enabled solutions to support success through productivity, accuracy and mobility.

Serving customers worldwide, Wolters Kluwer Law & Business products include those under the Aspen Publishers, CCH, Kluwer Law International, Loislaw, ftwilliam.com and MediRegs family of products.

CCH products have been a trusted resource since 1913, and are highly regarded resources for legal, securities, antitrust and trade regulation, government contracting, banking, pension, payroll, employment and labor, and healthcare reimbursement and compliance professionals.

Aspen Publishers products provide essential information to attorneys, business professionals and law students. Written by preeminent authorities, the product line offers analytical and practical information in a range of specialty practice areas from securities law and intellectual property to mergers and acquisitions and pension/benefits. Aspen's trusted legal education resources provide professors and students with high-quality, up-to-date and effective resources for successful instruction and study in all areas of the law.

Kluwer Law International products provide the global business community with reliable international legal information in English. Legal practitioners, corporate counsel and business executives around the world rely on Kluwer Law journals, looseleafs, books, and electronic products for comprehensive information in many areas of international legal practice.

Loislaw is a comprehensive online legal research product providing legal content to law firm practitioners of various specializations. Loislaw provides attorneys with the ability to quickly and efficiently find the necessary legal information they need, when and where they need it, by facilitating access to primary law as well as state-specific law, records, forms and treatises.

ftwilliam.com offers employee benefits professionals the highest quality plan documents (retirement, welfare and non-qualified) and government forms (5500/PBGC, 1099 and IRS) software at highly competitive prices.

MediRegs products provide integrated health care compliance content and software solutions for professionals in healthcare, higher education and life sciences, including professionals in accounting, law and consulting.

Wolters Kluwer Law & Business, a division of Wolters Kluwer, is headquartered in New York. Wolters Kluwer is a market-leading global information services company focused on professionals.

Dedication

For our students and families—thank you for helping us learn to be teachers!

Preface

Among us, we have over 60 years of experience practicing criminal law (both defense and prosecution on the state and federal level) and a comparable number of years of teaching experience. Our goal in preparing this textbook was to use that practical experience to create a student-friendly text that empowers students to learn criminal law more efficiently and comprehensively and prepares them to practice law as well. In aspiring to achieve this goal, we included cases, statutes, and problems. We have used many of the cases in our classes for years; however, we have edited them and provided our own notes to help students avoid common mistakes in interpretation. Given that a frequent student complaint is "too much jumping around" within a textbook, we have also spent considerable time organizing the cases in a clear and sensible manner.

Today, criminal law practitioners spend hours reading and interpreting statutes. Given this reality, this textbook offers numerous sample statutes (as well as Model Penal Code provisions) to provide students with the opportunity to engage in some "practice" statutory interpretation. We have found that students often better understand the key principles in the cases when they see how statutes have subsequently been modified or created to address the concerns stemming from those cases. Additionally, in an effort to more completely "fill the brain cells," we have provided practice problems in many chapters. In our experience, students more fully comprehend the basic concepts when they have an opportunity to apply them to actual problems.

As with any criminal law textbook, this book is intended to introduce students to basic principles and common criminal law trends. Keep in mind that the cases and statutes (as well as the laws within the problems) may or may not be complete. For this reason, we advise students not to rely on this textbook to provide the latest statement of the law.

Moreover, because many of our students practice law in Michigan, we have made an effort to periodically include a case, statute, or note pertaining to Michigan law. Keep in mind, however, that this book is not intended to teach Michigan law; instead, we incorporated the Michigan materials only when we believed inclusion would help students interested in practicing criminal law both within and outside of Michigan.

We embrace the idea of a limited amount of outside reading to enhance student learning. To this end, we have purposely avoided providing too much subject matter background, preferring instead to encourage students to consult certain outside resources when they need more information, such as Professor Joshua Dressler's *Understanding Criminal Law,* or Professor Wayne LaFave's *Criminal Law*.

Because this text is geared toward education, rather than scholastics, we have decided to stray from several scholarly conventions for identifying omissions. In editing the cases, we have used ellipses to designate deleted material and brackets to indicate added material; however, no signals have been used to indicate the omission of citations, headings, or footnotes. These elements have only been retained where we believed their inclusion would serve a sound instructive purpose. Also, footnotes within cases retain their original numbering system, whereas author footnotes are designated by an asterisk.

We welcome any feedback from both professors and students, including any ideas you have on how the book could be improved to better meet your needs. We plan to update the book as needed and will seriously consider any suggestions you send. Thank you in advance.

Patrick Corbett
Ronald Bretz
Alan Gershel

April 2015

Acknowledgments

After many years of teaching law—where we had the opportunity to see what worked, and what did not—we decided to create our own criminal law textbook. We want to thank all of our students, past and present, for helping us figure out the best way to present the materials in order to heighten comprehension of the subject matter. We appreciate our Research Assistants, Rachel Jordan Miller, Porscha Brown, and Christopher Schmidt, for the many hours they spent compiling the materials and editing our work. Rachel, in particular, was invaluable as our Student Editor; we so value her amazing skills. We are grateful for the assistance of Tara Chambers and Cynthia Brown in compiling the tables and index. We also want to acknowledge Librarians Jamie Baker and Michael Bird for the excellent research they provided, as well as their efforts in locating and cite checking many of the cases used in this textbook.

Additionally, we need to recognize two colleagues, Professors Dorean Koenig and John Nussbaumer. Several years ago, Professor Koenig created a criminal law textbook that several professors have used for many years. With her permission, many of her ideas have been incorporated into this new textbook. Professor Nussbaumer, on the other hand, served as a "mentor" to all three of us upon commencement of the teaching portion of our careers, helping each of us to learn to teach effectively. His words and thoughts are a large part of this book and we are very grateful to him. With his permission, we have reprinted many pages from his criminal law syllabus and supplement.

We also want to thank the following entities for permission to reprint portions of their work:

Model Penal Code §§1.13, 2.01–2.04, 2.06, 2.08–2.09, 2.13, 3.02, 3.04–3.07, 3.09, 4.01–4.03, 5.01–5.03, 210.1–210.4, 223.1, Copyright © 1985 by the American Law Institute. Reproduced with permission. All rights reserved.

Joshua Dressler, *Understanding Criminal Law* §§1.01[A][2], 27.06[A], 27.07[D], 29.01, 32.11 (6th ed. 2012), with permission. Copyright © 2012 LexisNexis, Inc. All rights reserved.

Nancy S. Erickson, *Final Report: "Sex Bias in the Teaching of Criminal Law,"* 42 Rutgers L. Rev. 309 (1989–1990).

Alan Gershel, *Utilitarianism vs. Retributivism* (from New York Times, Room for Debate (February 18, 2014), http://www.nytimes.com/roomfordebate/2014/02/18/affluenza-and-life-circumstances-in-sentencing/in-sentencing-utilitarianism-vs-retributivism).

Summary of Contents

Contents

Chapter 5
Rape and Criminal Sexual Conduct   155

Chapter 9
Necessity of an Act — 293

Chapter 15
Intoxication

Introduction

A.   Criminal Law Overview

Welcome to the study of criminal law—you are about to embark on a fascinating journey. Collectively, the authors of this textbook have devoted over 60 years to practicing criminal law, and a comparable number of years to teaching criminal law. That practical and educational experience has provided the foundation for this book.

A typical criminal law class is divided into three main parts: (1) the elements that the prosecution must prove in order to convict a defendant of particular crimes; (2) general principles that may come into play with regard to any of the particular crimes we will study; and (3) defenses that a defendant may raise in response to a criminal charge. Success requires that you not only master each of these three individual parts, but also understand how the different parts interact with and relate to each other. This textbook generally covers those three main parts.

There is no single, uniform code of criminal law that all jurisdictions follow. Instead, each jurisdiction is free to define what is or is not a crime, subject only to some very narrow constitutional limitations. As a result, there is considerable variation from one jurisdiction to another as far as the rules, definitions, and policies are concerned. The goal will not be to learn the law of any particular jurisdiction. Instead, this textbook will focus on common concepts and the major differences of opinion (i.e., splits of authority) that exist. The cases and statutes used in this textbook are merely "examples" of the various trends in criminal law. As such, it is important for students and lawyers to consult the most up-to-date law in their relevant jurisdiction when preparing for the bar exam.

The textbook will spend a fair amount of time reviewing the common law rules and definitions developed by the early English and American courts. This is necessary because the common law is the foundation upon which much of modern criminal law is built. The textbook will also examine modern statutory provisions, including provisions of the Model Penal Code and statutes from various states, encouraging discussion on how they differ from the common law. Finally, various problems throughout the text will provide you with the opportunity to apply what you have learned.

B. Latin Terms

When you run into Latin terms, look them up. Although their use is declining, some judges and lawyers still use them. Two such terms that you must know early on are: (1) actus reus—the act that must be committed and/or the harm or result that must occur in order to establish the existence of a crime; and (2) mens rea—the mental state or the degree of moral blameworthiness that must have existed concurrently with the actus reus in order to establish the existence of a crime.

You can use these terms as shorthand tools for organizing the elements of particular crimes. Generally speaking, each of the crimes we will be studying has an actus reus and a mens rea, although we will see some exceptions.

C. Familiarity with the Subject Matter

Sufficient familiarity with the subject matter involves much more than just memorizing rules and definitions. It requires knowing and understanding any applicable threshold triggering requirements that must be satisfied before the rules and definitions come into play, as well as the rationales behind the rules and definitions and any limitations or exceptions that apply. It requires you to have a deeper level of understanding that will enable you to use and apply the rules and definitions in new and unfamiliar fact situations. The main subjects that you will need to master and understand in this way are:

- **Utilitarian and Retributive Theories of Punishment**: the two basic theories as to why we inflict criminal punishment, and how they differ;
- **Homicide**: the elements of the different kinds of homicide and the distinctions between them;
- **Sexual Offenses**: the elements of rape, statutory rape, and one modern day equivalent known as criminal sexual conduct;
- **Miscellaneous Crimes**: the elements of other crimes such as battery, assault, kidnapping, burglary, and arson;
- **Theft Offenses**: the distinctions between the theft crimes of larceny, embezzlement, larceny by trick, false pretenses, and robbery, and the concept of consolidated theft;
- **Failure to Act:** the situations in which a person can be criminally prosecuted for a failure to act;
- **Inchoate Crimes**: the elements of the inchoate crimes of attempt, solicitation, and conspiracy, as well as the distinctions between them and the defenses and general principles related to them;
- **Accomplice Liability**: the situations outside of conspiracy in which a person can be held responsible for another person's criminal act;

- **Strict Liability**: the situations in which a person can be criminally prosecuted without proof of mens rea;
- **Transferred Intent**: the situations in which a person can be held responsible for harm to an unintended victim;
- **Motive**: what we mean by motive and how it is distinguishable from mens rea;
- **Concurrence Doctrine**: the relationship that must exist between the actus reus and the mens rea in order to successfully prosecute a person for a crime;
- **Mens Rea Defenses**: the defenses related to mens rea, or moral culpability, that may provide a person with a complete or partial defense to a criminal charge, such as insanity, diminished capacity, and intoxication;
- **Ignorance or Mistake of Law**: the situations when ignorance or mistake of law may provide a person with a defense to a criminal charge;
- **Ignorance or Mistake of Fact**: the situations when ignorance or mistake of fact may provide a person with a defense to a criminal charge;
- **Victim's Conduct**: the extent to which the victim's consent or condonation may provide a person with a defense to a criminal charge;
- **Excuses and Justifications**: the situations in which the reasons why the defendant engaged in conduct that we would otherwise consider criminal may excuse or justify that conduct, such as compulsion, crime prevention, defense of habitation, law enforcement, self-defense, and defense of others; and
- **Entrapment**: the situations in which entrapment may provide a defendant with a defense to a criminal charge.

Remember that learning these subjects is just the beginning of your task—not the end. You must also be able to use the knowledge that you have learned together with analytical thinking skills to solve particular, concrete legal problems not previously encountered.

D. Sources of the Criminal Law

American criminal law has deep roots that stretch far back into history. But, for practical purposes, it is fair to say that in the beginning there were judges, and the judges made the law.

Long before the rise of the English Parliament, judges appointed by the King or Queen defined what conduct should or should not be considered criminal on a case-by-case basis. There were no statutes to guide them, and they basically made the law up as they went along, reasoning largely by a process of analogy and distinction. When a new case came before them, the basic question they asked was "is this new case like or unlike the previous cases we have decided?" Over time, the opinions they wrote built up a body of precedent known as the common law, which was brought to America by the colonial settlers.

Gradually, however, a shift occurred. Legislatures began passing more and more statutes, some of which codified existing common law crimes, while others created new crimes. Today, the pendulum has swung to the point where most (but not all) of the criminal law is at least initially defined by the legislative branch through statutes, not by judges through the common law. But the common law remains important for two reasons: (1) legislatures have left the development of some parts of the criminal law to the judicial branch; and (2) the common law concepts have either shaped the statutory definitions or have been incorporated into them. Thus, in order to fully understand modern statutory definitions, you need to understand the common law antecedents.

E. The Role of Modern Courts

As a general rule, when a legislature talks through the passage of a statute, the courts are supposed to listen. Between these two branches of government, the legislature has the superior authority to define what should or should not be considered criminal. This is because the legislature generally is more responsive to and more representative of the will of the people through the electoral process.

This means that if the legislature chooses to exercise its authority by passing a statute, the role of the modern court is largely limited to determining what the legislature intended and applying that intent to the case before it. Judges are not supposed to deviate from the legislature's intent or substitute their view of what is best for society for that of the legislature. Instead, they are just supposed to interpret and apply the statute. The only time judges have the authority to reject what the legislature has done is if the statute violates a constitutional limitation on legislative power. As students, you will generally study these limitations in constitutional law courses, rather than in criminal law.

Whether judges strictly abide by these rules is a debatable proposition. It is not uncommon for judges to subtly change a statutory definition on a case-by-case basis through the process of interpretation and application. In addition, sometimes the legislature is unable to reach agreement on a particular issue and deliberately leaves that issue ambiguous. This may leave the door open to the courts to fill in the holes in the statute. Thus, even when the legislature has spoken through the passage of a statute, the development of the criminal law retains a common law flavor through the interpretational process.

F. Felonies and Misdemeanors

At common law, as Professor Joshua Dressler notes, "[t]he list of felonies was short: felonious homicide (later divided by statute into murder and manslaughter), arson, mayhem, rape, robbery, larceny, burglary, prison escape, and (perhaps) sodomy. All other criminal offenses were misdemeanors." Joshua Dressler, *Understanding Criminal Law* §1.01[A][2] (6th ed. 2012). Dressler further notes that "[a]ll common law felonies were punishable by death." *Id.*

There are many more felonies today than existed at common law. Typically, offenses punishable by death or imprisonment for a term exceeding one year are treated as felonies; crimes that are not felonies are misdemeanors. See, e.g., M.C.L. §761.1.

G. Vagueness Doctrine

One constitutional limitation you need to be familiar with as a student of criminal law is the vagueness doctrine. This doctrine is based on the 14th Amendment due process clause and the fundamental proposition that individuals should not be punished for their conduct unless they had fair notice of what was prohibited.

In theory, the vagueness doctrine says that the definition of a crime must be sufficiently clear so that a person of ordinary intelligence could determine its meaning. In practice, however, it is unusual for a court to find that a statute is unconstitutionally vague, unless the language of the statute gives the authorities virtually complete and unconstrained discretion to pick and choose who should be prosecuted.

H. Principle of Legality

A basic premise of criminal law is that conduct—even if immoral or harmful—is not a crime unless the law provides that it is a crime. Additionally, it must be deemed a crime *before* the person commits the act. The net result: periodically, bad conduct might go unpunished. For more information, see Joshua Dressler, *Understanding Criminal Law* §§5.01–5.04 (6th ed. 2012).

I. Rules of Statutory Interpretation

There are many so-called "rules" of statutory interpretation. But it is more accurate to think of these as guides rather than as hard and fast rules that judges must apply. A few guides that you should be familiar with at the outset are: (1) when the legislature uses a common law term, it ordinarily intends to incorporate the common law definition; (2) if a statute is ambiguous, the ambiguity should be resolved in the defendant's favor, in order to avoid fair notice problems (usually referred to as the rule of lenity); and (3) when a term is undefined by the legislature and is not a common law term, courts typically look to the ordinary meaning of the words in order to understand the term.

J. Procedural Terminology

This textbook is for a substantive criminal law class, not a criminal procedure course (which generally examines how the Constitution limits what police can and cannot do in interacting with people). There are certain procedural terms, however, that you need to be familiar with in order to fully understand the cases in this textbook. Among them are the following:

- **Indictment**: the charging document issued by a grand jury;
- **Grand Jury**: the body of people charged with the duty of hearing evidence to determine whether probable cause exists justifying the issuance of an indictment;
- **Preliminary Hearing or Examination**: an early court hearing at which the prosecution must present evidence establishing probable cause to believe that a crime has been committed and that the defendant committed it;
- **Information**: the charging document issued by a prosecuting attorney after a preliminary hearing or examination where the court finds the existence of probable cause (in a jurisdiction that does not require grand jury approval);
- **Motion to Dismiss or Reduce the Charge (AKA a Demurrer or a Motion to Quash)**: a pretrial motion filed by the defense arguing that there is not enough evidence to require the defendant to stand trial on a particular charge;
- **Bench Trial**: a trial in which the parties have waived a jury and elected to have the judge decide the case;
- **Trial Jury**: the body of people responsible for hearing the evidence at trial and determining the criminal liability of the charged defendant;
- **Motion for a Directed Verdict of Acquittal**: a mid-trial motion filed by the defense (usually after the prosecution has rested its case), arguing that there is not enough evidence to support a particular charge and that the judge should therefore enter a directed verdict of not guilty;
- **Jury Charge or Instructions**: the applicable law that the jury must use in deciding the case, communicated by the judge to the jury (usually orally in language that is often difficult for the jurors to understand);
- **Burden of Proof**: which side has to prove something or else lose if they do not (usually the burden rests on the prosecution in a criminal

case, but there are some exceptions, especially as it concerns certain defenses);

- **Standard of Proof**: how much evidence the party with the burden must present in order to win (usually the standard in criminal cases is beyond a reasonable doubt, but again there are some exceptions);
- **Lesser-Included Offenses**: less serious charges related to the main charge that the parties may ask the judge to submit to the jury;
- **Motion for a New Trial**: a post-trial motion filed by a convicted defendant arguing that some error in the trial requires that a new trial be granted (based, for example, on the ground that the instructions to the jury failed to properly define the applicable law);
- **Motion for a Judgment of Acquittal (JNOV)**: a post-trial motion filed by a convicted defendant arguing that there was insufficient evidence to support the guilty verdict and that the judge should therefore substitute a verdict of not guilty.

K.   Standards of Review

Standards of review are the standards by which a higher court reviews a lower court's decision. The standards differ depending on the issue. One standard of review that commonly arises in criminal law cases is the standard used to review a defendant's contention that there was insufficient evidence to support his or her conviction.

When a defendant appeals on this ground, the appellate judges are not supposed to start from scratch on a clean slate, giving no weight at all to the jury's verdict, and deciding what they personally would have done if they had been the fact finder. Instead, they are supposed to view the evidence in the light most favorable to the winning party (i.e., the prosecution), and ask whether any rational jury could have found the defendant guilty beyond a reasonable doubt.

The reason for this standard of review is to give due deference to the jury's decision. The jury speaks as the voice of the community, and it usually is in the best position to determine which evidence is believable and which is not because of its opportunity to actually see and hear the witnesses testify firsthand.

As a result of this standard of review, many appellate case decisions focus on the evidence supporting the prosecution's theory. This is not necessarily because the courts are inherently biased in favor of the prosecution. Instead, it is because the prosecution has already convinced a jury beyond a reasonable doubt that the defendant is guilty, and the appellate court is giving due deference to the jury's decision.

This does not mean that an appellate court will always affirm a jury's verdict. But it does mean that the defendant has the heavy burden of convincing the appellate court that, even viewing the evidence in the light most favorable to the prosecution, no rational jury could have found him or her guilty beyond a reasonable doubt.

Another standard of review we will run into is the standard used to review a defendant's contention that the trial judge should have instructed the jury on a lesser-included offense or a particular defense. When a defendant requests such an instruction, the trial judge acts as a gatekeeper of sorts, making the initial decision on whether there is sufficient evidence to support giving the instruction.

But because the defendant has a constitutional right to a jury trial, the judge is not supposed to weigh the credibility or believability of the testimony in deciding whether to give the instruction. Weighing the credibility or believability of the testimony is the jury's job, not the judge's. Thus, on appeal, the rule in most jurisdictions is that the appellate court will view the evidence in the light most favorable to the defendant, and ask whether a rational view of the evidence would support the defendant's request.

L. Model Penal Code

The Model Penal Code (MPC) is a suggested code of criminal laws originally drafted during the 1950s and the 1960s by a respected legal think-tank known as the American Law Institute. It is not "the law" in any jurisdiction, except to the extent that a court or a legislature has chosen to formally adopt it. Each jurisdiction is free to pick and choose those parts of the MPC that it finds persuasive. Some parts of it have been widely adopted, while other parts have not. This textbook will cover the parts that have been the most influential.

M. Holmesisms

Supreme Court Justice Oliver Wendell Holmes, Jr. once said two things that all new law students must learn to understand if they are to become lawyers. One is that "a word is but the skin of a living thought." The other is that "the life of the law has not been logic, it has been experience." By the end of your criminal law course, you should understand what both of these sayings mean.

Chapter 1
Theories of Punishment

A. Introduction

1. Purposes of the Criminal Law

The general purpose of the criminal law is to maintain an acceptable degree of social order by requiring adherence to certain commonly agreed upon standards of conduct. We attempt to do this through various means. Among the more important ones are:

- **Specific Deterrence**: punishing an individual who has broken the law to specifically deter him or her from breaking the law in the future;
- **General Deterrence**: punishing an individual who has broken the law as an example to generally deter other members of society from engaging in similar behavior;
- **Incapacitation:** physically or otherwise preventing individuals from perpetrating future crimes (i.e. prison, the death penalty, etc.);
- **Retribution**: giving an individual who has broken the law his or her "just desserts," in part because this is the right thing to do morally, and in part to channel the human instinct for revenge through the criminal justice process so as to limit vigilantism;
- **Rehabilitation**: changing the behavior of those who have broken the law so that they will not commit more crimes when they are released.

These different purposes help shape what we define as criminal and what we think the appropriate social response to an individual's misconduct should be.

2. Theories of Punishment

There are two major theories of punishment that have dominated American criminal law. One is the utilitarian theory, which in general terms seeks to accomplish the greatest good for the greatest number. More specifically, this theory looks forward to the expected consequences of punishment, and argues that punishment is justifiable to the extent that it will reduce future crime.

This theory views the individual defendant more as a means to an end, and it focuses heavily on deterrence—punishment is justifiable to the extent that it can be expected to deter the defendant and others from committing future crimes; or, conversely, withholding punishment is justifiable if this incentive or reward will encourage the defendant and others to avoid future criminal behavior. This prong of utilitarian theory assumes that individuals think about the potential consequences of their actions before they act. This is an assumption that some people question, at least in certain contexts.

Utilitarian theory also emphasizes rehabilitation as a means of reducing future crime. This rehabilitation prong is premised on the assumption that individuals who break the law can be reformed through treatment, education, job training, and other means. Some people question this assumption, at least with regard to certain kinds of offenders. Utilitarian theory may also incorporate a retributive aspect, by emphasizing the need to channel the human instinct for revenge through the criminal justice process in order to reduce future vigilantism.

The other major theory that has dominated American criminal law is retributive theory. This theory looks backward to the offender's conduct, and argues that punishment is justifiable because the individual has broken the law, regardless of whether punishment or withholding punishment will reduce future crime. Punishment is viewed as the offender's "just desserts," and as morally justifiable on that basis alone. This theory focuses on the particular defendant's moral culpability, rather than on whether punishment will deter the defendant or others from engaging in similar behavior in the future.

Incapacitation can be justified on either utilitarian or retributive grounds. From a utilitarian perspective, incapacitation by imprisonment or otherwise can prevent the incapacitated individual from committing future crimes, can specifically deter that individual from committing future crimes, and can generally deter others from engaging in similar behavior. From a retributive perspective, the punitive aspects of incapacitation are a part of the offender's "just desserts."

In the real world, these two theories often overlap in the development of the criminal law. Punishment can serve both utilitarian and retributive ends. Whether one theory predominates often depends on the context and on the tenor of the times.

Two other concepts should be noted here. The first is free will. American criminal law is heavily premised on the assumption that individuals possess free will—i.e., that each of us has the ability to freely choose whether or not to obey the law. Some people question this assumption, arguing that our upbringing, our environment, or other factors external to ourselves determine our actions instead. The second concept is economics. Increasingly, today's debates about punishment focus on economic considerations, such as how much it will cost us as a society to build more prisons and incarcerate more offenders for longer periods of time, and what we will have to give up in order to do this.

B.   Traditional Theories of Punishment

1.   Utilitarian Theory

Of the Ends of Punishment—Jeremy Bentham (*from The Works of Jeremy Bentham, vol. 1 (Principles of Morals and Legislation, Fragment on Government, Civil Code, Penal Law)* [1843])

When any act has been committed which is followed, or threatens to be followed, by such effects as a provident legislator would be anxious to prevent, two wishes naturally and immediately suggest themselves to his mind: first, to obviate the danger of the like mischief in future: secondly, to compensate the mischief that has already been done.

The mischief likely to ensue from acts of the like kind may arise from either of two sources,—either the conduct of the party himself who has been the author of the mischief already done, or the conduct of such other persons as may have adequate motives and sufficient opportunities to do the like.

Hence the prevention of offences divides itself into two branches: *Particular prevention*, which applies to the delinquent himself; and *general prevention*, which is applicable to all the members of the community without exception.

Pain and pleasure are the great springs of human action. When a man perceives or supposes pain to be the consequence of an act, he is acted upon in such a manner as tends, with a certain force, to withdraw him, as it were, from the commission of that act. If the apparent magnitude, or rather value of that pain be greater than the apparent magnitude or value of the pleasure or good he expects to be the consequence of the act, he will be absolutely prevented from performing it. The mischief which would have ensued from the act, if performed, will also by that means be prevented.

With respect to a given individual, the recurrence of an offence may be provided against in three ways:—

1.   By taking from him the physical power of offending.
2.   By taking away the desire of offending.
3.   By making him afraid of offending.

In the first case, the individual can no more commit the offence; in the second, he no longer desires to commit it; in the third, he may still wish to commit it, but he no longer dares to do it. In the first case, there is a physical incapacity; in the second, a moral reformation; in the third, there is intimidation or terror of the law.

General prevention is effected by the denunciation of punishment, and by its application, which, according to the common expression, serves for an example. The punishment suffered by the offender presents to everyone an example of what he himself will have to suffer, if he is guilty of the same offence.

General prevention ought to be the chief end of punishment, as it is its real justification. If we could consider an offence which has been committed as an isolated fact, the like of which would never recur, punishment would be useless. It would be only adding one evil to another. But when we consider that an unpunished crime leaves the path of crime open, not only to the same delinquent, but also to all those who may have the same motives and opportunities for entering upon it, we perceive that the punishment inflicted on the individual becomes a source of security to all. That punishment which, considered in itself, appeared base and repugnant to all generous sentiments, is elevated to the first rank of benefits, when it is regarded not as an act of wrath or of vengeance against a guilty or unfortunate individual who has given way to mischievous inclinations, but as an indispensable sacrifice to the common safety.

With respect to any particular delinquent, we have seen that punishment has three objects: incapacitation, reformation, and intimidation. If the crime he has committed is of a kind calculated to inspire great alarm, as manifesting a very mischievous disposition, it becomes necessary to take from him the power of committing it again. But if the crime, being less dangerous, only justifies a transient punishment, and it is possible for the delinquent to return to society, it is proper that the punishment should possess qualities calculated to reform or to intimidate him. . . .

2. Retributive Theory

The Right of Punishing—Immanuel Kant, trans. W. Hastie (*from The Philosophy of Law: An Exposition of the Fundamental Principles of Jurisprudence as the Science of Right* [1796])

The right of administering punishment, is the right of the sovereign as the supreme power to inflict pain upon a subject on account of a crime committed by him. . . .

Judicial or juridical punishment (*pæna forensis*) is to be distinguished from natural punishment (*pæna naturalis*), in which crime as vice punishes itself, and does not as such come within the cognizance of the legislator. Juridical punishment can never be administered merely as a means for promoting another good either with regard to the criminal himself or to civil society, but must in all cases be imposed only because the individual on whom it is inflicted has committed a crime. For one man ought never to be dealt with merely as a means subservient to the purpose of another, nor be mixed up with the subjects of real right. Against such treatment his inborn personality has a right to protect him, even although he may be condemned to lose his civil personality. He must first be found guilty and punishable, before there can be any thought of drawing from his punishment any benefit for himself or his fellow-citizens. The penal law is a categorical imperative; and woe to him who creeps through the serpent-windings of utilitarianism to discover some advantage that may discharge him from the justice of punishment, or even from the due measure of it, according to the Pharisaic maxim: 'It is better that one man should die than that the whole people should perish.' For if justice and righteousness perish, human life would no longer have any value in the world.—What, then, is to be said of such a proposal as to keep a criminal alive who has been condemned to death, on his being given to understand that if he agreed to certain dangerous experiments being performed upon him, he would be allowed to survive if he came happily through them? It is argued that physicians might thus obtain new information that would be of value to the commonweal. But a court of justice would repudiate with scorn any proposal of this kind if made to it by the medical faculty; for justice would cease to be justice, if it were bartered away for any consideration whatever.

But what is the mode and measure of punishment which public justice takes as its principle and standard? It is just the principle of equality, by which the pointer of the scale of justice is made to incline no more to the one side than the other. It may be rendered by saying that the undeserved evil which any one commits on another, is to be regarded as perpetrated on himself. Hence it may be said: 'If you slander another, you slander yourself; if you steal from another, you steal from yourself; if you strike another, you strike yourself; if you kill another, you kill yourself.' This is the right of retaliation (*jus talionis*); and properly understood, it is the only principle which in regulating a public court, as distinguished from mere private judgment, can definitely assign both the quality and the quantity of a just penalty. All other standards are wavering and uncertain; and on account of other considerations involved in them, they contain no principle conformable to the sentence of pure and strict justice. It may appear, however, that difference of social status would not admit the application of the principle of retaliation, which is that of 'like with like.' But although the application may not in all cases be possible according to the letter, yet as regards the effect it may always be attained in practice, by due regard being given to the disposition and sentiment of the parties in the higher social sphere. Thus a pecuniary penalty on account of a verbal injury, may have no direct proportion to the injustice of slander; for one who is wealthy may be able to indulge himself in this offence for his own gratification. Yet the attack committed on the honour of the party aggrieved may have its equivalent in the pain inflicted upon the pride of the aggressor, especially if he is condemned by the judgment of the Court, not only to retract and apologize, but to submit to some meaner ordeal, as kissing the hand of the injured person. In like manner, if a man of the highest rank has violently assaulted an innocent citizen of the lower orders, he may be condemned not only to apologize but to undergo a solitary and painful imprisonment, whereby, in addition to the discomfort endured, the vanity of the offender would be painfully affected, and the very shame of his position would constitute an adequate retaliation after the principle of 'like with like.' But how then would we render the statement: 'If you *steal* from another, you steal from yourself'? In this way, that whoever steals anything makes the property of all insecure; he therefore robs himself of all security in property, according to the right of retaliation. Such a one has nothing, and can acquire nothing, but he has the will to live; and this is only possible by others supporting him. But as the state should not do this gratuitously, he must for this purpose yield his powers to the state to be used in penal labour; and thus he falls for a time, or it may be for life, into a condition of slavery.—But whoever has committed murder, must *die*. There is, in this case, no juridical substitute or surrogate, that can be given or taken for the satisfaction of justice. There is no *likeness* or proportion between life, however painful, and death; and therefore there is no equality between the crime of murder and the retaliation of it but what is judicially accomplished by the execution of the criminal. His death, however, must be kept free from all maltreatment that would make the humanity suffering in his person loathsome or abominable. Even if a civil society resolved to dissolve itself with the consent of all its members—as might be supposed in the case of a people inhabiting an island resolving to separate and scatter themselves throughout the whole world—the last murderer lying in the prison ought to be executed before the resolution was carried out. This ought to be done in order that every one may realize the desert of his deeds, and that bloodguiltiness may not remain upon the people; for otherwise they might all be regarded as participators in the murder as a public violation of justice.

The equalization of punishment with crime, is therefore only possible by the cognition of the judge extending even to the penalty of death, according to the right of retaliation. This is manifest from the fact that it is only thus that a sentence can be pronounced over all criminals proportionate to their internal wickedness. . . .

3. Recent Thoughts on Utilitarianism v. Retributivism

In a recent case, a 16-year-old boy who killed several people when he drove while intoxicated was given no jail time by the court as the judge found that his extraordinarily privileged upbringing was a significant reason for his mental and emotional state. *See Sentencing and the 'Affluenza' Factor*, New York Times, Room for Debate (February 18, 2014), http://www.nytimes.com/roomfordebate/2014/02/18/affluenza-and-life-circumstances-in-sentencing?emc=eta1. In response, Professor Alan Gershel offered the following opinion:

Utilitarianism vs. Retributivism—Alan Gershel
(*from* New York Times, Room for Debate (February 18, 2014),
http://www.nytimes.com/roomfordebate/2014/02/18/affluenza-and-life-
circumstances-in-sentencing/in-sentencing-utilitarianism-vs-retributivism)

A just sentence is a proportionate sentence. That is, a sentence that is appropriate to the offense, taking into account a multitude of discrete factors, including a person's life circumstances. A good judge does not have a linear sentencing philosophy. Judges sentence people, not robots, and every case presents with its own unique facts and circumstances.

A sentence should achieve proportionality. And striking the right balance depends oftentimes on competing sentencing philosophies: utilitarianism and retributivism. A utilitarian approach would tend to limit a person's life circumstances as a sentencing factor. The paramount concerns under this sentencing philosophy would be meting out a sentence that protects society and achieves general deterrence even if it is done at the expense of the offender. On the other hand, a retributivist is typically more concerned about a person's background since a central tenet is the offender's moral culpability and responsibility. These are complex issues that have confounded philosophers and jurists for thousands of years.

Within these two competing philosophies exist several sentencing theories, which are not necessarily compatible with each other. This includes the public's and the victim's demand for retribution ("just deserts"), incapacitation (if appropriate), deterrence, both specific and general, and rehabilitation. In weighing and evaluating these goals a relevant part of the sentencing calculus should include a person's life circumstances regardless of where he or she may fall on the socioeconomic scale. However, it should not be at the expense of proportionality especially when the crime is particularly serious. Unfortunately, the voices of victims, as well as the impact a particular crime may have had on the public's legitimate need to feel secure sometimes gets lost in the debate. A judge should strive to achieve balance in a sentence. This balance should include consideration of the above-mentioned sentencing concepts. A person's life circumstances are relevant but as a general rule should not tip the scales of justice so unevenly that the resulting sentence would seem to many as unjust. An unjust sentence, at either extreme, fuels the cynicism and mistrust many have for our criminal justice system.

4. Practice Problems on Utilitarian v. Retributive Theories

(1) Assume that a judge says: "Counsel, I'm concerned about the individual moral culpability of this particular defendant, not about how my decision will affect the future behavior of this or any other defendant. I don't think it's right to use a defendant as a means to an end. I think that we ought to decide whether this defendant is morally culpable for his actions, and, if so, how

culpable he was ought to determine what we decide in this case." Would this be an example of utilitarian or retributive theory? Why?

(2) Assume that a judge says: "Counsel, what I'm concerned about is how my decision in this case will affect other defendants in the future. I don't think that your client is a bad person or morally at fault for what happened here, but if I don't impose a substantial penalty, there are other people out there in the world who will get the impression that it's socially acceptable for people to do what your client did here. And I just cannot let that happen." Would this be an example of utilitarian or retributive theory? Why?

C. Cases

1. Death Penalty for Rape?

In reviewing *Coker v. Georgia*, consider whether the Supreme Court approaches the case from a retributive or utilitarian theory of punishment perspective.

Coker v. Georgia, 433 U.S. 584 (1977)

Mr. Justice WHITE announced the judgment of the Court and filed an opinion in which Mr. Justice STEWART, Mr. Justice BLACKMUN, and Mr. Justice STEVENS, joined. [Mr. Justice Brennan and Mr. Justice Marshall each filed separate opinions concurring in the judgment.]

Georgia Code Ann. §26–2001 (1972) provides that "(a) person convicted of rape shall be punished by death or by imprisonment for life, or by imprisonment for not less than one nor more than 20 years." Punishment is determined by a jury in a separate sentencing proceeding in which at least one of the statutory aggravating circumstances must be found before the death penalty may be imposed. Petitioner Coker was convicted of rape and sentenced to death. Both the conviction and the sentence were affirmed by the Georgia Supreme Court. Coker was granted a writ of certiorari, limited to the single claim, rejected by the Georgia court, that the punishment of death for rape violates the Eighth Amendment, which proscribes "cruel and unusual punishments" and which must be observed by the States as well as the Federal Government.

While serving various sentences for murder, rape, kidnaping, and aggravated assault, petitioner escaped from the Ware Correctional Institution near Waycross, Ga., on September 2, 1974. At approximately 11 o'clock that night, petitioner entered the house of Allen and Elnita Carver through an unlocked kitchen door. Threatening the couple with a "board," he tied up Mr. Carver in the bathroom, obtained a knife from the kitchen, and took Mr. Carver's money and the keys to the family car. Brandishing the knife and saying "you know what's going to happen to you if you try anything, don't you," Coker then raped Mrs. Carver. Soon thereafter, petitioner drove away in the Carver car, taking Mrs. Carver with him. Mr. Carver, freeing himself, notified the police; and not long thereafter petitioner was apprehended. Mrs. Carver was unharmed.

Petitioner was charged with escape, armed robbery, motor vehicle theft, kidnaping, and rape. Counsel was appointed to represent him. Having been found competent to stand trial, he was tried. The jury returned a verdict of guilty, rejecting his general plea of insanity. . . . The jury's verdict on the rape count was death by electrocution. . . .

. . . It is now settled that the death penalty is not invariably cruel and unusual punishment within the meaning of the Eighth Amendment; it is not inherently barbaric or an unacceptable mode of punishment for crime; neither is it always disproportionate to the crime for which it is imposed. . . .

. . . [In *Gregg v Georgia*, 428 U.S. 153 (1976)], the Court's judgment was that the death penalty for deliberate murder was neither the purposeless imposition of severe punishment nor a punishment grossly disproportionate to the crime. But the Court reserved the question of the constitutionality of the death penalty when imposed for other crimes.

That question, with respect to rape of an adult woman, is now before us. We have concluded that a sentence of death is grossly disproportionate and excessive punishment for the crime of rape and is therefore forbidden by the Eighth Amendment as cruel and unusual punishment.[4] . . .

We do not discount the seriousness of rape as a crime. It is highly reprehensible, both in a moral sense and in its almost total contempt for the personal integrity and autonomy of the female victim and for the latter's privilege of choosing those with whom intimate relationships are to be established. Short of homicide, it is the "ultimate violation of self." It is also a violent crime because it normally involves force, or the threat of force or intimidation, to overcome the will and the capacity of the victim to resist. Rape is very often accompanied by physical injury to the female and can also inflict mental and psychological damage. Because it undermines the community's sense of security, there is public injury as well.

Rape is without doubt deserving of serious punishment; but in terms of moral depravity and of the injury to the person and to the public, it does not compare with murder, which does involve the unjustified taking of human life.

---

[4] Because the death sentence is a disproportionate punishment for rape, it is cruel and unusual punishment within the meaning of the Eighth Amendment even though it may measurably serve the legitimate ends of punishment and therefore is not invalid for its failure to do so. We observe that in the light of the legislative decisions in almost all of the States and in most of the countries around the world, it would be difficult to support a claim that the death penalty for rape is an indispensable part of the States' criminal justice system.

Although it may be accompanied by another crime, rape by definition does not include the death of or even the serious injury to another person. The murderer kills; the rapist, if no more than that, does not. Life is over for the victim of the murderer; for the rape victim, life may not be nearly so happy as it was, but it is not over and normally is not beyond repair. We have the abiding conviction that the death penalty, which "is unique in its severity and irrevocability," is an excessive penalty for the rapist who, as such, does not take human life. . . .

So ordered.

2. Exploring Utilitarian and Retributive Theories of Punishment

When preparing to discuss *The Queen v. Dudley and Stephens*, it is important to know that the jury issued a "special verdict"—essentially an opinion finding certain facts—and that they asked the court to decide whether or not it is murder. The opinion below does not indicate whether the court thinks Dudley and Stephens are guilty of murder. After you read the opinion, consider these questions: Would punishing the defendants advance any of the purposes of the criminal law? If so, which ones and why? Would utilitarian theory support punishing the defendants? Why or why not? Will punishment result in the deterrence of future criminal conduct? Would retributive theory support punishing the defendants? Why or why not? What should be their "just desserts"? Who is morally culpable—and for what?

As you contemplate these questions, ask yourself how others might respond *and* how you might respond if faced with the same situation; further, how might these same defendants respond if the situation happened again on a subsequent journey.

The Queen v. Dudley and Stephens, 14 Q.B.D. 273 (1884)

LORD COLERIDGE, C.J.

The two prisoners, Thomas Dudley and Edwin Stephens, were indicted for the murder of Richard Parker on the high seas on the 25th of July in the present year. They were tried before my Brother Huddleston at Exeter on the 6th of November, and, under the direction of my learned Brother, the jury returned a special verdict, the legal effect of which has been argued before us, and on which we are now to pronounce judgment.

The special verdict . . . is as follows. . . .

. . . "[T]hat, on July 5, 1884, the prisoners, Thomas Dudley and Edward Stephens, with one Brooks, all able-bodied English seamen, and the deceased also an English boy, between seventeen and eighteen years of age, the crew of an English yacht, a registered English vessel, were cast away in a storm on the high seas 1600 miles from the Cape of Good Hope, and were compelled to put into an open boat belonging to the said yacht. That in this boat they had no supply of water and no supply of food, except two 1 lb. tins of turnips, and for three days they had nothing else to subsist upon. That on the fourth day they caught a small turtle, upon which they subsisted for a few days, and this was the only food they had up to the twentieth day when the act now in question was committed. That on the twelfth day the remains the turtle were entirely consumed, and for the next eight days they had nothing to eat. That they had no fresh water, except such rain as they from time to time caught in their oilskin capes. That the boat was drifting on the ocean, and was probably more than 1000 miles away from land. That on the eighteenth day, when they had been seven days without food and five without water, the prisoners spoke to Brooks as to what should be done if no succour came, and suggested that some one should be sacrificed to save the rest, but Brooks dissented, and the boy, to whom they were understood to refer, was not consulted. That on the 24th of July, the day before the act now in question, the prisoner Dudley proposed to Stephens and Brooks that lots should be cast who should be put to death to save the rest, but Brooks refused to consent, and it was not put to the boy, and in point of fact there was no drawing of lots. That on that day the prisoners spoke of their having families, and suggested it would be better to kill the boy that their lives should be saved, and Dudley proposed that if there was no vessel in sight by the morrow morning, the boy should be killed. That next day, the 25th of July, no vessel appearing, Dudley told Brooks that he had better go and have a sleep, and made signs to Stephens and Brooks that the boy had better be killed. The prisoner Stephens agreed to the act, but Brooks dissented from it. That the boy was then lying at the bottom of the boat quite helpless, and extremely weakened by famine and by drinking sea water, and unable to make any resistance, nor did he ever assent to his being killed. The prisoner Dudley offered a prayer asking forgiveness for them all if either of them should be tempted to commit a rash act, and that their souls might be saved. That Dudley, with the assent of Stephens, went to the boy, and telling him that his time was come, put a knife into his throat and killed him then and there; that the three men fed upon the body and blood of the boy for four days; that on the fourth day after the act had been committed the boat was picked up by a passing vessel, and the prisoners were rescued, still alive, but in the lowest state of prostration. That they were carried to the port of Falmouth, and committed for trial at Exeter. That if the men had not fed upon the body of the boy they would probably not have survived to be so picked up and rescued, but would within the four days have died of famine. That the boy, being in a much weaker condition, was likely to have died before them. That at the time of the act in question there was no sail in sight, nor any reasonable prospect of relief. That under these circumstances there appeared to the prisoners every probability that unless they then fed or very soon fed upon the boy or one of themselves they would die of starvation. That there was no appreciable chance of saving life except by killing some one for the others to eat. That assuming any necessity to kill anybody, there was no greater necessity for killing the boy than any of the other three men. But whether upon the whole matter by the jurors found the killing of Richard Parker by Dudley and Stephens be felony and murder the jurors are ignorant, and pray the advice of the Court thereupon, and if upon the whole matter the Court shall be of opinion that the killing of Richard Parker be felony and murder, then the jurors say that Dudley and Stephens were each guilty of felony and murder as alleged in the indictment." . . .

3. Modern Perspectives on Theories of Punishment

The *Blarek* decision makes clear that utilitarian and retributive theories of punishment remain quite relevant today.

United States v. Blarek, 7 F. Supp. 2d 192 (E.D.N.Y. 1998)

WEINSTEIN, Senior District Judge.

Introduction

This sentencing presents the unusual case of two talented decorators whose desires to rise in the ranks of their profession while having access to unlimited funding for their creative endeavors induced them to become the facilitators, through money washing, of a ruthless and notorious Colombian drug cartel's operations.

A long term of incarceration and severe monetary penalties that will strip defendants of all their assets is required. The sentences are designed to penalize the defendants for their criminal behavior and to deter other business and professional people from assisting drug traffickers.

Facts

Defendants Blarek and Pellecchia were arrested in March 1996. They were charged with Racketeering, Racketeering Conspiracy, and Conspiring to Launder Monetary Instruments, for their alleged involvement in the activities of the Santacruz faction of the Cali Colombia drug mob. Blarek was additionally charged with one count of Interstate Travel in Aid of Racketeering. By way of indictment, the government sought the forfeiture of defendants' property traceable to their alleged criminality. Both defendants pleaded not guilty. . . .

After a two week trial, in February, 1997, defendants were each found guilty of the Racketeering Conspiracy and Money Laundering Conspiracy counts. The jury also returned a verdict of Blarek's guilt of Interstate Travel in Aid of Racketeering.

Following trial, defendants entered into a stipulation with the government, forfeiting nearly all of their property, including their home in San Francisco worth over two millions dollars, three Harley Davidson motorcycles, a Mercedes Benz automobile, approximately $75,000 worth of jewelry, and hundreds of thousands of dollars in bank accounts and safe deposit boxes.

According to the Presentence Reports prepared by the United States Probation Office, . . . [Blarek's Sentencing] Guidelines imprisonment range . . . [is] 135 to 168 months. A fine range for Blarek's crimes of $20,000 to $14,473,063, as well as a required period of supervised release of at least two but not more than three years is also indicated.

Pellecchia's . . . imprisonment range . . . [is] 135 to 168 months. The Presentence Report also indicates a fine range of $17,500 to $14,473,063 and a required period of supervised release of at least two but not more than three years. . . .

[Defendants assert that the Sentencing Guidelines were not calculated properly in the Presentence Report due to inappropriate upward departures. Defendants also argue several reasons why the court should depart downward from the Sentencing Guidelines range].

Law
A.   *Sentencing Statute: 18 U.S.C. §3553*
1.   *Sufficient But Not Greater Than Necessary*

Congress restructured the federal sentencing law in the 1980's to create the current Guidelines-based system. It expressly stated that courts "shall impose a sentence sufficient, but not greater than necessary," to comply with the purposes of criminal sanctions. Harshness greater than that required is statutorily prohibited by this portion of the Sentencing Reform Act. Excessive leniency is also forbidden.

2.   *Seriousness of the Offense, Adequate Deterrence,*
Protection of the Public, and Correctional Treatment

The Sentencing Reform Act went on to explicitly delineate the purposes of criminal sanctions. Section 3551(a) provides that every defendant "shall be sentenced . . . so as to achieve the purposes set forth in subparagraphs (A) through (D) of section 3553(a)(2) to the extent that they are applicable in light of all the circumstances of the case."

Subparagraphs (A) through (D) of section 3553(a)(2) instruct courts to consider the necessity of the sentence imposed:

(A) to reflect the seriousness of the offense, to promote respect for the law, and to provide just punishment for the offense;

(B) to afford adequate deterrence to criminal conduct;

(C) to protect the public from further crimes of the defendant; and

(D) to provide the defendant with needed educational or vocational training, medical care, or other, correctional treatment in the most effective manner.

As [previously] analyzed . . . (A) above largely constitutes a summary of the just deserts theory and (B), (C), and (D) encompass utilitarian concerns. In creating the sentencing statutes, "Congress spelled out the four traditional justifications of the criminal sentence—deterrence, incapacitation, retribution and rehabilitation—and expressly instructed the sentencing court to keep these purposes in mind . . . ." . . .

To understand how these statutory provisions should be applied, a brief review of the theory and background of the purposes of criminal sentences is required.

B. *Traditional Sentencing Rationales*

Sentencing is a critical stage of a criminal prosecution. It represents an important moment in the law, a "fundamental judgment determining how, where, and why the offender should be dealt with for what may be much or all of his remaining life." It is significant not only for the individual before the court, but for his family and friends, the victims of his crime, potential future victims, and society as a whole.

Four core considerations, in varying degrees and permutations, have traditionally shaped American sentencing determinations: incapacitation of the criminal, rehabilitation of the offender, deterrence of the defendant and of others, and just deserts for the crime committed. . . .

Ascertaining priorities among these potentially conflicting notions has long been a point of contention amongst legislators, scholars, jurists, and practitioners. Somewhat oversimplifying, there are two basic camps. Retributivists contend that "just deserts" are to be imposed for a crime committed. Utilitarians, in their various manifestations, suggest that penalties need to be viewed more globally by measuring their benefits against their costs. "The debate between the desert justification and the various utilitarian justifications such as deterrence, incapacitation, and rehabilitation has continued to divide criminal law thinkers. . . ."

Implied in this debate are questions about our basic values and beliefs:

> Why do we impose punishment? Or is it properly to be named "punishment"? Is our purpose retributive? Is it to deter the defendant himself or others in the community from committing crimes? Is it for reform? rehabilitation? incapacitation of dangerous people? Questions like these have engaged philosophers and students of the criminal law for centuries.

In the nineteenth and most of the twentieth century American prison and punishment system reforms were designed primarily to rehabilitate the prisoner as a protection against further crime. In more recent years there has been a perception by many that attempts at rehabilitation have failed; a movement towards theoretically-based, more severe, fixed punishments, based upon the nature of the crime gained momentum. Two eighteenth and nineteenth century philosophers set the terms of the current late twentieth century debate.

1. *Kant's Retributive Just Deserts Theory*

Immanuel Kant, born in East Prussia in 1724, is regarded by some as "one of the most important philosophers in Western culture." On the ascendency of law, he wrote:

> Duty is the necessity to act out of reverence for the law. . . . Thus, the moral worth of an action does not depend on the result expected from it, and so too does not depend on any principle of action that needs to borrow its motive from this expected result . . . nothing but the idea of law in itself . . . can constitute that pre-eminent good which we call moral, a good which is already present in the person acting on this idea. . . .

It is said that "Kant accepted as fundamental the principle . . . that the only absolutely good thing in the universe is the human will governed by respect for the moral law or the consciousness of duty." . . . It follows from this position that the sole justification for criminal punishment is retribution or "jus talionis." . . .

For Kant and his adherents, "[p]unishment that gives an offender what he or she deserves for a past crime is a valuable end in itself and needs no further justification." . . . Kantian "just deserts" theory, therefore, focuses almost exclusively on the past to determine the level of punishment that should be meted out to right the wrong that has already occurred as a result of the defendant's delict.

Some softening of this cold and relentless rigidity by simultaneously integrating the Benthamite utilitarian approach is possible.

2. *Bentham's Utilitarian Theory*

Jeremy Bentham, an English philosopher born in 1748, advocated a far different, more prospective approach through his "Principle of Utility." For him, law in general, and criminal jurisprudence in particular, was intended to produce the "greatest happiness for the greatest number," a concept sometimes referred to as the "felicity calculus." . . .

Unlike his contemporary, Kant, Bentham was not interested in criminal punishment as a way of avenging or canceling the theoretical wrong suffered by society through a deviation from its norms. Rather, a criminal sanction was to be utilized only when it could help ensure the greater good of society and provide a benefit to the community. . . .

Under the Benthamite approach, deterring crime, as well as correction and reformation of the criminal, are primary aspirations of criminal law. While "the theory of retribution would impose punishment for its own sake, the utilitarian theories of deterrence and reformation would use punishment as a means to [a practical] end—the end being community protection by the prevention of crime." . . .

C.   *Utility and Retribution Under Sentencing Guidelines*

The Sentencing Guidelines, written by the United States Sentencing Commission pursuant to the Sentencing Reform Act, purport to comport with the competing theoretical ways of thinking about punishment. The Guidelines state that they provided "for the development of guidelines that will further the basic purposes of criminal punishment: deterrence, incapacitation, just punishment, and rehabilitation." A systematic, theoretical approach to these four purposes was not, however, employed by the Commission:

> A philosophical problem arose when the Commission attempted to reconcile the differing perceptions of the purposes of criminal punishment. Most observers of the criminal law agree that the ultimate aim of the law itself, and of punishment in particular, is the control of crime. Beyond this point, however, the consensus seems to break down. Some argue that appropriate punishment should be defined primarily on the basis of the principle of "just deserts." Under this principle, punishment should be scaled to the offender's culpability and the resulting harms. Others argue that punishment should be imposed primarily on the basis of practical "crime control" considerations. This theory calls for sentences that most effectively lessen the likelihood of future crime, either by deterring others or incapacitating the defendant.

The Commission decided not to create a solely retributivist or utilitarian paradigm, or "accord one primacy over the other." . . .

D.   *Deference to Sentencing Judge on Guidelines' Critical Sentencing Issues*

Since the Sentencing Commission did not say how competing rationales should shape individual sentencing decisions, courts are left to make that judgment. . . .

A fully comprehensive sentencing system that provides an absolute balance between the various sentencing rationales while permitting sentencing judges the appropriate level of discretion is probably not attainable. The creation of a flawless system is not a realistic goal. . . .

E.   *Application of the Guidelines*

Until broad-based transformation of the current complex federal system takes place, individual judges have a duty under the statutes to consider all traditional purposes of sentencing when determining an appropriate penalty. "Such [p]urpose-based analysis by judges may be the best hope for bringing justification to sentences imposed in the federal guideline system." . . .

Law Applied to Facts
A. *Guidelines Computations*

Based upon the evidence presented at trial and the sentencing hearing [in calculating the Sentencing Guidelines,] . . . Blarek faces a period of imprisonment of 121 to 151 months. Pellecchia faces 97 to 121 months' incarceration. . . .

B. *Traditional and Statutory Sentencing Rationales*
1. *Incapacitation*

Incapacitation seeks to ensure that "offenders . . . are rendered physically incapable of committing crime." . . .

In the instant case, incapacitation is not an important factor. First, these defendants have no prior criminal record indicating any propensity towards crime. Second, their connection to the criminal world, Santacruz, is now deceased. Third, it does not appear that long term restriction is necessary to ensure that defendants do not reenter a life of crime.

Consistent with utilitarian-driven analysis, little would be gained if the sentences emphasized incapacitation.

2. *Rehabilitation*

Rehabilitation is designed to instill "in the offender proper values and attitudes, by bolstering his respect for self and institutions, and by providing him with the means of leading a productive life. . . ." Neither of these men is wayward or in need of special instruction on the mores of civilized society. They have in place strong community support systems, as evidenced by the many letters submitted to the court by family and friends. They know how to live a law abiding life. It is not required that a penalty be fashioned that teaches them how to be moral in the future. This criterion, rehabilitation, therefore, is not one that is useful in assessing a penalty.

3. *Deterrence*

Of the two forms of deterrence that motivate criminal penalties—general and specific—only one is of substantial concern here.

Specific deterrence is meant to "disincline individual offenders from repeating the same or other criminal acts." Such dissuasion has likely already occurred. Defendants regret their actions. The ordeal of being criminally prosecuted and publically shamed by being denominated felons and the imposition of other penalties has taught them a sobering lesson.

General deterrence attempts to discourage the public at large from engaging in similar conduct. It is of primary concern in this case. Defendants' activities have gained a great deal of attention. Notorious cases are ideal vehicles for capturing the attention of, and conveying a message to, the public at large. While it is not appropriate under just deserts views for defendants in famous cases to be treated more harshly than defendants in less significant ones simply for the sake of making an example of them, under a utilitarian view the notoriety of a particular defendant may be taken into account by sentencing courts provided the punishment is not disproportionate to the crime.

4. *Retribution*

Retribution is considered by some to be a barbaric concept, appealing to a primal sense of vengeance. It cannot, however, be overlooked as an appropriate consideration. When there is a perception on the part of the community that the courts have failed to sensibly sanction wrongdoers, respect for the law may be reduced. This is a notion applicable under both just deserts and utilitarian balancing concepts that has had some resurgence with the current growth of the rights of victims to be heard at sentencing.

Should punishment fail to fit the crime, the citizenry might be tempted to vigilantism. This may be why, according to one group of scholars, "a criminal law based on the community's perceptions of just deserts, from a utilitarian perspective, [is] the more effective strategy for reducing crime." "White collar" "victimless" offenses, such as the ones committed by these defendants, are harmful to all society, particularly since drugs are involved. It is important, therefore, that the imposition of a penalty in this case capture, to some rational degree, the "worth" of defendants' volitional criminal acts.

5. *Sufficient But Not Greater Than Necessary*

Mercy is seldom included on the list of "traditional" rationales for sentencing. It is, however, evinced by the federal sentencing statute, which provides, as noted above, that the lowest possible penalty consistent with the goals of sentencing be imposed.

The notion that undue harshness should be avoided by those sitting in judgment has long been a part of the human fabric and spirit. Lenity is often the desirable route. . . .

Individual Sentences

. . . [The court then departed downward from the proposed Sentencing Guidelines range and sentenced Blarek to 68 months' incarceration, and a fine of $305,186, and sentenced Pellecchia to 48 months' incarceration and no fine.]

Conclusion

Defendants' money laundering, racketeering, and interstate travel in aid of racketeering did not involve weapons, direct physical injury to victims, or the taking of a life. Yet, these are serious crimes that have induced talented and intelligent individuals, including many business people, to enter the drug-trafficking world.

Blarek and Pellecchia did not aspire to become criminals, but they allowed themselves to be lured into felonies by the promise of prestige and money. The sentences imposed follow statutory and case law mandates requiring these defendants to be treated harshly, primarily to deter others.

Chapter 2
The Mens Rea of Crimes

A. Introduction

This chapter focuses primarily on the mens rea of crimes. Generally speaking, in establishing the existence of most crimes, the prosecutor must prove both an act, the "actus reus," and a particular mental state, the "mens rea." It is helpful to think of the actus reus and the mens reus as the basic "ingredients" for the "recipe" of most crimes. While there may be additional elements or "ingredients" to various crimes, the actus reus and the mens rea are the core elements. By way of illustration, review Pattern Jury Instruction 2.02 at the end of this chapter before reading the cases below.

B. Cases

1. Can a court require a prosecutor to prove a mental state that is not actually in the criminal statute used for the charge?

In reading *Morissette v. United States*, keep in mind that the federal statute involved, 18 U.S.C. §641, is based upon the common law crime of larceny. At common law, the mens rea for the crime of larceny required proof that the defendant intended to steal, or to permanently deprive the rightful possessor of his property. The *Morissette* case is a good example of how common law aids in interpreting a statute—even reading words into a statute that are not actually present.

Morissette v. United States, 342 U.S. 246 (1952)

Mr. Justice JACKSON delivered the opinion of the Court. . . .
On a large tract of uninhabited and untilled land in a wooded and sparsely populated area of Michigan, the Government established a practice bombing range over which the Air Force dropped simulated bombs at ground targets.

These bombs consisted of a metal cylinder about forty inches long and eight inches across, filled with sand and enough black powder to cause a smoke puff by which the strike could be located. At various places about the range signs read "Danger—Keep Out—Bombing Range." Nevertheless, the range was known as good deer country and was extensively hunted.

Spent bomb casings were cleared from the targets and thrown into piles "so that they will be out of the way." They were not stacked or piled in any order but were dumped in heaps, some of which had been accumulating for four years or upwards, were exposed to the weather and rusting away.

Morissette, in December of 1948, went hunting in this area but did not get a deer. He thought to meet expenses of the trip by salvaging some of these casings. He loaded three tons of them on his truck and took them to a nearby farm, where they were flattened by driving a tractor over them. After expending this labor and trucking them to market in Flint, he realized $84.

Morissette, by occupation, is a fruit stand operator in summer and a trucker and scrap iron collector in winter. An honorably discharged veteran of World War II, he enjoys a good name among his neighbors and has had no blemish on his record more disreputable than a conviction for reckless driving.

The loading, crushing and transporting of these casings were all in broad daylight, in full view of passers-by, without the slightest effort at concealment. When an investigation was started, Morissette voluntarily, promptly and candidly told the whole story to the authorities, saying that he had no intention of stealing but thought the property was abandoned, unwanted and considered of no value to the Government. He was indicted, however, on the charge that he "did unlawfully, wilfully and knowingly steal and convert" property of the United States of the value of $84, in violation of 18 U.S.C. §641, which provides that "whoever embezzles, steals, purloins, or knowingly converts" government property is punishable by fine and imprisonment.[2] Morissette was convicted and sentenced to imprisonment for two months or to pay a fine of $200. The Court of Appeals affirmed, one judge dissenting.

On his trial, Morissette, as he had at all times told investigating officers, testified that from appearances he believed the casings were cast-off and

---

[2] 18 U.S.C. § 641, so far as pertinent, reads:

> Whoever embezzles, steals, purloins, or knowingly converts to his use or the use of another, or without authority, sells, conveys or disposes of any record, voucher, money, or thing of value of the United States or of any department or agency thereof, or any property made or being made under contract for the United States or any department or agency thereof; . . .
>
> Shall be fined not more than $10,000 or imprisoned not more than ten years, or both; but if the value of such property does not exceed the sum of $100, he shall be fined not more than $1,000 or imprisoned not more than one year, or both.

abandoned, that he did not intend to steal the property, and took it with no wrongful or criminal intent. The trial court, however, was unimpressed, and ruled: "[H]e took it because he thought it was abandoned and he knew he was on government property. . . . That is no defense. . . . I don't think anybody can have the defense they thought the property was abandoned on another man's piece of property." The court stated: "I will not permit you to show this man thought it was abandoned. . . . I hold in this case that there is no question of abandoned property." The court refused to submit or to allow counsel to argue to the jury whether Morissette acted with innocent intention. It charged: "And I instruct you that if you believe the testimony of the government in this case, he intended to take it. . . . He had no right to take this property. . . . [A]nd it is no defense to claim that it was abandoned, because it was on private property. . . . And I instruct you to this effect: That if this young man took this property (and he says he did), without any permission (he says he did), that was on the property of the United States Government (he says it was), that it was of the value of one cent or more (and evidently it was), that he is guilty of the offense charged here. If you believe the government, he is guilty. . . . The question on intent is whether or not he intended to take the property. He says he did. Therefore, if you believe either side, he is guilty." Petitioner's counsel contended, "But the taking must have been with a felonious intent." The court ruled, however: "That is presumed by his own act."

The Court of Appeals suggested that "greater restraint in expression should have been exercised", but affirmed the conviction because, "As we have interpreted the statute, appellant was guilty of its violation beyond a shadow of doubt, as evidenced even by his own admissions." Its construction of the statute is that it creates several separate and distinct offenses, one being knowing conversion of government property. The court ruled that this particular offense requires no element of criminal intent. This conclusion was thought to be required by the failure of Congress to express such a requisite . . . .

I.

. . . The contention that an injury can amount to a crime only when inflicted by intention is no provincial or transient notion. It is as universal and persistent in mature systems of law as belief in freedom of the human will and a consequent ability and duty of the normal individual to choose between good and evil. A relation between some mental element and punishment for a harmful act is almost as instinctive as the child's familiar exculpatory "But I didn't mean to," and has afforded the rational basis for a tardy and unfinished substitution of deterrence and reformation in place of retaliation and vengeance as the motivation for public prosecution. Unqualified acceptance of this doctrine by English common law in the Eighteenth Century was indicated by Blackstone's sweeping statement that to constitute any crime there must first be a "vicious will." . . .

Crime, as a compound concept, generally constituted only from concurrence of an evil-meaning mind with an evil-doing hand, was congenial to an intense individualism and took deep and early root in American soil. As the state codified the common law of crimes, even if their enactments were silent on the subject, their courts assumed that the omission did not signify disapproval of the principle but merely recognized that intent was so inherent in the idea of the offense that it required no statutory affirmation. Courts, with little hesitation or division, found an implication of the requirement as to offenses that were taken over from the common law. The unanimity with which they have adhered to the central thought that wrongdoing must be conscious to be criminal is emphasized by the variety, disparity and confusion of their definitions of the requisite but elusive mental element. However, courts of various jurisdictions, and for the purposes of different offenses, have devised working formulae, if not scientific ones, for the instruction of juries around such terms as "felonious intent," "criminal intent," "malice aforethought," "guilty knowledge," "fraudulent intent," "wilfulness," "scienter," to denote guilty knowledge, or "mens rea," to signify an evil purpose or mental culpability. By use or combination of these various tokens, they have sought to protect those who were not blameworthy in mind from conviction of infamous common-law crimes. . . .

Stealing, larceny, and its variants and equivalents, were among the earliest offenses known to the law that existed before legislation; they are invasions of rights of property which stir a sense of insecurity in the whole community and arouse public demand for retribution, the penalty is high and, when a sufficient amount is involved, the infamy is that of a felony, which, says Maitland, is ". . . as bad a word as you can give to man or thing." State courts of last resort, on whom fall the heaviest burden of interpreting criminal law in this country, have consistently retained the requirement of intent in larceny-type offenses. If any state has deviated, the exception has neither been called to our attention nor disclosed by our research.

Congress, therefore, omitted any express prescription of criminal intent from the enactment before us in the light of an unbroken course of judicial decision in all constituent states of the Union holding intent inherent in this class of offense, even when not expressed in a statute. Congressional silence as to mental elements in an Act merely adopting into federal statutory law a concept of crime already so well defined in common law and statutory interpretation by the states may warrant quite contrary inferences than the same silence in creating an offense new to general law, for whose definition the courts have no guidance except the Act. . . .

The Government asks us by a feat of construction radically to change the weights and balances in the scales of justice. The purpose and obvious effect of doing away with the requirement of a guilty intent is to ease the prosecution's path to conviction, to strip the defendant of such benefit as he derived at common law from innocence of evil purpose, and to circumscribe the freedom heretofore allowed juries. Such a manifest impairment of the immunities of the individual should not be extended to common-law crimes on judicial initiative.

The spirit of the doctrine which denies to the federal judiciary power to create crimes forthrightly admonishes that we should not enlarge the reach of enacted crimes by constituting them from anything less than the incriminating components contemplated by the words used in the statute. And where Congress borrows terms of art in which are accumulated the legal tradition and meaning of centuries of practice, it presumably knows and adopts the cluster of ideas that were attached to each borrowed word in the body of learning from which it was taken and the meaning its use will convey to the judicial mind unless otherwise instructed. In such case, absence of contrary direction may be taken as satisfaction with widely accepted definitions, not as a departure from them.

We hold that mere omission from §641 of any mention of intent will not be construed as eliminating that element from the crimes denounced.

II.

It is suggested, however, that the history and purposes of §641 imply something more affirmative as to elimination of intent from at least one of the offenses charged under it in this case. The argument does not contest that criminal intent is retained in the offenses of embezzlement, stealing and purloining, as incorporated into this section. But it is urged that Congress joined with those, as a new, separate and distinct offense, knowingly to convert government property, under circumstances which imply that it is an offense in which the mental element of intent is not necessary.

Congress has been alert to what often is a decisive function of some mental element in crime. It has seen fit to prescribe that an evil state of mind, described variously in one or more such terms as "intentional," "wilful," "knowing," "fraudulent" or "malicious," will make criminal an otherwise indifferent act, or increase the degree of the offense or its punishment. Also, it has at times required a specific intent or purpose which will require some specialized knowledge or design for some evil beyond the common-law intent to do injury. The law under some circumstances recognizes good faith or blameless intent as a defense, partial defense, or as an element to be considered in mitigation of punishment. And treason—the one crime deemed grave enough for definition in our Constitution itself—requires not only the duly witnessed overt act of aid and comfort to the enemy but also the mental element of disloyalty or adherence to the enemy. In view of the care that has been bestowed upon the subject, it is significant that we have not found, nor has our attention been directed to, any instance in which Congress has expressly eliminated the mental element from a crime taken over from the common law.

The section with which we are here concerned was enacted in 1948, as a consolidation of four former sections of Title 18, as adopted in 1940, which in turn were derived from two sections of the Revised Statutes. . . . We find no other purpose in the 1948 re-enactment than to collect from scattered sources crimes so kindred as to belong in one category. Not one of these had been interpreted to be a crime without intention and no purpose to differentiate between them in the matter of intent is disclosed. No inference that some were and some were not crimes of intention can be drawn from any difference in classification or punishment. Not one fits the congressional classification of the petty offense; each is, at its least, a misdemeanor, and if the amount involved is one hundred or more dollars each is a felony. If one crime without intent has been smuggled into a section whose dominant offenses do require intent, it was put in ill-fitting and compromising company. The Government apparently did not believe that conversion stood so alone when it drew this one-count indictment to charge that Morissette "did unlawfully, wilfully and knowingly steal and convert to his own use." . . .

We find no grounds for inferring any affirmative instruction from Congress to eliminate intent from any offense with which this defendant was charged.

III.

As we read the record, this case was tried on the theory that even if criminal intent were essential its presence . . . should be . . . predicated upon the isolated act of taking rather than upon all of the circumstances. In [this respect] we believe the trial court was in error. . . .

. . . The court thought the only question was, "Did he intend to take the property?" That the removal of them was a conscious and intentional act was admitted. But that isolated fact is not an adequate basis on which the jury should find the criminal intent to steal or knowingly convert, that is, wrongfully to deprive another of possession of property. Whether that intent existed, the jury must determine, not only from the act of taking, but from that together with defendant's testimony and all of the surrounding circumstances.

Of course, the jury, considering Morissette's awareness that these casings were on government property, his failure to seek any permission for their removal and his self-interest as a witness, might have disbelieved his profession of innocent intent and concluded that his assertion of a belief that the casings were abandoned was an afterthought. Had the jury convicted on proper instructions it would be the end of the matter. But juries are not bound by what seems inescapable logic to judges. They might have concluded that the heaps of spent casings left in the hinterland to rust away presented an appearance of unwanted and abandoned junk, and that lack of any conscious deprivation of property or intentional injury was indicated by Morissette's good character, the openness of the taking, crushing and transporting of the casings, and the candor with which it was all admitted. They might have refused to brand Morissette as a thief. Had they done so, that too would have been the end of the matter.

Reversed.

2. "A crime may be established by direct evidence, circumstantial evidence, or a combination of the two."

In proving mens rea, a prosecutor rarely has direct evidence of exactly what a defendant was thinking at the time of a crime. Of course, a defendant could fully confess, including an admission that specifically concedes having the mental state required for a crime. Most of the time, however, a prosecutor must resort to circumstantial evidence, making common sense reasonable inferences from that evidence to prove the mens rea for the crime. *See, e.g., People v. Portellos*, 298 Mich. App. 431, 444–45 (2012) (allowing for reasonable inferences from the facts, court held sufficient evidence of malice to support defendant's conviction of second degree murder; although learning disabled, defendant knew she was pregnant, hid her pregnancy from her mother because she thought mother was going to be mad at her, read books on childbirth and delivery, and decided to deliver the baby herself without assistance; when she realized it was going to be a breech birth she did not call for assistance even though she had access to a cell phone; when the baby was born and did not cry, she wrapped it in a towel and left it in a garbage can).

The *Hall* decision gives a good example of how circumstantial evidence is used in the context of a murder case. In reading *Hall*, focus on how mens rea is proved, not on the specifics of a murder prosecution. Crimes of homicide will be reviewed in subsequent chapters.

State v. Hall, 2004 WL 443351 (Tenn. Crim. App. Sept. 7, 2004)

JAMES CURWOOD WITT, JR., J.

Michael Lenard Hall appeals from his Knox County Criminal Court conviction of first degree murder of his ex-wife, Pamela Hall. He claims that insufficient evidence supports his conviction . . . . Because we agree with the defendant that the state failed to present sufficient proof of premeditation, we modify the first degree murder conviction and impose a second degree murder conviction in its place. However, we are unpersuaded of error warranting a new trial. We remand for sentencing on the second degree murder conviction.

The defendant does not dispute that Pamela Hall suffered a brutal and grisly death. Ms. Hall was beaten to death in her own home. She died lying in a pool of her own blood, which was also smeared and spattered throughout the apartment in which she lived. The state theorized at trial that the defendant, distraught over the victim's rejection of him, killed her in an encounter on the afternoon of September 11, 1998. The defendant admitted that he had been to the victim's home that afternoon, but he claimed that he had not seen her there and that he did not kill her.

The state's case-in-chief established that the authorities were summoned to the victim's apartment home shortly after noon on September 12, 1998. The victim's body was on the floor, and there was blood on almost every surface in the room.

Doctor Sandra Elkins, the Knox County Medical Examiner, testified that the victim's death was caused by blunt force head injuries. Doctor Elkins opined that the victim had been dead for approximately 24 hours prior to her examination of the body on September 12, 1998 at 4:00 p.m. The victim had injuries on her arms that were consistent with defensive wounds, and she had injuries on her hands that were consistent with either offensive or defensive wounds. Doctor Elkins concluded after a visit to the scene that a struggle lasting at least one to two minutes had occurred prior to the victim being rendered unconscious and that the victim had been alive for two to six hours after the fatal blow was delivered to the back of the head.

Mary Booth, the manager of the apartment building in which the victim lived, testified that the defendant came to her door on September 12 with his son in his arms. He said that Pam had been hurt. The defendant was calm and was not crying. Mrs. Booth's husband went to check on the victim, and returned and told Mrs. Booth to call 911. During the time that the defendant was in Mrs. Booth's home, he said something like, "Oh God. God help her over the River Jordan."

Several items of physical evidence linked the defendant to the crime scene. Broken glass was found around the room in which the victim's body was discovered, and the glass was determined to have come from a broken globe from a chandelier that was hanging above the victim's body. On one of the pieces of glass, a fingerprint matching that of the defendant was identified. In addition, DNA evidence matching the victim's profile was present on a watch recovered from the defendant's car and a boot recovered from the home in which the defendant was living at the time of the victim's death.

Gloria King, with whom the defendant was living at the time of the victim's death, testified that the defendant was not at her house for several hours on the afternoon of September 11, 1998. He left around 1:00, and he returned at approximately 4:20. He was wearing the same clothing when he returned late that afternoon as he had been wearing when he departed earlier, and he and his toddler son were sweaty and red-faced as if they had been playing. Later that evening, the defendant burned some trash, which was not unusual, as there was no garbage collection at the residence. Ms. King heard the defendant come inside the house that night sometime after she retired to bed at 9:00 or 9:30, and she claimed that had he left during the night, she would have heard him. Ms. King testified that she recalled making an earlier statement to a detective that it was not unusual for the defendant to get up early in the morning to go look for the victim. Ms. King also recalled that the defendant had accused the victim of having sexual relations with other men and that he had been experiencing financial difficulties and was at odds with the victim over the issue of child support.

Carol Bounds, the victim's mother, testified that the defendant had been at her house at 5:45 a.m. a few days before the victim was killed. He struck up a conversation with Ms. Bounds, during which he expressed disapproval of the victim's parenting style and suggested that Ms. Bounds check the victim's handbag for condoms. Ms. Bounds claimed that the defendant told her, "Pam and [the defendant's child with the victim] is the same as dead to me."

One of the owners of the car dealership from which the victim's car was purchased testified that the defendant came to the dealership from time to time to make car payments on the victim's behalf. The defendant was there for that purpose on the afternoon of September 11, 1998 at 2:00 or 2:30. She identified the receipt found in the victim's pants pocket as the one she issued to the defendant on that date. She described the clothing that the defendant was wearing, and that description was at odds with the clothing that Gloria King described the defendant as wearing on that afternoon.

Investigator Mike Grissom of the Knox County Sheriff's Department testified that he had responded to the scene on September 12. He spoke with the defendant at length. The defendant told Investigator Grissom that he had been to the victim's apartment on the afternoon of September 11 to talk the victim, but she was not home. He left a plastic bag with diapers and some children's clothing between the screen and inner doors of the apartment. The defendant did not mention leaving a receipt for the victim's car payment inside the bag. The defendant detailed his activities of September 11 for Investigator Grissom, but he did not mention having made the victim's car payment for her. The defendant claimed that he had come to the victim's apartment on the morning of September 12. After knocking and receiving no response, he noticed that the door was cracked and went inside. He saw the victim on the floor, checked her pulse, and then stepped over her and went to the sink to wash his hands. He saw some car keys in the sink, which he retrieved. He placed a blanket over the victim's body. As he left, he tossed the keys he had found in the sink onto a washing machine that was near the front door. The defendant did not explain why he had moved the keys. The defendant claimed that he still loved the victim. He said that he had been intimate with the victim earlier in the week that she had been killed, and he claimed that he was only afforded this opportunity when he made her car payment for her.

In his case-in-chief, the defendant presented evidence calculated to contradict the state's proof that he was the victim's killer.

The owner of a neighborhood grocery store testified that the defendant and his toddler son had been in the store at approximately 3:00 on the afternoon of September 11. . . .

The defendant testified that he left Gloria King's house around noon or 1:00 p.m. on September 11. After making two stops, he went to make the victim's car payment. He denied that he changed clothes that afternoon before returning to Ms. King's home. He admitted that he sometimes went to check on the victim early in the morning, and he attributed this activity to their young son's desire to see his mother.

The defendant admitted that he had been to the victim's apartment the afternoon of September 11, and he claimed that he left a plastic bag with diapers, children's clothing, and a receipt for the victim's car payment there. After leaving the victim's home, he and his son went to a grocery store, a gas station, and then returned to Ms. King's home at 4:20 p.m. or 4:25 p.m. Later that evening, the defendant burned some trash, which he claimed he did three or four times a week.

The defendant testified that he returned to the victim's apartment in the early afternoon of September 12. The victim did not open the door when the defendant knocked. The door was ajar, and the defendant went inside. He discovered the victim's body, attempted to check her pulse, and found that she was cold. He became distraught, covered the victim's body with a blanket, stepped over her body, and washed his hands in the sink. He noticed some keys in the sink and a watch belonging to his and the victim's son on the counter. He took the keys and the watch, stepped back over the victim's body, and headed for the door. As he was leaving, he threw the keys onto the washer or dryer. The defendant said he was not sure why he had picked up the keys.

The defendant claimed that he still loved the victim at the time of her death and denied that he had killed her. In an attempt to explain why her blood was on his boots, he claimed that the victim had cut her finger a few weeks before her death while he was helping her move her washer and dryer, and she had slung her finger so that blood flew onto him.

The defendant denied that he had told the victim's mother to check the victim's purse for condoms. He likewise denied that he had told the victim's mother that the victim and their son were as good as dead to him.

The defendant claimed that he had told Investigator Grissom about having taken his son's watch from the victim's apartment. He testified that he told Investigator Grissom this during a taped conversation, but the tape had been damaged.

After receiving the evidence, the jury found the defendant guilty of first degree murder. The defendant then perfected this appeal.

. . . [Defendant] claims that the state failed to prove that the victim's murder was premeditated . . . .

The standard of review for sufficiency claims is a familiar one. When an accused challenges the sufficiency of the convicting evidence, this court must review the record to determine if the evidence adduced at trial is sufficient "to support the finding by the trier of fact of guilt beyond a reasonable doubt." This rule is applicable to findings of guilt based upon direct evidence, circumstantial evidence, or a combination of direct and circumstantial evidence.

In determining the sufficiency of the convicting evidence, this court does not re-weigh or re-evaluate the evidence. Nor may this court substitute its inferences for those drawn by the trier of fact from circumstantial evidence. To the contrary, this court is required to afford the state the strongest legitimate view of the evidence contained in the record as well as all reasonable and legitimate inferences which may be drawn from the evidence. . . .

A crime may be established by direct evidence, circumstantial evidence, or a combination of the two. Before an accused may be convicted of a criminal offense based upon circumstantial evidence, the facts and the circumstances "must be so strong and cogent as to exclude every other reasonable hypothesis save the guilt of the defendant, and that beyond a reasonable doubt." "A web of guilt must be woven around the defendant from which he cannot escape and from which facts and circumstances the jury could draw no other reasonable inference save the guilt of the defendant beyond a reasonable doubt."

We consider first the defendant's claim that he was improperly convicted of first degree murder because the state failed to prove that the crime was premeditated. First degree murder, as relevant here, is "[a] premeditated and intentional killing of another." " '[P]remeditation' is an act done after the exercise of reflection and judgment." The defendant claims that the state's proof was insufficient to overcome the presumption that the crime was second degree murder.

Proof of premeditation is inherently circumstantial. The trier of fact cannot speculate what was in the killer's mind, so the existence of premeditation must be determined from the defendant's conduct in light of the circumstances surrounding the crime. Thus, in evaluating the sufficiency of proof of premeditation, the appellate court may look to the circumstances surrounding the killing. Such circumstances may include "the use of a deadly weapon upon an unarmed victim; the particular cruelty of the killing; declarations by the defendant of an intent to kill; evidence of procurement of a weapon; preparations before the killing for concealment of the crime, and calmness immediately after the killing." Although the infliction of multiple blows to the victim is not alone sufficient to establish premeditation, repeated blows that evidence the particularly brutal nature of the killing are supportive of a jury's finding of premeditation.

Pamela Hall suffered an attack by an armed perpetrator; there is no evidence to indicate whether she was likewise armed. The killing was a brutal bludgeoning. A few days before the homicide, the defendant made a statement to the victim's mother that the victim and their child were "the same as dead" to him. There is no evidence to demonstrate that the defendant procured a weapon or made prior preparations to conceal the crime. The evidence regarding the defendant's demeanor in the late afternoon and evening of September 11, 1998 is not remarkable. Given the scant evidence from which premeditation may be inferred, we hold that the evidence cannot sustain a conviction of premeditated first degree murder.

This conclusion is buttressed by the position the state itself took at trial. The state theorized that the defendant went to the victim's house with the expectation of receiving sexual favors for having made the victim's car payment for her, as was consistent with their usual custom. However, according to the state's theory, the agreement went awry that day, and the defendant responded by beating the victim with an unidentified object, thereby killing her. Even if the state's postulation is accredited, it does not foster a conclusion that a premeditated murder occurred. The state's own theory is itself more consistent with a knowing killing or unpremeditated, intentional killing, that is, second degree murder. Accordingly, the defendant's conviction of first degree murder must be modified to the lesser offense of second degree murder. . . .

Having found insufficient proof of premeditation, we modify the defendant's first degree murder conviction to one of second degree murder. . . .

C.   Pattern Jury Instructions

Jury instructions include the applicable law that the jury must use in deciding the case, usually communicated to the jury by the judge. In a typical case, the prosecutor and defense attorney agree on many of the jury instructions, especially those that represent clear rules of law or guiding principles (such as those provided below) that both sides may rely on in presenting arguments to the jury. As you review the instructions herein, consider how the principles enunciated in the instructions help guide the determination of whether the mens rea for a crime has or has not been satisfied. These instructions (and other instructions) can be accessed from the website for the United States Court of Appeals for the Sixth Circuit at http://www.ca6.uscourts.gov/internet/crim_jury_insts.htm.

1.03 PRESUMPTION OF INNOCENCE, BURDEN OF PROOF, REASONABLE DOUBT

(1)   As you know, the defendant has pleaded not guilty to the crime charged in the indictment. The indictment is not any evidence at all of guilt. It is just the formal way that the government tells the defendant what crime he is accused of committing. It does not even raise any suspicion of guilt.

(2)   Instead, the defendant starts the trial with a clean slate, with no evidence at all against him, and the law presumes that he is innocent. This presumption of innocence stays with him unless the government presents evidence here in court that overcomes the presumption, and convinces you beyond a reasonable doubt that he is guilty.

(3)   This means that the defendant has no obligation to present any evidence at all, or to prove to you in any way that he is innocent. It is up to the government to prove that he is guilty, and this burden stays on the government from start to finish. You must find the defendant

not guilty unless the government convinces you beyond a reasonable doubt that he is guilty.

(4) The government must prove every element of the crime charged beyond a reasonable doubt. Proof beyond a reasonable doubt does not mean proof beyond all possible doubt. Possible doubts or doubts based purely on speculation are not reasonable doubts. A reasonable doubt is a doubt based on reason and common sense. It may arise from the evidence, the lack of evidence, or the nature of the evidence.

(5) Proof beyond a reasonable doubt means proof which is so convincing that you would not hesitate to rely and act on it in making the most important decisions in your own lives. If you are convinced that the government has proved the defendant guilty beyond a reasonable doubt, say so by returning a guilty verdict. If you are not convinced, say so by returning a not guilty verdict.

Use Note

Paragraph (3) should be modified when an affirmative defense is raised which the defendant has the burden of proving, for example, insanity and justification. In these circumstances, paragraph (3) should be changed to explain that while the government has the burden of proving the elements of the crime, the defendant has the burden of proving the defense.

1.04 EVIDENCE DEFINED

(1) You must make your decision based only on the evidence that you saw and heard here in court. Do not let rumors, suspicions, or anything else that you may have seen or heard outside of court influence your decision in any way.

(2) The evidence in this case includes only what the witnesses said while they were testifying under oath; the exhibits that I allowed into evidence; [the stipulations that the lawyers agreed to]; [and the facts that I have judicially noticed].

(3) Nothing else is evidence. The lawyers' statements and arguments are not evidence. Their questions and objections are not evidence. My legal rulings are not evidence. And my comments and questions are not evidence.

(4) During the trial I did not let you hear the answers to some of the questions that the lawyers asked. I also ruled that you could not see some of the exhibits that the lawyers wanted you to see. And sometimes I ordered you to disregard things that you saw or heard, or I struck things from the record. You must completely ignore all of these things. Do not even think about them. Do not speculate about

what a witness might have said or what an exhibit might have shown. These things are not evidence, and you are bound by your oath not to let them influence your decision in any way.

(5)   Make your decision based only on the evidence, as I have defined it here, and nothing else.

Use Note

In paragraph (2), provisions on stipulations and judicial notice are bracketed and should be used only if relevant. If the court has taken judicial notice of a fact, Instruction 7.19 should be given later in the instructions.

Paragraph (4) should also be tailored depending on what has happened during the trial.

1.05 CONSIDERATION OF EVIDENCE

You should use your common sense in weighing the evidence. Consider it in light of your everyday experience with people and events, and give it whatever weight you believe it deserves. If your experience tells you that certain evidence reasonably leads to a conclusion, you are free to reach that conclusion.

1.06 DIRECT AND CIRCUMSTANTIAL EVIDENCE

(1)   Now, some of you may have heard the terms "direct evidence" and "circumstantial evidence."

(2)   Direct evidence is simply evidence like the testimony of an eyewitness which, if you believe it, directly proves a fact. If a witness testified that he saw it raining outside, and you believed him, that would be direct evidence that it was raining.

(3)   Circumstantial evidence is simply a chain of circumstances that indirectly proves a fact. If someone walked into the courtroom wearing a raincoat covered with drops of water and carrying a wet umbrella, that would be circumstantial evidence from which you could conclude that it was raining.

(4)   It is your job to decide how much weight to give the direct and circumstantial evidence. The law makes no distinction between the weight that you should give to either one, or say that one is any better evidence than the other. You should consider all the evidence, both direct and circumstantial, and give it whatever weight you believe it deserves.

2.02 DEFINITION OF THE CRIME

(1) Count ___ of the indictment accuses the defendant of _____ in violation of federal law. For you to find the defendant guilty of this crime, you must be convinced that the government has proved each and every one of the following elements beyond a reasonable doubt:
 (A) First, that the defendant [fully define the prohibited acts and/or results required to convict].
 (B) Second, that the defendant did so [fully define the precise mental state required to convict].
 [(C) Third, that [fully define any other elements required to convict].]
[(2) Insert applicable definitions of terms used here.]
(3) If you are convinced that the government has proved all of these elements, say so by returning a guilty verdict on this charge. If you have a reasonable doubt about any one of these elements, then you must find the defendant not guilty of this charge.
[(4) Insert applicable explanations of any matters not required to convict here.]

Use Note

Definitions of the precise mental state required for various federal offenses are provided in the elements instructions in Chapters 10 *et seq*.

Bracketed paragraph (1)(C) should be included when the crime cannot be broken down neatly into two elements. Additional paragraphs should be added as needed to cover all the elements.

Bracketed paragraph (2) should be included when terms used in paragraphs (1)(A-C) require further explanation.

Bracketed paragraph (4) should be included when it would be helpful to explain matters that need not be proved in order to convict. When used, a final sentence should be included for balance emphasizing what it is that the government must prove to convict.

2.08 INFERRING REQUIRED MENTAL STATE

(1) Next, I want to explain something about proving a defendant's state of mind.
(2) Ordinarily, there is no way that a defendant's state of mind can be proved directly, because no one can read another person's mind and tell what that person is thinking.
(3) But a defendant's state of mind can be proved indirectly from the surrounding circumstances. This includes things like what the

defendant said, what the defendant did, how the defendant acted, and any other facts or circumstances in evidence that show what was in the defendant's mind.

(4) You may also consider the natural and probable results of any acts that the defendant knowingly did [or did not do], and whether it is reasonable to conclude that the defendant intended those results. This, of course, is all for you to decide.

Use Note

The bracketed language in paragraph (4) should be used only when there is some evidence of a potentially probative failure to act.

Chapter 3
The Corpus Delicti

A.   Introduction

Corpus delicti is a Latin term meaning "the body of the crime." It refers to the requirement that the necessary elements of a crime must be proven before an individual can be tried for the crime. In the context of a criminal homicide prosecution, the prosecutor initially must prove, by evidence independent of any out-of-court confession by the defendant (1) that a person has died (i.e., death) (2) as a result of another's criminal act (i.e., criminal agency).

Extra-judicial confessions are excluded based upon concerns regarding the manner in which the police may have obtained the confession. It is not unheard of for a person to confess to a crime he did not commit. Once the corpus delicti has been established, the prosecution can then seek to introduce the confession.

B.   Cases

1.   Proving Corpus Delicti

Can the corpus delicti be established by circumstantial evidence? Can the court consider statements made by the defendant to the police to establish the corpus delicti?

Downey v. People, 121 Colo. 307 (1950)

MOORE, Justice.

David Albert Downey, the defendant in the lower court and to whom we hereinafter refer as defendant, or by name, was charged by information filed in the district court of El Paso county on July 28, 1947, with having "feloniously, wilfully and of his malice aforethought" killed and murdered one Lolly Lila Downey. Defendant entered a plea of not guilty and the cause came on for trial

October 7, 1947. The jury returned a verdict of guilty of murder in the first degree and fixed the penalty at "life imprisonment at hard labor in the State Penitentiary." Motion for new trial was thereafter filed, argued, and denied, and appropriate judgment was entered by the court. Defendant brings the cause here by writ of error, and relies for reversal upon alleged errors of the lower court in the conduct of the trial as follows: . . .

. . . The court erred in refusing to strike the testimony of Dr. Henry W. Maly as the same related to the injuries to the larynx of the deceased.

. . . The court erred in overruling defendant's motion for a directed verdict upon the ground that the corpus delicti had not been established. . . .

Between one and two o'clock in the afternoon of July 18, 1947, a Dr. Wilson was driving on the Rampart Range road when he observed the defendant being assisted into a car by a Mr. Hubbard from Texas. Dr. Wilson stopped his automobile and noticed blood on the left side of defendant's shirt. He testified that defendant stated, "I am not hurt—that is my wife's blood. . . . She may be dead." Dr. Wilson and Mr. Hubbard were unable to find Mrs. Downey and returned to defendant's automobile and he thereupon assisted them in locating the body. According to Dr. Wilson the body was not disarranged. It was placed out very carefully. Mrs. Downey was dead but the body was warm. Defendant complained of injuries received from a fall, police authorities were notified, and defendant was taken to a hospital in Colorado Springs where he remained until Saturday, July 19, when he was lodged in the county jail. Dr. Wilson testified that while at the hospital defendant asked him, "if her tongue was out" and when the doctor asked the reason for the question defendant stated, "She seemed to be strangling and I tried to remove her tongue." The terrain where the body was found was rugged, being a mass of rocks and boulders. It was not, however, a dangerous area as to being precipitous. The body was lying at the foot of a ledge of rock about three feet in height, on the surface of which there was a considerable amount of blood. About thirty-four feet up the hill from the point where the body was found there was some evidence that a scuffle had occurred. An autopsy was performed which disclosed superficial scratches and bruises. There was a two inch wound in the back of the head which penetrated the scalp but did no further damage and was not the cause of death, which, as testified by the experts performing the autopsy, was asphyxia due to strangulation. . . .

Questions to be Determined . . .
Was the corpus delicti sufficiently established by the evidence?

At the close of all the evidence the defendant moved for a directed verdict of not guilty "for the reason that the corpus delicti has not been established without recourse to the alleged confession of the defendant." The motion was overruled and error is assigned on the ruling.

In Bruner v. People, 156 P.2d 111, 117, we said: "It is well settled in this jurisdiction that the corpus delicti consists of two components: death as a result and the criminal agency of another as the means, and it is equally settled that the corpus delicti may be established by either direct or circumstantial evidence."

The Bruner case is authority for the rule prevailing in this jurisdiction that circumstantial evidence is sufficient to establish the corpus delicti in a homicide case if it is such as to prove the essentials thereof to a reasonable certainty.

In Lowe v. People, 234 P. 169, 173, we stated:

> Proof that one charged committed a felonious homicide involves three elements; First, the death; Second, the criminal agency of another as the cause; third, the identity of the accused as that other. The first two constitute what is known in law as the corpus delicti. . . . Each of these elements must be established by the prosecution to the satisfaction of the jury beyond a reasonable doubt. The court, however, is not the judge of the weight of the evidence. When sufficient has been produced to justify a submission to the jury and support a verdict of guilty, should such a verdict be returned thereon, the requirements of the law have been met. This rule applies to each of the elements of the corpus delicti as it does to the proof of the identity of the accused as the perpetrator; no more no less.

> That proof may be made by any legal evidence, the same as proof of other facts.

It is true that a conviction of crime cannot be upheld where it is based upon the uncorroborated confession of the person accused. There must be evidence of the corpus delicti apart from the statements contained in the confession. In the case at bar there is ample evidence, apart from the confession, from which the jury might properly find that the wife of defendant was dead, and that her death was brought about by "the criminal agency of another as the means." Defendant was the sole companion of his wife at the time of her death. There was blood on his shirt, which he stated was that of his wife. He directed those first upon the scene to the place where her body was found. The body was still warm. The position of the body, the fact that her clothing was not disarranged, the fact that pressure had been applied to both of her wrists and her throat, the general topography of the terrain where she was found, were all inconsistent with the theory of accidental death. The ragged scalp wound in the back of the head of deceased corroborated the statement of defendant that he struck her a blow with a "rock about the size of two teacups." The defendant directed an inquiry to Dr. Wilson as to whether deceased's tongue was out when he first observed the body, and this unusual question was wholly the thought of defendant. The doctors who performed the autopsy testified that the cause of death was strangulation produced by pressure applied to the throat. Competent evidence tending to establish these facts was sufficient to establish the corpus delicti of the crime of murder, and the trial court did not commit error in overruling defendant's motion for a directed verdict on the ground that the corpus delicti had not been sufficiently proven. . . .

The defendant was capably represented at the trial, and here, by counsel of ability and experience, and we are persuaded that he was afforded a fair trial in accordance with established rules of law. The assignments upon which he relies for reversal are overruled, and accordingly the judgment is affirmed.

Note

In *People v. LaRosa*, 293 P.3d 567 (Colo. 2013), the Colorado Supreme Court abrogated *Downey*. The court rejected the rule requiring the prosecution to establish the corpus delicti without consideration of the defendant's confession. Rather, the court adopted what has become known as the trustworthy standard, which permits the use of the defendant's confession if there is corroborating evidence establishing the reliability of the confession.

2. Is the exclusion of an uncorroborated confession to establish the corpus delicti limited to statements made to the police?

Hicks v. Sheriff, Clark County, 86 Nev. 67 (1970)

BATJER, Justice:

Appellant was charged with the murder of Glenn E. Christiernsson. After an extensive preliminary examination the charge was dismissed because the state had failed to prove the corpus delicti and has also failed to prove that Christiernsson's death was caused by the criminal agency of the appellant. Thereafter, the state filed a petition in the district court for leave to file an information against the appellant under NRS 173.035(2), attaching to the petition the transcript of the testimony taken at the preliminary examination. Also attached to the petition was an affidavit of a Ronald Elton King, who had been a cellmate of the appellant in the Clark County jail. The affidavit of King alleged that the appellant, while in jail, had admitted to him, the killing of Christiernsson. There was also attached to the petition an affidavit of a deputy district attorney which recited that the appellant had been discharged after preliminary examination, but alleged that the testimony adduced was sufficient compliance with NRS 173.035(2), and that it contained sufficient facts to justify the issuance of an information against the appellant.

The district court granted leave to file the information; the appellant was rearrested and then applied for a writ of habeas corpus which was denied by the district court.

This appeal is taken from the order denying the writ of habeas corpus. We reverse the order of the district court.

Counsel for both the state and the appellant urge this court to determine this appeal on the question of the state's compliance or noncompliance with the provisions of NRS 173.035(2), as well as the question of its constitutionality.

We do not reach either the question of the degree of compliance necessary to enable the state to take advantage of that statute nor the question of its constitutionality.

The only question before us is whether the facts laid before the district court, prior to the filing of the information, established a corpus delicti and probable cause to believe that the appellant committed the crime as charged.

The record of the preliminary examination is absolutely devoid of proof of the corpus delicti to support the filing of an information charging the crime of murder. The appellant was properly discharged by the justice of the peace on the evidence presented at that hearing.

Except in the affidavit of King, we find no testimony or other evidence about the cause of death of Christiernsson. All that we find relating to his death is testimony that his body was found on December 6, 1967, in the desert; that it was identified by a military service identification tag and a thumb print, and that the body was partially clothed. There is absolutely no evidence before either the justice's court or the district court that a criminal agency of the appellant or anyone else was responsible for the alleged victim's death.

The affidavit of the appellant's fellow prisoner to the effect that the appellant admitted to him that he had murdered the victim, does not supply the proof necessary to show that death was caused by criminal means. Only after the corpus delicti has been proved by lawful evidence may confessions and admissions be considered in establishing probable cause to show that the accused was the criminal agency causing the death. In re Kelly, 83 P. 223 (1905). In Kelly, . . . this court said: ". . . It is not requisite, however, that the crime charged be conclusively established by evidence independent of the confession or admission. It is sufficient if there be other competent evidence tending to establish the fact of the commission of the crime." Here there is absolutely no evidence independent of the appellant's purported admission.

The testimony at the preliminary examination establishing that the deceased and the appellant were seen together shortly before the deceased's disappearance on or about October 9, 1967, as well as testimony concerning the appellant's behavior prior to arrest, and the fact that he was driving Christiernsson's car at the time of his arrest would only have been material to show probable cause that the appellant was guilty of the crime of murder if the corpus delicti of that crime had been established.

In Azbill v. State . . . we held: "If, in considering all the evidence admissible upon the element of corpus delicti, it cannot be said there was sufficient evidence to make it appear the death resulted from another's criminal agency the state has failed in its burden and the person charged may not be held to stand trial on that charge."

At the very least there must be established, independent of any confession or admission by the accused, the fact of death and that it resulted from the criminal agency of another and not from natural causes, accident or suicide.

In his affidavit, King swore that the appellant told him that he beat Christiernsson to death and then stabbed him to make sure he was dead. If King is telling the truth there surely must have been some evidence on the body of the decedent showing bruises, contusions, abrasions, wounds or fractures.

Neither the justice of the peace, the district court judge, who ordered the information to be filed pursuant to NRS 173.035(2), the district court judge who denied habeas corpus, nor this court "may speculate that a criminal agency caused the death. There must be sufficient proof of the hypothesis of death by criminal means."

The evidence before the district court is insufficient to show probable cause of the corpus delicti of the crime of murder. Accordingly we reverse the order of the district court, and order that appellant be freed from custody under the information charging murder unless within a reasonable time the state elects to bring a new charge against him for that crime.

People v. Borrelli, 463 Mich. 930 (2000)

On order of the Court, the application for leave to appeal from the June 19, 2000 decision of the Court of Appeals is considered, and it is DENIED, because we are not persuaded that the question presented should be reviewed by this Court.

CORRIGAN, J., concurs and states as follows:

I join in the order denying leave to appeal, but write separately to express my concern with the application of the corpus delicti rule to the crime of knowingly filing a false police report, M.C.L. §750.411a; MSA 28.643(1).

Defendant lost his car in the early morning hours while driving home from a bar. When he could not find it the next day, he reported to the police that he had been carjacked by a dark complected [sic] African-American male. Three weeks later, during a follow-up interview with the police, defendant admitted that he had no memory of how he had become separated from his car and that he had no knowledge of ever being carjacked. Defendant was then charged with knowingly filing a false police report in violation of M.C.L. §750.411a; MSA 28.643(1). At defendant's preliminary examination, the prosecution admitted that it had no evidence of the falsity of the police report apart from defendant's own admission. Accordingly, the district court dismissed the charges on the basis of Michigan's common law corpus delicti rule. The circuit court then affirmed and the Court of Appeals denied the prosecutor's application for leave to appeal.

In Michigan, the common law corpus delicti rule provides that a defendant's confession may not be admitted as evidence unless there is direct or circumstantial evidence independent of the confession establishing the occurrence of a specific injury (for example, death in cases of homicide) and some criminal agency as the source of the injury. The prosecutor now argues that we should abandon Michigan's common law rule in favor of the less stringent federal rule set forth in *Opper v. United States,* 348 U.S. 84, (1954). While there may be good reasons to adopt the federal rule, the prosecution's argument was considered and rejected by this Court in *People v. McMahan,* 451 Mich. 543, (1996). Therefore, the principle of *stare decisis* counsels against reconsidering the argument again at this time.

Although the prosecution's argument does not provide a sound reason for this Court to grant its application for leave to appeal, the facts of this case aptly demonstrate the substantial cost of applying the common law corpus delicti rule to crimes involving false statements. To overcome the common law corpus delicti rule where the defendant is charged with violating M.C.L. §750.411a; MSA 28.643(1), the prosecution must present independent evidence establishing the *falsity* of the police report at issue. This imposes an extremely onerous burden, because it effectively requires the prosecution to produce independent evidence of a negative fact. Here, for example, the prosecution would have to prove, through independent evidence, that defendant was *not* the victim of a car jacking. Such evidence would not likely exist absent extraordinary police efforts.

False police reports are a significant societal problem because they require the police to expend time and effort investigating "crimes" that did not occur. To expect the police to continue to investigate a nonexistent "crime" *after* the complainant has admitted that the report was false seems to ask too much of law enforcement. On the other hand, to allow persons making false reports to escape conviction does little to deter false police reports. Accordingly, I urge the Legislature to consider whether the cost of the corpus delicti rule is justified in the context of M.C.L. §750.411a; MSA 28.643(1).

3. Is it necessary to have a body to establish the corpus delicti?

If corpus delicti means the body of the crime, how could a court find it was established in the absence of a body? As you read the *Warmke* case, consider how it differs from *Hicks*. In addition, notice that the court in *Warmke* considered the defendant's statement. Does the use of the defendant's statement run counter to the prohibition regarding the exclusion of confessions to establish the corpus delicti?

Warmke v. Commonwealth, 297 Ky. 649 (1944)

FULTON, Chief Justice.

This appeal is from a manslaughter sentence of nine years imposed on the appellant in connection with the death of her infant child. The sole ground urged for reversal was that the corpus delicti was not sufficiently shown.

The appellant resided in Utica, a village in Davies County. Some weeks prior to July 8, 1943 she went to Louisville and there gave birth to an illegitimate child. On July 8, 1943 she traveled to Cloverport, in Breckenridge County, by bus arriving about 8 o'clock p.m. It was raining very hard and she went into a drug store for shelter. A. T. Couch, an employee of the store, loaned her a coat in which to wrap her baby. She went out leaving her suitcase in the store. She called Couch by telephone about 10:30, requesting him to come to the store so that she might get her suitcase. When she met Couch at the store she did not have the baby but returned the borrowed coat. Early the next morning she went to the home of a kinswoman, Mrs. Pate. The town marshal, having learned that the baby was missing, went to Mrs. Pate's home and questioned the appellant. She told him that after she left the drug store she started to cross a railroad trestle near the town in an effort to get to the home of a friend and that while she was crossing a train approached and she crawled over on the edge of the ties and accidently dropped the baby. The town marshal and a highway patrolman then took the appellant to the trestle and she pointed out where the baby had been dropped. There was a creek under the trestle at this point. It was flooded and the current was swift. A baby's cap was found on the bank of the creek and the appellant exclaimed, "There is my little baby's cap". The baby's body was never found.

When the officers returned to town with the appellant she told them, after some questioning, that she purposely threw the baby into the creek because she was unable to face the humiliation of going home with an illegitimate child.

On the trial she repudiated the confession she had made to the officers and testified that she dropped the baby accidentally, in the manner she first told the officers. She testified that she was scared and excited and didn't remember saying she dropped the baby purposely. She said that after she dropped the baby she wandered around all night barefooted and in a dazed condition and that in the morning she put on her shoes and stockings and went to Mrs. Pate's. She gave as a reason for stopping off at Cloverport that it was her father's home town and that she desired to talk to a friend, Mrs. Atwill, and obtain advice. She did not see Mrs. Atwill but says that she was looking for her house when she dropped the baby and that thereafter she remembered nothing until early morning.

It is axiomatic that the corpus delicti must be shown. This term means the body of the offense, the substance of the crime. Proof of the corpus delicti in homicide cases involves two principal facts, namely, that the person is dead and that he died as a result of the injury alleged to have been received. In short, there must be proof of a death and proof that such death was caused by the criminal agency of the accused.

But the law does not subscribe to the rigid formula that the body must be found or seen after death. The death may be established by circumstantial evidence. 26 Amer.Juris. 376. As said in 13 R.C.L. 737, the death may be shown "by proof of criminal violence adequate to produce death and which accounts for the disappearance of the body. In short, the body must be found or there must be proof of death which the law deems to be equivalent to direct evidence that it was found."

We think there was sufficient proof of the death of the baby in the case before us. It was dropped, either purposely or accidentally, by the appellant from the railroad trestle into the flooded creek below and was never found. It seems beyond the bounds of possibility that the baby survived this ordeal and was never thereafter heard of. At least, we think the evidence was ample to justify the jury's finding that death ensued.

It is argued for the appellant, however, that the corpus delicti must be established by evidence other than the confession of the accused out of court and that there was no other evidence here. The soundness of the legal proposition thus advanced may be admitted. There must be proof of the component elements of the corpus delicti, a death and the criminal agency of the accused, by proof in addition to the confession of the accused made out of court. But, as indicated above, the appellant testified that the baby was dropped into the creek. Thus there was proof of the death independent of the appellant's confession made out of court.

The remaining question is whether there was proof, in addition to the appellant's confession made out of court, of her criminal agency in causing the death. Her agency in causing the death was admitted from the witness stand. Was there evidence, independent of her confession out of court, that this agency was criminal? We think there was an abundance of such evidence. Such independent evidence may be circumstantial as well as direct.

Circumstances pointing clearly to the fact that the appellant purposely dropped the baby from the trestle may be thus summarized. She had an impelling motive, concealment of the birth of the illegitimate child. Her reason for going to Cloverport instead of her home is rather vague and unsatisfactory. This reason was that she decided to consult her friend, Mrs. Atwill, yet she never did so. She eventually wound up at Mrs. Pate's and not at Mrs. Atwill's. But, most illuminating of all is her failure to notify any one that she had dropped the baby from the trestle, if it was dropped accidentally. She accounts for this by saying she was in a dazed condition, nevertheless she called Mr. Couch by telephone to come to the drug store so that she might get her suitcase. She returned the coat to him. She had borrowed this coat to wrap the baby in. It is singular that she would have accidentally dropped the baby without dropping the coat. It is even more singular that she never notified Mrs. Pate, her kinswoman, the next morning of the loss of the baby. These circumstances and the justifiable inferences to be drawn from them, amply warranted the jury in finding that the dropping of the baby from the trestle was purposely, and not accidentally, done by the appellant.

Affirmed.

C. Practice Problems on the Corpus Delicti

The problems below should take you 30 minutes or less to answer. Try preparing your answers under test-like conditions (i.e., after studying your outline, no notes or interruptions).

(1) Defendant has been charged with murder. At trial, the prosecution presents evidence that the victim's body was found in a park and that the cause of death was three stab wounds to the heart. But the only evidence establishing that Defendant was the perpetrator came from her out-of-court confession to the police, which was obtained under suspicious circumstances.

At the close of the prosecution's proofs, Defendant's lawyer asks the judge to grant a motion for a directed verdict of not guilty. The trial judge should:

(a) Grant the motion, because the corpus delicti must be proved by evidence independent of Defendant's out-of-court statements;

(b) Grant the motion, because Defendant's confession was obtained under suspicious circumstances;

(c) Deny the motion, because the corpus delicti was sufficiently established;

(d) Deny the motion, because murder is a serious felony and public justice requires that the judge allow the case to proceed.

(2) Which of the following different kinds of evidence *would least likely* be sufficient to establish the corpus delicti of homicide?

(a) Testimony from a medical examiner that she examined the victim's body and found that the cause of death was a single gunshot wound to the head;

(b) Statements made by Defendant on cross-examination at trial in response to questions asked by the prosecution admitting that he shot and killed the victim, but claiming that it was self-defense;

(c) Purely circumstantial evidence that the victim had disappeared and had never been heard from again, and that Defendant had a possible motive to kill the victim;

(d) Testimony from a 20-year-veteran detective that Defendant had admitted to him at the time of his arrest that he had killed the victim because the victim had threatened him with a knife.

(3) Defendant was tried for murder. At trial the prosecution introduced Defendant's out-of-court confession (in which he admitted killing the victim) at the very beginning of the case, without first establishing the corpus delicti. Although the prosecution was never able to produce any evidence that the victim's body was ever found, it was able to present testimony that the victim was a very conscientious single mother of three young children who failed to pick her children up from school one day and was never heard from again. The defense presented other testimony that the victim was severely depressed, had talked to friends about how difficult it was to raise children alone, and had

written entries in her diary about running away by herself to Alaska. Blood stains, a bloody knife, and other forensic evidence found in the victim's home established that a violent struggle had occurred in the kitchen the day the victim disappeared. The jury eventually found Defendant guilty of murder, and he has appealed his conviction to the Cooley Court of Appeals.

If Defendant argues to the Court of Appeals that his conviction should be reversed because of a violation of the corpus delicti rule, the Court of Appeals should:

(a) Affirm the conviction, if the Court of Appeals decides after an independent review of the facts that the testimony presented by the prosecution was more persuasive;

(b) Affirm the conviction, if, in viewing the evidence in the light most favorable to the prosecution, the Court of Appeals decides that a rational jury could have found Defendant guilty beyond a reasonable doubt;

(c) Reverse the conviction, because Defendant's confession was admitted into evidence first before any evidence of a death was presented;

(d) Reverse the conviction, because without a body there can never be proof beyond a reasonable doubt that a death has, in fact, occurred.

(4) A nine-year-old child disappeared without a trace. She was last seen entering a car that was eventually linked to Defendant. Detective interviewed Defendant with his consent at his home. Defendant's family attorney was present throughout the interview to assist and counsel Defendant. Detective fully advised Defendant of his Miranda rights before asking him any questions and Defendant voluntarily agreed to speak with her. He told her that he has a sexual problem he cannot control, and that he kidnapped, raped, and murdered the child. He said that he then dumped her body off the back of his fishing boat into the deepest part of Lake Michigan. No body was ever recovered. Detective tape recorded the entire conversation to make sure that she got it down verbatim.

With Defendant's consent, the police searched his boat. In the sleeping berth, they found human hairs that matched the child's hair exactly.

Assume that you represent Defendant. What arguments would you make on his behalf based on the corpus delicti rule? Assume now that you represent the prosecution. How would you respond?

Chapter 4
Homicide Offenses

A. Introduction

This chapter explores the crimes of homicide. It is important to understand that the word homicide is a general term used to describe all killings—criminal law students need to understand when homicide is criminal and, hence, a crime. Beginning with a discussion of common law murder and manslaughter (emphasizing the differences between involuntary and voluntary manslaughter), the chapter then weaves in a discussion of codified crimes of homicide and Model Penal Code homicide.

A primary concern regarding criminal homicide is the mens rea, i.e., the mental state, the defendant possessed in relation to the act of killing. The importance of the mens rea can be summed up by the following quote from *Maher v. People*, 10 Mich. 212, 217 (1862):

> Homicide, or the mere killing of one person by another, does not, of itself, constitute murder; it may be murder, or manslaughter, or excusable, or justifiable homicide, and therefore entirely innocent, according to the circumstances, or the disposition or state of mind or purpose, which induced the act. It is not, therefore, the act which constitutes the offense, or determines its character; but the *quo animo,* the disposition, or state of mind, with which it is done.

As you can see, the mental state of the defendant determines the severity of the crime of homicide and whether a crime has even been committed. By understanding the specific mental state required for the varying crimes of homicide presented in this chapter, you will be able to distinguish one crime of homicide from another.

B.   Causation in Homicide Context

Of course, in all crimes of homicide, there must be an act causing the death of a human being (the actus reus of the crime of homicide). The defendant's act, however, must also have *caused* the death. The *Lewis* case explores the question of causation in the context of a manslaughter prosecution.

People v. Lewis, 124 Cal. 551 (1899)

TEMPLE, J.

The defendant was convicted of manslaughter, and appeals from the judgment and from an order refusing a new trial. . . .

Upon a motion for a new trial questions of law may be presented in regard to the legal sufficiency of the evidence, and such questions may be reviewed here. . . . The evidence upon which these points are based is not conflicting, and, of course, there is no substantial disagreement in regard thereto. . . . Defendant and deceased were brothers-in-law, and not altogether friendly, although they were on speaking and visiting terms. On the morning of the homicide the deceased visited the residence of the defendant, was received in a friendly manner, but after a while an altercation arose, as a result of which defendant shot deceased in the abdomen, inflicting a wound that was necessarily mortal. Farrell fell to the ground, stunned for an instant, but soon got up, and went into the house, saying: "Shoot me again. I shall die anyway." His strength soon failed him, and he was put to bed. Soon afterwards,—about how long does not appear, but within a very few minutes,—when no other person was present except a lad about 9 years of age, nephew of the deceased, and son of defendant, the deceased procured a knife, and cut his throat, inflicting a ghastly wound, from the effect of which, according to the medical evidence, he must necessarily have died in five minutes. The wound inflicted by the defendant severed the mesenteric artery, and medical witnesses testified that under the circumstances it was necessarily mortal, and death would ensue within one hour from the effects of that wound alone. Indeed, the evidence was that usually the effect of such a wound would be to cause death in less time than that, but possibly the omentum may have filled the wound, and thus, by preventing the flow of the blood from the body, have stayed its certain effect for a short period. Internal hemorrhage was still occurring, and, with other effects of the gunshot wound, produced intense pain. The medical witnesses thought that death was accelerated by the knife wound. Perhaps some of them considered it the immediate cause of death. Now, it is contended that this is a case where one languishing from a mortal wound is killed by an intervening cause, and therefore deceased was not killed by Lewis. To constitute manslaughter, the defendant must have killed some one, and if, though mortally wounded by the defendant, Farrell actually died from an independent intervening cause, Lewis, at the most, could only be guilty of a felonious attempt. He was as effectually prevented from killing as he would have been if some obstacle had turned aside the bullet from its course, and left Farrell unwounded. And they contend that the intervening act was the cause of death, if it shortened the life of Farrell for any period whatever. The attorney general does not controvert the general proposition here contended for, but argues that the wound inflicted by the defendant was the direct cause of the throat-cutting, and therefore defendant is criminally responsible for the death. He illustrates his position by supposing a case of one dangerously wounded, and whose wounds had been bandaged by a surgeon. He says, suppose, through the fever and pain consequent upon the wound, the patient becomes frenzied, and tears away the bandage, and thus accelerates his own death, would not the defendant be responsible for a homicide? Undoubtedly he would be, for in the case supposed the deceased died from the wound, aggravated, it is true, by the restlessness of the deceased, but still the wound inflicted by the defendant produced death. Whether such is the case here is the question. . . .

. . . [T]he test is—or, at least, one test—whether, when the death occurred, the wound inflicted by the defendant did contribute to the event. If it did, although other independent causes also contributed, the causal relation between the unlawful acts of the defendant and the death has been made out. Here, when the throat was cut, Farrell was not merely languishing from a mortal wound; he was actually dying; and after the throat was cut he continued to languish from both wounds. Drop by drop the life current went out from both wounds, and at the very instant of death the gunshot wound was contributing to the event. If the throat-cutting had been by a third person, unconnected with the defendant, he might be guilty; for, although a man cannot be killed twice, two persons, acting independently, may contribute to his death, and each be guilty of a homicide. A person dying is still in life, and may be killed; but, if he is dying from a wound given by another, both may properly be said to have contributed to his death.

. . . The judgment is affirmed.

C. Common Law Crimes of Homicide

As the common law underlies so much of the criminal laws of the United States, it is important to have an understanding of how the common law treated murder and manslaughter. As has been discussed, common law crimes are, in the absence of some other statutory direction, defined by reference to the common law.

This section will begin with the *Comber* case, which provides a useful backdrop to the discussion. Importantly, while the issue in the *Comber* case involved jury instructions (which the court found to be erroneous), the case is only presented here to aid you in understanding the historical development of the common law crimes of homicide and their relationship to modern statutes.

Note that some concepts will be discussed in *Comber*—such as justification, excuse, and self-defense—that will not be fully explored until the point in the class when defenses are studied.

Comber v. United States, 584 A.2d 26 (D.C. App. 1990)

STEADMAN, Associate Judge:

. . . [W]e are faced with the immediate question of what jury instructions for the crime of manslaughter are appropriate where a person dies as a result of bare-fisted blows to the face. Like an unraveling string, this inquiry has led to and necessitated a more general examination of the law of manslaughter and particularly its division in our jurisdiction into "voluntary" and "involuntary" components. . . .

THE CRIME OF MANSLAUGHTER
A. *Historical background*

Although D.C.Code §22–2405 (1989) establishes the penalty for manslaughter, "there is no statutory definition of manslaughter in the District of Columbia." "[M]anslaughter is defined, rather, by reference to the common law." Accordingly, in resolving the issues before us, a brief review of the common law emergence of the crime of manslaughter will be useful.

1. The division of criminal homicide into murder and manslaughter

"What we now know as murder and manslaughter constituted just one offense under the common law of England. At the turn of the sixteenth century, all homicides, with the exception of accidental homicides, homicides committed in self-defense, or homicides committed "in the enforcement of justice," "were deemed unlawful and were punished by death." The harsh effects of this regime were mitigated, however, by the extension of ecclesiastic jurisdiction. Ecclesiastic courts, which retained jurisdiction to try clerics accused of criminal offenses, did not impose capital punishment. Rather, under ecclesiastic law, a person who committed an unlawful homicide "received a one-year sentence, had his thumb branded and was required to forfeit his goods." The transfer of a case from the secular to the ecclesiastic jurisdiction, a procedural device known as "benefit of clergy," thus "resulted in leniency of the most important sort." Moreover, "[b]y the fifteenth century, the courts began to accept proof of literacy as the test for clerical status, with the result that benefit of clergy became a 'massive fiction' that 'tempered in practice the harshness of the common law rule that virtually all felonies were capital offenses.' "

Perhaps because of concern about "the accretion of ecclesiastic jurisdiction at the expense of the secular," or perhaps because "the number of serious offenses appeared to increase," England's monarchs, beginning in the late fifteenth century and into the first half of the sixteenth, enacted a series of statutes which excluded a class of the most heinous homicides from benefit of clergy. These killings were referred to in the various statutes as "wilful prepense murders," "murder upon malice prepensed," and "murder of malice prepensed." Unlawful homicides that were committed without such malice were designated 'manslaughter,' and their perpetrators remained eligible for benefit of clergy." The offenses encompassed by the new statutes were designated "murder"; perpetrators of these offenses were subject to secular jurisdiction and capital punishment. This distinction between murder and manslaughter persisted "[e]ven after ecclesiastic jurisdiction was eliminated for all secular offenses." These early statutory developments thus

> led to the division of criminal homicides into murder, which retained its status as a capital crime, and the lesser offense of manslaughter. The courts defined murder in terms of the evolving concept of "malice aforethought" and treated manslaughter as a residual category for all other criminal homicides.

Thus, manslaughter, "[i]n its classic formulation . . . consisted of homicide without malice aforethought on the one hand and without justification or excuse on the other." This definition has been adopted in the District of Columbia. A homicide which constitutes manslaughter is distinguished from murder by the absence of malice, and is distinguished from a killing to which no homicide liability attaches by the absence of factors which would excuse or justify the homicide. Manslaughter is thus a "catch-all" category, defined essentially by reference to what it is not.

2. The division of manslaughter into
voluntary and involuntary manslaughter

The broad and undifferentiated early definition of manslaughter created pressure for refinement. In the same way that the early common law concept of unlawful homicide had evolved into murder and manslaughter, so too did manslaughter divide into separate categories of voluntary and involuntary manslaughter, depending on the type of conduct involved. The distinction between the two varieties of manslaughter was noted by Blackstone as early as 1769.[7] . . .

Both voluntary and involuntary manslaughter may still be accurately defined as "homicide[s] without malice aforethought on the one hand and without justification or excuse on the other." The two offenses are

---

[7] According to Blackstone, involuntary manslaughter resulted where one killed unintentionally in the course of a non-felonious unlawful act, or "where a person does an act, lawful in itself, but in an unlawful manner, and without due caution and circumspection." Voluntary manslaughter occurred "if upon a sudden quarrel two persons fight, and one of them kills the other."

distinguishable by virtue of the perpetrator's state of mind; specifically, the difference between the two offenses lies in the basis for concluding that the perpetrator acted without malice aforethought. As explained below, in all voluntary manslaughters, the perpetrator acts with a state of mind which, but for the presence of legally recognized mitigating circumstances, would constitute malice aforethought, as the phrase has been defined for purposes of second-degree murder. All involuntary manslaughters, in contrast, are killings in which the perpetrator's state of mind, without any consideration of any issues of mitigation, would not constitute malice aforethought.

B.   *"Malice aforethought" for purposes of second-degree murder*

Because of the relationship between voluntary manslaughter and murder, an understanding of the scope of the offense of voluntary manslaughter requires an examination of the states of mind which would make an unlawful killing second-degree murder. At common law, an unjustified or unexcused homicide rose to the level of murder if it was committed with malice aforethought. This definition continues in effect in the District of Columbia. D.C.Code §22–2403.

For purposes of second-degree murder, "malice aforethought" has evolved into "a term of art" embodying several distinct mental states. As the commentary to the Model Penal Code explains:

> Whatever the original meaning of [the] phrase [malice aforethought], it became over time an "arbitrary symbol" used by judges to signify any of a number of mental states deemed sufficient to support liability for murder. Successive generations added new content to "malice aforethought" until it encompassed a variety of mental attitudes bearing no predictable relation to the ordinary sense of the two words.

Following the common law trend, this court has recognized that malice aforethought, in the District of Columbia, "denotes four types of murder, each accompanied by distinct mental states."

First, a killing is malicious where the perpetrator acts with the specific intent to kill. Second, a killing is malicious where the perpetrator has the specific intent to inflict serious bodily harm. Third, "an act may involve such a wanton and willful disregard of an unreasonable human risk as to constitute malice aforethought even if there is not actual intent to kill or injure. In *Byrd v. United States,* 500 A.2d 1376, 1385 n 9 (D.C. 1985), we referred to this kind of malicious killing as "depraved heart" murder.

Although not all jurisdictions are in agreement on the matter, in the District of Columbia, such depraved heart malice exists only where the perpetrator was subjectively aware that his or her conduct created an extreme risk of death or serious bodily injury, but engaged in that conduct nonetheless.[12] . . .

Historically, a fourth kind of malice existed when a killing occurred in the course of the intentional commission of a felony. Under this "felony-murder" rule, "[m]alice, an essential element of murder, is implied from the intentional commission of the underlying felony even though the actual killing might be accidental." . . .

C. *Justification, excuse, and mitigation*

Even where an individual kills with one of the four states of mind described above, the killing is not malicious if it is justified, excused, or committed under recognized circumstances of mitigation. Implicit in the notion of malice aforethought is "the absence of every sort of justification, excuse or mitigation." The absence of justification, excuse, or mitigation is thus an essential component of malice, and in turn of second-degree murder, on which the government bears the ultimate burden of persuasion. For example, even an intentional killing, if it comports with legally accepted notions of self-defense, is not malicious; it is excused and accordingly no crime at all.

Unlike circumstances of justification or excuse, legally recognized mitigating factors do not constitute a total defense to a murder charge. Such circumstances may, however, serve to "reduc[e] the degree of criminality" of a homicide otherwise committed with an intent to kill, an intent to injure, or in conscious and wanton disregard of life. Though such mitigating circumstances most frequently arise "where the killer has been provoked or is acting in the heat of passion, with the latter including fear, resentment and terror, as well as rage and anger," mitigation may also be found in other circumstances, such as "when excessive force is used in self-defense or in defense of another and '[a] killing [is] committed in the mistaken belief that one may be in mortal danger.' " The mitigation principle is predicated on the legal system's recognition of the "weaknesses" or "infirmity" of human nature . . . . Legally recognized mitigating factors serve to extenuate or "dampen[ ]," the otherwise malicious nature of the perpetrator's mental state, and thus serve as a bar to a conviction for murder.

---

[12] The fact that a reasonable person would have been aware of the risk will not sustain a finding of malice, though it may sustain a conviction for manslaughter. As Judge Leventhal explained in *United States v. Dixon,* 135 U.S.App.D.C. 401, (1969), "[t]he difference between that recklessness which displays depravity and such extreme and wanton disregard for human life as to constitute 'malice' and that recklessness that amounts only to manslaughter lies in the quality of the awareness of the risk." Along similar lines, we stated in *United States v. Bradford,* 344 A.2d 208, 215 n. 22 (D.C.1975): "In terms of the actor's awareness of the risk to life, if he is aware of risk, the crime is murder and not involuntary manslaughter. If he is not aware . . . and he should have been aware, the crime is involuntary manslaughter."

D. *Voluntary manslaughter*

In this jurisdiction, a homicide constitutes voluntary manslaughter where the perpetrator kills with a state of mind which, but for the presence of legally recognized mitigating circumstances, would render the killing murder. This definition of voluntary manslaughter reflects the traditional common law view and the prevailing national norm, as indicated by the formulations in numerous criminal law treatises. . . .

. . . [I]n every reported case we have found from a jurisdiction which divides manslaughter into its voluntary and involuntary forms discussing killings resulting from the delivery of a single or a few blows, not administered with intent to kill or inflict serious bodily injury, such killings are classified as involuntary, rather than voluntary manslaughter. . . .

We must conclude, in conformity with the overwhelming weight of authority on the matter, that voluntary manslaughter involves only those homicides where the perpetrator's state of mind would constitute malice aforethought and the homicide murder, but for the presence of legally recognized mitigating circumstances. If the perpetrator's state of mind is not one which would constitute malice, the fact that he or she intends to inflict non-serious injury or otherwise direct force against the victim does not render a killing voluntary manslaughter. Thus, to the extent that a death resulting from conduct accompanied by an intent to cause something less than serious bodily injury rises to the level of an unlawful homicide, it is governed by the involuntary manslaughter doctrines to which we now turn.

E. *Involuntary manslaughter*

As described in the preceding subsection, voluntary manslaughter is a killing committed with an intent to kill or do serious bodily injury, or with a conscious disregard of an extreme risk of death or serious bodily injury, where the presence of mitigating factors precludes a determination that the killing was malicious. The absence of malice under these circumstances thus reduces the offense to one form of manslaughter. In contrast, where a killing is not committed with a specific intent to kill or do serious bodily injury, or in conscious disregard of an extreme risk of death or serious bodily injury, there is no question that the killing was without malice. However, even such an unintentional or accidental killing is unlawful, and thus constitutes involuntary manslaughter, unless it is justifiable or excusable. Indeed, it is the absence of circumstances of justification or excuse which renders a non-malicious killing "unlawful." Accordingly, one key to distinguishing those unintentional killings which are unlawful, and hence manslaughter, from those to which no homicide liability attaches is determining the circumstances under which a killing will be legally excused.

Generally, at common law, where a person kills another in doing a "lawful act in a lawful manner," the homicide is excusable. As this phrase implies, two categories of unintentional killings were not excused and thus were manslaughter: killings in the course of lawful acts carried out in an unlawful, *i.e.*, criminally negligent,[29] fashion, and killings in the course of unlawful, *i.e.*, criminal, acts.

1. Criminal-negligence involuntary manslaughter

The law pertaining to the first category, which may be labelled "criminal-negligence" manslaughter, has undergone considerable transformation, and the cases have steadily narrowed the range of conduct deemed sufficiently culpable to sustain a manslaughter conviction. In the thirteenth century, it appears that even a person who caused death "by misadventure," or in a completely non-negligent fashion, had no legal defense to a homicide charge. By the mid-eighteenth century, however, if a death-producing act "was done with due caution, or was accompanied only by slight negligence," the perpetrator lacked the "culpable negligence" required to render the homicide manslaughter.

Under current law in the District of Columbia, one who unintentionally causes the death of another as the result of non-criminal conduct is guilty of involuntary manslaughter only where that conduct both creates "extreme danger to life or of serious bodily injury," and amounts to "a gross deviation from a reasonable standard of care." Thus, provided it does not fall within the scope of the misdemeanor-manslaughter doctrine, conduct resulting in death is excused unless it creates an extreme risk of death or serious bodily injury. Indeed, in our jurisprudence the only difference between risk-creating activity sufficient to sustain a "depraved heart" murder conviction and an involuntary reckless manslaughter conviction "lies in the quality of [the actor's] awareness of the risk. The gravity of the risk of death or serious bodily injury required in each case is the same.[32]

---

[29] As used here, "criminally negligent" is a generic term used to describe the appropriate degree of negligence required to render a killing involuntary manslaughter. As discussed below, the law has evolved to demand increasingly heightened levels of negligence for an involuntary manslaughter conviction. Additionally, jurisdictions today differ on the degree of negligence required to render an unintentional or accidental killing involuntary manslaughter.

[32] In this regard, the law in the District of Columbia differs from the prevailing approach to "criminal-negligence" manslaughter. Most jurisdictions appear to permit the imposition of involuntary manslaughter liability on death-producing conduct involving something less than an "extreme" risk of death or serious bodily [sic]; a "high degree of risk of death or serious bodily injury" will suffice. Moreover, the "modern view, evidenced by the position taken in most of the recent comprehensive criminal codes, is to require for involuntary manslaughter a consciousness of risk." Accordingly, generally it is the gravity of the risk created by the actor, rather than his or her awareness of that risk, which serves as the principal distinguishing feature between "depraved heart" murder and involuntary manslaughter. However, many of these jurisdictions have also enacted negligent homicide statutes which permit imposition of at least minor homicide

2. Misdemeanor involuntary manslaughter

The second category of unexcused unintentional homicides are those occurring in the course of certain unlawful acts. Centuries ago, the "unlawful act" category of involuntary manslaughter included all killings occurring in the course of a criminal act not amounting to a felony, *i.e.,* a misdemeanor. The doctrine became known as the "misdemeanor-manslaughter rule," something of an analogue to the felony-murder rule. As time passed, however, the misdemeanor-manslaughter rule "came to be considered too harsh," and "the courts began to place limitations upon it. Thus, in many jurisdictions, a homicide occurring in the course of a misdemeanor is involuntary manslaughter only if the offense is *malum in se,* rather than *malum prohibitum.*[34] Where the misdemeanor manslaughter doctrine applies, involuntary manslaughter liability attaches even where the defendant does not act with the degree of recklessness ordinarily required for involuntary manslaughter predicated on criminally negligent behavior. In effect, the defendant's intentional commission of a misdemeanor supplies the culpability required to impose homicide liability. . . .

[The court then proceeded to find the jury instructions erroneous, remanding the cases for new trials].

Reversed and remanded.

D. Common Law Murder

As noted in the *Comber* case, common law murder is the killing of a human being with malice aforethought. Malice aforethought, i.e., malice, could be proved by one of the following: (1) intent to kill; (2) intent to inflict grievous bodily harm; (3) knowing creation, or conscious disregard, of a very high risk of death or great bodily harm (depraved heart); or (4) intent to commit a felony where a death results during the commission or attempted commission of the felony (felony-murder).[*] Although the word "aforethought" suggests that the person carefully thought about the killing ahead of time—and it may have

---

liability even in cases where the perpetrator did not realize the risk created by his or her conduct.

[34] *Malum in se* is defined as "[a] wrong in itself. . . . An act is said to be *malum in se* when it is inherently and essentially evil, that is, immoral in its nature and injurious in its consequences, without any regard to the fact of its being noticed or punished by the law of the state." BLACK'S LAW DICTIONARY 865 (5th ed. 1979). *Malum prohibitum* is defined as "[a] wrong prohibited . . .; an act which is not inherently immoral, but becomes so because its commission is expressly forbidden by positive law. . . ." *Id.*

[*] Felony murder will be discussed in a separate section of this chapter.

meant that at some point in history—that is not required for murder as it developed in American law. For more information, see Joshua Dressler, *Understanding Criminal Law* §§31.01–31.10 (6th ed. 2012).

While statutes discussing degrees of murder will be reviewed later in this chapter, it is helpful to know that when a statute (e.g., second degree murder) refers to the crime of murder without separately redefining it, the crime derives its meaning from the common law.

E. "Depraved Heart" Form of Common Law Murder

If intent to kill or intent to inflict grievous bodily harm is present, it is generally not difficult to see (e.g., a person shoots a bullet at another's head or at a less vital part of the body). The more difficult situation is presented in ascertaining whether the act of killing should be punished as "depraved heart" murder. With depraved heart murder, the defendant (1) created a very high degree of risk of death or great bodily harm and (2) he was subjectively aware of that risk (generally viewed as a *knowing* creation, or *conscious* disregard, of a very high risk of death or great bodily harm)—all in the absence of any excuse, justification, or provocation.

As you read through the *Banks* case, think about when the defendant crossed the line and committed depraved heart murder. Does the court note any analogous situations? Would it still be murder if the defendant was a passenger and as he stood up he lost his balance, his gun falling on the floor and killing the brakeman upon discharge?

Banks v. State, 85 Tex. Crim. 165 (1919)

LATTIMORE, J.

In this case appellant was convicted in the district court of Polk county of the offense of murder, and his punishment fixed at death.

On his appeal but one question is presented and but one question was contained in the motion for new trial, namely, that the evidence does not show appellant guilty of that character of homicide which should be punished by the extreme penalty of death.

It appears from the record that on the night of the homicide, and while at his post of duty on a moving railroad train one Hawkins, a negro brakeman, was shot and killed by some member of a party of negroes who were walking along a dirt road near to the railroad track. No reason is assigned for such shooting, and it does not appear that appellant or any member of the party was acquainted with any of the parties on the train, and that any specific malice could be directed toward the deceased, but under our law the same is not necessary.

One who deliberately uses a deadly weapon in such reckless manner as to evince a heart regardless of social duty and fatally bent on mischief, as is shown by firing into a moving railroad train upon which human beings necessarily are, cannot shield himself from the consequences of his acts by disclaiming malice. Malice may be toward a group of persons as well as toward an individual. It may exist without former grudges or antecedent menaces. The intentional doing of any wrongful act in such manner and under such circumstances as that the death of a human being may result therefrom is malice. In the instant case the appellant admits his presence and participation in the shooting which resulted in the death of the deceased. His written statement, introduced in evidence, is as follows: . . .

"On last Sunday night, Sept. 29th, in company with John L. Davis and Garnett Davis, I was going from New Willard to Leggett, Texas, and was walking the dirt road that runs parallel with the railroad track, and just a short way from New Willard we saw a train coming south on the H. E. & W. T. track, and just before the engine passed us, John L. Davis said, 'Less shoot into that train,' and I said, 'No, less don't do that,' and then Garnett Davis said, 'Yes, less shoot into it,' and just before the engine passed us John L. Davis handed me his pistol and said, 'Here, take this, and you can burn it,' and I said, 'No,' but I took the pistol and just as the train passed I shot into the ground by the wire fence, and looked around, and I saw Garnett Davis shoot into the engine, and as the caboose passed I shot again into the ground, and Garnett Davis shot into the caboose, and we walked on by the side of the road a little in the bushes, and soon we met two automobiles, and I said, 'Less shoot into these cars,' and John L. said, 'No, you have all shot enough,' and I said, 'Yes, but I did not hit anybody, for I shot into the ground.' We then crossed the dirt road and through the wire fence and on to the railroad, and while we were walking along, both Garnett and John L. took the empty shells out of their guns. We all walked the railroad until we came to the place where Garnett left the railroad, and there we separated, and John L. and myself walked on to Leggett, and I never saw Garnett any more until Tuesday, and I went to his house and we talked about the shooting, and he told me he had not heard of the man being killed until Monday at dinner time. I told him then that I did not shoot at the train, but that I shot at the ground, and he said, 'I shot at the gangway,' and he asked me not to say anything about it, and I told him I would not unless they put me in jail and made me tell it, and then I was going to tell the truth. The gun I shot was the gun that John L. Davis had with him that night, and was a .38 long, and the gun Garnett was shooting was a .45 caliber. John L. Davis did not shoot at the train, and the shooting was done by myself and Garnett Davis. Garnett and myself were close together when we did the shooting and John L. was a little behind us. [Signed] Tom Banks, Jr. . . ."

An examination of this statement shows a deliberate unprovoked shooting into a moving train, an act which could reasonably result in the destruction of human life. No excuse or justification is pleaded, or shown in the evidence for the act. . . . In this case the proof shows that two pistols were used, and appellant so states in his statement above, and also he therein says that the pistol he used was a .38 caliber and the one used by his companion was a .45

caliber. It was conclusively shown by the other evidence that the bullet which killed deceased at the front end of the moving train, and also the one which entered the caboose at the rear of the same train, were .38-caliber bullets. This evidence negatives the fact that the fatal shot was fired by appellant's companion, and fully justified the jury in concluding that the portion of appellant's statement in which he says that he fired into the ground was untrue, and also fully sustained the conclusion of the jury that his were the shots which took the life of deceased. Nor can we see that the jury was not justified in assessing the extreme penalty of the law. That man who can coolly shoot into a moving train, or automobile, or other vehicle in which are persons guiltless of any wrongdoing toward him or provocation for such attack is, if possible, worse than the man who endures insult or broods over a wrong, real or fancied, and then waylays and kills his personal enemy. . . . Of kindred spirit is he who can shoot in the darkness into houses, crowds, or trains and recklessly send into eternity those whom he does not know and against whom he has no sort of reason for directing his malevolence.

The only contention here being that the evidence does not support the verdict, with which we are unable to agree, and there being no errors shown in the charge of the court or otherwise, we direct that the judgment of the lower court be affirmed.

The judgment of the lower court is affirmed.

F.   Degrees of Murder Approach

Common law murder treated all murderers in the same way—it made no difference whether the defendant was a serial killer or someone like Mr. Banks. When state legislatures started codifying common law murder, many felt that there were some crimes of homicide that were worse than others; hence, the degrees of murder model developed.

It is important to remember that every state that has adopted a degrees of murder approach has its own statute. Because the statutes often vary from state to state, it is essential to carefully read your state's statute to see how it varies from the Pennsylvania model. For more information, see Joshua Dressler, *Understanding Criminal Law* §§31.02–31.03 (6th ed. 2012).

1.   Pennsylvania Degrees of Murder Model

The *Drum* case introduces the degrees of murder approach by providing an early statute from the State of Pennsylvania that became a model for much of the country. This approach is often referred to as the "degrees of murder model" or the "Pennsylvania model." In addition, the *Drum* case provides jury instructions (affirmed by the court), which are helpful in understanding the terms in both first degree and second degree murder. Do not worry that you cannot find the facts of the case—other than noting that the case involves the killing of a David Mohigan, no facts are provided in this excerpt.

After reading the *Drum* case, break down the statute ("Act of 31st March 1860") and determine the various theories for prosecuting a person for both first and second degree murder.

Commonwealth v. Drum, 58 Pa. 9 (1868)

. . . Justice AGNEW charged the jury as follows: . . .

The law of our state has made wilful, deliberate and premeditated murder a capital crime. Sworn, as we are, to obey that law, we must know no other guide, remembering that the powers that be are ordained of God, and that we needs must be subject to them, not only for the wrath they may invoke, but for our own conscience' sake. Then hold the balance firmly, that justice may be done both to the Commonwealth and to the prisoner; such words as rich and poor, high and low, should have no place in your thoughts. You would not willingly err, but you must endeavor not to err. Search your consciences for the source of every judgment. Let your convictions, carefully and deliberately formed, be such that you may follow them to their fountain in the hidden depths of the heart where the Unseen Eye alone can penetrate, and there, in that dread presence, challenge their true source.

A life has been taken. The unfortunate David Mohigan has fallen into an untimely grave; struck down by the hand of violence; and it is for you to determine whose was that hand, and what its guilt. The prisoner is in the morning of life; as yet so fresh and fair. As you sat and gazed into his youthful face, you have thought, no doubt, most anxiously thought, is his that hand? Can he, indeed, be a murderer? This, gentlemen, is the solemn question you must determine upon the law and the evidence.

At the common law murder is described to be, when a person of sound memory and discretion unlawfully kills any reasonable creature in being and under the peace of the Commonwealth, with malice aforethought, expressed or implied. The distinguishing criterion of murder is malice aforethought. But it is not malice in its ordinary understanding alone, a particular ill-will, a spite or a grudge. Malice is a legal term, implying much more. It comprehends not only a particular ill-will, but every case where there is wickedness of disposition, hardness of heart, cruelty, recklessness of consequences, and a mind regardless of social duty, although a particular person may not be intended to be injured. Murder, therefore, at common law embraces cases where no intent to kill existed, but where the state or frame of mind termed malice, in its legal sense, prevailed.

In Pennsylvania, the legislature, considering that there is a manifest difference in the degree of guilt, where a deliberate intention to kill exists, and where none appears, distinguished murder into two grades--murder of the first and murder of the second degree; and provided that the jury before whom any person indicted for murder should be tried, shall, if they find him guilty thereof, ascertain in their verdict whether it be murder of the first or murder of the second degree. By the Act of 31st March 1860, "all murder which shall be perpetrated by means of poison, or by lying in wait, or by any other kind of wilful, deliberate and premeditated killing, or which shall be committed in the perpetration of, or attempt to perpetrate any arson, rape, robbery or burglary, shall be deemed murder of the first degree; and all other kinds of murder shall be deemed murder of the second degree."

In this case we have to deal only with that kind of murder in the first degree described as "wilful, deliberate, and premeditated." Many cases have been decided under this clause, in all of which it has been held that the *intention* to kill is the essence of the offence. Therefore, if an intention to kill exists, it is wilful; if this intention be accompanied by such circumstances as evidence a mind fully conscious of its own purpose and design, it is deliberate; and if sufficient time be afforded to enable the mind fully to frame the design to kill, and to select the instrument, or to frame the plan to carry this design into execution, it is premeditated. The law fixes upon no length of time as necessary to form the intention to kill, but leaves the existence of a fully formed intent as a fact to be determined by the jury, from all the facts and circumstances in the evidence.

A learned judge (Judge Rush, in Commonwealth v. Richard Smith) has said: "It is equally true both in fact and from experience, that *no* time is too short for a wicked man to frame in his mind his scheme of murder, and to contrive the means of accomplishing it." But this expression must be qualified, lest it mislead. It is true that such is the swiftness of human thought, that no time is so short in which a wicked man may not form a design to kill, and frame the means of executing his purpose; yet this suddenness is opposed to premeditation, and a jury must be well convinced upon the evidence that there was time to deliberate and premeditate. The law regards, and the jury must find, the actual intent; that is to say, the fully formed purpose to kill, with so much time for deliberation and premeditation, as to convince them that this purpose is not the immediate offspring of rashness and impetuous temper, and that the mind has become fully conscious of its own design. If there be time to frame in the mind, fully and consciously, the intention to kill, and to select the weapon or means of death, and to think and know beforehand, though the time be short, the use to be made of it, there is time to deliberate and to premeditate.

The proof of the intention to kill, and of the disposition of mind constituting murder in the first degree, under the Act of Assembly, lies on the Commonwealth. But this proof need not be express or positive. It may be inferred from the circumstances. If, from all the facts attending the killing, the jury can fully, reasonably, and satisfactorily infer the existence of the intention to kill, and the malice of heart with which it was done, they will be warranted in so doing. He who uses upon the body of another, at some vital part, with a manifest intention to use it upon him, a deadly weapon, as an axe, a gun, a knife or a pistol, must, in the absence of qualifying facts, be presumed to know that his blow is likely to kill; and, knowing this, must be presumed to intend the death which is the probable and ordinary consequence of such an act. He who so uses a deadly weapon without a sufficient cause of provocation, must be presumed to do it wickedly, or from a bad heart. Therefore, he who takes the life of another with a deadly weapon, and with a manifest design thus to use it upon him, with sufficient time to deliberate, and fully to form the conscious purpose of killing, and without any sufficient reason or cause of extenuation, is guilty of murder in the first degree.

All murder not of the first degree, is necessarily of the second degree, and includes all unlawful killing under circumstances of depravity of heart, and a disposition of mind regardless of social duty; but where no intention to kill exists or can be reasonably and fully inferred. Therefore, in all cases of murder, if no intention to kill can be inferred or collected from the circumstances, the verdict must be murder in the second degree. . . .

You will now take the case and render such a verdict as the evidence warrants; one which will do justice to the Commonwealth and to the prisoner.

2. First Degree Murder

The *Perez* case explores what kind of evidence is sufficient to find that the killing was willful, deliberate, and premeditated[*] under a first degree murder statute. In a more subtle way, the case is also instructive in ascertaining the necessary mens rea absent a confession. How is the jury to know whether a defendant's conduct meets these three elements? How can the fact finder discern what is in the defendant's mind?

As you read the case, keep in mind that the standard of review on appeal for sufficiency of evidence questions is "whether *any* rational trier of fact could have been persuaded beyond a reasonable doubt that defendant premeditated the murder." The appellate court does not start from scratch on a clean slate—it is not supposed to decide the case based on what it would have decided as the fact finder.

People v. Perez, 2 Cal. 4th 1117 (1992) (In Bank)

PANELLI, Justice.

We granted review in this case after a divided Court of Appeal reduced defendant's first degree murder conviction to second degree murder for

---

[*] In proving premeditation and deliberation in Michigan, a prosecutor needs only to show that the defendant had time to "take a second look" before the ultimate killing. *See People v. Unger*, 278 Mich. App. 210 (2008).

insufficient evidence of premeditation and deliberation. As explained hereafter, we conclude that the judgment of the Court of Appeal should be reversed.

FACTS

Defendant killed Victoria Mesa in her home in Garden Grove on the morning of September 30, 1988. There is no question that he was the perpetrator. The only question is the circumstances under which the murder occurred—that is, whether it was premeditated and deliberate.

Michael Mesa, the victim's husband, testified that he left for work about 5:40 a.m. on the morning of the murder, while Victoria was still asleep. As part of their morning ritual he would leave her a note and call her before she left for work. Victoria was four months' pregnant, and Michael was concerned about her condition. This was to be their first child after years of unsuccessful attempts to have a child. In order to protect the pregnancy, Victoria's cervix had been sewn shut, and she could not have sexual relations. Michael called Victoria the morning of the murder about 7:35 a.m., before she left for work. She usually left for work around 8 a.m. He heard the sound of an automobile engine running in the background. The engine could have been his wife's car.

A neighbor who generally left for work at the same time as Victoria noticed Victoria's car in the driveway with exhaust coming from it. He also noticed that the front door to the house was open. The neighbor thought that it was about 8:05 a.m. when he drove by.

Victoria's employer called Michael about 9:45 a.m. to tell him that Victoria had not come to work. Michael called a neighbor to ask her to check on Victoria. The neighbor enlisted the aid of a gas company meter reader who, upon approaching the house, found the front door slightly ajar; he entered, found Victoria's body, and immediately left to call the police.

Police officers arrived about 9:50 a.m. and found Victoria's fully clothed body lying face down with her arms under her head in the bathroom and her legs extending into the hallway. A broken dish and dog food were lying near the body. A six-inch blade of a serrated steak knife was found under Victoria's head. A broken piece of knife handle was near her feet. The wood appeared to be the same as the handles of knives in the kitchen drawer. There was no sign of a forced entry, and the only unlocked door was the front door.

There was a large pool of blood beneath Victoria's body and splatters all over the adjacent walls and carpet. Blood was found in every room except the nursery. There were blood drippings throughout the floor of the master bedroom. Dresser drawers were open, and drops of blood were on the clothing inside the drawers. Jewelry boxes were open and had drops of blood inside. There was blood on the sink in the master bathroom. Four Band-Aid wrappers were lying on the counter; a folded Band-Aid saturated with blood was found in the entry of the master bedroom. A guest bedroom had bloodstains in the doorway of the room almost on a direct line with the light switch.

The entire kitchen was peppered with blood spots. There were drops of blood on the refrigerator and counter top and smeared blood around the handles of cupboards and drawers. Many of the cupboards and drawers were open. There were drops of blood inside some of the drawers, including one containing knives.

Victoria's purse was on top of a table in the kitchen. The contents of the purse were lying on the table. A removable car stereo was also on the table. All of the items had drops of blood on them.

The victim's husband found nothing missing from the house except for one of his dress shirts.

According to the pathologist who performed the autopsy, Victoria bled to death. She had sustained blunt force trauma to her eyes, nose and lips, probably from a fist. There were about 38 knife wounds, including 26 stab and slash wounds and 12 puncture wounds. There were deep stab and slash wounds about the head, face, and neck, in the carotid artery, around the spinal column, and on the back of the arms. There were defensive wounds on her forearms, wrists, and hands. The injuries to the front part of the body were inflicted before the injuries to the back of the body. Two different knives were used. Most of the wounds were inflicted by a single-blade knife consistent with the one found under the victim's body. Three wounds in the back were inflicted by a double-edged knife. These wounds appeared to have been inflicted after the victim was dead.

The only connection between defendant and the victim and her husband was that they had attended the same high school some 10 years earlier. Defendant had played sports with Michael Mesa. Defendant lived about two and a quarter miles away and would drive by the Mesa house about twice a week in the early evening and wave to Michael as the latter was working in the yard. Defendant's fingerprint was found on the wall in the hallway near the victim's body and on a bloody Band-Aid wrapper found in the master bathroom. Analysis of blood scrapings from the master bedroom, wall phone, kitchen floor, blood-soaked towel on the water cooler, and blood-soaked Band-Aid from the master bedroom revealed that they were consistent with 1 percent of the population, which includes defendant. To Michael Mesa's knowledge, defendant had never been in his house before.

Defendant's sister testified that he arrived home about 9 a.m. on the day of the murder. His hand was cut, and he was sweaty and pale. Defendant told her he had cut his hand on a saw. Defendant said he was going to drive to his father's jobsite. His sister offered to drive him, but defendant declined.

At 9:20 a.m. the same day, defendant was treated at a hospital emergency room for severe cuts on his right hand and smaller cuts on his left hand. Defendant told the nurse that he had cut himself with a Skil Saw. Based on her experience, the nurse did not believe that defendant's injury was the result of having been cut by a Skil Saw.

As a result of information learned from the hospital, police officers went to defendant's home that night. Defendant told the officers he had injured himself at a jobsite at a private residence in Anaheim while using a Skil Saw. Defendant was unable to show the officers where the jobsite was. Defendant's father produced for officers the shirt that Michael Mesa identified as the one missing from his house.

Defendant did not testify, and he made no statements about the offense. In argument, defense counsel challenged the sufficiency of the evidence of first degree murder and suggested that whoever killed Victoria had acted in a rage. The jury returned a verdict of guilty of first degree, premeditated and deliberate murder. As previously mentioned, a divided Court of Appeal reduced the conviction to second degree murder.

DISCUSSION
Sufficiency of Evidence of Premeditation and Deliberation

The People contend that the Court of Appeal erred in finding the evidence of premeditation and deliberation insufficient to support the judgment. Before proceeding to that question, we find it helpful to review the definition of premeditation and deliberation that was given to the jury, CALJIC No. 8.20, which we have found to be a correct statement of the law. CALJIC No. 8.20 defines premeditated and deliberate murder as follows:

> All murder which is perpetrated by any kind of willful, deliberate and premeditated killing with express malice aforethought is murder of the first degree.
>
> The word 'willful' as used in this instruction, means intentional.
>
> The word 'deliberate' means formed or arrived at or determined upon as a result of careful thought and weighing of considerations for and against the proposed course of action. The word 'premeditated' means considered beforehand.
>
> If you find that the killing was preceded and accompanied by a clear, deliberate intent on the part of the defendant to kill, which was the result of deliberation and premeditation, so that it must have been formed upon pre-existing reflection and not under a sudden heat of passion or other condition precluding the idea of deliberation, it is murder of the first degree.
>
> The law does not undertake to measure in units of time the length of the period during which the thought must be pondered before it can ripen into an intent to kill which is truly deliberate and premeditated. The time will vary with different individuals and under varying circumstances.

> The true test is not the duration of time, but rather the extent of the reflection. A cold, calculated judgment and decision may be arrived at in a short period of time, but a mere unconsidered and rash impulse, even though it included an intent to kill, is not such deliberation and premeditation as will fix an unlawful killing as murder of the first degree.
>
> To constitute a deliberate and premeditated killing, the slayer must weigh and consider the question of killing and the reasons for and against such a choice and, having in mind the consequences, he decides to and does kill.

Review on appeal of the sufficiency of the evidence supporting the finding of premeditated and deliberate murder involves consideration of the evidence presented and all logical inferences from that evidence in light of the legal definition of premeditation and deliberation that was previously set forth. Settled principles of appellate review require us to review the entire record in the light most favorable to the judgment below to determine whether it discloses substantial evidence—that is, evidence which is reasonable, credible, and of solid value—from which a reasonable trier of fact could find that the defendant premeditated and deliberated beyond a reasonable doubt. . . .

In challenging the Court of Appeal's reversal of the first degree murder conviction, the People argue that there is sufficient evidence to support the jury's verdict of premeditated and deliberate murder under traditional standards of review and that the Court of Appeal majority misapplied *People v. Anderson* (1968) 70 Cal.2d 15, in reaching a contrary determination. We agree.

In *People v. Anderson,* this court surveyed a number of prior cases involving the sufficiency of the evidence to support findings of premeditation and deliberation. From the cases surveyed, the court distilled certain guidelines to aid reviewing courts in analyzing the sufficiency of the evidence to sustain findings of premeditation and deliberation. The *Anderson* analysis was intended only as a framework to aid in appellate review; it did not propose to define the elements of first degree murder or alter the substantive law of murder in any way. Nor did *Anderson* change the traditional standards of appellate review that we have set forth above. The *Anderson* guidelines are descriptive, not normative. The goal of *Anderson* was to aid reviewing courts in assessing whether the evidence is supportive of an inference that the killing was the result of preexisting reflection and weighing of considerations rather than mere unconsidered or rash impulse.

In identifying categories of evidence bearing on premeditation and deliberation, *Anderson* did not purport to establish an exhaustive list that would exclude all other types and combinations of evidence that could support a finding of premeditation and deliberation. From the cases surveyed, the *Anderson* court identified three categories of evidence pertinent to the determination of premeditation and deliberation: (1) planning activity, (2) motive, and (3) manner of killing. Regarding these categories, *Anderson* stated: "Analysis of the cases will show that this court sustains verdicts of first degree murder typically when there is evidence of all three types and otherwise requires at least extremely strong evidence of (1) or evidence of (2) in conjunction with either (1) or (3)." It is thus evident from the court's own words that it was attempting to do no more than catalog common factors that had occurred in prior cases. The *Anderson* factors, while helpful for purposes of review, are not a sine qua non to finding first degree premeditated murder, nor are they exclusive. . . .

. . . From the evidence presented, the jury reasonably could have inferred the following: Defendant surreptitiously entered the house while Victoria was warming up her car; there were no signs of forced entry or of the presence of an additional car. Defendant surprised her as she was carrying the dog food; the broken dog dish and dog food were strewn about the floor. Defendant first beat Victoria about the head and neck with his fists. Then he stabbed her with a steak knife obtained from the victim's kitchen; the handle and blade were consistent with knives in the kitchen drawer. When that knife broke, cutting him, defendant went in search of another knife; drippings of defendant's blood were found all over the kitchen, including a drawer containing knives. Regardless of defendant's motive for entering the house, once confronted by Victoria, who knew him and could identify him, he determined to kill her to avoid identification.

As so viewed, the evidence is sufficient to support the jury's findings of premeditation and deliberation. Evidence of planning activity is shown by the fact that defendant did not park his car in the victim's driveway, he surreptitiously entered the house, and he obtained a knife from the kitchen. As to motive, regardless of what inspired the initial entry and attack, it is reasonable to infer that defendant determined it was necessary to kill Victoria to prevent her from identifying him. She was acquainted with him from high school and obviously would have been able to identify him. The manner of killing is also indicative of premeditation and deliberation. The evidence of blood in the kitchen knife drawer supports an inference that defendant went to the kitchen in search of another knife after the steak knife broke. This action bears similarity to reloading a gun or using another gun when the first one has run out of ammunition.

Thus, though the evidence is admittedly not overwhelming, it is sufficient to sustain the jury's finding. As we have stated, the relevant question on appeal is not whether *we* are convinced beyond a reasonable doubt, but whether *any* rational trier of fact could have been persuaded beyond a reasonable doubt that defendant premeditated the murder. We have previously observed that premeditation can occur in a brief period of time. "The true test is not the duration of time as much as it is the extent of the reflection. Thoughts may follow each other with great rapidity and cold, calculated judgment may be arrived at quickly . . . ."

Defendant challenges the strength of the inferences we have set forth, claiming that they are speculative and insubstantial. He asserts that it is speculative that the steak knife came from the kitchen. We disagree. Although one might think of other possibilities, the most reasonable inference is that the knife came from the kitchen, because it matched the kitchen knives and the victim's husband testified that he and Victoria were well-organized and kept everything in its place. Defendant dismisses reliance on the use of the second knife by noting that the coroner's testimony indicated that the wounds inflicted by it were post-mortem and in nonvital areas. There is no indication, however, that it would have been readily apparent, at the time of the assault, that the victim was already dead. She was knocked to the ground and lay bleeding to death; defendant would not have known the precise moment of death or which wound would cause it. Moreover, the jury could reasonably infer that the post-mortem wounds were inflicted to make certain the victim was dead. Given that the post-mortem wounds were inflicted after defendant had broken the first knife and used a second knife to inflict these wounds, it is difficult to characterize defendant's conduct as "mere rash and unconsidered impulse." Some period of time necessarily must have elapsed between the first and second set of wounds. While this conduct, in itself, may not necessarily support a finding of premeditation, in conjunction with the manner of killing, it could easily have led the jury to infer premeditation and deliberation.

Additionally, the conduct of defendant *after* the stabbing, such as the search of dresser drawers, jewelry boxes, kitchen drawers and the changing of a Band-Aid on his bloody hand, would appear to be inconsistent with a state of mind that would have produced a rash, impulsive killing. Here, defendant did not immediately flee the scene. Again, while not sufficient in themselves to establish premeditation and deliberation, these are facts which a jury could reasonably consider in relation to the manner of killing. . . .

Accordingly, we conclude that the evidence is sufficient to sustain the jury's finding of premeditation and deliberation and that the judgment of the Court of Appeal should be reversed. . . .

CONCLUSION

The judgment of the Court of Appeal is reversed.

3. Common Law Murder and Second Degree Murder

In enacting statutes, legislatures are the source of most criminal laws today. Remember that, in interpreting statutes based on a common law crimes, courts look to the common law to give meaning to the crime (unless the legislature separately redefines the crime).

In the *Edwards* case, the defendant was convicted of second degree murder for driving drunk and killing another. As you know from the *Drum* case, second degree murder is a statutory crime often defined as follows: "All other murder is second degree murder." Since "murder" is a common law crime and no separate statutory definition is given, we must look to common law to give meaning to this crime. What form of common law murder did the court examine in *Edwards*?

For an interesting contrast, be sure to revisit the *Edwards* case after reading *Commonwealth v. McLaughlin* contained within the manslaughter section of this chapter.

Edwards v. State, 202 Tenn. 393 (1957)

TOMLINSON, Justice.

While State Highway Patrolman Morris was standing on the edge of State Highway No. 70 he was struck and instantly killed by an automobile then being driven by James Edwards, who was drunk. Edwards was convicted of murder in the second degree, and has appealed.

A homicide of this character, generally speaking, is either involuntary manslaughter, or second degree murder, dependent upon the facts of each particular case. It is insisted in behalf of Edwards that there are no facts in this case from which the jury could reasonably infer malice; therefore, that Edwards' offense is involuntary manslaughter. The theory of this insistence is that Edwards was so drunk at the time as not to know what he was doing; hence, that, necessarily, the element of malice is absent.

In a homicide case "it is murder though the perpetrator was drunk. . . . Hence a party cannot show that he was so drunk as not to be capable of entertaining a malicious feeling. The conclusion of law is against him." Therefore, the question here is whether facts justifiably deducible from the evidence permit a finding by the jury of malice upon the part of Edwards.

At a point on State Highway No. 70 a short distance west of the corporate limits of the town of Lebanon, Patrolman Morris accompanied by a friend, Tommy Knowles, stopped for an official purpose a car driven east by soldier Sanford. When the soldier's car was brought to a stop its left rear wheel was thirteen inches south of the edge of the paved portion of the highway, and facing east, towards Lebanon. The car driven by patrolman Morris was parked behind it faced in the same direction and about the same distance from the paved portion of the highway. Knowles remained seated therein.

Patrolman Morris stood on the ground at the left front door of the soldier's car and examined his driver's license, etc. He had just returned these documents when there passed traveling towards Lebanon an automobile at a speed estimated at between 50 to 60 miles per hour.

It passed the patrol car "with a great gust" at a speed which "raised the side of it up". It then struck and knocked patrolman Morris a distance of 45 feet east of the soldier's car. Before striking Morris, as Morris stood on the ground at the left front door of the soldier's automobile, Edwards' automobile scraped the left rear fender of the soldier's car and on up the body of the soldier's car to where the patrolman was standing. It necessarily, therefore, was traveling with its right wheels on the right shoulder of the highway since the left wheels of the soldier's car were thirteen and fourteen inches, respectively, over on that car's right hand shoulder of the road.

Edwards did not stop his car though he told the sheriff the next morning that he "knew he hit something but didn't know what".

Edwards was pursued by Knowles in the patrol car, but was unsuccessful in efforts to stop him, until he forced Edwards' car to the shoulder of the road. Edwards was so drunk that the officers doubt that he understood what was then being said. It was there that his wife said "I tried to get you to stop and you wouldn't do it",—a remark to which Edwards made no response.

Since the court is permitted to know what the general public knows, it takes judicial knowledge of the fact that Highway No. 70 leading from Nashville to Lebanon and on east is a paved highway upon which traffic is very heavy. This highway from the point where Morris was struck is level for a distance west (towards Nashville) for more than a mile. It was from the west that Edwards was driving. The rear lights of the two parked automobiles, and the spot light of the patrol car, were burning. It was between 11 and 11:30 P.M.

Since no evidence was offered in behalf of Edwards other than in an unsuccessful effort to establish a reputation of sobriety, it is not known as to when Edwards began on this occasion to drink. It is permissible, however, to conclude (1) from the evidence of the character witnesses offered by him that he lived somewhere in the vicinity of Lebanon and (2) was thus returning to his home at the time he ran Morris down.

It is inconceivable that a man can get as drunk as Edwards was on that occasion without previously realizing that he would get in that condition if he continued to drink. But he did continue to drink and presumably with knowledge that he was going to drive his car back to, or close to, Lebanon over this heavily traveled highway. He knew, of course, that such conduct would be directly perilous to human life. From his conduct in so doing, it was permissible for the jury to imply "such a high degree of conscious and willful recklessness as to amount to that malignity of heart constituting malice."

The facts mentioned brought into the deliberations of the jury the rule that: "The act of a motorist may fall within the cases of murder in such a manner as to evince a depraved mind, as where one voluntarily becomes intoxicated while driving a car, and then drives on the streets of a city at a high rate of speed, heedless of pedestrians or of his acts." . . .

Edwards requested the Court to instruct the jury that he could not be convicted of second degree murder because he was so drunk "at the time as not to know what he or she was doing". The action of the Court in refusing to so instruct the jury is assigned as error. Counsel made this request for Edwards under a misconception of the law, as hereinbefore set out. . . .

It is said that the Court erred in charging the jury that the wilfully becoming drunk, or partly so, and driving an automobile while in that condition "with knowledge that driving in such a condition was perilous to human life would constitute murder in the second degree". This is assigned as error on the ground that it was for the jury to determine from all the circumstances whether the element of malice essential to murder in the second degree might be implied.

Here again is demonstrated the attorney's erroneous opinion that the presence of malice is negatived by the fact that "there was abundant evidence that he was so drunk as not to be conscious of any impending peril at the time of the alleged homicide".

The instruction so given was correct. Immediately following it is the instruction as to the circumstances under which the act of Edwards may be involuntary manslaughter.

When the charge as a whole is considered, rather than isolated clauses therein, it is clear that the jury was given to understand that it was for it to determine whether Edwards' act amounted to second degree murder or involuntary manslaughter, or no offense at all. The jury could not have been misled by the instructions, and its verdict is not contrary to the preponderance of the evidence. . . .

Affirmed.

G. Manslaughter

This section looks at the two forms of manslaughter that developed from common law, involuntary and voluntary manslaughter. Jury instructions from *Commonwealth v. Drum*, 58 Pa. 9, 17 (1868), provide a good introduction:

> Manslaughter is defined to be the unlawful killing of another without malice expressed or implied; which may be voluntarily in a sudden heat, or involuntarily, but in the commission of an unlawful act. Voluntary manslaughter often so nearly approaches murder, it is necessary to distinguish it clearly. The difference is this: manslaughter is never attended by legal malice or depravity of heart—that condition or frame of mind before spoken of, exhibiting wickedness of disposition, recklessness of consequences or cruelty. Being sometimes a wilful act (as the term voluntary denotes) it is necessary that the circumstances should take away every evidence of cool depravity of heart or wanton cruelty. Therefore, to reduce an intentional blow, stroke or wounding, resulting in death, to voluntary manslaughter, there must be sufficient cause of provocation, and a state of rage or passion, without time to cool, placing the prisoner beyond the control of his reason, and suddenly impelling him

to the deed. If any of these be wanting—if there be provocation without passion, or passion without a sufficient cause of provocation, or there be time to cool, and reason has resumed its sway, the killing will be murder.

Insulting or scandalous words are not sufficient cause of provocation; nor are actual indignities to the person of a light and trivial kind. Whenever the act evidences a deadly revenge, and not the mere heat of blood; whenever it is the result of a devilish disposition, and not merely the phrensy of rage, it is not manslaughter, but murder.

1. Involuntary Manslaughter

Common law courts have used many terms to explain involuntary manslaughter, including "gross negligence," "criminal negligence," and "culpable negligence." With some variation between jurisdictions, these terms are generally referring to the crime of involuntary manslaughter. The following principles or concepts are often addressed by the courts when analyzing the crime of involuntary manslaughter: (1) Did the defendant's conduct create a high risk of death?; (2) Was the risk of death reasonably foreseeable?; (3) Was the defendant's conduct unreasonable (socially unacceptable from a public policy perspective)?; and (4) Was the defendant's conduct a substantial departure from how an ordinary person would act? Generally, no intent or awareness is necessary for this crime (but there are a growing number of states which have incorporated some level of awareness as an element of involuntary manslaughter).

Courts often refer to involuntary manslaughter as the "catch-all" homicide crime. Consider the comments of the Michigan Supreme Court in *People v. Holtschlag*, 471 Mich. 1, 6–7 (2004):

> Involuntary manslaughter has, first and foremost, always been considered the "catch-all" homicide crime. Thus, in [*People v. Datema*, 448 Mich. 585, 594–95 (1995)], we explained, quoting Perkins & Boyce, Criminal Law (3d ed), p 105, that "[i]nvoluntary manslaughter is a catch-all concept including all manslaughter not characterized as voluntary: 'Every unintentional killing of a human being is involuntary manslaughter if it is neither murder nor voluntary manslaughter nor within the scope of some recognized justification or excuse.' " Thus, the catch-all crime of involuntary manslaughter is typically characterized in terms of what it is *not,* and ascertaining whether a homicide is involuntary manslaughter requires essentially questioning first whether it is murder, voluntary manslaughter, or a

justified or excused homicide. If it is none of those, then the homicide, generally, is involuntary manslaughter.

In general, involuntary manslaughter involves something less than "depraved heart" murder from common law (a knowing creation, or conscious disregard of a very high risk of death or great bodily harm), but more than ordinary (i.e., tort) negligence. In studying the cases in this section, note how the courts often struggled with making this determination. For more information, see Joshua Dressler, *Understanding Criminal Law* §§31.05, 31.08–31.09 (6th ed. 2012).

a. Playing with Guns

In preparing to read the *Hardie* case, it is important to note that the prosecutor chose to charge the defendant with manslaughter and not depraved heart murder or any other form of murder. Why? If the prosecutor chose a murder charge, what difficulties would arise?

State v. Hardie, 47 Iowa 647 (1878)

ROTHROCK, CH. J.

It appears from the evidence that the defendant was a boarder in the family of one Gantz, who is his brother-in-law. On the day of the homicide defendant was engaged in varnishing furniture. Mrs. Sutfen, a neighbor, called at the house, and after some friendly conversation she went into the kitchen. When she came back defendant picked up a tack hammer and struck on the door. She said, "My God, I thought it was a revolver." A short time afterwards she went into the yard to get a kitten. Defendant said he would frighten her with the revolver as she came in. He took a revolver from a stand drawer and went out of the room, and was in the kitchen when the revolver was discharged. He immediately came in and said to Mrs. Gantz, his sister, "My God, Hannah, come and see what I have done." His sister went out and found Mrs. Sutfen lying on the sidewalk at the side of the house, with a gunshot wound in the head, and in a dying condition. A physician was immediately called and made an examination of the deceased, took the revolver from the defendant, and informed him that nothing could be done for the deceased, whereupon the defendant became violent, said the shot was accidental, and exclaimed several times that he would kill himself. It became necessary to secure him, which was done by tying him with ropes.

The revolver had been in the house for about five years. It was found by Gantz in the road. There was one load in it when found. Some six months after it was found Gantz tried to shoot the load from it and it would not go off. He tried to punch the load out, but could not move it. He then laid it away, thinking it was harmless. The defendant was about the house and knew the condition of the revolver. Upon one occasion Gantz said he would try to kill a cat with the revolver. Defendant being present said he would not be afraid to allow it to be snapped at him all day. The revolver remained in the same condition that it was when found, no other load having been put into it, and it was considered by the family as well as defendant as entirely harmless.

The foregoing is the substance of all the evidence.

The State did not claim that the defendant was guilty of murder, but that he was guilty of manslaughter because of criminal carelessness. The defendant insisted that there was no such carelessness as to render the act criminal, and that it was homicide by misadventure, and therefore excusable.

The court instructed the jury as follows: "5. And on the charge of manslaughter, I instruct you that if the defendant used a dangerous and deadly weapon, in a careless and reckless manner, by reason of which instrument so used he killed the deceased, then he is guilty of manslaughter, although no harm was in fact intended."

Other instructions of like import were given, and the question of criminal carelessness was submitted to the jury, as follows: "8th. And in this case I submit to you to find the facts of recklessness and carelessness under the evidence, and if you find that the death of the party was occasioned through recklessness and carelessness of the defendant then you should convict him, and if not you should acquit. And by this I do not mean that defendant is to be held to the highest degree of care and prudence in handling a dangerous and deadly weapon, but only such care as a reasonably prudent man should and ought to use under like circumstances, and if he did not use such care he should be convicted, otherwise he should be acquitted."

There can be no doubt that the instructions given by the court embody the correct rule as to criminal carelessness in the use of a deadly weapon. Counsel for defendant insist that the instructions of the court do not go far enough, and upon the trial asked that the court give to the jury the following instruction:

"3. Although the deceased came to her death from the discharge of a pistol in the hands of the defendant, yet if the defendant had good reason to believe, and did believe, that the pistol which caused her death was not in any manner dangerous, but was entirely harmless, and if he did nothing more than a man of ordinary prudence and caution might have done under like circumstances, then the jury should find him not criminally liable and should acquit."

This instruction and others of like import were refused by the court, and we think the ruling was correct. That the revolver was in fact a deadly weapon is conclusively shown by the terrible tragedy consequent upon defendant's act in firing it off. If it had been in fact unloaded no homicide would have resulted, but the defendant would have been justly censurable for a most reckless and imprudent act in frightening a woman by pretending that it was loaded, and that he was about to discharge it at her. No jury would be warranted in finding that men of ordinary prudence so conduct themselves. On the contrary, such conduct is grossly reckless and reprehensible, and without palliation or excuse. Human life is not to be sported with by the use of firearms, even though the person using them may have good reason to believe that the weapon used is not loaded, or that being loaded it will do no injury. When persons engage in such reckless sport they should be held liable for the consequences of their acts.

It is argued that the evidence does not show the defendant guilty of criminal carelessness, because it does not appear that the defendant pointed the pistol at the deceased, or how it happened to be discharged. The fact that defendant took the weapon from the drawer with the avowed purpose of frightening the deceased, and while in his hands it was discharged with fatal effect, together with his admission that he did the act, fully warranted the jury in finding that he purposely pointed the pistol and discharged it at the deceased.

AFFIRMED.

Note

In *State v. Kernes*, 262 N.W.2d 602, 604 (Iowa 1978), the Supreme Court of Iowa criticized *Hardie* and other decisions for the "indiscriminate blurring" of words like "negligence," "careless," and "reckless." Nevertheless, the facts of *Hardie* continue to provide a good example of involuntary manslaughter.

b. Manslaughter and Drunk Driving

Recall *Edwards v. State of Tennessee*, 202 Tenn. 393 (1957), a drunk driving case that was pursued as second degree murder. Other jurisdictions have treated drunk driving resulting in death as a second degree murder. *See, e.g., People v. Goecke*, 457 Mich. 442 (1998) (evidence was sufficient to bind over and convict defendants for malice second degree murder for death caused by drunk driving and speeding, which evidenced wanton disregard for human life). In reading *McLaughlin*, consider whether manslaughter is a more appropriate charge.

Commonwealth v. McLaughlin, 293 Pa. 218 (1928)

SCHAFFER, J.

Defendant, a young man 20 years of age at the time of the occurrence we are to deal with, appeals from his conviction and sentence for murder of the second degree, contending that the evidence produced against him did not establish this crime.

With two companions he was driving his father's automobile, about half past 10 o'clock at night, along Northampton street in Wilkes-Barre township in the county of Luzerne. His progress was down grade and was at the rate of 20 or 25 miles an hour. The highway was well lighted. Frank Ravitt and his wife were walking in the cartway of the street ahead of and in the same direction as the automobile, their presence within the street limits and not on the sidewalk being due to the pavement's bad condition. They were to the right-hand side of the center of the cartway, the wife in or near the street car track, the husband to her right, [h]e was pushing a baby coach in which was their infant child. Defendant so drove his automobile that it struck the group in the cartway, killing the husband and the baby and seriously injuring the wife. The impact was with such force as to knock the bodies of the man and woman a distance of from 25 to 50 feet and the child out of the coach and over onto the pavement. There was a dispute in the testimony as to whether the lights on the automobile were lit, and as to whether defendant sounded his horn as he approached the stricken people; whether he was intoxicated was likewise a controverted fact.

One of the commonwealth's most material witnesses, Lawrence Brosinski, the only person except defendant and the two others who were in the car with him who actually saw the tragedy, testified that if defendant "had swung his machine toward the side instead of the middle of the road he would never have struck these people." Defendant's story in amplification of this was that he blew his horn and noticed the two persons walking in the center of the road, that he had ample room to pass them to the right, that when he blew his horn "they seemed to be going to the left, and all of a sudden they veered to the right, and as they did I applied my brakes, but it was too late. I had already struck them— he [the husband] seemed to dart to the right quicker than I could get the machine stopped." In this recital he was corroborated by the two young men who were in the car with him. The automobile ran some distance, perhaps 200 feet beyond the point of the collision. Defendant and his companions ascribed this to the circumstance that in his excitement he took his foot off the brake. It appeared in the prosecution's case by the testimony of more than one witness that the brakes were applied, as they heard their screeching before the crash. Immediately after the automobile stopped, defendant ran back, picked up the woman and aided in placing her and the husband in automobiles, one of them in his own, to convey them to the hospital. Upon this evidence the jury found defendant guilty of murder of the second degree, and the question to be decided is whether that finding can be sustained.

"Murder," as defined by the common law, consists of the unlawful killing of a human being with malice aforethought, express or implied. Malice is a legal term which comprehends not only a particular ill will, but every case where there is wickedness of disposition, hardness of heart, cruelty, recklessness of consequences, or a mind regardless of social duty. In this state the Legislature has divided the common-law crime of murder into two degrees. The statute defines murder of the first degree, and then provides that "all other kinds of murder shall be deemed murder of the second degree." Act of March 31, 1860, P. L. 382, §74 (Pa. St. 1920, §7974). Thus murder of the second degree is common-law murder, but the killing is not accompanied by the distinguishing features of murder of the first degree. . . . It is apparent, therefore, that malice is a necessary element of the crime of murder of the second degree, and it was with this in view that we recently said:

"It is rarely that the facts in a motor vehicle accident will sustain a charge of murder. The element of malice is usually missing. 'There must be a consciousness of peril or probable peril to human life imputed to the operator of a car before he can be held for murder.'"

In the present case, one of the things which seems to have been given much weight by the court below in its opinion sustaining the conviction was defendant's failure to see the people on the road in time to avoid striking them. This negatives any specific intent to injure them. Unless he intended to strike them, which we think it manifest from the evidence he did not, or was recklessly disregardful of their safety, which the testimony does not establish, he could not legally be convicted of murder. Malice may be inferred from the wanton and reckless conduct of one who kills another from wicked disregard of the consequences of his acts, but here defendant's actions after the collision negative the idea of wickedness of disposition or hardness of heart. He endeavored as best he knew how to care for those he had injured. Moreover, it cannot be implied from the circumstances of the accident that defendant was driving his car with wanton disregard of the rights and safety of others upon the highway. The mere fact that he was intoxicated (conceding this to have been proved), without more being shown, would not sustain the conviction. Consequently, we are of the opinion that it could not properly be found, upon the evidence presented, that defendant either purposely, intentionally, recklessly, or wantonly drove his car upon the deceased, and therefore that he should not have been convicted of murder.

If defendant was guilty of any crime, it was that of involuntary manslaughter, which consists in "the killing of another without malice and unintentionally, but in doing some unlawful act not amounting to a felony nor naturally tending to cause death or great bodily harm, or in negligently doing some act lawful in itself, or by the negligent omission to perform a legal duty."

. . .

The first assignment of error is sustained and the judgment of sentence is reversed without prejudice to the commonwealth's right to proceed against defendant for the crime of involuntary manslaughter.

SIMPSON, J. (dissenting).

The majority opinion states that defendant, while driving his father's automobile, struck three persons who were traveling in front of him and going in the same direction he was, killing two of them and greatly injuring the third; that the car then ran some 200 feet further, after which he returned and helped convey two of the three to the hospital, and from this concludes that "defendant's actions after the collision negative the idea of wickedness of disposition or hardness of heart." With all due respect, the jury and trial judge, who saw the witnesses when they testified, and the colleagues of the latter, who obtained from him a clear picture of their conduct on the witness stand, were far better able to draw the true inferences than the judges of this court who must rely upon what appears in cold type only. At least as possible an inference from the facts above stated is that the defendant, while running the 200 feet beyond the place of the accident, concluded he would be better off if he came back than if he fled further, and hence the fact of his return did not negative the conclusion, which the jury drew from all the evidence, that defendant's "wanton and reckless conduct . . . [*at the time of the accident* shows his] wicked disregard of the consequences of his acts," and this, if found to be true, as it was, the majority agree would be sufficient to sustain the verdict and sentence. For this reason I dissent.

The Chief Justice concurred in this dissent.

Note

Many states have specialized statutes that criminalize homicides committed with motor vehicles. *See, e.g.,* M.C.L. §257.625(4) ("A person, whether licensed or not, who operates a motor vehicle in violation of . . . [this law] and by operation of that motor vehicle causes the death of another person is guilty of a crime . . ." punishable by 15–20 years in prison). While often providing a penalty similar to that for manslaughter, these statutes frequently ease the burden of proof of the prosecutor by requiring proof of neither malice nor criminal negligence. Typically, the general murder statutes are not preempted by vehicular manslaughter and death from vehicular manslaughter could be prosecuted as second degree murder. *See, e.g., People v. Watson,* 30 Cal.3d 290 (1981). Courts have ruled that dual prosecutions for both vehicular manslaughter and murder are permitted. *See, e.g., People v. Werner,* 254 Mich. App. 528, 535 (2002) (affirming conviction of second degree murder, M.C.L. §750.317; operating a motor vehicle while under the influence of intoxicating liquor (OUIL) causing death, M.C.L. §257.625(4); OUIL causing serious impairment of a bodily function, M.C.L. §257.625(5); and driving with a suspended license, second offense, M.C.L. §257.904(1)).

c.   Raising Children and the Foreseeability of Harm

How should a prosecutor charge a defendant when death results from bad choices on the part of a parent? In *Rodriguez,* the mother locked her kids in the home and, while she was gone, a fire in the home killed one of her children. Is this murder? Manslaughter? Mere negligence? *Cf. People v. Ogg,* 26 Mich. App. 372 (1970) (involuntary manslaughter conviction affirmed for death of kids when parent left kids in small, windowless room, without proper heat, light, food, clothing, and means of escape); *Delay v. Brainard,* 182 Neb. 509 (1968) (involuntary manslaughter when mother locked the children in the house and went to join her paramour in his apartment).

Do you think the answer to these questions might vary depending on what the parent is doing while away from the kids? Or whether the parental decision was reasonable given the time in history when the case occurred? Or whether the parent had notice of the child's propensity to touch dangerous objects?

People v. Rodriguez, 186 Cal. App. 2d 433 (1960)

VALLEE, Justice.

By information defendant was accused of manslaughter in that on November 8, 1959 she did wilfully, unlawfully, feloniously, and without malice kill Carlos Quinones. In a nonjury trial she was found guilty of involuntary manslaughter. A new trial was denied. She appeals from the judgment and the order denying a new trial.

In November 1959 defendant was living with her four children in a single-family residence at 130 South Clarence Street, Los Angeles. The oldest child was 6 years of age. Carlos Quinones was the youngest, either 2 or 3 years of age.

Olive Faison lived across the street from defendant. About 10:45 p. m. on November 8, 1959 Miss Faison heard some children calling, "Mommy, mommy." For about 15 or 20 minutes she did not "pay too much attention." She noticed the cries became more shrill. She went to the front window and saw smoke coming from defendant's house. She "ran across the street and commenced to knock the door in and started pulling the children out." There was a screen door on the outside and a wooden door inside the screen door. The screen door was padlocked on the outside. The other door was open. She broke the screen door and with the help of neighbors pulled three of the children out of the house. She tried to get into the house through the front door but could not because of the flames. A neighbor entered through the back door but could not go far because of the flames. Miss Faison took the three children to her apartment and shortly thereafter returned to the scene of the fire. She remained "until after the little boy was brought out and revived and sent to the hospital." Miss Faison did not see defendant around the house or the neighborhood at the time of the fire.

Firemen arrived at the scene some time after 10 p. m. The front door was open; there was no obstruction. Fireman Hansen went inside and found a baby boy in the back bedroom near the bed. The fire was about 3 feet away from the boy. Hansen took the boy out of the house. "He appeared to be dead at the time." The child was Carlos Quinones.

Around 4 or 4:30 p. m. on November 8, 1959, defendant was in "Johnny's Place." She was at the bar drinking "coke." She stayed about an hour. As John Powers, one of the bartenders, was closing the place about 2:30 a. m. on the morning of November 9, he saw defendant outside the building. He had not seen her inside before that time.

Maria Lucero, defendant's sister, went to defendant's home about 12 p. m. on November 8, 1959. She went looking for defendant. She found her about 2 or 2:30 a. m. in the same block as "Johnny's Place." Defendant was nervous and frightened, said she knew about the fire and that she went over to tell Johnny Powers about it. Defendant had not been drinking.

Carlos Quinones died from "thermal burns, second and third degree involving 50 to 60 per cent of the body surface." Defendant did not testify. . . .

"Manslaughter is the unlawful killing of a human being without malice. It is of three kinds: . . . 2. Involuntary—in the commission of an unlawful act, not amounting to felony; or in the commission of a lawful act which might produce death, in an unlawful manner, or without due caution and circumspection . . . ." (Pen. Code, §192.) "In every crime or public offense there must exist a union, or joint operation of act and intent, or criminal negligence." (Pen. Code, §20.) Section 20 of the Penal Code makes the union of act and wrongful intent or criminal negligence an invariable element of every crime unless it is excluded expressly or by necessary implication. Section 26 of the Penal Code lists, among the persons incapable of committing crimes, "[p]ersons who committed the act or made the omission charged through misfortune or by accident, when it appears that there was no evil design, intention, or culpable negligence." Thus the question is: Was there any evidence of criminal intent or criminal negligence? . . .

It appears from the record that guilt was predicated on the alleged "commission of a lawful act which might produce death, in an unlawful manner, or without due caution and circumspection." (Pen. Code, §192.) . . .

It is generally held that an act is criminally negligent when a man of ordinary prudence would foresee that the act would cause a high degree of risk of death or great bodily harm. The risk of death or great bodily harm must be great. Whether the conduct of defendant was wanton or reckless so as to warrant conviction of manslaughter must be determined from the conduct itself and not from the resultant harm. Criminal liability cannot be predicated on every careless act merely because its carelessness results in injury to another. The act must be one which has knowable and apparent potentialities for resulting in death. Mere inattention or mistake in judgment resulting even in death of another is not criminal unless the quality of the act makes it so. The fundamental requirement fixing criminal responsibility is knowledge, actual or imputed, that the act of the accused tended to endanger life.

In a case of involuntary manslaughter the criminal negligence of the accused must be the proximate cause of the death.

It clearly appears from the definition of criminal negligence stated in *People v. Penny*, 44 Cal.2d 861, that knowledge, actual or imputed, that the act of the slayer tended to endanger life and that the fatal consequences of the negligent act could reasonably have been foreseen are necessary for negligence to be criminal at all. Must a parent never leave a young child alone in the house on risk of being adjudged guilty of manslaughter if some unforeseeable occurrence causes the death of the child? The only reasonable view of the evidence is that the death of Carlos was the result of misadventure and not the natural and probable result of a criminally negligent act. There was no evidence from which it can be inferred that defendant realized her conduct would in all probability produce death. There was no evidence as to the cause of the fire, as to how or where it started. There was no evidence connecting defendant in any way with the fire. There was no evidence that defendant could reasonably have foreseen there was a probability that fire would ignite in the house and that Carlos would be burned to death. The most that can be said is that defendant may have been negligent; but mere negligence is not sufficient to authorize a conviction of involuntary manslaughter.

The judgment and order denying a new trial are reversed.

d.   Misdemeanor Manslaughter

As a general matter, the common law classified a death that occurred during the commission of an unlawful act (not amounting to a felony) as involuntary manslaughter, regardless of whether the prosecution could prove that the defendant's conduct was grossly negligent. Recall the words of *Comber v. United States*, 584 A.2d 26, 49 (D.C. 1990):

> The second category of unexcused unintentional homicides are those occurring in the course of certain unlawful acts. Centuries ago, the "unlawful act" category of involuntary manslaughter included all killings occurring in the course of a criminal act not amounting to a felony, *i.e.*, a misdemeanor. The doctrine became known as the "misdemeanor-manslaughter rule," something of an analogue to the felony-murder rule. As time passed, however, the misdemeanor-manslaughter rule "came to be considered too harsh," and "the courts began to place limitations upon it. Thus, in many jurisdictions, a homicide occurring in the course of a misdemeanor is involuntary manslaughter only if the offense is *malum in se,* rather than *malum prohibitum.*[34] Where the misdemeanor manslaughter doctrine applies, involuntary manslaughter liability attaches even where the defendant does not act with the degree of recklessness ordinarily required for involuntary manslaughter predicated on criminally negligent behavior. In effect, the defendant's intentional commission

---

[34] *Malum in se* is defined as "[a] wrong in itself. . . . An act is said to be *malum in se* when it is inherently and essentially evil, that is, immoral in its nature and injurious in its consequences, without any regard to the fact of its being noticed or punished by the law of the state." BLACK'S LAW DICTIONARY 865 (5th ed. 1979). *Malum prohibitum* is defined as "[a] wrong prohibited . . .; an act which is not inherently immoral, but becomes so because its commission is expressly forbidden by positive law. . . ." *Id.*

of a misdemeanor supplies the culpability required to impose homicide liability.

Also known as "unlawful-act manslaughter," the breadth of this crime varies from state to state. For more information, see Joshua Dressler, *Understanding Criminal Law* §31.09 (6th ed. 2012).

2. Voluntary Manslaughter

When and under what circumstances will the law reduce what would otherwise be called murder down to manslaughter? This section explores the law of voluntary manslaughter.[*] It helps to think of voluntary manslaughter as an intentional killing committed under legally adequate (i.e., reasonable) provocation—due to the mitigation stemming from the provocation, what would otherwise be murder is reduced to voluntary manslaughter.

Sometimes referred to as the "provocation defense," the common law defined voluntary manslaughter as a killing that occurred in a "state of passion" as a result of legally adequate (i.e., reasonable) provocation where the defendant did not have a reasonable amount of time to cool off. At common law, only a limited number of acts, such as observation of adultery by a spouse or the commission of a serious crime against a close relative, constituted legally adequate provocation. *See* Joshua Dressler, *Understanding Criminal Law* §31.07[B][2][a] (6th ed. 2012) (providing a small, fixed list of what constituted legally adequate provocation at common law). As for the cooling off question, common law typically involved a *sudden* heat of passion. Today, what constitutes reasonable provocation and the reasonable cooling off period is often left to the jury. Additionally, to successfully assert the provocation defense, the reason for the killing has to be due to the provocation. For more information, see Joshua Dressler, *Understanding Criminal Law* §31.07 (6th ed. 2012).

a. Legally Adequate Provocation

In the *Troila* case, the defendant asserts that homosexual advances should constitute legally adequate provocation and that the judge should have

---

[*] Some courts allow a murder charge to be reduced to the crime of voluntary manslaughter when most, but not all, of the elements of a defense like self-defense are satisfied. This is often referred to as an "imperfect" self-defense claim. *See, e.g., State v. Sety*, 121 Ariz. 354 (1979) (affirming reduction of murder to voluntary manslaughter when defendant used excessive force in self-defense). *But see People v. Reese*, 491 Mich. 127 (2012) ("We hold that the doctrine of imperfect self-defense does not exist in Michigan law as a freestanding defense mitigating murder to voluntary manslaughter, although we recognize that factual circumstances that have been characterized imperfect self-defense may negate the malice element of second-degree murder.").

instructed the jury to consider voluntary manslaughter. Does that sound reasonable?

Commonwealth v. Troila, 410 Mass. 203 (1991)

NOLAN, Justice.

The defendant appeals from his conviction of murder in the first degree. He argues that . . . [*inter alia*] the judge improperly instructed the jury. We determine that the . . . instructions to the jury were appropriate.

At approximately 10 A.M., on May 2, 1987, two children discovered a body in a lot behind their home in the Roxbury section of Boston. The victim had been stabbed several times. A medical examiner testified that two of the stab wounds to the heart were fatal and that a third, to the neck, was potentially fatal. Time of death was set sometime within twenty-four hours of the body's discovery.

The defendant, Matthew Troila, was indicted for murder in the first degree and brought to trial. Several witnesses testified to having seen the defendant and the victim together on the evening of May 1, 1987, the night before the body was discovered. The jury heard a tape recording of the defendant being interrogated by Boston police in connection with the murder. In addition, three witnesses testified that the defendant had, on separate occasions, admitted to the killing.

One witness, Margaret Wilson, testified that she was with both the defendant and the victim on May 1 and into the early morning hours of May 2. She testified that, at that time, she was dating the defendant's brother, Joseph Troila. According to Wilson, she, Joseph, the defendant, and the victim traveled in her automobile to and from various gathering places. At one point, Wilson testified, she was directed to drive to the place where the body was subsequently found. Wilson was told to stay in her automobile while the three men went off in search of drugs. Approximately fifteen minutes later, Joseph returned, followed shortly by the defendant. Wilson testified that she then asked where the victim was, to which the defendant replied that he had killed him because the victim had "made a pass" at him.

Another witness, Debra Miele, with whom the defendant was living at the time of the murder, testified at trial that, on the morning of May 2, 1987, the defendant told her, "I think I killed somebody last night." When asked why, the defendant allegedly said that the victim was a homosexual and "had tried something on him sexually." The defendant's sister also testified that, about one week after the murder, the defendant said to her that he thought he killed somebody but was not sure.

There was corroboration of aspects of this testimony. The victim's sister testified that the victim was a homosexual. Several witnesses testified that they saw the victim in the company of the defendant, Joseph, and Wilson.

The jury convicted the defendant of murder in the first degree on the theory of extreme atrocity or cruelty. The defendant now appeals from that conviction. . . .

The defendant . . . contends that the judge erred by failing to instruct the jury that, if they found that the defendant had been provoked by the victim and committed the crime in the heat of passion, they could find him guilty of manslaughter rather than murder. The defendant contends that the jury could find that, because the victim allegedly made homosexual overtures to him, the defendant was reasonably provoked such that the severity of the crime ought to be reduced. We disagree.

"Voluntary manslaughter is 'a killing from a sudden transport of passion or heat of blood, upon a reasonable provocation and without malice, or upon sudden combat.' " The only evidence of provocation was the defendant's alleged statement that the victim "made a pass" at him. No jury could find on the basis of this evidence that reasonable provocation existed. On this record, no manslaughter instruction was necessary. . . .

Judgment affirmed.

b. Legally Adequate Provocation and Words

The *Guebara* case explores whether words, standing alone, constitute legally adequate provocation.

State v. Guebara, 236 Kan. 791 (1985)

PRAGER, Justice:

This is a direct appeal in a criminal action in which the defendant-appellant, Paul Guebara, was convicted of murder in the first degree (K.S.A. 21–3401). It was undisputed that the defendant shot and killed his wife, Genny Guebara. The defendant admitted the homicide in his testimony at the trial. The only issue raised on the appeal is that the trial court erred by failing to instruct the jury on the lesser included offense of voluntary manslaughter as defined in K.S.A. 21–3403.

At the trial, the factual circumstances were not greatly in dispute and essentially were as follows: Defendant Paul Guebara and Genny Guebara were common-law husband and wife, having declared themselves married in 1980. There were two children living with the couple: Sylvia Dawn Guebara, the natural child of the defendant, and Candice Ann Virgil, the natural child of Genny. Their marital relationship was characterized by frequent arguments and occasional violence. In February 1983, Genny filed for divorce. About the same time she also filed criminal charges against the defendant alleging misdemeanor battery and misdemeanor theft. On February 15, 1983, the defendant was served with a misdemeanor warrant by Ms. Anna Gallardo, a Finney County deputy sheriff who is related to the Guebara family by marriage. She testified that she had a conversation with defendant at the sheriff's office on the day before the shooting. She first saw him in the morning when he came to inquire where his divorce hearing was going to be held. She showed him a copy of the warrant and told him what the misdemeanor charges were. She told him to come back to the office at 2:30 p.m. to take care of the warrant and appear before the court.

He returned and appeared before the magistrate at 2:30 p.m. that afternoon. Following the hearing, she had a conversation with him in the sheriff's conference room. They discussed the divorce, and defendant told her he was very upset that the divorce was going on. He said that it made him very angry. He told her at different points in the conversation that he was going to kill Genny and that, if he did, he was not going to fight it—that he was going to turn himself in to the sheriff. He told her that he did not want to kill Genny but, when she made him angry, he could not hold back. Following the conversation, Ms. Gallardo concluded that he was not serious and was not really going to do anything. She did not report the conversation to anyone.

On February 16, 1983, the date of the shooting, Sylvia Dawn Guebara was staying with defendant at defendant's parents' house in accordance with an agreed visitation schedule. Genny and two of her friends arrived at the house to pick Sylvia up. Genny and another woman left the pickup truck and approached defendant, who was standing on the porch. At that point, defendant handed Genny the criminal process papers. According to defendant's testimony, when he handed Genny the papers, she stated that she tried to drop the charges but the assistant county attorney would not let her. The defendant testified that he immediately became angry, pulled out his gun, and started shooting her. According to defendant, he did not think about the act; it was a sudden impulse to shoot without reflection. A prosecution witness testified that Genny attempted to walk past defendant to the house after defendant refused to accept back the process papers. He grabbed her arm and turned her around towards him, displaying a gun. Genny turned her head and defendant fired the gun at her. Genny then stepped back, brought her hands up, and defendant fired the gun again. Then Genny turned and ran or stumbled toward the pickup truck. Defendant followed her into the street firing several additional shots. As Genny was lying in the street, defendant ran toward the house, throwing the gun at the house and immediately ran to the Finney County Law Enforcement Center where he turned himself in to a sheriff's employee.

Edwin C. Knight, Jr., a Garden City police officer who investigated the shooting, was advised that defendant Guebara was at the law enforcement center. Defendant had been placed under arrest by the sheriff's department. According to the officer, he advised defendant of his *Miranda* rights and defendant signed an acknowledgment and a waiver. The officer then took a statement from defendant. Defendant advised him that he had been having problems with his wife, referring to the pending divorce and to the fact that Genny had implicated him in misdemeanor theft and battery charges.

Defendant stated that he was depressed and upset. The officer asked defendant if he had shot his wife, and defendant admitted it. Defendant stated to the officer that he had thought about shooting her the day before and that he had thought about shooting her just prior to her arrival at the house. The officer asked defendant whether he intended to shoot her, and defendant replied that he had planned to shoot her.

On cross-examination the police officer testified that defendant told him defendant had smoked one and one-half joints of marijuana just before his wife arrived on the scene. Defendant informed him that, when he first pulled the gun out, he did not intend to shoot his wife and did not intend to shoot her with the first shot. The evidence presented by the defense at the trial sought to prove that the defendant was a person who, when put into pressure situations, was likely to respond in a violent, impulsive, quick manner. Defendant was characterized as a person who showed indications of gross thought disorder which might lead to an inability to assess reality accurately and respond to it accordingly. Defendant was described as an action-oriented person who could act in an assaultive manner.

The defense called to the witness stand a staff psychiatrist at Larned State Security Hospital who diagnosed defendant to have an anti-social personality disorder. She testified that, when a person with an anti-social personality disorder uses drugs such as marijuana, it is possible for the individual to have altered judgment and maladaptive behavior. The use of marijuana by such a person would have a tendency to worsen the individual's judgment, and if the individual had an aggressive personality, the use of the drugs would probably make the person more aggressive. Although defendant testified he had smoked marijuana shortly before the shooting, there was no evidence he was under the influence of drugs.

Defendant's father, mother, and a cousin testified that defendant was a quick-tempered person who typically reacted violently when put in pressure situations. His mother testified, in substance, that her son would make threats but never carried out his threats. Simply stated, defendant sought to prove that his actions were the result of an emotional state of mind characterized by anger and resentment which caused defendant to act on impulse without reflection. It was the position of the defense that the actions of the defendant were provoked by his wife's inability to arrange for the dismissal of the criminal charges which she had initiated against her husband and that his response to the situation was impulsive and not premeditated. Hence, the defense argued, he could only be found guilty of voluntary manslaughter.

At the close of the evidence, the defendant's counsel requested the trial court to instruct the jury on the lesser included offense of voluntary manslaughter as defined by K.S.A. 21–3403. The trial court instructed the jury on murder in the first and second degree but refused to give the requested instruction on voluntary manslaughter. In making its ruling, the trial court reasoned that two elements must exist to prove voluntary manslaughter: First, there must be evidence of an emotional state constituting heat of passion and, second, there must be a sufficient provocation. The trial court concluded that the refusal of a person to dismiss misdemeanor criminal charges arising from a domestic squabble was not a sufficient legal provocation to kill. The case was submitted to the jury and defendant was convicted of murder in the first degree. Defendant then appealed and, as noted above, the sole issue is whether the trial court erred in failing to instruct the jury on the lesser included offense of voluntary manslaughter. . . .

The basic issue before us is whether there was sufficient evidence presented in the case to support the defendant's theory that the killing was committed in the heat of passion under such circumstances as to require the requested instruction on voluntary manslaughter. At the outset, it would be helpful to review some of the Kansas cases on the subject and to note the general principles of law which have been applied in resolving the issue presented. These general principles may be summarized as follows:

(1) Voluntary manslaughter is the intentional killing in the heat of passion as a result of severe provocation. As a concession to human frailty, a killing, which would otherwise constitute murder, is mitigated to voluntary manslaughter.

(2) "Heat of passion" means any intense or vehement emotional excitement of the kind prompting violent and aggressive action, such as rage, anger, hatred, furious resentment, fright, or terror. Such emotional state of mind must be of such a degree as would cause an ordinary man to act on impulse without reflection.

(3) In order to reduce a homicide from murder to voluntary manslaughter, there must be provocation, and such provocation must be recognized by the law as adequate. A provocation is adequate if it is calculated to deprive a reasonable man of self-control and to cause him to act out of passion rather than reason. In order for a defendant to be entitled to a reduced charge because he acted in the heat of passion, his emotional state of mind must exist at the time of the act and it must have arisen from circumstances constituting *sufficient provocation.*

(4) The test of the sufficiency of the provocation is objective, not subjective. The provocation, whether it be "sudden quarrel" or some other form of provocation, must be sufficient to cause an ordinary man to lose control of his actions and his reason. In applying the objective standard for measuring the sufficiency of the provocation, the standard precludes consideration of the innate peculiarities of the individual defendant. The fact that his intelligence is not high and his passion is easily aroused will not be considered in this connection.

(5) Mere words or gestures, however insulting, do not constitute adequate provocation, but insulting words when accompanied by other conduct, such as assault, may be considered.

(6) An assault or battery resulting in a reasonable belief that the defendant is in imminent danger of losing his life or suffering great bodily harm may be of sufficient provocation to reduce the killing to voluntary manslaughter.

(7) If two persons engage in mutual combat, the blows given by each are adequate provocation to the other; thus, if one kills the other, the homicide may be reduced to voluntary manslaughter.

With these basic principles in mind, we now turn to a consideration of the factual circumstances of this case as set forth above in detail. We have concluded that the trial court did not err in refusing to give the defendant's requested instruction on voluntary manslaughter. We agree with the trial court that, although the requisite emotional state necessary to constitute heat of passion was present, the evidence in the record does not show that the defendant's emotional state of mind arose from circumstances constituting sufficient provocation. The record is devoid of any evidence that on February 16, 1983, Genny Guebara was quarrelsome or that she committed any aggressive acts or physical threats directed toward the defendant. The evidence was undisputed that, after defendant handed her the warrant in the criminal proceeding, she simply handed it back to him and turned to leave and that defendant immediately pulled his gun and fired the shots. Genny Guebara made no attempt to strike her husband or to interfere with his movements in any way. In fact, there was no evidence that she ever used abusive or insulting words toward him. . . .

As this court has held many times before, a court must apply an objective standard for measuring the sufficiency of the provocation. In doing so, the court should not consider the innate peculiarities of the individual defendant. We hold that the trial court did not err in refusing to instruct on voluntary manslaughter.

The judgment of the district court is affirmed.

Note

While *Guebara* states the general rule that words alone are not enough, not all courts agree. *See, e.g., People v. Pouncey*, 437 Mich. 382, 391 (1991) (while verbal exchange held insufficient, court "decline[d] to issue a rule that insulting words per se are never adequate provocation"); *Commonwealth v. Berry*, 461 Pa. 233 (1975) ("While words of an insulting and scandalous nature are not sufficient cause of provocation, *Commonwealth v. Drum*, 58 Pa. at 17, words conveying information of a fact which constitutes adequate provocation when that fact is observed would constitute sufficient provocation."); *State v. Grugin*, 147 Mo. 39 (1898) (words that amounted to an admission that the victim raped defendant's daughter justified jury instruction on voluntary manslaughter). For more information, see Joshua Dressler,

Understanding Criminal Law §31.07[B][2][b][i] (6th ed. 2012); Wayne LaFave, *Criminal Law* §15.2 (5th ed. 2010).

H. Felony Murder

A person goes into a store, with his gun drawn, with the intent to rob it. He approaches the clerk, an elderly man, who sees what is about to happen and has a fatal heart attack. Is this murder?

It is generally understood that the common law classified any death resulting from conduct during the commission, or attempted commission, of any felony, as common law murder, regardless of whether the defendant intended to kill, intended to do great bodily harm, or knowingly created (or consciously disregarded) a very high risk that death or great bodily harm would occur. The felony murder rule allows a prosecutor to prove murder based on the intent to commit the underlying felony.

For reasons that will be explored in the cases below, this can be a harsh rule as it allows the prosecutor to obtain a conviction for the most serious crime in our criminal justice system by proof of the mens rea for a less serious crime. As will be seen in this section, many jurisdictions have taken steps to limit the application of the felony-murder doctrine. For more information, see Joshua Dressler, *Understanding Criminal Law* §31.06 (6th ed. 2012).

1. Requiring Malice to Prove First Degree Felony Murder

In the *Aaron* case, the Michigan Supreme Court offers a vigorous criticism of the felony murder rule and then proceeds to limit the application of the rule in the context of first degree felony murder under Michigan law, holding that "the issue of malice must always be submitted to the jury." After reading the opinion, think about whether—even with the limitation—the prosecutor's job in getting a first degree felony murder conviction is less difficult if the felony murder theory is pursued. In creating this limitation, *Aaron* represents the minority approach to first degree felony murder.

People v. Aaron, Thompson, and Wright, 409 Mich. 672 (1980)

FITZGERALD, Justice.

The existence and scope of the felony-murder doctrine have perplexed generations of law students, commentators and jurists in the United States and England, and have split our own Court of Appeals. In these cases, we must decide whether Michigan has a felony murder rule which allows the element of malice required for murder to be satisfied by the intent to commit the underlying felony or whether malice must be otherwise found by the trier of fact. We must also determine what is the mens rea required to support a conviction under Michigan's first-degree murder statute.

FACTS

In *Thompson*, defendant was convicted by a jury of first-degree felony murder as the result of a death which occurred during an armed robbery. The trial judge instructed the jury that it was not necessary for the prosecution to prove malice, as a finding of intent to rob was all that was necessary for the homicide to constitute first-degree murder. The Court of Appeals held that reversible error resulted from the trial court's failure to instruct the jury on the element of malice in the felony-murder charge.

In *Wright*, defendant was convicted by a jury of two counts of first-degree felony murder for setting fire to a dwelling causing the death of two people. The trial court instructed the jury that proof that the killings occurred during the perpetration of arson was sufficient to establish first-degree murder. The Court of Appeals reversed the convictions, holding that it was error to remove the element of malice from the jury's consideration.

Defendant Aaron was convicted of first-degree felony murder as a result of a homicide committed during the perpetration of an armed robbery. The jury was instructed that they could convict defendant of first-degree murder if they found that defendant killed the victim during the commission or attempted commission of an armed robbery. . . .

HISTORY OF THE FELONY MURDER DOCTRINE

Felony murder has never been a static, well-defined rule at common law, but throughout its history has been characterized by judicial reinterpretation to limit the harshness of the application of the rule. Historians and commentators have concluded that the rule is of questionable origin and that the reasons for the rule no longer exist, making it an anachronistic remnant, "a historic survivor for which there is no logical or practical basis for existence in modern law." . . .

. . . [A]n examination of the felony-murder rule indicates that the doctrine is of doubtful origin. Derived from the misinterpretation of case law, it went unchallenged because of circumstances which no longer exist. The doctrine was continuously modified and restricted in England, the country of its birth, until its ultimate rejection by Parliament in 1957.

LIMITATION OF THE FELONY MURDER DOCTRINE IN THE UNITED STATES

While only a few states have followed the lead of Great Britain in abolishing felony murder, various legislative and judicial limitations on the doctrine have effectively narrowed the scope of the rule in the United States. Perkins states that the rule is "somewhat in disfavor at the present time" and that "courts apply it where the law requires, but they do so grudgingly and tend to restrict its application where circumstances permit". . . .

The numerous modifications and restrictions placed upon the common-law felony-murder doctrine by courts and legislatures reflect dissatisfaction with the harshness and injustice of the rule. Even though the felony-murder doctrine survives in this country, it bears increasingly less resemblance to the traditional felony-murder concept. To the extent that these modifications reduce the scope and significance of the common-law doctrine, they also call into question the continued existence of the doctrine itself.

THE REQUIREMENT OF INDIVIDUAL CULPABILITY FOR CRIMINAL RESPONSIBILITY
"If one had to choose the most basic principle of the criminal law in general . . . it would be that criminal liability for causing a particular result is not justified in the absence of some culpable mental state in respect to that result . . . ."

The most fundamental characteristic of the felony-murder rule violates this basic principle in that it punishes all homicides, committed in the perpetration or attempted perpetration of proscribed felonies whether intentional, unintentional or accidental, without the necessity of proving the relation between the homicide and the perpetrator's state of mind. This is most evident when a killing is done by one of a group of co-felons. The felony-murder rule completely ignores the concept of determination of guilt on the basis of individual misconduct. The felony-murder rule thus "erodes the relation between criminal liability and moral culpability."

The felony-murder rule's most egregious violation of basic rules of culpability occurs where felony murder is categorized as first-degree murder. All other murders carrying equal punishment require a showing of premeditation, deliberation and willfulness while felony murder only requires a showing of intent to do the underlying felony. Although the purpose of our degree statutes is to punish more severely the more culpable forms of murder, an accidental killing occurring during the perpetration of a felony would be punished more severely than a second-degree murder requiring intent to kill, intent to cause great bodily harm or wantonness and willfulness.[87] Furthermore, a defendant charged with felony murder is permitted to raise defenses only to the mental element of the felony, thus precluding certain defenses available to a defendant charged with premeditated murder who may raise defenses to the mental

---

[87] A good example of this point is provided by the one of the cases involved here. In *People v. Wright*, 409 Mich. 672 (1980), the trial judge instructed that as to the intent element of the possible verdicts, first-degree murder required intent to commit the crime of arson, second-degree murder required intent to kill or that defendant "consciously created a very high degree of risk of death to another with knowledge of its probable consequences", and involuntary manslaughter involved willful, wanton and reckless disregard of the consequences. Thus, a higher degree of culpability was required for second-degree murder and involuntary manslaughter than for first-degree murder.

element of murder (*e. g.*, self-defense, accident). Certainly, felony murder is no more reprehensible than premeditated murder.

LaFave and Scott explain the felony-murder doctrine's failure to account for a defendant's moral culpability as follows:

> The rationale of the doctrine is that one who commits a felony is a bad person with a bad state of mind, and he has caused a bad result, so that we should not worry too much about the fact that the fatal result he accomplished was quite different and a good deal worse than the bad result he intended. Yet it is a general principle of criminal law that one is not ordinarily criminally liable for bad results which differ greatly from intended results.

Termed as a "somewhat primitive rationale" it is deserving of the observation made by one commentator that "the felony-murder doctrine gives rise to what can only be described as an emotional reaction, not one based on logical and abstract principles".

Another writer states:

> It is an excuse based on the rough moral notion that a man who intentionally commits a felony must have a wicked heart, and therefore 'ought to be punished' for the harm which he has done accidentally. It is to guard against this kind of reasoning that our modern rules of evidence exclude in most cases any communication to the jury of a prisoner's previous misdeeds.

This Court has previously recognized this principle in a context analogous to the felony-murder situation:

> Every assault involves bodily harm. But any doctrine which would hold every assailant as a murderer where death follows his act, would be barbarous and unreasonable.

While it is understandable that little compassion may be felt for the criminal whose innocent victim dies, this does not justify ignoring the principles underlying our system of criminal law. As Professor Hall argues in his treatise on criminal law:

> The underlying rationale of the felony-murder doctrine—that the offender has shown himself to be a 'bad actor,' and that this is enough to exclude the niceties bearing on the gravity of the harm actually committed—might have been defensible in early law. The survival of the felony-murder doctrine is a tribute to the tenacity of legal conceptions rooted in simple moral attitudes. For as long ago as 1771 the doctrine was severely criticized by Eden [Baron Auckland], who felt that it 'may be reconciled to the philosophy of slaves; but it is surely repugnant to that noble,

and active confidence, which a free people ought to possess in the laws of their constitution, the rule of their actions.' "

The United States Supreme Court has reaffirmed on several occasions the importance of the relationship between culpability and criminal liability.

[T]he criminal law . . . is concerned not only with guilt or innocence in the abstract but also with the degree of criminal culpability. *Mullaney v. Wilbur*, 421 U.S. 684, 697–698 (1975).

The contention that an injury can amount to a crime only when inflicted by intention is no provincial or transient notion. It is as universal and persistent in mature systems of law as belief in freedom of the human will and a consequent ability and duty of the normal individual to choose between good and evil. A relation between some mental element and punishment for a harmful act is almost as instinctive as the child's familiar exculpatory 'But I didn't mean to,' and has afforded the rational basis for a tardy and unfinished substitution of deterrence and reformation in place of retaliation and vengeance as the motivation for public prosecution. *Morissette v. United States*, 342 U.S. 246, 250–251 (1952).

Whether a death results in the course of a felony (thus giving rise to felony-murder liability) turns on fortuitous events that do not distinguish the intention or moral culpability of the defendants. *Lockett v. Ohio*, 438 U.S. 586, 620 (1978) (Mr. Justice Marshall's concurring opinion.)

The failure of the felony-murder rule to consider the defendant's moral culpability is explained by examining the state of the law at the time of the rule's inception. The concept of culpability was not an element of homicide at early common law. The early definition of malice aforethought was vague. The concept meant little more than intentional wrongdoing with no other emphasis on intention except to exclude homicides that were committed by misadventure or in some otherwise pardonable manner. Thus, under this early definition of malice aforethought, an intent to commit the felony would in itself constitute malice. Furthermore, as all felonies were punished alike, it made little difference whether the felon was hanged for the felony or for the death.

Thus, the felony-murder rule did not broaden the concept of murder at the time of its origin because proof of the intention to commit a felony met the test of culpability based on the vague definition of malice aforethought governing at that time. Today, however, malice is a term of art. It does not include the nebulous definition of intentional wrongdoing. Thus, although the felony-murder rule did not broaden the definition of murder at early common law, it does so today. We find this enlargement of the scope of murder unacceptable, because it is based on a concept of culpability which is "totally incongruous with the general principles of our jurisprudence" today.

As Professor Hall observed in his treatise on criminal law:

> The modern tendency has been to oppose policy-formation such as that embodied in or extended from the felony-murder doctrine. It has insisted on a decent regard for the facts and on sanctions that represent fair evaluation of these facts and not of the supposed character of the offender. Most emphatically the progressive tendency has been to repudiate the imposition of severe penalties where bare chance results in an unsought harm." . . .

CONCLUSION

Whatever reasons can be gleaned from the dubious origin of the felony-murder rule to explain its existence, those reasons no longer exist today. Indeed, most states, including our own, have recognized the harshness and inequity of the rule as is evidenced by the numerous restrictions placed on it. The felony-murder doctrine is unnecessary and in many cases unjust in that it violates the basic premise of individual moral culpability upon which our criminal law is based.

We conclude that Michigan has no statutory felony-murder rule which allows the mental element of murder to be satisfied by proof of the intention to commit the underlying felony. Today we exercise our role in the development of the common law by abrogating the common-law felony-murder rule. We hold that in order to convict a defendant of murder, as that term is defined by Michigan case law, it must be shown that he acted with intent to kill or to inflict great bodily harm or with a wanton and willful disregard of the likelihood that the natural tendency of his behavior is to cause death or great bodily harm. We further hold that the issue of malice must always be submitted to the jury.

The first-degree murder statute will continue to operate in that all murder committed in the perpetration or attempted perpetration of the enumerated felonies will be elevated to first-degree murder. . . .

COLEMAN, C. J., and MOODY, LEVIN and KAVANAGH, JJ., concur.

RYAN, Justice (concurring in part, dissenting in part).

Note

Michigan's criminal homicide statute is provided in greater detail later in this chapter. In light of the *Aaron* case, however, consider Michigan's first degree felony murder rule, M.C.L. §750.316(1)(b):

> Murder committed in the perpetration of, or attempt to perpetrate, arson, criminal sexual conduct in the first, second, or third degree, child abuse in the first degree, a major controlled substance offense, robbery, carjacking,

breaking and entering of a dwelling, home invasion in the first or second degree, larceny of any kind, extortion, kidnapping, vulnerable adult abuse in the first or second degree under section 145n, torture under section 85, or aggravated stalking under section 411i.

How is this provision different from the first degree felony murder provision in the Pennsylvania degrees of murder model discussed in the *Drum* case? In light of *Aaron*, is proving that a death occurred during the commission of one of the enumerated offenses enough to prove felony murder under M.C.L. §750.316(1)(b)? How have Michigan courts applied *Aaron*? *See, e.g., People v. Nowack*, 462 Mich. 392 (2000); *People v. Carines*, 460 Mich. 750, 760 (1999); *People v. McCrady*, 244 Mich. App. 27 (2000).

2. During the Commission of a Felony

The *Mayle* case provides a basic application of the felony murder rule and raises an interesting question: If this killing occurs after the felon robs another, but before the felon has arrived to a place of safety, did the killing occur during the commission of the felony?

State v. Mayle, 178 W.Va. 26 (1987)

BROTHERTON, Justice:

This is an appeal from a judgment of felony murder by the Circuit Court of Cabell County in December, 1982. The jury trial was held in Fayette County, West Virginia, due to a change of venue motion, before Judge Alfred E. Ferguson. We find no error in the proceedings and affirm.

On December 14, 1981, at 1:15 a.m. two men entered a McDonald's restaurant in Chesapeake, Ohio. One was a tall, white man, the other was a shorter, black man. They wore dark blue or black ski masks over their faces. The pair demanded that the employees give them the combination to the safe. The employees did not know the combination, so the robbers took the keys to one of the employee's cars, a 1972 Matador, and left in the stolen car. The car was later found in Huntington, West Virginia, with a tape deck and some tapes missing.

Approximately one-half hour after the Ohio robbery, Officer Byard of the Huntington Police Department observed a possible breaking and entering by two men at a gasoline station. He notified Officer Harman, a few blocks away. Harman indicated over the radio "I've got 'em over here." A few minutes later, Officer Byard heard a gunshot and started running to Harman's aid. He heard more gunshots, and saw two men running west down Jefferson Street in Huntington. Officer Harman had been fatally wounded by several hard blows to the head and five gunshot wounds from his service revolver. Officer Byard observed the men getting into a green Buick and leaving the scene.

One witness, Ted Norman, looked out the window of his home and saw Officer Harman on the ground with a man on top of him trying to take something from the officer. The man raised up and shot Harman several times. Mr. Norman turned on his porch light and clearly saw the man's face at a distance of between eight and ten feet. He later identified the man as Bobby Stacy. Other witnesses saw two men running from the area, one white and the other a shorter, fair-skinned black man.

A short time after the shooting, Officer Leroy Campbell of the Kenova Police Department passed a car driven by a black man travelling west. Officer Campbell turned around and followed the vehicle and then passed it. As he passed it, the driver turned his head toward Campbell. The driver was later identified by Campbell as Wilbert Mayle. At this time the officer learned of the shooting of Officer Harman over his radio. When he received a description of the vehicle and the suspects, he realized that it was the car he had just passed. The officer blocked the Kenova-Catlettsburg bridge on Route 60 leading into Kentucky. The car's occupants obviously saw the roadblock and turned left off Route 60 onto 23rd Street in Kenova. Officer Campbell followed, and found the vehicle abandoned on Sycamore Street, which is a dead-end street by the river.

Kathy Pearson, a resident of Columbus, Ohio, had been a friend of Bobby Stacy for several years and was acquainted with Wilbert Mayle. Pearson was told by Stacy at 6:00 p.m. on the night of the shooting that "he had to go meet Jackie and pick him up and go to the hills and take care of business." Jackie was Wilbert Mayle's nickname. It is undisputed that Stacy and Mayle were good friends and had been for a long time.

The automobile found on Sycamore Street was registered in the name of Bobby Stacy and contained a tape deck and tapes stolen from the Matador in Ohio, a black ski mask, and Officer Harman's gun. Wilbert Mayle's fingerprints were found on the steering wheel. An analysis of hair samples found in two ski masks (the one found in the car and another found near the car) revealed that one mask had hair consistent with Mayle's hair and the other had hair consistent with Bobby Stacy's and Mayle's. . . .

At the end of the evidence, the jury found Wilbert Mayle guilty of first degree murder, with a recommendation of mercy. He appeals to this Court . . . .

. . . Mr. Mayle claims that the State failed to meet its burden in proving felony murder under W.Va.Code §61–2–1 (1984), which provides: "Murder by poison, lying in wait, imprisonment, starving, or by any willful, deliberate and premeditated killing, or in the commission of, or attempt to commit, arson, rape, robbery or burglary, is murder of the first degree." The State is not required in a felony murder case to prove any specific intent to kill, premeditation, or malice. Instead, "the elements which the State is required to prove to obtain a conviction of felony murder are: (1) The commission of, or attempt to commit, one or more of the enumerated felonies; (2) the defendant's participation in such commission or attempt; and (3) the death of the victim as a result of injuries received during the course of such commission or attempt."

We will look at each of the three elements individually, starting with the commission or attempt to commit a felony. A felony was unquestionably committed in this case. A robbery, which is one of the enumerated felonies in §61–2–1, was committed when the two men took car keys at gunpoint from an employee of a McDonald's restaurant in Chesapeake, Ohio.

The defendant's participation in such commission or attempt was also satisfactorily proved. In this case, one of the robbers was a short, black man who fit Mayle's general description. He was wearing a ski mask. A ski mask similar to the one used in the robbery was found in Bobby Stacy's car, and another was found near the car. Both had hair similar to Mayle's hair in them. The car, which Mayle was seen driving shortly after the robbery, was quickly abandoned when a police officer came to investigate, and contained articles stolen from a car which was taken during the McDonald's robbery. While individually each item of evidence presented above would be quite weak evidence, taken together it is strong evidence pointing toward Mayle's guilt from which a jury could easily conclude that there was no reasonable hypothesis of innocence.

Finally, there was sufficient evidence to support the jury's determination that Officer Harman was killed during the commission of the felony. The act of robbing had been completed several minutes earlier, but the incident was not complete. The robbers had yet to return home to a place of safety. The distance from the McDonald's in Chesapeake to the scene of the shooting was only 2.1 miles. The loot had not been distributed, but remained in the trunk of Stacy's car. Whether the robbers were conducting their escape or were moving on to another crime, their activities were a part of "one continuous transaction."

In *State v. Wayne*, 169 W.Va. 785 (1982), the defendant was convicted of first degree murder in a felony murder situation. His claim of error to this Court was that the underlying felony of the robbery had been completed prior to the murder. After an examination of the law of several other jurisdictions, we concluded that the felony murder statute does apply where the robbery was complete but the defendants were still in the act of escape. We noted with approval the case of *State v. Squire*, 292 N.C. 494 (1977), where a car containing bank robbers was stopped by a state policeman for a traffic violation ten miles from the scene of the robbery. As the state policeman approached the car, he was killed. Despite the distance from the scene, the North Carolina court found that the robbers were still in the act of escape and applied the felony murder rule. In the present case, the escape was not complete. Wilbert Mayle and Bobby Stacy were still "in the hills taking care of business." They were still involved in the chain of events surrounding the robbery. Therefore the felony murder rule was properly applied.[6]

For the above reasons, the judgment of the Circuit Court of Cabell County is affirmed.

   Affirmed.

3. Independent Felony (Merger) Limitation

Jurisdictions have taken a variety of steps to limit the application of the felony murder rule. As has already been seen in studying the Pennsylvania degrees of murder model (in the *Drum* case), many legislatures have chosen to limit the felony murder rule to specifically enumerated felonies (e.g., first degree felony murder under the Pennsylvania model is limited to arson, rape, robbery, or burglary).

As will be seen in the *Ireland* case, California law at the time of the *Ireland* decision limited first degree felony murder to six specific felonies, allowing for second degree felony murder if the killing occurred during an unspecified "felony inherently dangerous to human life." In exploring what kind of felony qualified as inherently dangerous to human life, the *Ireland* case makes clear that a felony that is closely related to the means of death cannot serve as the underlying felony in a felony murder prosecution (i.e., the underlying felony must be independent of the homicide).

Known as the independent felony or merger doctrine, it is not applied in all jurisdictions. *See*, *e.g.*, *People v. Jones*, 209 Mich. App. 212, 214–15 (1995) (merger doctrine did not apply because felony murder statute requires proof of malice). For more information, see Joshua Dressler, *Understanding Criminal Law* §31.06[C][2] (6th ed. 2012).

---

[6] The defense relies heavily on the fact that much of this evidence is circumstantial. Circumstantial evidence is not per se less reliable than direct evidence. It is merely a different class of evidence which has its special dangers and its special advantages. In many cases circumstantial evidence can be stronger than direct evidence. A fingerprint found on a shelf would probably be stronger evidence that the owner of the fingerprint put his finger on the shelf than a witness swearing that it had not happened. Further, a dog track in the mud would be far more likely to convince the average man that a dog had come by than a host of witnesses swearing that no dog had passed. In this case, the defense put on direct testimony that Mr. Mayle was clean shaven on the night of the murder, and the prosecution's introduction of a photograph showing him a few hours later with a mustache and goatee was merely circumstantial evidence that Mr. Mayle was not clean shaven at the time of the murder. Nevertheless, it was very powerful evidence, and the jury apparently believed it over the testimony of two witnesses to the contrary.

People v. Ireland, 70 Cal.2d 522 (1969)

SULLIVAN, Justice.

Defendant Patrick Ireland was charged by indictment with the murder of Ann Lucille Ireland, his wife. He entered pleas of not guilty and not guilty by reason of insanity and, after a trial by jury, was found guilty of murder in the second degree. Defendant's plea of not guilty by reason of insanity was personally withdrawn by him, and he was sentenced to imprisonment for the term prescribed by law. He appeals from the judgment.

Defendant, a high school teacher, and Ann Lucille Ireland, the deceased, were married in 1957 while defendant was attending college. They had two children, born in 1958 and 1960, respectively. In 1963 they began to experience marital difficulties and Ann entered into the first of a series of secret extramarital affairs. Defendant soon began to doubt his wife's fidelity and to make accusations against her. Ann at first denied her involvement, and defendant's accusations resulted in a number of violent physical encounters between them in which Ann sustained injuries. The relationship continued in this turbulent and unhappy state for several years.

Early in 1967, Ann consulted an attorney and commenced an action for divorce. The parties continued to live together, however, and undertook several attempts to revive their marriage. Their efforts were unsuccessful, and Ann soon became involved in an extramarital relationship with the salesman for a company which had installed a swimming pool at the Ireland residence. Defendant was informed of this by a family friend, and when he accused Ann she admitted her involvement and shortly thereafter promised to sever the relationship in the interest of the family. Defendant, in order to make certain that Ann would keep her promise, hired a private detective to follow her. Apparently Ann's relationship with the salesman was terminated by the latter when he learned of the private detective, but this did not result in improved relations between the Irelands.

During this period defendant began to suffer from headaches, nervousness, and fatigue, and consulted a doctor who prescribed medication for these conditions.

On April 24, 1967, the Irelands met with a conciliation counsellor attached to the county conciliation court. As a result of this meeting defendant and Ann agreed to seek the services of the Western Behavioral Institute in a last effort to save their marriage; apparently Ann's consent to this step was obtained with some reluctance on her part. After the meeting defendant suggested that they have lunch together but Ann was not willing to do so and they returned to their home. Ann went out to her hairdresser that afternoon, and when she had returned and the children had been put to bed the Irelands discussed their meeting with the conciliation counsellor and their future appointment at the Western Behavioral Institute. Defendant agreed to undertake certain changes in their relationship such as diminishing the influence of his parents, who lived nearby, and allowing Ann to assume a more positive role in the family. Ann again expressed to defendant a willingness to make efforts in the interest of renewed family harmony.

On the morning of April 25, Ann displayed a sullen and incommunicative attitude in response to defendant's attempts to engage in conversation with her. Defendant made efforts to be relieved from his teaching duties but was unsuccessful in doing so and taught five classes during the day. When he returned home between 3:30 and 4 p.m., Ann was not at home, but shortly thereafter she returned from the market where she had been shopping. During the day defendant had taken the various medications which had been prescribed for him, and prior to Ann's return from the market he drank two coffee mugs of wine. Upon her return defendant, Ann, and their daughter went out to purchase chlorine for their pool and to do other errands, and on their way home defendant suggested that they have dinner at the home of a friend. Ann did not wish to do so, and they returned home where she prepared dinner for the family. Defendant at this time had another coffee mug of wine and took a rest until he was called for dinner. After dinner defendant lay down again and had another coffee mug of wine.

Sometime between 7:30 and 8:30 p.m. on April 25, 1967, defendant shot and killed his wife Ann by firing into her at close range two .38 caliber bullets from a pistol which he usually kept in his bedroom. Defendant himself testified that he had no memory of the actual shooting or of certain events occurring thereafter, and the only known details of the homicide were provided at trial by the testimony of his six-year-old daughter, Terry, in whose presence the shooting took place.

Terry testified that after she had gone to bed on the evening in question she heard her parents talking in the den where her mother had been watching television; that she asked her parents what they were talking about and they replied that they were talking about the television program; that her parents were really "talking about who was going to leave first"; that defendant shortly thereafter "got the gun in his pocket," returned to the den, and asked Ann to go outside by the swimming pool and talk; that Ann refused to go and defendant pulled her off the couch where she was lying; that Ann fell to the floor and she, Terry, then went into the room and began crying; the defendant then sat down in a chair and Ann climbed back upon the couch; that defendant then took the gun from his pocket, and said "Now what, Ann?" and fired three shots at Ann; that the first shot went into the window and the second and third shots struck Ann in the eye and chest; that defendant then went into the front room and "was sitting and rocking and crying"; and that she, Terry, then stayed on the couch with her mother Ann, until neighbors arrived. . . .

Defendant . . . contends that it was error, in the circumstances of this case, to instruct the jury on second degree felony murder. In the alternative he contends that, if second degree felony murder instructions were appropriate in this case, the court should have given an instruction requested by him which purported to cure any confusion which might result from the giving of such instructions. Because we agree with the former of these contentions we need not address ourselves to the latter.

The felony-murder rule operates (1) to posit the existence of malice aforethought in homicides which are the direct causal result of the perpetration or attempted perpetration of *all* felonies inherently dangerous to human life, and (2) to posit the existence of malice aforethought *and* to classify the offense as murder of the first degree in homicides which are the direct causal result of those six felonies specifically enumerated in section 189 of the Penal Code. Thus, "[a] homicide that is a direct causal result of the commission of a felony inherently dangerous to human life (other than the six felonies enumerated in Pen. Code, §189) constitutes at least second degree murder." Accordingly, the giving of a second degree felony-murder instruction in a murder prosecution has the effect of "reliev(ing) the jury of the necessity of finding one of the elements of the crime of murder", to wit, malice aforethought.

The jury in this case was given an instruction based upon CALJIC No. 305 (Revised). The instruction given provided in relevant part: ". . . the unlawful killing of a human being with malice aforethought is murder of the second degree in any of the following cases: . . . Three, when the killing is a direct causal result of the perpetration or attempt to perpetrate a felony inherently dangerous to human life, such as an assault with a deadly weapon." The court then went on to instruct upon the elements of the crime of assault with a deadly weapon in the terms of CALJIC No. 604.

This instruction might have been understood by the jury in either of two ways. First, the jury might have concluded therefrom that it should find defendant guilty of second degree murder if it *first* found that defendant harbored malice aforethought and *then* found that the homicide had occurred in the perpetration of the crime of assault with a deadly weapon. If the jury had understood the instruction in this way it would have misconceived the doctrine of second degree felony murder as we have explained it above. Second, if the jury derived from the instruction the correct meaning of the doctrine in question, it would have concluded that it should find defendant guilty of second degree murder if it found only that the homicide was committed in the perpetration of the crime of assault with a deadly weapon. This, the proper understanding of the instruction, would have relieved the jury from a specific finding of malice aforethought.

We have concluded that the utilization of the felony-murder rule in circumstances such as those before us extends the operation of that rule "beyond any rational function that it is designed to serve." To allow such use of the felony-murder rule would effectively preclude the jury from considering the issue of malice aforethought in all cases wherein homicide has been committed as a result of a felonious assault—a category which includes the great majority of all homicides. This kind of bootstrapping finds support neither in logic nor in law. We therefore hold that a second degree felony-murder instruction may not properly be given when it is based upon a felony which is an integral part of the homicide and which the evidence produced by the prosecution shows to be an offense included *in fact* within the offense charged.

A similar limitation upon the felony-murder rule has been recognized in New York and other states. Although we are not at this time prepared to say that the limitation which we have above articulated, when applied to fact situations not now before us, will come to assume the exact outlines and proportions of the so-called "merger" doctrine enunciated in these other jurisdictions, we believe that the reasoning underlying that doctrine is basically sound and should be applied to the extent that it is consistent with the laws and policies of this state. . . .

The judgment is reversed.

4.   Inherently Dangerous Felony Limitation

In *Ireland*, a prosecutor could pursue second degree murder using a felony murder theory if the underlying felony was "inherently dangerous to human life." The *Patterson* case examines, in more detail, the meaning of an inherently dangerous felony. For more information, see Joshua Dressler, *Understanding Criminal Law* §31.06[C][1] (6th ed. 2012).

People v. Patterson, 49 Cal.3d 615 (1989)

KENNARD, Justice.

The issue before us is whether the second degree felony-murder doctrine applies to a defendant who, in violation of Health and Safety Code section 11352, furnishes cocaine to a person who dies as a result of ingesting it. We reaffirm the rule that, in determining whether a felony is inherently dangerous to human life under the second degree felony-murder doctrine, we must consider "the elements of the felony in the abstract, not the particular 'facts' of the case." While Health and Safety Code section 11352 includes drug offenses other than the crime of furnishing cocaine, which formed the basis for the prosecution's theory of second degree felony murder here, we conclude that the inquiry into inherent dangerousness must focus on the felony of furnishing cocaine, and not on section 11352 as a whole. We further hold that—consistent with the established definition of the term "inherently dangerous to life" in the context of implied malice as an element of second degree murder—a felony is inherently dangerous to life when there is a high probability that its commission will result in death.

We reverse the decision of the Court of Appeal affirming the trial court's ruling that, as a matter of law, the second degree felony-murder doctrine was inapplicable to this case. We direct the Court of Appeal to remand the matter to the trial court.

FACTUAL AND PROCEDURAL BACKGROUND

According to the testimony at the preliminary hearing, victim Jennie Licerio and her friend Carmen Lopez had been using cocaine on a daily basis in the months preceding Licerio's death. On the night of November 25, 1985, the two women were with defendant in his motel room. There, all three drank "wine coolers," inhaled "lines" of cocaine, and smoked "coco puffs" (hand-rolled cigarettes containing a mixture of tobacco and cocaine). Defendant furnished the cocaine. When Licerio became ill, Lopez called an ambulance. Defendant stayed with the two women until the paramedics and the police arrived. The paramedics were unable to revive Licerio, who died of acute cocaine intoxication.

The People filed an information charging defendant with one count each of murder (Pen. Code, §187), possession of cocaine (Health & Saf. Code, §11350), and possession of cocaine for sale (Health & Saf. Code, §11351). Defendant was also charged with three counts of violating Health and Safety Code section 11352, in that he "did willfully, unlawfully and feloniously transport, import into the State of California, sell, furnish, administer, and give away, and attempt to import into the State of California and transport a controlled substance, to-wit: cocaine."

Defendant moved under Penal Code section 995 to set aside that portion of the information charging him with murder, contending the evidence presented at the preliminary hearing did not establish probable cause to believe he had committed murder. In opposing the motion, the People did not suggest the murder charge was based on a theory of implied malice. Instead, they relied solely on the second degree felony-murder doctrine. They argued that by furnishing cocaine defendant committed an inherently dangerous felony, thus justifying application of the rule. The trial court denied the motion. However, when the case was reassigned for trial, the court dismissed the murder charge under Penal Code section 1385. In compliance with Penal Code section 1385's requirement that "[t]he reasons for the dismissal must be set forth in an order entered upon the minutes," the court gave this explanation in its minute order: "Court finds that violation of 11351 H & S and 11352 H & S are not inherently dangerous to human life and on the Courts [sic] own motion orders count 1 of the information dismissed in the interest of justice under section 1385 P.C."

Following the dismissal, defendant entered a negotiated plea of guilty to the three counts of violating Health and Safety Code section 11352. In his written plea form, defendant specifically admitted he had "furnished a controlled substance, to wit: cocaine, knowing it was cocaine." The remaining charges were dismissed, and defendant was placed on probation for three years, with credit for the time he had already spent in custody. The People appealed the dismissal of the murder charge.

The Court of Appeal affirmed the dismissal of the murder count. Based on its review of the applicable decisions of this court, the Court of Appeal felt compelled to analyze Health and Safety Code section 11352 in its entirety (as opposed to only that portion of the statute actually violated in the present case) to determine whether defendant had committed an inherently dangerous felony. The court observed that section 11352 could be violated in various nonhazardous ways, such as transporting or offering to transport controlled substances.[4] As the court said, "The latter acts are obviously not inherently dangerous to human life." While recognizing that the murder charge against defendant rested on his *furnishing* cocaine to the victim, the court concluded that, viewing the statute "in the abstract," a violation of section 11352 could not be characterized as an inherently dangerous felony.

The Court of Appeal reached this conclusion reluctantly. The court noted that consideration of the entire statute, which included offenses unrelated to defendant's conduct, had brought the second degree felony-murder rule "to the brink of logical absurdity." The court suggested that "[i]f the rule is not abolished, it should be codified by the legislature with meaningful guidelines to effectuate its use."

As we shall explain, the Court of Appeal has interpreted our previous decisions in this area too broadly. In determining whether defendant had committed an inherently dangerous felony, the court should have considered only the particular crime at issue, namely, furnishing cocaine, and not the entire group of offenses included in the statute but not involved here. Thus, it is the offense of furnishing cocaine, not the statute as a whole, which must be examined "in the abstract."

DISCUSSION
1. Second degree felony-murder doctrine

There is no precise statutory definition for the second degree felony-murder rule.[5] In *People v. Ford* (1964) 60 Cal.2d 772, 795, we defined the

---

[4] Health and Safety Code section 11352 provides: "Except as otherwise provided in this division, every person who transports, imports into this state, sells, furnishes, administers, or gives away, or offers to transport, import into this state, sell, furnish, administer, or give away, or attempts to import into this state or transport (1) any controlled substance specified in subdivision (b), (c), or (e), or paragraph (1) of subdivision (f) of Section 11054, specified in paragraph (14), (15), or (20) of subdivision (d) of Section 11054, or specified in subdivision (b), (c), or (g) of Section 11055, or (2) any controlled substance classified in Schedule III, IV, or V which is a narcotic drug, unless upon the written prescription of a physician, dentist, podiatrist, or veterinarian licensed to practice in this state, shall be punished by imprisonment in the state prison for three, four, or five years." Cocaine is one of the numerous drugs covered by the statute. (Health & Saf. Code, § 11054, subd. (f)(1).)

[5] Penal Code section 189 provides in relevant part: "All murder which is perpetrated by means of a destructive device or explosive, knowing use of ammunition designed primarily to penetrate metal or armor, poison, lying in wait, torture, or by any other kind of willful, deliberate, and premeditated killing, or which is committed in the perpetration of, or attempt to perpetrate, arson, rape, robbery, burglary, mayhem, or

doctrine as follows: "A homicide that is a direct causal result of the commission of a felony inherently dangerous to human life (other than the six felonies enumerated in Pen. Code, §189) constitutes at least second degree murder. In determining whether the felony is inherently dangerous, "we look to the elements of the felony in the abstract, not the particular 'facts' of the case."

The Court of Appeal's opinion in this case criticized the second degree felony-murder rule in its present form, suggesting the doctrine should either be completely eliminated or considerably "reformed." In response, defendant and amici curiae on his behalf have urged us to abolish the rule. The People and their amici curiae, on the other hand, have asked that we "reform" the doctrine by looking solely to the actual conduct of a defendant, thereby dispensing with the requirement that the elements of the offense be viewed in the abstract. We decline both invitations for the reasons discussed below.

The second degree felony-murder doctrine has been a part of California's criminal law for many decades. In recent years, we have characterized the rule as "anachronistic" and "disfavored", based on the view of many legal scholars that the doctrine incorporates an artificial concept of strict criminal liability that "erodes the relationship between criminal liability and moral culpability." The Legislature, however, has taken no action to alter this judicially created rule, and has declined our more recent suggestion in *People v. Dillon* that it reconsider the rules on first and second degree felony murder and misdemeanor manslaughter. In this case, our limited purpose in granting the People's petition for review was to determine the applicability of the second degree felony-murder doctrine to the crime of furnishing cocaine. . . .

2.   *Determining "inherent dangerousness" of the felony of furnishing cocaine*
    . . . [I]n determining whether defendant committed an inherently dangerous felony, we must consider the elements of the felony "in the abstract." Because Health and Safety Code section 11352 also proscribes conduct other than that involved here (furnishing cocaine), the issue still to be resolved is whether we must consider only the specific offense of furnishing cocaine or the entire scope of conduct prohibited by the statute.

The Court of Appeal examined Health and Safety Code section 11352 in its entirety. It felt compelled to do so because of a series of recent cases where we held that, to determine a felony's inherent dangerousness, the statute as a whole had to be examined. However, unlike the situation here, each of those cases involved a statute that proscribed an essentially single form of conduct.
. . .

The fact that the Legislature has included a variety of offenses in Health and Safety Code section 11352 does not require that we treat them as a unitary entity. Rather, we must decide whether in "[r]eading and considering the

---

any act punishable under Section 288, is murder of the first degree; and all other kinds of murders are of the second degree."

statute as a whole in order to determine the true legislative intent . . . we find [a] basis for severing" the various types of conduct it forbids. There are more than 100 different controlled substances that fall within the confines of Health and Safety Code section 11352. To create statutes separately proscribing the importation, sale, furnishing, administration, etc., of each of these drugs, would require the enactment of hundreds of individual statutes. It thus appears that for the sake of convenience the Legislature has included the various offenses in one statute.

The determination whether a defendant who furnishes cocaine commits an inherently dangerous felony should not turn on the dangerousness of other drugs included in the same statute, such as heroin and peyote; nor should it turn on the danger to life, if any, inherent in the transportation or administering of cocaine. Rather, each offense set forth in the statute should be examined separately to determine its inherent dangerousness.

For the reasons discussed above, we hold the Court of Appeal and the trial court erred in concluding that Health and Safety Code section 11352 should be analyzed in its entirety to determine whether, in furnishing cocaine, defendant committed an inherently dangerous felony. Defendant, however, argues that even the more narrow offense of furnishing cocaine is not an inherently dangerous felony and therefore the trial court acted correctly in dismissing the murder charge, despite its faulty analysis. In countering that argument, the People have asked us to take judicial notice of various medical articles and reports that assertedly demonstrate that the offense of furnishing cocaine is sufficiently dangerous to life to constitute an inherently dangerous felony.

The task of evaluating the evidence on this issue is most appropriately entrusted to the trial court, subject, of course, to appellate review. We therefore direct the Court of Appeal to remand the matter to the trial court for further proceedings in light of this opinion. This remand does not foreclose a finding by the trial court that the crime of furnishing cocaine is not a felony inherently dangerous to life, thus justifying a dismissal of the murder charge. If, however, the trial court concludes the offense of furnishing cocaine is inherently dangerous and therefore the murder charge should not be dismissed, defendant must be allowed to withdraw his guilty plea to the charges of violating Health and Safety Code section 11352, with credit for any interim time served.

3. *Meaning of the term "inherently dangerous to human life"*

For the guidance of the trial court on remand, we shall elaborate on the meaning of the term "inherently dangerous to life" for purposes of the second degree felony-murder doctrine.

The felony-murder rule generally acts as a substitute for the *mental state* ordinarily required for the offense of murder. We observed in *People v. Satchell*, 6 Cal.3d at page 43: "Under well-settled principles of criminal liability a person who kills—whether or not he is engaged in an independent felony at the time—is guilty of murder *if he acts with malice aforethought*. The felony-murder doctrine, whose ostensible purpose is to deter those engaged in felonies from killing negligently or accidentally, operates to posit the existence of that crucial mental state—and thereby to render irrelevant evidence of actual malice or the lack thereof—when the killer is engaged in a felony whose inherent danger to human life renders logical an imputation of malice on the part of all who commit it." Ordinarily, when a defendant commits an unintentional killing, a murder conviction requires a showing that he acted with implied malice. (Pen. Code, §188.) With the felony-murder rule, however, such malice need not be shown.

Implied malice, for which the second degree felony-murder doctrine acts as a substitute, has both a physical and a mental component. The physical component is satisfied by the performance of "an act, the natural consequences of which are dangerous to life." The mental component is the requirement that the defendant "knows that his conduct endangers the life of another and . . . acts with a conscious disregard for life."

The second degree felony-murder rule eliminates the need for the prosecution to establish the *mental* component. The justification therefor is that, when society has declared certain inherently dangerous conduct to be felonious, a defendant should not be allowed to excuse himself by saying he was unaware of the danger to life because, by declaring the condut to be felonious, society has warned him of the risk involved. The *physical* requirement, however, remains the same; by committing a felony inherently dangerous to life, the defendant has committed "an act, the natural consequences of which are dangerous to life", thus satisfying the physical component of implied malice.

The definition of "inherently dangerous to life" in the context of the implied malice element of second degree murder is well established. An act is inherently dangerous to human life when there is "a *high probability* that it will result in death."

We therefore conclude—by analogy to the established definition of the term "dangerous to life" in the context of the implied malice element of second degree murder—that, for purposes of the second degree felony-murder doctrine, an "inherently dangerous felony" is an offense carrying "a high probability" that death will result. A less stringent standard would inappropriately expand the scope of the second degree felony-murder rule reducing the seriousness of the act which a defendant must commit in order to be charged with murder.

We share the concern Chief Justice Lucas has expressed in his dissent regarding the tragic effects that the abuse of illegal drugs, particularly "crack" cocaine, has on our society. However, it is the Legislature, rather than this court, that should determine whether expansion of the second degree felony-murder rule is an appropriate method by which to address this problem. In the absence of specific legislative action, we must determine the scope of the rule by applying the established definition of inherent dangerousness.

DISPOSITION

We reverse the decision of the Court of Appeal, and direct that court to remand the matter to the trial court for further proceedings consistent with this opinion.

5. Killings by a Non-Felon

A and B agree to rob a liquor store. An off-duty police officer intervenes and, while attempting to apprehend B, shoots and kills both A and a customer. Can B be held criminally responsible for both deaths? Can co-defendants be held criminally liable in a felony murder prosecution when the killing occurs during the felony but is done by a non-felon, such as an innocent bystander, victim, or police officer? Is a killing by a bystander, victim, or police officer "in furtherance" of the felony?

The *Campbell* case explores how various jurisdictions have handled these questions.

Campbell v. State, 293 Md. 438 (1982)

DAVIDSON, Judge.

This case concerns the criminal responsibility of felons for the lethal acts of others. More particularly, it presents the question whether, under Maryland Code (1957, 1982 Repl. Vol.), Art. 27, §410, Maryland's so-called "felony-murder" statute, the killing of a co-felon during an armed robbery, by either a police officer attempting to apprehend him, or by a victim resisting the armed robbery, constitutes murder in the first degree on the part of the surviving felon.

On 5 February 1980, in the Criminal Court of Baltimore, the appellant, Anthony Wilson Campbell, pled guilty to first degree felony murder of a co-felon [and other charges] . . . . A factual statement presented as the basis for the guilty pleas showed that on 19 September 1979, at approximately 12 midnight, the appellant and Rufus Branch (co-felon) entered a taxicab operated by Paul Alston (victim). The appellant sat in the back seat of the taxicab and the co-felon sat in the front seat. After requesting the victim to drive to a street in an area of deserted buildings, the co-felon pulled out a small caliber handgun, pointed it at the victim, and said, "This is a stick up." The co-felon then ordered the victim to hand him his money bag. The appellant said, "Do what he tells you. I have a gun too." The victim handed his money bag and his wallet to the co-felon and then looked at both the co-felon and the appellant. The appellant said, "He's seen our faces; we have to take him somewhere and kill him."

As the victim drove up the street, he saw two police cars. The victim drove alongside the police car of Officer Cruse and slammed on his brakes. At that point, the co-felon opened fire at the victim who returned the fire with his own handgun. Both the victim and the co-felon were wounded. Officer Heiderman, then on foot patrol, came to the victim's assistance and shot at the co-felon. The co-felon and the appellant then left the taxicab and began to run. The appellant hid in the vestibule of a nearby building.

Officer Heiderman and Officer Cruse chased the co-felon and ordered him to halt. The co-felon continued to run. Officer Heiderman hid behind a truck to reload his weapon. When Officer Heiderman emerged, the co-felon suddenly appeared from behind a vehicle and pointed his gun toward the officer. Officer Cruse shouted a warning to Officer Heiderman, who turned and shot the co-felon approximately four times. The co-felon fell to the ground, dead. An autopsy report revealed nine bullet wounds, five of which were potentially lethal. At least two of the nine wounds were inflicted by the victim. Under these circumstances, it is unclear whether the co-felon was killed by the victim or by the police officer.

A third police officer, Officer Steinman, arrested the appellant in the vestibule where he was hiding. After searching the appellant and finding that he did not have any weapons, Officer Steinman walked the appellant back to the victim's taxicab. At that time, the victim identified the appellant as one of his assailants. The victim's money bag and his wallet were found in the gutter of the street directly between the taxicab and the vestibule in which the appellant was found.

The trial court accepted the appellant's guilty pleas. Thereafter, the trial court convicted the appellant of first degree murder [and other charges] . . . sentenced him to concurrent terms of life (all but 15 years suspended), 15 years, and 10 years respectively. The appellant appealed to the Court of Special Appeals. We issued a writ of certiorari before consideration by that Court.

Maryland Code, Art. 27, §§407–410 provide that certain types of murder shall be murder in the first degree. More particularly, §410 provides in pertinent part:

> All murder which shall be committed in the perpetration of, or attempt to perpetrate . . . robbery . . . shall be murder in the first degree.

All murder not specified in §§407–410 is murder in the second degree. §411. These sections do not create any new statutory crimes, but rather divide the crime of murder, as known at common law, into degrees.

With respect to the crime of murder as known at common law, this Court has recently stated in *Jackson v. State*, 286 Md. 430 (1979):

> At the common law, to which the inhabitants of Maryland are entitled, Md. Const. Declaration of Rights, Art. 5, homicide is the killing of a human being by another human being; criminal homicide is homicide without lawful justification or excuse; criminal homicide with malice aforethought is murder; malice aforethought is established, *inter alia*, upon commission of criminal homicide in the perpetration of, or in the attempt to

perpetrate, a felony. *Thus, at common law, homicide arising in the perpetration of, or in the attempt to perpetrate, a felony is murder whether death was intended or not, the fact that the person was engaged in such perpetration or attempt being sufficient to supply the element of malice.* 'The [felony-murder] doctrine has repeatedly been recognized and applied in this country, and is to be regarded as still in force, except where it has been expressly abrogated by statute.'

The doctrine has not been abrogated by statute in this State.

This Court has held that under the felony-murder doctrine a participating felon is guilty of murder when a homicide has been committed by a co-felon. We have also held that under the felony-murder doctrine a participating felon is guilty of murder when a hostage is accidentally killed by a police officer attempting to apprehend robbers fleeing from the scene of an armed robbery. However, this Court has not previously considered whether under the felony-murder doctrine a participating felon is guilty of murder when, during an armed robbery, a police officer kills a fleeing co-felon in an attempt to apprehend him, or a victim kills a co-felon in an attempt to resist the armed robbery. . . .

Courts in some jurisdictions that have considered the precise question here have relied on the agency theory and have held that a participating felon is not guilty of murder when a police officer kills a fleeing co-felon while attempting to apprehend him. Thus, in *Commonwealth v. Redline*, 391 Pa. 486 (1958), a felon and his co-felon were fleeing from the scene of an armed robbery when a police officer, attempting to apprehend them, killed the co-felon. Manifestly, the police officer's killing of the co-felon was committed to thwart the felony rather than to further it. The Supreme Court of Pennsylvania, employing the agency theory, stated:

> The mere coincidence of homicide and felony is not enough to satisfy the requirements of the felony-murder doctrine. 'It is necessary . . . to show that the conduct causing death was done in furtherance of the design to commit the felony. . . .
>
> [I]n order to convict for felony-murder, *the killing must have been done by the defendant or by an accomplice or confederate or by one acting in furtherance of the felonious undertaking. Redline*, 391 Pa. at 495–96 (emphasis in original).

That Court reversed the surviving felon's conviction of first degree murder.

Similarly, courts in some jurisdictions have held that under the felony-murder doctrine a participating felon is not guilty of murder when a victim kills a co-felon during the commission of a felony. More particularly, in *Sheriff, Clark County v. Hicks*, 89 Nev. 78 (1973), the victim of an attempted murder, in an effort to resist the perpetration of the crime, fatally shot one of three co-felons. As in *Redline*, the victim's killing of the co-felon was committed to thwart the felony rather than to further it. The Supreme Court of Nevada, employing the agency theory, stated:

> [T]he felony-murder rule does not apply when the killing is done by the victim of the crime, because in such a case the malice aforethought necessary for murder is not attributable to the accomplice felon. The killing in such an instance is done, not in the perpetration of, or an attempt to perpetrate, a crime, but rather in an attempt to thwart the felony. *Hicks*, 506 P.2d at 768.

That Court determined that the surviving felon was not guilty of murder.

In at least one jurisdiction, it has been held that under the felony-murder doctrine a participating felon is not guilty of murder when a bystander kills a co-felon fleeing from the scene of a felony. In *People v. Wood*, 8 N.Y.2d 48 (1960), the surviving felon and his co-felons, while patronizing a tavern, became embroiled in the near-fatal shooting of another party and a gun battle with an approaching police officer. When the felons attempted to escape, the owner of the tavern, in an effort to assist the police officer, killed one of the felons. As in *Redline*, and *Hicks*, the bystander's killing of the co-felon was committed to thwart the felony rather than to further it. The Court of Appeals of New York, employing the agency theory, stated:

> Thus, a felony murder embraces not any killing incidentally coincident with the felony but only those committed by one of the criminals in the attempted execution of the unlawful end. Although the homicide itself need not be within the common design, the *act* which results in death must be in furtherance of the unlawful purpose. *Wood*, 8 N.Y.2d at 51 (citations omitted) (emphasis in original).

That Court determined that the surviving felon was not guilty of murder.

Courts in still other jurisdictions have considered whether under the felony-murder doctrine a participating felon is guilty of murder when a person other than a co-felon has been killed during the commission of a felony. Such courts have held that under that doctrine a participating felon is not guilty of murder when a police officer attempting to thwart the felony accidentally kills the victim, and when a police officer attempting to thwart the felony accidentally kills another police officer. Additionally, courts in some jurisdictions have held that under the felony-murder doctrine a participating felon is not guilty of murder when a victim, attempting to resist the perpetration of the felony, accidentally kills an innocent bystander.

Courts in some jurisdictions have held that under the felony-murder doctrine a participating felon is guilty of murder when a killing is committed by a person other than the accused felon or his co-felons. The rationale underlying this rule is the "proximate cause" theory of felony murder.

A statement of the proximate cause theory appears in *Miers v. State*, 157 Tex.Cr.R. 572 (1952). There, a victim of an attempted robbery accidentally killed himself while he was attempting to resist the perpetration of the felony. Quoting from *Taylor v. State*, 41 Tex.Crim. 564, 572 (1900), the Court of Criminal Appeals of Texas stated:

> The whole question here is one of causal connection. If the appellant here set in motion the cause which occasioned the death of deceased, we hold it to be a sound doctrine that he would be as culpable as if he had done the deed with his own hands. *Miers*, 157 Tex.Cr.R. at 578.

That Court determined that the accused felon was guilty of murder.

This statement was amplified in *People v. Hickman*, 59 Ill.2d 89 (1974), *cert. denied*, 421 U.S. 913 (1975). There, a police officer killed another police officer while attempting to apprehend co-felons fleeing from the scene of a burglary. Quoting from *People v. Payne*, 359 Ill. 246, 255 (1935), a case in which a victim resisting a robbery was killed by a co-felon, the Supreme Court of Illinois stated:

> It reasonably might be anticipated that an attempted robbery would meet with resistance, during which the victim might be shot either by himself or some one else in attempting to prevent the robbery, and those attempting to perpetrate the robbery would be guilty of murder. *Hickman*, 59 Ill.2d at 93.

That Court determined that the accused felon was guilty of murder.

Employing the proximate cause theory, courts in these jurisdictions have held that under the felony-murder doctrine a participating felon is guilty of murder not only when a police officer attempting to thwart a felony accidentally kills another police officer, or when a victim, attempting to resist the felony, accidentally kills himself, or when a bystander, attempting to thwart the perpetration of the felony, accidentally kills another bystander, but also when a police officer kills a fleeing co-felon while attempting to apprehend him.

The present trend has been for courts to employ the agency theory and to limit criminal culpability under the felony-murder doctrine to lethal acts committed by the felons themselves or their accomplices, and not to employ the proximate cause theory to extend criminal culpability for lethal acts of nonfelons. Thus, courts in several jurisdictions have recently abandoned the proximate cause theory upon which they previously relied and have substituted the agency theory. Such courts now hold that under the felony-murder doctrine, criminal culpability is limited to lethal acts committed by felons and their accomplices and does not extend to the lethal acts of nonfelons.

One reason for declining to extend the felony-murder doctrine is that such an extension would not achieve the rule's basic purpose. Manifestly, the purpose of deterring felons from killing by holding them strictly responsible for killings they or their co-felons commit is not effectuated by punishing them for killings committed by persons not acting in furtherance of the felony.

Another reason to decline to extend the applicability of the felony-murder doctrine is that the tort liability concept of proximate cause has no proper place in prosecutions for criminal homicide. There is a difference between the underlying rationale of tort and criminal law. Tort law is primarily concerned with who shall bear the burden of loss, while criminal law is concerned with the imposition of punishment. "Tort concepts of foreseeability and proximate cause have shallow relevance to culpability for murder in the first degree." Because of the extreme penalty attaching to a conviction of felony murder, a closer and more direct causal connection between the felony and the killing is required than the causal connection ordinarily required under the tort concept of proximate cause. Because the tort liability concept of proximate cause is generally too broad and comprehensive to be appropriate in a criminal proceeding, the proximate cause theory ordinarily should not be employed to extend the applicability of the felony-murder doctrine.

We are persuaded that the felony-murder doctrine should not be extended beyond its traditional common law limitation. We now hold that ordinarily, under the felony-murder doctrine, criminal culpability shall continue to be imposed for all lethal acts committed by a felon or an accomplice acting in furtherance of a common design. However, criminal culpability ordinarily shall not be imposed for lethal acts of nonfelons that are not committed in furtherance of a common design.

Here, the factual statement presented to the trial court shows that in the course of an armed robbery, a fleeing co-felon was killed by either a police officer or a victim. Manifestly, the killing of the co-felon was committed to thwart the felony rather than to further it. Under Maryland's felony-murder doctrine, the surviving felon is not guilty of murder. Under these circumstances, the factual statement serving as the basis for the plea of first degree felony murder of a co-felon failed to demonstrate guilt of the crime to which the plea was entered. The plea was not properly accepted by the trial court. Accordingly, we shall reverse the conviction of first degree murder. . . .

AS TO FIRST DEGREE MURDER, JUDGMENT REVERSED.

6. Alternatives to Felony Murder in Agency Jurisdiction

As *Campbell* makes clear, in an "agency" jurisdiction, a co-felon cannot be successfully prosecuted using a felony murder theory for a killing by a non-felon. The *Caldwell* case explores an alternative that a prosecutor might consider. Additionally, note how important the question of causation is to the outcome of this case.

People v. Caldwell, 36 Cal.3d 210 (1984)

REYNOSO, Justice.

Convicted of robbery and murder, defendants Ernest Edward Caldwell and Warren Edwin Washington appeal, claiming that they should not have been found guilty of the murder of a co-felon killed by police in the course of a shootout. Defendants claim that the co-felon's death proximately resulted from his own provocative conduct, for which, under our decisions, they cannot be held vicariously liable. More broadly, they wish us to reconsider the now settled rule that, though the felony-murder rule does not extend to killings by victims or police, such killings which proximately result from provocative conduct by one of the felons which exhibits a conscious disregard for life and a high probability of resulting in death constitute murder without the necessity of any "imputation" of malice. The record discloses substantial evidence of malicious conduct by the defendants themselves, and we decline their invitation to reconsider settled decisional law. Accordingly, we will affirm.

I

At about 7:15 p.m. on January 28, 1980, a man wearing a gray overcoat and dark glasses, subsequently identified as Anthony Belvin (the murder victim), approached the patio window of a Church's Fried Chicken outlet and placed an order, indicating that a companion would pay. The latter was wearing a blue jacket and was later identified as defendant Washington. Washington approached the window, then walked to the rear of the building, returned to speak to Belvin, and then walked to another window as though intending to pay for the order. Belvin then revealed a sawed-off shotgun, pointed it at one of the employees, and announced a holdup. Belvin ordered the employees to lie down on the ground and forced one of them to open one of the cash registers and hand over the contents ($24). While the employee attempted to open a second register at Belvin's behest, Washington entered the building through one of the counter windows and approached the manager's office carrying a handgun. The manager was already in telephone contact with the sheriff's department, having retreated to his office when he saw the robbers (whom he thought he recognized from a previous robbery) approaching the place. When the manager failed to open his door, Washington returned to the front of the establishment and left with Belvin.

Within seconds after the men fled, a patrol car containing Deputies Morris Boothroyd and Ronald Trujillo arrived. After one of the employees indicated in which direction the robbers had gone, Deputy Boothroyd saw a man in a blue jacket entering a brown automobile, which pulled away from the curb very rapidly, so much so that the tires lost traction on the road's surface. The deputies activated their lights and siren and gave chase.

The brown car, driven without headlights, was pursued by an increasing number of patrol cars over a twisting course for 5 to 10 miles, at speeds up to 70 miles per hour. During the chase, it drove through several stop signs and red lights, once skidded out of control, and nearly collided with another car. At an intersection, the suspects' auto struck a sheriff's vehicle coming from a side street and continued. Two more radio cars containing Deputies Steven Maggiora and Robert Lopez and Deputies Milkey and Bruton, joined the pursuit.

A fourth sheriff's vehicle, carrying Deputies James McSweeney and Patrick Hunter, came on the scene in front of the suspects' car, traveling in the opposite direction. The brown car initially veered toward the patrol car, then slowed almost to a stop and pulled toward the opposite curb. Suddenly the deputies noticed that the passenger in the right front seat (Washington) was pointing a shotgun at them. Instinctively, Deputy Hunter accelerated and rammed the suspects' car head-on. The shotgun discharged and flew out of Washington's hands, skidding away from the auto. Deputy Boothroyd pulled up directly behind the brown car, which rolled backward a short distance and came to rest against the patrol car's front bumper. The other sheriffs' cars parked a little behind and to the right of Boothroyd's and Trujillo's car.

The deputies alighted immediately, and took cover with guns drawn. A moment later, they saw the rear-seat passenger (Belvin) lean forward and put his hand out the window with a revolver in it. At the same time, Deputy McSweeney saw the driver (defendant Caldwell) open his door and crouch behind it carrying a recognizable handgun. Deputy Hunter watched Washington as he took cover behind a door post and formed the impression that he, too, had a weapon, in view of the way he kept watching the deputy, rather than seeking better cover (but it is apparently undisputed that Washington was unarmed at this point). Belvin moved his gun back and forth in a sweeping motion, ignoring repeated orders to "freeze" and "drop the gun." When Belvin took aim at two of the deputies and failed to respond to a last order to drop his weapon, Deputy Hunter fired at him, then at Washington. The rest of the deputies also fired at the car at about the same time (though Hunter is the only one of those who testified who did not state that he heard one or more shots before firing). When the shooting started, Deputy McSweeney focused his attention on Caldwell, and shot at him when, instead of dropping his gun, he looked in the direction of McSweeney's partner. Estimates of the time between the ramming of the suspects' car to the firing of the first shot ranged from 5 to 40 seconds.

After the gunfire ended, the suspects were removed from their vehicle. Belvin had been wounded, and he died the next morning. Tests indicated that Deputy Lopez' gun probably fired the fatal bullet. Belvin's revolver had not been fired, and Caldwell's was not found.

Both defendants testified in their own defense. Washington testified that he passed out from a PCP cigarette at Belvin's residence sometime before the robbery and could recall nothing further until he woke up in the hospital several days later. Caldwell testified that Belvin induced him to drive him and Washington to the fried chicken outlet with a promise to pay Caldwell some money he owed him. Caldwell assertedly had no idea that Belvin had committed a robbery until the police arrived and Belvin pointed the shotgun at him and threatened to shoot him if he did not drive away in an effort to elude the police.

II

Defendants contend that their murder convictions are not supported by substantial evidence. Although the killing of their confederate, Belvin, occurred as a culmination of their unsuccessful attempt to escape after a robbery, it is conceded that the felony-murder rule has no application here, since Belvin was not killed by defendants, but by a deputy sheriff in the pursuit of his duty. Defendants correctly point out that they could be found guilty of murder based on such a killing only if one or both of them were shown to have intentionally committed acts which it was highly probable would result in death, manifesting a conscious disregard of human life, or malice. They assert that it was Belvin's act of pointing a gun out the window of the car that precipitated the deputies' fire, and that they themselves did nothing which could be characterized as likely to result in death; since they are not liable for Belvin's malicious conduct, they insist the murder convictions cannot stand.

Their argument fails because the major premise is inaccurate. The fundamental problem with defendants' contention is that it requires a misapplication of the "substantial evidence" rule to sustain it. In reviewing a claim of insufficiency of the evidence, an appellate court " 'must view the evidence in a light most favorable to the respondent and presume in support of the judgment the existence of every fact the trier could reasonably deduce from the evidence.' " " 'The test on appeal is whether substantial evidence supports the conclusion of the trier of fact, not whether the evidence proves guilt beyond a reasonable doubt. . . .' . . . Evidence, to be 'substantial' must be 'of ponderable legal significance . . . reasonable in nature, credible, and of solid value.' " A review of the record discloses substantial evidence of malicious conduct on the part of both defendants.

Washington's suggestion that he did not commit "any acts . . . which were likely to cause death" seems utterly fantastic. The record reflects that he pointed a shotgun at Deputies Hunter and McSweeney as their patrol car approached from the front and was, from all that appears, prevented from shooting them only by Hunter's reflexive acceleration and ramming of the suspects' automobile. In fact, as previously noted, the shotgun discharged at about the moment of impact, though no one was hit, and it flew out of Washington's hands and skittered across the pavement. (Washington's more plausible argument that, malicious or not, his action with the shotgun was not a proximate cause of the subsequent shooting is considered [below].)

Caldwell does not dispute the testimony that he drove the getaway car without headlights on a rainy evening at speeds up to 70 miles per hour and passed through a number of stop signs and red lights, losing control more than once and colliding with other cars. In view of the jury's implicit rejection of his duress defense, this in itself could constitute substantial evidence of malice. (Again, a more serious issue of proximate causation remains to be discussed.)

Beyond that, though, there is Deputy McSweeney's testimony that, after the car was finally stopped (by a head-on collision with the car in which the deputy was riding) and Washington lost the shotgun, there was movement in the car, following which Caldwell exited the car and took a position of cover behind the door post with a gun in his hand, and then proceeded to ignore various commands to drop his gun, just as Belvin was doing. When the shooting started, McSweeney fired at Caldwell in response to the latter's fixing his attention on McSweeney's partner's position. The jury could reasonably infer that by the foregoing conduct Caldwell and Belvin manifested a concerted determination not to surrender and a readiness instead to shoot it out with their pursuers. In *People v. Reed* (1969) 270 Cal.App.2d 37, the defendant was held to have initiated a gun battle by pointing his gun toward a policeman and toward the robbery victim, the appellate court remarking that "[s]uch aggressive actions required immediate reaction unless an officer is to be held to the unreasonable requirement that an armed robber be given the courtesy of the first shot." Although Caldwell was not given a chance to do more than look toward Deputy Hunter's position, the jury could reasonably conclude that he had already, by emerging from the car with a gun and taking cover, and then refusing to drop the gun, exhibited unambiguously his aggressive intentions, so that it was plain to Deputy McSweeney, observing him, that when he looked toward his (McSweeney's) partner, it was because he was about to fire at him.

Recognizing the damaging effect of Detective McSweeney's testimony, defendants diffidently suggest that we simply ignore it, since none of the other deputies who testified saw the gun, and it was not found at the scene. While the lack of corroboration undoubtedly might have affected the weight of the witness' testimony, it cannot be said that the fact that no gun was found renders it "physically impossible" or "inherently improbable." We note that three of the officers involved, including Deputy Lopez whose gun probably fired the fatal bullet, did not testify at trial. The incidents in question occurred on a rainy winter evening, so a handgun thrown away some distance from the suspect's car might conceivably have been missed.

The question remains whether the killing of Belvin was "attributable" to the malicious acts of either or both of the defendants—i.e., whether it *proximately resulted* from said conduct. Defendants insist that Belvin's actions, ignoring the commands to drop his gun, and aiming at two deputies, were the sole cause of his death, but for which the officers would not have fired. All of the deputies who testified cited Belvin's actions as forming at least part of their reasons for opening fire. The jury might have concluded on the evidence that there was more than one proximate cause of the killing, however.

A difficult problem is presented when we examine the causal relationship between Caldwell's dangerous getaway driving and Washington's malicious and provocatory act of aiming a shotgun at Deputies Hunter and McSweeney and the shootout that followed. On one hand, it is undisputed that the deputies did not begin firing immediately, but gave the robbers a chance to surrender. Two of the four deputies who testified, Boothroyd and Maggiora, specifically testified that Washington's act was not a motivating factor in their decisions to fire. Deputy McSweeney stated that Caldwell's actions *after* the car stopped were the reason he fired. Though Deputy Hunter was concerned that Washington might have rearmed himself, even he did not cite the aiming of the shotgun as one of his reasons for opening fire. Therefore, to conclude that Caldwell's driving or Washington's act was a "but for" cause of Belvin's death might require some rather heroic inferences on the part of the jury. On the other hand, as little as five or six seconds may have elapsed between the collision and Washington's dropping of the shotgun and the deputies' opening fire. Though the deputies did not begin firing immediately, but gave the suspects an opportunity to drop their guns, it can hardly be said that whatever provocative force the high-speed chase and Washington's apparent attempt to shoot two policemen may have had dissipated, or "come to rest in a position of apparent safety." The lull in the action was precarious and short-lived, and at least one deputy, Boothroyd, did count the chase and the fact that Washington had "produced" a weapon a few seconds before among his reasons for fearing for his and his compatriots' safety just after the suspects' car was stopped. Thus a reasonable trier of fact could have concluded that the officers' lethal response was provoked by a violent confrontation which was the product of the actions of both Caldwell and Washington, as well as those of Belvin.

The jury might also reasonably have inferred that Belvin would have been unwilling to provoke a gun battle if Caldwell had not similarly adopted an aggressive stance, refusing to drop his gun. It may have concluded that the co-felons' conduct reflected a common determination not to surrender, and the several acts of resistance were interdependent. Caldwell's acts may thus also have been a "but for" cause (in fact) of the gun battle and Belvin's death.

To be considered a *proximate* cause of Belvin's death, the acts of the defendants must have been a "substantial factor" contributing to the result. "[N]o cause will receive juridical recognition if the part it played was so infinitesimal or so theoretical that it cannot properly be regarded as a *substantial factor* in bringing about the particular result. This is merely a special application of the general maxim—'*de minimis non curat lex*' . . ." The fact that one of the deputies who testified was primarily concerned about Caldwell's actions after the car stopped, and that another reacted to Washington's brandishing of the shotgun, and their inferential importance to Belvin, militate in favor of recognizing said acts as a substantial factor in bringing about the gun battle and Belvin's death.

Decisions in cases involving conduct of more than one co-felon acting in concert reflect the settled view that the extent of an individual's contribution to the resulting death need not be minutely determined. . . .

. . . [D]efendants' malicious conduct of fleeing in a dangerous high-speed chase, confronting the officers with a dangerous weapon when the chase ended and further preparing to shoot it out with the deputies was a proximate cause of Belvin's death. Moreover, all of these acts were reasonably in furtherance of the robbery, as their evident purpose was to permit the robbers to escape. Consequently, the evidence supports a determination that Caldwell and Washington were liable for the murder of Belvin. . . .

The judgment is affirmed.

I.   Michigan's Criminal Homicide Statute

In reviewing Michigan's criminal homicide statute provided, in part,[*] below, note the similarities and differences with the Pennsylvania degrees of murder model discussed previously in the *Drum* case.

M.C.L. §750.316. First degree murder; penalty; definitions

(1) Except as provided in sections 25 and 25a of chapter IX of the code of criminal procedure, 1927 PA 175, MCL 769.25 and 769.25a, a person who commits any of the following is guilty of first degree murder and shall be punished by imprisonment for life without eligibility for parole:

(a) Murder perpetrated by means of poison, lying in wait, or any other willful, deliberate, and premeditated killing.

(b) Murder committed in the perpetration of, or attempt to perpetrate, arson, criminal sexual conduct in the first, second, or third degree, child abuse in the first degree, a major controlled substance offense, robbery, carjacking, breaking and entering of a dwelling, home invasion in the first or second degree, larceny of any kind, extortion, kidnapping, vulnerable adult abuse in the first or second degree under section 145n, torture under section 85, or aggravated stalking under section 411i.

(c) A murder of a peace officer or a corrections officer committed while the peace officer or corrections officer is lawfully engaged in the performance of any of his or her duties as a peace officer or corrections officer, knowing that the peace officer or corrections officer is a peace officer or corrections officer engaged in the performance of his or her duty as a peace officer or corrections officer.

(2) As used in this section:

(a) "Arson" means a felony violation of chapter X.

(b) "Corrections officer" means any of the following:

(*i*) A prison or jail guard or other prison or jail personnel.

---

[*] Michigan has many other statutory provisions pertaining to killings. *See* M.C.L. §§750.316–329a (15 separate statutes).

(*ii*)   Any of the personnel of a boot camp, special alternative incarceration unit, or other minimum security correctional facility.

(*iii*)   A parole or probation officer.

(c)   "Major controlled substance offense" means any of the following:

(*i*)   A violation of section 7401(2)(a)(*i*) to (*iii*) of the public health code, 1978 PA 368, MCL 333.7401.

(*ii*)   A violation of section 7403(2)(a)(*i*) to (*iii*) of the public health code, 1978 PA 368, MCL 333.7403.

(*iii*)   A conspiracy to commit an offense listed in subparagraph (*i*) or (*ii*).

(d)   "Peace officer" means any of the following:

(*i*)   A police or conservation officer of this state or a political subdivision of this state.

(*ii*)   A police or conservation officer of the United States.

(*iii*)   A police or conservation officer of another state or a political subdivision of another state.

M.C.L. §750.317. Second degree murder; penalty

All other kinds of murder shall be murder of the second degree, and shall be punished by imprisonment in the state prison for life, or any term of years, in the discretion of the court trying the same.

M.C.L. §750.321. Manslaughter

Any person who shall commit the crime of manslaughter shall be guilty of a felony punishable by imprisonment in the state prison, not more than 15 years or by fine of not more than 7,500 dollars, or both, at the discretion of the court.

J.   Practice Problems on Criminal Homicide

For the essay problems below, write an answer in 90 minutes or less (approximately 45 minutes for each essay). Prepare your answer under test-like conditions (i.e., after studying your outline, no notes or interruptions) and be sure to carefully read the call of the question.

(1)   A woman saw her husband struck by a car in front of their home, which was located in a quiet residential neighborhood. He had been jogging home in the middle of the street, at approximately 10:15 p.m. on a Sunday evening.

Traffic was light and few people were out. He was wearing a dark-colored running suit without any reflective material.

Student, 22, was the driver of the car that struck the man. He had been driving at approximately 35 miles per hour in a 25 mile per hour zone. Additionally, he had been drinking beer at a college fraternity party earlier that night, and had turned around to talk to a passenger in the back seat just before the collision. As a result, he did not see the man in time to avoid striking him. Student immediately stopped his car just a few houses down the street, and got out to check and see if the man was injured. He discovered that the man had struck his head on the cement curb, and was dead.

Assume that you are the law clerk for the assistant prosecuting attorney who has been assigned to determine what homicide charges, if any, should be filed against Student in this case. Fully explain to her whether these facts would reasonably support: (a) a depraved heart murder charge; and (b) a criminal negligence manslaughter charge.

(2) Victim and a friend were drinking and shooting pool in the local bar. Witnesses reported that the pool game escalated into an argument when victim accused the friend of cheating by moving the cue ball. The friend angrily denied cheating and said that victim had no right to attack his honor. Victim shouted back that the friend had no honor to attack. He also said that after last night, neither did the friend's wife. The friend appeared to become enraged at this last comment and said, "You've had it now." He grabbed his cue stick and struck Victim's head so hard that victim collapsed and died of a massive subdural hemorrhage. The friend immediately fell to his knees, cradled his lifelong pal's head, and said "I didn't mean to hurt you buddy."

Based on these facts, and using the statute provided below, discuss whether the friend can be convicted of any degree of murder and whether any type of a manslaughter verdict would be a possible alternative. Justify your answers by applying the facts to the elements of whatever offenses you choose.

§2501. Criminal Homicide

(a) Offense defined. A person is guilty of criminal homicide if he intentionally, knowingly, recklessly, or negligently causes the death of another human being.
(b) Classification. Criminal homicide shall be classified as murder, voluntary manslaughter, or involuntary manslaughter.

§2502. Murder

(a) Murder of the first degree. A criminal homicide constitutes murder of the first degree when it is committed by an intentional killing.

(b) Murder of the second degree. A criminal homicide constitutes murder of the second degree when it is committed while defendant was engaged as a principal or an accomplice in the perpetration of a felony.

(c) Murder of the third degree. All other kinds of murder shall be murder of the third degree. Murder of the third degree is a felony of the first degree.

(d) Definitions. As used in this section the following words and phrases shall have the meanings given to them in this subsection:

(1) "Fireman." Includes any employee or member of a municipal fire department or volunteer fire company.

(2) "Hijacking." Any unlawful or unauthorized seizure or exercise of control, by force or violence or threat of force or violence.

(3) "Intentional killing." Killing by means of poison, or by lying in wait, or by any other kind of willful, deliberate, and premeditated killing.

(4) "Perpetration of a felony." The act of the defendant in engaging in, or being an accomplice in the commission of, or an attempt to commit, or flight after committing, or attempting to commit, robbery, rape, or deviate sexual intercourse by force or threat of force, arson, burglary, or kidnapping.

(5) "Principal." A person who is the actor or perpetrator of the crime.

§2503. Voluntary Manslaughter

(a) General rule. A person who kills an individual without lawful justification commits voluntary manslaughter if at the time of the killing he is acting under a sudden and intense passion resulting from serious provocation by the individual killed.

(b) Grading. Voluntary manslaughter is a felony of the first degree.

§2504. Involuntary Manslaughter

(a) General rule. A person is guilty of involuntary manslaughter when, as a direct result of the doing of an unlawful act in a reckless or grossly negligent manner, or the doing of a lawful act in a reckless or grossly negligent manner, he causes the death of another person.

(b) Grading. Involuntary manslaughter is a misdemeanor in the first degree. Where the victim is under 12 years of age and is in the care, custody, or control of the person who caused the death, involuntary manslaughter is a felony of the second degree.

K. Model Penal Code

Portions of the Model Penal Code (MPC) have been adopted in several states; as such, it is important to study selected provisions of the MPC. As will become apparent upon review of the MPC in this textbook, the MPC puts a great deal of emphasis on the defendant's state of mind—both to punish severely when a defendant has a bad state of mind and to give breaks when a defendant has a change of heart. This section will examine MPC Criminal Homicide, offering several cases that explore state statutes based on various provisions of the MPC.

Before looking at the cases, it helps to review MPC §1.13, General Definitions; MPC §2.02, General Requirements of Culpability; and the MPC Criminal Homicide Provisions (MPC §§210.1–210.4). Keep in mind that MPC §§1.13 and 2.02 are *general* provisions applicable to all crimes defined in the MPC. Your job will be to figure out how these general provisions apply to the specific homicide crimes in MPC §§210.1–210.4.

1. Model Penal Code Provisions

§210.1. Criminal Homicide

> (1) A person is guilty of criminal homicide if he purposely, knowingly, recklessly or negligently causes the death of another human being.
>
> (2) Criminal homicide is murder, manslaughter or negligent homicide.

§210.2. Murder

> (1) Except as provided in Section 210.3(1)(b), criminal homicide constitutes murder when:
>> (a)   it is committed purposely or knowingly; or
>> (b)   it is committed recklessly under circumstances manifesting extreme indifference to the value of human life. Such recklessness and indifference are presumed if the actor is engaged or is an accomplice in the commission of, or an attempt to commit, or flight after committing or attempting to commit robbery, rape or deviate sexual intercourse by force or threat of force, arson, burglary, kidnapping or felonious escape.
>
> (2) Murder is a felony of the first degree [but a person convicted of murder may be sentenced to death, as provided in Section 210.6].

§210.3. Manslaughter

> (1) Criminal homicide constitutes manslaughter when:

(a) it is committed recklessly; or

(b) a homicide which would otherwise be murder is committed under the influence of extreme mental or emotional disturbance for which there is reasonable explanation or excuse. The reasonableness of such explanation or excuse shall be determined from the viewpoint of a person in the actor's situation under the circumstances as he believes them to be.

(2) Manslaughter is a felony of the second degree.

§210.4. Negligent Homicide

(1) Criminal homicide constitutes negligent homicide when it is committed negligently.

(2) Negligent homicide is a felony of the third degree.

§1.13. General Definitions

In this Code, unless a different meaning plainly is required:

(1) "statute" includes the Constitution and a local law or ordinance of a political subdivision of the State;

(2) "act" or "action" means a bodily movement whether voluntary or involuntary;

(3) "voluntary" has the meaning specified in Section 2.01;

(4) "omission" means a failure to act;

(5) "conduct" means an action or omission and its accompanying state of mind, or, where relevant, a series of acts and omissions;

(6) "actor" includes, where relevant, a person guilty of an omission;

(7) "acted" includes, where relevant, "omitted to act";

(8) "person," "he" and "actor" include any natural person and, where relevant, a corporation or an unincorporated association;

(9) "element of an offense" means (i) such conduct or (ii) such attendant circumstances or (iii) such a result of conduct as

(a) is included in the description of the forbidden conduct in the definition of the offense; or

(b) establishes the required kind of culpability; or

(c) negatives an excuse or justification for such conduct; or

(d) negatives a defense under the statute of limitations; or

(e) establishes jurisdiction or venue;

(10) "material element of an offense" means an element that does not relate exclusively to the statute of limitations, jurisdiction, venue, or to any other matter similarly unconnected with (i) the harm or evil, incident to conduct, sought to be prevented by the law defining the offense, or (ii) the existence of a justification or excuse for such conduct;

(11) "purposely" has the meaning specified in Section 2.02 and equivalent terms such as "with purpose," "designed" or "with design" have the same meaning;

(12) "intentionally" or "with intent" means purposely;

(13) "knowingly" has the meaning specified in Section 2.02 and equivalent terms such as "knowing" or "with knowledge" have the same meaning;

(14) "recklessly" has the meaning specified in Section 2.02 and equivalent terms such as "recklessness" or "with recklessness" have the same meaning;

(15) "negligently" has the meaning specified in Section 2.02 and equivalent terms such as "negligence" or "with negligence" have the same meaning;

(16) "reasonably believes" or "reasonable belief" designates a belief that the actor is not reckless or negligent in holding.

§2.02. General Requirements of Culpability

(1) Minimum Requirements of Culpability. Except as provided in Section 2.05, a person is not guilty of an offense unless he acted purposely, knowingly, recklessly or negligently, as the law may require, with respect to each material element of the offense.

(2) Kinds of Culpability Defined.

    (a) Purposely. A person acts purposely with respect to a material element of an offense when:

        (i) if the element involves the nature of his conduct or a result thereof, it is his conscious object to engage in conduct of that nature or to cause such a result; and

        (ii) if the element involves the attendant circumstances, he is aware of the existence of such circumstances or he believes or hopes that they exist.

    (b) Knowingly. A person acts knowingly with respect to a material element of an offense when:

        (i) if the element involves the nature of his conduct or the attendant circumstances, he is aware that his conduct is of that nature or that such circumstances exist; and

        (ii) if the element involves a result of his conduct, he is aware that it is practically certain that his conduct will cause such a result.

    (c) Recklessly. A person acts recklessly with respect to a material element of an offense when he consciously disregards a substantial and unjustifiable risk that the material element exists or will result from his conduct. The risk must be of such a nature and degree that, considering the nature and purpose of the actor's conduct and the circumstances known to him, its disregard involves a gross deviation from the standard of conduct that a law-abiding person would observe in the actor's situation.

(d) Negligently. A person acts negligently with respect to a material element of an offense when he should be aware of a substantial and unjustifiable risk that the material element exists or will result from his conduct. The risk must be of such a nature and degree that the actor's failure to perceive it, considering the nature and purpose of his conduct and the circumstances known to him, involves a gross deviation from the standard of care that a reasonable person would observe in the actor's situation.

(3) Culpability Required Unless Otherwise Provided. When the culpability sufficient to establish a material element of an offense is not prescribed by law, such element is established if a person acts purposely, knowingly or recklessly with respect thereto.

(4) Prescribed Culpability Requirement Applies to All Material Elements. When the law defining an offense prescribes the kind of culpability that is sufficient for the commission of an offense, without distinguishing among the material elements thereof, such provision shall apply to all the material elements of the offense, unless a contrary purpose plainly appears.

(5) Substitutes for Negligence, Recklessness and Knowledge. When the law provides that negligence suffices to establish an element of an offense, such element also is established if a person acts purposely, knowingly or recklessly. When recklessness suffices to establish an element, such element also is established if a person acts purposely or knowingly. When acting knowingly suffices to establish an element, such element also is established if a person acts purposely.

(6) Requirement of Purpose Satisfied if Purpose Is Conditional. When a particular purpose is an element of an offense, the element is established although such purpose is conditional, unless the condition negatives the harm or evil sought to be prevented by the law defining the offense.

(7) Requirement of Knowledge Satisfied by Knowledge of High Probability. When knowledge of the existence of a particular fact is an element of an offense, such knowledge is established if a person is aware of a high probability of its existence, unless he actually believes that it does not exist.

(8) Requirement of Wilfulness Satisfied by Acting Knowingly. A requirement that an offense be committed wilfully is satisfied if a person acts knowingly with respect to the material elements of the offense, unless a purpose to impose further requirements appears.

(9) Culpability as to Illegality of Conduct. Neither knowledge nor recklessness or negligence as to whether conduct constitutes an

offense or as to the existence, meaning or application of the law determining the elements of an offense is an element of such offense, unless the definition of the offense or the Code so provides.

(10) Culpability as Determinant of Grade of Offense. When the grade or degree of an offense depends on whether the offense is committed purposely, knowingly, recklessly or negligently, its grade or degree shall be the lowest for which the determinative kind of culpability is established with respect to any material element of the offense.

2.   Reckless Murder v. "Depraved Heart" Murder

King v. State, 505 So.2d 403 (Ala. Crim. App. 1987)

PATTERSON, Judge.

Appellant, Christopher Doyle King, was indicted by a two-count indictment for murder in violation of §13A–6–2, Code of Alabama 1975. Count one charged that appellant

> . . . did recklessly engage in conduct which manifested extreme indifference to human life and created a grave risk of death to a person other than the said Christopher Doyle King, and did thereby cause the death of Dwight Lee Reeves by shooting into an automobile in which the said Dwight Lee Reeves was a passenger and shooting the said Dwight Lee Reeves with a pistol, in violation of Section 13A–6–2[(a)(2)] of the Alabama Criminal Code . . . .

The case was tried to a jury, and on October 3, 1985, the jury returned a verdict of guilty of murder, as charged in count one. . . .

King appeals, raising one issue: "Whether or not the State of Alabama failed to prove that the appellant manifested extreme indifference to human life in general as required by Section 13A–6–2(a)(2) of the Alabama Code so as to support a conviction for reckless murder." This issue was properly preserved for our review by a motion for judgment of acquittal made at the conclusion of the State's case-in-chief and by motion for new trial, both of which were overruled.

The evidence presented by the State disclosed that on the evening of November 22, 1984, Dwight Lee Reeves and his cousin, Rodney Dunnaway, traveled from Fultondale to Birmingham to visit Trader Johns, a nightclub in east Birmingham. They traveled in Dunnaway's automobile. That same evening, appellant and a friend, Bobby Knight, visited the same club. They traveled in appellant's blue pickup truck. While at the club, appellant and Reeves apparently "bumped" into each other and exchanged words. Both were apparently upset by the encounter. Dunnaway and Reeves left the club around 1:30 a.m. to go home. Appellant and Knight left shortly before Dunnaway and Reeves. As Dunnaway and Reeves were pulling out of the parking lot of the club, a blue pickup truck pulled up closely behind Dunnaway's automobile and stopped for a short period. Dunnaway was driving, and Reeves was sitting on the passenger's side in the front seat of the automobile. Dunnaway drove away from the club, entered the interstate highway, and proceeded westward toward downtown Birmingham and Fultondale at a speed of approximately fifty-five miles per hour. Appellant and Knight left the parking lot of the club in the pickup truck, which appellant was driving, and after entering the interstate highway, proceeded westward in the same direction as Dunnaway was proceeding, and in the opposite direction from appellant's home. Appellant observed Dunnaway's automobile and recognized the passenger, Reeves, as the person with whom he had had the altercation at the club. Appellant drove his truck closely behind Dunnaway's automobile and, while blinking his truck's lights, "tailgated" it for several miles. Dunnaway reduced his speed several times to let the truck pass, but it continued closely behind him. As the vehicles approached the 31st Street exit, appellant pulled a .38-caliber pistol from under the seat of his truck, pulled up beside Dunnaway's automobile on the right side, fired two or three shots at the vehicle, and turned right on the off-ramp, leaving the interstate highway. Bullets struck the rear tires of Dunnaway's vehicle, causing them to immediately go flat, and the vehicle came to a halt some distance beyond the 31st Street exit. One bullet pierced the window on the passenger's side and struck Reeves in the head. He fell over into Dunnaway's lap. Reeves died from the head wound several hours later. Reeves and Dunnaway were unarmed and did nothing to provoke the shooting. Appellant went home immediately after the incident and did not report it. The police investigation ultimately led to his arrest some two months later. Appellant gave conflicting stories to several persons about the incident, and when arrested, falsely stated that he had no knowledge of the incident. He disposed of the pistol in a "dumpster," and it was never recovered. The State's case was primarily based upon the testimony of Dunnaway and Knight, and the testimony of each was essentially consistent with the other's.

Knight, testifying for the State, stated that, just before the incident, appellant stated that he was going to "mess with them and shoot the tires out." He further testified that, just after the shooting, appellant stated that he "might have messed up or he shot the window out." In substance, Knight testified that there was no provocation or excuse for appellant's actions.

This court interpreted the meaning of reckless homicide proscribed by §13A–6–2(a)(2), in *Northington v. State,* 413 So.2d 1169 (Ala.Cr.App.1981), cert. quashed, 413 So.2d 1172 (Ala. 1982). Therein, we stated the following:

> Reckless homicide manifesting extreme indifference to human life (13A–6–2(a)(2)) must be distinguished from purposeful or knowing murder (13A–6–2(a)(1)). See American Law Institute, Model Penal Code and Commentaries, Part II, Section 210.2 (1980). Under whatever name, the doctrine of universal malice, depraved heart murder, or reckless homicide manifesting extreme indifference to human life is intended to embrace those

cases where a person has no deliberate intent to kill or injure any particular individual. 'The element of "extreme indifference to human life," by definition, does not address itself to the life of the victim, but to human life generally.'

Id. at 1170–71. We also stated,

The function of this section is to embrace those homicides caused by such acts as driving an automobile in a grossly wanton manner, shooting a firearm into a crowd or moving train, and throwing a timber from a roof onto a crowded street.

Id. at 1172. The Supreme Court of Alabama subsequently adopted this interpretation. *Ex parte Washington,* 448 So.2d 404, 408 (Ala. 1984); *Ex parte McCormack,* 431 So.2d 1340 (Ala. 1983).

In *Ex parte Weems,* 463 So.2d 170, 172 (Ala. 1984), the Supreme Court, in an opinion by Justice Faulkner, stated the following:

Alabama's homicide statutes were derived from the Model Penal Code. In providing that homicide committed 'recklessly under circumstances manifesting extreme indifference to human life' constitutes murder, the drafters of the model code were attempting to define a degree of recklessness 'that cannot be fairly distinguished from homicides committed purposely or knowingly.' Model Penal Code and Commentaries, §210.02, Comment, 4 (1980). That standard was designed to encompass the category of murder traditionally referred to as 'depraved heart' or 'universal malice' killings. Examples of such acts include shooting into an occupied house or into a moving automobile or piloting a speedboat through a group of swimmers. See LaFave & Scott, *Criminal Law,* §70 (1972).

We find in a discussion of "depraved heart murder" in LaFave & Scott, *Criminal Law,* §70 (1972), the following:

For murder the degree of risk of death or serious bodily injury must be more than a mere unreasonable risk, more even than a high degree of risk. Perhaps the required danger may be designated a 'very high degree' of risk to distinguish it from those lesser degrees of risk which will suffice for other crimes. Such a designation of conduct at all events is more accurately descriptive than that flowery expression found in the old cases and occasionally incorporated into some modern statutes—i.e., conduct 'evincing a depraved heart, devoid of social duty, and fatally bent on mischief.' Although 'very high degree of risk' means something quite substantial, it is still something less than certainty or substantial certainty. The distinctions between an unreasonable risk and a high degree of risk and a very high degree of risk are, of course, matters of degree, and there is no exact boundary line between each category; they shade gradually like a spectrum from one group to another.

It should be noted, however, that for depraved-heart murder it is not a great amount of risk in the abstract which is decisive. The risk is exactly the same when one fires his rifle into a window of what appears to be an abandoned cabin in a deserted mining town as when one shoots the same bullet into the window of a well-kept city home, when in fact in each case one person occupies the room into which the shot is fired. In the deserted cabin situation it may not be, while in the occupied home situation it may be, murder when the occupant is killed. This illustrates that it is what the defendant should realize to be the degree of risk, in the light of the surrounding circumstances which he knows, which is important, rather than the amount of risk as an abstract proposition of the mathematics of chance.

Another matter to be noted is that the risk must not only be very high, as the defendant ought to realize in the light of what he knows, it must also under the circumstances be unjustifiable for him to take the risk. The motives for the defendant's risky conduct thus become relevant; or, to express the thought in another way, the social utility of his conduct is a factor to be considered. . . . Since the amount of risk which will do for depraved-heart murder varies with these two variable factors—the extent of the defendant's knowledge of the surrounding circumstances and the social utility of his conduct—the mathematical chances of producing death required for murder cannot be measured in terms of percentages.

The following types of conduct have been held, under the circumstances, to involve the very high degree of unjustifiable homicidal danger which will do for depraved-heart murder: firing a bullet into a room occupied, as the defendant knows, by several people; shooting into the caboose of a passing train or into a moving automobile, necessarily occupied by human beings; . . . driving a car at very high speeds along a main street. . . . Other sorts of extremely risky conduct may be imagined: throwing stones from the roof of a tall building onto the busy street below; piloting a speedboat through a group of swimmers; swooping an airplane as to risk the decapitation of the motorist. In any such case, if death actually results to an endangered person and occurs in a foreseeable way, the defendant's conduct makes him an eligible candidate for a murder conviction." (Footnotes omitted.)

In *Hill v. Commonwealth,* 239 Ky. 646 (1931), the court held that one who intentionally fires into an automobile which he knows is occupied and who kills someone therein is guilty of murder. *Hill* involved a traffic policeman firing at the tires of an occupied automobile without justification in an effort to stop it. The court stated the following:

> The most that can be said is that he intentionally fired into the car knowing that it was occupied by human beings. It has long been the law that if one voluntarily and recklessly fires into a crowd and kills any person, he is guilty of murder though he had no intention to kill or injure any one. . . . The reason for the rule is that such conduct establishes 'general malignity and recklessness of the lives and personal safety of others, which proceed from a heart void of just sense or social duty, and fatally bent on mischief. And whenever the fatal act is committed deliberately or without adequate provocation,' the jury has a right to presume it was done with malice. The rule has been applied where one having reason to believe that it was occupied by persons intentionally discharged a firearm into a dwelling house and killed some one therein. It has also been held that one who deliberately shoots into a railroad train, occupied by passengers, cannot avoid liability for the resulting homicide by disclaiming malice, but is guilty of murder. *Banks v. State,* 85 Tex.Cr.R. 165. As an automobile offers less protection than a railroad coach, there is every reason why the same rule should apply where one intentionally fires into an automobile, which he knows to be occupied by human beings, and kills someone therein.

Id. at 649. . . .

In the instant case, appellant questions the sufficiency of the State's evidence that he manifested extreme indifference to human life in general, an element of the offense charged which must be found to exist in order to sustain a conviction for reckless murder under §13A–6–2(a)(2). . . .

Section 13A–6–2(a)(2) requires the prosecution to prove conduct which manifests an extreme indifference to human life, and not to a particular person only. Its gravamen is the act of reckless [sic] by engaging in conduct which creates a grave or very great risk of death under circumstances "manifesting extreme indifference to human life." What amounts to "extreme indifference" depends on the circumstances of each case, but some shocking, outrageous, or special heinousness must be shown. A person acts recklessly when he is aware of and consciously disregards a substantial and unjustifiable risk. §13A–2–2(3).

"The risk must be of such nature and degree that disregard thereof constitutes a gross deviation from the standard of conduct that a reasonable person would observe in the situation." *Id.* To bring appellant's conduct within the murder statute, the State is required to establish that his act was imminently dangerous and presented a very high or grave risk of death to others and that it was committed under circumstances which evidenced or manifested extreme indifference to human life. The conduct must manifest extreme indifference to human life generally. The crime charged here differs from intentional murder in that it results not from a specific, conscious intent to cause the death of any particular person, but from an indifference to or disregard of the risks attending appellant's conduct.

The State's evidence of appellant's conduct in firing his pistol at the Dunnaway vehicle on the interstate highway without excuse or provocation, under the circumstances enumerated above, was sufficient for the jury to conclude that appellant was aware of a very great risk of death to others and consciously disregarded it. The evidence without question justifies a finding that appellant's conduct was unjustifiable and, because of the very great risk involved, that his conduct constituted a gross deviation from the standard of conduct that a reasonable person would observe. There was sufficient evidence presented for the jury to conclude that appellant's conduct manifested an extreme indifference to human life generally. The firing at the vehicle under the circumstances created a very great risk of death to Dunnaway, the driver, as well as his passenger, Reeves, and to anyone else who might have been using that portion of the interstate highway on that occasion. . . .

Accordingly, appellant's motions for judgment of acquittal and for a new trial based on the assertion of insufficient evidence were properly denied. The judgment in this case is due to be affirmed.

AFFIRMED.

All Judges concur.

3. Reckless Murder—Presumption of Recklessness

The defendant in the *Hokenson* case was charged with murder under an antiquated Idaho law that read:

I.C. §18–603. Murder

> (1) Except as provided in section 18–604(1)(b) of this code, criminal homicide constitutes murder when:
>   (a) it is committed purposely or knowingly; or
>   (b) it is committed recklessly under circumstances manifesting extreme indifference to the value of human life. Such recklessness and indifference are presumed if the actor is engaged or is an accomplice in the commission of, or an attempt

to commit, or flight after committing or attempting to commit robbery, rape, or deviate sexual intercourse by force or threat of force, arson, burglary, kidnaping or felonious escape.

(2) Murder is a felony of the first degree, but a person convicted of murder may be sentenced to death, as provided in section 18–607 of this code.

As you study *Hokenson*, think about how the provision at issue, section 18–603(1)(b), is different from common law felony murder.

State v. Hokenson, 96 Idaho 283 (1974)

DONALDSON, Justice.

Appellant Fred W. Hokenson, armed with a homemade bomb and a knife, entered Dean's Drug Center, Lewiston, on the evening of January 13, 1972 with the intent to commit robbery. The resulting course of events ended with the death of Officer Ross D. Flavel. In June, 1972, trial was held in the Second Judicial District Court for Nez Perce County and a jury found the appellant guilty of murder in the first degree. Judgment of conviction was entered and sentence of life imprisonment was imposed. This appeal is from that judgment.

On the evening of January 13, 1972, Kent Dean, owner and manager of Dean's Drug Center, Lewiston, received a call from an individual (later identified as appellant Fred W. Hokenson) asking him to return to the store and fill a prescription which was urgently needed. Upon agreeing to do so, Mr. Dean, accompanied by his wife and two small sons, returned to the store arriving shortly after 7:00 p.m. After a short wait, appellant Fred W. Hokenson entered the rear of the Drug Center wearing a gas mask and carrying a sack close to his shoulder in his right hand. He stated, "Nobody moves, nobody gets hurt."

Kent Dean immediately raced over to the appellant and grabbed him in a bear hug. The two men struggled, rolled against the counter, and Dean obtained a headlock on Hokenson. Hokenson then stated that he had a bomb. Mr. Dean asked his wife to call the police and to get his gun. While she was doing so, the two men fell to the ground and the appellant again mentioned the bomb. Dean managed to grasp the sack the appellant was holding and to slide it approximately ten feet away. Upon coming to rest, cylindrical rods could be seen protruding from the sack's top.

While both men were still on the floor Dean heard the appellant say, "Okay, I have a knife and this is it." Dean felt the knife at the back of his neck but changed his position and managed to wrestle it away.

Mrs. Dean called the police and returned to the rear of the store. She was holding a gun on the appellant and Mr. Dean was still grasping Hokenson in a headlock when the police arrived. Officer Ross D. Flavel entered the store through the rear door and upon learning the facts started handcuffing Hokenson. After securing appellant's left wrist, he told Mrs. Dean that another officer, Tom Saleen, was at the front of the store. Mrs. Dean promptly let him in and the two officers along with Mr. Dean completed the task of handcuffing Hokenson.

Officer Flavel then left the store and backed the patrol car to the rear door. Upon his return Mrs. Dean mentioned the bomb. Officer Flavel approached the device, picked it up and identified it as being a bomb. Some conflict then exists in the testimony concerning the following events. Officer Saleen testified that Officer Flavel began pulling wires out of the device and that Hokenson stated that it would make no difference since they only had thirty seconds to live. The Deans testified that Officer Flavel merely had his hands on the sack at the time of Hokenson's statement and subsequent explosion. Nonetheless, the device did explode killing Officer Flavel and injuring Officer Tom Saleen and Kent Dean.

The following morning two handwritten notes were found near the rear of the store. One established drugs as being the object of the robbery and the other contained a threat against Dean's family.

The appellant seeks reversal on the following grounds: . . .

Asserted error in denying appellant's motion for acquittal, or in the alternative, the verdict is contrary to the evidence.

Appellant argues that since he was under arrest and in custody at the time of the explosion, the attempted crime had been fully terminated and therefore he was not liable for the death under I.C. §18–603.

Idaho Code §18–603 provides that a criminal homicide is murder if it is committed recklessly under circumstances manifesting extreme indifference to the value of human life. This recklessness and indifference is presumed if the actor is engaged in the commission of, attempt to commit, or flight after committing or attempting to commit robbery. The state argues that the evidence presented showed beyond a reasonable doubt that the homicide was committed recklessly under circumstances manifesting extreme disregard to human life. As such, the state argues their case was established without the aid of the felony-murder presumption. We agree.

The statute requires no showing that the homicide took place during the attempted robbery. The appellant's act of carrying an active bomb into the store, knowing it to be extremely dangerous as shown by his handling, manifests extreme indifference to the value of human life. This act, coupled with the ensuing explosion and death, suffices without the presumption to establish murder under I.C. §18–603(1)(b).

Further, this Court cannot accept the appellant's contention that he should escape liability under the felony-murder rationale. The record shows that the appellant entered the store armed with a homemade bomb and a knife with the intent to commit robbery. His handling of the bomb illustrated his full cognizance of its characteristics. The fact he was met by resistance on the part of his intended victim, and in fact placed under arrest, does not release him from the final consequence of his act.

In the case of People v. Welch, 8 Cal.3d 106 (1972) the California Supreme Court stated:

> . . . homicide is committed in perpetration of the felony if the killing and the felony are parts of one continuous transaction . . . . The person killed need not be the object of the felony.
> 104 Cal.Rptr. at 225.

In Commonwealth v. Banks, 311 A.2d 576, 578 (1973) the court stated that liability would be imposed where the conduct causing the death was done in furtherance of the design to commit the felony.

The explosion causing the death of Officer Flavel clearly falls within the above two definitions. A person is criminally liable for the natural and probable consequences of his unlawful acts as well as unlawful forces set in motion during the commission of an unlawful act. The appellant voluntarily set in motion an instrumentality which carried a very real probability of causing great bodily harm. Death ensued, and the fact appellant was under arrest does not erase criminal liability. . . .

Judgment affirmed.

4. Extreme Mental or Emotional Disturbance Manslaughter

In studying the *Dumlao* case, make note of how different MPC extreme mental or emotional disturbance manslaughter is from common law voluntary manslaughter. Do not make the mistake of thinking these are the same crimes.

After reading *Dumlao*, take a second look at the *Guebara* case from the common law voluntary manslaughter section of this chapter. Given the defendant's documented illness in *Guebara*, how might the defendant in that case have fared in a MPC jurisdiction?

State v. Dumlao, 6 Haw. App. 173 (1986)

HEEN, Judge.

Defendant Vidado B. Dumlao (Dumlao) appeals from his conviction of murder. Hawaii Revised Statutes (HRS) §707–701 (1976).[1] He argues on appeal that the trial court erred in refusing to give his requested manslaughter instruction. Relying on *State v. O'Daniel,* 62 Haw. 518 (1980), he contends there was sufficient evidence that he shot his mother-in-law, Pacita M. Reyes (Pacita), while "under the influence of extreme mental or emotional disturbance for

---

[1] Hawaii Revised Statutes (HRS) § 707–701(1) (1976) defines murder as follows:
> Murder. (1) Except as provided in section 707–702, a person commits the offense of murder if he intentionally or knowingly causes the death of another person.

which there [was] a reasonable explanation" to support an instruction under HRS §707–702(2) (1976).[2] We agree and reverse.

The trial court instructed the jury that they could find Dumlao guilty of manslaughter if they concluded that he had recklessly shot Pacita to death, HRS §707–702(1)(a)(1976),[3] but refused to give the instruction Dumlao had requested.[4]

After a jury trial, Dumlao was convicted of murder for shooting Pacita . . . .

The questions presented are: (I) what is the meaning of the language of HRS §707–702(2); and (II) was there evidence to support the giving of Dumlao's requested instruction?

---

[2] HRS § 707–702(2) reads as follows:

> Manslaughter. . . . (2) In a prosecution for murder it is a defense, which reduces the offense to manslaughter, that the defendant was, at the time he caused the death of the other person, under the influence of extreme mental or emotional disturbance for which there is a reasonable explanation. The reasonableness of the explanation shall be determined from the view-point of a person in the defendant's situation under the circumstances as he believed them to be.

Although the statute refers to the mental state of a defendant as a defense, it is really a mitigating factor. "Intentionally killing while under the influence of extreme emotional disturbance does not present a true 'defense,' for the punishment is merely reduced through the mechanism of denominating the crime as 'manslaughter' rather than 'murder.' It could be considered a 'partial defense' in the sense that an acquittal of the charge of murder occurs when the jury finds that the defendant is guilty only of manslaughter." *State v. Ott,* 297 Or. 375, 377 n. 2 (1984).

[3] HRS § 707–702(1)(a) reads as follows:

> Manslaughter. (1) A person commits the offense of manslaughter if: (a) He recklessly causes the death of another person[.]

[4] The proffered instruction reads as follows:

> (1)   A person commits the offense of manslaughter if:
>
> (a)   He recklessly causes the death of another person.
>
> (2)   In a prosecution for murder it is a defense, which reduces the offense to manslaughter, that the defendant was, at the time he caused the death of the person, under the influence of extreme mental or emotional disturbance for which there is a reasonable explanation. The reasonableness of the explanation shall be determined from the view-point of a person in the defendant's situation under the circumstances as he believed them to be.

I. . . .
HRS §707–702(2)

Under HRS §707–702(2), the two principal elements of the extenuating factor are established: (1) extreme mental or emotional disturbance and (2) an objective/subjective test of the reasonableness of the explanation for the disturbance. However, the nature of those elements are not clear from the language of the statute, and neither the *Commentary* nor the legislative history indicates what considerations go into making up those elements.

Since HRS §707–702(2) is derived from MPC §210.3,[9] we may look to the commentaries and cases from other jurisdictions explaining and construing that section for insight into the meaning of the language of our statute. We will examine the first element of §707–702 first.

A.

"Extreme mental or emotional disturbance" sometimes is, but should not be, confused with the "insanity" defense. The point of the extreme emotional disturbance defense is to provide a basis for mitigation that differs from a finding of mental defect or disease precluding criminal responsibility. The disturbance was meant to be understood in relative terms as referring to a loss of self-control due to intense feelings. *Id.*

The extreme mental or emotional disturbance concept of the MPC must also be distinguished from the so-called "diminished capacity" defense.

> The doctrine of diminished capacity provides that evidence of an abnormal mental condition not amounting to legal insanity but tending to prove that the defendant could not or did not entertain the specific intent or state of mind essential to the offense should be considered for the purpose of determining whether the crime charged or a lesser degree thereof was in fact committed.

State v. Baker, 691 P.2d 1166, 1168 (1984).

Although the MPC does *not* recognize diminished capacity as a distinct category of mitigation, II Model Penal Code and Commentaries §210.3 at 72 (Official Draft and Revised Comments 1980) [hereafter cited as 1980 MPC Commentary], by placing more emphasis than does the common law on the

---

[9] Section 210.3 states in pertinent part as follows:

Manslaughter

(1) Criminal homicide constitutes manslaughter when: . . . (b) a homicide which would otherwise be murder is committed under the influence of extreme mental or emotional disturbance for which there is reasonable explanation or excuse. The reasonableness of such explanation or excuse shall be determined from the viewpoint of a person in the actor's situation under the circumstances as he believes them to be.

actor's subjective mental state, it also may allow inquiry into areas which have traditionally been treated as part of the law of diminished responsibility or the insanity defense.

Thus, the MPC is said to have in fact adopted an expanded concept of diminished capacity to reduce murder to manslaughter. *People v. Spurlin,* 156 Cal.App.3d 119, 127 n. 4 (1984).

> Diminished capacity involves a mental disturbance which peculiarly involves the killer. Heat of passion is a concession to human weakness, to a universal human condition. *Diminished capacity is an effort to reduce punishment because the actor is not like all humans, whereas heat of passion reduces punishment because the actor is, unfortunately, like most humans.* [Footnotes omitted and emphasis added.]

Dressler, *Rethinking Heat of Passion: A Defense in Search of a Rationale,* 73 J.Crim.L. and Criminology 421, 459–60 (1982) (hereafter *Dressler*).

The MPC merges the two concepts of heat of passion and diminished capacity.

> It is enough if the killing occurs while the defendant's capacity to form an intent to murder is diminished by an extreme mental or emotional *disturbance* deemed to have a reasonable explanation or excuse from the defendant's standpoint. [Emphasis included.]

Spurlin, supra.

An explanation of the term "extreme emotional disturbance" which reflects the situational or relative character of the concept was given in *People v. Shelton,* 385 N.Y.S.2d 708, 717 (1976), as follows:

> [T]hat extreme emotional disturbance is the emotional state of an individual, who: (a) has no mental disease or defect that rises to the level established by Section 30.05 of the Penal Law; and (b) is exposed to an extremely unusual and overwhelming stress; and (c) has an extreme emotional reaction to it, as a result of which there is a loss of self-control and reason is overborne by intense feelings, such as passion, anger, distress, grief, excessive agitation or other similar emotions.[12] [Footnotes added.]

---

[12] The extreme emotional disturbance defense is also broader than the heat of passion doctrine which it replaced, in that a cooling off period intervening between the fatal act and the disturbance does not negate the defense. *People v. Parmes,* 451 N.Y.S.2d 1015, 1017 (1982). "A spontaneous explosion is not required." *Id.* Rather, "a significant mental trauma" could have "affected a defendant's mind for a substantial period of time, simmering in the unknown subconscious and then inexplicably coming to the fore." *People v. Shelton,* 385 N.Y.S.2d 708, 715 (1976). *See also People v. Parmes, supra.*

It is clear that in adopting the "extreme mental or emotional disturbance" concept, the MPC intended to define the provocation element of manslaughter in broader terms than had previously been done. It is equally clear that our legislature also intended the same result when it adopted the language of the MPC.

We turn then to the second prong of our analysis, the test to determine the reasonableness of the explanation for the mental or emotional disturbance. It is here that the most significant change has been made in the law of manslaughter.

B.

The anomaly of the reasonable person test was corrected by the drafters of the MPC through the development of an objective/subjective test of reasonableness. *See* 1980 MPC Commentary, *supra. Dressler, supra*, at 431, explains that,

> it makes the test more, although not entirely, subjective, by requiring the jury to test the reasonableness of the actor's conduct, "from the viewpoint of a person in the actor's situation." Thus, the actor's sex, sexual preference, pregnancy, physical deformities, and similar characteristics are apt to be taken into consideration in evaluating the reasonableness of the defendant's behavior. (Footnotes omitted.)

This more subjective version of the provocation defense goes substantially beyond the common law by abandoning preconceptions of what constitutes adequate provocation, and giving the jury wider scope. *Id.*

Under the prior law of provocation, personal characteristics of the defendant were not to be considered. Under the MPC a change from the old provocation law and the reasonable person standard has been effected by requiring the factfinder to focus on a person in the defendant's situation. Thus, the MPC, while requiring that the explanation for the disturbance must be reasonable, provides that the reasonableness is determined from the defendant's viewpoint. The phrase "actor's situation," as used in §210.3(b) of the MPC, is designedly ambiguous and is plainly flexible enough to allow the law to grow in the direction of taking account of mental abnormalities that have been recognized in the developing law of diminished responsibility.

Moreover, the MPC does not require the provocation to emanate from the victim as was argued by the State here. In light of the foregoing discussion and the necessity of articulating the defense in comprehensible terms, we adopt the

---

The drafters of the Model Penal Code (MPC) found it "shocking" that the common law disregarded the fact that the passage of time sometimes served only to increase rather than diminish outrage. . . .

test enunciated by the New York Court of Appeals in *People v. Casassa,* 427 N.Y.S.2d 769, 775, *cert. denied,* 449 U.S. 842 (1980):

> [W]e conclude that the determination whether there was reasonable explanation or excuse for a particular emotional disturbance should be made by viewing the subjective, internal situation in which the defendant found himself and the external circumstances as he perceived them at the time, however inaccurate that perception may have been, and assessing from that standpoint whether the explanation . . . for his emotional disturbance was reasonable, so as to entitle him to a reduction of the crime charged from murder . . . to manslaughter. . . . [Footnote omitted.] . . .

Thus, we hold in the instant case that the trial court was required to instruct the jury as requested by Dumlao, if there was any evidence to support a finding that at the time of the offense he suffered an "extreme mental or emotional disturbance" for which there was a "reasonable explanation" when the totality of circumstances was judged from his personal viewpoint.

We turn now to the question of whether there was evidence to support the proffered instruction.

II.

In the instant case, there was evidence of the following: . . .

Dr. Golden diagnosed Dumlao as having unwarranted suspiciousness, one of the basic indicators of the "paranoid personality disorder." That unwarranted suspiciousness included pathological jealousy, which Dumlao suffered throughout his ten-year marriage. Dumlao harbored the belief that other males, including his wife's relatives, were somehow sexually involved with her. He could never figure out exactly who or where or how, yet this extreme suspiciousness persisted.

Dr. Golden described the second major sign of Dumlao's paranoid personality disorder as hypersensitivity, characterized by being easily slighted or quick to take offense, and a readiness to counterattack when a threat was perceived. . . .

Dumlao's extreme and irrational jealousy concerning his wife was known to all the family members. According to Agapito, they couldn't even talk to their sister in Dumlao's presence. "If we have to talk to her, we have to talk from a distance because he suspects us." Furthermore, Dumlao "never allowed us to talk in a group."

Dumlao's testimony, describing his own perceptions of the night in question, further confirms the nature of his extreme jealousy. Dumlao described how he became suspicious and jealous of his wife that night because of the way that Agapito looked at him:

> A. I had this feeling that something going to happen when I leave because the action that I seen—Agapito.

Q.   What action?. . .

A.   He look at me on, the kine. He make sure—he make sure that—I don't know, making sure if I stay—if I leave the house or I don't know so I got the bad feeling so I never leave. . . .

Q.   Why did you have this feeling that he would go into your wife's bedroom?

A.   Jealousy arose. . . .

Q.   What did you do? Did you do anything after you went back to your bedroom?

A.   I wake up my wife, questioned her. . . .

A.   If he—if she had something to do with my brother-in-law, Agapito.

Q.   What do you mean, had something to do with your brother-in-law, Agapito? . . .

A.   Sexual relation. . . .

Q.   What happened after you insisted on her answering you?

A.   She got up so I lay down—I laid down on the bedroom so I—I kick or push her on the side over there.

Dumlao went on to describe how, after his father had counseled him and he went back in the room, he could hear the voices of the others talking in the living room. He thought that they were talking about him. He then came out to "investigate" with his gun in his waistband. He saw "Pedrito with his eyes at me, burning eye, angry eye, angry," and he saw Eduardo and Agapito alongside Pedrito. Dumlao testified that Pedrito rushed at him, holding a knife in his hand, saying, "My sister suffer ten years. You going to pay. Now you going to pay". He testified that when he pulled his gun to "try and scare [Pedrito]," the gun went off, firing the bullet that struck and killed Pacita.

CONCLUSION

Reviewing the evidence within the context of the meaning of HRS §707–702(2), we conclude that it was sufficient to require the trial court to give Dumlao's requested instruction on manslaughter. There was evidence, "no matter how weak, inconclusive or unsatisfactory," that Dumlao killed Pacita while under the influence of "extreme emotional disturbance." Whether a jury will agree that there was such a disturbance or that the explanation for it was reasonable we cannot say. However, Dumlao was entitled to have the jury make that decision using the objective/subjective test.

The fact that the other witnesses contradicted his testimony concerning an attack by Pedrito, and that his testimony that he was only trying to scare Pedrito does not comport with the manslaughter defense, does not detract from Dumlao's right to the instruction based on the above evidence. Dumlao was entitled to an instruction on every theory of defense shown by the evidence. It was the jury's province to determine the weight and credibility of that evidence.

Reversed and remanded for new trial.

5.   Reckless Manslaughter

In *Duffy*, the prosecutor charged a defendant with reckless manslaughter for assisting another in committing a suicide. Note that while the opinion does not mention the MPC, it appears that the MPC is the original source.

People v. Duffy, 79 N.Y.2d 611 (1992)

TITONE, Judge.

This appeal calls upon us to address two related questions: whether a person may be convicted of second degree manslaughter for engaging in *reckless* conduct which results in another person's committing suicide and, if so, whether the conduct of the defendant in this case was a sufficiently direct cause of the victim's death to support his conviction. For the reasons that follow, we conclude that both these questions should be answered in the affirmative.

I

According to the evidence adduced below, Jason Schuhle—a 17–year–old youth—met defendant on a street in the Village of McGraw, New York, during the early morning hours of August 6, 1988. Schuhle—who, at the time, was extremely distraught over having recently broken-up with his girlfriend—immediately imparted to defendant his desire to kill himself. At defendant's invitation, Schuhle then accompanied him back to defendant's apartment. There, for approximately the next half hour or so, Schuhle—who had been drinking heavily—continued to express suicidal thoughts and repeatedly importuned defendant to shoot him. In response to these entreaties, defendant provided Schuhle with some more alcohol and challenged him several times to jump headfirst off the porch of his second-story apartment. Finally, defendant—who later explained to the police that he was "tired" of hearing Schuhle complain about wanting to die—told Schuhle that he had a gun which he could use to kill himself. Defendant then retrieved a British .303 caliber Enfield rifle from his gun cabinet, and handed it to Schuhle, along with a number of bullets. He then urged Schuhle to "put the gun in his mouth and blow his head off." Moments later, Schuhle loaded the rifle, pointed the barrel at himself and pulled the trigger. He later died as a result of the massive injuries he suffered.

Defendant was thereafter indicted for two counts of manslaughter in the second degree. The first count alleged that he had intentionally caused or aided Schuhle in committing suicide (*see,* Penal Law §125.15[3]), and the second alleged that he had recklessly caused Schuhle's death (*see,* Penal Law

§125.15[1]). After a jury trial, defendant was acquitted of the first count but convicted of the second.

On appeal, however, the Appellate Division reversed and dismissed the indictment. . . . A Judge of this Court subsequently granted the People leave to appeal. We now reverse.

II

At the outset, we note that the conduct with which defendant was charged clearly fell within the scope of section 125.15(1)'s proscription against recklessly causing the death of another person. As the People aptly observe, a person who, knowing that another is contemplating immediate suicide, deliberately prods that person to go forward *and* furnishes the means of bringing about death may certainly be said to have "consciously disregard[ed] a substantial and unjustifiable risk" that his actions would result in the death of that person (*see,* Penal Law §15.05[3]; §125.15[1]). Accordingly, . . . defendant's prosecution for reckless manslaughter cannot be said to have been improper.   . . .

III

Having concluded that a person may be convicted of second degree manslaughter for having engaged in reckless conduct which results in another person's committing suicide (*see,* Penal Law §125.15[1]), we now turn to the question whether defendant's conduct here was a "sufficiently direct cause" of Schuhle's death to subject him to criminal liability. Defendant, stressing the fact that it was Schuhle—not he—who loaded the rifle and pulled the trigger, urges us to answer this question in the negative. We find defendant's argument to be unpersuasive.

Generally speaking, a person will not be held criminally accountable for engaging in conduct which results in another person's death unless it can be demonstrated that his actions were "an actual contributory cause of death, in the sense that they 'forged a link in the chain of causes which actually brought about the death.' " The proof adduced below, when viewed in a light most favorable to the People, indicates that defendant gave Schuhle a rifle and a number of rounds of ammunition knowing full well that Schuhle had been drinking heavily and was in an extremely depressed and suicidal state, and that he then began taunting Schuhle to "put the gun in his mouth and blow his head off." In light of this evidence, we must disagree with defendant that Schuhle's act of loading the rifle and using it to kill himself constituted an intervening cause which—as a matter of law—relieved defendant of criminal responsibility. The jury could rationally have concluded that the risk of Schuhle's taking these actions was something which defendant should have, under the circumstances, plainly foreseen. There is therefore no basis, on this Court's review, to disturb the jury's verdict.

Accordingly, the order of the Appellate Division should be reversed and the case remitted to that court for consideration of the facts.

Chapter 5
Rape and Criminal Sexual Conduct

A. Introduction

This chapter will address traditional common law rape (i.e., forcible rape) and statutory rape, comparing them with more recent approaches to sexual assault. Michigan's criminal sexual conduct statute will be examined in detail, giving students the opportunity to both learn more about how the law in this area is developing and get some practice reading and applying statutes. While sexual assault is an uncomfortable topic, it is an essential part of any complete criminal law course—most lawyers working criminal cases in state courts will have some exposure to these crimes.

It helps to begin the discussion of rape with an understanding that this crime is one of the worst that a victim can endure. Consider the following excerpt:

> *Sexual Assaults: Rape*—Nancy S. Erickson (*from Final Report: "Sex Bias in the Teaching of Criminal Law,"* 42 Rutgers L. Rev. 309 (1989–1990) (footnotes omitted))

It is important to remember that all students need a solid foundation of facts upon which to base discussions of the law of rape. In order to assess the legal definition of rape, to determine appropriate penalties, to evaluate decisions concerning whether to prosecute, and to understand whether special evidentiary requirements are appropriate, the facts about the crime are essential. Yet many people lack knowledge of these facts.

The nature and severity of the harm suffered by victims of the crime are generally unrecognized. Many people do not realize that rape usually causes physical pain; they reason that if consensual sexual intercourse is not generally painful, then neither is forced intercourse. Some people even assume that rape must give some sexual pleasure to the victim; hence the jokes such as "rape is assault with a friendly weapon," and "he [the rapist] was just giving her a good time." Not surprisingly, this failure to accurately perceive the female victim's experience seems much more common among men than among women, and perhaps originates in physiological differences:

> Physiologically, male sexuality . . . is dependent upon penile reactions. Thus the male must experience some stimulation, and the result must be physically pleasurable even if the situation is psychologically distasteful. Therefore it may be difficult for a man to comprehend rape as anything but a basically sexual experience for anyone who is engaged in it . . . . The woman's claim that the rape was physically only painful and without any pleasurable sensation . . . may be unintelligible to a man . . . .

The truth about rape can be discovered only by listening to its victims:

> Forcible rape is not in any normal sense intercourse. In most cases, the lubrication . . . required for normal completed intercourse does not exist . . . . As a result of this crucial aspect, as well as the fact that the victim is usually in a traumatized state immediately preceding the rape and, thus, the muscles at the entrance to the vagina are not relaxed, penetration cannot either easily or immediately occur. What does happen is that the rapist repeatedly batters . . . the very delicate and sensitive features lying outside the vagina, causing the tissues to tear and to bleed. [After penetration,] . . . the tissues (this time, the lining of the vagina) are repeatedly, with each thrust, ripped and torn.
>
> As can be imagined, forcible rape is traumatically painful. I believe that it is the most physically painful ordeal that an individual can undergo and still live afterward. When I was being raped I felt as though I were being repeatedly stabbed with a knife in one of the most sensitive areas of my body. Near the end, I was in shock. I felt numb and could feel no pain, but I knew that the rapist was tearing me apart inside. Hours after the attack, the pain returned, and I felt as though I had been set on fire. Although I bled for only a few days, the pain lasted for weeks.
>
> "What harm does it do?" Some of the flesh of my external genitalia has been battered away. It simply does not exist anymore. Other areas are torn and snagged. Some of the flesh can be pulled apart. Most of my hymen has been obliterated . . . . Inside my vagina, the muscles at the entrance are damaged and I fear that this will adversely affect any future sexual intercourse that I engage in. Polyps have developed . . . . Also, the tissues of the lower part of my vaginal wall remain ripped. Thus, not only do people fail to comprehend the severe pain involved in a rape, or the length

> of time that the victim must suffer, they also do not understand that the physical damage done to the genital organs does not repair itself with time and that rape is a mutilating, disfiguring crime.

This rape victim sums it up by saying: "[T]here is no 'sex' in rape. There is only pain . . . ."

In addition to physical pain, the victim experiences severe psychological trauma. It would be useful for students to know that current studies show that "men and women share the same basic responses to rape—including depression, nightmares, flashbacks, self-blame, and a sometimes overwhelming sense of vulnerability . . . ." Such responses are understandable when one sees rape for what it really is—a violent crime that deprives a victim of feelings of autonomy, security, and personhood. Many women have also reported additional consequences that may be more common for female than male victims, such as fear of men in general. Whatever the particular effects of rape may be on an individual, it is clear that the psychological trauma is often severe and long-lasting.

Once a class is presented with the facts about rape, including an accurate picture of the harm suffered by the victim, any tendency to snicker, make jokes about the victim, or otherwise trivialize the crime will probably be dissipated, and a basis for analyzing traditional and current rape laws will be established.

B. Rape

Generally, traditional rape involves the penetration (penile-vaginal only) by a man against a woman *not* his wife, by force (or threat of death or serious bodily harm) and against her will (i.e., lack of consent). The defendant must act with a morally blameworthy state of mind regarding the female's lack of consent and the female must physically resist unless faced with a serious threat of death or great bodily harm.

Some states require that the victim's testimony be corroborated by other witnesses or circumstantial evidence. Several states, by statute, indicate that the testimony of a victim need not be corroborated. *See, e.g.,* M.C.L. §750.520h ("The testimony of a victim need not be corroborated in prosecutions under sections 520b to 520g.").

In interpreting "rape-shield" laws, [*] jurisdictions vary regarding the allowable scope of cross-examination of the victim concerning past sexual

---

[*] *See, e.g.,* Michigan's rape-shield law (M.C.L. 750.520(j)):

(1) Evidence of specific instances of the victim's sexual conduct, opinion evidence of the victim's sexual conduct, and reputation evidence of the victim's sexual conduct shall not be admitted under sections 520b to 520g unless and only to the extent that the judge finds that the following proposed evidence is material to a fact

history and reputation for chastity. *See, e.g., State v. Colbath*, 540 A.2d 1212 (N.H. 1988) (allowing introduction of evidence regarding victim's sexual behavior with other men in same location on same day as act in question); *People v. Wilhelm*, 190 Mich. App. 574 (1991) (excluding evidence of sexual behavior with others).

For a detailed discussion of common law rape and modern statutory variations, see Joshua Dressler, *Understanding Criminal Law* §§33.01–33.08 (6th ed. 2012).

C. Statutory Rape

Early common law rape did not cover sexual relations with children. Long ago, Parliament addressed this problem by creating the crime of statutory rape. Traditional statutory rape involved the sexual intercourse of a female child under the age of consent. Consent (or lack thereof) and force (or lack thereof) were not required. Today, the label of the crime and the statutory age of consent vary by state. For more information, see Wayne LaFave, *Criminal Law* §17.4(c) (5th ed. 2010).

One issue that periodically arises in the context of statutory rape involves the defendant's mistaken belief that the victim was "of age." That concern will be addressed in a separate section of the textbook involving the mistake of fact defense.

D. Statutory Variations on Common Law Rape

1. Is "force" proven if the victim says "no" throughout the encounter?

Occasionally, courts will use terms that are not familiar to the reader. The first sentence of the *Berkowitz* case includes the word "allocatur"—from the context, one can infer that allocatur means permission to appeal. It is a good habit to consult a legal dictionary when there is any doubt.

---

at issue in the case and that its inflammatory or prejudicial nature does not outweigh its probative value:

(a) Evidence of the victim's past sexual conduct with the actor.

(b) Evidence of specific instances of sexual activity showing the source or origin of semen, pregnancy, or disease.

(2) If the defendant proposes to offer evidence described in subsection (1)(a) or (b), the defendant within 10 days after the arraignment on the information shall file a written motion and offer of proof. The court may order an in camera hearing to determine whether the proposed evidence is admissible under subsection (1). If new information is discovered during the course of the trial that may make the evidence described in subsection (1)(a) or (b) admissible, the judge may order an in camera hearing to determine whether the proposed evidence is admissible under subsection (1).

How much force is necessary to prove the "forcible compulsion" element of the crime of rape under the Pennsylvania statute?

Commonwealth of Pennsylvania v. Berkowitz, 537 Pa. 143 (1994)

CAPPY, Justice.

We granted allocatur in this case to address the question of the precise degree of force necessary to prove the "forcible compulsion" element of the crime of rape. . . .

The Commonwealth appeals from an order of the Superior Court which overturned the conviction by a jury of Appellee, Robert A. Berkowitz, of one count of rape [and another charge]. . . . For the reasons that follow, we affirm the Superior Court's reversal of the conviction for rape . . . .

The relevant facts of this case are as follows. The complainant, a female college student, left her class, went to her dormitory room where she drank a martini, and then went to a lounge to await her boyfriend. When her boyfriend failed to appear, she went to another dormitory to find a friend, Earl Hassel. She knocked on the door, but received no answer. She tried the doorknob and, finding it unlocked, entered the room and discovered a man sleeping on the bed. The complainant originally believed the man to be Hassel, but it turned out to be Hassel's roommate, Appellee. Appellee asked her to stay for a while and she agreed. He requested a back-rub and she declined. He suggested that she sit on the bed, but she declined and sat on the floor.

Appellee then moved to the floor beside her, lifted up her shirt and bra and massaged her breasts. He then unfastened his pants and unsuccessfully attempted to put his penis in her mouth. They both stood up, and he locked the door. He returned to push her onto the bed, and removed her undergarments from one leg. He then penetrated her vagina with his penis. After withdrawing and ejaculating on her stomach, he stated, "Wow, I guess we just got carried away," to which she responded, "No, we didn't get carried away, you got carried away."

In reviewing the sufficiency of the evidence, this Court must view the evidence in the light most favorable to the Commonwealth as verdict winner, and accept as true all evidence and reasonable inferences that may be reasonably drawn therefrom, upon which, if believed, the jury could have relied in reaching its verdict. If, upon such review, the Court concludes that the jury could not have determined from the evidence adduced that all of the necessary elements of the crime were established, then the evidence will be deemed insufficient to support the verdict.

The crime of rape is defined as follows:

§3121. Rape

A person commits a felony of the first degree when he engages in sexual intercourse with another person not one's spouse:

(1) by forcible compulsion;

(2) by threat of forcible compulsion that would prevent resistance by a person of reasonable resolution;

(3) who is unconscious; or

(4) who is so mentally deranged or deficient that such person is incapable of consent.

18 Pa.C.S.A. §3121. The victim of a rape need not resist. 18 Pa.C.S.A. §3107. "The force necessary to support a conviction of rape . . . need only be such as to establish lack of consent and to induce the [victim] to submit without additional resistance. . . . The degree of force required to constitute rape is relative and depends on the facts and particular circumstance of the case."

In regard to the critical issue of forcible compulsion, the complainant's testimony is devoid of any statement which clearly or adequately describes the use of force or the threat of force against her. In response to defense counsel's question, "Is it possible that [when Appellee lifted your bra and shirt] you took no physical action to discourage him," the complainant replied, "It's possible." When asked, "Is it possible that [Appellee] was not making any physical contact with you . . . aside from attempting to untie the knot [in the drawstrings of complainant's sweatpants]," she answered, "It's possible." She testified that "He put me down on the bed. It was kind of like—He didn't throw me on the bed. It's hard to explain. It was kind of like a push but not—I can't explain what I'm trying to say." She concluded that "it wasn't much" in reference to whether she bounced on the bed, and further detailed that their movement to the bed "wasn't slow like a romantic kind of thing, but it wasn't a fast shove either. It was kind of in the middle." She agreed that Appellee's hands were not restraining her in any manner during the actual penetration, and that the weight of his body on top of her was the only force applied. She testified that at no time did Appellee verbally threaten her. The complainant did testify that she sought to leave the room, and said "no" throughout the encounter. As to the complainant's desire to leave the room, the record clearly demonstrates that the door could be unlocked easily from the inside, that she was aware of this fact, but that she never attempted to go to the door or unlock it.

As to the complainant's testimony that she stated "no" throughout the encounter with Appellee, we point out that, while such an allegation of fact would be relevant to the issue of consent, it is not relevant to the issue of force. In *Commonwealth v. Mlinarich,* 518 Pa. 247, (1988) (plurality opinion), this Court sustained the reversal of a defendant's conviction of rape where the alleged victim, a minor, repeatedly stated that she did not want to engage in sexual intercourse, but offered no physical resistance and was compelled to engage in sexual intercourse under threat of being recommitted to a juvenile detention center. The Opinion in Support of Affirmance acknowledged that physical force, a threat of force, or psychological coercion may be sufficient to support the element of "forcible compulsion", if found to be enough to "prevent resistance by a person of reasonable resolution." However, under the facts of

Mlinarich, neither physical force, the threat of physical force, nor psychological coercion were found to have been proven, and this Court held that the conviction was properly reversed by the Superior Court. Accordingly, the ruling in *Mlinarich* implicitly dictates that where there is a lack of consent, but no showing of either physical force, a threat of physical force, or psychological coercion, the "forcible compulsion" requirement under 18 Pa.C.S. §3121 is not met. . . .

Reviewed in light of the above described standard, the complainant's testimony simply fails to establish that the Appellee forcibly compelled her to engage in sexual intercourse as required under 18 Pa.C.S. §3121. Thus, even if all of the complainant's testimony was believed, the jury, as a matter of law, could not have found Appellee guilty of rape. Accordingly, we hold that the Superior Court did not err in reversing Appellee's conviction of rape. . . .

Accordingly, the order of the Superior Court reversing the rape conviction is affirmed. . . .

2. How limited is the traditional crime of forcible rape?

In *Alston*, the court explores the use of a threat to satisfy the force requirement in the context of a statute based on common law rape. Keep in mind when examining the opinion that the court found the victim did not consent to the intercourse.[*]

State v. Alston, 310 N.C. 399 (1984)

MITCHELL, Justice.

The defendant raises on appeal the question whether the evidence of his guilt of kidnapping and second degree rape was sufficient to support his convictions of those crimes. For reasons discussed herein, we conclude the evidence was insufficient to support his conviction of either crime.

The State's evidence tended to show that at the time the incident occurred the defendant and the prosecuting witness in this case, Cottie Brown, had been involved for approximately six months in a consensual sexual relationship. During the six months the two had conflicts at times and Brown would leave the apartment she shared with the defendant to stay with her mother. She testified that she would return to the defendant and the apartment they shared when he called to tell her to return. Brown testified that she and the defendant had sexual relations throughout their relationship. Although she sometimes enjoyed their sexual relations, she often had sex with the defendant just to accommodate him. On those occasions, she would stand still and remain

---

[*] Although not discussed in this chapter, it is worth noting that the *Alston* court also examined the kidnapping conviction, ultimately ruling that the trial court erred in denying the defendant's motion to dismiss the kidnapping charge.

entirely passive while the defendant undressed her and had intercourse with her.

Brown testified that at times their consensual sexual relations involved some violence. The defendant had struck her several times throughout the relationship when she refused to give him money or refused to do what he wanted. Around May 15, 1981, the defendant struck her after asking her for money that she refused to give him. Brown left the apartment she shared with the defendant and moved in with her mother. She did not have intercourse with the defendant after May 15 until the alleged rape on June 15. After Brown left the defendant, he called her several times and visited her at Durham Technical Institute where she was enrolled in classes. When he visited her they talked about their relationship. Brown testified that she did not tell him she wanted to break off their relationship because she was afraid he would be angry.

On June 15, 1981, Brown arrived at Durham Technical Institute by taxicab to find the defendant standing close to the school door. The defendant blocked her path as she walked toward the door and asked her where she had moved. Brown refused to tell him, and the defendant grabbed her arm, saying that she was going with him. Brown testified that it would have taken some effort to pull away. The two walked toward the parking lot and Brown told the defendant she would walk with him if he let her go. The defendant then released her. She testified that she did not run away from him because she was afraid of him. She stated that other students were nearby.

Brown stated that she and the defendant then began a casually paced walk in the neighborhood around the school. They walked, sometimes side by side, sometimes with Brown slightly behind the defendant. As they walked they talked about their relationship. Brown said the defendant did not hold her or help her along in any way as they walked. The defendant talked about Brown's "dogging" him and making him seem a fool and about Brown's mother's interference in the relationship. When the defendant and Brown left the parking lot, the defendant threatened to "fix" her face so that her mother could see he was not playing. While they were walking out of the parking lot, Brown told the defendant she wanted to go to class. He replied that she was going to miss class that day.

The two continued to walk away from the school. Brown testified that the defendant continually talked about their relationship as they walked, but that she paid little attention to what he said because she was preoccupied with her own thoughts. They passed several people. They walked along several streets and went down a path close to a wooded area where they stopped to talk. The defendant asked again where Brown had moved. She asked him whether he would let her go if she told him her address. The defendant then asked whether the relationship was over and Brown told him it was. He then said that since everyone could see her but him he had a right to make love to her again. Brown said nothing.

The two turned around at that point and began walking towards a street they had walked down previously. Changing directions, they walked in the same fashion they had walked before—side by side with Brown sometimes slightly behind. The defendant did not hold or touch Brown as they walked. Brown testified that the defendant did not say where they were going but that, when he said he wanted to make love, she knew he was going to the house of a friend. She said they had gone to the house on prior occasions to have sex. The defendant and Brown passed the same group of men they had passed previously. Brown did not ask for assistance because some of the men were friends of the defendant, and she assumed they would not help. The defendant and Brown continued to walk to the house of one of the defendant's friends, Lawrence Taylor.

When they entered the house, Taylor was inside. Brown sat in the living room while the defendant and Taylor went to the back of the house and talked. When asked why she did not try to leave when the defendant and Taylor were in the back of the house, Brown replied, "It was nowhere to go. I don't know. I just didn't." The defendant returned to the living room area and turned on the television. He attempted to fix a broken fan. Brown asked Taylor for a cigarette, and he gave her one.

The defendant began talking to Brown about another man she had been seeing. By that time Taylor had gone out of the room and perhaps the house. The defendant asked if Brown was "ready." The evidence tended to show that she told him "no, that I wasn't going to bed with him." She testified that she did not want to have sex with the defendant and did not consent to do so at any time on June 15.

After Brown finished her cigarette, the defendant began kissing her neck. He pulled her up from the chair in which she had been sitting and started undressing her. He noticed that she was having her menstrual period, and she sat down pulling her pants back up. The defendant again took off her pants and blouse. He told her to lay down on a bed which was in the living room. She complied and the defendant pushed apart her legs and had sexual intercourse with her. Brown testified that she did not try to push him away. She cried during the intercourse. Afterwards they talked. The defendant told her he wanted to make sure she was not lying about where she lived and that he would not let her up unless she told him.

After they dressed they talked again about the man Brown had been seeing. They left the house and went to the defendant's mother's house. After talking with the defendant's mother, Brown took a bus home. She talked with her mother about taking out a complaint against the defendant but did not tell her mother she and the defendant had had sex. Brown made a complaint to the police the same day.

The defendant continued to call Brown after June 15, but she refused to see him. One evening he called from a telephone booth and told her he had to talk. When he got to her apartment he threatened to kick her door down and

Brown let him inside. Once inside he said he had intended merely to talk to her but that he wanted to make love again after seeing her. Brown said she sat and looked at him, and that he began kissing her. She pulled away and he picked her up and carried her to the bedroom. He performed oral sex on her and she testified that she did not try to fight him off because she found she enjoyed it. The two stayed together until morning and had sexual intercourse several times that night. Brown did not disclose the incident to the police immediately because she said she was embarrassed.

The defendant put on no evidence and moved at the close of the State's evidence for dismissal of both charges based on insufficiency of evidence. The trial court denied the motions and the majority in the Court of Appeals affirmed the trial court.

Upon the defendant's motion to dismiss, the question for the court is whether substantial evidence was introduced of each element of the offense charged and that the defendant was the perpetrator. Substantial evidence is "such relevant evidence as a reasonable mind might accept as adequate to support a conclusion." . . .

. . . [T]he defendant contends there was no substantial evidence that the sexual intercourse between Brown and him was by force and against her will. He argues that the evidence was insufficient to allow the trial court to submit the issue of his guilt of second degree rape to the jury. After a review of the evidence, we find this argument to have merit.

Second degree rape involves vaginal intercourse with the victim both by force and against the victim's will. G.S. 14–27.3. Consent by the victim is a complete defense, but consent which is induced by fear of violence is void and is no legal consent.

A defendant can be guilty of raping even his mistress or a "common strumpet." This is so because consent to sexual intercourse freely given can be withdrawn at any time prior to penetration. If the particular act of intercourse for which the defendant is charged was both by force and against the victim's will, the offense is rape without regard to the victim's consent given to the defendant for prior acts of intercourse.

Where as here the victim has engaged in a prior continuing consensual sexual relationship with the defendant, however, determining the victim's state of mind at the time of the alleged rape obviously is made more difficult. Although inquiry in such cases still must be made into the victim's state of mind at the time of the alleged rape, the State ordinarily will be able to show the victim's lack of consent to the specific act charged only by evidence of statements or actions by the victim which were clearly communicated to the defendant and which expressly and unequivocally indicated the victim's withdrawal of any prior consent and lack of consent to the particular act of intercourse.

In the present case the State introduced such evidence. It is true, of course, that Brown gave no physical resistance to the defendant. Evidence of physical resistance is not necessary to prove lack of consent in a rape case in this jurisdiction. *State v. Hall*, 293 N.C. 559, 563, (1977). Brown testified unequivocally that she did not consent to sexual intercourse with the defendant on June 15. She was equally unequivocal in testifying that she submitted to sexual intercourse with the defendant only because she was afraid of him. During their walk, she told the defendant that their relationship was at an end. When the defendant asked her if she was "ready" immediately prior to having sexual intercourse with her, she told him "no, that I wasn't going to bed with him." Even in the absence of physical resistance by Brown, such testimony by her provided substantial evidence that the act of sexual intercourse was against her will.

The State did not offer substantial evidence, however, of the element of force. As we have stated, actual physical force need not be shown in order to establish force sufficient to constitute an element of the crime of rape. Threats of serious bodily harm which reasonably induce fear thereof are sufficient. In the present case there was no substantial evidence of either actual or constructive force.

The evidence in the present case tended to show that, shortly after the defendant met Brown at the school, they walked out of the parking lot with the defendant in front. He stopped and told Brown he was going to "fix" her face so that her mother could see he was not "playing." This threat by the defendant and his act of grabbing Brown by the arm at the school, although they may have induced fear, appeared to have been unrelated to the act of sexual intercourse between Brown and the defendant. More important, the record is devoid of evidence that Brown was in any way intimidated into having sexual intercourse with the defendant by that threat or any other act of the defendant on June 15. Brown said she did not pay a lot of attention to what the defendant said because she was thinking about other things. She specifically stated that her fear of the defendant was based on an experience with him prior to June 15 and that on June 15 he did not hold her down or threaten her with what would happen if she refused to submit to him. The State failed to offer substantial evidence of force used or threatened by the defendant on June 15 which related to his desire to have sexual intercourse on that date and was sufficient to overcome the will of the victim.

We note that the absence of an explicit threat is not determinative in considering whether there was sufficient force in whatever form to overcome the will of the victim. It is enough if the totality of the circumstances gives rise to a reasonable inference that the unspoken purpose of the threat was to force the victim to submit to unwanted sexual intercourse. The evidence introduced in the present case, however, gave rise to no such inference. Under the peculiar facts of this case, there was no substantial evidence that threats or force by the defendant on June 15 were sufficiently related to sexual conduct to cause Brown to believe that she had to submit to sexual intercourse with him or suffer harm. Although Brown's general fear of the defendant may have been justified by his conduct on prior occasions, absent evidence that the defendant used force or threats to overcome the will of the victim to resist the sexual intercourse alleged to have been rape, such general fear was not sufficient to show that the defendant used the force required to support a conviction of rape.

In summary, we think that the State's evidence was sufficient to show that the act of sexual intercourse in question was against Brown's will. It was not sufficient, however, to show that the act was accomplished by actual force or by a threat to use force unless she submitted to sexual intercourse. Since the State did not introduce substantial evidence of the element of force required to sustain a conviction of rape, the trial court erred in denying the defendant's motion to dismiss the case against the defendant for second degree rape.

For the foregoing reasons, we reverse the opinion of the Court of Appeals holding that there was no error in the defendant's trial for kidnapping and second degree rape and remand this action to the Court of Appeals . . . .

E. Criminal Sexual Conduct

In an effort to redraft traditional rape statutes, various states have passed criminal sexual conduct (hereinafter CSC) laws. Generally, the word "rape" is not found in these laws; rape is a common law crime and these statutes appear to have been written with the purpose of redefining the law.

Generally, CSC laws are quite different from the traditional crimes of rape and statutory rape. CSC laws are gender neutral—both as to the defendant and the victim—and include a wide variety of non-consensual sexual acts besides penile-vaginal penetration. These laws have eliminated or limited the scope of, *inter alia*: (1) corroboration of the victim's testimony; (2) the resistance requirement; (3) evidence of past sexual experiences; and (4) the marital privilege. *See, e.g.*, M.C.L. §§750.520a–520n.

The remainder of this chapter will explore CSC laws by examining a New Jersey case, reviewing excerpts from Michigan's CSC statute, and practicing some statutory analysis through various CSC problems.

F. Reforming Rape Laws with Criminal Sexual Conduct Statutes

How does the traditional crime of forcible rape differ from CSC? After reading the *M.T.S.* case, consider how the same set of facts would have been interpreted in a more traditional rape jurisdiction, like that of the *Berkowitz* case.

State in Interest of M.T.S., 129 N.J. 422 (1992)

HANDLER, J.
Under New Jersey law a person who commits an act of sexual penetration using physical force or coercion is guilty of second-degree sexual assault. The

sexual assault statute does not define the words "physical force." The question posed by this appeal is whether the element of "physical force" is met simply by an act of non-consensual penetration involving no more force than necessary to accomplish that result.

That issue is presented in the context of what is often referred to as "acquaintance rape." The record in the case discloses that the juvenile, a seventeen-year-old boy, engaged in consensual kissing and heavy petting with a fifteen-year-old girl and thereafter engaged in actual sexual penetration of the girl to which she had not consented. There was no evidence or suggestion that the juvenile used any unusual or extra force or threats to accomplish the act of penetration.

The trial court determined that the juvenile was delinquent for committing a sexual assault. The Appellate Division reversed the disposition of delinquency, concluding that non-consensual penetration does not constitute sexual assault unless it is accompanied by some level of force more than that necessary to accomplish the penetration. We granted the State's petition for certification.

I

The issues in this case are perplexing and controversial. We must explain the role of force in the contemporary crime of sexual assault and then define its essential features. We then must consider what evidence is probative to establish the commission of a sexual assault. The factual circumstances of this case expose the complexity and sensitivity of those issues and underscore the analytic difficulty of those seemingly-straightforward legal questions.

On Monday, May 21, 1990, fifteen-year-old C.G. was living with her mother, her three siblings, and several other people, including M.T.S. and his girlfriend. A total of ten people resided in the three-bedroom town-home at the time of the incident. M.T.S., then age seventeen, was temporarily residing at the home with the permission of the [sic] C.G.'s mother; he slept downstairs on a couch. C.G. had her own room on the second floor. At approximately 11:30 p.m. on May 21, C.G. went upstairs to sleep after having watched television with her mother, M.T.S., and his girlfriend. When C.G. went to bed, she was wearing underpants, a bra, shorts, and a shirt. At trial, C.G. and M.T.S. offered very different accounts concerning the nature of their relationship and the events that occurred after C.G. had gone upstairs. The trial court did not credit fully either teenager's testimony.

C.G. stated that earlier in the day, M.T.S. had told her three or four times that he "was going to make a surprise visit up in [her] bedroom." She said that she had not taken M.T.S. seriously and considered his comments a joke because he frequently teased her. She testified that M.T.S. had attempted to kiss her on numerous other occasions and at least once had attempted to put his hands inside of her pants, but that she had rejected all of his previous advances.

C.G. testified that on May 22, at approximately 1:30 a.m., she awoke to use the bathroom. As she was getting out of bed, she said, she saw M.T.S., fully clothed, standing in her doorway. According to C.G., M.T.S. then said that "he was going to tease [her] a little bit." C.G. testified that she "didn't think anything of it"; she walked past him, used the bathroom, and then returned to bed, falling into a "heavy" sleep within fifteen minutes. The next event C.G. claimed to recall of that morning was waking up with M.T.S. on top of her, her underpants and shorts removed. She said "his penis was into [her] vagina." As soon as C.G. realized what had happened, she said, she immediately slapped M.T.S. once in the face, then "told him to get off [her], and get out." She did not scream or cry out. She testified that M.T.S. complied in less than one minute after being struck; according to C.G., "he jumped right off of [her]." She said she did not know how long M.T.S. had been inside of her before she awoke.

C.G. said that after M.T.S. left the room, she "fell asleep crying" because "[she] couldn't believe that he did what he did to [her]." She explained that she did not immediately tell her mother or anyone else in the house of the events of that morning because she was "scared and in shock." According to C.G., M.T.S. engaged in intercourse with her "without [her] wanting it or telling him to come up [to her bedroom]." By her own account, C.G. was not otherwise harmed by M.T.S.

At about 7:00 a.m., C.G. went downstairs and told her mother about her encounter with M.T.S. earlier in the morning and said that they would have to "get [him] out of the house." While M.T.S. was out on an errand, C.G.'s mother gathered his clothes and put them outside in his car; when he returned, he was told that "[he] better not even get near the house." C.G. and her mother then filed a complaint with the police.

According to M.T.S., he and C.G. had been good friends for a long time, and their relationship "kept leading on to more and more." He had been living at C.G.'s home for about five days before the incident occurred; he testified that during the three days preceding the incident they had been "kissing and necking" and had discussed having sexual intercourse. The first time M.T.S. kissed C.G., he said, she "didn't want him to, but she did after that." He said C.G. repeatedly had encouraged him to "make a surprise visit up in her room."

M.T.S. testified that at exactly 1:15 a.m. on May 22, he entered C.G.'s bedroom as she was walking to the bathroom. He said C.G. soon returned from the bathroom, and the two began "kissing and all," eventually moving to the bed. Once they were in bed, he said, they undressed each other and continued to kiss and touch for about five minutes. M.T.S. and C.G. proceeded to engage in sexual intercourse. According to M.T.S., who was on top of C.G., he "stuck it in" and "did it [thrust] three times, and then the fourth time [he] stuck it in, that's when [she] pulled [him] off of her." M.T.S. said that as C.G. pushed him off, she said "stop, get off," and he "hopped off right away."

According to M.T.S., after about one minute, he asked C.G. what was wrong; she replied with a back-hand to his face. He recalled asking C.G. what was wrong a second time, and her replying, "how can you take advantage of me or something like that." M.T.S. said that he proceeded to get dressed and told

C.G. to calm down, but that she then told him to get away from her and began to cry. Before leaving the room, he told C.G., "I'm leaving . . . I'm going with my real girlfriend, don't talk to me . . . I don't want nothing to do with you or anything, stay out of my life . . . don't tell anybody about this . . . it would just screw everything up." He then walked downstairs and went to sleep.

On May 23, 1990, M.T.S. was charged with conduct that if engaged in by an adult would constitute second-degree sexual assault of the victim, contrary to *N.J.S.A.* 2C:14–2c(1). In addition, he faced unrelated charges for third-degree theft of movable property, contrary to *N.J.S.A.* 2C:20–3a, third-degree escape, contrary to *N.J.S.A.* 2C:29–5, and fourth-degree criminal trespass, contrary to *N.J.S.A.* 2C:18–3.

Following a two-day trial on the sexual assault charge, M.T.S. was adjudicated delinquent. After reviewing the testimony, the court concluded that the victim had consented to a session of kissing and heavy petting with M.T.S. The trial court did not find that C.G. had been sleeping at the time of penetration, but nevertheless found that she had not consented to the actual sexual act. Accordingly, the court concluded that the State had proven second-degree sexual assault beyond a reasonable doubt. On appeal, following the imposition of suspended sentences on the sexual assault and the other remaining charges, the Appellate Division determined that the absence of force beyond that involved in the act of sexual penetration precluded a finding of second-degree sexual assault. It therefore reversed the juvenile's adjudication of delinquency for that offense.

II

The New Jersey Code of Criminal Justice, *N.J.S.A.* 2C:14–2c(1), defines "sexual assault" as the commission "of sexual penetration" "with another person" with the use of "physical force or coercion."[1] An unconstrained reading

---

[1] The sexual assault statute, *N.J.S.A.* 2C:14–2c(1), reads as follows:

    c.   An actor is guilty of sexual assault if he commits an act of sexual penetration with another person under any one of the following circumstances:

        (1)   The actor *uses physical force or coercion*, but the victim does not sustain severe personal injury;

        (2)   The victim is one whom the actor knew or should have known was physically helpless, mentally defective or mentally incapacitated;

        (3)   The victim is on probation or parole, or is detained in a hospital, prison or other institution and the actor has supervisory or disciplinary power over the victim by virtue of the actor's legal, professional or occupational status;

        (4)   The victim is at least 16 but less than 18 years old and:

            (a)   The actor is related to the victim by blood or affinity to the third degree; or

            (b)   The actor has supervisory or disciplinary power over the victim; or

            (c)   The actor is a foster parent, a guardian, or stands in loco parentis within the household;

of the statutory language indicates that both the act of "sexual penetration" and the use of "physical force or coercion" are separate and distinct elements of the offense. Neither the definitions section of *N.J.S.A.* 2C:14–1 to –8, nor the remainder of the Code of Criminal Justice provides assistance in interpreting the words "physical force." The initial inquiry is, therefore, whether the statutory words are unambiguous on their face and can be understood and applied in accordance with their plain meaning. The answer to that inquiry is revealed by the conflicting decisions of the lower courts and the arguments of the opposing parties. The trial court held that "physical force" had been established by the sexual penetration of the victim without her consent. The Appellate Division believed that the statute requires some amount of force more than that necessary to accomplish penetration.

The parties offer two alternative understandings of the concept of "physical force" as it is used in the statute. The State would read "physical force" to entail any amount of sexual touching brought about involuntarily. A showing of sexual penetration coupled with a lack of consent would satisfy the elements of the statute. The Public Defender urges an interpretation of "physical force" to mean force "used to overcome lack of consent." That definition equates force with violence and leads to the conclusion that sexual assault requires the application of some amount of force in addition to the act of penetration.

Current judicial practice suggests an understanding of "physical force" to mean "any degree of physical power or strength used against the victim, even though it entails no injury and leaves no mark." Resort to common experience or understanding does not yield a conclusive meaning. The dictionary provides several definitions of "force," among which are the following: (1) "power, violence, compulsion, or constraint exerted upon or against a person or thing," (2) "a general term for exercise of strength or power, esp. physical, to overcome resistance," or (3) "strength or power of any degree that is exercised without justification or contrary to law upon a person or thing."

Thus, as evidenced by the disagreements among the lower courts and the parties, and the variety of possible usages, the statutory words "physical force" do not evoke a single meaning that is obvious and plain. Hence, we must pursue avenues of construction in order to ascertain the meaning of that statutory language. Those avenues are well charted. When a statute is open to conflicting interpretations, the court seeks the underlying intent of the legislature, relying on legislative history and the contemporary context of the statute. With respect to a law, like the sexual assault statute, that "alters or amends the previous law or creates or abolishes types of actions, it is important, in discovering the

---

(5)   The victim is at least 13 but less than 16 years old and the actor is at least 4 years older than the victim.

Sexual assault is a crime of the second degree.

legislative intent, to ascertain the old law, the mischief and the proposed remedy." . . .

The provisions proscribing sexual offenses found in the Code of Criminal Justice, *N.J.S.A.* 2C:14–2c(1), became effective in 1979, and were written against almost two hundred years of rape law in New Jersey. The origin of the rape statute that the current statutory offense of sexual assault replaced can be traced to the English common law. Under the common law, rape was defined as "carnal knowledge of a woman against her will." American jurisdictions generally adopted the English view, but over time states added the requirement that the carnal knowledge have been forcible, apparently in order to prove that the act was against the victim's will. As of 1796, New Jersey statutory law defined rape as "carnal knowledge of a woman, forcibly and against her will." Those three elements of rape—carnal knowledge, forcibly, and against her will—remained the essential elements of the crime until 1979.

Under traditional rape law, in order to prove that a rape had occurred, the state had to show both that force had been used and that the penetration had been against the woman's will. Force was identified and determined not as an independent factor but in relation to the response of the victim, which in turn implicated the victim's own state of mind. "Thus, the perpetrator's use of force became criminal only if the victim's state of mind met the statutory requirement. The perpetrator could use all the force imaginable and no crime would be committed if the state could not prove additionally that the victim did not consent." . . .

The presence or absence of consent often turned on credibility. To demonstrate that the victim had not consented to the intercourse, and also that sufficient force had been used to accomplish the rape, the state had to prove that the victim had resisted. According to the oft-quoted Lord Hale, to be deemed a credible witness, a woman had to be of good fame, disclose the injury immediately, suffer signs of injury, and cry out for help. 1 Matthew Hale, *History of the Pleas of the Crown* 633 (1st ed. 1847). Courts and commentators historically distrusted the testimony of victims, "assuming that women lie about their lack of consent for various reasons: to blackmail men, to explain the discovery of a consensual affair, or because of psychological illness." Evidence of resistance was viewed as a solution to the credibility problem; it was the "outward manifestation of nonconsent, [a] device for determining whether a woman actually gave consent."

The resistance requirement had a profound effect on the kind of conduct that could be deemed criminal and on the type of evidence needed to establish the crime. Courts assumed that any woman who was forced to have intercourse against her will necessarily would resist to the extent of her ability. In many jurisdictions the requirement was that the woman have resisted to the utmost. . . . Other states followed a "reasonableness" standard, while some required only sufficient resistance to make non-consent reasonably manifest. . . .

The judicial interpretation of the pre-reform rape law in New Jersey, with its insistence on resistance by the victim, greatly minimized the importance of the forcible and assaultive aspect of the defendant's conduct. Rape prosecutions turned then not so much on the forcible or assaultive character of the defendant's actions as on the nature of the victim's response. . . .

The resistance requirement had another untoward influence on traditional rape law. Resistance was necessary not only to prove non-consent but also to demonstrate that the force used by the defendant had been sufficient to overcome the victim's will. The amount of force used by the defendant was assessed in relation to the resistance of the victim. . . . Resistance, often demonstrated by torn clothing and blood, was a sign that the defendant had used significant force to accomplish the sexual intercourse. Thus, if the defendant forced himself on a woman, it was her responsibility to fight back, because force was measured in relation to the resistance she put forward. Only if she resisted, causing him to use more force than was necessary to achieve penetration, would his conduct be criminalized. . . .

The importance of resistance as an evidentiary requirement set the law of rape apart from other common-law crimes, particularly in the eyes of those who advocated reform of rape law in the 1970s. However, the resistance requirement was not the only special rule applied in the rape context. A host of evidentiary rules and standards of proof distinguished the legal treatment of rape from the treatment of other crimes. Many jurisdictions held that a rape conviction could not be sustained if based solely on the uncorroborated testimony of the victim. Often judges added cautionary instructions to jury charges warning jurors that rape was a particularly difficult charge to prove. Courts in New Jersey allowed greater latitude in cross-examining rape victims and in delving into their backgrounds than in ordinary cases. Rape victims were required to make a prompt complaint or have their allegations rejected or viewed with great skepticism. Some commentators suggested that there be mandatory psychological testing of rape victims.

During the 1970s feminists and others criticized the stereotype that rape victims were inherently more untrustworthy than other victims of criminal attack. Reformers condemned such suspicion as discrimination against victims of rape. They argued that "[d]istrust of the complainant's credibility [had] led to an exaggerated insistence on evidence of resistance," resulting in the victim rather than the defendant being put on trial. Reformers also challenged the assumption that a woman would seduce a man and then, in order to protect her virtue, claim to have been raped. If women are no less trustworthy than other purported victims of criminal attack, the reformers argued, then women should face no additional burdens of proving that they had not consented to or had actively resisted the assault.

To refute the misguided belief that rape was not real unless the victim fought back, reformers emphasized empirical research indicating that women who resisted forcible intercourse often suffered far more serious injury as a result. That research discredited the assumption that resistance to the utmost or to the best of a woman's ability was the most reasonable or rational response to a rape.

The research also helped demonstrate the underlying point of the reformers that the crime of rape rested not in the overcoming of a woman's will or the insult to her chastity but in the forcible attack itself—the assault on her person. Reformers criticized the conception of rape as a distinctly sexual crime rather than a crime of violence. They emphasized that rape had its legal origins in laws designed to protect the property rights of men to their wives and daughters. Although the crime had evolved into an offense against women, reformers argued that vestiges of the old law remained, particularly in the understanding of rape as a crime against the purity or chastity of a woman. The burden of protecting that chastity fell on the woman, with the state offering its protection only after the woman demonstrated that she had resisted sufficiently.

That rape under the traditional approach constituted a sexual rather than an assaultive crime is underscored by the spousal exemption. According to the traditional reasoning, a man could not rape his wife because consent to sexual intercourse was implied by the marriage contract. Therefore, sexual intercourse between spouses was lawful regardless of the force or violence used to accomplish it.

Critics of rape law agreed that the focus of the crime should be shifted from the victim's behavior to the defendant's conduct, and particularly to its forceful and assaultive, rather than sexual, character. Reformers also shared the goals of facilitating rape prosecutions and of sparing victims much of the degradation involved in bringing and trying a charge of rape. There were, however, differences over the best way to redefine the crime. Some reformers advocated a standard that defined rape as unconsented-to sexual intercourse; others urged the elimination of any reference to consent from the definition of rape. Nonetheless, all proponents of reform shared a central premise: that the burden of showing non-consent should not fall on the victim of the crime. In dealing with the problem of consent the reform goal was not so much to purge the entire concept of consent from the law as to eliminate the burden that had been placed on victims to prove they had not consented.

Similarly, with regard to force, rape law reform sought to give independent significance to the forceful or assaultive conduct of the defendant and to avoid a definition of force that depended on the reaction of the victim. Traditional interpretations of force were strongly criticized for failing to acknowledge that force may be understood simply as the invasion of "bodily integrity." In urging that the "resistance" requirement be abandoned, reformers sought to break the connection between force and resistance.

III

The history of traditional rape law sheds clearer light on the factors that became most influential in the enactment of current law dealing with sexual offenses. The circumstances surrounding the actual passage of the current law reveal that it was conceived as a reform measure reconstituting the law to address a widely-sensed evil and to effectuate an important public policy. Those circumstances are highly relevant in understanding legislative intent and in determining the objectives of the current law. . . .

. . . The new statutory provisions covering rape were formulated by a coalition of feminist groups assisted by the National Organization of Women (NOW) National Task Force on Rape. Both houses of the Legislature adopted the NOW bill, as it was called, without major changes and Governor Byrne signed it into law on August 10, 1978. The NOW bill had been modeled after the 1976 Philadelphia Center for Rape Concern Model Sex Offense Statute. The Model Sex Offense Statute in turn had been based on selected provisions of the Michigan Criminal Sexual Conduct Statute, *Mich.Stat.Ann.* §28.788(4)(b) (Callaghan 1990), [M.C.L.A. §750.520d] and on the reform statutes in New Mexico, Minnesota, and Wisconsin. The stated intent of the drafters of the Philadelphia Center's Model Statute had been to remove all features found to be contrary to the interests of rape victims. According to its proponents the statute would " 'normalize the law. We are no longer saying rape victims are likely to lie. What we are saying is that rape is just like other violent crimes.' "

Since the 1978 reform, the Code has referred to the crime that was once known as "rape" as "sexual assault." The crime now requires "penetration," not "sexual intercourse." It requires "force" or "coercion," not "submission" or "resistance." It makes no reference to the victim's state of mind or attitude, or conduct in response to the assault. It eliminates the spousal exception based on implied consent. It emphasizes the assaultive character of the offense by defining sexual penetration to encompass a wide range of sexual contacts, going well beyond traditional "carnal knowledge."[2] Consistent with the assaultive character, as opposed to the traditional sexual character, of the offense, the statute also renders the crime gender-neutral: both males and females can be actors or victims.

The reform statute defines sexual assault as penetration accomplished by the use of "physical force" or "coercion," but it does not define either "physical force" or "coercion" or enumerate examples of evidence that would establish

---

[2] The reform replaced the concept of carnal abuse, which was limited to vaginal intercourse, with specific kinds of sexual acts contained in a broad definition of penetration:

> Sexual penetration means vaginal intercourse, cunnilingus, fellatio or anal intercourse between persons or insertion of the hand, finger or object into the anus or vagina either by the actor or upon the actor's instruction. [*N.J.S.A.* 2C:14–1.]

those elements. Some reformers had argued that defining "physical force" too specifically in the sexual offense statute might have the effect of limiting force to the enumerated examples. The task of defining "physical force" therefore was left to the courts. . . .

. . . [T]he New Jersey Code of Criminal Justice does not refer to force in relation to "overcoming the will" of the victim, or to the "physical overpowering" of the victim, or the "submission" of the victim. It does not require the demonstrated non-consent of the victim. As we have noted, in reforming the rape laws, the Legislature placed primary emphasis on the assaultive nature of the crime, altering its constituent elements so that they focus exclusively on the forceful or assaultive conduct of the defendant.

The Legislature's concept of sexual assault and the role of force was significantly colored by its understanding of the law of assault and battery. As a general matter, criminal battery is defined as "the unlawful application of force to the person of another." The application of force is criminal when it results in either (a) a physical injury or (b) an offensive touching. Any "unauthorized touching of another [is] a battery." Thus, by eliminating all references to the victim's state of mind and conduct, and by broadening the definition of penetration to cover not only sexual intercourse between a man and a woman but a range of acts that invade another's body or compel intimate contact, the Legislature emphasized the affinity between sexual assault and other forms of assault and battery.

The intent of the Legislature to redefine rape consistent with the law of assault and battery is further evidenced by the legislative treatment of other sexual crimes less serious than and derivative of traditional rape. The Code redefined the offense of criminal sexual contact to emphasize the involuntary and personally-offensive nature of the touching. *N.J.S.A.* 2C:14–1(d). Sexual contact is criminal under the same circumstances that render an act of sexual penetration a sexual assault, namely, when "physical force" or "coercion" demonstrates that it is unauthorized and offensive. *N.J.S.A.* 2C:14–3(b). Thus, just as any unauthorized touching is a crime under traditional laws of assault and battery, so is any unauthorized sexual contact a crime under the reformed law of criminal sexual contact, and so is any unauthorized sexual penetration a crime under the reformed law of sexual assault.

The understanding of sexual assault as a criminal battery, albeit one with especially serious consequences, follows necessarily from the Legislature's decision to eliminate non-consent and resistance from the substantive definition of the offense. Under the new law, the victim no longer is required to resist and therefore need not have said or done anything in order for the sexual penetration to be unlawful. The alleged victim is not put on trial, and his or her responsive or defensive behavior is rendered immaterial. We are thus satisfied that an interpretation of the statutory crime of sexual assault to require physical force in addition to that entailed in an act of involuntary or unwanted sexual penetration would be fundamentally inconsistent with the legislative purpose to eliminate any consideration of whether the victim resisted or expressed non-consent.

We note that the contrary interpretation of force—that the element of force need be extrinsic to the sexual act—would not only reintroduce a resistance requirement into the sexual assault law, but also would immunize many acts of criminal sexual *contact* short of penetration. The characteristics that make a sexual contact unlawful are the same as those that make a sexual penetration unlawful. An actor is guilty of criminal sexual contact if he or she commits an act of sexual contact with another using "physical force" or "coercion." *N.J.S.A.* 2C:14–3(b). That the Legislature would have wanted to decriminalize unauthorized sexual intrusions on the bodily integrity of a victim by requiring a showing of force in addition to that entailed in the sexual contact itself is hardly possible.

Because the statute eschews any reference to the victim's will or resistance, the standard defining the role of force in sexual penetration must prevent the possibility that the establishment of the crime will turn on the alleged victim's state of mind or responsive behavior. We conclude, therefore, that any act of sexual penetration engaged in by the defendant without the affirmative and freely-given permission of the victim to the specific act of penetration constitutes the offense of sexual assault. Therefore, physical force in excess of that inherent in the act of sexual penetration is not required for such penetration to be unlawful. The definition of "physical force" is satisfied under *N.J.S.A.* 2C:14–2c(1) if the defendant applies any amount of force against another person in the absence of what a reasonable person would believe to be affirmative and freely-given permission to the act of sexual penetration.

Under the reformed statute, permission to engage in sexual penetration must be affirmative and it must be given freely, but that permission may be inferred either from acts or statements reasonably viewed in light of the surrounding circumstances. Persons need not, of course, expressly announce their consent to engage in intercourse for there to be affirmative permission. Permission to engage in an act of sexual penetration can be and indeed often is indicated through physical actions rather than words. Permission is demonstrated when the evidence, in whatever form, is sufficient to demonstrate that a reasonable person would have believed that the alleged victim had affirmatively and freely given authorization to the act.

Our understanding of the meaning and application of "physical force" under the sexual assault statute indicates that the term's inclusion was neither inadvertent nor redundant. The term "physical force," like its companion term "coercion," acts to qualify the nature and character of the "sexual penetration." Sexual penetration accomplished through the use of force is unauthorized sexual penetration. That functional understanding of "physical force" encompasses the notion of "unpermitted touching" derived from the Legislature's decision to redefine rape as a sexual assault. As already noted, under assault and battery doctrine, any amount of force that results in either physical injury or offensive touching is sufficient to establish a battery. Hence, as a description of the method of achieving "sexual penetration," the term "physical force" serves to define and explain the acts that are offensive, unauthorized, and unlawful.

That understanding of the crime of sexual assault fully comports with the public policy sought to be effectuated by the Legislature. In redefining rape law as sexual assault, the Legislature adopted the concept of sexual assault as a crime against the bodily integrity of the victim. Although it is possible to imagine a set of rules in which persons must demonstrate affirmatively that sexual contact is unwanted or not permitted, such a regime would be inconsistent with modern principles of personal autonomy. The Legislature recast the law of rape as sexual assault to bring that area of law in line with the expectation of privacy and bodily control that long has characterized most of our private and public law. In interpreting "physical force" to include any touching that occurs without permission we seek to respect that goal.

Today the law of sexual assault is indispensable to the system of legal rules that assures each of us the right to decide who may touch our bodies, when, and under what circumstances. The decision to engage in sexual relations with another person is one of the most private and intimate decisions a person can make. Each person has the right not only to decide whether to engage in sexual contact with another, but also to control the circumstances and character of that contact. No one, neither a spouse, nor a friend, nor an acquaintance, nor a stranger, has the right or the privilege to force sexual contact.

We emphasize as well that what is now referred to as "acquaintance rape" is not a new phenomenon. Nor was it a "futuristic" concept in 1978 when the sexual assault law was enacted. Current concern over the prevalence of forced sexual intercourse between persons who know one another reflects both greater awareness of the extent of such behavior and a growing appreciation of its gravity. Notwithstanding the stereotype of rape as a violent attack by a stranger, the vast majority of sexual assaults are perpetrated by someone known to the victim. One respected study indicates that more than half of all rapes are committed by male relatives, current or former husbands, boyfriends or lovers. Similarly, contrary to common myths, perpetrators generally do not use guns or knives and victims generally do not suffer external bruises or cuts. Although this more realistic and accurate view of rape only recently has achieved widespread public circulation, it was a central concern of the proponents of reform in the 1970s.

The insight into rape as an assaultive crime is consistent with our evolving understanding of the wrong inherent in forced sexual intimacy. It is one that was appreciated by the Legislature when it reformed the rape laws, reflecting an emerging awareness that the definition of rape should correspond fully with the experiences and perspectives of rape victims. Although reformers focused primarily on the problems associated with convicting defendants accused of violent rape, the recognition that forced sexual intercourse often takes place between persons who know each other and often involves little or no violence comports with the understanding of the sexual assault law that was embraced by the Legislature. Any other interpretation of the law, particularly one that defined force in relation to the resistance or protest of the victim, would directly undermine the goals sought to be achieved by its reform.

IV

In a case such as this one, in which the State does not allege violence or force extrinsic to the act of penetration, the factfinder must decide whether the defendant's act of penetration was undertaken in circumstances that led the defendant reasonably to believe that the alleged victim had freely given affirmative permission to the specific act of sexual penetration. Such permission can be indicated either through words or through actions that, when viewed in the light of all the surrounding circumstances, would demonstrate to a reasonable person affirmative and freely-given authorization for the specific act of sexual penetration.

In applying that standard to the facts in these cases, the focus of attention must be on the nature of the defendant's actions. The role of the factfinder is not to decide whether reasonable people may engage in acts of penetration without the permission of others. The Legislature answered that question when it enacted the reformed sexual assault statute: reasonable people do not engage in acts of penetration without permission, and it is unlawful to do so. The role of the factfinder is to decide not whether engaging in an act of penetration without permission of another person is reasonable, but only whether the defendant's belief that the alleged victim had freely given affirmative permission was reasonable.

In these cases neither the alleged victim's subjective state of mind nor the reasonableness of the alleged victim's actions can be deemed relevant to the offense. The alleged victim may be questioned about what he or she did or said only to determine whether the defendant was reasonable in believing that affirmative permission had been freely given. To repeat, the law places no burden on the alleged victim to have expressed non-consent or to have denied permission, and no inquiry is made into what he or she thought or desired or why he or she did not resist or protest.

In short, in order to convict under the sexual assault statute in cases such as these, the State must prove beyond a reasonable doubt that there was sexual penetration and that it was accomplished without the affirmative and freely-given permission of the alleged victim. As we have indicated, such proof can be based on evidence of conduct or words in light of surrounding circumstances and must demonstrate beyond a reasonable doubt that a reasonable person would not have believed that there was affirmative and freely-given permission. If there is evidence to suggest that the defendant reasonably believed that such permission had been given, the State must demonstrate either that defendant did not actually believe that affirmative permission had been freely-given or that such a belief was unreasonable under all of the circumstances. Thus, the State bears the burden of proof throughout the case.

In the context of a sexual penetration not involving unusual or added "physical force," the inclusion of "permission" as an aspect of "physical force" effectively subsumes and obviates any defense based on consent. *See N.J.S.A.* 2C:2–10c(3). The definition of "permission" serves to define the "consent" that otherwise might allow a defendant to avoid criminal liability. Because "physical force" as an element of sexual assault in this context requires the *absence* of affirmative and freely-given permission, the "consent" necessary to negate such "physical force" under a defense based on consent would require the *presence* of such affirmative and freely-given permission. Any lesser form of consent would render the sexual penetration unlawful and cannot constitute a defense.

In this case, the Appellate Division concluded that non-consensual penetration accomplished with no additional physical force or coercion is not criminalized under the sexual assault statute. It acknowledged that its conclusion was "anomalous" because it recognized that "a woman has every right to end [physically intimate] activity without sexual penetration." Thus, it added to its holding that "[e]ven the force of penetration might . . . be sufficient if it is shown to be employed to overcome the victim's unequivocal expressed desire to limit the encounter."

The Appellate Division was correct in recognizing that a woman's right to end intimate activity without penetration is a protectable right the violation of which can be a criminal offense. However, it misperceived the purpose of the statute in believing that the only way that right can be protected is by the woman's unequivocally-expressed desire to end the activity. The effect of that requirement would be to import into the sexual assault statute the notion that an assault occurs only if the victim's will is overcome, and thus to reintroduce the requirement of non-consent and victim-resistance as a constituent material element of the crime. Under the reformed statute, a person's failure to protest or resist cannot be considered or used as justification for bodily invasion.

We acknowledge that cases such as this are inherently fact sensitive and depend on the reasoned judgment and common sense of judges and juries. The trial court concluded that the victim had not expressed consent to the act of intercourse, either through her words or actions. We conclude that the record provides reasonable support for the trial court's disposition.

Accordingly, we reverse the judgment of the Appellate Division and reinstate the disposition of juvenile delinquency for the commission of second-degree sexual assault.

G. The Law in Transition

1. Michigan's Criminal Sexual Conduct Statute

Michigan has enacted a CSC statute that differs significantly from the traditional law of forcible and statutory rape. M.C.L. §§750.520a–520n. The CSC statute, partially excerpted below, covers both penetration (First and Third Degree CSC) as well as sexual contact (Second and Fourth Degree CSC). As you examine this statute, be sure to start with a general review of the definition section, as that will aid in your comprehension of the specifics of the statute.

M.C.L. §750.520a. Definitions

As used in this chapter:

(a) "Actor" means a person accused of criminal sexual conduct.

(b) "Developmental disability" means an impairment of general intellectual functioning or adaptive behavior which meets all of the following criteria:

(*i*) It originated before the person became 18 years of age.

(*ii*) It has continued since its origination or can be expected to continue indefinitely.

(*iii*) It constitutes a substantial burden to the impaired person's ability to perform in society.

(*iv*) It is attributable to 1 or more of the following:

(A) Mental retardation, cerebral palsy, epilepsy, or autism.

(B) Any other condition of a person found to be closely related to mental retardation because it produces a similar impairment or requires treatment and services similar to those required for a person who is mentally retarded.

(c) "Electronic monitoring" means that term as defined in section 85 of the corrections code of 1953, 1953 PA 232, MCL 791.285.

(d) "Intellectual disability" means that term as defined in section 100b of the mental health code, 1974 PA 258, MCL 330.1100b.

(e) "Intermediate school district" means a corporate body established under part 7 of the revised school code, 1976 PA 451, MCL 380.601 to 380.705.

(f) "Intimate parts" includes the primary genital area, groin, inner thigh, buttock, or breast of a human being.

(g) "Mental health professional" means that term as defined in section 100b of the mental health code, 1974 PA 258, MCL 330.1100b.

(h) "Mental illness" means a substantial disorder of thought or mood that significantly impairs judgment, behavior, capacity to recognize reality, or ability to cope with the ordinary demands of life.

(i)   "Mentally disabled" means that a person has a mental illness, is mentally retarded, or has a developmental disability.

(j)   "Mentally incapable" means that a person suffers from a mental disease or defect that renders that person temporarily or permanently incapable of appraising the nature of his or her conduct.

(k)   "Mentally incapacitated" means that a person is rendered temporarily incapable of appraising or controlling his or her conduct due to the influence of a narcotic, anesthetic, or other substance administered to that person without his or her consent, or due to any other act committed upon that person without his or her consent.

(l)   "Nonpublic school" means a private, denominational, or parochial elementary or secondary school.

(m)   "Physically helpless" means that a person is unconscious, asleep, or for any other reason is physically unable to communicate unwillingness to an act.

(n)   "Personal injury" means bodily injury, disfigurement, mental anguish, chronic pain, pregnancy, disease, or loss or impairment of a sexual or reproductive organ.

(o)   "Public school" means a public elementary or secondary educational entity or agency that is established under the revised school code, 1976 PA 451, MCL 380.1 to 380.1852.

(p)   "School district" means a general powers school district organized under the revised school code, 1976 PA 451, MCL 380.1 to 380.1852.

(q)   "Sexual contact" includes the intentional touching of the victim's or actor's intimate parts or the intentional touching of the clothing covering the immediate area of the victim's or actor's intimate parts, if that intentional touching can reasonably be construed as being for the purpose of sexual arousal or gratification, done for a sexual purpose, or in a sexual manner for:

  (*i*)   Revenge.

  (*ii*)   To inflict humiliation.

  (*iii*)   Out of anger.

(r)   "Sexual penetration" means sexual intercourse, cunnilingus, fellatio, anal intercourse, or any other intrusion, however slight, of any part of a person's body or of any object into the genital or anal openings of another person's body, but emission of semen is not required.

(s)   "Victim" means the person alleging to have been subjected to criminal sexual conduct.

M.C.L. §750.520b. Criminal sexual conduct in first degree

(1)   A person is guilty of criminal sexual conduct in the first degree if he or she engages in sexual penetration with another person and if any of the following circumstances exists:

(a)   That other person is under 13 years of age.

(b)   That other person is at least 13 but less than 16 years of age and any of the following:

> (*i*)   The actor is a member of the same household as the victim.
>
> (*ii*)   The actor is related to the victim by blood or affinity to the fourth degree.
>
> (*iii*) The actor is in a position of authority over the victim and used this authority to coerce the victim to submit.
>
> (*iv*) The actor is a teacher, substitute teacher, or administrator of the public school, nonpublic school, school district, or intermediate school district in which that other person is enrolled.
>
> (*v*)   The actor is an employee or a contractual service provider of the public school, nonpublic school, school district, or intermediate school district in which that other person is enrolled, or is a volunteer who is not a student in any public school or nonpublic school, or is an employee of this state or of a local unit of government of this state or of the United States assigned to provide any service to that public school, nonpublic school, school district, or intermediate school district, and the actor uses his or her employee, contractual, or volunteer status to gain access to, or to establish a relationship with, that other person.
>
> (*vi*) The actor is an employee, contractual service provider, or volunteer of a child care organization, or a person licensed to operate a foster family home or a foster family group home in which that other person is a resident, and the sexual penetration occurs during the period of that other person's residency. As used in this subparagraph, "child care organization", "foster family home", and "foster family group home" mean those terms as defined in section 1 of 1973 PA 116, MCL 722.111.

(c)   Sexual penetration occurs under circumstances involving the commission of any other felony.

(d)   The actor is aided or abetted by 1 or more other persons and either of the following circumstances exists:

> (*i*)   The actor knows or has reason to know that the victim is mentally incapable, mentally incapacitated, or physically helpless.
>
> (*ii*)   The actor uses force or coercion to accomplish the sexual penetration. Force or coercion includes, but is not limited to, any of the circumstances listed in subdivision (f).

(e)   The actor is armed with a weapon or any article used or fashioned in a manner to lead the victim to reasonably believe it to be a weapon.

(f)   The actor causes personal injury to the victim and force or coercion is used to accomplish sexual penetration. Force or coercion includes, but is not limited to, any of the following circumstances:

   (i)   When the actor overcomes the victim through the actual application of physical force or physical violence.

   (ii)   When the actor coerces the victim to submit by threatening to use force or violence on the victim, and the victim believes that the actor has the present ability to execute these threats.

   (iii)   When the actor coerces the victim to submit by threatening to retaliate in the future against the victim, or any other person, and the victim believes that the actor has the ability to execute this threat. As used in this subdivision, "to retaliate" includes threats of physical punishment, kidnapping, or extortion.

   (iv)   When the actor engages in the medical treatment or examination of the victim in a manner or for purposes that are medically recognized as unethical or unacceptable.

   (v)   When the actor, through concealment or by the element of surprise, is able to overcome the victim.

(g)   The actor causes personal injury to the victim, and the actor knows or has reason to know that the victim is mentally incapable, mentally incapacitated, or physically helpless.

(h)   That other person is mentally incapable, mentally disabled, mentally incapacitated, or physically helpless, and any of the following:

   (i)   The actor is related to the victim by blood or affinity to the fourth degree.

   (ii)   The actor is in a position of authority over the victim and used this authority to coerce the victim to submit.

(2)   Criminal sexual conduct in the first degree is a felony punishable as follows:

(a)   Except as provided in subdivisions (b) and (c), by imprisonment for life or for any term of years.

(b)   For a violation that is committed by an individual 17 years of age or older against an individual less than 13 years of age by imprisonment for life or any term of years, but not less than 25 years.

(c)   For a violation that is committed by an individual 17 years of age or older against an individual less than 13 years of age, by imprisonment for life without the possibility of parole if the person was previously convicted of a violation of this section or section 520c, 520d, 520e, or 520g committed against an individual less than 13 years of age or a violation of law of the United States, another state or political subdivision substantially corresponding to a violation of this section or section 520c, 520d, 520e, or 520g committed against an individual less than 13 years of age.

(d)   In addition to any other penalty imposed under subdivision (a) or (b), the court shall sentence the defendant to lifetime electronic monitoring under section 520n.

(3)   The court may order a term of imprisonment imposed under this section to be served consecutively to any term of imprisonment imposed for any other criminal offense arising from the same transaction.

M.C.L. §750.520c. Criminal sexual conduct in second degree

(1)   A person is guilty of criminal sexual conduct in the second degree if the person engages in sexual contact with another person and if any of the following circumstances exists:

(a)   That other person is under 13 years of age.

(b)   That other person is at least 13 but less than 16 years of age and any of the following:

(i)   The actor is a member of the same household as the victim.

(ii)   The actor is related by blood or affinity to the fourth degree to the victim.

(iii)   The actor is in a position of authority over the victim and the actor used this authority to coerce the victim to submit.

(iv) The actor is a teacher, substitute teacher, or administrator of the public school, nonpublic school, school district, or intermediate school district in which that other person is enrolled.

(v)   The actor is an employee or a contractual service provider of the public school, nonpublic school, school district, or intermediate school district in which that other person is enrolled, or is a volunteer who is not a student in any public school or nonpublic school, or is an employee of this state or of a local unit of government of this state or of the United States assigned to provide any service to that public school, nonpublic school, school district, or intermediate school district, and the actor uses his or her employee, contractual, or volunteer status to gain access to, or to establish a relationship with, that other person.

(*vi*) The actor is an employee, contractual service provider, or volunteer of a child care organization, or a person licensed to operate a foster family home or a foster family group home in which that other person is a resident and the sexual contact occurs during the period of that other person's residency. As used in this subdivision, "child care organization", "foster family home", and "foster family group home" mean those terms as defined in section 1 of 1973 PA 116, MCL 722.111.

(c)   Sexual contact occurs under circumstances involving the commission of any other felony.

(d)   The actor is aided or abetted by 1 or more other persons and either of the following circumstances exists:

(*i*)   The actor knows or has reason to know that the victim is mentally incapable, mentally incapacitated, or physically helpless.

(*ii*)   The actor uses force or coercion to accomplish the sexual contact. Force or coercion includes, but is not limited to, any of the circumstances listed in section 520b(1)(f).

(e)   The actor is armed with a weapon, or any article used or fashioned in a manner to lead a person to reasonably believe it to be a weapon.

(f)   The actor causes personal injury to the victim and force or coercion is used to accomplish the sexual contact. Force or coercion includes, but is not limited to, any of the circumstances listed in section 520b(1)(f).

(g)   The actor causes personal injury to the victim and the actor knows or has reason to know that the victim is mentally incapable, mentally incapacitated, or physically helpless.

(h)   That other person is mentally incapable, mentally disabled, mentally incapacitated, or physically helpless, and any of the following:

(*i*)   The actor is related to the victim by blood or affinity to the fourth degree.

(*ii*)   The actor is in a position of authority over the victim and used this authority to coerce the victim to submit.

(i)   That other person is under the jurisdiction of the department of corrections and the actor is an employee or a contractual employee of, or a volunteer with, the department of corrections who knows that the other person is under the jurisdiction of the department of corrections.

(j) That other person is under the jurisdiction of the department of corrections and the actor is an employee or a contractual employee of, or a volunteer with, a private vendor that operates a youth correctional facility under section 20g of the corrections code of 1953, 1953 PA 232, MCL 791.220g, who knows that the other person is under the jurisdiction of the department of corrections.

(k) That other person is a prisoner or probationer under the jurisdiction of a county for purposes of imprisonment or a work program or other probationary program and the actor is an employee or a contractual employee of or a volunteer with the county or the department of corrections who knows that the other person is under the county's jurisdiction.

(*l*) The actor knows or has reason to know that a court has detained the victim in a facility while the victim is awaiting a trial or hearing, or committed the victim to a facility as a result of the victim having been found responsible for committing an act that would be a crime if committed by an adult, and the actor is an employee or contractual employee of, or a volunteer with, the facility in which the victim is detained or to which the victim was committed.

(2) Criminal sexual conduct in the second degree is a felony punishable as follows:

(a) By imprisonment for not more than 15 years.

(b) In addition to the penalty specified in subdivision (a), the court shall sentence the defendant to lifetime electronic monitoring under section 520n if the violation involved sexual contact committed by an individual 17 years of age or older against an individual less than 13 years of age.

M.C.L. §750.520d. Criminal sexual conduct in third degree

(1) A person is guilty of criminal sexual conduct in the third degree if the person engages in sexual penetration with another person and if any of the following circumstances exist:

(a) That other person is at least 13 years of age and under 16 years of age.

(b) Force or coercion is used to accomplish the sexual penetration. Force or coercion includes but is not limited to any of the circumstances listed in section 520b(1)(f)(*i*) to (*v*).

(c) The actor knows or has reason to know that the victim is mentally incapable, mentally incapacitated, or physically helpless.

(d) That other person is related to the actor by blood or affinity to the third degree and the sexual penetration occurs under circumstances not otherwise prohibited by this chapter. It is an affirmative defense to a prosecution under this subdivision that the other person was in a position of authority over the defendant and used this authority to coerce the defendant to violate this subdivision. The defendant has the burden of proving this defense by a preponderance of the evidence. This subdivision does not apply if both persons are lawfully married to each other at the time of the alleged violation.

(e)   That other person is at least 16 years of age but less than 18 years of age and a student at a public school or nonpublic school, and either of the following applies:

(*i*)   The actor is a teacher, substitute teacher, or administrator of that public school, nonpublic school, school district, or intermediate school district. This subparagraph does not apply if the other person is emancipated or if both persons are lawfully married to each other at the time of the alleged violation.

(*ii*)   The actor is an employee or a contractual service provider of the public school, nonpublic school, school district, or intermediate school district in which that other person is enrolled, or is a volunteer who is not a student in any public school or nonpublic school, or is an employee of this state or of a local unit of government of this state or of the United States assigned to provide any service to that public school, nonpublic school, school district, or intermediate school district, and the actor uses his or her employee, contractual, or volunteer status to gain access to, or to establish a relationship with, that other person.

(f)   That other person is at least 16 years old but less than 26 years of age and is receiving special education services, and either of the following applies:

(*i*)   The actor is a teacher, substitute teacher, administrator, employee, or contractual service provider of the public school, nonpublic school, school district, or intermediate school district from which that other person receives the special education services. This subparagraph does not apply if both persons are lawfully married to each other at the time of the alleged violation.

(*ii*)   The actor is a volunteer who is not a student in any public school or nonpublic school, or is an employee of this state or of a local unit of government of this state or of the United States assigned to provide any service to that public school, nonpublic school, school district, or intermediate school district, and the actor uses his or her employee, contractual, or volunteer status to gain access to, or to establish a relationship with, that other person.

(g) The actor is an employee, contractual service provider, or volunteer of a child care organization, or a person licensed to operate a foster family home or a foster family group home, in which that other person is a resident, that other person is at least 16 years of age, and the sexual penetration occurs during that other person's residency. As used in this subdivision, "child care organization", "foster family home", and "foster family group home" mean those terms as defined in section 1 of 1973 PA 116, MCL 722.111.

(2) Criminal sexual conduct in the third degree is a felony punishable by imprisonment for not more than 15 years.

M.C.L. §750.520e. Criminal sexual conduct in fourth degree

(1) A person is guilty of criminal sexual conduct in the fourth degree if he or she engages in sexual contact with another person and if any of the following circumstances exist:

(a) That other person is at least 13 years of age but less than 16 years of age, and the actor is 5 or more years older than that other person.

(b) Force or coercion is used to accomplish the sexual contact. Force or coercion includes, but is not limited to, any of the following circumstances:

(i) When the actor overcomes the victim through the actual application of physical force or physical violence.

(ii) When the actor coerces the victim to submit by threatening to use force or violence on the victim, and the victim believes that the actor has the present ability to execute that threat.

(iii) When the actor coerces the victim to submit by threatening to retaliate in the future against the victim, or any other person, and the victim believes that the actor has the ability to execute that threat. As used in this subparagraph, "to retaliate" includes threats of physical punishment, kidnapping, or extortion.

(iv) When the actor engages in the medical treatment or examination of the victim in a manner or for purposes which are medically recognized as unethical or unacceptable.

(v) When the actor achieves the sexual contact through concealment or by the element of surprise.

(c) The actor knows or has reason to know that the victim is mentally incapable, mentally incapacitated, or physically helpless.

(d)   That other person is related to the actor by blood or affinity to the third degree and the sexual contact occurs under circumstances not otherwise prohibited by this chapter. It is an affirmative defense to a prosecution under this subdivision that the other person was in a position of authority over the defendant and used this authority to coerce the defendant to violate this subdivision. The defendant has the burden of proving this defense by a preponderance of the evidence. This subdivision does not apply if both persons are lawfully married to each other at the time of the alleged violation.

(e)   The actor is a mental health professional and the sexual contact occurs during or within 2 years after the period in which the victim is his or her client or patient and not his or her spouse. The consent of the victim is not a defense to a prosecution under this subdivision. A prosecution under this subsection shall not be used as evidence that the victim is mentally incompetent.

(f)   That other person is at least 16 years of age but less than 18 years of age and a student at a public school or nonpublic school, and either of the following applies:

(*i*)   The actor is a teacher, substitute teacher, or administrator of that public school, nonpublic school, school district, or intermediate school district. This subparagraph does not apply if the other person is emancipated or if both persons are lawfully married to each other at the time of the alleged violation.

(*ii*)   The actor is an employee or a contractual service provider of the public school, nonpublic school, school district, or intermediate school district in which that other person is enrolled, or is a volunteer who is not a student in any public school or nonpublic school, or is an employee of this state or of a local unit of government of this state or of the United States assigned to provide any service to that public school, nonpublic school, school district, or intermediate school district, and the actor uses his or her employee, contractual, or volunteer status to gain access to, or to establish a relationship with, that other person.

(g)   That other person is at least 16 years old but less than 26 years of age and is receiving special education services, and either of the following applies:

(*i*)   The actor is a teacher, substitute teacher, administrator, employee, or contractual service provider of the public school, nonpublic school, school district, or intermediate school district from which that other person receives the special education services. This subparagraph does not apply if both persons are lawfully married to each other at the time of the alleged violation.

(*ii*) The actor is a volunteer who is not a student in any public school or nonpublic school, or is an employee of this state or of a local unit of government of this state or of the United States assigned to provide any service to that public school, nonpublic school, school district, or intermediate school district, and the actor uses his or her employee, contractual, or volunteer status to gain access to, or to establish a relationship with, that other person.

(h) The actor is an employee, contractual service provider, or volunteer of a child care organization, or a person licensed to operate a foster family home or a foster family group home, in which that other person is a resident, that other person is at least 16 years of age, and the sexual contact occurs during that other person's residency. As used in this subdivision, "child care organization", "foster family home", and "foster family group home" mean those terms as defined in section 1 of 1973 PA 116, MCL 722.111.

(2) Criminal sexual conduct in the fourth degree is a misdemeanor punishable by imprisonment for not more than 2 years or a fine of not more than $500.00, or both.

Note

(1) Court held that definition of "sexual contact" under M.C.L. §750.520a(q), did not require the prosecutor to prove the defendant must have specifically intended the contact for sexual gratification. *People v. Piper*, 223 Mich. App. 642 (1997).

(2) Relation by affinity (i.e., by marriage) is sufficient; victim and defendant need not be related by blood. *People v. Russell*, 266 Mich. App. 307 (2005).

(3) There must be a nexus between the sexual penetration and the underlying felony to support a conviction under M.C.L. §750.520b(1)(c). *People v. Waltonen*, 272 Mich. App. 678 (2006).

(4) "Mental anguish" under the statute must be "extreme or excruciating pain, distress, or suffering of the mind." *People v. Petrella*, 424 Mich. 221, 227 (1985).

2. Practice Problems on Criminal Sexual Conduct

For the following problems,[*] read, interpret, and apply the Michigan CSC statute as provided in the textbook. For each fact pattern, think like a prosecutor and explore the statute, determining which specific offenses from the statute are chargeable and why.

(1) The victim testified that on October 4, at 3:30 a.m., on her way home from a friend's house, she stopped for a stop sign at Allen Road in Allen Park. Defendant got into her car, began choking her, and told her that he needed a ride. At Defendant's request, the victim drove Defendant to a side street in Lincoln Park where, after struggling with Defendant for her car keys, Defendant performed nonconsensual oral and vaginal sexual intercourse with her. The victim testified that she was afraid that if she did not do what Defendant demanded, Defendant would choke her to death.

(2) The 11-year-old victim testified that she lived with Defendant, her father, for a summer. During that time, Defendant asked the victim to go to his bedroom because he wanted to feel her tan. When she went into the bedroom, Defendant told her to pull her pants down. Defendant then penetrated her vagina with his penis, his tongue, and his finger. Defendant told her that he did not do anything wrong and not to tell anybody—that it was their secret. Defendant also indicated that he would get into a lot of trouble and go to prison if anyone found out.

(3) The 7-year-old victim testified that on the day of the incident, he arrived home from school and met Defendant, his second cousin, who was charged with responsibility for taking the victim to the home of Defendant's mother. It had been arranged that Defendant's mother would babysit the victim while the victim's mother was working. The victim testified that Defendant pulled the victim by his shirt into the victim's bedroom and pushed him onto the bed. A pillow was placed in the window. Defendant then pulled down both the child's pants and his own pants. Defendant obtained a jar of Vaseline from the bathroom and applied some "grease" "up [the victim's] behind." He then penetrated the victim by "put[ting] his private in [the victim's] behind." Defendant instructed the victim not to tell anybody because Defendant did not want to go to jail. Defendant cleaned both himself and the victim with paper towels and then took the victim over to his mother's residence.

---

[*] The facts in the problems are taken, in part, from the following cases: *People v. Purcell*, 174 Mich. App 126 (1989); *People v. Sharbnow*, 174 Mich. App. 94 (1989); *People v. Hackney*, 183 Mich. App. 516 (1990); *People v. Swinford*, 150 Mich. App. 507 (1986); and *People v. Lasky*, 157 Mich. App. 265 (1987).

(4)   The complainant testified that she finished her work shift at the U.S. Post Office at 4:00 a.m. on November 26, and left for home. While driving in a rural area, she noticed a car following closely behind her. She increased her speed to 80 miles per hour in an attempt to elude the vehicle. During this chase, the other car rammed the back of her car three or four times. She lost control of her car and spun off the road, finally coming to a halt 50 feet from the road in a field. At the same time, a car turned about in a driveway and returned to her location. A man, later identified as Defendant, exited from the car and approached the complainant. He grabbed her neck, choked her, stated that he was going to rape her, and threatened to kill her. Defendant pulled the complainant into the back seat of the car and proceeded to commit various acts of sexual conduct. After threatening to kill her, Defendant drove away in his car. The complainant sought assistance in a nearby farmhouse and was taken for a medical examination to a local hospital. The record indicated that the choking of the complainant left visible handprints which lasted several days and caused the complainant to have muscle spasms in her neck. A pelvic examination revealed that part of the complainant's vaginal areas were swollen and torn and would take up to two weeks to heal. It was indicated that these tears were consistent with "very, very, very forceful intercourse." As a result of the incident, the complainant regularly saw a therapist and experienced marital problems. She testified that she became fearful of working at night and relinquished her duties on the night shift, which resulted in a substantial pay cut.

(5)   The 13-year-old victim testified that on December 7, she was babysitting three children at the home of a woman. Defendant was the woman's guest and was sleeping in her bedroom when the woman and a friend who shared the apartment left for the evening. Defendant awoke approximately 20 minutes later and he thereafter left the apartment for a short period of time. He came back with a bottle of wine, which he consumed. He then left for a second time and returned to the apartment at 12:15 a.m. The victim further testified that when Defendant returned, the apartment was cold. The victim was wearing a winter coat and watching television. Defendant asked her whether she was cold. When she answered in the affirmative, he sat on her lap, stating, "Well, if I sit on your lap, maybe you will be warm." Although he complied with the victim's request to get up, after arising he stood before her and said, "Now you can sit on my lap." When the victim answered "No, that's okay" and slid from the chair to the floor, Defendant picked her up, placed her on his lap, and held her there. He asked if she was ticklish, placed his hand under her shirt, tickled her ribs and then touched one of her breasts. The victim escaped his grasp by slipping out of her coat, whereupon she returned to the floor. Her breast hurt. After she slid to the floor, Defendant stayed in the chair and left her alone. The woman and her roommate returned approximately 20 minutes later. The victim reported the incident to them at that time.

Chapter 6
Battery, Assault, and Kidnapping

A. Battery

1. Introduction

The crime of battery is ordinarily defined as an unlawful harmful or offensive contact caused by the defendant with the intent to cause a harmful or offensive contact or as the result of criminal negligence. States are split on whether the crime of battery can be achieved by criminal negligence. Michigan, for example, requires the touching to be intended. *See People v. Lakeman*, 135 Mich. App. 235 (1984); Michigan Model Criminal Jury Instructions §17.2 (ICLE 2014) (available at http://courts.mi.gov/courts/michigansupremecourt/criminal-jury-instructions/pages/default.aspx).

A person may consent to a harmful contact (e.g., a hockey player, a football player, etc.) or a harmful contact may be authorized by law (e.g., a policeman effectuating an arrest), making the contacts "lawful" or "privileged." Of course, a person may go beyond what is lawful, raising the likelihood that a criminal battery has occurred. Whether a contact is offensive is ordinarily judged by an objective standard (i.e., a reasonable person standard). The rationale of this crime is to protect personal bodily security and to prevent breaches of the peace. Some kind of unwanted physical contact is necessary for a battery. Generally, an aggravated battery occurs when there is a significant injury.

Notably, many jurisdictions will use the term "assault" to mean assault or battery. It is important to carefully read the statute at issue to see how the crime is labeled and defined. When a court uses the term "assault and battery," the court is typically referring to the crime of battery. For more information, see Wayne LaFave, *Criminal Law* §§16.1–16.2 (5th ed. 2010).

2. Cases

For a criminal battery to occur, the harmful or offensive contact has to be unlawful. Does the owner of a bar have the lawful right to forcibly eject unwanted persons from the premises? Does that have an impact on whether or not a battery has occurred? In reading the *Stull* case, note how the court refers to the crime as "assault" even though a physical contact clearly occurred.

Government of Virgin Island v. Stull, 280 F. Supp. 460 (1968)

WALTER A. GORDON, District Judge.

This is an appeal from a judgment of the Municipal Court of the Virgin Islands convicting the appellant, Ray Stull, of a violation of 14 VIC 299, simple assault and battery. The judgment of the court was entered on November 3, 1967, sentencing Stull to a suspended fine of $50.00. From that judgment and sentence he has appealed. For the reasons outlined in this opinion, the judgment of conviction is vacated and the case is remanded to the Municipal Court with instructions to enter a verdict of not guilty.

FACTS

Appellant is part owner and manager of Trader Dan's which in the words of his counsel is "a waterfront saloon and poolroom which cannot be expected to attract clientele always likely to maintain the highest degree of order." The record indicates that Stull considered the complaining witness, Matthew, to be a minor trouble maker and that on recent previous occasion had told Matthew to leave the establishment and not come back. It appears, however, that due to the intercession of a police officer, the complaining witness did not leave and was in fact allowed to return. On the night of August 10, when the alleged assault occurred, it appears that Stull heard a disturbance in the upstairs poolroom portion of the bar and upon entering saw the complaining witness standing at the bar arguing with another patron. Stull told him to leave and when Matthew objected, Stull, in his words, "grabbed him by the arm and led him to the door." Stull's characterization of the event is corroborated by the upstairs bartender, Ronald Lucas, who also testified that Matthew was involved in a loud argument with one of the pool players.

While there may be a question of creditability in the testimony of Stull and his employee, Lucas, this characterization of the event appears to have been accepted by the Municipal Court. This is especially true in light of that court's reduction of the charge from aggravated to simple assault based on the court's disbelief of the complaining witness's testimony that Stull had kicked him. The trial judge stated, "From the testimony . . . I can't find beyond a reasonable doubt that this complaining witness was kicked by the defendant. I do, however, find that there was simple assault and I do find that the techniques used by the defendant were unnecessary under the circumstances. . . ."

OPINION

The Municipal Court apparently recognized, as this court does, that the owner of a bar or other public or semipublic place has the right to eject unwanted or disorderly persons from the premises. Indeed, the law is rather clear on this point:

> The owner, occupant, or person in charge of any public or semi-public place of business may request the departure of a person who does not rightfully belong there or who by his conduct has forfeited his right to be there, and may treat him as a trespasser, using reasonable force to eject him from the premises. 1 Wharton's Crim.Law, Sec. 356.
>
> A person may lawfully eject another from his premises, after requesting him to leave, if he has no right to remain, and he may use such force in so doing as may reasonable be necessary without being guilty of an assault and battery. Clark and Marshall Crimes, Sec. 208.

The main thrust of the government's argument is that Stull's action was not predicated upon any investigation of the disturbance nor was Matthew's conduct sufficient to warrant the means used. While this Court's view of the facts differs slightly from that of the government, whether or not a saloon keeper could forcibly remove a patron for no cause whatsoever, after an ignored request to leave, seems relevant. Absent a statute to the contrary, it would appear that once a patron's license to remain on the premises has been terminated, for whatever cause or lack of it, he becomes a mere trespasser and is subject to being treated as one. This being so, it only serves to enforce the right of the proprietor to eject one who is causing a disturbance. . . .

Under the circumstances of the present case, the Court cannot see how appellant could have used any lesser degree of force in removing Matthew from the premises, an act which he had the right to do. Matthew, in Stull's view, was causing a disturbance. He was told to leave. He objected. Whereupon Stull took him by the arm and led him out. It was not incumbent upon Stull to argue or plead with Matthew. His license to remain on the premises had been terminated, and reasonably so, as the court views the facts. His failure to leave when requested to do so authorized Stull to exercise a reasonable degree of force. Had Stull kicked Matthew, as Matthew alleged, this would be a different case, but the taking of Matthew by the arm and pushing, pulling, or leading him to the door was, in the Court's opinion, entirely reasonable and in fact the minimal amount of force employable under the circumstances.

The judgment of conviction is vacated with instructions to enter a verdict of not guilty.

B. Assault

1. Introduction

The crime of assault originally was defined as an attempted, but unsuccessful battery (generally referred to as attempted battery-type assault). Over time it has been expanded to include cases where the defendant's conduct creates a reasonable apprehension in the victim that he or she is about to suffer an imminent battery (generally referred to as frightening-type assault or reasonable apprehension assault). Oftentimes, both types of assault will be present, but either theory will suffice.

With attempted battery-type assault, apprehension by the victim is not required and the attempt must come close to completion. States are split on whether the defendant has to have the actual present ability, thinks he or she has the present ability, or appears to have the present ability to cause the battery.

With frightening-type assault, the defendant's conduct must actually cause the victim to be apprehensive that the victim is about to suffer an imminent harmful or offensive contact and the victim's apprehension must be objectively reasonable.

Most states require the prosecution to prove that the defendant intended to cause a harmful or offensive contact, or intended to create a reasonable apprehension of an imminent battery (i.e., criminal negligence ordinarily is not enough to convict). Generally, all assaults are considered specific intent crimes. *See, e.g., People v. Johnson*, 407 Mich. 196 (1979) (defendants who pointed guns at complainants but did not fire shots could be convicted of assault upon proof of *either* intent to injure *or* intent to put victims in reasonable fear of apprehension of an immediate injury).

The rationale of this crime is similar to that of battery (i.e., to protect personal bodily security and to prevent breaches of the peace). An added rationale for frightening-type assault is that it is socially harmful to unnecessarily frighten others. For more information, see Wayne LaFave, *Criminal Law* §§16.1–16.3 (5th ed. 2010).

2. Cases

a. Where multiple people are present when a defendant engages in assaultive behavior, who is the "victim" of the assault?

The *Harrod* case is helpful in explaining the difference between attempted battery-type assault and frightening-type assault. In examining *Harrod*, think about how you might have approached the charging decision as a prosecutor in a different manner. Additionally, ask yourself what charge the prosecutor might have considered if the child in the case, Christopher, had actually been injured.

Harrod v. State, 65 Md. App. 128 (1985)

ALPERT, Judge.

We are called upon in this appeal to decide, *inter alia*, whether a person can be convicted of assaulting another who has suffered no harm and was never aware of the alleged assault. Appellant John G. Harrod was charged with two counts of assault and two counts of carrying a deadly weapon openly with intent to injure. He was convicted of these offenses on December 11, 1984, following a trial without a jury in the Circuit Court for Carroll County (Lerner, J., presiding), and sentenced on January 21, 1985, to two terms of two years' imprisonment for the assault convictions and two terms of one year's imprisonment for the weapons convictions, all sentences to run concurrently. On appeal to this court, appellant presents [the question of whether] . . . the evidence [was] sufficient to sustain the charge of assault upon James Christopher Harrod . . . .

The common law crime of assault encompasses two definitions: (1) an attempt to commit a battery or (2) an unlawful intentional act which places another in reasonable apprehension of receiving an immediate battery. The facts in the instant case present this court with an excellent opportunity to explain the distinctions between these two different types of assault.

The assault charges arose out of a confrontation among appellant, his wife Cheryl, and her friend Calvin Crigger. The only two witnesses at trial were appellant and Cheryl Harrod.

Cheryl testified that on September 15, 1983, Calvin Crigger came over to visit when she thought appellant had gone to work; that "all of a sudden [appellant] came out of the bedroom with a hammer in his hand, swinging it around, coming after me and my friend [Calvin]"; that Calvin ran out of the house and down the steps; that appellant "had thrown the hammer over top of [Christopher's] port-a-crib in the living room, and it went into the wall"; that appellant then reentered the bedroom and returned with a five-inch blade hunting knife; that appellant told Cheryl that he was going to kill her and that, if she took his daughter away from him, he was going to kill Christopher; that appellant put the knife into the bannister near Cheryl's arm; that appellant followed Cheryl out to Calvin's car and "went after Calvin, going around and around the car."

Appellant testified that he missed his ride to work that day; that he came back home around 10:00 a.m. and went to sleep in a back room; that he was awakened by Calvin's deep voice; that appellant picked up his hammer and, walking into the living room, told Calvin to leave; that Cheryl told Calvin he didn't have to leave; that he then told Calvin, "Buddy, if you want your head busted in, stand here; if you want to be healthy and leave, go." Appellant said that Calvin just stood there, so he swung the hammer, Calvin moved his head back, and the hammer struck the wall over Christopher's crib, which was near the door.

In rendering its verdict, the court stated:

> And, the Court finds beyond a reasonable doubt and to a moral certainty that Mr. Harrod . . . came after [Cheryl] and . . . Calvin; and that Mr. Harrod came out of his room swinging a . . . hammer, and ultimately threw it, not too far from the child, Christopher, and that he went after both Cheryl and Calvin, down the steps with a knife, with a blade of about four to five inches. The Court finds that he is guilty of [various counts including] . . . two counts of Assault; one against Cheryl and one against the minor child. . . .

A. *Two Types of Assault*

Appellant contends that there was insufficient evidence to demonstrate that he harbored a specific intent to injure Christopher when he threw the hammer. Further, he notes that there was no evidence that Christopher was injured by the hammer or that he was even aware that a hammer was thrown. Therefore, appellant claims that the trial court's finding that he committed a criminal assault upon Christopher was clearly erroneous. We agree for the reasons set forth below.

As we noted *supra*, an assault "is committed when there is *either* an attempt to commit a battery *or* when, by an unlawful act, a person is placed in reasonable apprehension of receiving an immediate battery." These two types of assault—*attempted battery* and *putting another in fear*—are indeed two distinct crimes that have been inadvertently overlapped and confused. One commentator explained this confusion:

> In the early law the word "assault" represented an entirely different concept in criminal law than it did in the law of torts. As an offense it was an attempt to commit a battery; as a basis for a civil action for damages it was an intentional act wrongfully placing another in apprehension of receiving an immediate battery. The distinction has frequently passed unnoticed because a misdeed involving either usually involves both. If, with the intention of hitting X, D wrongfully threw a stone that X barely managed to dodge, then D would have been guilty of a criminal assault because he had attempted to commit a battery, and he would also have been liable in a civil action of trespass for assault because he had wrongfully placed X in apprehension of physical harm.
>
> Some commentators have been so imbued with the tort theory of assault that they have had difficulty in

realizing that in the early law a criminal assault was an attempt to commit a battery and that only. . . .

B. *Attempted Battery*

The language in *Woods* [*v. State*, 14 Md. App. 627, 630 n. 3 (1972)] supports the proposition that in an attempted battery-type assault, the victim need not be aware of the perpetrator's intent or threat.

> If a person be struck from behind, or by stealth or surprise, or while asleep, he is certainly the victim of a battery. But if we accept the oft-repeated statement that every battery included or is preceded by an assault, and if there could be no assault without premonitory apprehension in the victim, then it could be argued that there was no battery. That is not the law.

In other words, because there may be committed a battery without the victim first being aware of the attack, an attempted battery-type assault cannot include a requirement that the victim be aware.

The facts in the case *sub judice* do not support a finding that appellant committed an attempted battery towards the infant, Christopher. An attempt to commit any crime requires a specific intent to commit that crime. An attempted battery-type assault thus requires that the accused harbor a specific intent to cause physical injury to the victim, and take a substantial step towards causing that injury.

Nowhere does the record indicate that appellant threw the hammer with the specific intent to injure Christopher. The court expressly stated that it found specific intent on behalf of appellant because he "[t]hrew that hammer within a very short distance" of the child. The court here is merely inferring a criminal intent from reckless or negligent acts of the appellant. This is not sufficient, especially where all of the evidence tends to the contrary: that appellant's intent was to injure Calvin. . . .

. . . The record indicates that appellant swung a hammer which struck the wall "not too far from" Christopher. Significantly, there is no evidence that Christopher was harmed. Further, the weight of the evidence shows that appellant's specific intent, if any, was to injure Calvin, not Christopher. Why the State charged appellant with assaulting Christopher, rather than Calvin, we will not speculate. There is clearly insufficient evidence to find that appellant committed an attempted battery-type assault upon Christopher.

C. *Assault by Placing One in Fear*

There is likewise insufficient evidence that appellant, by an unlawful intentional act, placed Christopher in reasonable apprehension of receiving an immediate battery. By definition the victim must be aware of the impending contact. This is consistent with the tort theory of assault.

There is no evidence in the record before us that Christopher was in fact aware of the occurrences in his home on the morning in question. Therefore, there was insufficient evidence to find appellant guilty of the putting victim in fear-type assault.

Because the trial court was clearly erroneous in finding appellant guilty of an assault on Christopher, we must reverse that conviction. . . .

JUDGMENT OF CONVICTION OF ASSAULT UPON JAMES CHRISTOPHER HARROD REVERSED AND SENTENCE VACATED; ALL OTHER JUDGMENTS AFFIRMED . . . .

b.   Is an assault present when the victim was not and could not have been placed in fear?

United States v. Bell, 505 F.2d 539 (7th Cir. 1974)

TONE, Circuit Judge.

The defendant Tommie Bell was convicted in a bench trial of assault with intent to commit rape at a place within the special territorial jurisdiction of the United States, in violation of 18 U.S.C. §113(a). On appeal he raises only one question, *viz.*, whether it is necessary to the offense of assault that the victim have a reasonable apprehension of bodily harm. We answer this question in the negative and affirm the conviction.

It is conceded that while defendant was a patient in the detoxification ward for alcoholic and drug addiction patients in the Veterans Administration Hospital, Downey, Illinois, he attempted to rape a female geriatric patient. It is also undisputed that the victim was suffering from a mental disease which made her unable to comprehend what was going on. Defendant's only asserted defense in the trial court and here is that, because the victim was incapable of forming a reasonable apprehension of bodily harm, there was no assault.

Defendant's contention is squarely contradicted by this court's statement in United States v. Rizzo, 409 F.2d 400, 403 (7th Cir. 1969), cert. denied, 396 U.S. 911 (1969). There, in sustaining a jury instruction defining assault (taken from W. Mathes and E. Devitt, Federal Jury Practice and Instructions §43.07 (1965)), the court recognized that there are two concepts of assault in criminal law, the first being an attempt to commit a battery and the second an act putting another in reasonable apprehension of bodily harm. While the second concept was applicable in that case, the court, said with respect to the first:

> There may be an attempt to commit a battery, and hence an assault, under circumstances where the intended victim is unaware of danger. Apprehension on the part of the victim is not an essential element of that type of assault.

We adhere to that statement of the law. When a federal criminal statute uses a common law term without defining it, the term is given its common law meaning. United States v. Turley, 352 U.S. 407, 411 (1957); Morissette v. United

States, 342 U.S. 246, 263 (1952). A criminal assault at common law was originally an attempt to commit a battery. . . .

Since an attempted battery is an assault, it is irrelevant that the victim is incapable of forming a reasonable apprehension. . . . There are many statements to the effect that an attempt upon an unconscious or otherwise insensitive victim is an assault, both in the cases, *e.g.*, People v. Lilley, 43 Mich. 521 (1880); People v. Pape, 66 Cal. 366 (1885); Ross v. State, 16 Wyo. 285 (1908); Woods v. State 14 Md.App. 627 (1972), and in the treatises.

Defendant's attempt to rape an insensitive victim was an assault under 18 U.S.C. §113(a). His conviction is affirmed. . . .

Affirmed.

c.   Statutory Variations on Assault—Stalking

In examining the *Matsos* case, note the relevancy of common law assault in interpreting the meaning of a modern stalking statute.

Commonwealth v. Matsos, 421 Mass. 391 (1995)

GREANEY, Justice.

The defendant challenges his conviction by a jury of six in the District Court under the so-called stalking statute, G.L. c. 265, §43, inserted by St.1992, c. 31.[1] The defendant argues that his motion for a required finding of not guilty should have been allowed because the Commonwealth's evidence was insufficient to prove that he had made a threat with the intent to place the victim in imminent fear of death or serious bodily injury. . . . We affirm the defendant's conviction.

The evidence in the Commonwealth's case would have warranted the jury in finding the following facts. The defendant and the victim, a black officer with the Salem police department, first met in early 1991. On May 18, 1992, the victim was walking to work when she was confronted by the defendant. The victim asked the defendant what he was doing there and told him to stop following her around. On May 21, 1992, the victim received the first in a series of letters from the defendant. From May 21, 1992, until March 16, 1993, he sent approximately forty letters to the victim. The letters repeatedly lamented the victim's perceived indifference toward the defendant, and were filled with sexual references. Several of the letters described in explicit detail the defendant's sexual fantasies about the victim. Many of the letters admitted in

---

[1] The statute provides, in relevant part, as follows:

> (*a*) Whoever willfully, maliciously, and repeatedly follows or harasses another person and who makes a threat with the intent to place that person in imminent fear of death or serious bodily injury shall be guilty of the crime of stalking. . . .

evidence expressed the defendant's anger with the victim, sometimes couched in racial terms. There were references to the defendant's dangerous acquaintances (including one old friend whom the United States Attorney said was responsible for five murders) and to guns. The letters also established that the defendant was following the victim during the relevant period, spying on her and her friends, and attempting to acquire information about her private life.

The victim first had initiated a complaint against the defendant for stalking in June, 1992. On July 17, 1992, the victim learned that the defendant had signed documents and forwarded them to her employer, the Salem police department, claiming that the victim had used drugs with him. The allegations prompted an extensive internal affairs investigation, including drug testing for the victim. The police department ultimately concluded the allegations were unfounded.

The victim testified that, at first, the letters made her feel uncomfortable. Later she became fearful, ceased opening the letters, and changed her residence. There was also testimony that she had obtained a special telephone service that permitted her to screen her telephone calls to ensure that incoming calls were not from the defendant.

Following the close of the Commonwealth's case, the defendant moved for a required finding of not guilty. He argues that this motion was improperly denied because the Commonwealth's proof was insufficient to show that he had made threats with the intent to place the victim in imminent fear of death or serious bodily injury. We reject the defendant's argument. . . .

. . . To obtain a conviction under G.L. c. 265, §43, the prosecution must prove that the defendant made a threat with the intent to place the victim in imminent fear of death or bodily injury. This element closely approximates the common law definition of the crime of assault, and we may presume that the Legislature was aware of this when it enacted the statute. Accordingly, we turn to the common law treatment of assault for purposes of examining the legislation.

In [*Commonwealth v. Gordon*, 407 Mass. 340, 349 (1990)], this court summarized the common law definition of criminal assault, as follows. "Under the common law, 'it is well established . . . that an act placing another in reasonable apprehension that force may be used is sufficient for the offense of criminal assault.' In determining whether an apprehension of anticipated physical force is reasonable, a court will look to the actions and words of the defendant in light of the attendant circumstances." In a case of simple criminal assault, the Commonwealth need not prove that the defendant actually intended to harm the victim, it need only prove that the defendant's threats were reasonably calculated to place the victim in imminent fear of bodily injury.

The defendant sent the victim more than forty letters during a ten-month period. These letters, which amounted to hundreds of pages, revealed the defendant's intense obsession with the victim and his anger at her rejection of him, and the letters chronicle a campaign of harassment mounted by him, which included a malicious attempt to interfere with the victim's employment. We disagree with the defendant's contention that the evidence did not provide a basis for a reasonable juror to conclude that the defendant had intentionally placed the victim in imminent fear of death or serious bodily injury. The defendant identified himself as "The Stalker" in a return address. Among other quite explicit threats, he warned the victim, "There is [going to come] a day when you are [going to] want to come and see me. . . . But you will never see me, your eyes will alway[s] be closed." He made references to guns and silencers, to dangerous friends, and to his own involvement in illegal activity. He made it clear that he was following the victim and would be able to find her, and his accusation against her of drug use demonstrated that he was prepared to act on his threats of harassment and violence. On the basis of the Commonwealth's evidence, the jury could have found that the defendant intended to place the victim in fear of imminent bodily injury, and that she was afraid of him. The judge correctly denied the defendant's motion for a required finding. . . .

Judgment affirmed.

C. Practice Problems on Assault and Battery

While states have codified assault and battery in a wide variety of ways, the common law still plays an important role in helping to interpret the meaning of statutes. Explore some modern statutes by writing an answer to the following essay problem.

Man was a 27-year-old certified public accountant. He lived with Woman, a 22-year-old student at State University. They shared a two-bedroom house on Maple Street that they had lived in together for about one year. The house was located approximately a block away from a bar where Woman worked part-time as a waitress. At approximately 1:30 a.m. on September 14, the City Police Department received a 911 call from Woman. She was crying and hysterical, but she managed to say that Man had just struck her in the face with a beer bottle. She reported that the bottle shattered when it struck her, and that she was bleeding pretty badly.

City Police Officers responded to this call. When they arrived at the Maple Street house, they found Man sitting on the front lawn. When he saw the officers, he stood up and told them that Woman "had it coming to her." When an Officer asked him what he meant, Man answered that he and Woman had gotten into an argument, and that he had "hit her just once in the face, hard enough to knock some sense into her, but not hard enough to really hurt her." Woman was taken to a hospital where she received fourteen stitches to close a wound on her forehead. The doctor who treated the wound told the police that it was serious, but not life-threatening.

A subsequent check of police records revealed that Man had one prior conviction for assaulting Woman approximately six months earlier. Woman gave a statement to the police indicating that although Man hit her "pretty hard" with the bottle, it did not appear to her that he had hit her as hard as he could.

The State Penal Code includes the following statutes:

§600.83

> Any person who shall assault or assault and batter another person with intent to commit the crime of murder shall be guilty of a felony punishable by imprisonment for life or any term of years.

§600.84

> Any person who shall assault or assault and batter another with intent to do great bodily harm less than the crime of murder shall be guilty of a felony punishable by imprisonment for not more than 10 years or a fine of not more than $5,000.00 or both.

Section 600.83 has been interpreted by the State Supreme Court as requiring proof that the defendant specifically intended to kill in order to convict.

Fully discuss Man's best argument as to why he cannot be prosecuted for a violation of §600.83. Also discuss the prosecution's best argument as to why Man could be convicted of violating §600.84. Limit your discussion to those issues that are reasonably in dispute given the facts, and make sure to fully explain your arguments by reference to the facts.

D. Kidnapping

1. Introduction

The common law crime of kidnapping was originally defined by Blackstone as "the forcible abduction or stealing away of man, woman, or child from their own country, and selling them into another." *State v. Avery*, 126 Ohio App. 3d 36 (1998) (quoting 4 Blackstone's Commentaries 219). The common law definition is now considered obsolete.

The crime of kidnapping is ordinarily defined as either forcible movement or secret confinement of the victim against the victim's will and without lawful authority. The rationale of this crime is to protect personal freedom of movement and freedom from confinement and to prevent more serious crimes that may occur when a victim is isolated from outside assistance.

The forcible movement or secret confinement can be done by force, fraud, deception, or threats. The confinement or movement is typically against the victim's will or against a victim who is unable to give lawful consent. While generally treated as a general intent crime, some state statutes require the defendant to have acted with an enhanced level of knowledge. *See, e.g.,* M.C.L. §750.349 ("A person commits the crime of kidnapping if he or she knowingly restrains another person with the intent to . . . [h]old that person for ransom or reward."). As with all modern crimes, it is important to read and construe each relevant statute to determine precisely what the prosecutor must prove. For more information, see Wayne LaFave, *Criminal Law* §§18.1–18.3 (5th ed. 2010).

2.   Cases

Can a person be deemed guilty of kidnapping for forcibly confining victims in their own home to facilitate a robbery? In studying the *Denmon* case, it is important to have a basic understanding of accomplice liability, a criminal law concept that will be more fully explored in a different section of the book. Stated simply, a person can be held fully criminally responsible for a crime even though that person may only have aided in the crime. Keep this in mind when considering defendant Denmon's criminal liability for first degree kidnapping.

State v. Denmon, 347 N.J. Super. 457 (2002)

WALLACE, Jr., J.A.D.

Defendant Lester Denmon was convicted by a jury of first degree kidnapping, *N.J.S.A.* 2C:13–1b [and other crimes]. . . .

The State presented evidence to show that in February 1997, defendant discussed with James Chester a plan to rob the home of James and Ethel Scott. Defendant told Chester he had worked at the Scotts' house in the past and believed the elderly couple kept a lot of money in a suitcase.

On March 1, 1997, defendant, along with Chester, drove his red Cadillac and parked it down the street from the Scotts' home. He gave Chester a gun and a set of handcuffs and instructed Chester to handcuff the couple before leaving the home. Chester knocked on the door. When James opened the door, Chester said he needed to use the telephone to call a tow truck for his car. James suggested that Chester call Triple A [sic] and invited him in the house. James went to his bedroom to look up the phone number while his wife Ethel escorted Chester into their home. When James returned with the telephone number, Chester pulled a gun, and said, "I don't want to hurt you. I just want your money." James replied that they did not keep money in the house. Chester then moved the couple into the bedroom where he removed $40 in cash and a Visa gold credit card from James's wallet. Chester next ordered the couple into the living room, where he handcuffed James to Ethel while they sat in a chair. Chester fled the house and returned to the car where defendant waited.

Once Chester left, the Scotts tried to get out of the chair, but were unable to do so because Ethel had recently had knee replacement surgery which made it difficult for her to maneuver. After struggling for over five minutes, James managed to get to the telephone and call the police. . . .

Defendant timely moved for a judgment of acquittal or for a new trial contending that the verdict of guilty on the first-degree kidnapping was against the weight of the evidence. He makes the same argument on appeal. Specifically, defendant argues that his conduct was not first degree kidnapping because the victims were not confined for a substantial period of time and were released unharmed and in a safe place.

N.J.S.A. 2C:13–1b provides:

> A person is guilty of kidnapping if he unlawfully removes another from his place of residence or business, or a substantial distance from the vicinity where he is found, or if he unlawfully confines another for a substantial period, with any of the following purposes:
>
> 1) To facilitate commission of any crime or flight thereafter.
> 2) To inflict bodily injury on or to terrorize the victim or another; or
> 3) To interfere with the performance of any governmental or political function.

Recently, in *State v. Soto,* 340 *N.J.Super.* 47, 73–4 (App.Div.2001), we noted that "[t]o support a conviction for kidnapping the confinement must be 'criminally significant in the sense of being more than merely incidental to the underlying crime.' " The determination of whether the confinement is substantial is not determined by its duration. Rather, the jury should look at the "enhanced risk of harm resulting from the confinement and isolation of the victim."

In *State v. Bryant,* 217 *N.J.Super.* 72, 80–82 (1987), we found that elderly victims were substantially confined when they were bound and gagged for 10 minutes because their confinement increased the risk of harm to the victims. We explained that "[h]ad the victims been unable to free themselves for an extended period of time . . ., there was a significant possibility of additional discomfort, physical injury or even death."

Thus, it is necessary to consider "whether the nature of the confinement and the duration of the victims' isolation made them more vulnerable to harm beyond that created by the robbery itself." Here, the victims were in their eighties and were handcuffed to facilitate Chester's flight after the robbery. In his testimony, James explained that it was difficult to move around with the handcuffs, "because my wife, she had replacement knees and it was a little rough for her to get up faster in order to get to the door, because you see she had to walk a little backwards or sideways or so to—in order for us to get there." Furthermore, there was no one to help them if they had health problems while they were confined. In our view, the evidence was sufficient for the jury to conclude that the conduct in handcuffing the elderly victims enhanced the risk of harm such that the elderly victims were substantially confined.

In sum, giving the State the benefit of its favorable testimony as well as all reasonable inferences, we conclude that a reasonable jury could find defendant guilty of first-degree kidnapping. The jury's verdict was not a miscarriage of justice under the law. . . .

. . . [W]e affirm.

3.   Kidnapping in Connection with Other Crimes

In the Rape and Criminal Sexual Conduct chapter of this book, the *Alston* case was examined for its exploration of the use of a threat to satisfy the force requirement in the context of a statute based on common law rape. The case is provided again in this chapter, edited to include only the discussion of the kidnapping charge.

In reviewing the *Alston* case, consider how significant the words of the statute were to the outcome of the case.

State v. Alston, 310 N.C. 399 (1984)

MITCHELL, Justice.

The defendant raises on appeal the question whether the evidence of his guilt of kidnapping and second degree rape was sufficient to support his convictions of those crimes. For reasons discussed herein, we conclude the evidence was insufficient to support his conviction of either crime.

The State's evidence tended to show that at the time the incident occurred the defendant and the prosecuting witness in this case, Cottie Brown, had been involved for approximately six months in a consensual sexual relationship. During the six months the two had conflicts at times and Brown would leave the apartment she shared with the defendant to stay with her mother. She testified that she would return to the defendant and the apartment they shared when he called to tell her to return. Brown testified that she and the defendant had sexual relations throughout their relationship. Although she sometimes enjoyed their sexual relations, she often had sex with the defendant just to accommodate him. On those occasions, she would stand still and remain entirely passive while the defendant undressed her and had intercourse with her.

Brown testified that at times their consensual sexual relations involved some violence. The defendant had struck her several times throughout the relationship when she refused to give him money or refused to do what he wanted. Around May 15, 1981, the defendant struck her after asking her for money that she refused to give him. Brown left the apartment she shared with the defendant and moved in with her mother. She did not have intercourse with the defendant after May 15 until the alleged rape on June 15. After Brown left the defendant, he called her several times and visited her at Durham Technical Institute where she was enrolled in classes. When he visited her they talked about their relationship. Brown testified that she did not tell him she wanted to break off their relationship because she was afraid he would be angry.

On June 15, 1981, Brown arrived at Durham Technical Institute by taxicab to find the defendant standing close to the school door. The defendant blocked her path as she walked toward the door and asked her where she had moved. Brown refused to tell him, and the defendant grabbed her arm, saying that she was going with him. Brown testified that it would have taken some effort to pull away. The two walked toward the parking lot and Brown told the defendant she would walk with him if he let her go. The defendant then released her. She testified that she did not run away from him because she was afraid of him. She stated that other students were nearby.

Brown stated that she and the defendant then began a casually paced walk in the neighborhood around the school. They walked, sometimes side by side, sometimes with Brown slightly behind the defendant. As they walked they talked about their relationship. Brown said the defendant did not hold her or help her along in any way as they walked. The defendant talked about Brown's "dogging" him and making him seem a fool and about Brown's mother's interference in the relationship. When the defendant and Brown left the parking lot, the defendant threatened to "fix" her face so that her mother could see he was not playing. While they were walking out of the parking lot, Brown told the defendant she wanted to go to class. He replied that she was going to miss class that day.

The two continued to walk away from the school. Brown testified that the defendant continually talked about their relationship as they walked, but that she paid little attention to what he said because she was preoccupied with her own thoughts. They passed several people. They walked along several streets and went down a path close to a wooded area where they stopped to talk. The defendant asked again where Brown had moved. She asked him whether he would let her go if she told him her address. The defendant then asked whether the relationship was over and Brown told him it was. He then said that since everyone could see her but him he had a right to make love to her again. Brown said nothing.

The two turned around at that point and began walking towards a street they had walked down previously. Changing directions, they walked in the same fashion they had walked before—side by side with Brown sometimes slightly behind. The defendant did not hold or touch Brown as they walked. Brown testified that the defendant did not say where they were going but that, when he said he wanted to make love, she knew he was going to the house of a friend. She said they had gone to the house on prior occasions to have sex. The defendant and Brown passed the same group of men they had passed previously. Brown did not ask for assistance because some of the men were friends of the defendant, and she assumed they would not help. The defendant and Brown continued to walk to the house of one of the defendant's friends, Lawrence Taylor.

When they entered the house, Taylor was inside. Brown sat in the living room while the defendant and Taylor went to the back of the house and talked. When asked why she did not try to leave when the defendant and Taylor were in the back of the house, Brown replied, "It was nowhere to go. I don't know. I just didn't." The defendant returned to the living room area and turned on the television. He attempted to fix a broken fan. Brown asked Taylor for a cigarette, and he gave her one.

The defendant began talking to Brown about another man she had been seeing. By that time Taylor had gone out of the room and perhaps the house. The defendant asked if Brown was "ready." The evidence tended to show that she told him "no, that I wasn't going to bed with him." She testified that she did not want to have sex with the defendant and did not consent to do so at any time on June 15.

After Brown finished her cigarette, the defendant began kissing her neck. He pulled her up from the chair in which she had been sitting and started undressing her. He noticed that she was having her menstrual period, and she sat down pulling her pants back up. The defendant again took off her pants and blouse. He told her to lay down on a bed which was in the living room. She complied and the defendant pushed apart her legs and had sexual intercourse with her. Brown testified that she did not try to push him away. She cried during the intercourse. Afterwards they talked. The defendant told her he wanted to make sure she was not lying about where she lived and that he would not let her up unless she told him.

After they dressed they talked again about the man Brown had been seeing. They left the house and went to the defendant's mother's house. After talking with the defendant's mother, Brown took a bus home. She talked with her mother about taking out a complaint against the defendant but did not tell her mother she and the defendant had had sex. Brown made a complaint to the police the same day.

The defendant continued to call Brown after June 15, but she refused to see him. One evening he called from a telephone booth and told her he had to talk. When he got to her apartment he threatened to kick her door down and Brown let him inside. Once inside he said he had intended merely to talk to her but that he wanted to make love again after seeing her. Brown said she sat and looked at him, and that he began kissing her. She pulled away and he picked her up and carried her to the bedroom. He performed oral sex on her and she testified that she did not try to fight him off because she found she enjoyed it. The two stayed together until morning and had sexual intercourse several times that night. Brown did not disclose the incident to the police immediately because she said she was embarrassed.

The defendant put on no evidence and moved at the close of the State's evidence for dismissal of both charges based on insufficiency of evidence. The trial court denied the motions and the majority in the Court of Appeals affirmed the trial court.

Upon the defendant's motion to dismiss, the question for the court is whether substantial evidence was introduced of each element of the offense charged and that the defendant was the perpetrator. Substantial evidence is "such relevant evidence as a reasonable mind might accept as adequate to support a conclusion." . . .

. . . [W]e examine first the evidence relating to the charge of kidnapping. Kidnapping is the unlawful restraint, confinement or removal of a person without that person's consent, if the person is 16 or over, for one of the following purposes:

(1) Holding such other person for ransom or as a hostage or using such other person as a shield; or

(2) Facilitating the commission of any felony or facilitating flight of any person following the commission of a felony; or

(3) Doing serious bodily harm to or terrorizing the person so confined, restrained or removed or any other person.

(4) Holding such other person in involuntary servitude in violation of G.S. 14–43.2.

G.S. 14–39(a). In order to convict the defendant of first degree kidnapping, the State must allege and prove as an additional element that "the person kidnapped either was not released by the defendant in a safe place or had been seriously injured or sexually assaulted. . . ." G.S. 14–39(b); *State v. Jerrett*, 309 N.C. 239 (1983).

The indictment for kidnapping in the present case alleged that the defendant removed Brown for the purpose of facilitating the commission of the felony of second degree rape. When such an indictment alleges an intent to commit a particular felony, the State must prove the particular intent alleged. In order to withstand the defendant's motion to dismiss, the State was, therefore, required to introduce substantial evidence tending to show that the defendant had the intent to rape Brown at the time he removed her.

The defendant argues that no substantial evidence was introduced tending to show either that he forcibly removed Brown or that he had the intent to rape her when he did so. Our review of the evidence introduced at trial leads us to the conclusion that, although there was substantial evidence of force, intimidation and removal of Brown by the defendant, the evidence was insufficient to show that the defendant removed her with the intent to commit rape.

The evidence tended to show that when he approached Brown at the school on June 15, the defendant blocked her way and grabbed her arm, forcing her to walk with him towards the parking lot. He questioned her about where she was living and expressed a desire to see her again. There was no evidence that while he held her he had an intent to have sex with her. He made no sexual remarks but expressed a desire to talk about their relationship. The two then embarked on a walk through the neighborhood. The defendant and Brown continued on their walk, staying slightly apart, with the defendant neither holding Brown nor threatening her in any way with what might happen if she tried to leave. They talked about their relationship as they walked.

The defendant made no sexual remarks at all until they reached a wooded area some distance from the school and stopped to talk. There Brown told the defendant that the relationship was over. For the first time the defendant spoke of sex and said he deserved another lovemaking session. They changed directions at that point. Brown said nothing but followed him to the house where the two had gone to have sex before.

There was no substantial evidence of an intent by the defendant to have sex until the time he made his statement about deserving sex. Ordinarily, the mere fact that a defendant removed and then raped the victim is substantial evidence that the defendant removed the victim with the intent to commit rape. Even when it is assumed arguendo that the defendant in this case raped Brown, however, all of the evidence tended to show that, at the time the defendant removed Brown, he had no reason to think that she would not engage in consensual sexual acts with him. To the contrary, all of the evidence tended to show that Brown's actions on June 15 prior to telling the defendant that their relationship was at an end were entirely consistent with the well established pattern of the couple's consensual sexual relationship. During that relationship she frequently remained entirely passive while the defendant at times engaged in some violence at the time of sexual intercourse. Brown's conduct on June 15, at least prior to her telling the defendant the relationship was over, was entirely consistent with her prior consensual sexual conduct. It in no way indicated to the defendant that he would have to rape Brown in order to have sexual intercourse with her. Therefore, there was no substantial evidence that the defendant had formed the intent to rape Brown at the time he forcibly removed her or that he removed her with the intent to facilitate any such crime.

All of the evidence tended to show that, after Brown told the defendant their relationship was over and he made his statement concerning sex, the defendant did not threaten Brown in any way and did not touch her again until he actually had sex with her at the Taylor house. Instead, all of the evidence tends to show that Brown followed the defendant to the Taylor house without protesting or giving any apparent indication that she went unwillingly. We think that such evidence was insufficient to show that the defendant knew or had any reason to know at the time he removed Brown from the school that she would not have consensual sexual intercourse with him as she always had in the past. Thus, there was no substantial evidence that the defendant had formed an intent to rape Brown at the time he removed her from the school.

Since there was no substantial evidence of forcible confinement, restraint or removal for the purpose of committing rape, the State failed to present substantial evidence of every element of the offense charged in the bill of indictment. We reverse the majority holding of the Court of Appeals on this issue and hold that the trial court erred in denying the defendant's motion to dismiss the kidnapping charge for insufficiency of the evidence. . . .

For the foregoing reasons, we reverse the opinion of the Court of Appeals holding that there was no error in the defendant's trial for kidnapping. . . and remand this action to the Court of Appeals . . . .

4. Michigan's Kidnapping Statute

M.C.L. §750.349. Kidnapping

(1) A person commits the crime of kidnapping if he or she knowingly restrains another person with the intent to do 1 or more of the following:

(a) Hold that person for ransom or reward.

(b) Use that person as a shield or hostage.

(c) Engage in criminal sexual penetration or criminal sexual contact with that person.

(d) Take that person outside of this state.

(e) Hold that person in involuntary servitude.

(2) As used in this section, "restrain" means to restrict a person's movements or to confine the person so as to interfere with that person's liberty without that person's consent or without legal authority. The restraint does not have to exist for any particular length of time and may be related or incidental to the commission of other criminal acts.

(3) A person who commits the crime of kidnapping is guilty of a felony punishable by imprisonment for life or any term of years or a fine of not more than $50,000.00, or both.

(4) This section does not prohibit the person from being charged with, convicted of, or sentenced for any other violation of law arising from the same transaction as the violation of this section.

M.C.L. §750.349a. Prisoner taking another as a hostage

A person imprisoned in any penal or correctional institution located in this state who takes, holds, carries away, decoys, entices away or secretes another person as a hostage by means of threats, coercion, intimidation or physical force is guilty of a felony and shall be imprisoned in the state prison for life, or any term of years, which shall be served as a consecutive sentence.

M.C.L. §750.349b. Unlawful imprisonment

(1) A person commits the crime of unlawful imprisonment if he or she knowingly restrains another person under any of the following circumstances:
    (a) The person is restrained by means of a weapon or dangerous instrument.
    (b) The restrained person was secretly confined.
    (c) The person was restrained to facilitate the commission of another felony or to facilitate flight after commission of another felony.
(2) A person who commits unlawful imprisonment is guilty of a felony punishable by imprisonment for not more than 15 years or a fine of not more than $20,000.00, or both.
(3) As used in this section:
    (a) "Restrain" means to forcibly restrict a person's movements or to forcibly confine the person so as to interfere with that person's liberty without that person's consent or without lawful authority. The restraint does not have to exist for any particular length of time and may be related or incidental to the commission of other criminal acts.
    (b) "Secretly confined" means either of the following:
        (*i*) To keep the confinement of the restrained person a secret.
        (*ii*) To keep the location of the restrained person a secret.
(4) This section does not prohibit the person from being charged with, convicted of, or sentenced for any other violation of law that is committed by that person while violating this section.

M.C.L. §750.350. Leading, taking, carrying away, decoying, or enticing away child under 14; intent; violation as felony; penalty; adoptive or natural parent

(1) A person shall not maliciously, forcibly, or fraudulently lead, take, carry away, decoy, or entice away, any child under the age of 14 years, with the intent to detain or conceal the child from the child's parent or legal guardian, or from the person or persons who have adopted the child, or from any other person having the lawful charge of the child. A person who violates this section is guilty of a felony, punishable by imprisonment for life or any term of years.
(2) An adoptive or natural parent of the child shall not be charged with and convicted for a violation of this section.

M.C.L. §750.350a. Taking or retaining child by adoptive or natural parent; intent; violation; penalty; restitution; probation; discharge and dismissal; proceedings open to public; nonpublic records; defense

(1) An adoptive or natural parent of a child shall not take that child, or retain that child for more than 24 hours, with the intent to detain or conceal the child from any other parent or legal guardian of the child who has custody or parenting time rights under a lawful court order at the time of the taking or retention, or from the person or persons who have adopted the child, or from any other person having lawful charge of the child at the time of the taking or retention.

(2) A parent who violates subsection (1) is guilty of a felony, punishable by imprisonment for not more than 1 year and 1 day, or a fine of not more than $2,000.00, or both.

(3) A parent who violates this section, upon conviction, in addition to any other punishment, may be ordered to make restitution to the other parent, legal guardian, the person or persons who have adopted the child, or any other person having lawful charge of the child for any financial expense incurred as a result of attempting to locate and having the child returned.

(4) When a parent who has not been convicted previously of a violation of section 349, 350, or this section, or under any statute of the United States or of any state related to kidnapping, pleads guilty to, or is found guilty of, a violation of this section, the court, without entering a judgment of guilt and with the consent of the accused parent, may defer further proceedings and place the accused parent on probation with lawful terms and conditions. The terms and conditions of probation may include participation in a drug treatment court under chapter 10A of the revised judicature act of 1961, 1961 PA 236, MCL 600.1060 to 600.1084. Upon a violation of a term or condition of probation, the court may enter an adjudication of guilt and proceed as otherwise provided. Upon fulfillment of the terms and conditions of probation, the court shall discharge from probation and dismiss the proceedings against the parent. Discharge and dismissal under this subsection shall be without adjudication of guilt and is not a conviction for purposes of disqualifications or disabilities imposed by law upon conviction of a crime, including any additional penalties imposed for second or subsequent convictions. There may be only 1 discharge and dismissal under this section as to an individual.

(5) All court proceedings under this section shall be open to the public. Except as provided in subsection (6), if the record of proceedings as to the defendant is deferred under this section, the record of proceedings during the period of deferral shall be closed to public inspection.

(6)   Unless the court enters a judgment of guilt under this section, the department of state police shall retain a nonpublic record of the arrest, court proceedings, and disposition of the criminal charge under this section. However, the nonpublic record shall be open to the following individuals and entities for the purposes noted:

(a)   The courts of this state, law enforcement personnel, the department of corrections, and prosecuting attorneys for use only in the performance of their duties or to determine whether an employee of the court, law enforcement agency, department of corrections, or prosecutor's office has violated his or her conditions of employment or whether an applicant meets criteria for employment with the court, law enforcement agency, department of corrections, or prosecutor's office.

(b)   The courts of this state, law enforcement personnel, and prosecuting attorneys for the purpose of showing either of the following:

(*i*)   That a defendant has already once availed himself or herself of this section.

(*ii*)   Determining whether the defendant in a criminal action is eligible for discharge and dismissal of proceedings by a drug treatment court under section 1076(5) of the revised judicature act of 1961, 1961 PA 236, MCL 600.1076.

(c)   The department of human services for enforcing child protection laws and vulnerable adult protection laws or ascertaining the preemployment criminal history of any individual who will be engaged in the enforcement of child protection laws or vulnerable adult protection laws.

(7) It is a complete defense under this section if a parent proves that his or her actions were taken for the purpose of protecting the child from an immediate and actual threat of physical or mental harm, abuse, or neglect.

Note

Re-read §§750.350 and 750.350a. Why would the Michigan Legislature carve out a separate parental kidnapping statute with lesser penalties? Why should a parent be treated in a more lenient manner? Alternatively, why did the legislature even make this conduct a crime?

In satisfying the movement requirement under a pre-2006 version of M.C.L. §750.349, the Michigan Supreme Court held that "it must be shown to be movement having significant independence of any accompanying offense" (not "merely incidental" to the commission of another offense). *People v. Barker*, 411 Mich. 291, 300 (1981). Look at M.C.L. §750.349 as provided in this chapter.

Is the "merely incidental" rule announced in *Barker* still relevant in light of the newly revised statute? Does the statute require movement in connection with criminal sexual conduct? For some recent reflections on this question, see *People v. Alzubaidy*, 2014 WL 1510050 (Mich. Ct. App. April 15, 2014).

Chapter 7
Burglary and Arson

A. Burglary

1. Introduction

At common law, burglary was an offense against habitation. Intended to protect the right of peaceful occupancy of one's dwelling, it was not considered to be a crime against property interests. The rationale of the crime was to protect the peace and security of the home against criminal intrusions and to prevent potentially dangerous nighttime breaches of the peace.

The crime of burglary was originally defined as the breaking and entering of the dwelling of another in the nighttime with the intent to commit a felony therein. "Breaking" was defined as any physical force, however slight, necessary to gain entry. Damage to the dwelling was not required. "Entry" was defined as any intrusion of any part of the body through a door, window, or other opening. "Dwelling" was defined as any structure used for human habitation, and it included any outbuildings within the curtilage of the home. Actual presence of the occupants was not required, as long as they intended to return at some point. "Of another" was defined as the lack of authorization to enter under the conditions that the defendant did. ""Nighttime was generally defined as after dusk but before dawn. Lastly, "intent to commit a felony therein" included the intent to commit any felony, not just larceny. For a detailed discussion, see Wayne LaFave, *Criminal Law* §21.1 (5th ed. 2010).

This chapter will explore the common law crime of burglary, focusing on early cases interpreting some of the elements. It is important to know that modern statutes have expanded on common law burglary in a wide variety of ways, e.g., eliminating the "breaking" and "nighttime" requirements (or retaining them as aggravating circumstances only), expanding the definition of "dwelling" to include a wide variety of locations, and broadening the intent element to include intent to commit a misdemeanor, or any theft offense, regardless of the value. It is still generally true, however, that whatever elements states retain from the common law continue to be defined by reference to common law. As such, it is essential to understand the common law crime of burglary.

2. Breaking

At common law, "breaking" was defined as any physical force, however slight, necessary to gain entry to the dwelling. Damage to the dwelling was not required. Breaking can be actual or constructive. "There is a constructive breaking when an entrance has been obtained by threat of violence, by fraud, or by conspiracy." *Davis v. Commonwealth*, 132 Va. 521 (1922).

a. What if the owner or occupier of the dwelling gives consent?

Davis v. Commonwealth, 132 Va. 521 (1922)

KELLY, P.

The defendant, Annie Davis, under indictment for burglary was convicted and sentenced to confinement in the penitentiary for a term of five years.

The indictment charged that in the nighttime she broke and entered the dwelling house of one E. P. Fowlkes, and "feloniously and burglariously" stole and carried away therefrom the sum of $412.50 belonging to one Dolly Wingfield.

The case is before us for review, and the sole assignment of error is that the court refused to set aside the verdict as being contrary to the law and the evidence.

. . . [T]he judgment will have to be reversed and a new trial awarded [because] . . . there was no "breaking" within the meaning of the familiar definition of burglary.

The evidence tends to show that, as contended by the commonwealth, the theft was committed in a house owned by Fowlkes, and in a room therein occupied and controlled by Dolly Wingfield, the owner of the stolen money. The testimony of Fowlkes and Dolly Wingfield conclusively shows that the defendant was and long had been their intimate associate and friend, and that with their consent and encouragement she carried a key to the house, was "just the same as at home there," was "over there day and night, and anything she wanted there she came and got it." She was not in any sense a servant or employee of the owners, nor a carekeeper or custodian of the property. Her relationship was that of a companion and friend, her right to enter the premises up to the time of the alleged theft being as free and unlimited as that of Dolly Wingfield herself. She came and went at will; she ate and slept there whenever she pleased; and, in short, as expressed by Fowlkes, she was "treated the same as home folks."

Breaking, as an element of the crime of burglary, may be either actual or constructive. There is a constructive breaking when an entrance has been obtained by threat of violence, by fraud, or by conspiracy. The entrance to the premises in the instant case was not obtained by either of these means, and cannot be classed as a constructive breaking.

Actual breaking involves the application of some force, slight though it may be, whereby the entrance is effected. Merely pushing open a door, turning the key, lifting the latch, or resort to other slight physical force is sufficient to constitute this element of the crime. But a breaking, either actual or constructive, to support a conviction of burglary, must have resulted in an entrance contrary to the will of the occupier of the house.

The modern authorities have gone quite far, and we believe properly so, in holding that if a servant or a caretaker, or one having a bare charge (not possession) of the premises, although fully authorized to enter for purposes within the scope of the employment or trust, actually enters for the purpose of carrying out a previously formed design to commit a felony, he will be guilty of burglary.

But in the instant case the right of the defendant to enter the premises as freely and unrestrictedly as either Fowlkes or Dolly Wingfield is undisputed, and it follows that she did not "break" and enter the house, and therefore cannot be convicted of the alleged burglary.

The following language of Judge Moncure . . . may well be applied here:

> We have seen no case, and think there has been none,
> in which the entry was by the voluntary act and consent of
> the owner or occupier of the house, which has been held to
> be burglary. . . .

Reversed.

b.   What if the defendant has a key to the dwelling?

Stowell v. People, 104 Colo. 255 (1939)

BURKE, Justice.

Plaintiff in error, hereinafter referred to as defendant, was convicted of burglary and sentenced to a term of three to seven years in the penitentiary. . . . The only question raised by the assignments, which we find it necessary to consider, may be thus stated: The information charging only burglary with force, was evidence that defendant entered by means of a key furnished him by the owner sufficient to support the charges?

The statute, so far as here applicable, reads: "Every person who shall wilfully, maliciously and forcibly break and enter, or wilfully and maliciously, without force, enter into any dwelling house, whether then occupied or not, . . . storehouse, ware-house, . . . with intent to commit . . . felony or misdemeanor, . . . shall be deemed guilty of burglary, and, upon conviction thereof, shall be punished by confinement in the penitentiary for a term not less than one year, nor more than ten years."

The information charged that defendant "did then and there feloniously, willfully, maliciously, burglariously and forcibly break and enter . . . with intent the personal property, . . . to steal, take and carry away. . . ."

Defendant was a freight conductor employed by the Rock Island railway. As such he was furnished with a "switch key" which he used in his work. It opened all switches and all depot and freight room doors on his division. There were no regulations governing its use. By means of it he entered the company's freight warehouse at Genoa and had taken therefrom two parcels of the value of $10, when he was arrested. The question here presented was raised by an instruction tendered and refused and by motion for a directed verdict at the close of all the evidence.

Had the switch key not been furnished defendant by the company, nor any authority given him under the terms of his employment to enter the building at the time and place in question, the evidence would have supported a conviction of burglary under the statute. For present purposes we assume, without deciding, that it would also have supported a conviction under this information. From the record it appears that defendant had a right to enter this warehouse at the time and in the manner he did, provided his intent in so doing was lawful. Hence this offense, if burglary, is raised to that grade solely by his unlawful intent. But intent alone is not always sufficient for that purpose. There is "no burglary, if the person entering has a right so to do, although he may intend to commit, and may actually commit, a felony, and although he may enter in such a way that there would be a breaking if he had no right to enter." Considering the history of the crime of burglary, and its evolution, this rule appears reasonable and necessary. The common law crime was an offense against habitation. Its purpose was to give security to the home when it was presumably least protected. Essential elements thereof were an actual *breaking*, in the *night time*, with intent to commit a *felony*. It has been extended by statute in most states to entry in any way, into any kind of building, at any time, for any unlawful purpose. Under the rule of strict construction of statutes in derogation of the common law courts must necessarily be careful not to extend such acts beyond the clear intent of the Legislature. For instance, among the buildings enumerated in our statute are "schoolhouses". Hence, but for the rule above stated, a school teacher, using the key furnished her by the district to re-open the schoolhouse door immediately after locking it in the evening, for the purpose of taking (but not finding) a pencil belonging to one of her pupils, could be sent to the penitentiary. . . .

. . . It follows that the evidence before us establishes no greater offense than petit larceny. . . .

The motion for an instructed verdict should have been sustained. The judgment is accordingly reversed.

c. **What is a "constructive breaking?"**

Nichols v. State, 68 Wis. 416 (1887) *used apparatus to enter*

CASSODAY, J.

There is undisputed testimony on the part of the state to the effect that Saturday, July 25, 1885, the plaintiff in error was stopping at a hotel in Black River Falls, having his name registered as W. H. Eldredge, and a room assigned him opposite thereto. He had then been there about three days. In the afternoon of the day named he had a box or chest taken from the depot to his room, weighing about 150 pounds. No evidence was given as to what was in it. About 3 o'clock in the afternoon of the same day he arranged with the local express agent for the sending of a box to Chicago, then at the hotel, and represented by him as weighing about 225 pounds. By his prearrangement, the box was brought to the depot just in time for the 7:50 P. M. Chicago train, and was shipped in the express car thereon by the local agent, as directed. Soon after the starting of the train, there seems to have been a suspicion as to the contents of the box. This suspicion was increased as telegraphs were received at different stations from Black River Falls respecting the box. Finally, being convinced by such dispatches that there was a man in the box, the train-men telegraphed forward to Elroy to secure the presence of an officer on the approach of the train to make the arrest. On reaching Elroy, in the night, this box in the express car was opened, and the plaintiff in error was found therein, with a revolver, billy, razor, knife, rope, gimlet, and a bottle of chloroform. There was also evidence tending to show that there were packages of money in the custody of the express agent on the car; that such agent had an assistant as far as Elroy; that from there to Chicago such car was usually in the charge of the man; that after the arrest, and when asked his object in being thus shipped in the box, the prisoner voluntarily admitted, in effect, that he had considered his chances carefully; that he went into the thing as a matter of speculation; that he needed money, and needed it quickly; that he expected to get fully fifty thousand dollars; that had he passed out of Elroy he would have got off with the money; that, in a case of that kind, if a human life stood in his way, it did not amount to a snap of the finger.

The motion in arrest of judgment was based upon the dissimilarity in the language employed in the second count in the information, under which the plaintiff in error was convicted, and the statute under which he was prosecuted.

That statute provides, in effect, that "any person who shall *enter in the night-time without breaking,* or shall *break and* enter in the day-time, any . . . railroad freight car, or passenger car, with intent to commit the crime of murder, rape, robbery, larceny, or other felony, shall be punished by imprisonment in the state prison not more than three years, nor less than one," etc. Section 4410. . . .

The question recurs whether the proofs show that there was a breaking in fact, within the meaning of the statute. Certainly not in the sense of picking a lock, or opening it with a key, or lifting a latch, or severing or mutilating the door, or doing violence to any portion of the car. On the contrary, the box was placed in the express car with the knowledge, and even by the assistance, of those in charge of the car. But it was not a passenger car, and the plaintiff in error was in no sense a passenger. The railroad company was a common carrier of passengers as well as freight. But the express company was exclusively a common carrier of freight; that is to say, goods, wares and merchandise. As such carrier, it may have at times transported animals, birds, etc., but it may be safely assumed that it never knowingly undertook to transport men in packages or boxes for special delivery. True, the plaintiff in error contracted with the local express agent for the carriage and delivery of such box, but neither he, nor anyone connected with the express car or the train, had any knowledge or expectation of a man being concealed within it. On the contrary, they each and all had the right to assume that the box contained nothing but inanimate substance,—goods, wares, or merchandise of some description. The plaintiff in error knew that he had no right to enter the express car at all without the consent of those in charge. The evidence was sufficient to justify the conclusion that he unlawfully gained an entrance without the knowledge or consent of those in charge of the car, by false pretenses, fraud, gross imposition, and circumvention, with intent to commit the crime of robbery or larceny, and, in doing so, if necessary, the crime of murder. This would seem to have been sufficient to constitute a constructive breaking at common law, as defined by Blackstone, thus: "To come down a chimney is held a burglarious entry; for that is as much closed as the nature of things will permit. So, also, to knock at the door, and, upon opening it, to rush in with a felonious intent; or, under pretense of taking lodgings, to fall upon the landlord and rob him; or to procure a constable to gain admittance, in order to search for traitors, and then to bind the constable, and rob the house. All these entries have been adjudged burglarious, though there was no actual breaking, for the law will not suffer itself to be trifled with by such evasions, especially under the cloak of legal process. And so, if a servant opens and enters his own master's chamber door with a felonious design; or if any other person, lodging in the same house, or in a public inn, opens and enters another's door, with such evil intent, it is burglary. Nay, if the servant conspires with a robber, and lets him into the house by night, this is burglary in both; for the servant is doing an unlawful act, and the opportunity afforded him of doing it with greater ease rather aggravates than extenuates the guilt."

So it has frequently been held in this country that, "to obtain admission to a dwelling-house at night, with the intent to commit a felony by means of artifice or fraud, or upon a pretense of business or social intercourse, is a constructive breaking, and will sustain an indictment charging a burglary by breaking and entering." . . . We must hold the evidence sufficient to support the charge of breaking. . . .

The judgment of the circuit court is affirmed.

3.   Entering

At common law, entry was defined as any intrusion of any part of the body through a door, window, or other opening. What if the entry is made with some kind of instrument?

Walker v. State, 63 Ala. 49 (1879)

BRICKELL, C. J.

The statute (Code of 1876, §4343) provides, that "any person who, either in the night or day time, with intent to steal, or to commit a felony, breaks into and enters a dwelling-house, or any building, structure or inclosure within the curtilage of a dwelling-house, though not forming a part thereof, or into any shop, store, warehouse, or other building, structure or inclosure in which any goods, merchandise, or other valuable thing is kept for use, sale, or deposit, *provided* such structure, other than a shop, store, ware-house or building, is specially constructed or made to keep such goods, merchandise, or other valuable thing, is guilty of burglary."

The defendant was indicted for breaking into and entering "a corn-crib of Noadiah Woodruff and Robert R. Peeples, a building in which corn, a thing of value, was at the time kept for use, sale, or deposit, with intent to steal." He was convicted; and the case is now presented on exceptions taken to instructions given, and the refusal of instructions requested, as to what facts will constitute a breaking into and entry, material constituents of the offense charged in the indictment. The facts, on which the instructions were founded, are: that in the crib was a quantity of shelled corn, piled on the floor; in April, or May, 1878, the crib had been broken into, and corn taken therefrom, without the consent of the owners, who had the crib watched; and thereafter the defendant was caught under it, and, on coming out, voluntarily confessed that, about three weeks before, he had taken a large auger, and, going under the crib, had bored a hole through the floor, from which the corn, being shelled, ran into a sack he held under it; that he then got about three pecks of corn, and with a cob closed the hole. On these facts, the City Court was of opinion, and so instructed the jury, that there was such a breaking and entry of the crib, as would constitute the offense, and refused instructions requested asserting the converse of the proposition. . . .

The statute employs the words, *"breaks into and enters;"* and these are borrowed from the common-law definition of burglary. They must be received with the signification, and understood in the sense, given them at common law. . . . The degree of force or violence which may be used is not of importance—it may be very slight. The lifting the latch of a door; the picking of a lock, or opening with a key; the removal of a pane of glass, and, indeed, the displacement or unloosing of any fastening, which the owner has provided as a security to the house, is a breaking—an *actual* breaking—within the meaning of the term as employed in the definition of burglary at common law, and as it is employed in the statute. In *Hughes' case* (1 Leach, C. C., case 178), the prisoner had bored a hole with a *centre-bit,* through the panel of the house-door, near to one of the bolts by which it was fastened; and some pieces of the broken panel were found within-side the threshold of the door; but it did not appear that any instrument, except the point of the *centre-bit,* or that any part of the prisoner's body, had been within-side the house, or that the aperture made was large enough to admit a man's hand. The court were of opinion, that there was a sufficient *breaking,* but not such an *entry,* as would constitute the offense.

The boring the hole through the floor of the crib, was a sufficient breaking; but with it there must have been an entry. Proof of a breaking, though it may be with an intent to steal, or the intent to commit a felony, is proof of one only of the facts making up the offense, and is as insufficient as proof of an entry through an open door, without breaking. If the hand, or any part of the body, is intruded within the house, the entry is complete. The entry may also be completed by the intrusion of a tool, or instrument, within the house, though no part of the body be introduced. Thus, "if A. breaks the house of B. in the night time, with intent to steal goods, and breaks the window, and puts in his hand, or puts in a hook, or other engine, to reach out goods; or puts a pistol in at the window, with an intent to kill, though his hand be not within the window, this is burglary."—1 Hale, 555. When no part of the body is introduced—when the only entry is of a tool, or instrument, introduced by the force and agency of the party accused, the inquiry is, whether the tool or instrument was employed solely for the purpose of *breaking,* and thereby effecting an *entry;* or whether it was employed not only to *break and enter,* but also to aid in the consummation of the criminal intent, and its capacity to aid in such consummation. Until there is a *breaking* and *entry,* the offense is not consummated. The offense rests largely in intention; and though there may be sufficient evidence of an attempt to commit it, which, of itself, is a crime, the attempt may be abandoned—of it there may be repentance, before the consummation of the offense intended. The *breaking* may be at one time, and the *entry* at another. The *breaking* may be complete, and yet an *entry* never effected. From whatever cause an *entry* is not effected, burglary has not been committed. When one instrument is employed to *break,* and is without capacity to aid otherwise than by opening a way of *entry,* and another instrument must be used, or the instrument used in the breaking must be used in some other way or manner to consummate the criminal intent, the intrusion of the instrument is not, of itself, an *entry.* But when, as in this case, the instrument is employed, not only to *break,* but to effect the only *entry* contemplated, and necessary to the consummation of the criminal intent; when it is intruded within the house, *breaking* it, effecting an *entry,* enabling the person introducing it to consummate his intent, the offense is complete. The instrument was employed, not only for the purpose of *breaking* the house, but to effect the larceny intended. When it was intruded into the crib, the burglar acquired dominion over the corn intended to be stolen. Such dominion did not require any other act on his part. When the auger was withdrawn from the aperture made with it, the corn ran into the sack he used in its asportation. There was a *breaking* and *entry,* enabling him to effect his criminal intent, without the use of any other means, and this satisfies the requirements of the law.

Let the judgment be affirmed.

4. Dwelling

A dwelling was defined as any structure currently used for human habitation. Included within the meaning of dwelling were any outbuildings within the curtilage of the home, such as garages, porches, etc. Curtilage has been defined as "the land immediately surrounding and associated with the home." *Oliver v. United States*, 466 U.S. 170, 180 (1984).

a. Is it a dwelling if nobody has moved in yet?

Woods v. State, 188 Miss. 463 (1939)

GRIFFITH, Justice.

Appellant was indicted and convicted under the charge of the burglary of a dwelling-house. The undisputed proof showed that the house in question, although intended for a dwelling-house, had been only recently erected and had not yet been occupied as a dwelling. It was vacant.

Appellant relies on Haynes v. State, 180 Miss. 291, wherein the court held that a house from which the occupants had permanently removed on the day before the night of the burglary was not a dwelling at the time of the commission of the alleged crime; and that proof of the burglary of such a house would not sustain the conviction under an indictment charging the burglary of a dwelling. Appellant submits that if a house from which the occupants have permanently removed is not a dwelling-house within the statutes on burglary, then, upon the same reasoning, a house into which no dwellers have ever yet moved is not a dwelling-house; and in this contention appellant is clearly correct. . . .

. . . [T]his presents the question whether an indictment charging the burglary of a dwelling can be amended during the trial so as to make it charge the burglary of some house other than a dwelling-house; and that question we must answer in the negative. An indictment cannot be amended at the trial so as to change the identity of the offense, and the burglary of a dwelling is an offense separate and distinct from that of the burglary of an unoccupied house, although both belong to the same class of felonies. They are dealt with under separate statutes, and these statutes contain separate and distinct elements to constitute the crimes therein denounced. . . .

Reversed and remanded.

b. Is an "outhouse" a dwelling and, if so, where must it be located to qualify as a dwelling?

State v. Neff, 122 W. Va. 549 (1940)

HATCHER, Judge.

The two Neffs were charged with burglariously breaking and entering in the night time a chicken house, an outhouse adjoining the dwelling house of J. A. Trent and belonging to him, and stealing from the chicken house his chickens valued at $30. The Neffs were found guilty of burglary and sentenced to the penitentiary.

The evidence is incomplete as to the size of the alleged chicken house and its proximity to the Trent dwelling. The former is described as a "small house", having a floor space of four and a half by five feet; but neither its height, nor evidence from which the height might be estimated, is shown. It had a hinged door fastened by a chain drawn through holes bored in the door and "the building face", respectively. The dwelling "sets back about" seventy-five feet from a public road; the chicken house is "out across" the road somewhere, but its distance from the road or the dwelling is not shown.

At common law burglary was "an offense against the habitation not against the property." But burglary could be committed on uninhabited structures, provided they were "parcel of" and within the same common fence as the mansion-house, though not contiguous to it. The Virginia Assembly modified the common law by restricting the burglary of a building other than the dwelling house to "any outhouse adjoining thereto and occupied therewith." That restriction remained in the Virginia statute until this state was formed and then we adopted it. West Virginia Acts 1882, Ch. 148, Sec. 11, substituted the alternative "or" for the connective "and", so that the phrase read "outhouse adjoining thereto (the dwelling house) or occupied therewith." . . .

All the words in the phrase are plain and well understood. No reason appears for not holding that they are used in their ordinary sense. We held in State v. Crites, 110 W.Va. 36, that the word "outhouse" was so used, and, in effect, that it meant a building constructed at least large enough for an adult to enter erect and to turn around comfortably within. The State, failing to show the height of the structure in question, did not prove it to be a house at all. But if we should concede that because the Trents called it a house, it should be taken as such, the State has still failed to make a case because the so-called house, being across the public road one hundred feet or more from the dwelling house, cannot, under any fair construction, be said to adjoin it. Since the statute limits the burglary of an outhouse not occupied in connection with the dwelling house, to one "adjoining" it, such contiguity must be proven. We are not advised of any decision on a statute like ours. But the statute, as amended in 1882, differs from the common law more in words than substance. And under the common law an outhouse across a public road from its owner's dwelling house is held to be not parcel thereof and not the subject of burglary. Curkendall v. People, 36 Mich. 309.

The judgment is reversed, the verdict set aside and a new trial awarded defendants.

Reversed and remanded.

5. Of Another

Generally, the dwelling is "of another" if the person entering is not authorized to enter under the conditions that existed at the time of entry. What if the entry is in an apartment within a larger building?

Daniels v. State, 78 Ga. 98 (1886)

HALL, Justice.

The indictment charges the defendant with breaking and entering the depot building of the Western and Atlantic Railroad Company, where valuable goods were contained, with intent to steal, etc. The proof showed that the outer door was left open, but that after getting into the building, which had numerous apartments, the doors to each of these, in which the postage stamps belonging to the company were deposited, were broken and entered and they were stolen and carried away by the defendant. It is now insisted that neither the charge in the indictment nor the facts in proof made out the offence of burglary against the defendant; that in order to fix legal guilt upon him, it should have been alleged and proved that he effected his entrance by breaking the door through which he got into the house, and not by showing that, after entering it, he broke either of the doors of the departments in it, where the valuables in question were found. Such, however, is not our apprehension of the law. It is well-settled, by a number of cases, that where a party is indicted for breaking and entering an out-house within the curtilage or protection of a mansion or dwelling, the burglary should be laid as having been done in the dwelling-house. If this be true as to an out-house within the protection of the mansion or dwelling-house, *a fortiori* would it be so as to an apartment in the house, a party's place of business in which his goods, wares, etc. were stored or contained, and which was broken and entered with an intent to commit a larceny upon the articles of value therein contained. This indictment does not allege in terms that the depot was the place of business of the railroad company, but no specific objection was taken to it on this account, and had there been one, we are not prepared to hold that it was tenable, as the offence, though not charged in the terms and language of the code, is so plainly set forth that its nature could be easily understood by the jury. It is always best, however, to avoid cavil or dispute, to conform to the very words of the statute on which the accusation is based. On this point, there was no error in the instruction given by the court. . . .

Judgment affirmed.

6. In the Nighttime

Generally, nighttime was defined as after dusk but before dawn. For more information, see Wayne LaFave, *Criminal Law* §21.1(d) (5th ed. 2010).

7. With Intent to Commit a Felony Therein

Often referred to as a specific intent crime, burglary involves the intent to commit a felony within the dwelling. The significance of the general intent/specific intent dichotomy will be explored in subsequent chapters; it suffices here to say that the crime is specific intent because it involves a heightened mental state above and beyond the knowledge that one is breaking and entering a dwelling.

The intent to commit a felony involves any felony, not just larceny. It is also important to understand that the mental state involves the intent to commit the felony *therein* (within the dwelling) and that the felonious intent must exist at the time of the breaking and entering. Importantly, however, the defendant does not have to actually commit the felony. When reading *Goldman*, consider whether intent may be inferred from the evidence.

Goldman v. Anderson, 625 F.2d 135 (6th Cir. 1980)

BOYCE F. MARTIN, Jr., Circuit Judge.

Petitioner is an inmate subject to the jurisdiction of the Michigan Department of Corrections. His incarceration is the result of a 1976 Michigan conviction of breaking and entering a real estate office with intent to commit larceny therein contrary to MCLA 750.110; MSA 28.305. Upon conviction in Detroit Recorder's Court by a jury, he was sentenced to a term of five to ten years in prison. Petitioner appeals to this Court from a judgment entered November 19, 1979 by the Honorable James P. Churchill in the United States District Court for the Eastern District of Michigan which dismissed his petition for habeas corpus . . . .

During the trial, a police officer testified that she responded at 5:00 a.m. to a call that a breaking and entering of a real estate office was in progress. When she arrived at the reported address, she saw the petitioner leaving the premises. He ran, but was later apprehended by a private citizen and returned to the scene. The officer further testified that petitioner had white plaster dust on his clothes. Another officer found a hole in the wall of the real estate office which was adjacent to a bar, and found a sledgehammer, crowbar, screwdriver, and flashlight near the hole. Nothing had been stolen from either establishment, perhaps because of the arrival of the police.

Petitioner testified that he was never in the building but that he had been arrested for running by the building near the time of the break-in; he denied ever having run from the police. . . .

Petitioner argues that . . . the evidence was insufficient to establish his intent to larcenize the real estate office, hence, his conviction was a denial of due process within the purview of *Jackson v. Virginia*, 443 U.S. 307 (1979) . . . .

Petitioner bases his argument regarding the sufficiency of the evidence upon the thesis that the evidence clearly showed intent to larcenize the adjacent bar and not the real estate office. Hence, he argues, evidence of intent to larcenize the real estate office had not been established and petitioner could not be convicted of MCLA 750.110. While petitioner's argument raises an interesting problem in conceptualization and may point out some ambiguity in the statute, we are constrained to note that "the relevant question is whether, after viewing the evidence in the light most favorable to the prosecution, *any* rational trier of fact could have found the essential elements of the crime beyond a reasonable doubt." (emphasis in the original) *Jackson v. Virginia* at 319. . . .

As in every case where intent is material, larcenous intent may be inferred from the surrounding circumstances. "Because such mischief is a normal incident to a breaking and entering, and because of the difficulty of proving the actor's state of mind, circumstantial evidence has been found sufficient to sustain the conclusion that the defendant entertained the requisite (larcenous) intent." *People v. Palmer*, 42 Mich.App. 549, 551–552 (1972). *See also People v. Jablonski*, 70 Mich.App. 218, 223 (1976).

Under Michigan law, intent to commit larceny may be inferred from the totality of circumstances disclosed by the testimony. Such intent may be inferred from the nature, time, or place of the defendant's acts before and during the breaking and entering. *People v. Saunders*, 25 Mich.App. 149 (1970). *People v. Hughes*, 27 Mich.App. 221 (1970).

Here, the testimony reveals that a real estate office was broken into at approximately 5:00 a.m. on Sunday, July 25, 1976. The real estate agency was an ongoing business, not open for business at the time, and the owner had given no one permission to enter that morning. A witness saw the petitioner inside the real estate office. Later, an officer apprehended him after he fled the building. A forced entry had been made into the real estate office. Further, the police discovered a crow bar, a screwdriver, a flashlight, and a sledgehammer inside the office as well as a hole in the wall separating the office from an adjacent bar.

Appellant argues that whoever broke into the real estate office did so for the purpose of breaking a hole in the party wall so that entry could be gained into the bar next door, and that an intent to break through the party wall leading to the bar was incompatible with an intent to commit larceny in the real estate office. But nothing precluded petitioner from having both the intent to commit larceny within the office and in the bar next door. Based on the hour, the nature of the business involved, the burglar tools used, and the unexplained presence of petitioner inside the building, the jury could well have inferred that petitioner intended to steal anything of value within either the real estate office or the bar. To this extent, we agree with the district court that there was sufficient evidence in the record to leave the jury verdict undisturbed. . . .

Accordingly, the petition for a writ of habeas corpus is denied.

8. Statutory Variations on Common Law Burglary

States have codified burglary in a wide variety of ways. Should it be burglary if the defendant breaks into a Salvation Army drop box?

State v. Mann, 129 Ariz. 24 (1981)

HOWARD, Judge.

Is the Salvation Army collection box a "structure" within the meaning of A.R.S. Sec. 13–1506(A) and Sec. 13–1501(8)? We hold that it is and affirm appellants' conviction of burglary, third-degree.

Appellants were caught by the police while they were removing used clothing from a Salvation Army collection box. The box in question was located on a corner of the intersection of Ft. Lowell Road and Dodge Boulevard in Tucson. It was approximately six feet high and four feet deep by four feet wide, made of tin metal. About four feet from the bottom of one side it had an unlockable chute-like door for depositing items. The items in the box were regularly collected about every 36 hours. The Salvation Army removed the articles through a locked trap door located near the bottom of another side. Mary Lou Mann removed the clothing by reaching into the unlocked chute.

A.R.S. Sec. 13–1506 provides in part:

> A. A person commits burglary in the third degree by entering or remaining unlawfully in a non-residential structure . . . with the intent to commit any theft . . . therein.

The word structure is defined in A.R.S. Sec. 13–1501(8):

> 'Structure' means any building, object, vehicle, railroad car or place with sides and a floor, separately securable from any other structure attached to it and used for lodging, business, transportation, recreation or storage.

Appellants contend that the trial court erred when it instructed the jury that the Salvation Army collection box was a non-residential structure as a matter of law. They claim that this was a question of fact for the jury. We do not agree. The box had sides and a floor and it was used for storage. There were no facts in dispute and its nature was a question of law for the court. The trial court did not err in its instruction.

Appellants next contend the trial court erred in refusing to give their Instruction No. 14 which stated that abandoned property cannot be the subject of a theft. Appellants' contention that the clothing inside the Salvation Army collection box was abandoned, however, is without merit. The property was not abandoned but was donated to the Salvation Army and in its possession. . . .

Affirmed.

9. Michigan's Breaking and Entering Statute

Michigan's breaking and entering statute codifies the common law, but it also adds much more. Note that the statutes in the following practice problem are based, in part, on the Michigan statute (but modified to simplify the problem).

After reviewing the Michigan statute, can you explain the differences between home invasion in the first, second, and third degrees? What is the difference between breaking and entering, entering without breaking, and home invasion?

M.C.L. §750.110. Breaking and entering

(1) A person who breaks and enters, with intent to commit a felony or a larceny therein, a tent, hotel, office, store, shop, warehouse, barn, granary, factory or other building, structure, boat, ship, shipping container, or railroad car is guilty of a felony punishable by imprisonment for not more than 10 years.
(2) As used in this section and section 111, "shipping container" means a standardized, reusable container for transporting cargo that is capable of integrating with a railcar flatbed or a flatbed semitrailer.

M.C.L. §750.110a. Definitions; breaking and entering a dwelling; crime of home invasion

(1) As used in this section:
(a) "Dwelling" means a structure or shelter that is used permanently or temporarily as a place of abode, including an appurtenant structure attached to that structure or shelter.
(b) "Dangerous weapon" means 1 or more of the following:
(*i*) A loaded or unloaded firearm, whether operable or inoperable.
(*ii*) A knife, stabbing instrument, brass knuckles, blackjack, club, or other object specifically designed or customarily carried or possessed for use as a weapon.

(*iii*) An object that is likely to cause death or bodily injury when used as a weapon and that is used as a weapon or carried or possessed for use as a weapon.

(*iv*) An object or device that is used or fashioned in a manner to lead a person to believe the object or device is an object or device described in subparagraphs (*i*) to (*iii*).

(c) "Without permission" means without having obtained permission to enter from the owner or lessee of the dwelling or from any other person lawfully in possession or control of the dwelling.

(2) A person who breaks and enters a dwelling with intent to commit a felony, larceny, or assault in the dwelling, a person who enters a dwelling without permission with intent to commit a felony, larceny, or assault in the dwelling, or a person who breaks and enters a dwelling or enters a dwelling without permission and, at any time while he or she is entering, present in, or exiting the dwelling, commits a felony, larceny, or assault is guilty of home invasion in the first degree if at any time while the person is entering, present in, or exiting the dwelling either of the following circumstances exists:

(a) The person is armed with a dangerous weapon.

(b) Another person is lawfully present in the dwelling.

(3) A person who breaks and enters a dwelling with intent to commit a felony, larceny, or assault in the dwelling, a person who enters a dwelling without permission with intent to commit a felony, larceny, or assault in the dwelling, or a person who breaks and enters a dwelling or enters a dwelling without permission and, at any time while he or she is entering, present in, or exiting the dwelling, commits a felony, larceny, or assault is guilty of home invasion in the second degree.

(4) A person is guilty of home invasion in the third degree if the person does either of the following:

(a) Breaks and enters a dwelling with intent to commit a misdemeanor in the dwelling, enters a dwelling without permission with intent to commit a misdemeanor in the dwelling, or breaks and enters a dwelling or enters a dwelling without permission and, at any time while he or she is entering, present in, or exiting the dwelling, commits a misdemeanor.

(b) Breaks and enters a dwelling or enters a dwelling without permission and, at any time while the person is entering, present in, or exiting the dwelling, violates any of the following ordered to protect a named person or persons:

(*i*) A probation term or condition.

(*ii*) A parole term or condition.

(*iii*) A personal protection order term or condition.

(*iv*) A bond or bail condition or any condition of pretrial release.

(5) Home invasion in the first degree is a felony punishable by imprisonment for not more than 20 years or a fine of not more than $5,000.00, or both.

(6) Home invasion in the second degree is a felony punishable by imprisonment for not more than 15 years or a fine of not more than $3,000.00, or both.

(7) Home invasion in the third degree is a felony punishable by imprisonment for not more than 5 years or a fine of not more than $2,000.00, or both.

(8) The court may order a term of imprisonment imposed for home invasion in the first degree to be served consecutively to any term of imprisonment imposed for any other criminal offense arising from the same transaction.

(9) Imposition of a penalty under this section does not bar imposition of a penalty under any other applicable law.

M.C.L. §750.111. Entering without breaking

Any person who, without breaking, enters any dwelling, house, tent, hotel, office, store, shop, warehouse, barn, granary, factory or other building, boat, ship, shipping container, railroad car or structure used or kept for public or private use, or any private apartment therein, with intent to commit a felony or any larceny therein, is guilty of a felony punishable by imprisonment for not more than 5 years or a fine of not more than $2,500.00.

M.C.L. §750.112. Burglary with explosives

Any person who enters any building, and for the purpose of committing any crime therein, uses or attempts to use nitro-glycerine, dynamite, gunpowder or any other high explosive, shall be guilty of a felony, punishable by imprisonment in the state prison not less than 15 years nor more than 30 years.

M.C.L. §750.113. Opening or attempting to open receptacle maintained for payment for merchandise or services by public; obtaining or attempting to obtain money or thing of value deposited in receptacle

A person who maliciously and willfully, by and with the aid and use of any key, instrument, device, or explosive, blows or attempts to blow, or forces or attempts to force an entrance into any coin box, depository box, or other receptacle established and maintained for the convenience of the public, or of any person or persons, in making payment for any article of merchandise or service, wherein is contained any money or thing of value, or extracts or obtains, or attempts to extract or obtain, therefrom any such money or thing of value so deposited or contained therein, is guilty of a misdemeanor punishable by imprisonment for not more than 6 months or a fine of not more than $750.00.

M.C.L. §750.114. Breaking or entering outside showcase or other enclosed counter with intent to commit larceny

A person who shall break and enter, or enter without breaking, at any time, any outside showcase or other outside enclosed counter used for the display of goods, wares, or merchandise, with intent to commit the crime of larceny, is guilty of a misdemeanor punishable by imprisonment for not more than 6 months or a fine of not more than $750.00.

M.C.L. §750.115. Breaking and entering or entering without breaking; buildings, tents, boats, railroad cars; entering public buildings when expressly denied

(1) Any person who breaks and enters or enters without breaking, any dwelling, house, tent, hotel, office, store, shop, warehouse, barn, granary, factory or other building, boat, ship, railroad car or structure used or kept for public or private use, or any private apartment therein, or any cottage, clubhouse, boat house, hunting or fishing lodge, garage or the out-buildings belonging thereto, any ice shanty with a value of $100.00 or more, or any other structure, whether occupied or unoccupied, without first obtaining permission to enter from the owner or occupant, agent, or person having immediate control thereof, is guilty of a misdemeanor.
(2) Subsection (1) does not apply to entering without breaking, any place which at the time of the entry was open to the public, unless the entry was expressly denied. Subsection (1) does not apply if the breaking and entering or entering without breaking was committed by a peace officer or an individual under the peace officer's direction in the lawful performance of his or her duties as a peace officer.

M.C.L. §750.116. Burglar's tools, possession

Any person who shall knowingly have in his possession any nitroglycerine, or other explosive, thermite, engine, machine, tool or implement, device, chemical or substance, adapted and designed for cutting or burning through, forcing or breaking open any building, room, vault, safe or other depository, in order to steal therefrom any money or other property, knowing the same to be adapted and designed for the purpose aforesaid, with intent to use or employ the same for the purpose aforesaid, shall be guilty of a felony, punishable by imprisonment in the state prison not more than 10 years.

Note

In *People v. Osby*, 291 Mich. App. 412 (2011), the court limited the burglar's tools statute, M.C.L. §750.116, to tools used to open a building, room, safe, or other depository (i.e., vehicle). Why might a court pose such a limitation?

In *People v. Powell*, 278 Mich. App. 318 (2008), the court held that an owner's temporary absence or a structure's habitability will not automatically preclude a structure from being a "dwelling" under the statute.

10. Practice Problems on Breaking and Entering

While states have codified burglary in a wide variety of ways, the common law still plays an important role in helping to interpret the meaning of statutes. Explore some modern statutes by writing an answer to the following problem.

At approximately 4:20 a.m. on October 1, the City Police Department received a telephone call from a woman who reported that she had just seen someone walking around inside the home of her neighbors, a retired couple who were out of town for the weekend.

When the officers investigated this call, they entered the backyard of the home and found a sliding glass door to the house standing wide open. When the officers walked inside, they found a man hiding in a walk-in closet in one of the bedrooms upstairs. When an officer opened the closet door, the man tried to run past him and escape, but the officer grabbed him and wrestled him to the floor. A thorough search by the officer revealed that the man was not armed, but on the floor of the closet near the man was a pile of approximately 30 compact discs. The search also revealed that the man was carrying a key ring with approximately a dozen different house keys on it, and a driver's license with a home address approximately 15 miles away.

Subsequent investigation revealed that the disks belonged to the retired couple and were ordinarily stored downstairs in the living room. In addition, fingerprints found on the discs matched the man's prints. The police also learned that the retired couple had mistakenly left the patio door standing wide open when they left town. The man later told the detectives in charge of the case that he had seen the door wide open and had just walked into the house to see if anything was wrong, and he had no intention of stealing anything. He was unable, however, to provide the detective with any explanation of why he was in this specific neighborhood.

The Penal Code includes these statutes:

§750.110a

> Any person who breaks and enters a dwelling with intent to commit a felony, larceny, or assault in the dwelling; a person who enters a dwelling without permission with intent to commit a felony, larceny, or assault in the dwelling; or a person who breaks and enters a dwelling or enters a dwelling without permission and, at any time while he or she is entering, present in, or exiting the dwelling, commits a felony, larceny, or assault is guilty of home invasion in the first degree if at any time while the person is entering, present in, or exiting the dwelling either of the following circumstances exists:
>   (1)   The person is armed with a dangerous weapon.
>   (2)   Another person is lawfully present in the dwelling.

§750.110b

> Any person who breaks and enters a dwelling with the intent to commit a felony or larceny in the dwelling or a person that enters a dwelling without permission with the intent to commit a felony or a larceny in the dwelling is guilty of home invasion in the second degree.

In addition, the State Supreme Court held in a previous decision that police officers who are investigating a home invasion do not satisfy the requirement under §750.110a that another person be lawfully present in the dwelling.

Assume that "trespassing" is not a felony. Fully discuss the prosecution's best argument why an intent to steal by the man (the required mental state for larceny) can be proven based on these facts. Also, fully discuss whether the man should be charged with a violation of §750.110a or §750.110b.

B.   Arson

1.   Introduction

Similar to burglary, the crime of arson is an offense against habitation, which is the right to peacefully occupy one's dwelling. One rationale of this crime is to protect the peace and security of the home. Another is to protect the occupants and others from the dangers of fire.

The common law crime of arson was originally defined as the malicious burning of the dwelling of another. "Malicious" was defined as either the intent to burn *or* the reckless disregard of a very high risk (implying knowledge of the risk being taken) that burning would occur. "Burning" was defined as any consumption of any part of the structure by fire. "Dwelling" was defined the same as it was in the crime of burglary—any structure currently used for human habitation, including any outbuildings within the curtilage of the home such as garages and porches (note that this did not include a business). "Of another" was defined as a dwelling other than the defendant's own home. For a detailed discussion, see Wayne LaFave, *Criminal Law* §21.3 (5th ed. 2010).

As with burglary, it is important to know that modern statutes have expanded on common law arson in a variety of ways, e.g., expanding the definition of "dwelling" to include a wide variety of structures (including a business), and eliminating the "of another" requirement (making it possible to charge someone with arson for burning their own property). It remains true, however, that elements states retain from the common law are defined by reference to common law. As such, it is essential to understand the common law crime of arson.

2. Cases

Richmond v. State explores the meaning of "dwelling" as well as the required mental state for the crime of common law arson. Contending that the burning of three separate apartments inside one building should only be one offense, the defendant asserts violation of the Double Jeopardy Clause of the United States Constitution because he was sentenced for three separate arsons. In reading the case, know that the double jeopardy discussion has been edited out—it is not relevant to the general discussion of common law arson and you, as a student of criminal law, do not need to fully understand double jeopardy to understand the common law crime of arson.

Richmond v. State, 326 Md. 257 (1992)

KARWACKI, Judge.

. . . On February 5, 1987, a fire broke out in a two story apartment building located at Dallas Place in Temple Hills. The building contained approximately ten units. The fire originated in the ground floor apartment of Martha Gobert and quickly spread to the apartment located across a common hallway, occupied by Wanda Pfeiffer, and to the apartment located above the Gobert unit, occupied by Evelyn Saunders. All three apartment units were substantially damaged before the fire could be extinguished.

An official investigation of the fire disclosed that Guy L. Richmond, Jr., the appellant, had arranged for three of his confederates to set fire to Gobert's apartment. Richmond and Gobert worked for the same employer, and Richmond recently had been suspended from his job because of a work place grievance filed against him by Gobert.

On October 19, 1987, after a bench trial before the Circuit Court for Prince George's County, Richmond was convicted of three separate counts of an indictment, charging violation of Maryland Code (1957, 1982 Repl.Vol.) Article 27, §6[8] for procuring the burning of the "dwelling houses" of Gobert, Pfeiffer, and Saunders. . . .

Richmond contends that the burning of three apartments was the result of one criminal act, that it is but one offense proscribed by Art. 27, §6, and that the imposition of multiple sentences for this one offense violates double jeopardy principles. The Double Jeopardy Clause of the Fifth Amendment protects against a second prosecution for the same offense after acquittal, a second prosecution for the same offense after conviction, and multiple punishments for the same offense. . . .

It is manifest from the language employed in Art. 27, §6 that the General Assembly intended the unit of prosecution to be "any dwelling house" burned. The issue before us is not thereby resolved, however, because the term "dwelling house" is not defined in the statute; we must determine whether each individual apartment unit burned constitutes a separate dwelling house.

. . . Maryland has retained the common law definition of arson in Art. 27, §6.[4] Sir William Blackstone explained the reasons why arson is considered such a serious crime:

> ARSON, *ab ardendo,* is the malicious and wilful burning of the house or outhouses of another man. This is an offence of very great malignity, and much more pernicious to the public than simple theft: because, first, it is an offence against that right, of habitation, which is acquired by the law of nature as well as by the laws of society; next, because of

---

[8] Article 27, § 6 provides:

> Any person who wilfully and maliciously sets fire to or burns or causes to be burned or who aids, counsels or procures the burning of any dwelling house, or any kitchen, shop, barn, stable or other outhouse that is parcel thereof, or belonging to or adjoining thereto, whether the property of himself, or of another, shall be guilty of arson, and upon conviction thereof, be sentenced to the penitentiary for not more than thirty years.

[4] Furthermore, if a term such as "dwelling house" is not otherwise defined by statute, the common law meaning is assumed to be intended. 3 C. Torcia, *Wharton's Criminal Law* § 352 (14th ed. 1980).

the terror and confusion that necessarily attends it; and, lastly, because in simple theft the thing stolen only changes it's [sic] master, but still remains *in esse* for the benefit of the public, whereas by burning the very substance is absolutely destroyed.

Thus, at common law, arson is an offense against the security of habitation or occupancy, rather than against ownership or property. Expounding on what constitutes a "dwelling house," Blackstone stated that "if a landlord or reversioner sets fire to his own house, of which another is in possession under a lease from himself or from those whose estate he hath, it shall be accounted arson; for, during the lease, the house is the property of the tenant." Thus, since each leased apartment is the property of a separate tenant, and a burning of that property, whether by the landlord or some other individual, constitutes arson, each separate apartment burned constitutes a separate unit of prosecution. . . .

Generally, a structure which qualifies as a dwelling house for the purpose of burglary also qualifies as a dwelling house for the purpose of arson. In describing what places could be subjects of a burglary, Blackstone observed, "[a] chamber in a college or an inn of court, where each inhabitant hath a distinct property, is, to all other purposes as well as this, the mansion-house of the owner."

Several cases dealing with convictions for breaking and entering a dwelling house indicate that one separate portion of a building can independently be a dwelling house subject to being invaded by the offender. In *Jones v. State,* 2 Md.App. 356 (1967), Jones broke into a building where two floors were occupied by a club and one floor was used as an apartment by an individual. The Court of Special Appeals held that the part of the building used as an apartment was a dwelling house and the part used as a club was a storehouse. In *Herbert v. State,* 31 Md.App. 48 (1976), the defendant walked down a row of motel rooms, entered Room 66 for several minutes, and then attempted to enter Room 76. He was convicted of burglary of Room 66 and attempted storehouse breaking of Room 76. The court upheld his conviction for burglary of Room 66 because the State had proven that one room of the motel to be a dwelling house. Thus, for the purposes of satisfying a necessary element of the crime of burglary, a separate unit of a building may be a separate dwelling house. These cases support the conclusion that each separate apartment is a dwelling house under Art. 27, §6. . . .

Richmond next contends that the State was required to prove that he possessed the specific intent to burn, or *mens rea* that the act of burning shall have been "wilful and malicious" as to each apartment unit. The intent requirement as stated by Perkins and Boyce undermines that proposition:

> Lord Coke, writing in the early 1600's said that the 'law doth sometime imply, that the house was burnt maliciously and voluntarily,' giving as an illustration the instance of a fire

spreading and causing damage beyond that actually intended. It is not common-law arson for a dweller to burn his own dwelling, and this has given rise to the outstanding example of unintentional arson; for if such a fire obviously creates an unreasonable fire hazard for other nearby dwellings, and any of these is actually burned, common-law arson has been committed even if the wrongdoer did not actually intend the consequence and may have hoped it would not happen. An intentional act creating an obvious fire hazard to the dwelling of another, done without justification, excuse or mitigation, might well be characterized as 'wilful' (a word of many meanings), and would certainly be malicious, but as the law has developed it is a mistake to assume that the phrase 'wilful and malicious,' when found in the definition of common-law arson, adds some distinct requirement not included in the word 'malicious' alone.

R. Perkins and R. Boyce, *Criminal Law* 274–75 (3d ed. 1982). Consequently, setting a fire with reckless and wanton disregard for the consequences satisfies the wilful and malicious requirement of Art. 27, §6. Clearly, setting fire to one apartment in a multiple unit apartment building satisfies this requirement. Moreover, the fact that Richmond was convicted of procuring the arson is of no consequence. Richmond's act of procuring is, in itself, a substantive offense, and he is subject to the same punishment as though he, himself, had actually perpetrated the burning. . . .

For all of the foregoing reasons, Richmond's convictions and sentences for procuring the burning of three separate apartments within one apartment building do not offend the Double Jeopardy Clause.

JUDGMENTS AFFIRMED, WITH COSTS TO BE PAID BY APPELLANT.

3. Michigan's Arson and Burning Statute

Michigan's Arson and Burning statutes M.C.L. §§750.71–78, represent a typical way in which states have codified the common law crime of arson. Below are four sections of the statute—the definition section and the sections covering first degree, second degree, and third degree arson. In reviewing the statute, note how the meaning of "dwelling" has been expanded.

M.C.L. §750.71. Definitions

Unless the context requires otherwise, the following terms have the following meanings:
(a) "Building" includes any structure regardless of class or character and any building or structure that is within the curtilage of that

building or structure or that is appurtenant to or connected to that building or structure.

(b) "Burn" means setting fire to, or doing any act that results in the starting of a fire, or aiding, counseling, inducing, persuading, or procuring another to do such an act.

(c) "Damage", in addition to its ordinary meaning, includes, but is not limited to, charring, melting, scorching, burning, or breaking.

(d) "Dwelling" includes, but is not limited to, any building, structure, vehicle, watercraft, or trailer adapted for human habitation that was actually lived in or reasonably could have been lived in at the time of the fire or explosion and any building or structure that is within the curtilage of that dwelling or that is appurtenant to or connected to that dwelling.

(e) "Individual" means any individual and includes, but is not limited to, a firefighter, law enforcement officer, or other emergency responder, whether paid or volunteer, performing his or her duties in relation to a violation of this chapter, or performing an investigation of a violation of this chapter.

(f) "Personal property" includes any personally owned property regardless of class, character, or value.

(g) "Physical injury" means an injury that includes, but is not limited to, the loss of a limb or use of a limb; loss of a foot, hand, finger, or thumb, or loss of use of a foot, hand, finger, or thumb; loss of an eye or ear or loss of use of an eye or ear; loss or substantial impairment of a bodily function; serious visible disfigurement; a comatose state that lasts for more than 3 days; measurable brain or mental impairment; a skull fracture or other serious bone fracture; subdural hemorrhage or subdural hematoma; loss of an organ; heart attack; heat stroke; heat exhaustion; smoke inhalation; a burn including a chemical burn; or poisoning.

(h) "Prior conviction" means a previous conviction for a violation of this chapter that arises out of a separate transaction, whether under this chapter, a local ordinance substantially corresponding to this chapter, a law of the United States substantially corresponding to this chapter, or a law of another state substantially corresponding to this chapter, but does not include a violation of section 79(1)(a).

M.C.L. §750.72. First degree arson

(1) A person who willfully or maliciously burns, damages, or destroys by fire or explosive any of the following or its contents is guilty of first degree arson:

(a) A multiunit building or structure in which 1 or more units of the building are a dwelling, regardless of whether any of the units are occupied, unoccupied, or vacant at the time of the fire or explosion.

(b) Any building or structure or other real property if the fire or explosion results in physical injury to any individual.

(c) A mine.

(2) Subsection (1) applies regardless of whether the person owns the dwelling, building, structure, or mine or its contents.

(3) First degree arson is a felony punishable by imprisonment for life or any term of years or a fine of not more than $20,000.00 or 3 times the value of the property damaged or destroyed, whichever is greater, or both imprisonment and a fine.

M.C.L. §750.73. Second degree arson

(1) Except as provided in section 72, a person who willfully or maliciously burns, damages, or destroys by fire or explosive a dwelling, regardless of whether it is occupied, unoccupied, or vacant at the time of the fire or explosion, or its contents, is guilty of second degree arson.

(2) Subsection (1) applies regardless of whether the person owns the dwelling or its contents.

(3) Second degree arson is a felony punishable by imprisonment for not more than 20 years or a fine of not more than $20,000.00 or 3 times the value of the property damaged or destroyed, whichever is greater, or both imprisonment and a fine.

M.C.L. §750.74. Third degree arson

(1) Except as provided in sections 72 and 73, a person who does any of the following is guilty of third degree arson:

(a) Willfully or maliciously burns, damages, or destroys by fire or explosive any building or structure, or its contents, regardless of whether it is occupied, unoccupied, or vacant at the time of the fire or explosion.

(b) Willfully and maliciously burns, damages, or destroys by fire or explosive any of the following or its contents:

(i) Any personal property having a value of $20,000.00 or more.

(ii) Any personal property having a value of $1,000.00 or more if the person has 1 or more prior convictions.

(2) Subsection (1) applies regardless of whether the person owns the building, structure, other real property or its contents, or the personal property.

(3) Third degree arson is a felony punishable by imprisonment for not more than 10 years or a fine of not more than $20,000.00 or 3 times the value of the property damaged or destroyed, whichever is greater, or both imprisonment and a fine.

Chapter 8
Theft Offenses

A. Introduction

This chapter will explore the common law theft offenses of larceny, embezzlement, and false pretenses. They are all specific intent crimes. At very early common law, only forcible appropriations of property (i.e., robbery) were prosecuted. As England became more commercial and trade increased, various economic pressures led to the common law development of additional theft offenses in order to respond to the varying types of dishonest conduct. Eventually, it became apparent that the crime of larceny was not sufficient to address the various types of theft. This led to the development of the additional theft offenses. However, this development was neither seamless nor necessarily logical. Inasmuch as larceny was punishable by death, the possibility of capital punishment may have influenced the development of the law. Thus, rather than creating new theft crimes, the common law courts often engaged in a strained interpretation of larceny.

Unfortunately, what we are left with is a complicated body of law concerning the theft offenses. The distinctions can be very thin. In order to assist you in determining which theft offense is applicable, the following questions may be helpful. They include: (1) whether the initial taking of the owner's rights was trespassory (larceny); (2) whether the trespassory taking was fraudulent (larceny by trick); (3) whether the defendant legally had possession (embezzlement) or merely custody (larceny/larceny by trick) and then later converted the property; and (4) whether the defendant fraudulently obtained title (false pretenses) or merely possession (larceny by trick).

B. Larceny

Larceny is defined as the trespassory taking and carrying away of the personal property of another with the intent to permanently deprive. The actus reus of this crime is the trespassory taking and carrying away of the personal property of another. The mens rea is the intent to permanently deprive.

1. Trespassory Taking

Because the first element can be the most challenging, it is important that you focus on the initial transfer of the property, as this will define the eventual crime, if any. The focus of this first element, therefore, is whether the defendant obtained possession of the rightful owner's property without her consent.

There are three ways to satisfy the trespass requirement. They are: (1) asks, but lies; (2) takes without asking; and (3) mistaken transfer with knowledge of the mistake at the time of transfer.

a. "Asks, but lies."

Assume *A* asks to borrow a watch from *B* and promises to return it by the end of the day. In fact, *A* intends to keep the watch. As you read *Pear*, consider what the defendant tells the owner of the horse at the time he rented it and what his actual intent was with respect to the use of the horse.

The King v. Pear, 168 Eng. Rep. 208 (1779)

This case was reserved by Mr. Justice Ashhurst, at the Old Bailey in September Session 1779.

The prisoner was indicted for stealing a black horse, the property of Samuel Finch. It appeared in evidence that Samuel Finch was a Livery-Stable-keeper in the Borough; and that the prisoner, on the 2d of July 1779, hired the horse of him to go to *Sutton*, in the county of *Surry*, and back again, saying on being asked where he lived, that he lodged at No. 25 in King-street, and should return about eight o'clock the same evening. He did not return; and it was proved that he had sold the horse on the very day he had hired it, to one *William Hollist*, in Smithfield Market; and that he had no lodging at the place to which he had given the prosecutor directions.

The learned judge said: There had been different opinions on the law of this class of cases; that the general doctrine then was that if a horse be let for a particular portion of time, and after that time is expired, the party hiring, instead of returning the horse to its owner, sell it and convert the money to his own use, it is felony, because there is then no *privity of contract* subsisting between the parties; that in the present case the horse was hired to take a journey into *Surry*, and the prisoner sold him the same day, without taking any such journey; that there were also other circumstances which imported that at the time of the hiring the prisoner had it in intention to sell the horse, as his saying that he lodged at a place where in fact he was not known. He therefore left it with the Jury to consider, Whether the prisoner meant *at the time of the hiring* to take such journey, but was *afterwards* tempted to sell the horse? for if so he must be acquitted; but that if they were of opinion that at the time of the hiring the journey was a mere pretence to get the horse into his possession, and he had no intention to take such journey but intended to sell the horse, they would find that fact specially for the opinion of the Judges.

The Jury found that the facts above stated were true; and also that the prisoner had hired the horse with a fraudulent view and intention of selling it immediately.

The question was referred to the Judges, Whether the delivery of the horse by the prosecutor to the prisoner, had so far changed the possession of the property, as to render the subsequent conversion of it a mere breach of trust, or whether the conversion was felonious?

The Judges differed greatly in opinion on this case; and delivered their opinions *seriatim* upon it at Lord Chief Justice DeGray's house on 4th February 1780 and on the 22nd of the same month Mr. Baron Perryn delivered their opinion on it.[a1] The majority of them thought, That the question, as to the original intention of the prisoner in hiring the horse, had been properly left to the jury; and as they had found, that his view in so doing was fraudulent, the parting with the *property* had not changed the nature of the *possession*, but that it remained unaltered in the prosecutor at the time of the conversion; and that the prisoner was therefore guilty of felony.[a2]

b. "Takes without asking."

In *Pear*, the property was obtained by fraud and not returned (larceny by trick). As you read *Banks,* consider how *Banks* differs from *Pear* and what the "loophole," or gap, in the law is that prevented Banks's conviction.

[a1] This Judgment it seems was settled, and approved by several of the Judges before it was delivered . . . .

[a2] At the Old Bailey in October Session, 1729, *John Tunnard* was tried before Lord Chief Justice Raymond, present Mr. Baron Hale and Mr. Justice Denton, for stealing a brown mare, the property of *Henry Smith*. It appeared in evidence, that the prosecutor lived in the Isle of Ely; that he lent the prisoner the mare to ride to a place three miles distant; but that instead of riding the three miles according to the agreement, the prisoner rode her up to London, and sold her. Lord Chief Justice Raymond left it with the Jury *quo animo* he had ridden the mare to *London*, and they found him guilty.—The Court. The finding of the Jury will make this case felony, because he rode the mare farther than he had agreed to do; for if there had been no special agreement the privity would have remained, and it could not have been felony.

Rex v. Banks, 168 Eng. Rep. 887 (1821)

The prisoner was tried and convicted before Mr. Justice Bayley, at the Lancaster Lent assizes, in the year 1821, for horse-stealing.

It appeared that the prisoner borrowed a horse, under pretence of carrying a child to a neighbouring surgeon. Whether he carried the child thither did not appear; but the day following, after the purpose for which he borrowed the horse was over, he took the horse in a different direction and sold it.

The prisoner did not offer the horse for sale, but was applied to to [sic] sell it, so that it was possible he might have had no felonious intention till that application was made.

The jury thought the prisoner had no felonious intention when he took the horse; but as it was borrowed for a special purpose, and that purpose was over when the prisoner took the horse to the place where he sold it, the learned judge thought it right upon the authority of 2 Russ. 1089, 1090,[a] to submit to the consideration of the judges, whether the subsequent disposing of the horse, when the purpose for which it was borrowed was no longer in view, did not in law include in it a felonious taking?

In Easter term, 1821, the judges met and considered this case. They were of opinion that the doctrine laid down on this subject in 2 Russ. 1089 & 1090, was not correct. They held that if the prisoner had not a felonious intention when he originally took the horse, his subsequent withholding and disposing of it did not constitute a new felonious taking, or make him guilty of felony; consequently the conviction could not be supported.

c. Mistaken Transfer with Knowledge of the Mistake at the Time of Transfer

The third method for establishing a trespassory taking concerns a situation where the victim mistakenly gives the defendant possession of property. Critically, the defendant *must* be aware of the mistake at the time the property is transferred for it to be considered a trespassory taking. You should focus on this issue as you study *Cooper.*

---

[a] In 2 Russ. 1089, it is said that, "In the case of a delivery of a horse upon hire or loan, if such delivery were obtained *bona fide,* no subsequent wrongful conversion pending the contract will amount to felony; and so of other goods. But when the purpose of the hiring, or loan, for which the delivery was made, has been ended, felony may be committed by a conversion of the goods."

Cooper et al. v. Commonwealth, 110 Ky. 123 (1901)

O'REAR, J.

Appellants, Grant Cooper, Fred Cooper, Thomas Harris, and Sandy Waggener, were convicted in the Union circuit court of the crime of grand larceny, under the following state of facts: The four named had been shucking corn, and were paid $6 for their services. In order to divide the money equally among themselves, they went to the Bank of Uniontown to have $2 of the money changed into smaller denominations. Appellant Sandy Waggener went into the bank and to the cashier's counter, handed him the $2, and asked for the change. The cashier handed him two half dollars and a roll of small-sized coin wrapped in paper, saying, "There are twenty nickels." Waggener, without unwrapping the coins, and not knowing what was in the paper, except from the statement of the cashier, rejoined his companions; and the four together went a distance of some four squares, to a more secluded spot, to divide their money. On opening the package they discovered it contained 20 5-dollar gold coins, instead of nickels. Waggener remarked, "Boys, banks don't correct mistakes," and the money was divided among the four and appropriated by them. Upon this evidence the court gave the jury the following instruction: "If you believe from the evidence, to the exclusion of a reasonable doubt, that in this county, and prior to the finding of the indictment herein, the defendants, Grant Cooper, Fred Cooper, and Thos. [sic] Harris, and Sandy Waggener, sought to have some money changed at the Bank of Uniontown in order to get twenty nickels, or some small change, and that Chas. Kelleners, the assistant cashier of said bank, in making said change delivered by mistake to the defendants twenty five-dollar gold pieces, wrapped in a paper, believing at the time that he was giving them twenty nickels, and that the defendants, sharing in that belief, shortly thereafter opened said paper, and found therein twenty five-dollar gold pieces, and failed to return said gold pieces to said bank—Now, if you further believe from the evidence, to the exclusion of a reasonable doubt, that when said defendants unwrapped said paper, and found therein, and in their possession, the said five-dollar gold pieces, they knew that same had been delivered to them by said Kelleners through mistake, and knew or had the means of ascertaining that the bank was the owner of said gold pieces, but thereupon nevertheless feloniously converted the same to their own use, intending to permanently deprive the owner thereof, you will find them guilty as charged; and in your verdict you will fix their punishment at confinement in the penitentiary for not less than one nor more than five years." Appellants objected to the foregoing, and asked the court to give the jury these instructions: "(a) The court instructs the jury that, to find the defendants guilty of larceny, they must believe that at the time they received the money from Chas. Kelleners they must have then had the purpose and intent to convert the excess which they received over and above what was justly due them as change to their own use and benefit, and to deprive the bank of its money feloniously; that, unless the felonious intent was proven at the time of the receiving of the money, the law is for the defendants, and the jury will so find. (b) The court instructs the jury that the felonious intent must exist at the time of receiving the money, and that no felonious intent, subsequent or wrongful conversion, will amount to a felony,"—which were rejected by the court.

It was held in Elliott v. Com., 12 Bush, 176, that where the possession of the goods was obtained by the accused for a particular purpose, with the intent then, however, on the part of the accused, to convert them to his own use, which he subsequently did, it would constitute larceny. In Snapp v. Com., 82 Ky. 173, we held that, where money came into the hands of the accused lawfully, his subsequent felonious conversion would not be larceny. In the last-named case the court said it devolved upon the commonwealth to show an unlawful taking of this money from the city (the owner) by the accused with a felonious intent, and that "the money had been received without fraud and as a matter of right, and in such a case, although he may have the animus furandi afterwards, and convert it to his own use, he was not guilty of larceny." In Smith v. Com., 96 Ky. 87, this court announced, "The general and common-law rule is that when property comes lawfully into the possession of a person, either as agent, bailee, part owner, or otherwise, a subsequent appropriation of it is not larceny, unless the intent to appropriate it existed in the mind of the taker at the time it came into his hands." Whart. Cr. Law, §958, says, "To constitute larceny in receiving an overpayment, the defendant must know at the time of the overpayment, and must intend to steal." The authorities seem to be agreed that, to constitute the crime of larceny, there must be a simultaneous combination of an unlawful taking, an asportation, and a felonious intent.

We conclude that the instructions asked by appellants should have been given to the jury, and that the idea expressed in the first instruction given,—that if appellants received the money under a mutual mistake, and after discovering it feloniously converted it,—should not have been given. Judgment reversed and cause remanded for a new trial, and for proceedings consistent herewith.

d. Continuing Trespass

Typically, the specific intent to steal coincided with a trespassory taking. What about a situation when the intent to steal comes *after* there has been a trespassory taking? Is that still larceny? As you read *Coombs*, consider (1) if there had been a trespassory taking and (2) when the intent to steal developed.

State v. Coombs, 55 Me. 477 (1868)

DICKERSON, J.

Exceptions. The prisoner was indicted for the larceny of a horse, sleigh and buffalo robes. The jury were instructed that, if the prisoner obtained possession of the team by falsely and fraudulently pretending that he wanted it to drive to a certain place, and to be gone a specified time, when in fact he did not intend to go to such place, but to a more distant one, and to be absent a longer time, without intending at the time to steal the property, the team was not lawfully in his possession, and that a subsequent conversion of it to his own use, with a felonious intent while thus using it, would be larceny.

It is well settled that where one comes lawfully into possession of the goods of another, with his consent, a subsequent felonious conversion of them to his own use, without the owner's consent, does not constitute larceny, because the felonious intent is wanting at the time of the taking.

But how is it when the taking is fraudulent or tortious, and the property is subsequently converted to the use of the taker with a felonious intent? Suppose one takes his neighbor's horse from the stable, without consent, to ride him to a neighboring town, with the intention to return him, but subsequently sells him and converts the money to his own use, without his neighbor's consent, is he a mere trespasser, or is he guilty of larceny? In other words, must the felonious intent exist at the time of the original taking, when that is fraudulent or tortious, to constitute larceny?

When property is thus obtained, the taking or trespass is continuous. The wrongdoer holds it all the while without right, and against the right and without the consent of the owner. If at this point no other element is added, there is no larceny. But, if to such taking there be subsequently superadded a felonious intent, that is, an intent to deprive the owner of his property permanently without color of right, or excuse, and to make it the property of the taker without the owner's consent, the crime of larceny is complete. "A felonious intent," observes Baron PARKE, in *Regina v. Holloway*, 2 Cor. & Kir., 61 E. C. L., 944, "means to deprive the owner, not temporarily, but permanently of his own property, without color of right or excuse for the act, and to convert it to the taker's use without the consent of the owner."

The case of *Regina v. Steer*, 61 E. C. L., 988, is in harmony with this doctrine. The prosecutor let the prisoner have his horse to sell for him; he did not sell it, but put it at a livery stable. The prosecutor directed the keeper of the stable not to give up the horse to the prisoner, and told the prisoner he must not have the horse again, to which the prisoner replied, "well." The prisoner got possession of the horse by telling a false story to the servant of the keeper of the stable, and made off with him. The case was reserved, and the Court held the prisoner guilty of larceny. *Commonwealth v. White*, 11 Cush., 483.

In the case at bar, the prisoner obtained possession of the property by fraud. This negatives the idea of a contract, or that the possession of the prisoner was a lawful one, when he sold the horse. He was not the bailee of the owner, but was a wrongdoer from the beginning; and the owner had a right to reclaim his property at any time. It has been decided that when a person hires a horse to go to a certain place, and goes beyond that place, that the subsequent act is tortious and that trover may be maintained, on the ground of a wrongful taking and conversion. *Morton v. Gloster*, 46 Maine, 520.

In contemplation of law, the wrongful act was continuous, and, when to that act the prisoner subsequently added the felonious intent, that is, the purpose to deprive the owner of his property permanently, without color of right or excuse, and to convert it to his own use without the consent of the owner, the larceny became complete from that moment. The color of consent to the possession obtained by fraud, does not change the character of the offence from larceny to trespass or other wrongful act. In such case it is not necessary that the felonious intent should exist at the time of the original taking to constitute larceny, the wrongful taking being all the while continuous.

It is to be observed that this principle does not apply in cases where the owner parted with his property and not the possession merely, as in the case of a sale procured by fraud or false pretences. In such instances there is no larceny, however gross the fraud by which the property was obtained. *Mawrey v. Walsh*, 8 Cowen, 238; *Ross v. The People*, 5 Hill, 294. "It is difficult to distinguish such a case from larceny," remarks Mr. Justice COWEN, in *Ross v. The People*; "and were the question res nova in this Court, I, for one, would follow the decision in *Rex v. Campbell*, 1 Mood. Cr. Cases, 179. The decisions, however, are the other way, even in England, with the single exception of that case, and they have long been followed here. There is nothing so palpably absurd in this as to warrant our overruling them."

We are unable to discover any error in the instructions of the presiding Judge.

Exceptions overruled.
Judgment for the State.

Note

How does *Coombs* compare to *Pear*? Did both cases involve a trespassory taking? When did each defendant develop the intent to steal? Did the defendant in *Coombs* commit larceny?

Coombs illustrates one of the legal fictions that developed at common law. As noted at the beginning of this chapter, larceny was a crime punishable by death at common law. As a result, this may have influenced the way judges considered larceny. The continuous trespass doctrine thus broadened the reach of the crime of larceny and arguably the application of the death penalty.

2. Carrying Away

The defendant must gain possession of the property either directly or through an agent or instrumentality. In addition, the defendant must make some movement (asportation) for the purpose of carrying it away. In *Thompson*, as well as the subsequent case of *People v. Khoury*, the courts considered how much control and asportation is necessary.

Thompson v. State, 94 Ala. 535 (1892)

WALKER, J.

The witness for the state testified that he held out his open hand, with two silver dollars therein, showing the money to the defendant; that the defendant struck witness' hand, and the money was either knocked out of his hand, or was taken by the defendant, he could not tell positively which. It was after 12 o'clock at night, and the witness did not see the money either in defendant's possession or on the ground. The court charged the jury: "If the jury find from the evidence that the defendant, with a felonious intent, grabbed for the money, but did not get it, but only knocked it from the owner's hand with a felonious intent, this would be a sufficient carrying away of the money, although defendant never got possession at any time of said money." This charge was erroneous. To constitute larceny, there must be a felonious taking and carrying away of personal property. There must be such a caption that the accused acquires dominion over the property, followed by such an asportation or carrying away as to supersede the possession of the owner for an appreciable period of time. Though the owner's possession is disturbed, yet the offense is not complete if the accused fails to acquire such dominion over the property as to enable him to take actual custody or control. It is not enough that the money was knocked out of the owner's hand, if it fell to the ground, and the defendant never got control of it. The defendant was not guilty of larceny, if he did not get the money under his control. If the attempt merely caused the money to fall from the owner's hand to the ground, and the defendant ran off without getting it, the larceny was not consummated, as the dominion of the trespasser was not complete. Charge No. 1 was a proper statement of the law as applicable to the evidence above referred to, and it should have been given. Reversed and remanded.

People v. Khoury, 166 Cal. Rptr. 705 (1980)

FAINER, J.

Defendant appeals his conviction, by jury trial, for violation of Penal Code section 487, subdivision 1 (grand theft). The pertinent facts of this case were that defendant, after being observed for several hours pushing a shopping cart around a Fed Mart Store, was seen pushing a cart, with a large cardboard chandelier box on it, up to a checkstand in the store. An alert cashier at the checkstand, noticing that the box was loosely taped, stated that he would have to open and check the contents of the box before he would allow defendant to pay the price marked and remove the box from the store. Defendant then walked back through the checkstand and into the store, leaving the box with the cashier. Defendant was arrested by store security after the box was opened, disclosing in excess of $900 worth of store items, consisting of batteries, tools, and chain saws, but no chandelier.

Defendant contends that these facts were insufficient evidence to convict him of grand theft. More specifically, defendant contends that the evidence was insufficient to show an asportation or carrying away of the personal property of the Fed Mart Store and therefore was, at most, an attempt to commit grand theft.

Our function on appeal in this case is to determine first the applicable law of theft by larceny, which is the theft for which defendant was specifically charged, and then to examine the record to ascertain whether there was substantial evidence of the disputed element of the crime to support the judgment of conviction.

The crime of larceny is the stealing or taking of the property of another. (Pen. Code, §484.) "The completed crime of larceny—as distinguished from an attempt—requires asportation or carrying away, in addition to the taking. [Citations omitted.]" "The element of asportation is not satisfied unless it is shown that 'the goods were severed from the possession or custody of the owner, and in the possession of the thief, though it be but for a moment.' " (*Ibid.*)

The other element of theft by larceny is the specific intent in the mind of the perpetrator ". . . to deprive the owner permanently of his property . . . ."

The sufficiency of the evidence to support a finding of intent is not a claim of error on this appeal but is important in reviewing the jury's determination of the existence of the element of asportation or carrying away, a question of fact. The jury was instructed that "[I]n order to constitute a carrying away, the property need not be . . . actually removed from the premises of the owner. Any removal of the property from the place where it was kept or placed by the owner, done with the specific intent to deprive the owner permanently of his property . . . , whereby the perpetrator obtains possession and control of the property for any period of time, is sufficient to constitute the element of carrying away." (CALJIC No. 14.03.)

The cases make a distinction between fact patterns in which the defendant takes possession of the owner's property and moves it with the intent to carry it away, so that it is not attached to any other property of the owner and those cases in which a thief is frustrated in his attempt to carry the property away. All of the cases cited above make it clear that the property does not have to be actually removed from the premises of the owner. The jury was properly instructed as to the necessary elements of the crime of theft by larceny. They were not told that there could be no taking or carrying away or asportation unless defendant was able to get the chandelier box containing other store property past the cashier. This was a factor to be considered by the jury, as the trier of fact, in determining whether there was or was not an asportation.

The defendant was seen pushing a shopping cart carrying a carton or container for packaging a chandelier; the chandelier had been removed from the carton and the items already described, of a value of $900, were in the carton. The carton was taped. It was the recent taping of the carton that prompted the cashier not to permit the defendant to go through the check stand until the contents of the carton were checked. The defendant, on being informed of this, walked back into the store, leaving the carton behind. These facts, and the reasonable inferences which can be drawn therefrom support the jury's finding of asportation by substantial evidence.

The intent to permanently deprive the store of its merchandise was clear. The defendant in this appeal does not even attempt to negate the element of intent by proof of innocence [sic] though careless mistake.

The judgment of conviction is affirmed.

3. Personal Property

At common law, the theft must be of personal property. Real estate was not protected inasmuch as it could not be taken and carried away. Similarly it did not extend to intangible personal property, such as labor or services. *See* Wayne Lafave, *Criminal Law* §19.4 (5th ed. 2010).

4. Of Another

The common law required that the defendant must invade a superior possessory interest in the property. Thus, notwithstanding ownership of the property, a person may be convicted of larceny if, for example, a landlord takes and carries away personal property from leased premises which he owns.

State v. Cohen, 196 Minn. 39 (1935)

HOLT, Justice.

Defendant was charged and convicted of the crime of grand larceny in the second degree and appeals from the judgment.

The main assignment of error is that the verdict is not supported by the evidence and that it is contrary to law. There is evidence from which the jury could find substantially as follows: In November, 1934, defendant owned a Hudson seal fur coat, which needed certain alterations and repairs, such as to be made longer and more ample in girth, and new lining and a new collar. Her husband engaged one Mellon, a furrier, to do the work and furnish the materials needed for $50. In the negotiations the husband represented that the owner of the coat was a customer by the name of Mrs. Sbroe. When the work was done Mellon and his brother made efforts to deliver the coat and get the money. Defendant found fault with the way the alterations were made. At one time when Mellon's brother brought the coat to her home and demanded the money she wanted to keep the coat, but at last surrendered possession, when he told her he would be held responsible. Finally, on January 2, 1935, Mellon took it to her home for the fourth time and requested payment. She tried the coat on, thought it was too long, and stated she desired to go back in her apartment where there was a long mirror to see how it looked. She went back, but returned without the coat, and when Mellon demanded the coat or his money she told him he could have neither. A detective and Mellon's lawyer were called and came. Defendant refused to tell what she had done with the coat. The apartment was searched, but the coat was not found there. On the trial she gave this testimony concerning the matter:

"Q. Where did you take the coat? A. Well, it is my coat. Can't I do anything I want?

"Q. I am asking you where you took it? A. I don't know where I took it. It was in the house.

"Q. Where in the house? A. I don't know; around the house.

"Q. In your house, in your flat? A. Yes.

"Q. Where? A. Well what do you mean where?

"Q. Don't you know what 'where' means? Where did you put it? A. Well, I did not have it in the house.

"Q. Where did you take it? A. I just took it.

"Q. Where? A. I locked it up in a closet."

This kind of testimony continued for some time without divulging where she took the coat. The next day it was in the possession of a downtown store, where it was kept until the trial. The jury could well conclude that from the start defendant and her husband planned to obtain the work and labor on the coat and repossess it without paying therefor. The jury was well justified in not believing a witness who thus evades and contradicts herself upon a matter of which she could not be ignorant. She got possession of the coat by subterfuge and fraud and carried it away and concealed it. We think she could be found guilty. Her felonious intent to deprive Mellon of his lien is apparent from her actions.

The verdict is not contrary to law. A person may be guilty of larceny of his own property, if taken from the possession of one who has a lien thereon under which possession may lawfully be retained until the lien is discharged. Sections 8507 and 8508, Mason's Minn.St. 1927, gave a possessory lien to Mellon, and the way defendant procured the coat to see how it looked on her person does not, as a matter of law, bring her within the protection of section 10372, Mason's Minn.St. 1927. On the contrary, the jury had warrant for finding that defendant's scheme of trying on the coat and disappearing with it was with the felonious intent of depriving Mellon of his lien and his right of possession until the lien was discharged. An owner of personal property may be found guilty of larceny thereof when he wrongfully takes it from a pledgee or from one whom he has given possession for the purpose of having it cared for or repaired under statutes such as ours giving a lien therefor and the right to retain possession until the lien is paid. State v. Hubbard, 126 Kan. 129, where the authorities are cited, and this conclusion therefrom is stated: "If personal property in the possession on one other than the general owner by virtue of some special right or title is taken from him by the general owner, such taking is larceny if it is done with the felonious intent of depriving such person of his rights or of charging him with the value of the property." . . .

The conviction is affirmed.

Note

What if the victim had no right to possess the property? Can a thief steal from a thief? *See, e.g., People v. Otis*, 235 N.Y. 421 (1923).

5. Intent to Permanently Deprive

The mens rea required for larceny is intent to permanently deprive the victim of his or her possessory interest.

People v. Brown, 105 Cal. 66 (1894)

GAROUTTE, J.

The appellant was convicted of the crime of burglary, alleged by the information to have been committed in entering a certain house with intent to commit grand larceny. The entry is conceded, and also it is conceded that appellant took therefrom a certain bicycle, the property of the party named in the information, and of such a value as to constitute grand larceny. The appellant is a boy of seventeen years of age, and for a few days immediately prior to the taking of the bicycle was staying at the place from which the machine was taken, working for his board. He took the stand as a witness, and testified: "I took the wheel to get even with the boy, and of course I didn't intend to keep it. I just wanted to get even with him. The boy was throwing oranges at me in the evening, and he would not stop when I told him to, and it made me mad, and I left Yount's house Saturday morning. I thought I would go back and take the boy's wheel. He had a wheel, the one I had the fuss with. Instead of getting hold of his, I got Frank's, but I intended to take it back Sunday night; but before I got back they caught me. I took it down by the grove, and put it on the ground, and covered it with brush, and crawled in, and Frank came and hauled off the brush and said: 'What are you doing here'? Then I told him . . . I covered myself up in the brush so that they could not find me until evening, until I could take it back. I did not want them to find me. I expected to remain there during the day, and not go back until evening." Upon the foregoing state of facts the court gave the jury the following instruction: "I think it is not necessary to say very much to you in this case. I may say, generally, that I think counsel for the defense here stated to you in this argument very fairly the principles of law governing this case, except in one particular. In defining to you the crime of grand larceny he says it is essential that the taking of it must be felonious. That is true; the taking with the intent to deprive the owner of it; but he adds the conclusion that you must find that the taker intended to deprive him of it permanently. I do not think that is the law. I think in this case, for example, if the defendant took this bicycle, we will say for the purpose of riding twenty-five miles, for the purpose of enabling him to get away, and then left it for another to get it, and intended to do nothing else except to help himself away for a certain distance, it would be larceny, just as much as though he intended to take it all the while. A man may take a horse, for instance, not with the intent to convert it wholly and permanently to his own use, but to ride it to a certain distance, for a certain purpose he may have, and then leave it. He converts it to that extent to his own use and purpose feloniously." This instruction is erroneous, and demands a reversal of the judgment. If the boy's story be true he is not guilty of larceny in taking the machine; yet, under the instruction of the court, the words from his own mouth convicted him. The court told the jury that larceny may be committed, even though it was only the intent of the party taking the property to deprive the owner of it temporarily. We think the authorities form an unbroken line to the effect that the felonious intent must be to deprive the owner of the property permanently. The illustration contained in the instruction as to the man taking the horse is too broad in its terms as stating a correct principle of law. Under the circumstances depicted by the illustration the man might, and again he might not, be guilty of larceny. It would be a pure question of fact for the jury, and dependent for its true solution upon all the circumstances surrounding the transaction. But the test of law to be applied to these circumstances for the purpose of determining the ultimate fact as to the man's guilt or innocence is, did he intend to permanently deprive the owner of his property? If he did not intend so to do, there is no felonious intent, and his acts constitute but a trespass. While the felonious intent of the party taking need not necessarily be an intention to convert the property to his own use, still it must in all cases be an intent to wholly and permanently deprive the owner thereof. For the foregoing reasons it is ordered that the judgment and order be reversed and the cause remanded for a new trial.

C. Statutory Gap Fillers

1. Embezzlement

Larceny is a common law offense that requires a trespassory taking. Unlike larceny, embezzlement is not a common law offense. It involves a situation where the defendant was already in *lawful* possession of the property. Because larceny did not cover this situation, economic crimes like embezzlement and false pretenses were legislatively created. Although embezzlement is not a traditional common law offense, it is so old that it is treated as being one. The elements for this offense are: (1) fraudulent conversion, that is, the defendant has taken some action to permanently deprive the owner of his property (e.g., sells the property); (2) of personal property; (3) of another; (4) by a defendant in lawful possession, that is, substantial discretion and control over the property, as a result of a trust relationship; (5) with intent to permanently deprive (often referred to as "fraudulently" or with the intent to use the property in a manner inconsistent with the trust relationship).

a. Embezzlement Is Not Larceny

Is it common law larceny for a bank teller to accept a customer's money for the bank and then take it for himself? The court in *Bazeley* was faced with this issue.

The King v. Bazeley, 168 Eng. Rep. 517 (1799)

At the Old Bailey in February Session 1799, *Joseph Bazeley* was tried before John Silvester, Esq. *Common Serjeant* of the city of *London*, for feloniously stealing on the 18th January preceding, a Bank-note of the value of one hundred pounds, the property of *Peter Esdaile, Sir Benjamin Hammett, William Esdaile,* and *John Hammett*.

The following facts appeared in evidence. The prisoner, *Joseph Bazeley*, was the principal teller at the house of Messrs. *Esdaile's* and *Hammett's*, bankers, in *Lombard-street*, at the salary of £100 a year, and his duty was to receive and pay money, notes, and bills, at the counter. The manner of conducting the business of this banking-house is as follows: There are four tellers, each of whom has a separate money-book, a separate money-drawer, and a separate bag. The prisoner being the chief teller, the total of the receipts and payments of all the other money-books were every evening copied into his, and the total balance or rest, as it is technically called, struck in his book, and the balances of the other money-books paid, by the other tellers, over to him. When any monies, whether in cash or notes, are brought by customers to the counter to be paid in, the teller who receives it counts it over, then enters the Bank-notes or drafts, and afterwards the cash, under the customer's name, in his book; and then, after casting up the total, it is entered in the customer's book. The money is then put into the teller's bag, and the Bank-notes or other papers, if any, put into a box which stands on a desk behind the counter, directly before another clerk, who is called the cash book-keeper, who makes an entry of it in the received cash-book in the name of the person who has paid it in, and which he finds written by the receiving teller on the back of the bill or note so placed in the drawer. The prisoner was treasurer to an association called "The Ding Dong Mining Company"; and in the course of the year had many bills drawn on him by the Company, and many bills drawn on other persons remitted to him by the Company. In the month of January 1799, the prisoner had accepted bills on account of the Company, to the amount of £112, 4s. 1d. and had in his possession a bill of £166, 7s. 3d. belonging to the

Company, but which was not due until the 9th February. One of the bills, amounting to £100, which the prisoner had accepted, became due on 18th January. Mr. *William Gilbert*, a grocer, in the Surry-road, Black-friars, kept his cash at the banking-house of the prosecutors, and on the 18th January 1799, he sent his servant, *George Cock*, to pay in £137. This sum consisted of £122 in Bank-notes, and the rest in cash. One of these Bank-notes was the note which the prisoner was indicted for stealing. The prisoner received this money from *George Cock*, and after entering the £137 in Mr. *Gilbert's* Bank-book, entered the £15 cash in his own money-book, and put over the £22 in Bank-notes into the drawer behind him, keeping back the £100 Bank-note, which he put into his pocket, and afterwards paid to a banker's clerk the same day at a clearing-house in *Lombard-street*, in discharge of the £100 bill which he had accepted on account of the Ding Dong Mining Company. To make the sum in Mr. *Gilbert's* Bank-book, and the sum in the book of the banking-house agree, it appeared that a unit had been added to the entry of £37 to the credit of Mr. *Gilbert*, in the book of the banking-house, but it did not appear by any direct proof that this alteration had been made by the prisoner; it appeared however that he had made a confession, but the confession having been obtained under a promise of favour, it was not given in evidence.

Const and Jackson, *the prisoner's Counsel*, submitted to the Court, that to constitute a larceny, it was necessary in point of law that the property should be taken from *the possession* of the prosecutor, but that it was clear from the evidence in this case, that the Bank-note charged to have been stolen, never was either in the actual or the constructive possession of *Esdaile and Hammett*, and that even if it had been in their possession, yet that from the manner in which it had been secreted by the prisoner, it amounted only to a breach of trust.

The Court left the facts of the case to the consideration of the Jury, and on their finding the prisoner Guilty, the case was reserved for the opinion of the Twelve Judges on a question, whether under the circumstances above stated, *the taking* of the Bank-note was in law a *felonious taking*, or only a *fraudulent breach of trust*.

The case was accordingly argued before nine of the Judges in the Exchequer Chamber on Saturday, 27th April 1799, by Const *for the prisoner*, and by Fielding *for the Crown* . . . .

The Judges, it is said, were of opinion, upon the authority of *Rex v. Waite*, that this Bank-note never was in the legal custody or possession of the prosecutors, Messrs. *Esdailes* and *Hammett*; but no opinion was ever publicly delivered; and the prisoner was included in the Secretary of State's letter as a proper object for a pardon.

b.   What is the key distinction between larceny and embezzlement?

Shortly after the *Bazeley* case, Parliament enacted the first general embezzlement statute. What if the dishonest teller had placed the money in a cash draw and then took it? Would the result have been the same? In *Morgan v. Commonwealth*, the court explores the distinction between having lawful possession and converting the property (embezzlement) and merely having custody and thereafter keeping it (larceny).

Morgan v. Commonwealth, 242 Ky. 713 (1932)

DIETZMAN, C. J.

Appellant was convicted of the offense of grand larceny, sentenced to serve two years in the penitentiary, and appeals.

The undisputed facts in this case are these: The Western Union Telegraph Company has for a number of years maintained a local office in Irvine, Ky. In February, 1930, the appellant was put in full charge of this office. It is not clear how many employees were under him, but at least it is shown that there were a porter and a young lady employee who worked under his direction. The office was equipped with a safe. At the time appellant was put in charge of the office, the combination on this safe was reset and he was given a copy of it. Another copy of the combination was sealed in an envelope and sent to the main office of the company in Nashville, where it was placed among the archives not to be opened unless the appellant severed his connection with the company and it became necessary to ascertain what the combination was in order to get into the safe. Thus although the company could, by opening this sealed envelope, apprise itself of what the combination was, yet so long as appellant continued in its employ it remained in actual ignorance of the combination to the safe and the appellant was the only one who had actual access to the safe. Inside of the safe was a small portable steel vault or box, the keys to which were intrusted to appellant. In this steel vault or box appellant placed at night the funds which came into the office during the day, and in the morning took them out either for use as change, for deposit in bank, or to be forwarded to the company. On the morning of July 5, 1930, the safe was discovered open. Its handle and dial were broken off, and the steel vault or box which had in it approximately $90 of the funds of the company was missing. It was later discovered empty in a field near by appellant's boarding house. We shall assume for the purpose of the decision of this case, and without detailing the facts at length, that the commonwealth's proof made out a case to go to the jury that the abstraction of the steel vault from the safe and the conversion of the funds that it contained were done by the appellant. Appellant was indicted, as stated, for the offense of grand larceny, and he insists on this appeal that his motion for a peremptory instruction should have been sustained because the proof shows that if any offense was committed it was that of embezzlement and not larceny.

The main distinction between embezzlement and larceny in cases like the instant one turns on the distinction between custody and possession. We quote from the case of Warmoth v. Commonwealth, 81 Ky. 135:

"A distinction exists where a servant has merely the custody and where he has the possession of the goods. In the former case the felonious appropriation of the goods is larceny; in the latter it is not larceny, but embezzlement.

"The custody alluded to is such as that of a butler or house servant of household goods, a hired hand of the plow and horses of the farmer for whom he is laboring, etc., and the possession mentioned is an actual or constructive possession of the master or employer at the time the goods are taken. What constitutes such a possession in many cases requires some nicety of analysis to determine.

"Generally, where the agent has received goods or money to carry, deliver, control, or manage for the principal, unless the agent parts with the manual possession, and delivers the property to the principal or another for him, or places it in some depository, such as a drawer or safe provided for the purpose, and to which the principal or superior agents have access, or over which they have control, he cannot be convicted of larceny for a felonious appropriation of the goods or money, the offense being embezzlement. (Johnson v. Commonwealth, 5 Bush, page 431.)"

In 20 C. J. 410, it is said: "Embezzlement differs from larceny in that it is the wrongful appropriation or conversion of property where the original taking was lawful, or with the consent of the owner, while in larceny the taking involves a trespass, and the felonious intent must exist at the time of such taking. Thus, a bailee who obtains possession of property without fraudulent intent is not guilty of larceny where he subsequently converts it. So long as he has lawful possession he cannot commit a trespass with respect to the property. But where a person enters into a contract of bailment and obtains possession of the property with felonious intent, existing at the time, to appropriate or apply the property to his own use, he is guilty of a trespass and larceny, and not embezzlement, and if one enters into a contract of bailment fraudulently, but without felonious intent, and afterward converts the property, his offense is larceny and not embezzlement. If for any reason a bailment is terminated, so that the possession of the property vests again constructively in the owner, its subsequent conversion by the bailee before the owner has obtained actual possession, will amount to a trespass and larceny, and not embezzlement. It has been held, however, that where money has been voluntarily delivered to accused as agent, the fact that he formed the intent to appropriate it at or before the time he received it does not prevent a prosecution for embezzlement, although the offense may also constitute larceny. Since, therefore, larceny at common law involves the element of an original wrongful taking or trespass, it cannot apply to the stealing or wrongful conversion of property by an agent or bailee, or by a servant having the possession, as distinguished from the mere custody, or by anyone else intrusted with the possession of the property; and to remedy this defect and prevent an evasion of justice in such cases, statutes of embezzlement were passed."

Under the peculiar facts of this case, we are constrained to the view that at the time the appellant converted the funds here involved (as we have assumed the evidence so establishes) he had the possession as distinguished from the custody of such funds. They were in the safe, the combination of which was known actually only by him. It was intended, in the absence of some untoward circumstance, that at least until he forwarded these funds to the company they should be in his possession. They came into his possession as the servant of the Western Union. He was in full charge of the office. It was he who locked the safe at night and it was only he who could open it in the morning. Although the company had the right to demand the funds of him at any time, and although the company could potentially enter the safe by opening the sealed envelope and apprising itself of the combination, yet it was not intended by the company that it should interfere with appellant's control and possession of the contents of this safe and the funds of the company unless and until some condition which had not occurred in this case at the time of the conversion had come to pass. It is quite manifest that the possession of these funds at the time they were converted was in the appellant and that it had not yet become that of the Western Union. This being true, the conversion amounted to an embezzlement and not larceny. Warmoth v. Commonwealth, supra. The two offenses are not degrees of one another. They are distinct offenses. 20 C. J. 412. Hence appellant could not be convicted of the offense of larceny when it was shown that what he did constituted embezzlement and not larceny. It follows that appellant's motion for a peremptory instruction should have been sustained. Judgment reversed, with instructions to grant the appellant a new trial in conformity with this opinion.

c. Embezzlement and Larceny Distinguished

This matter of "larceny v. embezzlement" is again at issue in the following case. As you read *Stahl*, consider whether the defendant had merely custody or possession of the receptacles from where he was accused of stealing.

State v. Stahl, 93 N.M. 62 (1979)

WOOD, Chief Judge.

Defendant was convicted of embezzling over $100. To have embezzled the money, defendant must have been entrusted with the money. Section 30–16–8, N.M.S.A.1978. Defendant contends there is no evidence that he was entrusted with over $100. We agree.

Defendant was a clerk at a store. The store had two cash registers and a drop-box. There was a slit in the counter; money pushed through this slit went into the drop-box. The drop-box was locked with two padlocks, the keys to which were retained by the manager. When money accumulated in the registers, portions of the accumulation were placed in the drop-box through the slit in the counter.

About 7:30 p. m. on the night in question, the manager removed the money from the drop-box. About 11:00 p. m. the clerk on duty closed down one of the registers, placing the money from that register into the drop-box. When defendant went on duty at midnight, the one register being used contained $50 to $75. Defendant's shift was from midnight to 8:00 a.m. At 3:00 a.m., defendant was absent from the store. The drop-box had been pried open and its money removed. There is evidence that defendant took a total of $612 from the drop-box and the register being used.

Defendant was the only clerk on duty when the money was taken; he was "in charge of the whole store" and "responsible for the entire store." The register being used, and its contents, were for defendant's use in performing his duties. Defendant does not claim that he was not entrusted with the money in this register and does not contend that the money he took from this register was not embezzlement. However, there is no proof that the money taken from the register was over $100, and no proof that the amount of money in the register, plus money from sales after defendant went on duty, ever amounted to $100.

The State asserts that defendant was also entrusted with money which defendant took from the register and placed in the drop-box. We need not answer this contention because there is no evidence that defendant placed any money into the drop-box.

To reach a monetary amount over $100, the money taken from the drop-box must be included. Under the evidence, the money in the drop-box was put there by another clerk, and before defendant was on duty. Defendant did not have the keys to the drop-box, he had no permission or authority to get any money out of the box, he had no permission to have possession of the money in the drop-box, or "use it for change or anything . . . ." The only one supposed to take money from the drop-box was the manager. These facts are not disputed.

The trial court denied defendant's motion for a directed verdict on the charge of embezzlement over $100. Because defendant was in charge of the store, the trial court was of the view that defendant had been entrusted with "everything there on the premises" including the drop-box. We disagree; defendant had not been entrusted with the contents of the drop-box.

"Entrust" means to commit or surrender to another with a certain confidence regarding his care, use or disposal of that which has been committed or surrendered. The money in the drop-box would not have been entrusted to defendant unless the money came into defendant's possession by reason of his employment.

2 Wharton's Criminal Law and Procedure, §468 (1957) states:

> A clerk taking money or goods from his employer's safe,
> till or shelves is guilty of larceny unless he is authorized to

dispose of such money or goods at his discretion. An employee who feloniously appropriates to his own use property of his master or employer to which he has access only by reason of a mere physical propinquity as an incident of the employment, and not by reason of any charge, care, or oversight of the property entrusted to him, may be guilty of larceny by such act the same as any stranger.

In *State v. Peke*, 70 N.M. 108 (1962), the defendant's employment duties involved checks, the proceeds of which defendant converted. In *State v. Konviser*, 57 N.M. 418 (1953), the defendant was the manager of the property which he converted.

Although defendant was in charge of the entire store, the undisputed facts show that the money in the drop-box was not committed or surrendered to defendant's care, use or disposal; that money was to be handled exclusively by the manager. Defendant was excluded from having anything to do with that money. Defendant's offense, as to the money in the drop-box, was larceny, not embezzlement, because he had not been entrusted with that money.

Because of an absence of evidence showing that defendant was entrusted with over $100 of the money he took, his embezzlement conviction is reversed.

IT IS SO ORDERED.

Note

The distinction between "custody" and "possession" as discussed in *Morgan* and *Stahl* involved a discussion of "possession" as a legal term of art. Knowing the distinction is critical in deciding whether there was larceny (merely custody) or embezzlement (possession). You must consider whether the defendant was given substantial discretion and control over the property in question. If the defendant has substantial discretion and control over the property, he is in possession; if he converts the property to his own use, the offense is embezzlement. Conversely, if the defendant is given little discretion and control he is in custody; if he then takes the property without consent it is likely larceny.

2. False Pretenses

The crime of false pretenses is another "gap filler" created by statute. The elements are: (1) obtaining title (i.e., the ownership interest); (2) to personal property; (3) of another; (4) by way of a knowing misrepresentation; (5) of a material; (6) past or existing fact; (7) with intent to defraud.

The first six elements constitute the actus reus of the offense and the last element is the mens rea requirement. Whereas larceny is a crime against possession, false pretense is a crime against title. The offense is similar to larceny by trick *except* the crime of false pretenses causes the owner to pass title (i.e., ownership).

a.   False Pretenses Requires Passing of Title

As you read *Regina v. Prince,* look to the intent of the owner of the property. Ask yourself whether the bank official, because of the customer's deceit, intended to pass ownership of the customer's funds.

Regina v. Prince, L.R. 1 C.C.R. 150 (1868)

[Mrs. Allen forged her husband's name in order to draw funds from their joint bank account. After withdrawing the funds, Ms. Allen gave some of the money to Prince, who was convicted of receiving stolen property.]

Where a servant is entrusted with his master's property with a general authority to act for his master in his business, and is induced by fraud to part with his master's property, the person who is guilty of the fraud and so obtains the property, is guilty of obtaining it by false pretenses, and not of larceny, because to constitute larceny there must be a taking against the will of the owner, or of the owner's servant duly authorized to act generally for the owner.

But where a servant has no such general authority from his master, but is merely entrusted with the possession of his goods for a special purpose, and is tricked out of that possession by fraud, the person who is guilty of the fraud and so obtains the property is guilty of larceny, because the servant has no authority to part with the property in the goods except to fulfil the special purpose for which they were entrusted to him.

The cashier of a bank is a servant having a general authority to conduct the business of the bank, and to part with its property on the presentation of a genuine order from a customer; and if he is deceived by a forged order, and parts with the money of the bank, he parts, intending so to do, with the property in the money, and the person knowingly presenting such forged order is guilty of obtaining the money by false pretenses, and not of larceny.

The following ease was stated by the Common Serjeant:—

The prisoner was tried before me at the August session of the Central Criminal Court on an indictment charging him, in the first count, with stealing money to the amount of £100, the property of Henry Allen; in the second count, with receiving the same, knowing it to have been stolen; and in two other counts the ownership of the money was laid in the London and Westminster Bank.

It appeared in evidence that the prosecutor, Henry Allen, had paid moneys amounting to £900 into the London and Westminster Bank on a deposit account in his name, and on the 27th of April, 1868, that sum was standing to his credit at that bank. On that day the wife of Henry Allen presented at the bank a forged order purporting to be the order of the said Henry Allen for payment of the deposit, and the cashier at the bank, believing the authority to be genuine, paid to her the deposit and interest in eight bank-notes of £100 each, and other notes. Among the notes of £100 was one numbered 72,799, dated the 19th of November, 1867.

On the 1st of July, 1868, the wife of Henry Allen left him and his house, and she and the prisoner were shortly afterwards found on board a steamboat at Queenstown on its way from Liverpool to New York, passing as Mr. and Mrs. Prince, Mrs. Allen then having in her possession nearly all the remainder of the notes obtained from the bank. The note for £100, No. 72,799, was proved to have been paid away by the prisoner in payment for some sheep in May, 1868, and he said he had it from Mrs. Allen.

Upon this evidence it was objected by prisoner's counsel that the counts alleging the property to be in Henry Allen must fail, as the note had never been in his possession; and that, as to the other counts, the evidence did not shew any larceny of the note from the bank by the wife, but rather an obtaining by forgery or false pretences by her, and that the receipt by the prisoner from her was not a receipt of stolen property. I held, however, that the forged order presented by the wife was, under the circumstances, a mere mode of committing a larceny against the London and Westminster Bank, and that the prisoner was liable to be convicted on the fourth count.

The jury found the prisoner guilty on that count, and I respited judgment, and reserved for the consideration of the Court the question whether the obtaining the note from the bank by Mrs. Allen, under the circumstances stated, was a larceny by her; if not, the conviction must be reversed.

BLACKBURN, J.

I also am of the same opinion. I must say I cannot but lament that the law now stands as it does. The distinction drawn between larceny and false pretences, one being made a felony and, the other a misdemeanour—and yet the same punishment attached to each—seems to me, I must confess, unmeaning and mischievous. The distinction arose in former times, and I take it that it was then held in favour of life that in larceny the taking must be against the will of the owner, larceny then being a capital offence. However, as the law now stands, if the owner intended the property to pass, though he would not so have intended had he known the real facts, that is sufficient to prevent the offence of obtaining another's property from amounting to larceny; and where the servant has an authority co-equal with his master's, and parts with his master's property, such property cannot be said to be stolen, inasmuch as the servant intends to part with the property in it. If, however, the servant's authority is limited, then he can only part with the possession, and not with the property; if he is tricked out of the possession, the offence so committed will be larceny. In *Reg. v. Longstreeth*, the carrier's servant had no authority to part with the goods, except to the right consignee. His authority was not generally to act in his master's business, but limited in that way. The offence was in that case held to be larceny on that ground, and this distinguishes it from the pawnbroker's case, which the same judges, or at any rate some of them, had shortly before decided. There the servant, from whom the goods were obtained, had a general authority to act for his master, and the person who obtained the goods was held not to be guilty of larceny. So, in the present case, the cashier holds the money of the bank with a general authority from the bank to deal with it. He has authority to part with it on receiving what he believes to be a genuine order. Of the genuineness he is the judge; and if under a mistake he parts with money, he none the less intends to part with the property in it, and thus the offence is not, according to the cases, larceny, but an obtaining by false pretences. The distinction is inscrutable to my mind, but it exists in the cases. There is no statute enabling a count for larceny to be joined with one for false pretences; and as the prisoner was indicted for the felony, the conviction must be quashed.

b. Distinguishing False Pretenses from Larceny

The court in *Prince* found that the victim teller had the authority to part with both title (i.e., money) and possession. Contrast the theft offenses of larceny by trick and false pretenses. How are they alike? How do they differ? Again, the line separating these two offenses is not always clear. Compare *Regina v. Prince* with *The King v. Pear*.

What distinguishes larceny from false pretenses? In *Regina v. Prince* the bank teller had the authority to pass title. Is that a requirement of the crime of false pretenses? Consider this issue as you read *Wilkinson v. State*.

Wilkinson v. State, 215 Miss. 327 (1952)

[Ferguson found stray cattle that belonged to Leonard. Some of Whittington's cattle had also strayed. Whittington and his hired hand, defendant Wilkinson, went to Ferguson's farm to see the strays. Defendant convinced his employer, Whittington, to claim all of them as his. Ferguson gave the strays to the employer, Whittington, mistakenly thinking that he (Whittington) owned them. Whittington then sold the cattle and gave some of the proceeds from the sale to his hired hand, defendant Wilkinson.]

ETHRIDGE, Justice.

Appellant, Fred Wilkinson, was indicted and convicted at the January 1952 term of the Circuit Court of Franklin County of grand larceny, consisting of the theft of three head of cattle. He argues here that the conviction was against the great weight of the evidence, was based upon the uncorroborated testimony of an accomplice, and that he was indicted and convicted under the wrong statute.
. . .

. . . [T]he indictment was properly found under the grand larceny statute, Sec. 2240. The general rule is set forth in 32 Am.Jur., Larceny, Sec. 33: "Although there is some authority to the contrary, the better rule is that one who falsely personates another and in such assumed character receives property intended for such other person is guilty of larceny if he does so with the requisite felonious intent, provided the transaction does not involve the passing of title to the property from the owner to him. Although express statutes to this effect exist in some jurisdictions, it is larceny at common law for a person to pretend that he is the owner or person entitled to personal property in order to obtain possession thereof with the felonious intent of converting it to his own use and depriving the owner of it. Subject to this rule, one who fraudulently claims an estray from the person taking it up or lost property from the finder may be convicted of larceny."

The distinction, a rather fine one, between the crimes of obtaining property by false pretenses and that of larceny through obtaining possession by fraud seems to rest in the intention with which the owner parts with possession. Thus if the possession is obtained by fraud and the owner intends to part with his title as well as his possession, the crime is that of obtaining property by false pretenses, provided the means by which it is acquired comply therewith. But if the possession is fraudulently obtained with a present intent on the part of the person obtaining it to convert the property to his own use, and the owner intends to part with his possession merely and not with the title, the offense is larceny. These same cases also support the rule that the fact that defendant obtained possession openly and not secretly and surreptitiously does not negative the felonious character of the act, provided the requisite elements of the crime exist.

At common law, for a person to pretend that he was the owner of the property in order to get possession of it with the felonious intent of converting it to his own use constituted larceny. Accordingly convictions of larceny have been sustained where a person has fraudulently claimed an estray from the person taking it up, and where a person has claimed to be the owner of lost property from the finder. . . .

The foregoing authorities support the conviction under the general grand larceny statute, Sec. 2240. The distinction rests upon the intention with which the owner or possessor parts with possession. Here the possessor of the estrays, Ferguson, obviously had no intent to part with any title to the estrays. . . . Ferguson thought he was transferring simply the possession back to the true owner. This accords with the principle that if possession is fraudulently obtained, with present intent on the part of the person obtaining it, to convert the property to his own use, and the owner or possessor intends to part with his possession merely and not with the title, the offense is larceny. The crime for which appellant was convicted constitutes grand larceny both at common law and under Code Sec. 2240. Moreover, Sec. 2146, even if applicable, does not exclude the use of the grand larceny statute as to facts constituting that crime at common law.

Another reason why Code Sec. 2146 is not applicable to this crime is that the terms and apparent purposes of that act are not pertinent to the instant facts. Appellant did not "falsely represent . . . another". He did not pretend to be the agent of anyone. He simply advised Ferguson, who held the estrays, that he was the owner. Nor did appellant "falsely . . . personate another, and, in such assumed character" obtain possession of the cattle. He did not, for example, tell Ferguson that he was Douglas Leonard, who was the true owner, or someone else. There was no impersonation of any assumed, particular person. . . .

Affirmed.

3. Consolidated Theft Offenses

The distinctions between larceny, embezzlement, and false pretenses can be very fine. Assuming the punishment for these offenses is roughly the same, do they make sense? In selecting the appropriate charge, the prosecutor had to know what was in the minds of the parties at the time personal property was transferred. For example, was the defendant in lawful possession of the property or did he obtain it by fraud? What was the intent of the defendant at the time he obtained the property? Did the victim intend to pass title or simply transfer possession? The prosecutor was required to allege the specific form of theft and could not obtain a conviction for another. The result was frequently the reversal of a conviction because the incorrect theft offense was charged.

To solve this problem, many states have enacted consolidated theft offenses or umbrella offenses. The various common law theft crimes have been consolidated into an offense often called simply "theft."

State v. Saylor, 228 Kan. 498 (1980)

PRAGER, Justice:

This is a direct appeal from a conviction of theft by deception (K.S.A. 1979 Supp. 21-3701[b]). The Court of Appeals in a published opinion, *State v. Saylor*, 4 Kan.App.2d 563 (1980), reversed and remanded with directions to grant the defendant a new trial on the lesser included offense of attempt to commit theft by deception. We granted review on petition of the State.

The facts in the case are well summarized in the opinion of the Court of Appeals. On September 27, 1978, in the city of Lawrence, a K-Mart store security officer observed the defendant, Glenn Lee Saylor, as he made numerous trips through the store placing items in his shopping cart. He would go to the hardware department with items in the cart, but would leave that department with an empty cart. The security officer observed the defendant move about in one particular area, but was unable to see exactly what he was doing. She saw him take a bottle of glue to the area, use it, and then return it to a counter. The defendant then made a minor purchase and left the store. The security officer notified her supervisor. On investigation, she found in the hardware department a cardboard box which should have been located in the toy department and which ordinarily would contain a $13.97 plastic pig toy chest. The cover of the box had recently been resealed with glue. The security officer did not move or otherwise touch the box. When the defendant returned to the store later that evening, the security officer and the police were on hand. The defendant went to the hardware department where he placed the box in a shopping cart. He proceeded to the checkout counter and paid for two items—a quart of oil and a plastic pig toy chest priced at $13.97. The checkout cashier did not suspect there was anything wrong. The defendant was arrested outside the store in the parking lot. There the box was opened and found to contain several chain saws, metal rules, cigarettes, heavy duty staple guns, and record albums, with a total value in excess of $500. The defendant was arrested for theft. He was charged with and convicted of theft by deception under K.S.A. 1979 Supp. 21–3701(*b*).

The defendant appealed raising several points of alleged error. The Court of Appeals reversed the conviction, finding error in the trial court's failure to instruct the jury on attempted theft by deception. Noting this court's decision in *State v. Finch*, 223 Kan. 398 (1978), the Court of Appeals held that, since there had been no actual reliance by or actual deception of the corporate victim, K-Mart, the defendant could only be guilty of attempted theft by deception. The Court of Appeals reversed the conviction and directed a new trial on attempted theft by deception.

On petition for review, the State of Kansas urges this court to reconsider the elements of theft by deception as enumerated by *Finch*, claiming that by interpreting 21–3701(*b*) to require reliance by or actual deception of the owner, the court added to the offense of theft an element not contained in the statutory definition. Alternatively, the State argues that the present case is distinguishable from *Finch*, claiming that there was actual deception in this case, at least in part, since the checkout cashier was totally unaware of defendant's larcenous intent and no one within the employment of K-Mart had more than a suspicion of defendant's scheme at the time defendant purchased the merchandise and left the store with the box. The State finally argues that, under the consolidated theft statute, a conviction of theft should be sustained, even though the burden of proof is not met as to the offense specified in the indictment or information, if the evidence supports conviction of theft under any other subsection of K.S.A. 1979 Supp. 21–3701.

We have reconsidered the rule announced in *State v. Finch*, and have concluded that it is a correct statement of the law. The syllabus in *Finch* states the rule which is consistent with prior decisions of this court and with the rule generally accepted throughout the United States:

> In order to convict a defendant of theft by deception under K.S.A. 21–3701(*b*) the state must prove that the

> defendant with the required intent obtained control over another's property by means of a false statement or representation. To do so the state must prove that the victim was actually deceived and relied in whole or in part upon the false representation.

The rationale of the rule and the reasons why it was adopted by this court are discussed in depth in that opinion. We have concluded, however, that, under its particular facts, the present case is distinguishable from *Finch*, in that the K-mart checkout cashier, who permitted the defendant to leave the store premises with the box, was completely unaware of the true contents hidden in the box and relied upon the deception practiced by the defendant at that time.

The State argues that the defendant could have properly been charged under section (*a*) of K.S.A. 1979 Supp. 21–3701, since the evidence established that the defendant, with intent to deprive the owner permanently of the possession, use, or ownership of the owner's property, exerted unauthorized control over the property by concealing the articles in the cardboard box. We agree with the State. It is clear to us that where a customer in a self-service store conceals on his person, or in a box or receptacle, property of the store and has the requisite specific criminal intent, that customer has committed a theft under subsection (*a*) of K.S.A. 1979 Supp. 21–3701. The specific criminal intent is difficult to prove, however, unless the customer actually fails to make proper payment for the property at the cashier's desk and leaves the store with the same remaining concealed. In this case, the defendant was not specifically charged under subsection (*a*) of K.S.A. 1979 Supp. 21–3701. The State did not seek to amend the information to include that subsection, nor was an appropriate instruction on that subsection given to the jury. The State thus relied only on proving theft by deception under subsection (*b*). The conviction of the defendant must stand or fall on the sufficiency of the evidence to show that the defendant, with the required specific intent, obtained control over the property by deception. We have concluded that the evidence was sufficient and that an instruction on attempted theft was not required.

In concluding that the evidence established a completed theft by deception, the trial court pointed out that the security employees of K-Mart had only a suspicion that the defendant was planning to steal articles of merchandise from the store. The actual merchandise taken was not determined until the box was opened following the defendant's arrest in the parking lot. We think it also important to note that the act of deception and false representation did not actually occur until the defendant deceived the cashier into believing that the box contained a plastic pig toy chest of a value of $13.97.

The rule of *Finch* simply requires the State to prove that the victim was actually deceived and relied wholly or in part upon the false representation made by the defendant. We note that this same result was reached under similar factual circumstances in *Lambert v. State*, 55 Ala. App. 242, cert. denied 294 Ala. 763 (1975). In *Lambert*, it was held that reliance upon a misrepresentation was proved in a prosecution for false pretense, although the evidence showed that numerous persons in the store knew of defendant's scheme to change price tags on merchandise, where the checkout girl to whom defendant took the falsely priced merchandise relied upon the false representation as to those prices and parted with the merchandise, having no knowledge of the defendant's scheme. Since the undisputed evidence in this case showed the cashier at the checkout counter at K-Mart relied upon the false representation made by the defendant as to the contents of the box and permitted defendant to take control of the box and its contents outside the confines of the store, we hold that the trial court did not err in concluding that there was the required reliance and thus an instruction on the lesser offense of attempted theft by deception was not required.

We now address the contention of the State that, under the consolidated statute, K.S.A. 1979 Supp. 21–3701, a conviction of theft may be upheld even though the burden of proof is not sustained as to the particular subsection specified in the information, if the evidence supports the conviction of theft under any one of the other subsections. We agree with the State that the primary purpose of the consolidated theft statute was to eliminate the complexities of pleading and proving the vague historical distinctions in the various types of theft. See comment, Judicial Council, 21–3701 (1968). Professor Paul E. Wilson, in his article, *Thou Shalt Not Steal: Ruminations on the New Kansas Theft Law*, 20 Kan.L.Rev. 385 (1972), makes the following observation:

> [C]onsolidation should eliminate the procedural difficulties that sometimes result from the fact that boundaries between the traditional theft crimes are obscure and the defendant who is charged with one crime cannot be convicted by proving another. An inexperienced—or even an experienced—prosecutor may have difficulty in determining whether a given set of facts indicates larceny, false pretense, or embezzlement. And even though the right charge is selected, a conviction based on borderline facts is more likely to be challenged on appeal. The objective, then, has been to define the crime broadly enough to include all vaguely separated theft offenses, so that evidence of appropriation by any of the forbidden methods will support the charge. p. 393.

Likewise, the Model Penal Code, §223.1 (Proposed Off. Draft, May 4, 1962), provides:

> (1) *Consolidation of Theft Offenses.* Conduct denominated theft in this Article constitutes a single offense embracing the separate offenses heretofore known as larceny, embezzlement, false pretense, extortion, blackmail, fraudulent conversion, receiving stolen property, and the like. An accusation of theft may be supported by evidence

> that it was committed in any manner that would be theft under this Article, notwithstanding the specification of a different manner in the indictment or information, subject only to the power of the Court to ensure fair trial by granting a continuance or other appropriate relief where the conduct of the defense would be prejudiced by lack of fair notice or by surprise.

Under the former Kansas code as it existed prior to the adoption of the present code, effective July 1, 1970, the crime of false pretenses was covered by K.S.A. 21–551 and 21–552 (Corrick 1964). The legislature recognized the difficulties of proof in this area by enacting K.S.A. 21–553 (Corrick 1964):

> 21–553. Conviction of larceny under 21–551, 21–552. If upon the trial of any person indicted for any offense prohibited in the last two sections, it should be proved that he obtained the money or other thing in question in such manner as to amount in law to a larceny, he shall not by reason thereof be entitled to an acquittal, but he shall be convicted and punished as if the offense had been proved as charged.

In *Talbot v. Wulf*, 122 Kan. 1, 5 (1926), this court stated that G.S. 21–553 was designed to prevent a failure of justice on account of a variance between pleading and proof dependent on the distinction between the crime of larceny and the crime of obtaining property by false pretense.

It is obvious to us that one of the purposes of the enactment of the consolidated theft statute, K.S.A. 21–3701, was to avoid the pitfalls of pleading where a defendant might escape a conviction for one type of theft by proof that he had committed another type of theft. There is now only the single crime of theft which is complete when a man takes property not his own with the intent to take it and deprive the owner thereof. A defendant may be convicted of theft upon proof of facts establishing either embezzlement, larceny, receiving stolen property, or obtaining property by false pretense. It has long been the law of Kansas that an accusatory pleading in a criminal action may, in order to meet the exigencies of proof, charge the commission of the same offense in different ways. In such a situation, a conviction can be upheld only on one count, the function of the added counts in the pleading being to anticipate and obviate fatal variance between allegations and proof. Thus, it has been held proper to charge by several counts of an information the same offense committed in different ways or by different means to the extent necessary to provide for every possible contingency in the evidence. *Williams v. Darr*, 4 Kan.App.2d 178, 180–81 (1979); *State v. Hagan*, 3 Kan.App.2d 558 (1979); *State v. Pierce et al.*, 205 Kan. 433 (1970); *State v. Emory*, 116 Kan. 381 (1924); and *State v. Harris*, 103 Kan. 347 (1918).

Where there is a question in the mind of the prosecutor as to what the evidence will disclose at trial, the correct procedure is to charge the defendant in the alternative under those subsections to K.S.A. 1979 Supp. 21–3701 which may possibly be established by the evidence. This may properly be done under Kansas law by charging several counts in the information to provide for every possible contingency in the evidence. By so doing, the jury may properly be instructed on the elements necessary to establish the crime of theft under any of the subsections charged and the defendant will have no basis to complain that he has been prejudiced in his defense.

It should also be noted that, under K.S.A. 1979 Supp. 22–3201(4), a trial court may permit a complaint or information to be amended at any time before verdict or finding if no additional crime is charged and if substantial rights of the defendant are not prejudiced. Following that statute, we have a number of decisions which hold that it is proper for the State to amend the information during trial by adding words which change the method by which the particular crime was committed in the particular case. For example in *State v. Lamb*, 215 Kan. 795, 798 (1974), the State was permitted to amend a charge of kidnapping by adding the words "or deception" to the allegation "by means of force," since there was evidence presented in the case that the kidnapping was accomplished both through force and deception. In *State v. Bell*, 224 Kan. 105, 106 (1978), the State was permitted to amend certain counts in the information, charging kidnapping, to add the words "by force and deception" to make the information conform to the evidence presented. See also *State v. Rives*, 220 Kan. 141, 144–45 (1976) (where the information was amended to charge that the defendant took the purloined property "from the presence of" a named individual rather than "from the person of" the same individual); *State v. Ferguson*, 221 Kan. 103, 105 (1976) (where the State was permitted to amend the date of the violation originally charged in the information). In this case, as mentioned above, the State did not seek to amend the charge of theft contained in the information to include an allegation of theft under subsection (*a*) of K.S.A. 1979 Supp. 21–3701 and the jury was not instructed on that charge. Thus, the jury could not properly consider the question of defendant's guilt or innocence of the crime of theft under subsection (*a*).

In closing, it should be noted that we have considered the other point of complained error raised in defendant's brief that the district court erred in allowing the State to introduce certain rebuttal testimony. We find this point to be without merit.

For the reasons set forth above, we hold that the judgment of the district court upholding the conviction of the defendant for theft by deception (K.S.A. 1979 Supp. 21–3701[*b*]) is affirmed. It is further ordered that the judgment of the Court of Appeals is reversed for the reasons set forth in the opinion.

Note

Section 223.1 of the MPC allows a prosecutor to prove a different type of theft than was alleged in the indictment as long as the defendant's right to a fair trial (i.e., fair notice) has not been compromised. The MPC also permits the prosecutor to charge in the alternative, that is, to allege more than one type of theft. In *Saylor*, however, the court held that the defendant could not be charged with a theft offense that was not included in the charging document.

4.   Robbery

The elements of common law robbery include the elements of common law larceny, plus (1) the taking of the property must be from the victim's person or in the victim's presence; and (2) the taking must be accomplished by the use of actual physical force, or an immediate threat of physical force.

In *People v. Nasir*, 255 Mich. App. 38 (2003), the court held that a brief struggle over a purse is enough to satisfy the "by force" requirement for unarmed robbery.

5.   Claim of Right Defense   *Christopher taking his coat*

What if, in either a larceny or robbery prosecution, the defendant thought he or she was entitled to take the property? Will such a belief, even if mistaken, negate the necessary mens rea? Consider this issue as you read *Tufunga*.

People v. Tufunga, 21 Cal.4th 935 (1999)

BAXTER, J.

The claim-of-right defense provides that a defendant's good faith belief, even if mistakenly held, that he has a right or claim to property he takes from another negates the felonious intent necessary for conviction of theft or robbery. At common law, a claim of right was recognized as a defense to larceny because it was deemed to negate the *animus furandi*, or intent to steal, of that offense. (See 4 Blackstone, Commentaries 230 (Blackstone).) Since robbery was viewed as an aggravated form of larceny, it was likewise subject to the same claim-of-right defense. (*Id.* at pp. 241–243.)

In *People v. Butler* (1967) 65 Cal.2d 569, we reaffirmed that a claim-of-right defense can negate the requisite felonious intent of robbery as codified in Penal Code section 211 and extended the availability of the defense to forcible takings perpetrated to satisfy, settle or otherwise collect on a debt, liquidated or unliquidated.

In light of the strong public policy considerations disfavoring self-help through force or violence, including the forcible recapture of property, we granted review in this case to consider whether claim of right should continue to be recognized as a defense to robbery in California. Since *Butler* was decided over 30 years ago, courts around the nation have severely restricted, and in some cases eliminated altogether, the availability of the defense in prosecutions for robbery. As will be explained, however, the "felonious taking" required for robbery under section 211, as well as that for theft under section 484, is a taking accomplished with felonious intent, that is, the intent to steal, a state of mind that California courts for over 150 years have recognized as inconsistent with a good faith belief that the specific property taken is one's own. When our Legislature incorporated this mental state element into the definition of robbery upon codifying the offense in 1872, it effectively recognized claim of right as a defense to that crime. This court is therefore not free to expand the statutorily defined mens rea of robbery by eliminating claim of right as a defense altogether on policy grounds.

Since the Legislature incorporated the claim-of-right doctrine into the statutory definition of robbery over a century ago, the question whether it continues to reflect sound public policy as we enter the 21st century must be addressed to that body and not to this court. (Cal. Const., art. III, §3 [guaranteeing the separation of powers of the legislative and judicial branches].) Nonetheless, as will further be explained, we find nothing in the language of section 211 to suggest the Legislature intended to incorporate into the robbery statute *Butler*'s broad extension of the claim-of-right defense to forcible takings perpetrated to satisfy, settle or otherwise collect on a debt, liquidated or unliquidated. To the extent *Butler*'s expansion of the claim-of-right defense in that regard is unsupported by the language of the robbery statute and contrary to sound public policy, it is overruled.

I.   FACTUAL AND PROCEDURAL BACKGROUND

An amended four-count information charged defendant Halaliku Kaloni Tufunga with assault with a deadly weapon or force likely to produce great bodily injury (§245, subd. (a)(1)), residential robbery (§§211–212.5, subd. (a)), spousal abuse (the victim being the mother of his child) (§273.5), and making terrorist threats (§422) based on an episode of violence against his former wife, Shelly Tufunga. A jury found him guilty as charged on all but the first count (assault with a deadly weapon or force likely to produce great bodily injury), on which it convicted him of the lesser offense of battery (§242). An allegation that defendant had used a deadly or dangerous weapon (scissors) (§12022, subd. (b)) was found true in connection with the conviction of making terrorist threats, but not true in connection with the conviction of spousal abuse. Defendant was sentenced to state prison for the middle term of four years for robbery plus a subordinate term of one year for spousal abuse, with the enhancement finding stricken and all remaining terms to run concurrent with the aggregate five-year prison sentence.

Shelly Tufunga (Shelly) testified that around 5:00 p.m. on January 16, 1996, defendant, who is her former husband, his first wife Pelenaise (or Pele), and his daughter Lokelomi (or Loni) from that marriage came to Shelly's residence, pushed their way inside, and started yelling obscenities at her. Pele and Loni accused her of having made derogatory comments about Pele's younger daughter Helen's sexual promiscuity.

Defendant pushed Shelly to the floor and kicked her in the hip and thigh. He then threw her onto the couch and ordered the other women out of the residence, saying he would "take care of" her. After they left, defendant straddled Shelly on the couch, slapped and hit her, grabbed a pair of nine- or ten-inch scissors and, making overhead stabbing motions toward her face, forehead and neck, said he was going to "mess up her face," shove the scissors up her "big fat ass" and "make it so that nobody would be able to look at" her. Afraid for her life, Shelly begged him to stop. She dodged stabs at her eyes but suffered scratches to her forehead, neck and arms before defendant finally stopped, put the scissors down, and got off of her. He continued to yell, at one point breaking a lamp in the home.

Shelly's mother Josephine arrived at the house while defendant was still there. Initially unaware of the fracas, she handed Shelly $200 in cash for Shelly to use to purchase medicine and vitamins for her. Shelly testified she kept track of her mother's finances and routinely purchased vitamins and medicines the mother needed for her illness. Shelly put the money down on the coffee table, excused herself, and retired to the bathroom. When she reemerged, Josephine noticed her face was bruised, said, "My God, what happened?," and confronted defendant. Reminding him that she had said she was not going to stand for any more of this, Josephine picked up the phone to call the police. Defendant screamed at her and grabbed her by the arm, knocking the phone out of her hand. When Shelly intervened, defendant grabbed Shelly by the neck, shaking and choking her while screaming at them both.

Defendant then ran out the front door. Josephine yelled, "Shelly, he took the money," and tried to stop him. Shelly ran outside, wrote down the license number of the car defendant was driving, and called 911. That evening she filed a police report detailing the incident. After the incident but prior to his arrest, defendant returned to Shelly's apartment on several occasions; she did not call the police at those times out of fear for her safety.

Jurors saw photos of Shelly's injuries taken that same day. Responding police officers testified she was crying and appeared bruised and scratched. She reported that defendant had held the scissors against the bridge of her nose. She thought he had taken the money off the couch.

Shelly testified further that in April 1995 she had gotten a restraining order against defendant after being forced to move into a battered women's shelter with her daughter for a month because he was physically hitting and abusing her. At that time defendant had been coming over to her apartment, kicking the door in, hitting and pushing her, and wrecking the place.

Josephine also testified at trial, corroborating most of Shelly's account. She recalled that when defendant grabbed the phone he had unplugged it and threatened to kill her. When he choked Shelly, Josephine hit him on the head with the phone, without effect. Josephine thought Shelly had the $200 in her hand when she returned from the bathroom and dropped it on the table as defendant started choking her. Defendant hit Shelly a couple of times, grabbed the money off the table and left, pushing Josephine when she tried to stop him. Josephine called the police after defendant ran from the apartment.

Defendant testified in his own behalf and, after acknowledging prior felony convictions for forgery and grand theft, gave a different account of the incident leading to his arrest. He, and occasionally his daughters as well, had been living in Shelly's apartment around that time (Shelly testified defendant occasionally stayed at her home against her will, explaining defendant was very big and that she could not stop him from coming over). On the date in question he was paid $200 in cash by his employer/relative Hermasi Latu, who testified for the defense to corroborate that fact. Defendant claimed he knew Shelly had a bill due on the 19th of the month and had promised to bring her money to help with it. He brought the $200 over to Shelly's apartment that afternoon and put it down on the coffee table, stating it was to help pay for the bill. He claimed he and Shelly were watching television without incident when his former wife Pele and their daughter Loni arrived and the argument ensued. Defendant testified he told Pele and Loni to leave, which they did, after which he and Shelly themselves began arguing about the accusations his former wife was making against her. Defendant told Shelly he believed her mother Josephine was causing trouble between them and with his children by Pele. Defendant admitted the argument grew loud and that he broke a vase in the apartment, but he claimed he did not strike Shelly.

Josephine soon arrived at the apartment. When she asked Shelly why she was upset, Shelly told her defendant brought Pele and Loni to the apartment and they had tried to hit her. Defendant tried to explain, but Josephine said, "I'm sick and tired because you're hitting my daughter all the time," and went to the phone to call 911. Defendant and Josephine knew there was a warrant outstanding for defendant's arrest and he believed she was calling the police to have him arrested. He tried to talk Josephine out of it and told her to stay out of the argument between Shelly and him. At that point Shelly reached down, picked up the $200 from the coffee table and put it in her bra. Defendant believed the two were out to take the money, as this had happened before, and that Shelly would give it to her mother. Defendant demanded the money back and, when Shelly refused, wrestled with her, reached into her bra and took it back. As he walked out the door Josephine hit him with the phone. Shelly followed him outside and got the license plate number of the car he was driving as he drove off. Defendant testified he did not threaten, strike or push Shelly that day and had not broken into her apartment or stayed against her will. Defendant testified that three days later he and Shelly made up, and that he at that time gave her $160 to help pay her bills.

Pele and Loni testified for the defense, corroborating the story that Shelly had made accusations about Pele's daughter Helen and claiming they had come to Shelly's residence on the date in question and found defendant already there. Shelly appeared upset and looked as though she had been crying, but neither visitor saw defendant assault her. Twelve-year-old Helen also testified, confirming she had been living in Shelly's apartment with defendant and testifying further that, while defendant and Shelly would argue on occasion, he did not hit her.

Called in rebuttal, Shelly testified defendant never brought her money and in fact knew her paydays, regularly beat her and took her money, and continually threatened her and her family members.

II. DISCUSSION

At trial, the defense requested instruction on a claim-of-right defense to the charge of robbery. The trial court concluded the facts would not support the defense and refused to instruct on it. On appeal, defendant urged that even if he had used force to take back his $200, that fact is immaterial to the existence of his bona fide belief in his right to take back the money he conditionally gave to Shelly, once he concluded in good faith that she was not going to use it to pay bills and would instead turn it over to her mother. The People responded that defendant furnished no substantial evidence of a bona fide belief in his right to reclaim the money. Although the source of the money present in the apartment during the incident was therefore disputed at trial—Shelly claiming her mother brought over the money, which defendant then stole from them; defendant claiming he had brought over the $200 to give to Shelly to pay bills, then took it back upon concluding she would not use it for the purpose for which it was offered—it was not disputed that the same $200 in currency was at the heart of the controversy. In other words, if defendant's version of the incident was believed, there was no further evidence or claim by the People that Shelly had commingled the specific currency he gave her with her own funds before he grabbed it back and fled from the apartment.

We recently summarized the nature and scope of a claim-of-right defense to robbery after this court's decision in *Butler, supra,* as follows: "In [*Butler*], the defendant was accused of felony murder based on the underlying crime of robbery. At trial, the defendant testified he had been employed by the victim, who had not paid him for some work. The defendant, armed with a gun, went to the victim's home one evening to collect payment. Although the victim had at one point agreed to pay the defendant, he subsequently changed his mind and approached the defendant with a pistol. During the ensuing scuffle, the defendant shot and killed the victim, and also shot another person present in the victim's home. After quickly searching the home for money and finding none, the defendant grabbed a wallet and ran from the house. In recounting the events, the defendant claimed he did not intend to commit robbery when he went to the house, but intended only to recover the money he was owed. Over the defendant's objection, the prosecutor was permitted to argue to the jury that a robbery had been committed even if the defendant honestly believed the victim owed him money. The jury convicted the defendant of first degree felony murder and fixed the penalty at death.

"A majority of this court reversed, concluding: 'Although an intent to steal may ordinarily be inferred when one person takes the property of another, particularly if he takes it by force, proof of the existence of a state of mind incompatible with an intent to steal precludes a finding of either theft or robbery. It has long been the rule in this state and generally throughout the country that a bona fide belief, even though mistakenly held, that one has a right or claim to the property negates felonious intent. A belief that the property taken belongs to the taker, or that he had a right to retake goods sold is sufficient to preclude felonious intent. Felonious intent exists only if the actor intends to take the property of another without believing in good faith that he has a right or claim to it.' "

a.   *Sufficient evidence supported the giving of a claim-of-right instruction*

At the threshold we must determine whether the evidence warranted the giving of a claim-of-right instruction in the first instance. The Court of Appeal found that it did. We agree.

Defendant's account of the source of the $200 in the victim's residence during the criminal episode, and the manner in which he allegedly took it back upon fleeing from the residence, was sharply at odds with the victim's and victim's mother's testimony. Notably, however, it was defendant's testimony, not Shelly's or Josephine's, that most directly established a *forcible* taking of the $200 from the person of the victim: defendant claimed Shelly picked up the money and put it in her bra, and that he forcibly grabbed the money from her bra moments before he fled from the residence, whereas Josephine testified defendant took the money from the coffee table as he was fleeing.

Generally, "[a] party is not entitled to an instruction on a theory for which there is no supporting evidence." "[A] trial court is not required to instruct on a claim-of-right defense unless there is evidence to support an inference that [the defendant] acted with a subjective belief he or she had a lawful claim on the property."

Here, defendant's own testimony constituted such evidence. He claimed he brought the $200 into the residence to give to Shelly to pay bills and took it back upon concluding she was not going to use it for that purpose but would instead give it to her mother. He produced a witness (Hermasi Latu) who testified defendant had been paid $200 in cash on that same day. As explained, the prosecution did not attempt to argue that if defendant's testimony that he brought $200 into the residence was believed, there was further evidence that the $200 he took upon fleeing was different currency.

" 'In evaluating the evidence to determine whether a requested instruction should be given, the trial court should not measure its substantiality by weighing the credibility [of the witnesses]. . . . Doubts as to the sufficiency of the evidence to warrant instructions should be resolved in favor of the accused. [Citations.]' " In [*People v. Barnett* (1998) 17 Cal.4th 1044], we evaluated the necessity of giving a claim-of-right instruction under the defendant's account of events.

In *Butler* we observed that a forcible taking of property from another "ordinarily" allows an inference of an intent to steal, as opposed to a claim of right. (*Butler, supra*). Here, however, if defendant's version of the events was believed, even his self-admitted use of force did not preclude his raising a claim-of-right defense to the robbery charge, given his further testimony that he brought $200 into the victim's home and took back the same currency upon fleeing. Although defendant's and the victim's respective versions of the events differed considerably, defendant's testimony, together with that of the other defense witnesses, constituted sufficient evidence to warrant the giving of a claim-of-right instruction.

   b.   *A good faith claim of right to title or ownership of specific property taken from another can negate the element of felonious taking (a taking accomplished with intent to steal) necessary to establish theft (§484) or robbery (§211)*

At common law, claim of right was recognized as a defense to the crime of larceny because it was deemed to negate the *animus furandi*—or felonious intent to steal—of that offense. (See 4 Blackstone, *supra*, at p. 230.) Because robbery was viewed as simply an aggravated form of larceny, it was likewise subject to the same claim-of-right defense. (4 Blackstone, *supra*, at pp. 241–243.)

When the Legislature created the first statutory scheme codifying this state's criminal law in 1850, it incorporated portions of the then-existing common law into the new statutes. Thus, the 1850 robbery statute (Stats. 1850, ch. 99, §59, p. 235) closely tracked the definition of robbery set out in Blackstone's Commentaries. (Compare §59 of the Crimes and Punishments Act of 1850 ["Robbery is the *felonious* and violent *taking* of money, goods, or other valuable thing from the person of another, by force or intimidation." (Stats. 1850, ch. 99, §59, p. 235, italics added.)], with 4 Blackstone, *supra*, at p. 242 [robbery "is the *felonious* and forceful *taking* from the person of another of goods or money to any value, by violence or putting him in fear" (italics added)].) From this historical perspective alone, it can be inferred that the Legislature intended to incorporate the common law recognition of the defense of claim of right as negating the felonious taking or *animus furandi* element common to theft and robbery when it first codified those offenses in the 1850 statutes.

Moreover, the fact that the Legislature used the same terminology, i.e., "felonious taking," in both the larceny and robbery statutes of 1850 (Stats. 1850, ch. 99, §§59, 60–61, p. 235) most reasonably indicates an intent to ascribe the same meaning to that element which is common to both offenses, that is, recognition of the common law claim-of-right defense as applying to both theft and robbery. Put differently, by adopting the identical phrase "felonious taking" as used in the common law with regard to both offenses, the Legislature in all likelihood intended to incorporate the same meanings attached to those phrases at common law.

Thirteen years later, . . . this court held that property feloniously taken must belong to someone other than the defendant in order to constitute robbery: "The owner of property is not guilty of robbery in taking it from the person of the possessor, though he may be guilty of another public offense." [This court] held that an indictment charging robbery was deficient for failing to affirmatively allege that the property did not belong to the defendant. In so holding, the . . . court looked to the actual title or ownership of the property taken and essentially read into the 1850 robbery statute (Stats. 1850, ch. 99, §59, p. 235) an affirmative requirement, derived from the common law rule of larceny, that the thief (or robber) must take property belonging to someone other than himself ("another") in order to be guilty of robbery.) Similarly, this court found the same common law rule applicable to the 1850 theft statutes (Stats. 1850, ch. 99, §§60–61, p. 235). (See *People v. Stone* (1860) 16 Cal. 369, 371 ["It is not every trespass that is a larceny. The felony is in the intent to appropriate another's property, *the taker knowing that he had no right or claim to it.*" (Italics added.)]

In 1872, nine years [later], the Legislature enacted the first comprehensive Penal Code establishing a finite list of crimes punishable under California law. As part of this complete codification, the Legislature enacted section 211, the current robbery provision which has remained unchanged since first enacted 127 years ago. Section 211 provides: "Robbery is the *felonious taking* of personal property in the possession of another, from his person or immediate presence, and against his will, accomplished by means of force or fear." (Italics added.) As with the 1850 robbery statute (Stats. 1850, ch. 99, §59, p. 235), the most logical inference is that by use of the identical term "felonious taking" in section 211, the Legislature was yet again incorporating into the 1872 robbery statute the affirmative requirement, derived from the common law rule applicable to larceny and robbery, that the thief or robber has to intend to take property belonging to someone other than himself in order to be guilty of theft or robbery, that is to say, the common law recognition of the defense of claim of right.

Decisions, including those of this court, postdating the 1872 codification of the crime of robbery in section 211, continued to follow the 1863 holding . . . to wit, that the earlier robbery statute had incorporated the common law rule that a felonious taking does not occur when the defendant has a good faith claim of right to the specific property taken. (See, e.g., *People v. Hicks* (1884) 66 Cal. 103, 104 [information charging robbery not deficient because it sufficiently identified owner of property as other than defendant].

Also significant is a note accompanying section 211 in the first annotated edition of the 1872 Penal Code that plainly reflects the Legislature's intent to incorporate the common law claim-of-right defense as part and parcel of the *animus furandi* element found in the current robbery statute. The note cites this court's decision . . . for the proposition that "the owner of property is not guilty of robbery in taking it from the possession of the possessor."

As recently as last year, in *People v. Davis* (1998) 19 Cal.4th 301, in the course of discussing the elements of larceny, we cited Perkins and Boyce, Criminal Law (3d ed. 1982) at pages 326–327 (Perkins), for the well-settled principle that "[t]he intent to steal or *animus furandi* is the intent, *without a good faith claim of right,* to permanently deprive the owner of possession." (second italics added.)

Lastly, it has long been recognized that " '[t]heft is a lesser included offense of robbery, which includes the additional element of force or fear,' " and that robbery " 'is a species of aggravated larceny.' " (*Ibid.,* citing Perkins, *supra* at p. 350.) A conclusion here that a claim of right, for policy reasons, should no longer be recognized as a defense to robbery—even where the defendant can establish that he is taking back specific property to which he has lawful title or a bona fide claim of ownership—would mean such a defendant could be convicted of robbery *based on theft of his own property,* a proposition that would stand in patent conflict with both the commonsense notion that someone cannot steal his own property, and the corollary rule that "theft," the taking of "the personal property of *another*" (§484, italics added), is a lesser included offense at the core of every robbery. Wholesale elimination of the claim-of-right defense in such cases would stand in sharp conflict with these basic legal principles, principles that have their roots in the early common law, have recently been affirmed by this court, and have never seriously been questioned as a matter of California law.

The People make several additional arguments in support of their position that there is a sound legal basis for eliminating the claim-of-right defense to robbery in its entirety, none of which we find persuasive. They argue that upon enactment of section 211 in the Penal Code of 1872, the reclassification of robbery as a *crime against the person,* whereas larceny remained classified as a *crime against property* (compare Pen. Code, pt. 1, tit. 8 [Of Crimes Against The Person] with Pen. Code, pt. 1, tit. 13 [Of Crimes Against Property]), reflects the Legislature's belief that the predominant characteristic of robbery for purposes of assessing culpability and punishment, and for effectuating deterrence under our criminal statutory scheme, is the use of force or fear, rather than the taking of personal property. But the fact remains that a felonious taking, that is, a taking done with the intent to steal another's property, is a required element at the core of every robbery, and the fact that robbery is chaptered along with other crimes against the person in the Penal Code does not mean it does not share common elements of crimes against property as well. Moreover, section 10004, enacted in 1941, provides that "Division, chapter, article, and section headings contained [in the Penal Code] shall not be deemed to govern, limit, modify or in any manner affect the scope, meaning or intent of the provisions of any division, chapter, article or section hereof."

The People also observe that "[c]ommentators who favor retention of the claim of right defense for robbery have attempted to counter the compelling public policy concerns regarding the use of self-help involving violence or threat of violence by suggesting that even if the defendant could successfully argue that he was acting under an actual claim of right and therefore did not commit robbery, he would still face criminal liability, namely he would be guilty of assault. (See, e.g., 2 LaFave & Scott, Substantive Criminal Law (1986) §8.11(b), p. 442 ['Of course, one who collects debts or borrows property or perpetrates jokes by use of violence or intimidation, though he is not guilty of robbery, need not go free: for he is guilty of at least simple battery if he uses force, and of simple assault if he uses intimidation, and of aggravated assault or battery (e.g., assault with a deadly weapon) under appropriate circumstances.' (fns. omitted.)].)" The People disagree with the reasoning of such commentators and urge that this "rationalization represents a fundamental misapprehension of California jurisprudence" because "under California law assault is not a lesser included offense of robbery." The People assert that some robberies may be committed through use of force or threats of violence that would not be independently actionable as assault if a claim-of-right defense otherwise applied to preclude conviction of robbery, such as where the defendant robs another with a toy gun, unloaded gun, or simulated gun, which fact would support a conviction of robbery but not assault. (See *People v. Wolcott* (1983) 34 Cal.3d 92, 98–100 ["[B]ecause a defendant can commit robbery without attempting to inflict violent injury, and without the present ability to do so, robbery does not include assault as a lesser offense."].)

The point is unavailing for purposes of deciding the issue before us. We think it unlikely a large number of defendants charged with robbery will have a bona fide claim of right in the actual ownership of or title to the property taken from the person of the victim. In many if not most such cases, as in the instant case, the defendant likely will have committed various separately chargeable assaultive crimes through utilization of the force or fear necessary to support the charge of robbery. Here, for example, in addition to the charged robbery, defendant was convicted of battery, spousal abuse, and making terrorist threats. Simple or aggravated assault and false imprisonment also come readily to mind as charges that might be brought against persons who use unlawful force in seeking to take back property they in good faith believe belongs to them. None of these crimes is a lesser included offense of robbery; this does not lessen their availability to charge a robbery suspect for the use of unlawful force or threats of violence. It is difficult to hypothesize facts whereby a defendant who has used sufficient force or threats of violence to regain what he in good faith believes is his own property, thereby exposing himself to a charge of robbery but also possibly qualifying him to interpose a claim-of-right defense, has not also acted in a sufficiently forceful, violent or threatening manner as would separately expose him to prosecution and punishment for assaultive conduct against the robbery victim.

In sum, we find that the Legislature over 100 years ago codified in the current robbery statute the common law recognition that a claim-of-right defense can negate the *animus furandi* element of robbery where the defendant is seeking to regain specific property in which he in good faith believes he has a bona fide claim of ownership or title. Whatever be our views on the wisdom of the Legislature's chosen delineation of the mental state necessary for robbery, the separation of powers clause (Cal. Const., art. III, §3) prohibits this court from abolishing the claim-of-right defense altogether on policy grounds, as such would effectively alter a statutorily defined element of that offense by judicial fiat. The Legislature of course remains free to amend section 211 to preclude a claim-of-right defense in robbery prosecutions. The question whether such amendment would better reflect sound public policy is one properly addressed to that body rather than to this court.

c. *Expansion of the claim-of-right defense to robberies perpetrated to satisfy, settle or collect on a debt*

As noted above, *Butler* broadly held that "a bona fide belief, even though mistakenly held, that one has a right or claim to the property [taken in a robbery] negates felonious intent [Citations.]." *Butler* was a felony-murder case in which the defendant, a former employee of the victim, believed the victim owed him money, went armed with a gun to the victim's home "to collect payment," shot and killed the victim (and also shot another person present in the victim's home) during an ensuing scuffle, searched the home for money and found none, and finally "took a wallet and ran from the house." (*Id.* at p. 572.) The *Butler* court reversed defendant's murder conviction, concluding a claim-of-right defense could negate the felonious intent required for robbery on those facts.

In furtherance of the public policy of discouraging the use of forcible self-help, a majority of cases from other jurisdictions decided after *Butler* that have addressed the question whether claim of right should be available as a defense to robbery have rejected *Butler*'s expansive holding that a good faith belief by a defendant that he was entitled to the money or possessions of the victim to satisfy or collect on a debt is a defense to robbery.

In *Barnett, supra,* we confronted claims of instructional error, ineffective assistance of counsel and prosecutorial misconduct stemming from the trial court's failure to instruct on a claim-of-right defense as to one of two robbery victims in a capital case in which a robbery-murder special circumstance was alleged. After reviewing the rationale and holding of *Butler, supra,* we made the following observations regarding the policy implications of permitting a claim-of-right defense to robbery:

"In his dissent in *Butler,* Justice Mosk took a dim view of the majority's apparent authorization of armed robbery as a self-help measure. Pointing out that the statutory provision defining robbery (§211) raised no issue of ownership of property forcibly taken, but only its possession, Justice Mosk saw no statutory basis for the defense. Moreover, noting that the leading cases permitting forcible recapture of property were all decided before the turn of the century, Justice Mosk concluded that a six-shooter was no longer 'an acceptable device for do-it-yourself debt collection' and that the 'might-makes-right' doctrine of the previous century was of 'dubious adaptability' to modern times.

"Since Butler was decided, a number of other jurisdictions have rejected the claim-of-right defense for public policy reasons in cases where force, violence, or weapons are used for self-help debt collection. [Citations.] As several courts have observed, the proposition that a claim of right negates the felonious intent in robbery ' "not only is lacking in sound reason and logic, but it is utterly incompatible with and has no place in an ordered and orderly society such as ours, which eschews self-help through violence. Adoption of the proposition would be but one step short of accepting lawless reprisal as an appropriate means of redressing grievances, real or fancied." ' [Citations.]" (*Barnett,* 17 Cal.4th at pp. 1143–1144.)

In *Barnett* we were not asked by the People "to revisit *Butler*'s increasingly anachronistic authorization of the claim-of-right defense in the context of armed robbery." (Barnett, 17 Cal.4th at p. 1146.) However, noting "the obvious public policy reasons for strictly circumscribing the circumstances under which persons should be permitted *to enforce their debt demands* at gunpoint [citations], we conclude[d] the defense is not available *where the claimed debt* is uncertain and subject to dispute." (*Ibid.,* italics added.)

The People in this case urge that "[t]he rationale for declining to permit a defendant to assert a claim of right defense in a robbery case is quite simple: An ordered society founded on the rule of law does not countenance self-help when it is accomplished by the use of fear, intimidation, or violence."

Justice Mosk espoused a similar viewpoint in regard to the *Butler* majority's application of the claim-of-right defense to the facts there in issue: "[T]he question is ultimately one of basic public policy, which unequivocally dictates that the proper forum for resolving *debt disputes* is a court of law, pursuant to legal process—not the street, at the business end of a lethal weapon. Had this defendant been entrusted with the contents of the deceased's wallet, and had he appropriated them to his own use, believing he was entitled to keep the funds in payment of wages or a debt, that belief would have furnished him no defense to a charge of embezzlement (Pen. Code, §511; *People v. Proctor* (1959) 169 Cal.App.2d 269, 277). By parity of rationale, the claim of offset denied to the trusted employee who dips into the company cashbox should be denied to one who, like this defendant, enforces his demands at gunpoint. To hold otherwise would be to constitute him judge and jury in his own cause." (*Butler* (dis. opn. of Mosk, J.), italics added.)

" 'It is a general principle that one who is or believes he is injured or deprived of what he is lawfully entitled to must apply to the state for help. Self-help is in conflict with the very idea of social order. It subjects the weaker to risk of the arbitrary will or mistaken belief of the stronger. Hence the law in general forbids it.' " (*Daluiso v. Boone* (1969) 71 Cal.2d 484, 500, quoting 5 Pound, Jurisprudence (1959) §142, pp. 351–352.)

In *State v. Ortiz* (1973) 124 N.J.Super. 189, the New Jersey appellate court quoted the holding in *Butler* and criticized the decision for failing to acknowledge the fundamental policy against encouraging resort to force, fear, or violence to gain possession of money or goods, even when acting under a claim of right. The *Ortiz* court observed that, "A review of the authorities . . . reveals that the proposition so espoused by the California court is little more than a relic of days long past, which did not then and does not now enjoy anything like the universal acceptance suggested by the sweeping language of the majority opinion in *Butler*." (*Id.* at p. 801.) The *Ortiz* court found that allowing a claim-of-right defense to robbery, as provided in *Butler,* was antithetical to an "ordered and orderly society," and concluded by "reject[ing] . . . out of hand" the availability of the defense to robbery. (*Id.* at p. 802.)

In *State v. Mejia* (1995) 141 N.J. 475, the New Jersey Supreme Court quoted the decision in *State v. Ortiz* and concluded, in part "for sound reasons of public policy," that the New Jersey Legislature, in enacting a statutory claim-of-right defense to *theft,* did not intend to extend that affirmative defense to robbery.

The legitimacy of the need for our laws to discourage forcible or violent self-help as a remedy seems beyond question. Defendant himself acknowledges the strong public policy considerations militating against retention of the claim-of-right defense for robbery. Unlike the court in *Mejia, supra,* 141 N.J. 475, however, we have concluded that California's Legislature incorporated the common law claim-of-right doctrine into the statutorily defined mens rea element of robbery when it codified that offense over 100 years ago, and that consequently, we are not free to judicially abolish it and thereby effectively expand the statutory definition of the crime. (§6).

We nonetheless conclude that *Butler* went well beyond the basic underlying notion that a thief or robber must intend to steal *another's* property when, on the facts before it, the court extended the availability of a claim-of-right defense to perpetrators who rob their victims assertedly to settle, satisfy, or otherwise collect on a debt. Specifically, we find nothing in the language of section 211 to suggest the Legislature intended to incorporate such a broad and expansive extension of the claim-of-right doctrine into the robbery statute.

Many of the out-of-state decisions that have rejected *Butler's* expansive extension of the claim-of-right defense to so-called "debt collection" robbery cases have retained it as a viable defense where the defendant takes *specific property* in which he has a bona fide claim of ownership or title.

The Wisconsin Supreme Court in [*Edwards v. State* (1970) 49 Wis.2d 105, 181 N.W.2d 383, 388], cogently set forth the rationale for rejecting a claim-of-right defense to robberies involving forcible debt collection: "The distinction between specific personal property and money in general is important. A debtor can owe another $150 but the $150 in the debtor's pocket is not the specific property of the creditor. One has the intention to steal when he takes money from another's possession against the possessor's consent even though he also intends to apply the stolen money to a debt. The efficacy of self-help by force to enforce a bona fide claim for money does not negate the intent to commit robbery. Can one break into a bank and take money so long as he does not take more than the balance in his savings or checking account? Under the majority rule [as it then existed, allowing a claim of right defense to any robbery] the accused must make change to be sure he collects no more than the amount he believes is due him on the debt. A debt is a relationship and in respect to money seldom finds itself embedded in specific coins and currency of the realm. Consequently, taking money from a debtor by force to pay a debt is robbery. The creditor has no such right of appropriation and allocation."

We agree with the rationale of *Edwards v. State, supra*, and similar decisions drawing a distinction for debt collection cases. Indeed, the *Butler* majority appears to have overlooked this court's earlier decision in *People v. Beggs* (1918) 178 Cal. 79, an extortion case (§518) in which we explained that because of the strong public policy militating against self-help by force or fear, courts will not recognize a good faith defense to the satisfaction of a debt when accomplished by the use of force or fear. . . .

We therefore hold that to the extent *Butler* extended the claim-of-right defense to robberies perpetrated to satisfy, settle or otherwise collect on a debt, liquidated or unliquidated—as opposed to forcible takings intended to recover specific personal property in which the defendant in good faith believes he has a bona fide claim of ownership or title—it is unsupported by the statutory language, further contrary to sound public policy, and in that regard is overruled. . . .

III. CONCLUSION

The judgment of the Court of Appeal affirming defendant's conviction of robbery is reversed, the judgment affirmed in all other respects, and the matter remanded to that court for further proceedings consistent with the views expressed herein.

D. Practice Problems on Theft Offenses

(1) Defendant walked into a grocery store and spent approximately 10 minutes walking up and down the aisles, suspiciously looking around to see if anyone was watching him. At one point, he asked one of the employees if the store carried frozen seafood and was told where to find it. Defendant then took some frozen shrimp up to the counter and paid for it with a credit card. After he signed the charge slip, he asked the cashier if she could give him change for a $20 bill and handed her what he knew was a counterfeit $20. He then waited

while she counted out a $10, $5, four $1s, and $1 in change. He took the money, walked out the door, and was arrested a short time later.

Which of the following would be the most appropriate theft charge against Defendant based on these facts:

(a) Larceny by trick;

(b) Larceny;

(c) False pretenses;

(d) Embezzlement.

(2) Which of the following would be *most distinguishable* from the *Morgan* case, in which the defendant was the manager of the Western Union Office and took money from the safe that was under his control:

(a) Defendant was the Vice President at a bank (in charge of all the bank's funds and supervisor of the entire staff) and he took some money from his secretary's wallet while she was away from her desk;

(b) Defendant was the chief foreman of an automobile assembly plant and took some spare parts from a storage area for use on his own car;

(c) Defendant was the chief accountant for a major corporation and transferred funds from the corporation's bank account to his own personal account;

(d) Defendant was a part-time cashier at a local convenience store and took some money out of her cash register during her shift.

(3) Defendant was desperate for money to feed her drug habit. She decided to pose as a prostitute and steal whatever she could from any customers whom she was able to pick up. A short time after she walked to a local street corner, a man stopped his car and asked her if she was interested in sex for cash, and she said yes. She got into his car and they drove to a secluded parking lot. Once there, she demanded payment in advance, intending to grab the money and then jump out of the car. But when she grabbed for the cash that the man held out, he grabbed her wrist and said, "Not so fast." She then slapped him in the face hard enough to momentarily stun him, pried the money out of his hands, and jumped out of the car.

Which of the following would be the most appropriate theft charge against Defendant based on these facts?

(a) Larceny by trick;

(b) Larceny;

(c) False pretenses;

(d) Robbery.

(4) Defendant worked as a payroll clerk for a large construction company. His job was to print out the paychecks for all the employees, which would then be signed by the President. Defendant's job also included electronically forwarding amounts designated by the employees to their banks for direct deposit. On payday, he printed out all the checks with the correct amounts. But he then

transferred $35,000 in company funds to a bank account that he had set up in a false name. The next day, he went to the bank, wrote out a withdrawal slip for the entire $35,000, and cleaned out the account, receiving a cashier's check for $34,500, plus $500 in cash. When the construction company audited its books, the theft was discovered, and Defendant was eventually arrested.

Assume that the State has theft crimes of larceny, false pretenses, embezzlement, larceny by trick, and robbery. Fully discuss the most appropriate charge based on these facts.

Chapter 9
Necessity of an Act

A. Introduction

The basic elements of a crime include the actus reus, the mens rea, the concurrence of both, and causation. The actus reus is the deed that makes up the physical components of the crime. The mens rea is the mental state, if any, required for the offense. Furthermore, it is not sufficient that both the mens rea and actus reus are present. They must occur concurrently; that is, the mens rea has to be the reason for the actus reus. Finally, the actus reus must proximately cause the prohibited harm.

It is a fundamental principle that no matter how overwhelming the evidence is that a person intended to commit a crime, the law will not impute criminal liability to that person unless there has been some overt act towards putting the intent into effect. The one exception (discussed later in this chapter) involves those limited and specific situations where a person has a legal duty to act and a failure to do so may result in criminal liability.

B. Cases

The required act must be a conscious and voluntary one. For example, *A* picks up a baseball bat and hits *B* over the head, killing him. Thus, *A* has engaged in a voluntary act causing the death of *B*. However, what result if *A* wished that *B* was dead, planned to hit him with a baseball bat, but before doing so, *B* died of a heart attack? The absence of the actus reus precludes criminal liability. People are not punished for their bad thoughts, no matter how evil or immoral. Consider the applicability of this principle in the *Quick* case. At the conclusion, ask yourself if you agree with the result.

1. "Mere guilty intention."

State v. Quick, 199 S.C. 256 (1942)

FISHBURNE, Justice.

The defendant was convicted of the unlawful manufacture of intoxicating liquor under Section 1829, Code 1932, and amendments thereto. The main question in the case, as we see it, is whether the lower Court erred in refusing to direct a verdict of acquittal, a motion therefor having been made at the close of the evidence offered by the State.

On the morning of May 12, 1941, certain officers of Marlboro County found two stills on the property of the defendant in that county, with complete paraphernalia for the distillation of intoxicating liquor. These stills were located about 100 yards from the dead end of a road which led from the state highway into the woods. A pathway ran from the end of the road to the site of the stills. After watching and waiting around the stills for some time, they went to their car, which was parked in the bushes, and backed out upon the road to which we have referred. This road was narrow, and as they started forward they met an approaching automobile owned by the defendant, Shuford Quick, and occupied by him and two young men, and two little children. This car contained 500 pounds of sugar, a sack of mill feed, and three cases of yeast cakes. The appellant and the two young men were promptly arrested and placed in jail. The officers stated that neither of the stills was in operation. One, however, contained mash, and the other appeared to have been recently operated. Two cases of fruit jars were found at the stills, and a little whiskey or wine in a fruit jar. The officers further testified that they did not know to whom the stills belonged. They were located, as already stated, upon land owned by the appellant, and it was testified that his home was in the opposite part of the county.

We think there can be no doubt but that the evidence overwhelmingly tends to show an intention on the part of the appellant to manufacture liquor; certainly such inference may reasonably be drawn. But intent alone, not coupled with some overt act toward putting the intent into effect, is not cognizable by the Courts. The law does not concern itself with mere guilty intention, unconnected with any overt act.

No definite rule as to what constitutes an overt act can safely be laid down in cases of this kind. Each case must depend largely upon its particular facts and the inferences which the jury may reasonably draw therefrom, subject to general principles applied as nearly as can be, with a view to working substantial justice.

It is well settled that the "act" is to be liberally construed, and in numerous cases it is said to be sufficient that the act go far enough toward accomplishment of the crime to amount to the commencement of its consummation. While the efficiency of a particular act depends on the facts of the particular case, the act must always amount to more than mere preparation, and move directly toward the commission of the crime. In any event, it would seem, the act need not be the last proximate step leading to the consummation of the offense. 22 C.J.S., Criminal Law, §75, page 139.

In the case of State v. Ravan, 91 S.C. 265, the defendant was convicted of the unlawful manufacture of intoxicating liquor. Upon appeal the judgment was sustained, but upon a statement of facts different from the facts in the case at bar. In that case the testimony for the State was as follows: "We went to the distillery about 6 o'clock in the morning; no one was there; the still was in the furnace; and we hid ourselves in the bushes around there in sight of the distillery, and at 8:30 Mr. Ravan came with a _____ [sic] under one arm and kindling under the other. The still was full of water, and he let the water out of the still and picked up a piece of copper about the size of that (indicating) and was scraping in the still, and we rushed in on him. . . . We found seven fermenters, and I reckon fully 700 or 800 gallons of beer."

The Court held that this testimony justified the trial Court in its refusal to direct a verdict, and held that, "To constitute the offense of manufacturing liquor it is not necessary that the product of the manufacturer should be complete. Manufacture is 'the process of making by art or reducing materials into form fit for use, by the hand or by machinery;' and one employed in this process is manufacturing."

It will be noted that in the foregoing case the proof showed that the defendant was actually present at the still, in the act of taking out the water, cleaning out the still, and with a bundle of kindling under his arm. But in the case which is now before us, the defendant was 100 yards away from the still, in an automobile, and there is no evidence that he had taken any initial step, or performed any overt act looking toward the commission of the crime of unlawfully manufacturing, unless it can be held that the presence and possession of the sugar, meal, and yeast cakes found in his automobile constituted such overt act.

While the term "overt act" should be given a liberal construction so as to carry into effect the purpose of the law, we do not think that liberality can go so far under the facts in this case, so as to hold the defendant guilty of unlawfully manufacturing intoxicating liquor. There is a wide difference between the preparation for the commission of an offense and the commission of the offense itself, or even the attempt to commit. The preparation consists in devising or arranging the means or measures necessary for the commission of the crime; the attempt or overt act is the direct movement toward the commission, after the preparations are made. People v. Murray, 14 Cal. 159.

In the case at bar, the defendant was not at the stills, and it cannot be said under the facts of this case that he was engaged in the process of manufacturing. The testimony shows nothing more than an act on his part merely preparatory to the commission of the crime, and not an act proximately leading to its consummation, as was evident in the case of State v. Ravan, supra, where the defendant had engaged in manual operations connected with the mechanics of the manufacturing plant.

The appellant likewise raises the issue that the lower Court erred in refusing his motion for a new trial. This assignment of error relates to the instructions given by the Court to the jury. The charge objected to was given in the following language: "Mr. Foreman, as I told you in the beginning, if you conclude that these defendants went out there for the common enterprise of getting ready or doing anything for the manufacture of whiskey, then they would all be guilty if any one of them was guilty. However, if you find that there was some difference between why they were there and what they were there for, why, then, of course, your verdict would be, as to them, different, if you conclude that they were not taking part or intending to take part in the manufacture of whiskey."

It is contended that by this instruction the jury was told that the intention to manufacture intoxicating liquors illegally constituted a violation of the statute of the State, and that if any one or all of the defendants did engage in the manufacture, or intended to engage in the manufacture of liquor, such an act or intention constituted a violation of the law.

We think this charge went too far, and in our opinion it was prejudicial. Nor can we find in the entire charge any statement of the law which would correct it. Our statute makes it unlawful, except under certain conditions and requirements, to manufacture liquor. But it does not constitute an offense to intend to manufacture liquor. No person can lawfully be convicted of an offense merely because he intended to commit it, but did nothing in execution of such intention.

In our opinion the defendant is entitled to a new trial in any event. But because of the error in overruling his motion for a directed verdict the judgment is reversed, with direction to enter a verdict of not guilty.

Note

What is the rationale and justification for not punishing people for their bad thoughts? What are the practicalities if the requirement was otherwise? How much deterrent effect would there be?

2. What makes an act voluntary?

When reading *Decina*, consider whether the requirement of a voluntary act is satisfied when the actor, because of a preexisting medical condition, loses consciousness and causes the death of several people. Does that constitute criminal negligence?

People v. Decina, 2 N.Y.2d 133 (1956)

FROESSEL, Judge.

At about 3:30 p. m. on March 14, 1955, a bright, sunny day, defendant was driving, alone in his car, in a northerly direction on Delaware Avenue in the city of Buffalo. The portion of Delaware Avenue here involved is 60 feet wide. At a point south of an overhead viaduct of the Erie Railroad, defendant's car swerved to the left, across the center line in the street, so that it was completely in the south lane, traveling 35 to 40 miles per hour.

It then veered sharply to the right, crossing Delaware Avenue and mounting the easterly curb at a point beneath the viaduct and continued thereafter at a speed estimated to have been about 50 or 60 miles per hour or more. During this latter swerve, a pedestrian testified that he saw defendant's hand above his head; another witness said he saw defendant's left arm bent over the wheel, and his right hand extended towards the right door.

A group of six schoolgirls were walking north on the easterly sidewalk of Delaware Avenue, two in front and four slightly in the rear, when defendant's car struck them from behind. One of the girls escaped injury by jumping against the wall of the viaduct. The bodies of the children struck were propelled northward onto the street and the lawn in front of a coal company, located to the north of the Erie viaduct on Delaware Avenue. Three of the children, 6 to 12 years old, were found dead on arrival by the medical examiner, and a fourth child, 7 years old, died in a hospital two days later as a result of injuries sustained in the accident . . . .

We turn first to the subject of defendant's cross appeal, namely, that his demurrer should have been sustained, since the indictment here does not charge a crime. The *indictment* states essentially that defendant, *knowing* "that he was subject to epileptic attacks or other disorder rendering him likely to lose consciousness for a considerable period of time", was culpably negligent "in that he *consciously* undertook to and *did operate* his Buick sedan on a public highway" (emphasis supplied) and "while so doing" suffered such an attack which caused said automobile "to travel at a fast and reckless rate of speed, jumping the curb and driving over the sidewalk" causing the death of 4 persons. In our opinion, this clearly states a violation of section 1053–a of the Penal Law. The statute does not require that a defendant must deliberately intend to kill a human being, for that would be murder. Nor does the statute require that he knowingly and consciously follow the precise path that leads to death and destruction. It is sufficient, we have said, when his conduct manifests a "disregard of the consequences which may ensue from the act, and indifference to the rights of others. No clearer definition, applicable to the hundreds of varying circumstances that may arise, can be given. Under a given state of facts, whether negligence is culpable is a question of judgment."

Assuming the truth of the indictment, as we must on a demurrer, this defendant knew he was subject to epileptic attacks and seizures that might strike *at any time*. He also knew that a moving motor vehicle uncontrolled on public highway is a highly dangerous instrumentality capable of unrestrained destruction. With this *knowledge*, and without anyone accompanying him, he deliberately took a chance by making a conscious choice of a course of action, in disregard of the consequences which he knew might follow from his conscious act, and which in this case did ensue. How can we say as a matter of law that this did not amount to culpable negligence within the meaning of section 1053–a?

To hold otherwise would be to say that a man may freely indulge himself in liquor in the same hope that it will not affect his driving, and if it later develops that ensuing intoxication causes dangerous and reckless driving resulting in death, his unconsciousness or involuntariness at that time would relieve him from prosecution under the statute. His awareness of a condition which he knows may produce such consequences as here, and his disregard of the consequences, renders him liable for culpable negligence, as the courts below have properly held. To have a sudden sleeping spell, an unexpected heart or other disabling attack, without any prior knowledge or warning thereof, is an altogether different situation, and there is simply no basis for comparing such cases with the flagrant disregard manifested here. . . .

Accordingly, the Appellate Division properly sustained the lower court's order overruling the demurrer, as well as its denial of the motion in arrest of judgment on the same ground. . . .

Accordingly, the order of the Appellate Division should be affirmed.

Note

On what basis does the court find the "necessity of an act" requirement has been met? What result if the defendant was not aware he was prone to seizures? If the defendant had been on medication to control his epilepsy, then had a seizure while driving his car and killed a pedestrian, would the result be different from *Decina*?

3. Failure to Act

As a general rule, an omission or failure to act does not provide a basis for holding a person criminally responsible. While circumstances may create an arguable moral duty to act, subject to a few exceptions, there is no corresponding legal duty to act. Consider an Olympic swimmer who sees a child drowning and takes no steps to save her. The swimmer incurs no criminal liability, even though he could have saved her. The criminal law subscribes to the maxim that we are not our brothers' keepers. Most states—if not all—have

Good Samaritan laws that generally protect medical professionals from civil liability when acting in good faith to assist injured people.[*]

In *Jones*, the court considers the circumstances where a failure to act may result in criminal liability. Which of those are present in the case itself?

Jones v. United States, 308 F.2d 307 (D.C. Cir. 1962)

[Shirley Green, the mother of the two children mentioned in the case, arranged to have the appellant, a family friend, transport one of her newborn children from the hospital to her parents' home where she was then living. When it was time for the child to leave the hospital, the appellant took him to her own home rather than to Shirley Green's. The child stayed with the appellant for several months. While Shirley Green paid the appellant $72 a month for the care of her first child, there seems to have been no monetary agreement between Shirley Green and the appellant for her second child. There was evidence that the second child suffered substantial abuse while in the appellant's home and eventually died.]

WRIGHT, Circuit Judge.

Appellant, together with one Shirley Green, was tried on a three-count indictment charging them jointly with (1) abusing and maltreating Robert Lee Green, (2) abusing and maltreating Anthony Lee Green, and (3) involuntary manslaughter through failure to perform their legal duty of care for Anthony Lee Green, which failure resulted in his death. At the close of evidence, after trial to a jury, the first two counts were dismissed as to both defendants. On the third count, appellant was convicted of involuntary manslaughter. Shirley Green was found not guilty.

Appellant urges several grounds for reversal. We need consider but two. First, appellant argues that there was insufficient evidence as a matter of law to warrant a jury finding of breach of duty in the care she rendered Anthony Lee. Alternatively, appellant argues that the trial court committed plain error in failing to instruct the jury that it must first find that appellant was under a legal obligation to provide food and necessities to Anthony Lee before finding her guilty of manslaughter in failing to provide them. The first argument is without merit. Upon the latter we reverse . . . .

Appellant . . . takes exception to the failure of the trial court to charge that the jury must find beyond a reasonable doubt, as an element of the crime, that appellant was under a legal duty to supply food and necessities to Anthony Lee. Appellant's attorney did not object to the failure to give this instruction, but urges here the application of Rule 52(b).

---

[*] Although there is no general duty to assist injured people, Michigan provides a number of instances where those rendering aid in good faith are protected from civil liability. *See* M.C.L. 691.1501.

The problem of establishing the duty to take action which would preserve the life of another has not often arisen in the case law of this country. The most commonly cited statement of the rule is found in *People v. Beardsley*, 150 Mich. 206 (1907):

> The law recognizes that under some circumstances the omission of a duty owed by one individual to another, where such omission results in the death of the one to whom the duty is owing, will make the other chargeable with manslaughter. . . . This rule of law is always based upon the proposition that the duty neglected must be a legal duty, and not a mere moral obligation. It must be a duty imposed by law or by contract, and the omission to perform the duty must be the immediate and direct cause of death. . . .

There are at least four situations in which the failure to act may constitute breach of a legal duty. One can be held criminally liable: first, where a statute imposes a duty to care for another; second, where one stands in a certain status relationship to another; third, where one has assumed a contractual duty to care for another; and fourth, where one has voluntarily assumed the care of another and so secluded the helpless person as to prevent others from rendering aid.

It is the contention of the Government that either the third or the fourth ground is applicable here. However, it is obvious that in any of the four situations, there are critical issues of fact which must be passed on by the jury—specifically in this case, whether appellant had entered into a contract with the mother for the care of Anthony Lee or, alternatively, whether she assumed the care of the child and secluded him from the care of his mother, his natural protector. On both of these issues, the evidence is in direct conflict, appellant insisting that the mother was actually living with appellant and Anthony Lee, and hence should have been taking care of the child herself, while Shirley Green testified she was living with her parents and was paying appellant to care for both children.

In spite of this conflict, the instructions given in the case failed even to suggest the necessity for finding a legal duty of care. The only reference to duty in the instructions was the reading of the indictment, which charged, inter alia, that the defendants "failed to perform their legal duty." A finding of legal duty is the critical element of the crime charged and failure to instruct the jury concerning it was plain error. . . .

Reversed and remanded.

4. Assuming a Duty to Act

What about a person who is not required to provide care for someone, but assumes care for that individual? Does his or her subsequent failure to provide the necessary care result in a breach of a legal duty? A parent has a legal duty to care for a minor child, but does an adult child have a legal obligation to care for a parent? Even if the answer is no, are there circumstances where the law will recognize that an adult child's failure to provide care for a parent will result in criminal liability? Consider this issue as you read *Davis*.

Davis v. Commonwealth, 230 Va. 201 (1985)

STEPHENSON, Justice.

In a bench trial, Mary B. Davis was convicted of involuntary manslaughter of her mother, Emily B. Carter, and sentenced to 10 years in the penitentiary. The trial court found that Carter's death resulted from Davis' criminal negligence in failing to provide her mother with heat, food, liquids, and other necessaries.

The principal issues in this appeal are: (1) whether Davis had a legal duty to care for Carter, and if so, (2) whether she breached the duty by conduct constituting criminal negligence. . . .

On November 29, 1983, a paramedic with the Lynchburg Fire Department responded to a call at a house located at 1716 Monroe Street in the City of Lynchburg. The house was occupied by Davis and Carter. The paramedic arrived about 5:35 p.m. and found Carter lying on a bed. It was a cold day, and there was no heat in Carter's room. The only source of heat was a tin heater, and it was not being used. The only food in the house was two cans of soup, a can of juice, and an open box of macaroni and cheese. Two trash cans were found behind the house. One contained 11 or 12 empty vegetable cans, and the other was full of empty beer cans. An operable stove, a supply of firewood and a color television were found in Davis' upstairs bedroom.

Carter was admitted to a hospital that evening. . . .

A forensic pathologist with the Chief Medical Examiner's Office conducted an autopsy on Carter's body. He concluded that the causes of death were "pneumonia and freezing to death due to exposure to cold with a chronic state of starvation." He stated that any one of these conditions alone could have caused her death.

Additionally, the pathologist testified that a body temperature of 80 degrees was extremely low and that, except in rare, isolated cases involving children or young people, "no one survives" such a low body temperature. He estimated that it would take nine hours for a dead body to reach a temperature of 82 degrees in a room temperature of 67 degrees and that a living person would require a longer exposure to the cold to reach that temperature.

The pathologist further testified that when a person's dehydration reaches a five to seven percent range, it suggests that she has received no liquids for at least two days. He described Carter's condition as "bone dry." He also testified that Carter's physical condition at the time of the autopsy indicated that she had eaten "no food whatsoever" for at least 30 days.

For a number of years, Carter had been senile and totally disabled. The attending physician testified that Davis said her mother was "not able to feed herself at all; that she was not able to care for her personal needs and that she had to wear diapers and had to have total care." Moreover, Davis informed a number of people that she was responsible for the total care of Carter.

Carter signed a writing naming Davis her authorized representative to apply for, receive, and use her food stamps. Relying on this document, the Department of Social Services awarded Davis additional food stamp benefits of $75 per month and exempted her from the requirement of registering for outside employment as a requisite to receiving these benefits.

Davis also was the representative payee of Carter's social security benefits in the amount of $310 per month. Davis' household expenses were paid exclusively from Carter's social security. Davis also received $23 per month in food stamps for her mother. . . .

. . . [W]e determine whether, under the facts and circumstances presented, Davis was under a legal duty to care for her mother. This presents an issue which we have not addressed previously.

A legal duty is one either "imposed by law, or by contract." When a death results from an omission to perform a legal duty, the person obligated to perform the duty may be guilty of culpable homicide. If the death results from a malicious omission of the performance of a duty, the offense is murder. On the other hand, although no malice is shown, if a person is criminally negligent in omitting to perform a duty, he is guilty of involuntary manslaughter.

Davis acknowledges the accuracy of the foregoing legal principles. She contends, however, that the evidence fails to establish that she had a legal duty to care for her mother, asserting that the evidence proved at most a moral duty. We do not agree.

The evidence makes clear that Davis accepted sole responsibility for the total care of Carter. This became her full-time occupation. In return, Carter allowed Davis to live in her home expense free and shared with Davis her income from social security. Additionally, Carter authorized Davis to act as her food stamp representative, and for this Davis received food stamp benefits in her own right. From this uncontroverted evidence, the trial court reasonably could find the existence of an implied contract. Clearly, Davis was more than a mere volunteer; she had a legal duty, not merely a moral one, to care for her mother.

Finally, we consider whether the evidence is sufficient to support the trial court's finding of criminal negligence. . . .

When the proximate cause of a death is simply ordinary negligence, *i.e.*, the failure to exercise reasonable care, the negligent party cannot be convicted of involuntary manslaughter. To constitute criminal negligence essential to a conviction of involuntary manslaughter, an accused's conduct "must be of such reckless, wanton or flagrant nature as to indicate a callous disregard for human life and of the probable consequences of the act."

Davis contends that she cared for her mother as best she could under the circumstances. She points to the testimony of her four sisters and her boyfriend who stated that everything seemed normal and that they observed nothing to suggest that Carter was being neglected. These witnesses stated that the house always was heated properly and that sufficient food was available at all times.

Against this testimony, however, was the scientific evidence that Carter died of starvation and freezing. The evidence indicates that Carter had received no food for at least 30 days. She lay helpless in bed in an unheated room during cold weather. The trial court, as the trier of fact, determines the weight of the evidence and the credibility of the witnesses. Obviously, the court, as it had the right to do, accepted the Commonwealth's evidence and gave little or no weight to the testimony of the defendant and her witnesses. The court reasonably could conclude that Carter could not have starved or frozen to death unless she had been neglected completely for a protracted period of time.

We hold, therefore, that the evidence supports the trial court's finding that Davis' breach of duty was so gross and wanton as to show a callous and reckless disregard of Carter's life and that Davis' criminal negligence proximately caused Carter's death. Accordingly, we will affirm the judgment of the trial court.

Affirmed.

5. Criminal Liability of Employers

Is an employer ever criminally responsible for the acts of his or her employees? What if the employer is not present when the acts occur?

Moreland v. State, 164 Ga. 467 (1927)

[The owner of a car and its driver were charged with murder. The driver was operating the vehicle at a high rate of speed in inclement weather. The owner was present in the vehicle but took no steps to require the driver to slow down. There was a crash resulting in the death of the driver of another vehicle and the owner was convicted of involuntary manslaughter.]

HILL, J. . . .

Pen. Code 1910, §67, provides that:

> Involuntary manslaughter shall consist in the killing of a human being without any intention to do so, but in the commission of an unlawful act, or a lawful act, which probably might produce such a consequence, in an unlawful manner: Provided, that where such involuntary killing shall happen in the commission of an unlawful act which, in its consequences, naturally tends to destroy the life of a human being, or is committed in the prosecution of a riotous intent, or of a crime punishable by death or confinement in the

penitentiary, the offense shall be deemed and adjudged to be murder. . . .

. . . Under the above definition of what constitutes involuntary manslaughter in the commission of an unlawful act, there can be no question that that offense was committed by whomever was responsible for the operation of the automobile in question at the time of the unfortunate homicide. Whoever was responsible, it cannot be questioned under the facts as stated by the Court of Appeals that the automobile of Moreland was being operated in violation of the law of this state. It was being run at a rate of 50 miles per hour, when the law says that it could be run upon the public highway at a rate not exceeding 30 miles per hour. It was in violation of the law which prevents one vehicle passing another on the wrong side of the road. It was violating the law in running at a rate of speed in violation of a penal statute which provides that on a sharp curve that an automobile shall not exceed the speed of 10 miles per hour. And the sole question to be decided is, Is Moreland, the owner of the automobile, liable for the acts of his chauffeur done in his presence? He was present, and there is nothing to indicate that he remonstrated with the chauffeur, or attempted to prevent him from running at the high rate of speed of 50 miles per hour, around a curve, while it was raining. Under these circumstances, we are of the opinion that the owner of the car was in control thereof, and that he should have seen to it that his chauffeur did not operate the car in such a manner contrary to law as might produce such a consequence in an unlawful manner as that which happened on this fateful occasion. It must be held, therefore, that the owner of the car must have known, and did know, that it was being operated contrary to law, and that he did consent and agree to the running of the car at such a high rate of speed; and that being true, he is responsible for what happened in consequence of such violation of the law. It would be the owner's duty, when he saw that the law was being violated and that his machine was being operated in such a way as to be dangerous to the life and property of others on the highway, to curb and restrain one in his employment and under his control, and prevent him from violating the law with his own property. The owner of the automobile was bound to know that it was very dangerous for his chauffeur to run and operate the car at 50 miles per hour during a rainstorm along a public highway and at a dangerous curve. He was bound to know that a car operated at such a place and in such a manner was liable to come in collision and injure occupants of other automobiles upon the highway; and, that being so, he was equally guilty with his employee in causing the homicide in question, although he may have had no intention of injuring or killing the woman in question. It is not insisted that the operator of the car or the owner willfully intended to kill the party named in the indictment. As already stated, it is a question of intentional neglect not to curb the operator of the car when he was violating the highway law of the state. Nor is it a question here that the owner and operator of the car entered into a conspiracy to kill the party so killed, or any one else. The question of conspiracy is not involved.

So we reach the conclusion that the question propounded by the Court of Appeals must be answered in the affirmative.

Rex v. Huggins, 92 Eng. Rep. 518 (1730)

[The warden and his deputy were charged with the murder of a prisoner. The deputy assaulted the prisoner and kept him in an "unwholesome room" where he eventually died. The court considered whether to affirm the conviction of the warden based upon his position as supervisor of the deputy.]

In this case two questions have been made. 1. What crime the facts found upon Barnes in the special verdict will amount to? 2. Whether the prisoner at the Bar is found guilty of the same offence with Barnes?

1. As to the first question, it is very plain that the facts found upon Barnes do amount to murder in him. Murder may be committed without any stroke. The law has not confined the offence to any particular circumstances or manner of killing; but there are as many ways to commit murder, as there are to destroy a man, provided the act be done with malice, either express or implied. . . . In this case the jury have found the malice express: for the facts charged on Barnes are laid in the indictment to be *ex malitia sua praecogitata*, to wit, that he having the custody of Arne assaulted him, and carried him to this unwholesome room, and confined him there by force against his will, and without his consent, and without proper support, *ex malitia sua praecogitata*; by means of which he languished and died. And the jury have found that Barnes did all these facts, *modo et forma prout in indictamento praedicto specificatur*. . . .

2. The next question is, whether the prisoner Higgins [sic] is found guilty of the same offence as Barnes; or how far it appears by this special verdict, that he has been aiding and assisting to Barnes in the committing of these facts. . . .

The Judges are all unanimously of opinion, that the facts found in this special verdict do not amount to murder in the prisoner at the Bar; but as this special verdict is found, they are of opinion, that he is not guilty. Though he was warden, yet it being found, that there was a deputy; he is not, as warden, guilty of the facts committed under the authority of his deputy. He shall answer as superior for his deputy civilly, but not criminally. It has been settled, that though a sheriff must answer for the offences of his gaoler civilly, that is, he is subject in an action, to make satisfaction to the party injured; yet he is not to answer criminally for the offences of his under-officer. He only is criminally punishable, who immediately does the act, or permits it to be done. Hale's P.C. 114. So that if an act be done by an under-officer, unless it is done by the command or direction, or with the consent of the principal, the principal is not criminally punishable for it. In this case the fact was done by Barnes; and it no where appears in the special verdict, that the prisoner at the Bar ever commanded, or directed, or consented to this duress of imprisonment, which was the cause of Arne's death. 1. No command or direction is found. And 2. It is not found, that Huggins knew of it. That which made the duress in this case was, 1. Barnes's carrying, and putting, and confining Arne in this room by force and against his consent. 2. The situation and condition of this room. Now it is not found that Huggins knew these several circumstances, which made the duress. 1. It is not found, that he knew anything of Barnes's carrying Arne thither. 2. Nor that he was there without his consent, or without proper support. 3. As to the room, it is found by the verdict, 1. That the room was built of brick and mortar. 2. That the walls were valde humidae. 3. That the room was situate on the common sewer of the prison, and near the place where the filth of the prison and excrement of the prisoners were usually laid, ratione quorum the room was very unwholesome, and the life of any man kept there was in great danger. But all that is found with respect to the prisoner's knowledge is, that for fifteen days before Arne's death he knew that the room was then lately built, recenter, that the walls were made of brick and mortar, and were then damp. But it is not found, nor does it appear, that he knew, they were dangerous to a man's life, or that there was a want of necessary support. Nor is it found, that he directed, or consented, that Arne should be kept or continued there . . . .

Upon the whole, there is no authority against the Court's giving judgment of acquittal, upon a verdict that is not sufficient to convict; and therefore this verdict, not finding facts sufficient to make the prisoner guilty of murder, he must be adjudged not guilty. And he was discharged.

Note

Is criminal intent alone sufficient to convict a defendant of a crime? What else is necessary? When may a failure to act satisfy the actus reus of a criminal offense?

What are the five ways in which a legal duty to act may arise? What are the two most common examples of a legal duty arising from a status relationship? Can an innocent passerby who has no legal duty to act, but who may have a moral obligation to do so, be held criminally responsible for harm resulting from his or her failure to act?

In addition to a failure to act when there was a legal duty to do so, what else must the prosecution prove in order to convict a defendant based on a failure to act?

C. Model Penal Code Provisions

§2.01. Requirement of Voluntary Act; Omission as Basis of Liability

(1)   A person is not guilty of an offense unless his liability is based on conduct that includes a voluntary act or the omission to perform an act of which he is physically capable.

(2)   The following are not voluntary acts within the meaning of this Section:

   (a)   a reflex or convulsion;

   (b)   a bodily movement during unconsciousness or sleep;

   (c)   conduct during hypnosis or resulting from hypnotic suggestion;

   (d)   a bodily movement that otherwise is not a product of the effort or determination of the actor, either conscious or habitual.

(3)   Liability for the commission of an offense may not be based on an omission unaccompanied by action unless:

   (a)   the omission is expressly made sufficient by the law defining the offense; or

   (b)   a duty to perform the omitted act is otherwise imposed by law.

Chapter 10
Attempt and Solicitation

A.   Introduction

As discussed in Chapter 9, a fundamental principle of Anglo-American law is that no matter how overwhelming the evidence that a person intended to commit a crime, the law will not impute criminal liability to that person unless there has been some overt act towards putting his or her intent into effect. There are generally three inchoate (or incomplete) crimes: (1) attempt, (2) solicitation, and (3) conspiracy. This chapter will focus on attempt and solicitation; conspiracy will be addressed in a later chapter.

Because all three crimes deal with the gray area between merely thinking about the commission of a crime and actually completing the offense, some tension occasionally develops between the police and the prosecutor. Generally, the police seek an earlier intervention to protect potential victims, whereas the prosecutor seeks a later intervention to ensure that the defendant has taken a sufficient number of steps to demonstrate a seriousness of purpose (so as not to punish innocent conduct). This begs the question: How far does the crime have to proceed before it merits official sanction?

B.   Attempt Crimes

The inchoate (or incomplete) crime of attempt involves situations where the actor has, in addition to forming the mens rea, completed a sufficient number of overt acts (i.e., actus reus) towards the completion of the offense. Attempt crimes are punished because, at that point in time, the actor has already manifested danger to the community. The crime is not "attempt" standing alone, but rather "attempted murder," "attempted rape," etc.

Attempt crimes are considered a lesser offense than the completed substantive crime. If the substantive crime is committed, the attempt merges into the completed offense. Generally, most jurisdictions punish attempts less severely than the completed crime.

1. **Is attempt a specific intent or general intent crime?**

As you read the *Thacker* case, consider what the court held was necessary to establish the mens rea for attempted murder.

Thacker v. Commonwealth, 134 Va. 767 (1922)

WEST, J.

This writ of error is to a judgment upon the verdict of a jury finding John Thacker, the accused, guilty of attempting to murder Mrs. J. A. Ratrie, and fixing his punishment at two years in the penitentiary.

The only assignment of error is the refusal of the trial court to set aside the verdict as contrary to the law and the evidence.

The accused, in company with two other young men, Doc Campbell and Paul Kelly, was attending a church festival in Alleghany county, at which all three became intoxicated. They left the church between 10 and 11 o'clock at night, and walked down the county road about 1½ miles, when they came to a sharp curve. Located in this curve was a tent in which the said Mrs. J. A. Ratrie, her husband, four children, and a servant were camping for the summer. The husband, though absent, was expected home that night, and Mrs. Ratrie, upon retiring, had placed a lighted lamp on a trunk by the head of her bed. After 11 o'clock she was awakened by the shots of a pistol and loud talking in the road near by, and heard a man say, "I am going to shoot that Goddamned light out;" and another voice said, "Don't shoot the light out." The accused and his friends then appeared at the back of the tent, where the flaps of the tent were open, and said they were from Bath county and had lost their way, and asked Mrs. Ratrie if she could take care of them all night. She informed them she was camping for the summer, and had no room for them. One of the three thanked her, and they turned away, but after passing around the tent the accused used some vulgar language and did some cursing and singing. When they got back in the road, the accused said again he was going to shoot the light out, and fired three shots, two of which went through the tent, one passing through the head of the bed in which Mrs. Ratrie was lying, just missing her head and the head of her baby, who was sleeping with her. The accused did not know Mrs. Ratrie, and had never seen her before. He testified he did not know any of the parties in the tent, and had no ill will against either of them; that he simply shot at the light, without any intent to harm Mrs. Ratrie or any one else; that he would not have shot had he been sober, and regretted his action.

The foregoing are the admitted facts in the case.

An attempt to commit a crime is composed of two elements: (1) The intent to commit it; and (2) a direct, ineffectual act done towards its commission. The act must reach far enough towards the accomplishment of the desired result to amount to the commencement of the consummation.

The law can presume the intention so far as realized in the act, but not an intention beyond what was so realized. The law does not presume, because an assault was made with a weapon likely to produce death, that it was an assault with the intent to murder. And where it takes a particular intent to constitute a crime, that particular intent must be proved either by direct or circumstantial evidence, which would warrant the inference of the intent with which the act was done.

When a statute makes an offense to consist of an act combined with a particular intent, that intent is just as necessary to be proved as the act itself, and must be found as a matter of fact before a conviction can be had; and no intent in law or mere legal presumption, differing from the intent in fact, can be allowed to supply the place of the latter.

In discussing the law of attempts, Mr. Clark in his work on Criminal Law says, at page 111:

> The act must be done with the specific intent to commit a particular crime. This specific intent at the time the act is done is essential. To do an act from general malevolence is not an attempt to commit a crime, because there is no specific intent, though the act according to its consequences may amount to a substantive crime. **To do an act with intent to commit one crime cannot be an attempt to commit another crime, though it might result in such other crime.** To set fire to a house and burn a human being who is in it, but not to the offender's knowledge, would be murder, though the intent was to burn the house only; but to attempt to set fire to the house under such circumstances would be an attempt to commit arson only and not an attempt to murder. A man actuated by general malevolence may commit murder, though there is no actual intention to kill; to be guilty of an attempt to murder there must be a specific intent to kill.

Mr. Bishop, in his Criminal Law, vol. 1 (8th Ed.), at section 729, says:

> When the law makes an act, whether more or less evil in itself, punishable, though done simply from general malevolence, if one takes what, were all accomplished, would be a step towards it, yet if he does not mean to do the whole, no court can justly hold him answerable for more than he does. And when the thing done does not constitute a substantive crime, there is no ground for treating it as an attempt. So that necessarily an act prompted by general malevolence, or by a specific design to do something else, is not an attempt to commit a crime not intended. . . . When we say that a man attempted to do a given wrong, we mean that he intended to do specifically it, and proceeded a

certain way in the doing. The intent in the mind covers the thing in full; the act covers it only in part. Thus (section 730) to commit murder, one need not intend to take life, but to be guilty of an attempt to murder, he must so intend. It is not sufficient that his act, had it proved fatal, would have been murder. Section 736. We have seen that the unintended taking of life may be murder, yet there can be no attempt to murder without the specific intent to commit it— a rule the latter branch whereof appears probably in a few of the states to have been interfered with by statutes (citing Texas cases). For example, if one from a housetop recklessly throws down a billet of wood upon the sidewalk where persons are constantly passing, and it falls upon a person passing by and kills him, this would be the common-law murder, but if, instead of killing, it inflicts only a slight injury, the party could not be convicted of an assault with attempt to commit murder, since, in fact, the murder was not intended.

The application of the foregoing principles to the facts of the instant case shows clearly, as we think, that the judgment complained of is erroneous. While it might possibly be said that the firing of the shot into the head of Mrs. Ratrie's bed was an act done towards the commission of the offense charged, the evidence falls far short of proving that it was fired with the intent to murder her.

However averse we may be to disturb the verdict of the jury, our obligation to the law compels us to do so.

The judgment complained of will be reversed, the verdict of the jury set aside, and the case remanded for a new trial therein, if the commonwealth shall be so advised.

Reversed.

2. **What are the common law tests to determine whether the actor has committed a sufficient number of overt acts to constitute attempt?**

a. **Dangerous Proximity**

Neither the common law nor most states provide a clear vision of the *actus reus* of a criminal attempt. . . . [C]ourts have developed a myriad of sometimes overlapping rules or tests meant to identify the point, or line, past which conduct constitutes a criminal attempt. [Joshua Dressler, *Understanding Criminal Law* §27.06[A] (6th ed. 2012).]

Compare what constitutes "dangerous proximity" under the common law, as discussed in *Rizzo,* with the approach taken by the MPC, as discussed in *Young v. State,* immediately following *Rizzo.*

How close did you get to completion.

People v Rizzo, 246 N.Y. 334 (1927)

CRANE, J.

The police of the city of New York did excellent work in this case by preventing the commission of a serious crime. It is a great satisfaction to realize that we have such wide-awake guardians of our peace. Whether or not the steps which the defendant had taken up to the time of his arrest amounted to the commission of a crime, as defined by our law, is, however, another matter. He has been convicted of an attempt to commit the crime of robbery in the first degree and sentenced to State's prison. There is no doubt that he had the intention to commit robbery if he got the chance. An examination, however, of the facts is necessary to determine whether his acts were in preparation to commit the crime if the opportunity offered, or constituted a crime in itself, known to our law as an attempt to commit robbery in the first degree. Charles Rizzo, the defendant, appellant, with three others, Anthony J. Dorio, Thomas Milo and John Thomasello, on January 14th planned to rob one Charles Rao of a payroll valued at about $1,200 which he was to carry from the bank for the United Lathing Company. These defendants, two of whom had firearms, started out in an automobile, looking for Rao or the man who had the payroll on that day. Rizzo claimed to be able to identify the man and was to point him out to the others who were to do the actual holding up. The four rode about in their car looking for Rao. They went to the bank from which he was supposed to get the money and to various buildings being constructed by the United Lathing Company. At last they came to One Hundred and Eightieth street and Morris Park avenue. By this time they were watched and followed by two police officers. As Rizzo jumped out of the car and ran into the building all four were arrested. The defendant was taken out from the building in which he was hiding. Neither Rao nor a man named Previti, who was also supposed to carry a payroll, were at the place at the time of the arrest. The defendants had not found or seen the man they intended to rob; no person with a payroll was at any of the places where they had stopped and no one had been pointed out or identified by Rizzo. The four men intended to rob the payroll man, whoever he was. They were looking for him, but they had not seen or discovered him up to the time they were arrested.

Does this constitute the crime of an attempt to commit robbery in the first degree? The Penal Law, §2, prescribes,

> An act, done with intent to commit a crime, and tending but failing to effect its commission, is 'an attempt to commit that crime.'

The word "tending" is very indefinite. It is perfectly evident that there will arise differences of opinion as to whether an act in a given case is one *tending* to commit a crime. "Tending" means to exert activity in a particular direction. Any act in preparation to commit a crime may be said to have a tendency towards its accomplishment. The procuring of the automobile, searching the streets looking for the desired victim, were in reality acts tending toward the commission of the proposed crime. The law, however, has recognized that many acts in the way of preparation are too remote to constitute the crime of attempt. The line has been drawn between those acts which are remote and those which are proximate and near to the consummation. The law must be practical, and, therefore, considers those acts only as tending to the commission of the crime which are so near to its accomplishment that in all reasonable probability the crime itself would have been committed but for timely interference. The cases which have been before the courts express this idea in different language, but the idea remains the same. The act or acts must come or advance very near to the accomplishment of the intended crime. In People v. Mills, 178 N. Y. 274, 284, it was said:

> Felonious intent alone is not enough, but there must be
> an overt act shown in order to establish even an attempt. An
> overt act is one done to carry out the intention, and it must
> be such as would naturally effect that result, unless
> prevented by some extraneous cause.

In Hyde v. U. S., 225 U. S. 347, it was stated that the act amounts to an attempt when it is so near to the result that the danger of success is very great. "There must be dangerous proximity to success." Halsbury in his "Laws of England," vol. 9, p. 259, says:

> An act in order to be a criminal attempt must be
> immediately, and not remotely, connected with and directly
> tending to the commission of an offence.

Commonwealth v. Peaslee, 177 Mass. 267, refers to the acts constituting an attempt as coming *very near* to the accomplishment of the crime.

The method of committing or attempting crime varies in each case so that the difficulty, if any, is not with this rule of law regarding an attempt, which is well understood, but with its application to the facts. As I have said before, minds differ over proximity and the nearness of the approach.

How shall we apply this rule of immediate nearness to this case? The defendants were looking for the payroll man to rob him of his money. This is the charge in the indictment. Robbery is defined in section 2120 of the Penal Law as "the unlawful taking of personal property, from the person or in the presence of another, against his will, by means of force, or violence, or fear of injury, immediate or future, to his person;" and it is made robbery in the first degree by section 2124 when committed by a person aided by accomplices actually present. To constitute the crime of robbery the money must have been taken from Rao by means of force or violence, or through fear. The crime of attempt to commit robbery was committed if these defendants did an act tending to the commission of this robbery. Did the acts above described come dangerously near to the taking of Rao's property? Did the acts come so near the commission of robbery that there was reasonable likelihood of its accomplishment but for the interference? Rao was not found; the defendants were still looking for him; no attempt to rob him could be made, at least until he came in sight; he was not in the building at One Hundred and Eightieth street and Morris Park avenue. There was no man there with the payroll for the United Lathing Company whom these defendants could rob. Apparently no money had been drawn from the bank for the payroll by anybody at the time of the arrest. In a word, these defendants had planned to commit a crime and were looking around the city for an opportunity to commit it, but the opportunity fortunately never came. Men would not be guilty of an attempt at burglary if they had planned to break into a building and were arrested while they were hunting about the streets for the building not knowing where it was. Neither would a man be guilty of an attempt to commit murder if he armed himself and started out to find the person whom he had planned to kill but could not find him. So here these defendants were not guilty of an attempt to commit robbery in the first degree when they had not found or reached the presence of the person they intended to rob.

For these reasons, the judgment of conviction of this defendant, appellant, must be reversed and a new trial granted. . . .

b. Substantial Step   MPC

According to *Rizzo*, what would have been necessary before the police arrested the defendants? Would it have been sufficient if they saw the intended victim? How close would they need to get to the intended victim? Is the court's decision good public policy? Now consider the approach taken in the *Young* decision.

Young v. State, 303 Md. 298 (1985)

ORTH, Judge. . . .

Usually a criminal conviction is predicated upon the completion of the crime; the conduct of the accused has satisfied the elements necessary to establish the offense and he has actually committed the act as proscribed. But what if the conduct of the accused has not progressed to the point where a crime has been committed, that is, he has tried to commit the offense but for some reason he has not been successful?

> [T]here is just as much need to stop, deter and reform a person who has unsuccessfully attempted or is attempting to commit a crime than one who has already committed such an offense.

This is why the law of attempts exists. . . .

The offense of criminal attempt has long been accepted as a part of the criminal law of Maryland. We recognized a criminal attempt as a common law misdemeanor in *Mitchell v. State*, 82 Md. 527, 534 (1896). We have had surprisingly little to say, however, about the nature of the offense. *Mitchell* concerned an attempted rape, but the appeal was dismissed for procedural reasons and the Court had no occasion to elaborate on the crime. Almost 70 years later, in *Wiley v. State,* 237 Md. 560 (1965), we defined criminal attempt without citation to a prior decision of this Court. We said:

> An attempt to commit a crime consists of an intent to commit it, the performance of some act toward its commission, and failure to consummate its commission. . . .

Our opinions leave much unanswered. The application of particular facts to the law of criminal attempts frequently gives rise to problems in one or more of three aspects:

> (1) The determination of the overt act which is beyond mere preparation in furtherance of the commission of the crime.
>
> (2) At what point may the attempt to commit the intended crime be abandoned so as to escape liability.
>
> (3) What is the effect on culpability of impossibility to commit the intended crime. . . .

Such was the posture of the law of Maryland regarding criminal attempts when Raymond Alexander Young, also known as Morris Prince Cunningham and Prince Alexander Love, was found guilty by a jury in the Circuit Court for Prince George's County of . . . the attempted armed robbery of the manager of the Fort Washington, Md. branch of the First National Bank of Southern Maryland (the Bank) . . . .

There is no dispute as to the circumstances which led to the indictment of Young. Several banks in the Oxon Hill-Fort Washington section of Prince George's County had been held up. The Special Operations Division of the Prince George's Police Department set up a surveillance of banks in the area. In the early afternoon of 26 November 1982 the police team observed Young driving an automobile in such a manner as to give rise to a reasonable belief that he was casing several banks. They followed him in his reconnoitering. At one point when he left his car to enter a store, he was seen to clip a scanner onto his belt. The scanner later proved to contain an operable crystal number frequency that would receive Prince George's County uniform patrol transmissions. At that time Young was dressed in a brown waist-length jacket and wore sunglasses.

Around 2:00 p.m. Young came to rest at the rear of the Fort Washington branch of the First National Bank of Southern Maryland. Shortly before, he had driven past the front of the Bank and parked in the rear of it for a brief time. He got out of his car and walked hurriedly beside the Bank toward the front door. He was still wearing the brown waist-length jacket and sunglasses, but he had added a blue knit stocking cap pulled down to the top of the sunglasses, white gloves and a black eyepatch. His jacket collar was turned up. His right hand was in his jacket pocket and his left hand was in front of his face. As one of the police officers observing him put it, he was "sort of duck[ing] his head."

It was shortly after 2:00 p.m. and the Bank had just closed. Through the windows of his office the Bank Manager saw Young walking on the "landscape" by the side of the Bank toward the front door. Young had his right hand in his jacket pocket and tried to open the front door with his left hand. When he realized that the door was locked and the Bank was closed, he retraced his steps, running past the windows with his left hand covering his face. The Bank Manager had an employee call the police.

Young ran back to his car, yanked open the door, got in, and put the car in drive "all in one movement almost," and drove away. The police stopped the car and ordered Young to get out. . . .

A criminal attempt requires specific intent; the specific intent must be to commit some other crime. The requisite intent need not be proved by direct evidence. It may be inferred as a matter of fact from the actor's conduct and the attendant circumstances. Young concedes that "evidence is present . . . from which it is possible to infer that [he] may have intended to commit a crime inside the bank. . . ." He suggests, however, that this evidence is not "compelling. . . ." We think that it is most compelling. We believe that it is more than legally sufficient to establish beyond a reasonable doubt that Young had the specific intent to commit an armed robbery as charged. . . .

. . . Of course, if the person's conduct has not progressed beyond mere preparation, in other words, he has not performed the requisite overt act, he would not be culpable in any event. . . .

The determination of the overt act which is beyond mere preparation in furtherance of the commission of the intended crime is a most significant aspect of criminal attempts. If an attempt is to be a culpable offense serving as the basis for the furtherance of the important societal interests of crime prevention and the correction of those persons who have sufficiently manifested their dangerousness, the police must be able to ascertain with reasonable assurance when it is proper for them to intervene. It is not enough to say merely that there must be "some overt act beyond mere preparation in furtherance of the crime" as the general definition puts it. . . .

. . . As we have seen, bad thoughts do not constitute a crime, and so it is not enough that a person merely have intended and prepared to commit a crime. "There must also be an act, and not any act will suffice." LaFave & Scott, §59, at 431. What act will suffice to show that an attempt itself has reached the stage of a completed crime has persistently troubled the courts. They have applied a number of approaches in order to determine when preparation for the commission of a crime has ceased and the actual attempt to commit it has begun. . . .

"The Model Penal Code Approach" looks to §5.01 of the Model Penal Code (Proposed Official Draft 1962) to solve the problem. Under subsection (1)(c) a person is guilty of an attempt to commit a crime if, acting with the kind of culpability otherwise required for commission of the crime, he

> purposely does or omits to do anything which, under the circumstances as he believes them to be, is an act or omission constituting a *substantial step* in a course of conduct planned to culminate in his commission of the crime. (emphasis added).

Each of these approaches is not without advantages and disadvantages in theory and in application, as is readily apparent from a perusal of the comments of various text writers and of the courts.

We believe that the preferable approach is one bottomed on the "substantial step" test as is that of Model Penal Code. We think that using a "substantial step" as the criterion in determining whether an overt act is more than mere preparation to commit a crime is clearer, sounder, more practical and easier to apply to the multitude of differing fact situations which may occur.
. . .

Convinced that an approach based on the "substantial step" test is the proper one to determine whether a person has attempted to commit a crime, and that §110.00 of the Md. Proposed Criminal Code best expressed it, we adopt the provisions of that section:

> A person is guilty of an attempt to commit a crime when, with intent to commit a crime, he engages in conduct which constitutes a substantial step toward the commission of that crime whether or not his intention be accomplished. .
> . .

When the facts and circumstances of the case *sub judice* are considered in the light of the overt act standard which we have adopted, it is perfectly clear that the evidence was sufficient to prove that Young attempted the crime of armed robbery as charged. As we have seen, the police did not arrive on the scene after the fact. They had the advantage of having Young under observation for some time before his apprehension. They watched his preparations. They were with him when he reconnoitered or cased the banks. His observations of the banks were in a manner not usual for law-abiding individuals and were under circumstances that warranted alarm for the safety of persons or property. Young manifestly endeavored to conceal his presence by parking behind the Bank which he had apparently selected to rob. He disguised himself with an eyepatch and made an identification of him difficult by turning up his jacket collar and by donning sunglasses and a knit cap which he pulled down over his forehead. He put on rubber surgical gloves. Clipped on his belt was a scanner with a police band frequency. Except for the scanner, which he had placed on his belt while casing the Bank, all this was done immediately before he left his car and approached the door of the Bank. As he walked towards the Bank he partially hid his face behind his left hand and ducked his head. He kept his right hand in the pocket of his jacket in which, as subsequent events established, he was carrying, concealed, a loaded handgun, for which he had no lawful use or right to transport. He walked to the front door of the Bank and tried to enter the premises. When he discovered that the door was locked, he ran back to his car, again partially concealing his face with his left hand. He got in his car and immediately drove away. He removed the knit hat, sunglasses, eyepatch and gloves, and placed the scanner over the sun visor of the car. When apprehended, he was trying to take off his jacket. His question as to how much time he could get for attempted bank robbery was not without significance.

It is clear that the evidence which showed Young's conduct leading to his apprehension established that he performed the necessary overt act towards the commission of armed robbery, which was more than mere preparation. Even if we assume that all of Young's conduct before he approached the door of the Bank was mere preparation, on the evidence, the jury could properly find as a fact that when Young tried to open the bank door to enter the premises, that act constituted a "substantial step" toward the commission of the intended crime. It was strongly corroborative of his criminal intention. . . .

We think that the evidence adduced showed directly, or circumstantially, or supported a rational inference of, the facts to be proved from which the jury could fairly be convinced, beyond a reasonable doubt, of Young's guilt of attempted armed robbery as charged. Therefore, the evidence was sufficient in law to sustain the conviction. We so hold.

JUDGMENTS OF THE COURT OF SPECIAL APPEALS AFFIRMED. . . .

Note

Is the approach taken by the court in *Young* more utilitarian or retributive? Would the overt acts taken by the defendant have been sufficient under "dangerous proximity"? As a matter of public policy, which is the better test: "substantial step" or "dangerous proximity"? It is noteworthy that *Young* only uses some of the MPC language. A jurisdiction that adopts both §§5.01(1) and 5.01(2) (reproduced below) would have the same result but a different analysis than followed in *Young*.

c. Sufficiency of the Evidence under "Substantial Step"

As you read *Harper*, consider the requirements of "substantial step," as well as how a court of appeals is required to review sufficiency of the evidence. Also, as you are reading this case, compare *Young* with *Harper*. If you were the prosecutor assigned to *Harper* and the police called you asking for your advice as to what else you believed was necessary to establish attempt, what guidance would you have given them?

United States v. Harper, 33 F.3d 1143 (9th Cir. 1994)

CANBY, Circuit Judge:

Trina Devay Harper and Aziz Sharrieff appeal their convictions for conspiracy in violation of 18 U.S.C. §371, attempted bank robbery in violation of 18 U.S.C. §2113(a), and carrying a firearm during and in relation to a crime of violence in violation of 18 U.S.C. §924(c). [The defendants] assert . . . that there was insufficient evidence to support any of the verdicts. . . .

We reverse the attempt convictions, affirm the other convictions and remand for resentencing.

BACKGROUND

Police officers in Buena Park, California found appellants and one other codefendant, Carlos Munoz, sitting in a rented car in the parking lot of the Home Savings Bank shortly after 10:00 p.m. on the evening of September 21, 1992. The officers searched the defendants, the vehicle and the surrounding area. They found two loaded handguns—a .44 caliber Charter Arms Bulldog and a .357 magnum Smith and Wesson—under a bush located five or six feet from the car, where a witness had earlier seen one of the car's occupants bending over. In the car, the police discovered a roll of duct tape in a plastic bag, a stun gun, and a pair of latex surgical gloves. They found another pair of latex surgical gloves in the pocket of Munoz's sweat pants. They also found six rounds of .357 magnum ammunition in the pocket of his shorts, which he wore under his sweat pants. Some of this ammunition came from either the same box or the same lot as the ammunition in the loaded .357 magnum handgun. The defendants had a total of approximately $182 in cash among them and Sharrieff was carrying an automated teller machine (ATM) card which bore the name of Kimberly Ellis.

Harper had used the ATM card belonging to Kimberly Ellis shortly before 9:00 p.m. that evening in an ATM at the Buena Park branch of the Bank of America, which was located adjacent to the Home Savings parking lot in which the defendants were parked. The ATM's camera photographed Harper. Harper had requested a twenty dollar withdrawal from the ATM, but had not removed the cash from the cash drawer. This omission had created what is known as a "bill trap." When a bill trap occurs, the ATM shuts itself down and the ATM supply company that monitors the ATM contacts its ATM service technicians to come and repair the ATM. These facts were known to Harper, who had previously worked for both Bank of America and one of its ATM service companies.

On the basis of this evidence, Harper, Sharrieff and Munoz were indicted for conspiracy to rob a federally insured bank, attempted bank robbery, and carrying a firearm during and in relation to a crime of violence. The prosecution's theory was that Harper had intentionally caused the bill trap to summon the ATM service technicians who would have to open the ATM vault to clear the trap. At that time, the theory went, the defendants planned to rob the technicians of the money in the ATM. The three defendants were convicted of all charges.

DISCUSSION . . . .
Sufficiency of the Evidence

Harper and Sharrieff assert that there was insufficient evidence to support their convictions for the charged offenses. "[T]he relevant question is whether, after viewing the evidence in the light most favorable to the prosecution, *any* rational trier of fact could have found the essential elements of the crime beyond a reasonable doubt." *Jackson v. Virginia*, 443 U.S. 307, 319 (1979). We conclude that there was insufficient evidence to support the attempt convictions, but that there was sufficient evidence to support the conspiracy and firearm convictions.

Attempted Bank Robbery

To obtain a conviction for attempted bank robbery the prosecution must prove (1) culpable intent and (2) conduct constituting a substantial step toward the commission of the crime. Here, there was sufficient evidence to permit a jury to find that the defendants intended to rob the Bank of America. We conclude, however, that under the law of this circuit there was insufficient evidence that the defendants took a substantial step toward commission of the robbery.

It is admittedly difficult to draw the line between mere preparation to commit an offense, which does not constitute an attempt, and the taking of a substantial step toward commission of the crime, which does. Various theories have been propounded for determining when the activities of one who intends to commit a crime ripen into an attempt, and they yield varying results in a case like this. We must draw our guidance from our own precedent, however, and we conclude that the activities of the defendants, viewed in the light most favorable to the prosecution, fail to qualify as an attempt.

Our primary authorities are *Buffington* and *Still*. In *Buffington*, the defendants had driven past the supposed target bank twice. One of the three male defendants then entered a store near the bank and observed the bank. The two other defendants, one dressed as a woman, exited their vehicle in the bank parking lot, stood near the vehicle and focused their attention on the bank. They were armed. We held that the evidence was insufficient both as to the defendants' intent to rob the bank, and as to the existence of conduct constituting a substantial step towards the commission of the crime. With regard to the latter element, we observed:

> Not only did appellants not take a single step toward the bank, they displayed no weapons and no indication that they were about to make an entry. Standing alone, their conduct did not constitute that requisite "appreciable fragment" of a bank robbery, nor a step toward commission of the crime of

such substantiality that, unless frustrated, the crime would have occurred.

The same may be said of the defendants in this case. True, Harper had left money in the ATM, causing a bill trap that would eventually bring service personnel to the ATM. That act, however, is equivocal in itself. The robbery was in the future and, like the defendants in *Buffington,* the defendants never made a move toward the victims or the Bank to accomplish the criminal portion of their intended mission. They had not taken a step of "such substantiality that, unless frustrated, the crime would have occurred." Their situation is therefore distinguishable from that of the defendant in *United States v. Moore,* 921 F.2d 207 (9th Cir.1990), upon which the government relies. In *Moore,* the defendant was apprehended "walking toward the bank, wearing a ski mask, and carrying gloves, pillowcases and a concealed, loaded gun." These actions were a true commitment toward the robbery, which would be in progress the moment the would-be robber entered the bank thus attired and equipped. That stage of the crime had not been reached by Harper and Sharrieff; their actual embarkation on the robbery lay as much as 90 minutes away from the time when Harper left money in the ATM, and that time had not expired when they were apprehended.

Still provides further support for our conclusion. There, we relied upon *Buffington* to reverse a similar conviction for attempted bank robbery. The defendant in that case was seen sitting in a van approximately 200 feet from the supposed target bank. In the van he had a fake bomb, a red pouch with note demanding money attached to it, a police scanner, and a notebook containing drafts of the note. He also had been seen putting on a blonde wig while sitting in the van. The defendant's intent was clear; he told police that he had been about to rob the bank and "[t]hat's what [he] was putting the wig on for." We concluded, however, that the evidence was insufficient to establish that the defendant had taken a substantial step toward commission of the offense. "Our facts do not establish either actual movement toward the bank or actions that are analytically similar to such movement." Defendant Still, like the defendants here, was sitting in his vehicle when the police approached. As in *Still,* we conclude that the crime was too inchoate to constitute an attempt.

When criminal intent is clear, identifying the point at which the defendants' activities ripen into an attempt is not an analytically satisfying enterprise. There is, however, a substantial difference between causing a bill trap, which will result in the appearance of potential victims, and moving toward such victims with gun and mask, as in *Moore.* Making an appointment with a potential victim is not of itself such a commitment to an intended crime as to constitute an attempt, even though it may make a later attempt possible. Little more happened here; this case is more like *Buffington* and *Still* than it is like *Moore.* Accordingly, we reverse the appellants' convictions for attempted bank robbery. . . .

CONCLUSION

We reverse both Harper's and Sharrieff's convictions for attempted bank robbery. We affirm their convictions for conspiracy and use of a firearm during and in relation to a crime of violence. We also conclude that Harper is not subject to an upward adjustment in sentencing for use of a special skill. Moreover, the district judge on remand shall not impose an upward adjustment for her role in the offense without making a proper finding that she was an organizer, leader, or manager or supervisor in criminal activity.

AFFIRMED in part, REVERSED in part, and REMANDED for resentencing. . . .

3. Model Penal Code Provisions

As noted in *Young*, MPC §5.01 requires that the defendant take substantial steps towards the completion of the object crime. The focus is on the defendant's state of mind and whether he has completed enough acts to corroborate his intent. Unlike "dangerous proximity," which focuses on what remains to be done, the MPC considers what the defendant has already done. Thus, it takes many more acts to constitute attempt under "dangerous proximity" than under "substantial step."

> Section 5.01 has had significant impact on American attempt law. Most of the federal courts apply its doctrines, although Congress has not enacted the provision; and a large number of states [at least 25] have adopted the MPC provision in its entirety or in part. [Joshua Dressler, Understanding Criminal Law §27.09[A] (6th ed. 2012).]

§5.01. Criminal Attempt

(1) Definition of Attempt. A person is guilty of an attempt to commit a crime if, acting with the kind of culpability otherwise required for commission of the crime, he:

(a) purposely engages in conduct that would constitute the crime if the attendant circumstances were as he believes them to be; or

(b) when causing a particular result is an element of the crime, does or omits to do anything with the purpose of causing or with the belief that it will cause such result without further conduct on his part; or

(c) purposely does or omits to do anything that, under the circumstances as he believes them to be, is an act or omission constituting a substantial step in a course of conduct planned to culminate in his commission of the crime.

(2) Conduct That May Be Held Substantial Step Under Subsection (1)(c). Conduct shall not be held to constitute a substantial step under

Subsection (1)(c) of this Section unless it is strongly corroborative of the actor's criminal purpose. Without negating the sufficiency of other conduct, the following, if strongly corroborative of the actor's criminal purpose, shall not be held insufficient as a matter of law:

(a) lying in wait, searching for or following the contemplated victim of the crime;

(b) enticing or seeking to entice the contemplated victim of the crime to go to the place contemplated for its commission;

(c) reconnoitering the place contemplated for the commission of the crime;

(d) unlawful entry of a structure, vehicle or enclosure in which it is contemplated that the crime will be committed;

(e) possession of materials to be employed in the commission of the crime, that are specially designed for such unlawful use or that can serve no lawful purpose of the actor under the circumstances;

(f) possession, collection or fabrication of materials to be employed in the commission of the crime, at or near the place contemplated for its commission, if such possession, collection or fabrication serves no lawful purpose of the actor under the circumstances;

(g) soliciting an innocent agent to engage in conduct constituting an element of the crime.

C. Defenses to Attempt Crimes

1. Impossibility

A attempts to pick someone's pocket, but it is empty. *B* shoots his intended victim, however, the victim had already died from unrelated causes. *C* wants to scalp tickets to a sporting event not realizing that the statute, which proscribed the conduct, had been repealed. *D* makes arrangements to buy stolen auto parts not knowing that the police had recovered the property. Are *A*, *B*, *C*, and *D* guilty of attempt?

These situations raise the defense of impossibility. The common law distinguished between "legal impossibility" and "factual impossibility." The common law rules regarding impossibility are relatively easy to explain, but their application to specific cases has been the subject of debate. Factual impossibility is not a defense, whereas legal impossibility is a defense.

With respect to factual impossibility, the actor's goal is a crime; however, because of circumstances of which he is unaware, the crime cannot be consummated (e.g. a pickpocket who puts his hand into an empty pocket). As a matter of policy, this has not been recognized as a defense inasmuch as the defendant has demonstrated that he is a danger to society. For example, shooting at someone who resembles the president with the intent to assassinate the president is a violation of 18 U.S.C. §1751. *See United States v. Duran*, 884 F. Supp. 577 (1995).

Legal impossibility, on the other hand, involves a situation where the actor believes he is committing a crime, but the law does not prohibit the conduct. Within the category of legal impossibility is a subcategory known as "hybrid legal impossibility."

> Hybrid legal impossibility (or what some courts typically call, simply, "legal impossibility") exists if the actor's goal is illegal, but commission of the offense is impossible due to a *factual* mistake (and not simply a misunderstanding of the law) regarding the *legal* status of some attendant circumstance that constitutes an element of the charged offense. [Joshua Dressler, *Understanding Criminal Law* §27.07[D][3][a] (6th ed. 2012).]

An example of hybrid legal impossibility includes offering a bribe to a non-juror. *See, e.g., State v. Taylor*, 345 Mo. 325 (1939). Although hybrid legal impossibility can be a defense, the trend has been to reject it inasmuch as the actor has demonstrated dangerousness and. Thus, it is considered as factual impossibility, which, as noted, is not a defense.

a. Pure Legal Impossibility

As you read *Wilson*, consider all the steps he took to commit forgery and why the court concluded this was not a crime.

Wilson v. State, 85 Miss. 687 (1905)

CALHOON, J.

Wilson was convicted of an attempt to commit forgery, the court below properly charging the jury that it could not convict of the crime itself. The instrument of which attempt to commit forgery is predicated is a draft for "two and $^{50}/_{100}$ dollars," as written out in the body of it, having in the upper right-hand corner the figures "$2.$^{50}/_{100}$," as is customary in checks, drafts, and notes, and having plainly printed and stamped on the face of the instrument the words "Ten Dollars or Less." Wilson, with a pen, put the figure "1" before the figure "2" in the upper right-hand corner, making these immaterial figures appear "$12.50" instead of "$2.50," and undertook to negotiate it as $12.50. This was not forgery, because it was an immaterial part of the paper, and because it could not possibly have injured anybody. In order to constitute the crime, there must be not only the intent to commit it, but also an act of alteration done to a material part, so that injury might result. These authorities might be numerously added to, but it is enough to say now that they sustain what we have said, and establish also that an instrument void on its face is not the subject of forgery, and that, in order to be so subject, it must have been capable of working injury if it had been genuine, and that the marginal numbers and figures are not part of the instrument, and their alteration is not forgery.

This being true, can the conviction of an attempt to commit forgery be sustained in the case before us? We think not. No purpose appears to change anything on the paper except the figures in the margin, and this could not have done any hurt. Our statute (Code 1892, §1106) confines the crime of forgery to instances where "any person may be affected, bound, or in any way injured in his person or property." This is not such a case, and section 974 forbids convicting of an attempt "when it shall appear that the crime intended or the offense attempted was perpetrated." In this record the innocuous prefix of the figure "1" on the margin was fully accomplished, and no other effort appears, and, if genuine, could have done no harm; and so the appellant is guiltless, in law, of the crime of which he was convicted.

Reversed and remanded.

b. Applying Impossibility to Attempt

Does the defense of impossibility apply to attempt offenses in all jurisdictions? For example, assume the target of an investigation wants to meet with an individual he met online and believes to be a minor for the purpose of having sex, which is obviously a crime. However, the individual he believes to be a minor is actually a police officer. Consider this type of situation as you read *People v. Thousand*.

People v. Thousand, 465 Mich. 149 (2001)

YOUNG, J.

We granted leave in this case to consider whether the doctrine of "impossibility" provides a defense to a charge of attempt to commit an offense prohibited by law under M.C.L. §750.92 . . . . The circuit court granted defendant's motion to quash and dismissed all charges against him on the basis that it was legally impossible for him to have committed any of the charged crimes. We conclude that the concept of impossibility, which this Court has never adopted as a defense, is not relevant to a determination whether a defendant has committed attempt under M.C.L. §750.92, and that the circuit court therefore erred in dismissing the charge of attempted distribution of obscene material to a minor on the basis of the doctrine of legal impossibility. . . . Accordingly, we reverse in part and affirm in part the decision of the Court of Appeals and remand this matter to the circuit court for proceedings consistent with this opinion.

I.   FACTUAL AND PROCEDURAL BACKGROUND

Deputy William Liczbinski was assigned by the Wayne County Sheriff's Department to conduct an undercover investigation for the department's Internet Crimes Bureau. Liczbinski was instructed to pose as a minor and log onto "chat rooms" on the Internet for the purpose of identifying persons using the Internet as a means for engaging in criminal activity.

On December 8, 1998, while using the screen name "Bekka," Liczbinski was approached by defendant, who was using the screen name "Mr. Auto-Mag," in an Internet chat room. Defendant described himself as a twenty-three-year-old male from Warren, and Bekka described herself as a fourteen-year-old female from Detroit. Bekka indicated that her name was Becky Fellins, and defendant revealed that his name was Chris Thousand. During this initial conversation, defendant sent Bekka, via the Internet, a photograph of his face.

From December 9 through 16, 1998, Liczbinski, still using the screen name "Bekka," engaged in chat room conversation with defendant. During these exchanges, the conversation became sexually explicit. Defendant made repeated lewd invitations to Bekka to engage in various sexual acts, despite various indications of her young age.

During one of his online conversations with Bekka, after asking her whether anyone was "around there," watching her, defendant indicated that he was sending her a picture of himself. Within seconds, Liczbinski received over the Internet a photograph of male genitalia. Defendant asked Bekka whether she liked and wanted it and whether she was getting "hot" yet, and described in a graphic manner the type of sexual acts he wished to perform with her. Defendant invited Bekka to come see him at his house for the purpose of engaging in sexual activity. Bekka replied that she wanted to do so, and defendant cautioned her that they had to be careful, because he could "go to jail." Defendant asked whether Bekka looked "over sixteen," so that if his roommates were home he could lie.

The two then planned to meet at an area McDonald's restaurant at 5:00 p.m. on the following Thursday. Defendant indicated that they could go to his house, and that he would tell his brother that Bekka was seventeen. Defendant instructed Bekka to wear a "nice sexy skirt," something that he could "get [his] head into." Defendant indicated that he would be dressed in black pants and shirt and a brown suede coat, and that he would be driving a green Duster. Bekka asked defendant to bring her a present, and indicated that she liked white teddy bears.

On Thursday, December 17, 1998, Liczbinski and other deputy sheriffs were present at the specified McDonald's restaurant when they saw defendant inside a vehicle matching the description given to Bekka by defendant. Defendant, who was wearing a brown suede jacket and black pants, got out of the vehicle and entered the restaurant. Liczbinski recognized defendant's face from the photograph that had been sent to Bekka. Defendant looked around for approximately thirty seconds before leaving the restaurant. Defendant was then taken into custody. Two white teddy bears were recovered from defendant's vehicle. Defendant's computer was subsequently seized from his home. A search of the hard drive revealed electronic logs of Internet conversations matching those printed out by Liczbinski from the Wayne County-owned computer he had used in his Internet conversations with defendant.

Following a preliminary examination, defendant was bound over for trial on charges of solicitation to commit third-degree criminal sexual conduct, attempted distribution of obscene material to a minor, and child sexually abusive activity.

Defendant brought a motion to quash the information, arguing that, because the existence of a child victim was an element of each of the charged offenses, the evidence was legally insufficient to support the charges. The circuit court agreed and dismissed the case, holding that it was legally impossible for defendant to have committed the charged offenses. The Court of Appeals affirmed the dismissal of the charges of solicitation and attempted distribution of obscene material to a minor, but reversed the dismissal of the charge of child sexually abusive activity.

We granted the prosecution's application for leave to appeal.

II.   STANDARD OF REVIEW

We must determine in this case whether the circuit court and the Court of Appeals properly applied the doctrine of "legal impossibility" in concluding that the charges against defendant of attempt and solicitation must be dismissed. The applicability of a legal doctrine is a question of law that is reviewed de novo. Similarly, the issue whether "impossibility" is a cognizable defense under Michigan's attempt and solicitation statutes presents questions of statutory construction, which we review de novo.

III.   ANALYSIS
A.   THE "IMPOSSIBILITY" DOCTRINE

The doctrine of "impossibility" as it has been discussed in the context of inchoate crimes represents the conceptual dilemma that arises when, because of the defendant's mistake of fact or law, his actions could not possibly have resulted in the commission of the substantive crime underlying an attempt charge. Classic illustrations of the concept of impossibility include: (1) the defendant is prosecuted for attempted larceny after he tries to "pick" the victim's empty pocket; (2) the defendant is prosecuted for attempted rape after he tries to have nonconsensual intercourse, but is unsuccessful because he is impotent; (3) the defendant is prosecuted for attempting to receive stolen property where the property he received was not, in fact, stolen; and (4) the defendant is prosecuted for attempting to hunt deer out of season after he shoots at a stuffed decoy deer. In each of these examples, despite evidence of the defendant's criminal intent, he cannot be prosecuted for the *completed* offense of larceny, rape, receiving stolen property, or hunting deer out of season, because proof of at least one element of each offense cannot be derived from his objective actions. The question, then, becomes whether the defendant can be prosecuted for the *attempted* offense, and the answer is dependent upon whether he may raise the defense of "impossibility."

Courts and legal scholars have drawn a distinction between two categories of impossibility: "factual impossibility" and "legal impossibility." It has been said that, at common law, legal impossibility is a defense to a charge of attempt, but factual impossibility is not. See Perkins & Boyce, Criminal Law (3d ed.), p. 632; Dressler, Understanding Criminal Law (1st ed.), §27.07[B], p. 349. However, courts and scholars alike have struggled unsuccessfully over the years to articulate an accurate rule for distinguishing between the categories of "impossibility."

"Factual impossibility," which has apparently never been recognized in any American jurisdiction as a defense to a charge of attempt, "exists when [the defendant's] intended end constitutes a crime but she fails to consummate it because of a factual circumstance unknown to her or beyond her control." Dressler, *supra*, §27.07[C][1], p. 350. An example of a "factual impossibility" scenario is where the defendant is prosecuted for attempted murder after pointing an unloaded gun at someone and pulling the trigger, where the defendant believed the gun was loaded.

The category of "legal impossibility" is further divided into two subcategories: "pure" legal impossibility and "hybrid" legal impossibility. Although it is generally undisputed that "pure" legal impossibility will bar an attempt conviction, the concept of "hybrid legal impossibility" has proven problematic. As Professor Dressler points out, the failure of courts to distinguish between "pure" and "hybrid" legal impossibility has created confusion in this area of the law. Dressler, *supra*, §27.07[D][1], p. 351.

"*Pure legal impossibility* exists if the criminal law does not prohibit *D's* conduct or the result that she has sought to achieve." *Id.*, §27.07[D][2], p. 352 emphasis in original). In other words, the concept of pure legal impossibility applies when an actor engages in conduct that he believes is criminal, but is not actually prohibited by law: "There can be no conviction of criminal attempt based upon *D's* erroneous notion that he was committing a crime." Perkins & Boyce, *supra*, p. 634. As an example, consider the case of a man who believes that the legal age of consent is sixteen years old, and who believes that a girl with whom he had consensual sexual intercourse is fifteen years old. If the law actually fixed the age of consent at fifteen, this man would not be guilty of attempted statutory rape, despite his mistaken belief that the law prohibited his conduct. See Dressler, *supra*, §27.07[D][2], pp. 352–353, n. 25.

When courts speak of "legal impossibility," they are generally referring to what is more accurately described as "hybrid" legal impossibility.

> Most claims of legal impossibility are of the hybrid variety. *Hybrid legal impossibility* exists if *D's* goal was illegal, but commission of the offense was impossible due to a

factual mistake by her regarding the legal status of some factor relevant to her conduct. This version of impossibility is a "hybrid" because, as the definition implies and as is clarified immediately below, D's impossibility claim includes both a legal and a factual aspect to it.

Courts have recognized a defense of legal impossibility or have stated that it would exist if D receives unstolen property believing it was stolen; tries to pick the pocket of a stone image of a human; offers a bribe to a "juror" who is not a juror; tries to hunt deer out of season by shooting a stuffed animal; shoots a corpse believing that it is alive; or shoots at a tree stump believing that it is a human.

Notice that each of the mistakes in these cases affected the legal status of some aspect of the defendant's conduct. The status of property as "stolen" is necessary to commit the crime of "receiving stolen property with knowledge it is stolen"—i.e., a person legally is incapable of committing this offense if the property is not stolen. The status of a person as a "juror" is legally necessary to commit the offense of bribing a juror. The status of a victim as a "human being" (rather than as a corpse, tree stump, or statue) legally is necessary to commit the crime of murder or to "take and carry away the personal property *of another.*" Finally, putting a bullet into a stuffed deer can never constitute the crime of hunting out of season.

On the other hand, in each example of hybrid legal impossibility *D* was mistaken about a fact: whether property was stolen, whether a person was a juror, whether the victims were human or whether the victim was an animal subject to being hunted out of season. [Dressler, *supra,* §27.07[D][3][a], pp. 353–354 (emphasis in original).]

As the Court of Appeals panel in this case accurately noted, it is possible to view virtually any example of "hybrid legal impossibility" as an example of "factual impossibility":

> *Ultimately any case of hybrid legal impossibility may reasonably be characterized as factual impossibility.* . . . [B]y skillful characterization, one can describe virtually any case of hybrid legal impossibility, which is a common law defense, as an example of factual impossibility, which is *not* a defense. . . .

It is notable that "the great majority of jurisdictions have now recognized that legal and factual impossibility are 'logically indistinguishable' . . . and have abolished impossibility as a defense." For example, several states have adopted statutory provisions similar to Model Penal Code §5.01(1), which provides:

A person is guilty of an attempt to commit a crime if, acting with the kind of culpability otherwise required for commission of the crime, he:

(a) purposely engages in conduct which would constitute the crime if the attendant circumstances were as he believes them to be; or

(b) when causing a particular result is an element of the crime, does or omits to do anything with the purpose of causing or with the belief that it will cause such result without further conduct on his part; or

(c) purposely does or omits to do anything which, under the circumstances as he believes them to be, is an act or omission constituting a substantial step in a course of conduct planned to culminate in his commission of the crime.

In other jurisdictions, courts have considered the "impossibility" defense under attempt statutes that did not include language explicitly abolishing the defense. Several of these courts have simply declined to participate in the sterile academic exercise of categorizing a particular set of facts as representing "factual" or "legal" impossibility, and have instead examined solely the words of the applicable attempt statute.

B.   ATTEMPTED DISTRIBUTION OF OBSCENE MATERIAL TO A MINOR

The Court of Appeals panel in this case, after examining Professor Dressler's exposition of the doctrine of impossibility, concluded that it was legally impossible for defendant to have committed the charged offense of attempted distribution of obscene material to a minor. The panel held that, because "Bekka" was, in fact, an adult, an essential requirement of the underlying substantive offense was not met (dissemination to a minor), and therefore it was legally impossible for defendant to have committed the crime.

We begin by noting that the concept of "impossibility," in either its "factual" or "legal" variant, has never been recognized by this Court as a valid defense to a charge of attempt. In arguing that impossibility is a judicially recognized defense in Michigan, defendant relies heavily on our statement in *People v. Tinskey*, 394 Mich. 108 (1975), that

[i]t is possible, *although we need not decide,* that defendants could not have been convicted of attempted abortion; at common law the general rule is that while factual impossibility is not a defense, legal impossibility is a defense.

As is readily apparent, our statement in *Tinskey* regarding "legal impossibility" as a defense to an attempt charge is nothing more than obiter dictum. The defendants in *Tinskey* were not charged with attempt; rather, they were charged with statutory conspiracy. Moreover, we *specifically declined* in

Tinskey to express any opinion regarding the viability of the "impossibility" defense in the context of attempts. No other Michigan Supreme Court case has referenced, much less adopted, the impossibility defense.

Finding no recognition of impossibility in our common law, we turn now to the terms of the statute. MCL 750.92 provides, in relevant part:

> Any person who shall attempt to commit an offense prohibited by law, and in such attempt shall do any act towards the commission of such offense, but shall fail in the perpetration, or shall be intercepted or prevented in the execution of the same, when no express provision is made by law for the punishment of such attempt, shall be punished as follows: . . .
>
> . . . If the offense so attempted to be committed is punishable by imprisonment in the state prison for a term less than 5 years, or imprisonment in the county jail or by fine, the offender convicted of such attempt shall be guilty of a misdemeanor . . . .

Under our statute, then, an "attempt" consists of (1) an attempt to commit an offense prohibited by law, and (2) any act towards the commission of the intended offense. We have further explained the elements of attempt under our statute as including "an intent to do an act or to bring about certain consequences which would in law amount to a crime; and . . . an act in furtherance of that intent which, as it is most commonly put, goes beyond mere preparation."

In determining whether "impossibility," were we to recognize the doctrine, is a viable defense to a charge of attempt under M.C.L. §750.92, our obligation is to examine the statute in an effort to discern and give effect to the legislative intent that may reasonably be inferred from the text of the statute itself. "When a legislature has unambiguously conveyed its intent in a statute, the statute speaks for itself and there is no need for judicial construction; the proper role of a court is simply to *apply* the terms of the statute to the circumstances in a particular case." Accordingly, if our Legislature has indicated its intent to criminalize certain conduct despite the actor's mistake of fact, this Court does not have the authority to create and apply a substantive defense based upon the concept of "impossibility."

We are unable to discern from the words of the attempt statute any legislative intent that the concept of "impossibility" provide any impediment to charging a defendant with, or convicting him of, an attempted crime, notwithstanding any factual mistake—regarding either the attendant circumstances or the legal status of some factor relevant thereto—that he may harbor. The attempt statute carves out no exception for those who, possessing the requisite criminal intent to commit an offense prohibited by law and taking action toward the commission of that offense, have acted under an extrinsic misconception.

Defendant in this case is not charged with the substantive crime of distributing obscene material to a minor in violation of M.C.L. §722.675. It is unquestioned that defendant could not be convicted of that crime, because defendant allegedly distributed obscene material not to "a minor," but to an adult man. Instead, defendant is charged with the distinct offense of attempt, which requires only that the prosecution prove intention to commit an offense prohibited by law, coupled with conduct toward the commission of that offense. The notion that it would be "impossible" for the defendant to have committed the *completed* offense is simply irrelevant to the analysis. Rather, in deciding guilt on a charge of attempt, the trier of fact must examine the unique circumstances of the particular case and determine whether the prosecution has proven that the defendant possessed the requisite specific intent and that he engaged in some act "towards the commission" of the intended offense.

Because the nonexistence of a minor victim does not give rise to a viable defense to the attempt charge in this case, the circuit court erred in dismissing this charge on the basis of "legal impossibility." . . .

IV.   CONCLUSION

This Court has never recognized the doctrine of impossibility. Moreover, we are unable to discern any legislative intent that the doctrine may be advanced as a defense to a charge of attempt under M.C.L. §750.92. Accordingly, the circuit court erred in dismissing this charge on the basis that it was "legally impossible" for defendant to have committed the crime.

Furthermore, although we do not agree with the circuit court or the Court of Appeals that "legal impossibility" was properly invoked by defendant as a defense to the charge of solicitation, we nevertheless affirm the dismissal of this charge. There is no evidence that defendant solicited anyone "to commit a felony" or "to do or omit to do an act which if completed would constitute a felony."

Accordingly, we reverse in part, affirm in part [while the Court found that the Circuit Court and the Michigan Court of Appeals erred by concluding the defense of legal impossibility was properly invoked by the defendant to the charge of solicitation, there was, nonetheless, insufficient evidence to support the charge of solicitation], and remand this matter to the circuit court for proceedings consistent with this opinion. We do not retain jurisdiction.

c.   Factual Impossibility

As noted, factual impossibility is not a defense to attempt. Consider the policy reasons in support of this rule as you read *Mitchell*.

State v. Mitchell, 170 Mo. 633 (1902)

GANTT, J.

Defendant was tried upon an information filed by the prosecuting attorney of Clinton county at the May term, 1901, and convicted of an attempt to murder John O. Warren. His punishment was assessed at five years in the penitentiary.
. . .

The first insistence is that the first count in the information is so defective that it will not sustain the sentence. Whether the objection is well taken or not depends upon what constitutes the offense and what is essential to be proven. The statute provides that "every person who shall attempt to commit an offense prohibited by law and in such an attempt shall do any act towards the commission of such offense, but shall fail in the perpetration thereof or be intercepted or prevented from executing the same," etc., shall be punished as therein provided. Section 2360, Rev. St. 1899. Murder is an offense prohibited. When the defendant armed himself with a loaded revolver, and went to the window of the room in which he believed John O. Warren was sleeping, from his knowledge acquired by visiting his family, and fired his pistol at the place where he thought Warren was lying, he was attempting to assassinate and murder him. The fact that Warren was not there, as he believed him to be, did not make it any the less an attempt to murder. Our statute on this subject is substantially like that of Massachusetts construed in Com. v. McDonald, 5 Cush. 365, and Com. v. Sherman, 105 Mass. 169, in which it was held "that neither allegation nor proof was necessary that there was any property capable of being stolen in the pocket or upon the person of the one against whom the attempt to commit larceny was made." And the same conclusion was reached in Com. v. Bonner, 97 Mass. 587, in which the objection was distinctly made that it was equivocal and insufficient in its description of the overt act. "A man may make an attempt—an effort—to steal by breaking open a trunk, and be disappointed in not finding the object of pursuit, and so not steal in fact." "So a man may make an attempt—an experiment—to pick a pocket by thrusting his hand into it, and not succeed, because there happens to be nothing in the pocket. Still he has clearly made the attempt, and done the act towards the commission of the offense." The court concludes: "It not being necessary to allege that there was anything in the pocket of the unknown person, and as all that part of the indictment may be stricken out, the ruling of the court that there need be no evidence of any property in the pocket of the person was correct, and is fully supported by authority. Rosc. Cr. Ev. 100." . . . In Com. v. Jacobs, 9 Allen, 274, Mr. Justice Gray, speaking for the court, said: "Whenever the law makes one step towards the accomplishment of an unlawful object, with the intent or purpose of accomplishing it, criminal, a person taking that step with that intent or purpose, and himself capable of doing every act on his part to accomplish that object, cannot protect himself from responsibility by showing that, by reason of some fact unknown to him at the time of his criminal attempt, it could not be fully carried into effect in the particular instance. Kunkle v. State, 32 Ind. 220; 1 Bishop, New Cr. Law, §§75-753. So in this case the intent evidenced by the firing into the bedroom with a deadly weapon, accompanied by a present capacity in defendant to murder Warren if he were in the room, and the failure to do so only because Warren happily retired upstairs instead of in the bed into which defendant fired, made out a perfect case of an attempt within the meaning of the statute, and the information is sufficient. The evidence conclusively supported the information. It discloses a deliberate and dastardly attempt at assassination, which was only averted by the intended victim's going upstairs to bed that night. . . .

We find no error in the record, and affirm the judgment.

d. Legal and Hybrid Legal Impossibility

What type of impossibility did *Mitchell* present? As you read *Rojas* and *Booth*, consider and compare the courts' rationale for coming to two different conclusions based upon an almost identical set of facts. It is important to note which type of impossibility the court relies on in each of these cases.

People v. Rojas, 55 Cal.2d 252 (1961)

[handwritten: Conduit was not Stolen at the moment Rojas bought it.]

[Defendant was convicted of receiving stolen property. He worked out an arrangement with another defendant to sell him electrical materials. This other defendant stole $4,500 worth of conduit. The thief was arrested and the property was recovered. Thereafter, the thief agreed to cooperate with the police and arranged to sell the conduit to Rojas. Rojas was arrested after he obtained the conduit.]

SCHAUER, Justice.

In a trial by the court, after proper waiver of jury, defendants Rojas and Hidalgo were found guilty of a charge of receiving stolen property. Defendants' motions for new trial were denied. Rojas was granted probation without imposition of sentence and Hidalgo was sentenced to state prison. They appeal, respectively, from the order granting probation, the judgment, and the orders denying the motions for new trial.

Defendants urge that they were guilty of no crime (or, at most, of an attempt to receive stolen property) because when they received the property it had been recovered by the police and was no longer in a stolen condition. The attorney general argues that because the thief stole the property pursuant to prearrangement with defendants he took it as their agent, and the crime of receiving stolen property was complete when the thief began its asportation toward defendants and before the police intercepted him and recovered the property. We have concluded that defendants are guilty of attempting to receive stolen goods; that other matters of which they complain do not require a new trial; and that the appeal should be disposed of by modifying the finding that defendants are guilty as charged to a determination that they are guilty of attempting to receive stolen property, and by reversing with directions to the trial court to enter such judgments or probation orders as it deems appropriate based upon the modified finding. . . .

The offense with which defendants were charged and of which they were convicted was receiving "property which has been *stolen* . . ., *knowing the same to be so stolen*." Defendants, relying particularly upon People v. Jaffe (1906), 185 N.Y. 497, 501, urge that they neither received stolen goods nor criminally attempted to do so because the conduit, when defendants received it, was not in a stolen condition but had been recovered by the police. In the Jaffe case the stolen property was recovered by the owner while it was en route to the would-be receiver and, by arrangement with the police, was delivered to such receiver as a decoy, not as property in a stolen condition. The New York Court of Appeals held that there was no attempt to receive stolen goods "because neither [defendant] nor anyone else in the world could know that the property was stolen property inasmuch as it was not in fact stolen property. . . . If all which an accused person intends to do would if done constitute no crime it cannot be a crime to attempt to do with the same purpose a part of the thing intended."

Defendants also cited People v. Zimmerman, (1909), 11 Cal.App. 115, 118, which contains the following dictum concerning a state of facts like that in the Jaffe case: "The circumstances of the transaction . . . did not constitute an offense, as the goods were taken to the defendant's house with the consent and at the request of the owner."

As pointed out by the District Court of Appeal in Faustina v. Superior Court (1959), 174 Cal.App.2d 830, 833, "The rule of the Jaffe case has been the subject of much criticism and discussion." . . .

The situation here is materially like those considered in People v. Camodeca (1959), 52 Cal.2d 142, 146–147 (attempted theft by false pretenses); and People v. Lavine (1931), 115 Cal.App. 289, 300–301 (attempted extortion). Each of those cases is decided on the hypothesis that the defendants had the specific intent to commit the substantive offense and that under the circumstances as the defendants reasonably saw them they did the acts necessary to consummate the substantive offense; but because of circumstances unknown to defendants, essential elements of the substantive crime were lacking. Here, the goods did not have the status of stolen property and therefore defendants, although *believing* them to be stolen, could not have had *actual knowledge* of that condition. . . .

In the case at bench the criminality of the attempt is not destroyed by the fact that the goods, having been recovered by the commendably alert and efficient action of the Los Angeles police, had, unknown to defendants, lost their "stolen" status, any more than the criminality of the attempt in the case of In re Magidson (1917), 32 Cal.App. 566, 568, was destroyed by impossibility caused by the fact that the police had recovered the goods and taken them from the place where the would-be receiver went to get them. In our opinion the consequences of intent and acts such as those of defendants here should be more serious than pleased amazement that because of the timeliness of the police the projected criminality was not merely detected but also wiped out. (. . . [T]he Jaffe decision [has been explained as] a case "like selling oil stock and being surprised to discover that oil was actually in the ground where the accused vendor had represented but not believed it to be"—conduct which the New York Court of Appeals apparently feels is not criminal.) . . .

The orders denying defendants' motions for new trial are affirmed. The trial court's finding that defendants are guilty as charged is modified to find them **guilty of the offense of attempting to receive stolen property**. The judgment and probation order are reversed and the cause is remanded to the trial court for further proceedings not inconsistent with the views hereinabove expressed, and with directions to enter such lawful judgment or order against each defendant, based on the modified finding, as the court deems appropriate.

Booth v. State, 398 P.2d 863 (Ok. Cr. 1964)

[The defendant agreed to buy a stolen coat from a thief. They made arrangements for Booth to buy it for $20.00. Before they could meet, the thief was arrested, confessed, and agreed to cooperate with the police by following through with his plan to sell the coat to the defendant. The defendant was arrested after meeting with the thief. He was convicted of attempt to receive stolen property.]

NIX, Judge. . . .

. . . The rule, well stated, is to be found in U. S. v. Cawley, 255 F.2d 338:

When stolen goods are recovered by owner or his agent before they are sold, goods are no longer to be considered stolen, and purchaser cannot be convicted of receiving stolen goods.

In People v. Finkelstein, 197 N.Y.S.2d 31, (1960) the court said:

A defendant may not be convicted for receiving stolen property if property is no longer in category of stolen property when he receives it.

The law seems to be clear on this point, leaving the only question to be decided as whether or not the defendant could be convicted of an attempt to receive stolen property in such cases. It is the defendant's contention that if he could not be convicted of the substantive charge, because the coat had lost its character as stolen property; neither could he be convicted of an attempt because the coat was not in the category of stolen property at the time he received it.

The briefs filed in the case, and extensive research has revealed that two states have passed squarely on the question—New York and California. It is definitely one of first impression in Oklahoma.

The New York Court, in passing upon the question, laid down the following rule in the case of People v. Jaffe, 185 N.Y. 497, on the following facts:

> A clerk stole goods from his employer under an agreement to sell them to accused, but before delivery of the goods the theft was discovered and the goods were recovered. Later the employer redelivered the goods to the clerk to sell to accused, who purchased them for about one-half of their value, believing them to have been stolen.
>
> Held, that the goods had lost their character as stolen goods at the time defendant purchased them, and that his criminal intent was insufficient to sustain a conviction for an attempt to receive stolen property, knowing it to have been stolen.

The Jaffe case, supra, was handed down in 1906, and has prevailed as the law in New York state 58 years without modification—being affirmed in [three subsequent cases].

The State of California has passed upon the question several times and up until 1959, they followed the rule laid down in the Jaffe case, supra.

In 1959, in the case of People v. Camodeca, 52 Cal.2d 142, the California Court abandoned the Jaffe rationale that a person accepting goods which he believes to have been stolen, but which was not in fact stolen goods, is not guilty of an attempt to receive stolen goods, and imposed a liability for the attempt, overruling its previous holding to the contrary in the above cited cases. . . .

Though the instant case, insofar as it pertains to the specific crime of attempting to receive stolen property is one of first impression in Oklahoma. This Court held in the Nemecek v. State, 72 Okl. Cr. 195, involving attempting to receive money by false pretenses:

> An accused cannot be convicted of an attempt to commit a crime unless he could have been convicted of the crime itself if his attempt had been successful. Where the act, if accomplished, would not constitute the crime intended, there is no indictable attempt.

In the Nemecek case, supra, the Court quotes with approval, In re Schurman, 40 Kan. 533; wherein the Kansas Court said:

> With reference to attempt, it has also been said that 'if all which the accused person intended would, had it been done, constitute no substantive crime, it cannot be a crime, under the name 'attempt,' to do, with the same purpose, a part of this thing.'

The two paramount cases of latest date; Rojas of Calif. 1961, [55 Cal.2d 252], and Rollino of New York 1962, [233 N.Y.S. 580]; present two rationales directly contrary to each other relative to an attempt to receive stolen property after it had been recovered by the police. . . .

In this country it is generally held that a defendant may be charged with an attempt where the crime was not completed because of "physical or factual impossibility", whereas a "legal impossibility" in the completion of the crime precludes prosecution for an attempt. . . .

The reason for the "impossibility" of completing the substantive crime ordinarily falls into one of two categories: (1) Where the act if completed would not be criminal, a situation which is usually described as a "legal impossibility", and (2) where the basic or substantive crime is impossible of completion, simply because of some physical or factual condition unknown to the defendant, a situation which is usually described as a "factual impossibility".

The authorities in the various states and the text-writers are in general agreement that where there is a "legal impossibility" of completing the substantive crime, the accused cannot be successfully charged with an attempt, whereas in those cases in which the "factual impossibility" situation is involved, the accused may be convicted of an attempt. Detailed discussion of the subject is unnecessary to make it clear that it is frequently most difficult to compartmentalize a particular set of facts as coming within one of the categories rather than the other. Examples of the so-called "legal impossibility" situations are:

(a) A person accepting goods which he believes to have been stolen, but which were not in fact stolen goods, is not guilty of an attempt to receive stolen goods. *[Legal impossibility]*

(b) It is not an attempt to commit subornation of perjury where the false testimony solicited, if given, would have been immaterial to the case at hand and hence not perjurious.

(c) An accused who offers a bribe to a person believed to be a juror, but who is not a juror, is not guilty of an attempt to bribe a juror.

(d) An official who contracts a debt which is unauthorized and a nullity, but which he believes to be valid, is not guilty of an attempt to illegally contract a valid debt.

(e) A hunter who shoots a stuffed deer believing it to be alive is not guilty of an attempt to shoot a dear out of season.

Examples of cases in which attempt convictions have been sustained on the theory that all that prevented the consummation of the completed crime was a "factual impossibility" are:

(a) The picking of an empty pocket.

(b) An attempt to steal from an empty receptacle.

(c)   Where defendant shoots into the intended victim's bed, believing he is there, when in fact he is elsewhere.

(d)   Where the defendant erroneously believing that the gun is loaded points it at his wife's head and pulls the trigger.

(e)   Where the woman upon whom the abortion operation is performed is not in fact pregnant.

Your writer is of the opinion that the confusion that exists as a result of the two diverse rationales laid down in the Rollino case (NY) supra, and the Rojas case (Calif) supra, was brought about by the failure to recognize the distinction between a factual and a legal impossibility to accomplish the crime. In the Camodeca case (Calif) supra, the facts revealed a prevention of the crime because of a factual situation as stated on page 906, 338 P.2d:

> In the present case there was not a legal but only a factual impossibility of consummating the intended offense . . . .

In the Rojas case, supra, wherein was adopted the departure from the Jaffe case, by saying:

> The situation here is materially like those considered in People v. Camodeca.

The Rojas case was definitely not materially the same. In the Rojas case the facts reveal a legal and not factual impossibility.

In the case at bar the stolen coat had been recovered by the police for the owner and consequently had, according to the well-established law in this country, lost its character as stolen property. Therefore, a legal impossibility precluded defendant from being prosecuted for the crime of Knowingly Receiving Stolen Property.

It would strain reasoning beyond a logical conclusion to hold contrary to the rule previously stated herein, that,

> If all which the accused person intended would, had it been done, constituted no substantive crime, it cannot be a crime under the name 'attempt' to do, with the same purpose, a part of this thing. . . .

The rule is well stated by the English Court in the case of R. v. Percy, Ltd. 33 Crim.App.R. 102 (1949):

> Steps on the way to the commission of what would be a crime, if the acts were completed, may amount to attempts to commit that crime, to which, unless interrupted, they would have led; but steps on the way to the doing of something, which is thereafter done, and which is no crime, cannot be regarded as attempts to commit a crime.

Sayre, 41 Harvard Law Review 821, 853–54 (1928) states the rationale in this manner:

> It seems clear that cases (where none of the intended consequences is in fact criminal) cannot constitute criminal

attempts. If none of the consequences which the defendant sought to achieve constitute a crime, surely his unsuccessful efforts to achieve his object cannot constitute a criminal attempt. The partial fulfillment of an object not criminal cannot itself be criminal. If the whole is not criminal, the part cannot be.

The defendant in the instant case leaves little doubt as to his moral guilt. The evidence, as related by the self-admitted and perpetual law violator indicates defendant fully intended to do the act with which he was charged. However, it is fundamental to our law that a man is not punished merely because he has a criminal mind. It must be shown that he has, with that criminal mind, done an act which is forbidden by the criminal law.

Adhering to this principle, the following example would further illustrate the point.

A fine horse is offered to A at a ridiculously low price by B, who is a known horse thief. A, believing the horse to be stolen, buys the same without inquiry. In fact, the horse had been raised from a colt by B and was not stolen. It would be bordering on absurdity to suggest that A's frame of mind, if proven, would support a conviction of an attempt. It would be a "legal impossibility".

Our statute provides that defendant must attempt to *Knowingly* Receive Stolen Property before a conviction will stand. How could one know property to be stolen when it was not? The statute needs to be changed so it would be less favorable to the criminal. . . .

Reversed

. . . The Clerk of this Court is requested to send a copy of this decision to the Legislative Council for consideration, as our Court can only adjudicate, it cannot legislate.

In view of our statutory law, and the decisions herein related, it is our duty to Reverse this case, with orders to Dismiss, and it is so ordered. However, there are other avenues open to the County Attorney which should be explored.

Note

Although the court refers to this as legal impossibility, it is more accurate to refer to *Booth* as being an example of hybrid legal impossibility. Inasmuch as the defendant's goal to possess stolen property is a crime, the commission of the offense is impossible because he makes a factual mistake regarding the legal status of the offense that constitutes an element of the crime (i.e., the property was stolen). *Booth* was explicitly rejected by the New Mexico Supreme Court in *State v. Lopez*, 669 P.2d 1086 (N.M. 1983).

Rojas represents the majority view regarding hybrid legal impossibility as a defense to attempt crimes. *See* Joshua Dressler, *Understanding Criminal Law* §27.07[D][3][b]. *See also People v. Thousand*, 465 Mich. 149, 162 (2001). Is this sound public policy?

2. Abandonment

In addition to impossibility, another possible defense to attempt crimes is known as abandonment. Assume the defendant has committed a sufficient number of overt acts to constitute an attempt offense; if she decides to stop before the actual offense is committed, does she have a viable defense of abandonment? For example, assume a defendant plans to rob a bank. She has purchased a weapon, surveilled the bank, and walked up to a teller with the intent to rob the bank. At the last second, she changes her mind. Does she have a defense of abandonment?

Stewart v. State, 85 Nev. 388 (1969)

MOWBRAY, Justice.

A jury found Ernest Stewart guilty of attempted robbery. He has appealed to this court, seeking a reversal, on the sole ground that the evidence received during his trial was insufficient to support the jury's verdict.

Marvin Luedtke, who was the victim of the crime, and two police officers appeared for the State. Their testimony stands uncontroverted. It shows that the appellant, Stewart, approached Luedtke, a service station operator, and after brandishing a loaded .32 caliber automatic pistol, said, "I want all of your money." When Luedtke told him that the money was kept in a cash box located near the fuel pumps in front of the station, Stewart demanded the contents of Luedtke's wallet, which Luedtke promptly produced. It was at this juncture that the two police officers drove into the station. One of the officers actually saw the pistol in Stewart's hand. When Stewart saw the officers, he directed Luedtke to bring him two cans of oil and to act as though he, Stewart, were purchasing the oil. Luedtke gave him the oil. Stewart took one can, put his pistol in Luedtke's desk drawer, and attempted to leave the station. He was immediately apprehended by the officers.

Stewart argues that the attempted robbery was not proved because the evidence shows that he had abandoned his intent to commit the crime when he put down the pistol and left the station. We do not agree. The attempted robbery of Luedtke was completed when Stewart produced his pistol and demanded the money. The fact that Luedtke was apprehended on the spot does not lessen his guilt. As the court said in People v. Robinson, 4 Cal.Rptr. 679, 682 (1960), ". . . once an intent to commit a crime has been formed and overt acts toward the commission of that crime have been committed by a defendant he is then guilty of an attempt, whether he abandoned that attempt because of the approach of other persons or because of a change in his intentions due to a stricken conscience."

Affirmed.

Note

Does the result in *Stewart* make sense from a public policy standpoint? Although there is disagreement on the matter, most scholars believe that abandonment was not a common law defense to attempt, and many courts continue to decline to recognize the defense. "To the extent that a defense of abandonment is recognized today, however, it applies only if the defendant *voluntarily* and *completely* renounces her criminal purpose." Joshua Dressler, *Understanding Criminal Law* §27.08 (6th ed. 2012) (emphasis in original). In *People v. Kimball*, 109 Mich. App. 273 (1981), the court held that voluntary abandonment can be a defense to attempt crimes if it is voluntarily made and not as the result of extraneous factors such as resistance. The defendant bears the burden of demonstrating voluntary abandonment by a preponderance of the evidence.

The Model Penal Code allows for the defense of abandonment if the decision is voluntary. Section 5.01(4) provides:

> When the actor's conduct would otherwise constitute an attempt under Subsection (1)(b) or (1)(c) of this Section, it is an affirmative defense that he abandoned his effort to commit the crime or otherwise prevented its commission under circumstances manifesting a complete and voluntary renunciation of his criminal purpose. The establishment of such defense does not, however, affect the liability of an accomplice who did not join in such abandonment or prevention.
>
> Within the meaning of this Article, renunciation of criminal purpose is not voluntary if it is motivated, in whole or in part, by circumstances, not present or apparent at the inception of the actor's course of conduct, which increase the probability of detection or apprehension or which make more difficult the accomplishment of the criminal purpose. Renunciation is not complete if it is motivated by a decision to postpone the criminal conduct until a more advantageous time or to transfer the criminal effort to another but similar objective or victim.

Is the MPC good public policy? Consider the issue from both a utilitarian and retributive viewpoint? Would the MPC approach have provided Mr. Stewart with a defense?

D. Solicitation

The common law crime of solicitation involves a situation where one person asks another person to commit a crime. It generally applied only to felonies and serious misdemeanors. Like attempt, it is an inchoate crime and requires specific intent. This means the defendant must specifically intend that the other person commit the crime.

The actus reus for the crime of solicitation occurs when *A* asks *B* to kill *C*. There is no requirement that *C* take any overt act towards the completion of the offense. In fact, the crime is complete even if *B* rejects *A*'s request. If the crime is consummated, the crime of solicitation merges with the completed offense. Further, if *B* agrees to kill *C*, the common law crime of conspiracy is committed and the crime of solicitation again merges into the conspiracy. For more information, see Joshua Dressler, *Understanding Criminal Law* §§28.01–28.03 (6th ed. 2012).

1. Cases

As you read *Blechman*, consider the following questions: Could Blechman have been charged with attempt to commit arson? Why not? What is the rationale behind the crime of solicitation?

State v. Blechman, 135 N.J.L. 99 (1946)

[Defendant asked another person to burn a building for the purpose of collecting insurance on the building. He was convicted of solicitation and argues on appeal that solicitation requires the offense be committed.]

HEHER, Justice. . . .

Although we have but a meager description of the content of the indictment, it would seem, as said, that it accuses plaintiff-in-error merely of counseling another to set fire to the dwelling house; and it is urged at the outset that such is not an offense denounced by the cited statute unless the wrongful act thus counseled is done, and the insured property is actually burned. We do not so read the statute. It plainly classifies as a high misdemeanor the counseling or solicitation of another to set fire to or burn any insured building, ship or vessel, or goods, wares, merchandise or other chattels, with intent to prejudice or defraud the insurer; and in this regard the statute is primarily declaratory of the common law.

At common law, it is a misdemeanor for one to counsel, incite or solicit another to commit either a felony or a misdemeanor, certainly so if the misdemeanor is of an aggravated character, even though the solicitation is of no effect, and the crime counseled is not in fact committed. The gist of the offense is the solicitation. It is not requisite that some act should be laid to have been done in pursuance of the incitement. While the bare intention to commit evil is not indictable, without an act done, the solicitation, itself, is an act done toward the execution of the evil intent and therefore indictable. An act done with a criminal intent is punishable by indictment. It was said by an eminent common-law judge (Lawrence, J., in Rex v. Higgins, [2 East 5]) that under the common law all offenses of a public nature, i.e. "all such acts or attempts as tend to the prejudice of the community," are indictable; and it goes without saying that an attempt to incite another to commit arson or a kindred offense is prejudicial to the community and public in its nature. . . .

The solicitation constitutes a substantive crime in itself, and not an abortive attempt to perpetrate the crime solicited. It falls short of an attempt, in the legal sense, to commit the offense solicited. An attempt to commit a crime consists of a direct ineffectual overt act toward the consummation of the crime, done with an intent to commit the crime. Neither intention alone nor acts in mere preparation will suffice. There must be an overt act directly moving toward the commission of the designed offense—such as will apparently result, in the usual and natural course of events, if not hindered by extraneous causes, in the commission of the crime itself.

Of course, at common law one who counsels, incites or solicits another to commit a felony, is indictable as a principal or an accessory before the fact, if the designed felony is accomplished, depending upon his presence and participation or absence at the time of its commission.

Plaintiff-in-error sets great store upon the case of Wimpling v. State, 171 Md. 362. But it is not in point. The statute there under review was substantially different; it defined the offense of "arson" in terms that clearly signified an actual burning of the property as an indispensable ingredient of the crime.

We think that, apart from the statutory recognition of a subsisting common-law offense, the prime, if not the exclusive, purpose of the legislative act in question was the classification as a high misdemeanor of what would otherwise be a misdemeanor. . . .

Let the judgment be affirmed.

2. Model Penal Code Provisions

How does the common law differ from the MPC? The MPC's definition of solicitation is more expansive than the common law. Explore §5.02 to determine how the MPC is different from the common law.

§5.02. Criminal Solicitation

(1) Definition of Solicitation. A person is guilty of solicitation to commit a crime if with the purpose of promoting or facilitating its commission he commands, encourages or requests another person to engage in specific conduct that would constitute such crime or an attempt to commit such crime or would establish his complicity in its commission or attempted commission.

(2) Uncommunicated Solicitation. It is immaterial under Subsection (1) of this Section that the actor fails to communicate with the person

he solicits to commit a crime if his conduct was designed to effect such communication.

(3)   Renunciation of Criminal Purpose. It is an affirmative defense that the actor, after soliciting another person to commit a crime, persuaded him not to do so or otherwise prevented the commission of the crime, under circumstances manifesting a complete and voluntary renunciation of his criminal purpose.

Chapter 11
Conspiracy

A. Introduction

The third of the inchoate crimes is conspiracy. *A* and *B* agree to kill *C*, but no overt act is taken by either towards killing *C*. At common law, this would be enough to charge *A* and *B* with conspiracy to kill *C*. "A common law conspiracy is an agreement by two or more persons to commit a criminal act or series of criminal acts, or to accomplish a legal act by unlawful means." Joshua Dressler, *Understanding Criminal Law* §29.01 (6th ed. 2012). The agreement is the actus reus and the specific intent to commit the object crime is the mens rea.

Prosecutors frequently use a conspiracy charge, especially in the federal system. In *Harrison v. United States*, 7 F.2d 259, 263 (2d Cir. 1925), Judge Learned Hand characterized it as "that darling of the prosecutor's nursery." Notwithstanding its widespread use, conspiracy is a controversial crime. A policy concern regarding its use includes the vagueness of the offense. The defendant may be guilty before doing anything to accomplish the object crime; thus, it comes close to prosecuting someone for his mere thoughts. Policy arguments in support of the application of conspiracy include addressing the increased danger inherent in having groups of people agreeing to commit a crime, and, from a utilitarian paradigm, allowing earlier police intervention to benefit society, even before there is sufficient evidence to charge an attempt crime.

Unlike solicitation, which merges with the consummated offense, conspiracy at common law is a stand-alone offense that can be charged along with the completed object crime. Also, as you will see, the potential scope of liability for the co-conspirators can be extensive. The following issues, and more, will be considered in this chapter: (1) what constitutes a conspiracy; (2) the scope of liability for conspirators; (3) how to establish whether there is more than one conspiracy, and why that is important; (4) whether a conspirator can withdraw from a conspiracy, and, if so, what consequences that entails; (5) what the elements for conspiracy are under the MPC; and (6) the differences between the common law and the MPC.

B. Cases

1. Scope of Conspiracy Liability (*Pinkerton* Liability)

Suppose *A* and *B* agree to rob a bank. *B*'s role is to be the getaway driver. During the actual robbery, *A* shoots and kills an off-duty policeman who tried to prevent the robbery. Is *B* also liable for the murder? Further, as they are making their escape, *B*, driving at a very high rate of speed, runs through a red light and kills a pedestrian in the crosswalk. Is *A* responsible along with *B*? Consider this issue of conspiratorial liability as you read *Pinkerton v. United States*. Also, ask yourself whether substantive crimes (the actual underlying crime(s)) committed as part of the conspiracy can be prosecuted as separate crimes, or whether they all merge into a single conspiracy charge.

Pinkerton v. United States, 328 U.S. 640 (1946)

Mr. Justice DOUGLAS delivered the opinion of the Court.

Walter and Daniel Pinkerton are brothers who live a short distance from each other on Daniel's farm. They were indicted for violations of the Internal Revenue Code. The indictment contained ten substantive counts and one conspiracy count. The jury found Walter guilty on nine of the substantive counts and on the conspiracy count. It found Daniel guilty on six of the substantive counts and on the conspiracy count. Walter was fined $500 and sentenced generally on the substantive counts to imprisonment for thirty months. On the conspiracy count he was given a two year sentence to run concurrently with the other sentence. Daniel was fined $1,000 and sentenced generally on the substantive counts to imprisonment for thirty months. On the conspiracy count he was fined $500 and given a two year sentence to run concurrently with the other sentence. The judgments of conviction were affirmed by the Circuit Court of Appeals. The case is here on a petition for a writ of certiorari which we granted because one of the questions presented involved a conflict between the decision below and United States v. Sall, 116 F.2d 745 (1940), decided by the Circuit Court of Appeals for the Third Circuit.

A single conspiracy was charged and proved. Some of the overt acts charged in the conspiracy count were the same acts charged in the substantive counts. Each of the substantive offenses found was committed pursuant to the conspiracy. . . .

. . . It has been long and consistently recognized by the Court that the commission of the substantive offense and a conspiracy to commit it are separate and distinct offenses. . . .

Moreover, it is not material that overt acts charged in the conspiracy counts were also charged and proved as substantive offenses. As stated in Sneed v. United States, 298 F. 911, 913 (1924), "If the overt act be the offense which was the object of the conspiracy, and is also punished, there is not a double punishment of it." The agreement to do an unlawful act is even then distinct from the doing of the act.

It is contended that there was insufficient evidence to implicate Daniel in the conspiracy. But we think there was enough evidence for submission of the issue to the jury.

There is, however, no evidence to show that Daniel participated directly in the commission of the substantive offenses on which his conviction has been sustained, although there was evidence to show that these substantive offenses were in fact committed by Walter in furtherance of the unlawful agreement or conspiracy existing between the brothers. The question was submitted to the jury on the theory that each petitioner could be found guilty of the substantive offenses, if it was found at the time those offenses were committed petitioners were parties to an unlawful conspiracy and the substantive offenses charged were in fact committed in furtherance of it.

Daniel relies on United States v. Sall, supra. That case held that participation in the conspiracy was not itself enough to sustain a conviction for the substantive offense even though it was committed in furtherance of the conspiracy. The court held that, in addition to evidence that the offense was in fact committed in furtherance of the conspiracy, evidence of direct participation in the commission of the substantive offense or other evidence from which participation might fairly be inferred was necessary.

We take a different view. We have here a continuous conspiracy. There is here no evidence of the affirmative action on the part of Daniel which is necessary to establish his withdrawal from it. . . . "[H]aving joined in an unlawful scheme, having constituted agents for its performance, scheme and agency to be continuous until full fruition be secured, until he does some act to disavow or defeat the purpose he is in no situation to claim the delay of the law. As the offense has not been terminated or accomplished, he is still offending. And we think, consciously offending,—offending as certainly, as we have said, as at the first moment of his confederation, and consciously through every moment of its existence." And so long as the partnership in crime continues, the partners act for each other in carrying it forward. It is settled that "an overt act of one partner may be the act of all without any new agreement specifically directed to that act." Motive or intent may be proved by the acts or declarations of some of the conspirators in furtherance of the common objective. A scheme to use the mails to defraud, which is joined in by more than one person, is a conspiracy. Yet all members are responsible, though only one did the mailing. The governing principle is the same when the substantive offense is committed by one of the conspirators in furtherance of the unlawful project. The criminal intent to do the act is established by the formation of the conspiracy. Each conspirator instigated the commission of the crime. The unlawful agreement contemplated precisely what was done. It was formed for the purpose. The act done was in execution of the enterprise. The rule which holds responsible one who counsels, procures, or commands another to commit a crime is founded on the same principle. That principle is recognized in the law of conspiracy when the overt act of one partner in crime is attributable to all. An overt act is an essential ingredient of the crime of conspiracy under §37 of the Criminal Code, 18 U.S.C. §88, 18 U.S.C.A. §88. If that can be supplied by the act of one conspirator, we fail to see why the same or other acts in furtherance of the conspiracy are likewise not attributable to the others for the purpose of holding them responsible for the substantive offense.

A different case would arise if the substantive offense committed by one of the conspirators was not in fact done in furtherance of the conspiracy, did not fall within the scope of the unlawful project, or was merely a part of the ramifications of the plan which could not be reasonably foreseen as a necessary or natural consequence of the unlawful agreement. But as we read this record, that is not this case.

Affirmed.

2. Requirements for a Conspiracy

At common law, must the conspirators know each other? Must the conspirators be aware of all of the details surrounding the conspiracy? Is an overt act required? Consider these issues as you read *Rosado-Fernandez*.

United States v. Rosado-Fernandez, 614 F.2d 50 (5th Cir. 1980)

AINSWORTH, Circuit Judge:

Appellants Jose Eligio Borges and Angel Oscar Rosado-Fernandez, along with two other defendants, were convicted of conspiracy to possess with intent to distribute cocaine, 21 U.S.C. §846, and possession with intent to distribute cocaine, 21 U.S.C. §846, 18 U.S.C. §2. Rosado was also convicted of use of a communication facility during the course of and in the commission of a felony, in violation of 21 U.S.C. §§841(a)(1), 846, 843(b). On appeal, Borges contends that there is insufficient evidence to convict him of the conspiracy charge, and also contends that he cannot be found guilty of the possession charge since he never had actual possession of the cocaine in question. Rosado contends that the Government failed to prove that the cocaine involved in the attempted drug transaction was "L" cocaine rather than purportedly legal "D" cocaine. The contentions of both appellants are meritless and we affirm.

On January 3, 1979, Agent John Lawler of the Drug Enforcement Agency (DEA), acting in an undercover capacity as a New York cocaine buyer, went to the residence of appellant Borges. Lawler informed Borges that he wanted to buy three kilos of cocaine. Borges quoted a price, and stated that delivery could be arranged. During the conversation Borges was sifting a white powder on his kitchen table. He stated the cocaine would be better than that on the table. Borges then made a phone call in Spanish and told Lawler to return later that evening. When Lawler returned the parties agreed to meet still later at a nearby restaurant. Borges indicated he would bring his supplier to the restaurant.

Later that evening, Borges came to the restaurant accompanied by appellant Rosado, and Rosado's stepfather. Borges introduced Rosado to Lawler, and Lawler stated he was interested in purchasing three kilos of cocaine. Rosado stated it would be no problem as he had 40 kilos in the area. Borges was present during this entire conversation. Rosado then made a phone call and told Lawler the cocaine would be delivered to an apartment. Rosado and Lawler discussed delivery and agreed that they would be the only ones present during the actual transaction. Borges concurred in this arrangement. No actual delivery took place that evening.

The next day Lawler and Rosado had a series of telephone conversations, which were recorded and played for the jury. During the conversations, Rosado apologized for the delay and stated the price would be $46,000 per kilo. Lawler and Rosado later met at the home of the third codefendant Nelson Garcia. A quantity of white powder was produced, and Lawler tested it. The test indicated that the powder was cocaine. Shortly thereafter arrests were made. While Garcia and Rosado were being arrested, the fourth codefendant Zayas took the cocaine and dumped it into the swimming pool. Agent Lawler dove in the pool and recovered samples of the water and the cocaine, as well as a sample from the table inside. All samples were found to contain cocaine.

Borges does not deny that he introduced Agent Lawler to codefendant Rosado, but he contends that he had no part of the final drug transaction involving Rosado and codefendant Garcia. He argues that the Rosado-Garcia drug transaction is a separate conspiracy, as the purchase arranged by him was to involve Rosado and a drug source other than Garcia. The fact that Rosado eventually obtained the cocaine from a source not originally contemplated by Borges, however, is not sufficient to exonerate Borges.

To be convicted of conspiracy, a defendant must have knowledge of the conspiracy, and must intend to join or associate himself with the objectives of the conspiracy. Knowledge, actual participation and criminal intent must be proved by the Government. Participation, however, need not be proved by direct evidence; a common purpose and plan may be inferred from a pattern of circumstantial evidence. The essential elements of a criminal conspiracy are an agreement among the conspirators to commit an offense attended by an overt act by one of them in furtherance of the agreement. However, under the provisions of the drug conspiracy statute involved here, it is not necessary that an overt act be alleged or proved.

The facts at trial established a conspiracy between Borges and Rosado to sell cocaine to Lawler. They agreed to commit an offense against the United States. Borges was the organizer of the venture. He set up the meeting, and was present during the negotiations for the sale of the cocaine. The conspirators need not know each other nor be privy to the details of each enterprise comprising the conspiracy as long as the evidence is sufficient to show that each defendant possessed full knowledge of the conspiracy's general purpose and scope. Borges knew that Lawler wanted to buy cocaine. Borges knew that Rosado would obtain the cocaine for Lawler from one of Rosado's several sources. Under these circumstances the conspiracy was proved.

Borges next contends that he cannot be convicted of possession since the evidence shows he never had physical control of the cocaine involved in the transaction. It is undisputed, however, that Rosado had possession of the drug. A party to a continuing conspiracy may be responsible for a substantive offense committed by a coconspirator in furtherance of the conspiracy even though that party does not participate in the substantive offense or have any knowledge of it. As we stated recently in *United States v. Michel*, 588 F.2d 986, 999 (5th Cir. 1979):

> Once the conspiracy and a particular defendant's knowing participation in it has been established beyond a reasonable doubt, the defendant is deemed guilty of substantive acts committed in furtherance of the conspiracy by any of his criminal partners. This principle has been repeatedly applied by this circuit in cases involving drug conspiracies and substantive drug violations. . . .

There being no error in the trial, the convictions of appellants Jose Eligio Borges and Angel Oscar Rosado-Fernandez are

AFFIRMED; REMANDED for correction of appellant Rosado's sentence.

Note

The federal drug conspiracy statute used in *Rosado-Fernandez* did not require an overt act. The court also referenced a general conspiracy statute that did require an overt act. If a jurisdiction requires an overt act, what sort of act will suffice? Why require an overt act at all?

3. Single Conspiracy v. Multiple Conspiracies

Often it will be unclear if there is more than a single conspiracy. For example, *A* and *B* agree to commit an offense, then *B* subsequently agrees with *C* to commit that same crime. Are there one or two conspiracies?

There are several significant reasons why this issue matters. Whether there is one conspiracy or multiple conspiracies directly affects (1) the breadth and reach of the *Pinkerton* doctrine; (2) the number of substantive counts each conspirator may be liable for; and (3) whether there will be one trial or separate trials.

Read the following fact pattern and consider whether more than one conspiracy is present:

> During the first week of May, President of the Finance Company agreed to help Client 1 obtain a loan from the

Federal Housing Administration by fraudulently misrepresenting that the proceeds of the loan would be used to build low-income housing. In fact, Client 1 intended to use the proceeds to pay off his gambling debts. President knew this, and, because of the risk of criminal prosecution, he charged Client 1 triple the normal fee for helping to arrange the loan. Over the next three months, President entered into similar fraudulent arrangements with Client 2 and Client 3. President secretly solicited each of these clients and none of them knew about any of the others. Each of them dealt exclusively with President. The government has charged President, Client 1, Client 2, and Client 3 with a single conspiracy to defraud the government.

This fact pattern is based upon *Kotteakos v. United States*, 328 U.S. 750 (1946), where the United States Supreme Court held that President had a separate agreement with all three individuals; he was the hub of a wheel and the three clients were spokes in that wheel. Aside from President, however, none of the individuals had a relationship with one another—they were not connected by the "rim" of the wheel. Why do you think the Court reached that conclusion? Does the Court's conclusion mean there was only one conspiracy? Or multiple conspiracies?

How does *Kotteakos* compare to *Rosado-Fernandez*? If any member of the *Rosado-Fernandez* conspiracy failed to perform his job, what would have been the likely implications for the goal of selling cocaine to a specifically agreed upon individual? By comparison, what would have happened to the loan arrangement President had with Client 1, if, for example, either of the other two clients decided to not complete their agreed upon arrangements?

4. Abandonment and Withdrawal

If the elements of a conspiracy have been established, can abandonment or withdrawal be a defense to the crime of conspiracy? If not, are there still consequences for the defendant? Consider this last issue as you read *Peterson*.

State v. Peterson, 213 Minn. 56 (1942)

PETERSON, Justice.

Defendant was convicted of arson in the second degree, and appeals.

The indictment charges her with burning her dwelling house on October 30, 1940. The house was at Lake Minnetonka in Hennepin county.

The state claimed, and its evidence was to the effect, that she did not personally set the fire, but caused it to be set by an accomplice, one August Anderson. There was no dispute as to Anderson's having set the fire. Defendant stoutly maintained that she did not have anything to do with the burning of her house and that she not only directed Anderson not to go to the house on the occasion when the fire was set, but that she tried to persuade him before he set the fire to leave the premises to which he had gone contrary to her directions. . . .

. . . [Defendant asserts] that, assuming the truth of the state's evidence that Anderson and defendant were accomplices, defendant is not liable because she withdrew before the fire was set. . . .

It is important to bear in mind that defendant is not charged with the crime of conspiracy. A conspiracy to commit arson is a misdemeanor. A conspiracy to commit a crime is a separate offense from the crime which is the object of the conspiracy.

One who has procured, counseled, or commanded another to commit a crime may withdraw before the act is done and avoid criminal responsibility by communicating the fact of his withdrawal to the party who is to commit the crime. . . .

By her efforts . . . to induce Anderson to leave the premises before he set the fire and to go immediately to her in the hospital where she was then confined, the defendant in the instant case took the most effective measures within her power to arrest the execution of the plan, if there was one, to burn the house. Anderson must have known that if she wanted him to comply with her request to leave the premises before he set the fire she did not want him to burn the house. She not only withdrew in ample time from any plan to burn the house, but made that fact known to Anderson in an unmistakable manner. By withdrawing, defendant avoided criminal responsibility. Anderson was solely criminally responsible for the fire which he set. The facts being undisputed on this point, the verdict cannot stand.

Reversed.

C. Pattern Jury Instructions

The following are sample jury instructions used in conspiracy cases. You will see that these instructions reflect the case law. Note that these instructions are tailored to the law in the jurisdiction where the conspiracy charge is brought. For example, not every state recognizes *Pinkerton* liability.

3.01A CONSPIRACY TO COMMIT AN OFFENSE—BASIC ELEMENTS

(1) Count ___ of the indictment accuses the defendants of a conspiracy to commit the crime of _____ in violation of federal law. It is a crime for two or more persons to conspire, or agree, to commit a criminal act, even if they never actually achieve their goal.

(2) A conspiracy is a kind of criminal partnership. For you to find any one of the defendants guilty of the conspiracy charge, the government

must prove each and every one of the following elements beyond a reasonable doubt:

(A) First, that two or more persons conspired, or agreed, to commit the crime of _____.

(B) Second, that the defendant knowingly and voluntarily joined the conspiracy.

(C) And third, that a member of the conspiracy did one of the overt acts described in the indictment for the purpose of advancing or helping the conspiracy.

(3) You must be convinced that the government has proved all of these elements beyond a reasonable doubt in order to find any one of these defendants guilty of the conspiracy charge.

3.02 AGREEMENT

(1) With regard to the first element—a criminal agreement—the government must prove that two or more persons conspired, or agreed, to cooperate with each other to commit the crime of _____.

(2) This does not require proof of any formal agreement, written or spoken. Nor does this require proof that everyone involved agreed on all the details. But proof that people simply met together from time to time and talked about common interests, or engaged in similar conduct, is not enough to establish a criminal agreement. These are things that you may consider in deciding whether the government has proved an agreement. But without more they are not enough.

(3) What the government must prove is that there was a mutual understanding, either spoken or unspoken, between two or more people, to cooperate with each other to commit the crime of _____. This is essential.

(4) An agreement can be proved indirectly, by facts and circumstances which lead to a conclusion that an agreement existed. But it is up to the government to convince you that such facts and circumstances existed in this particular case.

[(5) One more point about the agreement. The indictment accuses the defendants of conspiring to commit several federal crimes. The government does not have to prove that the defendants agreed to commit all these crimes. But the government must prove an agreement to commit at least one of them for you to return a guilty verdict on the conspiracy charge.]

3.03 DEFENDANT'S CONNECTION TO THE CONSPIRACY

(1) If you are convinced that there was a criminal agreement, then you must decide whether the government has proved that the

defendants knowingly and voluntarily joined that agreement. You must consider each defendant separately in this regard. To convict any defendant, the government must prove that he knew the conspiracy's main purpose, and that he voluntarily joined it intending to help advance or achieve its goals.

(2)   This does not require proof that a defendant knew everything about the conspiracy, or everyone else involved, or that he was a member of it from the very beginning. Nor does it require proof that a defendant played a major role in the conspiracy, or that his connection to it was substantial. A slight role or connection may be enough.

(3)   But proof that a defendant simply knew about a conspiracy, or was present at times, or associated with members of the group, is not enough, even if he approved of what was happening or did not object to it. Similarly, just because a defendant may have done something that happened to help a conspiracy does not necessarily make him a conspirator. These are all things that you may consider in deciding whether the government has proved that a defendant joined a conspiracy. But without more they are not enough.

(4)   A defendant's knowledge can be proved indirectly by facts and circumstances which lead to a conclusion that he knew the conspiracy's main purpose. But it is up to the government to convince you that such facts and circumstances existed in this particular case.

3.04 OVERT ACTS

(1)   The third element that the government must prove is that a member of the conspiracy did one of the overt acts described in the indictment for the purpose of advancing or helping the conspiracy.

(2)   The indictment lists overt acts. The government does not have to prove that all these acts were committed, or that any of these acts were themselves illegal.

(3)   But the government must prove that at least one of these acts was committed by a member of the conspiracy, and that it was committed for the purpose of advancing or helping the conspiracy. This is essential.

[(4) One more thing about overt acts. There is a limit on how much time the government has to obtain an indictment. This is called the statute of limitations. For you to return a guilty verdict on the conspiracy charge, the government must convince you beyond a reasonable doubt that at least one overt act was committed for the purpose of advancing or helping the conspiracy after.]

3.09 MULTIPLE CONSPIRACIES—FACTORS IN DETERMINING

(1) In deciding whether there was more than one conspiracy, you should concentrate on the nature of the agreement. To prove a single conspiracy, the government must convince you that each of the members agreed to participate in what he knew was a group activity directed toward a common goal. There must be proof of an agreement on an overall objective.

(2) But a single conspiracy may exist even if all the members did not know each other, or never sat down together, or did not know what roles all the other members played. And a single conspiracy may exist even if different members joined at different times, or the membership of the group changed. These are all things that you may consider in deciding whether there was more than one conspiracy, but they are not necessarily controlling.

(3) Similarly, just because there were different sub-groups operating in different places, or many different criminal acts committed over a long period of time, does not necessarily mean that there was more than one conspiracy. Again, you may consider these things, but they are not necessarily controlling.

(4) What is controlling is whether the government has proved that there was an overall agreement on a common goal. That is the key.

3.10 PINKERTON LIABILITY FOR SUBSTANTIVE OFFENSES COMMITTED BY OTHERS

(1) Count ____ of the indictment accuses the defendants of committing the crime of _____.

(2) There are two ways that the government can prove the defendants guilty of this crime. The first is by convincing you that they personally committed or participated in this crime. The second is based on the legal rule that all members of a conspiracy are responsible for acts committed by the other members, as long as those acts are committed to help advance the conspiracy, and are within the reasonably foreseeable scope of the agreement.

(3) In other words, under certain circumstances, the act of one conspirator may be treated as the act of all. This means that all the conspirators may be convicted of a crime committed by only one of them, even though they did not all personally participate in that crime themselves.

(4) But for you to find any one of the defendants guilty of _____ based on this legal rule, you must be convinced that the government has proved each and every one of the following elements beyond a reasonable doubt:

(A) First, that the defendant was a member of the conspiracy charged in Count ___ of the indictment.

(B) Second, that after he joined the conspiracy, and while he was still a member of it, one or more of the other members committed the crime of _____.

(C) Third, that this crime was committed to help advance the conspiracy.

(D) And fourth, that this crime was within the reasonably foreseeable scope of the unlawful project. The crime must have been one that the defendant could have reasonably anticipated as a necessary or natural consequence of the agreement.

(5) This does not require proof that each defendant specifically agreed or knew that the crime would be committed. But the government must prove that the crime was within the reasonable contemplation of the persons who participated in the conspiracy. No defendant is responsible for the acts of others that go beyond the fair scope of the agreement as the defendant understood it.

(6) If you are convinced that the government has proved all of these elements, say so by returning a guilty verdict on this charge. If you have a reasonable doubt about any one of them, then the legal rule that the act of one conspirator is the act of all would not apply.

3.11A WITHDRAWAL AS A DEFENSE TO CONSPIRACY

(1) One of the defendants, _____, has raised the defense that he withdrew from the agreement before any overt act was committed. Withdrawal can be a defense to a conspiracy charge. But _____ has the burden of proving to you that he did in fact withdraw.

(2) To prove this defense, _____ must prove each and every one of the following things:

(A) First, that he completely withdrew from the agreement. A partial or temporary withdrawal is not enough.

(B) Second, that he took some affirmative step to renounce or defeat the purpose of the conspiracy. An affirmative step would include an act that is inconsistent with the purpose of the conspiracy and is communicated in a way that is reasonably likely to reach the other members. But some affirmative step is required. Just doing nothing, or just avoiding the other members of the group, would not be enough.

(C) Third, that he withdrew before any member of the group committed one of the overt acts described in the indictment. Once an overt act is committed, the crime of conspiracy is complete. And any withdrawal after that point is no defense to the conspiracy charge.

(3) If _____ proves these three factors by a preponderance of the evidence, then you must find him not guilty. Preponderance of the evidence is defined as "more likely than not." In other words, the defendant must convince you that the three factors are more likely true than not true.

(4) The fact that _____ has raised this defense does not relieve the government of its burden of proving that there was an agreement, that he knowingly and voluntarily joined it, and that an overt act was committed. Those are still things that the government must prove in order for you to find _____ guilty of the conspiracy charge.

3.11B WITHDRAWAL AS A DEFENSE TO SUBSTANTIVE OFFENSES COMMITTED BY OTHERS

(1) One of the defendants, _____, has raised the defense that he withdrew from the conspiracy before the crime of _____ was committed. Withdrawal can be a defense to a crime committed after the withdrawal. But _____ has the burden of proving to you that he did in fact withdraw.

(2) To prove this defense, _____ must prove each and every one of the following things:

(A) First, that he completely withdrew from the conspiracy. A partial or temporary withdrawal is not sufficient.

(B) Second, that he took some affirmative step to renounce or defeat the purpose of the conspiracy. An affirmative step would include an act that is inconsistent with the purpose of the conspiracy and is communicated in a way that is reasonably likely to reach the other members. But some affirmative step is required. Just doing nothing, or just avoiding the other members, would not be enough.

(C) Third, that he withdrew before the crime of _____ was committed. Once that crime was committed, any withdrawal after that point would not be a defense.

(3) If _____ proves these three factors by a preponderance of the evidence, then you must find him not guilty. Preponderance of the evidence is defined as "more likely than not." In other words, the defendant must convince you that the three factors are more likely true than not true.

(4) Withdrawal is not a defense to the conspiracy charge itself. But the fact that _____ has raised this defense does not relieve the government of proving that there was an agreement, that he knowingly and voluntarily joined it, that an overt act was committed, that the crime of _____ was committed to help advance the conspiracy and that this crime was within the reasonably foreseeable

scope of the unlawful project. Those are still things that the government must prove in order for you to find _____ guilty of _____.

D. Model Penal Code Provisions

§5.03. Criminal Conspiracy

(1) Definition of Conspiracy. A person is guilty of conspiracy with another person or persons to commit a crime if with the purpose of promoting or facilitating its commission he:

(a) agrees with such other person or persons that they or one or more of them will engage in conduct that constitutes such crime or an attempt or solicitation to commit such crime; or

(b) agrees to aid such other person or persons in the planning or commission of such crime or of an attempt or solicitation to commit such crime.

(2) Scope of Conspiratorial Relationship. If a person guilty of conspiracy, as defined by Subsection (1) of this Section, knows that a person with whom he conspires to commit a crime has conspired with another person or persons to commit the same crime, he is guilty of conspiring with such other person or persons, whether or not he knows their identity, to commit such crime.

(3) Conspiracy with Multiple Criminal Objectives. If a person conspires to commit a number of crimes, he is guilty of only one conspiracy so long as such multiple crimes are the object of the same agreement or continuous conspiratorial relationship.

(4) Joinder and Venue in Conspiracy Prosecutions.

(a) Subject to the provisions of paragraph (b) of this Subsection, two or more persons charged with criminal conspiracy may be prosecuted jointly if:

(i) they are charged with conspiring with one another; or

(ii) the conspiracies alleged, whether they have the same or different parties, are so related that they constitute different aspects of a scheme of organized criminal conduct.

(b) In any joint prosecution under paragraph (a) of this Subsection:

(i) no defendant shall be charged with a conspiracy in any county [parish or district] other than one in which he entered into such conspiracy or in which an overt act pursuant to such conspiracy was done by him or by a person with whom he conspired; and

(ii) neither the liability of any defendant nor the admissibility against him of evidence of acts or declarations of another shall be enlarged by such joinder; and

(iii) the Court shall order a severance or take a special verdict as to any defendant who so requests, if it deems it necessary or appropriate to promote the fair determination of his guilt or innocence, and shall take any other proper measures to protect the fairness of the trial.

(5) Overt Act. No person may be convicted of conspiracy to commit a crime, other than a felony of the first or second degree, unless an overt act in pursuance of such conspiracy is alleged and proved to have been done by him or by a person with whom he conspired.

(6) Renunciation of Criminal Purpose. It is an affirmative defense that the actor, after conspiring to commit a crime, thwarted the success of the conspiracy, under circumstances manifesting a complete and voluntary renunciation of his criminal purpose.

(7) Duration of Conspiracy. For purposes of Section 1.06(4):

(a) conspiracy is a continuing course of conduct that terminates when the crime or crimes that are its object are committed or the agreement that they be committed is abandoned by the defendant and by those with whom he conspired; and

(b) such abandonment is presumed if neither the defendant nor anyone with whom he conspired does any overt act in pursuance of the conspiracy during the applicable period of limitation; and

(c) if an individual abandons the agreement, the conspiracy is terminated as to him only if and when he advises those with whom he conspired of his abandonment or he informs the law enforcement authorities of the existence of the conspiracy and of his participation therein.

Note

What are the differences between common law conspiracy and the MPC's version? In particular, compare the overt act requirement, the requirement regarding the minimum number of participants, and withdrawal. In addition, note that §2.06 of the MPC rejects *Pinkerton* liability, which is consistent with the MPC's overall subjectivist approach to criminal liability.

Chapter 12
Accomplice Liability

A. Introduction

D1 and *D2* agree to rob a bank. *D1* commits the robbery and *D2* is the getaway driver. *D3* provided the car to *D2* and *D4* drove everyone to Canada after the robbery was completed. Neither *D3* nor *D4* was present at the time of the robbery. During the robbery, *D1* shot and killed a bank security guard who attempted to intercede. Is *D2* liable, even though he did not personally shoot the guard?

This chapter will consider the liability of a person who did not actually commit the crime, but may be held criminally accountable nonetheless. This concept is referred to as accomplice liability. Unlike conspiracy, accomplice liability is not a separate crime at common law. Rather, it is a theory of liability or prosecution that allows for vicarious or derivative liability for those who assist in the commission of a crime.

Often, accomplice liability involves a conspiracy and can be charged as such. As noted in the previous chapters, there are some significant advantages to a prosecutor's use of a conspiracy charge (e.g., *Pinkerton* liability). A key distinction between accomplice liability and conspiracy is the existence of an agreement. Also, a conspirator is not required to render actual assistance, whereas accomplice liability generally requires the actor to somehow actively assist in the commission of the crime. Ordinarily, criminal liability is potentially much greater as a conspirator than as an accomplice.

1. Common Law

At one time, accomplice liability was based upon distinctions involving the participation and involvement of the parties. The principal in the first degree (*P1*) was the person who physically committed the offense. The principal in the second degree (*P2*) was someone who was present, actually or constructively, and assisted in the commission in the offense (e.g., the getaway driver in the example above). At common law, both *P1* and *P2* had to specifically intend the commission of the crime.

The "accessory before the fact" is similar to *P2*, except he is neither actually nor constructively present during the commission of the offense. Typically, the accessory before the fact was involved in the planning of the offense, obtained the necessary tools, counseled *P1*, etc. In the above example, *D3* would be considered an accessory before the fact because he obtained the getaway car for *D2* and he was not present when the offense was committed. The "accessory after the fact," on the other hand, is one who did not participate in the commission of the offense, but, with knowledge of the criminal act, intentionally assisted the participants in avoiding capture. Thus, in the above example, *D4* would be derivatively liable as an accessory after the fact because, with knowledge of the bank robbery after its commission, he drove all of the participants to Canada to avoid arrest. For more information, see Joshua Dressler, *Understanding Criminal Law* §30.03 (6th ed. 2012).

2. Modern Statutes

With the possible exception of accessory after the fact, most states today no longer follow these common law distinctions and have promulgated statutes wherein all participants are considered principals or accessories. Many modern statutes collapsed these distinctions into what is now known as "aiding and abetting." As for the accessory after the fact, most jurisdictions treat this as a less severe crime, separate from the crime committed by the principal or accessory. This crime is often referred to as obstruction of justice.[*] *See* Joshua Dressler, *Understanding Criminal Law* §§30.04–30.05 (6th ed. 2012).

B. Aiding and Abetting

What is the necessary mens rea to establish aiding and abetting? Is it enough that the aider and abettor act with knowledge regarding the perpetrator's intent? Or does it also require the aider and abettor to act with the intent to commit the crime, or at least facilitate its commission? Consider this significant mens rea issue as you read *Beeman*.

---

[*] *People v Perry*, 460 Mich. 55, 62 (1999), states that "an accessory after the fact is 'one who, with knowledge of the other's guilt, renders assistance to a felon in the effort to hinder his detection, arrest, trial or punishment.' Perkins, *Criminal Law* (2d ed.), p. 667, quoted in *People v. Lucas*, 402 Mich. 302, 304 (1978). The crime of accessory after the fact is akin to obstruction of justice. *United States v. Brenson*, 104 F.3d 1267 (C.A.11 1997)."

People v. Beeman, 35 Cal.3d 547 (1984)

[Burk and Gray robbed Beeman's sister-in-law of valuable jewelry. Beeman was not present during the commission of the robbery, but was arrested six days after the offense. He had in his possession some of the jewelry that was taken during the robbery. Burk and Gray pled guilty. Beeman went to trial. Burk and Gray testified that Beeman was extensively involved in the planning of the robbery, but Beeman's testimony contradicted the testimony of Burk and Gray. He claimed that while he provided information regarding the type of jewelry owned by the victim and details regarding where she lived, he did not do so as part of a plan to rob her. The prosecution's theory was based upon Beeman's aiding and abetting Burk and Gray. Beeman was convicted of the robbery and related offenses.]

REYNOSO, J.

Timothy Mark Beeman appeals from a judgment of conviction of robbery, burglary, false imprisonment, destruction of telephone equipment and assault with intent to commit a felony. Appellant was not present during commission of the offenses. His conviction rested on the theory that he aided and abetted his acquaintances James Gray and Michael Burk.

The primary issue before us is whether the standard California Jury Instructions (CALJIC Nos. 3.00 and 3.01) adequately inform the jury of the criminal intent required to convict a defendant as an aider and abettor of the crime.

We hold that instruction No. 3.01 is erroneous. Sound law, embodied in a long line of California decisions, requires proof that an aider and abettor rendered aid with an intent or purpose of either committing, or of encouraging or facilitating commission of, the target offense. It was, therefore, error for the trial court to refuse the modified instruction requested by appellant. Our examination of the record convinces us that the error in this case was prejudicial and we therefore reverse appellant's convictions. . . .

Appellant requested that the jury be instructed in accord with *People v. Yarber* (1979) 90 Cal.App.3d 895, that aiding and abetting liability requires proof of intent to aid. The request was denied.

After three hours of deliberation, the jury submitted two written questions to the court: "We would like to hear again how one is determined to be an accessory and by what actions can he absolve himself"; and "Does inaction mean the party is guilty?" The jury was reinstructed in accord with the standard instructions, CALJIC Nos. 3.00 and 3.01. The court denied appellant's renewed request that the instructions be modified as suggested in *Yarber*, explaining that giving another, slightly different instruction at this point would further complicate matters. The jury returned its verdicts of guilty on all counts two hours later.

I

Penal Code section 31 provides in pertinent part: "All persons concerned in the commission of a crime, . . . whether they directly commit the act constituting the offense, or aid and abet in its commission, or, not being present, have advised and encouraged its commission, . . . are principals in any crime so committed." Thus, those persons who at common law would have been termed accessories before the fact and principals in the second degree as well as those who actually perpetrate the offense, are to be prosecuted, tried and punished as principals in California. (See Pen. Code, §971.) The term "aider and abettor" is now often used to refer to principals other than the perpetrator, whether or not they are present at the commission of the offense.

CALJIC No. 3.00 defines principals to a crime to include "Those who, with knowledge of the unlawful purpose of the one who does directly and actively commit or attempt to commit the crime, aid and abet in its commission . . ., or . . . Those who, whether present or not at the commission or attempted commission of the crime, advise and encourage its commission . . . ." CALJIC No. 3.01 defines aiding and abetting as follows: "A person aids and abets the commission of a crime if, with knowledge of the unlawful purpose of the perpetrator of the crime, he aids, promotes, encourages or instigates by act or advice the commission of such crime."

Prior to 1974 CALJIC No. 3.01 read: "A person aids and abets the commission of a crime if he knowingly and with criminal intent aids, promotes, encourages or instigates by act or advice, or by act and advice, the commission of such crime."

Appellant asserts that the current instructions, in particular CALJIC No. 3.01, substitute an element of knowledge of the perpetrator's intent for the element of criminal intent of the accomplice, in contravention of common law principles and California case law. He argues that the instruction given permitted the jury to convict him of the same offenses as the perpetrators without finding that he harbored either the same criminal intent as they, or the specific intent to assist them, thus depriving him of his constitutional rights to due process and equal protection of the law. . . .

The People argue that the standard instruction properly reflects California law, which requires no more than that the aider and abettor have knowledge of the perpetrator's criminal purpose and do a voluntary act which in fact aids the perpetrator. . . .

II

There is no question that an aider and abettor must have criminal intent in order to be convicted of a criminal offense. Decisions of this court dating back to 1898 hold that "the word 'abet' includes knowledge of the wrongful purpose of the perpetrator and counsel and encouragement in the crime" and that it is therefore error to instruct a jury that one may be found guilty as a principal if one aided *or* abetted. The act of encouraging or counseling itself implies a purpose or goal of furthering the encouraged result. "An aider and abettor's fundamental purpose, motive and intent is to aid and assist the perpetrator in the latter's commission of the crime."

The essential conflict in current appellate opinions is between those cases which state that an aider and abettor must have an intent or purpose to commit or assist in the commission of the criminal offenses and those finding it sufficient that the aider and abettor engage in the required acts with knowledge of the perpetrator's criminal purpose. . . .

We agree with the *Yarber* court that the facts from which a mental state may be inferred must not be confused with the mental state that the prosecution is required to prove. Direct evidence of the mental state of the accused is rarely available except through his or her testimony. The trier of fact is and must be free to disbelieve the testimony and to infer that the truth is otherwise when such an inference is supported by circumstantial evidence regarding the actions of the accused. Thus, an act which has the effect of giving aid and encouragement, and which is done with knowledge of the criminal purpose of the person aided, may indicate that the actor intended to assist in fulfillment of the known criminal purpose. However, as illustrated by *Hicks v. U.S.* (1893) 150 U.S. 442 (conviction reversed because jury not instructed that words of encouragement must have been used with the intention of encouraging and abetting crime in a case where ambiguous gesture and remark may have been acts of desperation) and *People v. Bolanger* (1886) 71 Cal. 17 (feigned accomplice not guilty because lacks common intent with the perpetrator to unite in the commission of the crime), the act may be done with some other purpose which precludes criminal liability. . . .

Thus, we conclude that the weight of authority and sound law require proof that an aider and abettor act with knowledge of the criminal purpose of the perpetrator *and* with an intent or purpose either of committing, or of encouraging or facilitating commission of, the offense.

When the definition of the offense includes the intent to do some act or achieve some consequence beyond the *actus reus* of the crime, the aider and abettor must share the specific intent of the perpetrator. By "share" we mean neither that the aider and abettor must be prepared to commit the offense by his or her own act should the perpetrator fail to do so, nor that the aider and abettor must seek to share the fruits of the crime. Rather, an aider and abettor will "share" the perpetrator's specific intent when he or she knows the full extent of the perpetrator's criminal purpose and gives aid or encouragement with the intent or purpose of facilitating the perpetrator's commission of the crime. The liability of an aider and abettor extends also to the natural and reasonable consequences of the acts he knowingly and intentionally aids and encourages.

CALJIC No. 3.01 inadequately defines aiding and abetting because it fails to insure that an aider and abettor will be found to have the required mental state with regard to his or her own act. While the instruction does include the word "abet," which encompasses the intent required by law, the word is arcane and its full import unlikely to be recognized by modern jurors. Moreover, even if jurors were made aware that "abet" means to encourage or facilitate, and implicitly to harbor an intent to further the crime encouraged, the instruction does not *require* them to find that intent because it defines an aider and abettor as one who "aids, promotes, encourages *or* instigates" (emphasis added). Thus, as one appellate court recently recognized, the instruction would "technically allow a conviction if the defendant knowing of the perpetrator's unlawful purpose, negligently or accidentally aided the commission of the crime." . . .

The convictions are reversed.

Note

Would it have been sufficient to convict Beeman of aiding and abetting the robbery if he knew of the offense in advance? Pursuant to *Beeman*, what is the necessary mens rea to convict a person of aiding and abetting? Is the rule in *Beeman* good policy?

C. Statutes

18 U.S.C. §2. Principals

(a) Whoever commits an offense against the United States or aids, abets, counsels, commands, induces or procures its commission, is punishable as a principal.

(b) Whoever willfully causes an act to be done which if directly performed by him or another would be an offense against the United States, is punishable as a principal.

18 U.S.C. §3. Accessory after the fact

Whoever, knowing that an offense against the United States has been committed, receives, relieves, comforts or assists the offender in order to hinder or prevent his apprehension, trial or punishment, is an accessory after the fact.

Except as otherwise expressly provided by any Act of Congress, an accessory after the fact shall be imprisoned not more than one-half the maximum term of imprisonment or (notwithstanding section 3571) fined not more than one-half the maximum fine prescribed for the punishment of the principal, or both; or if the principal is punishable by life imprisonment or death, the accessory shall be imprisoned not more than 15 years.

D. Pattern Jury Instructions

4.01 AIDING AND ABETTING

(1)   For you to find _____ guilty of _____, it is not necessary for you to find that he personally committed the crime. You may also find him guilty if he intentionally helped [or encouraged] someone else to commit the crime. A person who does this is called an aider and abettor.

(2)   But for you to find _____ guilty of _____ as an aider and abettor, you must be convinced that the government has proved each and every one of the following elements beyond a reasonable doubt:

    (A)   First, that the crime of _____ was committed.

    (B)   Second, that the defendant helped to commit the crime [or encouraged someone else to commit the crime].

    (C)   And third, that the defendant intended to help commit [or encourage] the crime.

(3)   Proof that the defendant may have known about the crime, even if he was there when it was committed, is not enough for you to find him guilty. You can consider this in deciding whether the government has proved that he was an aider and abettor, but without more it is not enough.

(4)   What the government must prove is that the defendant did something to help [or encourage] the crime with the intent that the crime be committed.

(5)   If you are convinced that the government has proved all of these elements, say so by returning a guilty verdict on this charge. If you have a reasonable doubt about any one of these elements, then you cannot find the defendant guilty of _____ as an aider and abettor.

4.02 ACCESSORY AFTER THE FACT

(1)   _____ is not charged with actually committing the crime of _____. Instead, he is charged with helping someone else try to avoid being arrested, prosecuted or punished for that crime. A person who does this is called an accessory after the fact.

(2)   For you to find _____ guilty of being an accessory after the fact, the government must prove each and every one of the following elements beyond a reasonable doubt:

    (A)   First, that the defendant knew someone else had already committed the crime of _____.

    (B)   Second, that the defendant then helped that person try to avoid being arrested, prosecuted or punished.

(C)   And third, that the defendant did so with the intent to help that person avoid being arrested, prosecuted or punished.

(3)   If you are convinced that the government has proved all of these elements, say so by returning a guilty verdict on this charge. If you have a reasonable doubt about any one of these elements, then you must find the defendant not guilty of this charge.

E.   Practice Problems on Accomplice Liability

Is the defendant criminally liable in each of the following hypotheticals based upon the following Michigan statute (M.C.L. §767.39), which defines accomplice liability? As you consider each hypothetical, also determine what type of principal or accessory, if any, the defendant would have been considered based upon the common law distinctions. Assume there is no preexisting agreement.

M.C.L. §767.39.

Every person concerned in the commission of an offense, whether he directly commits the act constituting the offense or procures, counsels, aids or abets in its commission may hereafter be prosecuted, indicted, tried and on conviction shall be punished as if he had directly committed such offense.

(1)   *D1* rapes a barmaid.
(2)   *D2* holds the barmaid's arms while she is being raped.
(3)   *D3* is present and yells, "Do it, do it."
(4)   *D4* is a customer. He likes what is happening, but does not say or do anything.
(5)   *D5* is a bartender. He does not say or do anything, but state statute requires reasonable efforts to control rowdy patrons.
(6)   *D6* is the owner of the bar. He is home watching TV.
(7)   *D7* is a drunk that is standing outside the bar. He is unaware of what is happening inside. When a police officer walking his beat asks if everything is all right inside, *D7* says "all quiet on the western front."
(8)   *D8* shows up after the rape, is told what happened, and drives his friend *D1* across the border to Canada.

Note

In *People v. Robinson*, 475 Mich. 1 (2006), the court held that a defendant who intends to aid and abet the commission of a crime can be found guilty of that offense, as well as any other crimes that are the natural and probable consequences of that crime.

F.   Model Penal Code Provisions

The MPC defines those situations where one's conduct can be imputed to another, but it does not contain the common law distinctions of principal and accessory. Recall that the MPC does not allow for *Pinkerton* liability either.

§2.06. Liability for Conduct of Another; Complicity.

(1)   A person is guilty of an offense if it is committed by his own conduct or by the conduct of another person for which he is legally accountable, or both.
(2)   A person is legally accountable for the conduct of another person when:
(a)   acting with the kind of culpability that is sufficient for the commission of the offense, he causes an innocent or irresponsible person to engage in such conduct; or
(b)   he is made accountable for the conduct of such other person by the Code or by the law defining the offense; or
(c)   he is an accomplice of such other person in the commission of the offense.
(3)   A person is an accomplice of another person in the commission of an offense if:
(a)   with the purpose of promoting or facilitating the commission of the offense, he
(i)   solicits such other person to commit it, or
(ii)   aids or agrees or attempts to aid such other person in planning or committing it, or
(iii)   having a legal duty to prevent the commission of the offense, fails to make proper effort so to do; or
(b)   his conduct is expressly declared by law to establish his complicity.
(4)   When causing a particular result is an element of an offense, an accomplice in the conduct causing such result is an accomplice in the commission of that offense if he acts with the kind of culpability, if any, with respect to that result that is sufficient for the commission of the offense.
(5)   A person who is legally incapable of committing a particular offense himself may be guilty thereof if it is committed by the conduct of another person for which he is legally accountable, unless such

liability is inconsistent with the purpose of the provision establishing his incapacity.

(6)   Unless otherwise provided by the Code or by the law defining the offense, a person is not an accomplice in an offense committed by another person if:

(a)   he is a victim of that offense; or

(b)   the offense is so defined that his conduct is inevitably incident to its commission; or

(c)   he terminates his complicity prior to the commission of the offense and

(i)   wholly deprives it of effectiveness in the commission of the offense; or

(ii)   gives timely warning to the law enforcement authorities or otherwise makes proper effort to prevent the commission of the offense.

(7) An accomplice may be convicted on proof of the commission of the offense and of his complicity therein, though the person claimed to have committed the offense has not been prosecuted or convicted or has been convicted of a different offense or degree of offense or has an immunity to prosecution or conviction or has been acquitted.

Chapter 13
Various Mens Rea Issues

A. Introduction

In this chapter, consideration will be given to a number of issues related to the mens rea, or the intent requirements, associated with crimes. In previous chapters, you learned that certain crimes only require general intent (e.g., second degree murder, arson, kidnapping) and others require specific intent (e.g., first degree murder, theft offenses, inchoate crimes, burglary). Specific intent generally refers to the intent necessary to commit the particular offense. Thus, common law burglary requires a breaking and entering into the dwelling of another in the nighttime *with the intent to commit a larceny or felony*. General intent, on the other hand, only requires the intent to complete the actus reus for the offense with a morally blameworthy state of mind or with criminal negligence.

In this chapter, the following issues will be covered: (1) whether the actus reus and mens rea must occur simultaneously; (2) whether there can be a crime in the absence of mens rea; and (3) whether the actor's intent to commit one offense can be transferred to the actus reus of another offense.

B. Concurrence of the Actus Reus and Mens Rea

1. Introduction

Ordinarily, the necessary mens rea triggers the resulting actus reus, which means that they occur simultaneously or in close proximity to each other. If there is no temporal relationship between the two, there is no crime. This is known as the "concurrence doctrine." Thus, it is not a crime if *A* accidentally kills his neighbor when he is cleaning his gun and the next day is happy his neighbor is dead. As you read *Cooper*, consider the requirements of burglary and at what point the mens rea must be established in relation to the commission of the actus reus.

Cooper v. People, 973 P.2d 1234 (Colo. 1999)

Justice KOURLIS delivered the Opinion of the Court.

Defendant, Samuel W. Cooper, appeals from a judgment of conviction entered upon a jury verdict finding him guilty of second degree burglary under section 18–4–203, 6 C.R.S. (1998). The statute defines the offense of second degree burglary as an unlawful entry or unlawful presence in an occupied building coupled with the intent to commit some other crime on the premises (the "ulterior offense"). We granted certiorari to consider whether the trial court erred in instructing the jury that it could convict Cooper if it found that he had formed the intent to commit the underlying offense after his unlawful entry into the premises in question. The court of appeals found no error. *See People v. Cooper,* 950 P.2d 620 (Colo.App. 1997).

We now hold that, under section 18–4–203 and our precedent, burglary punishes the defendant who trespasses with the intent to do more harm once on the premises. Thus, to convict a defendant of burglary, a jury must conclude that the defendant had made up his mind to commit some other offense at the point at which he or she becomes a trespasser. If the defendant forms the intent to commit the crime after the trespass is under way, he or she may be guilty of that underlying crime (or attempt) and of trespass—but is not guilty of burglary. Both circumstances reflect criminal acts, but burglary is the more serious. Burglary is the crime that requires that the defendant have a criminal intent to do more than trespass. To hold otherwise would convert burglary into a sentence enhancer for any crime committed in tandem with a trespass. Although the General Assembly could so provide, we find no indication in the statute or legislative history to indicate that such was their intent. Hence, we reverse the decision of the court of appeals.

I.

In February 1995, Cooper and his seven-year-old daughter were living with Cooper's sixty-eight-year-old mother, Shirley Thorman. Cooper had borrowed money from his mother, and the two argued frequently about financial matters. On February 26, 1995, following one such argument, the police arrested Cooper for harassment of his mother. Two days later, the police released Cooper from custody subject to a temporary restraining order that prohibited him from contacting his mother or going to her home.

The following day, on March 1, 1995, defendant went to Thorman's home and entered through the rear door. Thorman and Cooper gave conflicting testimony at trial concerning the nature of this visit. Thorman testified that her son broke in uninvited and unannounced, immediately cursed her and threatened her life, and then threw her onto a bed and repeatedly "twisted" her legs and arms. She further testified that her son beat her over the head with two decorator pillows until they began to tear. Cooper testified that his mother had invited him to the house, and that he broke through the door in order to escape the cold when his mother failed to answer his knocks. He further testified that upon his entry, he argued with Thorman about financial matters. He admitted that he became angry in the course of this discussion, and pulled a light fixture out of the ceiling, but claimed that he never physically contacted his mother. Hence, the evidence was unclear as to whether Cooper had formed an intent to commit the ulterior offense of assaulting his mother when he entered her home.

The trial court instructed the jury that it could find Cooper guilty of second degree burglary if it found that Cooper knowingly and unlawfully entered the home with the intent to commit therein the crime of assault. Over defense objection, the trial court further instructed that "the intent to so commit a crime . . . can be formed either before entry into the dwelling or after entry into the dwelling." The jury convicted Cooper of second degree burglary and assault on the elderly, and Cooper appealed, arguing that the burglary instructions were improper.

II.

The second degree burglary statute, section 18–4–203(1), 6 C.R.S. (1998) provides: "A person commits second degree burglary if he knowingly breaks an entrance into, or enters, or remains unlawfully in a building or occupied structure with intent to commit therein a crime against person or property." The General Assembly inserted the language "remains unlawfully" when it repealed and reenacted the statute in 1971. *See* Ch. 121, sec. 1, §4–4–203, 1971 Colo. Sess. Laws 427. Cooper argued on appeal that because the trial court never instructed the jury that the defendant could be convicted under the unlawfully remains theory, it was improper for that court to instruct that his intent to assault Thorman could be formed after his entry. In overruling Cooper's similar objection at trial, the trial court indicated that there seemed to be "no evidence to suggest that Mr. Cooper lawfully entered, and was asked to leave, and remained unlawfully." On that basis, the trial court declined to include the remaining unlawfully instruction, but nonetheless did include the instruction concerning the timing of the formation of intent.

Citing *People v. Angell*, 917 P.2d 312 (Colo.App. 1995), and *People v. Trujillo*, 749 P.2d 441 (Colo.App. 1987), the court of appeals concluded that the 1971 amendment supported the trial court's jury instruction. The court of appeals in *Angell* and *Trujillo* held that "a person can be found guilty of second degree burglary if the intent to commit a further crime is formed after entry, but while the person is remaining unlawfully upon the premises." *Trujillo*, 749 P.2d at 442; *see also Angell*, 917 P.2d at 314. Based on these holdings, the court of appeals found no error in the trial court's jury instructions.

III. . . .

. . . [T]he specific purpose of burglary was to deter trespass against habitations by persons who intended to commit a felony therein. Trespass into a home coupled with the intent to steal from or assault the resident was viewed as egregious and dangerous. However, unless a person possessed the intent to commit a felony at the moment he broke and entered a dwelling, such a trespass was punishable only as mere civil trespass. . . . [I]t is clear that such breaking and entry must be with a felonious intent, otherwise it is only a trespass." . . .

As to the manner of trespass, our statute has always encompassed unlawful entry achieved in either of two manners: (1) a traditional common law breaking and entry or; (2) an unlawful, nonforced entry. *See, e.g.,* Colo.Crim.Code, Ch. 36, §1227 (1891) (codified as amended at 18–4–201 to –204, 6 C.R.S. (1998).

In 1971, however, the General Assembly added a third manner of trespass, when it reenacted the burglary statute to apply to suspects who entered or "remain[ed] unlawfully" in a structure. *See* Ch. 121, sec. 1, §4–4–203, 1971 Colo. Sess. Laws 427. For purposes of burglary and criminal trespass, the General Assembly defined "unlawfully enters or remains" in pertinent part as:

> A person "unlawfully enters or remains" in or upon premises when he is not licensed, invited, or otherwise privileged to do so. A person who, regardless of his intent, enters or remains in or upon premises which are at the time open to the public does so with license and privilege unless he defies a lawful order not to enter or remain, personally communicated to him by the owner of the premises or some other authorized person.

See Ch. 121, sec. 1, §4–4–201(3), 1971 Colo. Sess. Laws 426; §18–4–201, 6 C.R.S. (1998). The General Assembly commented that "[t]his section contains definitions of terms applicable to burglary, derived from Michigan proposal sections 2601, 2605, 2606, and 2607 which in turn are copied without material change from New York Code section 145.00 et seq. (See also Model Penal Code 221.0 to 221.3.)" 1971 Perm. Supp., §40–4–201 cmt. at 306. The scope and nature of the "remains unlawfully" clause lie at the heart of the present case.

IV.

Two fundamental questions arise in this context: (1) when must the defendant form the intent to commit an ulterior crime; and (2) what does "remains unlawfully" mean: specifically, does it refer only to someone who enters lawfully and thereafter remains unlawfully, or does it also include someone who enters unlawfully, thereafter automatically remaining unlawfully for the duration of his presence in the structure.

First, we address the fundamental question of when criminal intent must be formed for purposes of burglary under section 18–4–203. We are guided in this inquiry by basic principles of statutory interpretation. In construing a statute, we give effect to the intent of the General Assembly whenever possible. The statute should be construed as a whole, giving consistent, harmonious, and sensible effect to all of its parts. . . .

As such, we look to long-settled judicial precedent to guide our inquiry into the mens rea element of burglary. This court has always required proof that a burglary defendant had the intent to commit a crime at the time of trespass. *See Martinez v. People,* 163 Colo. 503, 506 (1967) ("One of the essential elements in a charge of burglary . . . is that the accused have the intent to commit a specific crime at the very time and place of breaking and entering.) This construction derived from the ancient common law and from settled burglary law in other jurisdictions, and it ensured that the serious penalties for burglary were reserved for trespasses accompanied by the intent to commit another crime.

. . . [W]e hold that the intent to commit a crime must co-exist with the moment of trespass, regardless of the manner of trespass. . . .

We hold that to convict a defendant under section 18–4–203, 6 C.R.S. (1998), a jury must find that the defendant either: (1) broke and entered or unlawfully entered with the intent to commit a crime therein; or (2) entered lawfully but subsequently remained unlawfully with the intent to commit a crime therein. . . .

The trial court in this case should have instructed the jury that it could convict Cooper only if it found beyond a reasonable doubt that he possessed the intent to assault Thorman at the moment he first trespassed by: (1) entering unlawfully; (2) breaking and entering unlawfully; or (3) remaining unlawfully. The instruction the trial court gave allowed the jury to convict Cooper upon a finding that he formed the intent to assault Thorman at any time before or after entry without reference to the moment of trespass.

The precise effects of this error are "unquantifiable and indeterminate." The jury may have believed that Cooper broke into Thorman's home uninvited with the intent to assault her. Alternatively, the jury may have decided that Cooper broke into Thorman's home with no such intent, but later decided to assault her during their argument. In sum, the trial court's jury instructions permitted a finding inconsistent with the requirements of the statute.

Because the trial court did not correctly instruct the jury on an essential element of a crime for which the jury convicted Cooper, we reverse the decision of the court of appeals and remand this case for further proceedings.

Justice RICE dissenting:
. . . I believe that our statute allows convictions for second degree burglary so long as the defendant formed the intent to commit a crime while unlawfully remaining on the premises, regardless of the legality of the entry. Hence, I respectfully dissent.

I turn first to the plain meaning of the statute. As the majority notes, the second degree burglary statute provides: "A person commits second degree burglary if he *knowingly breaks an entrance into, or enters, or remains unlawfully,* in a building or occupied structure *with intent to commit therein* a crime against person or property." §18–4–203(1) (emphasis added). The "remains unlawfully" language was added to the statute upon its repeal and reenactment in 1971. . . .

In my opinion, the plain meaning of the language of the statute lends no support to the majority's distinction between instances of unlawful as opposed to lawful entry. In fact, the statute does not distinguish between lawful and unlawful entries at all. Given the plain language of the statute, therefore, it does not follow that the "remaining unlawfully" provision is confined to those situations where the initial entry was lawful. Under the majority's interpretation of the statute, one who enters lawfully but then remains unlawfully and forms the intent to commit another crime therein is guilty of burglary, while one who enters unlawfully and thereafter forms that same intent is guilty only of trespass. To distinguish between equally culpable defendants in these two scenarios would create an anomalous result. Therefore, I would refuse to imply the distinction the majority advances.

While it is true that this issue is one of first impression before this court, the majority also fails to give due consideration to the fact that this issue has been previously addressed by other Colorado courts. In fact, the majority's holding would overrule two court of appeals decisions which approved jury instructions for second degree burglary after finding that the defendant could form the necessary intent while unlawfully remaining after entering unlawfully. *See People v. Angell,* 917 P.2d 312, 314 (Colo.App. 1995); *People v. Trujillo,* 749 P.2d 441, 442 (Colo.App. 1987). . . .

. . . Seven additional jurisdictions—the majority of those which have decided this issue—have held that the intent to commit the underlying crime may be formed after entry and while unlawfully remaining on the premises regardless of whether the entry was lawful. . . . I agree with the Utah Supreme Court's statement:

> [I]t does not necessarily follow that the "remaining unlawfully" provision is confined to those situations where the initial entry was lawful. We believe that such an interpretation would create an anomalous result. For instance, under [the defendant's] interpretation of the statute, one who enters lawfully but then remains unlawfully and forms the intent to commit another felony, theft, or assault is guilty of burglary while one who enters unlawfully and thereafter forms that same intent is guilty only of trespass. We are unable to see the distinction between the two scenarios. In our view, the actor in the second scenario is at least as dangerous and culpable as the actor in the first.

State v. Rudolph, 970 P.2d 1221, 1228–29 (Utah 1998). . . . .

For the foregoing reasons, I would affirm the court of appeals' determination that a defendant may form the requisite intent to commit a felony after an unlawful entry.

2. Satisfying the Concurrence Doctrine

The *Cali* case involves the burning of a building. If defendant Cali did not form the intent to defraud the insurance company until after the fire started, how is the concurrence doctrine satisfied?

Commonwealth v. Cali, 247 Mass. 20 (1923)

BRALEY, J.

The defendant having been indicted, tried and convicted under G. L. c. 266, §10, of burning a building in Leominster belonging to Maria Cali, which at the time was insured against loss or damage by fire, with intent to injure the insurer, the case is here on his exceptions to the denial of his motion for a directed verdict, and to rulings at the trial.

It is contended there was no evidence the building was insured by a valid policy at the time it was burned. But it was uncontroverted that when the defendant was the owner he mortgaged the property to the Fitchburg Co-operative Bank and procured and delivered a policy of insurance thereon payable to the mortgagee . . . .

The only evidence as to the origin, extent and progress of the fire were the statements of the defendant to the police inspector, and as a witness. The jury who were to determine his credibility and the weight to be given his testimony could find notwithstanding his explanations of its origin as being purely accidental, that when all the circumstances were reviewed he either set it, or after the fire was under way purposely refrained from any attempt to extinguish it in order to obtain the benefit of the proceeds of the policy, which when recovered, would be applied by the mortgagee on his indebtedness. If they so found, a specific intent to injure the insurer had been proved. The motion and the defendant's requests in so far as not given were denied rightly. The instructions to the jury that:

> If a man does start an accidental fire what is his conduct in regard to it? A question—as if after the fire has started accidentally, and he then has it within his power and ability to extinguish the fire and he realizes and knows that he can, and then he forms and entertains an intent to injure an insurance company, he can be guilty of this offense. It is not necessary that the intent be formed before the fire is started,

—also show no error of law. It is true as the defendant contends, that if he merely neglected in the emergency of the moment to act, his negligence was not proof of a purpose to commit the crime charged.

The intention, however, to injure could be formed after as well as before the fire started. On his own admissions the jury were to say whether when considered in connection with all the circumstances, his immediate departure form [sic] the premises for his home in Fitchburg, without giving any alarm, warranted the inference of a criminal intent or state of mind, that the building should be consumed.

Exceptions overruled.

3. What if the concurrence doctrine is not satisfied?

If there is no concurrence, must the charges be dismissed? Can a court divorce the requirement of concurrence when there are substantial public policy concerns? Consider this issue as you read *Jackson*.

Jackson v. Commonwealth, 18 Ky. L. Rptr. 795 (1896)

HAZELRIGG, J.

The appellant was jointly indicted with one Alonzo Walling in the Campbell circuit court [Kentucky] for the murder of Pearl Bryan, and on his separate trial was found guilty, and sentenced to be hanged. . . . On the morning of Saturday, February 1, 1896, the headless body of a woman was found on the farm of one Locke, near Newport, in Campbell county. Every effort to find the head proved futile, but the shoes the dead girl wore were marked "Lewis and Hoes, Greencastle, Ind.," and this circumstance led to the identification of the body as that of Pearl Bryan, a young girl of that city. Her clothes were saturated with blood, particularly about the neck, and a large quantity of it was found on the ground, near the neck, covering a circular spot some six or seven inches in diameter, and also a spot of a similar kind some feet away. Extending near to or over this last-named spot there were some privet bushes, the leaves of which were spattered with blood, and drops were discovered pending under the leaves, as though the blood had reached the underside of them by spurting from the neck, which it might do, as disclosed by the testimony, if the decapitation had taken place or been commenced at the spot near the bushes, and if the victim were alive at the time. These and other circumstances led the authorities to proceed on the theory that the murder—for such it evidently appeared to be—occurred in Campbell county. An autopsy disclosed that the girl was pregnant, and a healthy fœtus of some five months' development was found, which, in the opinion of the experts, was probably alive until the death of the mother. The inquiries which led to the identification developed the fact that appellant, Scott Jackson, a dental student at the Ohio Medical College, but who formerly lived at Greencastle, was probably the author of the girl's ruin. It was established beyond question that Pearl Bryan, after trying without success certain remedies prescribed by the appellant, left home on the Monday preceding her death, ostensibly to go to Indianapolis, to visit friends, but in fact to come to Cincinnati [Ohio], in order that appellant might in some way procure relief for her . . . .

. . . The conclusion is fairly deducible from certain portions of the testimony that an attempt was made to kill the girl by the administration of cocaine, while in Cincinnati, and that this was done by the defendant, or at his instance, but that she was not thereby killed. It is to be remembered that, according to the testimony of Jackson, he did not see the girl in life after Wednesday, and, according to Walling's, he did not see her after that day. But the proof conduces to show that they were both with her Friday night, when she was in the cab, and that they brought her over to Campbell county. If she was dead then, as might be supposed from her making no outcry, a verdict of guilty could not have been rendered; but, if she was then alive, though appearing to be dead, and by the cutting of her throat she was killed, while in Campbell county, then the jury might find a verdict of guilty, although the cutting off of the head was merely for the purpose of destroying the chance of identification, or for any other purpose. At best, the instruction does not authorize a verdict of conviction unless Jackson is shown to have cut off the head of his victim in Campbell county, and while she was in fact alive; and if he did this he was guilty of murder, though believing her already dead, if the act succeeded, and was but a part of, the felonious attempt to kill her in Cincinnati. Some of the facts on which this instruction is based do not appear as distinctly in proof as others, but there is some basis for the hypothesis put, and the whole arises naturally out of the circumstances in evidence. . . . The fifth [claim of improper jury instructions] is based on the theory that Jackson feloniously administered, or procured another to administer, drugs to Pearl Bryan for the purpose of producing an abortion, when she was so far gone with child as to make it necessarily dangerous to her life, or when the drugs were in themselves or in the manner of their administration dangerous to her life; and, though believing her to have been killed in this way, he cut her head off, in Campbell county, when she was in fact alive, yet he was guilty of murder. . . . Keeping in mind the purpose for which, as appears from the proof, the girl was brought to Cincinnati, the fact that cocaine was found in her stomach, and the defendant's inquiries with respect thereto, we think these instructions fairly suggested by the proof, and embody correct principles of law. . . . The eleventh [claim of improper jury instructions] was on the subject of voluntary manslaughter, and authorized such a finding if Jackson cut the throat of Pearl Bryan, in Campbell county, under the belief that she was already dead; and did so, not intending to kill her, but merely for the purpose of concealing her identity, unless he had theretofore himself attempted to kill her, or procured another to so attempt, or had administered drugs, or procured another to do so, for the purpose of procuring an abortion, in which event they were to "find as elsewhere instructed,"—meaning, it is evident, that if the attempt was to kill her, or if the drugs were administered when dangerous to her life, he was still guilty of murder as theretofore defined, or of voluntary manslaughter, if the drugs were administered when not dangerous. . . .

Upon the whole case, we are convinced that the accused has had a fair and impartial trial. . . . The judgment must be affirmed.

The court delivered the following response to the petition for rehearing February 13, 1897:

With great earnestness, force, and plausibility two contentions are made by the petitions for rehearing in this case and in the case of Walling v. Commonwealth: First. That no facts which occurred in the foreign jurisdiction of Ohio can be tacked onto facts which occurred in Kentucky for the purpose of supplying the elements necessary to constitute the crime of murder in Kentucky. Second. (And this appears to be the point chiefly relied on) that, in giving its instructions to the jury, the trial court is not authorized to refer to any fact which occurred in the foreign jurisdiction. Other suggestions are made in the petitions, but in our judgment do not require specific response.

These two contentions may be considered together, as the first is necessarily raised and considered in the decision of the second, and so treated in the petition. Reduced to its lowest terms, the claim of counsel is that an attempt to commit a murder in another state, supposed by the guilty party to have been there successful, but in reality completed in this state, though by an act not by him believed to be the consummation of his purpose, is not in this state punishable. Such is not, nor should it be, the law. By the law of this state a crime is punishable in the jurisdiction in which it has effect. Statutes in numbers have been passed by the general assembly of this commonwealth providing that jurisdiction should be had of crimes in the county in which the crime became effectual. St. Ky. c. 36, art. 2. Such we believe to have been the common law before such enactments. Assuming that what the jury found was true, in what state or district could the crime be punished? If not here, where? If we concede the claims of counsel for appellants, no serious crime was committed in Ohio. Nothing was there done but an ineffective attempt to murder. None was committed here. What was done in this jurisdiction was only the mutilation of a supposed corpse. And yet the fact, established by overwhelming testimony, remains that the crime has been committed. Not all the refinements of counsel can lead us from the conclusion that when a crime has been completed, the result of which is a death in this commonwealth, we can take jurisdiction of the offense.

Not for a moment can we admit as law the logical conclusion of counsel's argument, namely, that there is a variety of murder which, by reason of error in its commission, is not anywhere in any jurisdiction punishable; not in Ohio, for the reason that the attempt there made was not successful; not in Kentucky, for the reason that the act there done, and which accomplished and completed the actual killing, was done upon the supposition that the murder had already been accomplished. . . . We see no good reason why we should not consider the motive which inspired an attempted crime in another sovereignty, and the circumstances of the attempt, with the view to determine the character, criminal or not, of the ultimate fact which took place in this sovereignty. . . .

The petition for rehearing is overruled.

Note

Why was there no concurrence as to the charge of murder? If there was no concurrence, why was the guilty verdict upheld? As stated by Oliver Wendell Holmes, Jr., "The life of the law has not been logic, it has been experience." O. W. Holmes, Jr., *The Common Law* 1 (1881).

C. Strict Liability

1. Introduction

D owns a meat packaging facility. He makes every effort to keep the facility clean. In fact, he exceeds the standards imposed by the U.S. Department of Agriculture. However, despite his best efforts, an inspector finds a single package of spoiled meat and cites *D*. Is *D* liable to pay the fine? The short answer is "yes."

Strict liability offenses are committed upon the completion of the necessary actus reus. There is typically no mens rea requirement. There can be liability even in the absence of fault, without regard to the defendant's mental state and without regard to whether there was a morally blameworthy state of mind. Traditionally, these tend to be less serious offenses and are designed to protect the public's health and welfare. Typically, all the prosecution has to establish is (1) the commission of the prohibited act (regardless of the defendant's mental state); and, generally speaking, (2) proof that the defendant had knowledge of sufficient facts to alert him to the possibility that his conduct was subject to regulation.

In *Olshefski*, note the differences between those crimes considered *mala in se* and those considered *mala prohibita*. As a general matter, which of these two characterizations involve strict liability crimes? Also, does it matter that Olshefski had proof suggesting he was in compliance with the ordinance he was charged with violating? What would be the problem with enforcement if the prosecutor had to prove a morally culpable state of mind?

Commonwealth v. Olshefski, 64 Pa. D. & C. 343 (Quar. Sess. 1948)

Strict liability

KREISHER, P. J.

On February 6, 1948, John Fisher, a driver for above-named defendant, at the direction of defendant, purchased a load of coal at the Gilberton Coal Company colliery and had the same loaded upon a truck owned by defendant, which had a "U" tag on it, and which, under The Vehicle Code of May 1, 1929, P. L. 905, is permitted to weigh 15,000 pounds plus five percent, or a gross weight of 15,750 pounds. The load was weighed by a licensed weighmaster at the colliery and the weight was given at 15,200 pounds. Fisher drove the truck to the home of defendant, who was out of town at the time and then placed the weigh slip from the colliery in the compartment of the truck. The following day defendant went to the Danville National Bank to do some banking business and observed the Pennsylvania State Police at the Northern end of the river bridge checking on trucks. He then returned to his home and drove his truck with the load of coal to the northern end of the river bridge on his way to the borough water department scales for the purpose of having it weighed. He states that he was selling the coal in Danville, and pursuant to the requirements of an ordinance in Danville, he had to have a Danville weigh slip. Before reaching the water department's scales a State policeman stopped him and he was directed to the scales where his load was weighed by the officer and the weigh slip was signed by a licensed weigh master [sic], showing that his gross weight was 16,015, and that he was, therefore, overloaded 265 pounds. The officer lodged an information for his violation of The Vehicle Code. Defendant waived a hearing and the matter is now before us for disposition. . . .

It is also contended by counsel for defendant that this prosecution should be dismissed for the reason that defendant had in his possession a weigh bill for this particular load by a duly licensed weighmaster, which was weighed the day before, showing that the gross weight of the truck and the load was within the load allowed by law for this particular truck, and that defendant, relying upon this weigh bill, voluntarily drove to where he knew the police were weighing trucks, and was of the belief that his load was a legal load, and therefore, because of this belief, he is not guilty of the crime charged.

In criminal law we have two distinct types of crimes: The one type of crime being the common-law crimes, which are designated as crimes *mala in se*, which means that they are crimes because the act is bad in and of itself. The other type of crime which did not exist at common law covers those acts which are made criminal by statute, and are termed crimes *mala prohibita*, and simply means that they are crimes not because they are bad in and of themselves, but merely because the legislative authority makes the act criminal and penal.

In crimes that are *mala in se*, two elements are necessary for the commission of the crime, viz., the mental element and the physical element. In this type of crime intent is a necessary element, but in statutory crimes, which are simply *mala prohibita*, the mental element is not necessary for the commission of the crime, and one who does an act in violation of the statute and is caught and prosecuted, is guilty of the crime irrespective of his intent or belief. The power of the legislature to punish an act as a crime, even though it is not bad in and of itself, is an absolute power of the legislature, the only restriction being the constitutional restrictions, and it is the duty of the court to enforce these enactments irrespective of what the court might personally think about the prosecution or the wisdom of the act.

Except for constitutional limitations, the power of the State legislature is absolute. It may punish any act which in its judgment requires punishment, provided it violates no constitutional restriction, and its enactments must be enforced by the courts. The courts cannot review the discretion of the legislature, or pass upon the expediency, wisdom, or propriety of legislative action in matters within its powers. Neither can the courts pass upon the action of a prosecuting officer who prosecutes a person for the violation of a statute which is violated by that person, even though the court might be of the opinion that the officer should have not instituted the prosecution.

If the testimony shows, as in this case, that defendant violated the law, and is prosecuted for that violation, then the court is bound to enforce the legislative enactments, and cannot in good conscience set itself up as the legislature and excuse one person who has violated the law and find another person guilty for the same violation. It is true that this rule of law may seem harsh and unjustifiable, but the court is powerless to correct it, and, therefore, under our duty as judge, we are obliged to hold that this defendant violated The Vehicle Code by having his truck overloaded, and that he is guilty as charged. To this end we make the following.

And now, to wit, September 9, 1948, it is ordered, adjudged and decreed that Felix Olshefski is guilty as charged, and the sentence of the court is that he pay the costs of prosecution, and that he pay a fine of $25 to the Commonwealth of Pennsylvania for the use of the County of Montour, and in default of payment thereof, shall undergo imprisonment in the Montour County Jail for an indeterminate period of not less than one day nor more than two days. Said sentence to be complied with on or before September 15, 1948.

2. Is it strict liability if a statute lacks a mens rea requirement?

Recall *Morissette v. United States*, 342 U.S. 246, 250 (1952), discussed in Chapter 2, wherein the Court observed that:

> [t]he contention that an injury can amount to a crime only when inflicted by intention is no provincial or transient notion. It is as universal and persistent . . . as belief in freedom of the human will and a consequent ability and duty of the normal individual to choose between good and evil.

As you read *Staples*, consider whether the absence of a mens rea requirement in the statute meant that Congress determined one was not required. Also, note the analysis the Court engages in to determine whether, despite its omission, Congress must have intended an intent requirement.

Staples v. United States, 511 U.S. 600 (1994)

Justice THOMAS delivered the opinion of the Court.

The National Firearms Act makes it unlawful for any person to possess a machinegun that is not properly registered with the Federal Government. Petitioner contends that, to convict him under the Act, the Government should have been required to prove beyond a reasonable doubt that he knew the weapon he possessed had the characteristics that brought it within the statutory definition of a machinegun. We agree and accordingly reverse the judgment of the Court of Appeals.

I

The National Firearms Act (Act), 26 U.S.C. §§5801–5872, imposes strict registration requirements on statutorily defined "firearms." The Act includes within the term "firearm" a machinegun, §5845(a)(6), and further defines a machinegun as "any weapon which shoots, . . . or can be readily restored to shoot, automatically more than one shot, without manual reloading, by a single function of the trigger," §5845(b). Thus, any fully automatic weapon is a "firearm" within the meaning of the Act. Under the Act, all firearms must be registered in the National Firearms Registration and Transfer Record maintained by the Secretary of the Treasury. §5841. Section 5861(d) makes it a crime, punishable by up to 10 years in prison, see §5871, for any person to possess a firearm that is not properly registered.

Upon executing a search warrant at petitioner's home, local police and agents of the Bureau of Alcohol, Tobacco and Firearms (BATF) recovered, among other things, an AR–15 rifle. The AR–15 is the civilian version of the military's M–16 rifle, and is, unless modified, a semiautomatic weapon. The M–16, in contrast, is a selective fire rifle that allows the operator, by rotating a selector switch, to choose semiautomatic or automatic fire. Many M–16 parts are interchangeable with those in the AR–15 and can be used to convert the AR–15 into an automatic weapon. No doubt to inhibit such conversions, the AR–15 is manufactured with a metal stop on its receiver that will prevent an M–16 selector switch, if installed, from rotating to the fully automatic position. The metal stop on petitioner's rifle, however, had been filed away, and the rifle had been assembled with an M–16 selector switch and several other M–16 internal parts, including a hammer, disconnector, and trigger. Suspecting that the AR–15 had been modified to be capable of fully automatic fire, BATF agents seized the weapon. Petitioner subsequently was indicted for unlawful possession of an unregistered machinegun in violation of §5861(d).

At trial, BATF agents testified that when the AR–15 was tested, it fired more than one shot with a single pull of the trigger. It was undisputed that the weapon was not registered as required by §5861(d). Petitioner testified that the rifle had never fired automatically when it was in his possession. He insisted that the AR–15 had operated only semiautomatically, and even then imperfectly, often requiring manual ejection of the spent casing and chambering of the next round. According to petitioner, his alleged ignorance of any automatic firing capability should have shielded him from criminal liability for his failure to register the weapon. He requested the District Court to instruct the jury that, to establish a violation of §5861(d), the Government must prove beyond a reasonable doubt that the defendant "knew that the gun would fire fully automatically." 1 App. to Brief for Appellant in No. 91–5033 (CA10), p. 42.

The District Court rejected petitioner's proposed instruction and instead charged the jury as follows:

> The Government need not prove the defendant knows he's dealing with a weapon possessing every last characteristic [which subjects it] to the regulation. It would be enough to prove he knows that he is dealing with a dangerous device of a type as would alert one to the likelihood of regulation. Tr. 465.

Petitioner was convicted and sentenced to five years' probation and a $5,000 fine.

The Court of Appeals affirmed. . . . We granted *certiorari* to resolve a conflict in the Courts of Appeals concerning the *mens rea* required under §5861(d).

II

A

Whether or not §5861(d) requires proof that a defendant knew of the characteristics of his weapon that made it a "firearm" under the Act is a question of statutory construction. As we observed in *Liparota v. United States*, 471 U.S. 419 (1985), "[t]he definition of the elements of a criminal offense is entrusted to the legislature, particularly in the case of federal crimes, which are solely creatures of statute." (citing *United States v. Hudson*). Thus, we have long recognized that determining the mental state required for commission of a federal crime requires "construction of the statute and . . . inference of the intent of Congress." *United States v. Balint*, 258 U.S. 250 (1922).

The language of the statute, the starting place in our inquiry, provides little explicit guidance in this case. Section 5861(d) is silent concerning the *mens rea* required for a violation. It states simply that "[i]t shall be unlawful for any person . . . to receive or possess a firearm which is not registered to him in the National Firearms Registration and Transfer Record." 26 U.S.C. §5861(d). Nevertheless, silence on this point by itself does not necessarily suggest that Congress intended to dispense with a conventional *mens rea* element, which would require that the defendant know the facts that make his conduct illegal. See *Balint, supra*, at 251 (stating that traditionally, "*scienter*" was a necessary element in every crime). On the contrary, we must construe the statute in light of the background rules of the common law, in which the requirement of some *mens rea* for a crime is firmly embedded. As we have observed, "[t]he existence of a *mens rea* is the rule of, rather than the exception to, the principles of Anglo-American criminal jurisprudence." See also *Morissette v. United States*, 342 U.S. 246, 250 (1952) ("The contention that an injury can amount to a crime only when inflicted by intention is no provincial or transient notion. It is as universal and persistent in mature systems of law as belief in freedom of the human will and a consequent ability and duty of the normal individual to choose between good and evil").

There can be no doubt that this established concept has influenced our interpretation of criminal statutes. Indeed, we have noted that the common-law rule requiring *mens rea* has been "followed in regard to statutory crimes even where the statutory definition did not in terms include it." Relying on the strength of the traditional rule, we have stated that offenses that require no *mens rea* generally are disfavored, and have suggested that some indication of congressional intent, express or implied, is required to dispense with *mens rea* as an element of a crime.

According to the Government, however, the nature and purpose of the Act suggest that the presumption favoring *mens rea* does not apply to this case. The Government argues that Congress intended the Act to regulate and restrict the circulation of dangerous weapons. Consequently, in the Government's view, this case fits in a line of precedent concerning what we have termed "public welfare" or "regulatory" offenses, in which we have understood Congress to impose a form of strict criminal liability through statutes that do not require the defendant to know the facts that make his conduct illegal. In construing such statutes, we have inferred from silence that Congress did not intend to require proof of *mens rea* to establish an offense.

For example, in *Balint,* we concluded that the Narcotic Act of 1914, which was intended in part to minimize the spread of addictive drugs by criminalizing undocumented sales of certain narcotics, required proof only that the defendant knew that he was selling drugs, not that he knew the specific items he had sold were "narcotics" within the ambit of the statute. See *Balint*, *supra*. Cf. *United States v. Dotterweich*, 320 U.S. 277, 281 (1943) (stating in dicta that a statute criminalizing the shipment of adulterated or misbranded drugs did not require knowledge that the items were misbranded or adulterated). As we explained in *Dotterweich, Balint* dealt with "a now familiar type of legislation whereby penalties serve as effective means of regulation. Such legislation dispenses with the conventional requirement for criminal conduct—awareness of some wrongdoing."

Such public welfare offenses have been created by Congress, and recognized by this Court, in "limited circumstances." Typically, our cases recognizing such offenses involve statutes that regulate potentially harmful or injurious items. Cf. *United States v. International Minerals & Chemical Corp*, 402 U.S. 558, 564–565 (1971). In such situations, we have reasoned that as long as a defendant knows that he is dealing with a dangerous device of a character that places him "in responsible relation to a public danger," he should be alerted to the probability of strict regulation, and we have assumed that in such cases Congress intended to place the burden on the defendant to "ascertain at his peril whether [his conduct] comes within the inhibition of the statute." Thus, we essentially have relied on the nature of the statute and the particular character of the items regulated to determine whether congressional silence concerning the mental element of the offense should be interpreted as dispensing with conventional *mens rea* requirements.

B

The Government argues that §5861(d) defines precisely the sort of regulatory offense described in *Balint*. In this view, all guns, whether or not they are statutory "firearms," are dangerous devices that put gun owners on notice that they must determine at their hazard whether their weapons come within the scope of the Act. . . .

The Government seeks support for its position from our decision in *United States v. Freed*, 401 U.S. 601 (1971), which involved a prosecution for possession of unregistered grenades under §5861(d). The defendant knew that the items in his possession were grenades, and we concluded that §5861(d) did not require the Government to prove the defendant also knew that the grenades were unregistered. To be sure, in deciding that *mens rea* was not required with respect to that element of the offense, we suggested that the Act "is a regulatory measure in the interest of the public safety, which may well be premised on the theory that one would hardly be surprised to learn that possession of hand grenades is not an innocent act." Grenades, we explained, "are highly dangerous offensive weapons, no less dangerous than the narcotics involved in *United States v. Balint*." But that reasoning provides little support for dispensing with *mens rea* in this case.

As the Government concedes, *Freed* did not address the issue presented here. In *Freed*, we decided only that §5861(d) does not require proof of knowledge that a firearm is *unregistered*. The question presented by a defendant who possesses a weapon that is a "firearm" for purposes of the Act, but who knows only that he has a "firearm" in the general sense of the term, was not raised or considered. And our determination that a defendant need not know that his weapon is unregistered suggests no conclusion concerning whether §5861(d) requires the defendant to know of the features that make his weapon a statutory "firearm"; different elements of the same offense can require different mental states. Moreover, our analysis in *Freed* likening the Act to the public welfare statute in *Balint* rested entirely on the assumption that the defendant *knew* that he was dealing with hand grenades—that is, that he knew he possessed a particularly dangerous type of weapon (one within the statutory definition of a "firearm"), possession of which was not entirely "innocent" in and of itself. The predicate for that analysis is eliminated when, as in this case, the very question to be decided is *whether* the defendant must know of the particular characteristics that make his weapon a statutory firearm.

Notwithstanding these distinctions, the Government urges that *Freed's* logic applies because guns, no less than grenades, are highly dangerous devices that should alert their owners to the probability of regulation. But the gap between *Freed* and this case is too wide to bridge. In glossing over the distinction between grenades and guns, the Government ignores the particular care we have taken to avoid construing a statute to dispense with *mens rea* where doing so would "criminalize a broad range of apparently innocent conduct." In *Liparota*, 741 U.S. at 426, we considered a statute that made unlawful the unauthorized acquisition or possession of food stamps. We determined that the statute required proof that the defendant knew his possession of food stamps was unauthorized, largely because dispensing with such a *mens rea* requirement would have resulted in reading the statute to outlaw a number of apparently innocent acts. Our conclusion that the statute should not be treated as defining a public welfare offense rested on the commonsense distinction that a "food stamp can hardly be compared to a hand grenade." *Id.,* at 433.

Neither, in our view, can all guns be compared to hand grenades. Although the contrast is certainly not as stark as that presented in *Liparota,* the fact remains that there is a long tradition of widespread lawful gun ownership by private individuals in this country. Such a tradition did not apply to the possession of hand grenades in *Freed* or to the selling of dangerous drugs that we considered in *Balint*. In fact, in *Freed* we construed §5861(d) under the assumption that "one would hardly be surprised to learn that possession of hand grenades is not an innocent act." Here, the Government essentially suggests that we should interpret the section under the altogether different assumption that "one would hardly be surprised to learn that owning a gun is not an innocent act." That proposition is simply not supported by common experience. Guns in general are not "deleterious devices or products or obnoxious waste materials."

The Government protests that guns, unlike food stamps, but like grenades and narcotics, are potentially harmful devices. Under this view, it seems that *Liparota*'s concern for criminalizing ostensibly innocuous conduct is inapplicable whenever an item is sufficiently dangerous—that is, dangerousness alone should alert an individual to probable regulation and justify treating a statute that regulates the dangerous device as dispensing with *mens rea.* But that an item is "dangerous," in some general sense, does not necessarily suggest, as the Government seems to assume, that it is not also entirely innocent. Even dangerous items can, in some cases, be so commonplace and generally available that we would not consider them to alert individuals to the likelihood of strict regulation. As suggested above, despite their potential for harm, guns generally can be owned in perfect innocence. Of course, we might surely classify certain categories of guns—no doubt including the machineguns, sawed-off shotguns, and artillery pieces that Congress has subjected to regulation—as items the ownership of which would have the same quasi-suspect character we attributed to owning hand grenades in *Freed*. But precisely because guns falling outside those categories traditionally have been widely accepted as lawful possessions, their destructive potential, while perhaps even greater than that of some items we would classify along with narcotics and hand grenades, cannot be said to put gun owners sufficiently on notice of the likelihood of regulation to justify interpreting §5861(d) as not requiring proof of knowledge of a weapon's characteristics.

On a slightly different tack, the Government suggests that guns are subject to an array of regulations at the federal, state, and local levels that put gun owners on notice that they must determine the characteristics of their weapons and comply with all legal requirements. But regulation in itself is not sufficient to place gun ownership in the category of the sale of narcotics in *Balint*. . . . Roughly 50 percent of American homes contain at least one firearm of some sort, and in the vast majority of States, buying a shotgun or rifle is a simple transaction that would not alert a person to regulation any more than would buying a car.

If we were to accept as a general rule the Government's suggestion that dangerous and regulated items place their owners under an obligation to inquire at their peril into compliance with regulations, we would undoubtedly reach some untoward results. Automobiles, for example, might also be termed "dangerous" devices and are highly regulated at both the state and federal levels. Congress might see fit to criminalize the violation of certain regulations concerning automobiles, and thus might make it a crime to operate a vehicle without a properly functioning emission control system. But we probably would hesitate to conclude on the basis of silence that Congress intended a prison term to apply to a car owner whose vehicle's emissions levels, wholly unbeknownst to him, began to exceed legal limits between regular inspection dates. . . .

C

The potentially harsh penalty attached to violation of §5861(d)—up to 10 years' imprisonment—confirms our reading of the Act. Historically, the penalty imposed under a statute has been a significant consideration in determining whether the statute should be construed as dispensing with *mens rea*. Certainly, the cases that first defined the concept of the public welfare offense almost uniformly involved statutes that provided for only light penalties such as fines or short jail sentences, not imprisonment in the state penitentiary.

As commentators have pointed out, the small penalties attached to such offenses logically complemented the absence of a *mens rea* requirement: In a system that generally requires a "vicious will" to establish a crime, imposing severe punishments for offenses that require no *mens rea* would seem incongruous. Indeed, some courts justified the absence of *mens rea* in part on the basis that the offenses did not bear the same punishments as "infamous crimes," *Tenement House Dept. v. McDevitt*, 215 N.Y. 160, 168 (1915) (Cardozo, J.), and questioned whether imprisonment was compatible with the reduced culpability required for such regulatory offenses. See, *e.g.*, *People ex rel. Price v. Sheffield Farms–Slawson–Decker Co.*, 225 N.Y. 25, 32–33 (1918) (Cardozo, J.); (Crane, J., concurring) (arguing that imprisonment for a crime that requires no *mens rea* would stretch the law regarding acts *mala prohibita* beyond its limitations). Similarly, commentators collecting the early cases have argued that offenses punishable by imprisonment cannot be understood to be public welfare offenses, but must require *mens rea.*

In rehearsing the characteristics of the public welfare offense, we, too, have included in our consideration the punishments imposed and have noted that "penalties commonly are relatively small, and conviction does no grave damage to an offender's reputation." *Morissette,* 342 U.S., at 256. We have even recognized that it was "[u]nder such considerations" that courts have construed statutes to dispense with *mens rea.*

Our characterization of the public welfare offense in *Morissette* hardly seems apt, however, for a crime that is a felony, as is violation of §5861(d). After all, "felony" is, as we noted in distinguishing certain common-law crimes from public welfare offenses, " 'as bad a word as you can give to man or thing.' " . . .

We need not adopt such a definitive rule of construction to decide this case, however. Instead, we note only that where, as here, dispensing with mens rea would require the defendant to have knowledge only of traditionally lawful conduct, a severe penalty is a further factor tending to suggest that Congress did not intend to eliminate a *mens rea* requirement. In such a case, the usual presumption that a defendant must know the facts that make his conduct illegal should apply.

III

In short, we conclude that the background rule of the common law favoring *mens rea* should govern interpretation of §5861(d) in this case. Silence does not suggest that Congress dispensed with *mens rea* for the element of §5861(d) at issue here. Thus, to obtain a conviction, the Government should have been required to prove that petitioner knew of the features of his AR–15 that brought it within the scope of the Act.

We emphasize that our holding is a narrow one. As in our prior cases, our reasoning depends upon a commonsense evaluation of the nature of the particular device or substance Congress has subjected to regulation and the expectations that individuals may legitimately have in dealing with the regulated items. In addition, we think that the penalty attached to §5861(d) suggests that Congress did not intend to eliminate a mens rea requirement for violation of the section. As we noted in *Morissette:* "Neither this Court nor, so far as we are aware, any other has undertaken to delineate a precise line or set forth comprehensive criteria for distinguishing between crimes that require a mental element and crimes that do not." 342 U.S., at 260. We attempt no definition here, either. We note only that our holding depends critically on our view that if Congress had intended to make outlaws of gun owners who were wholly ignorant of the offending characteristics of their weapons, and to subject them to lengthy prison terms, it would have spoken more clearly to that effect.

For the foregoing reasons, the judgment of the Court of Appeals is reversed, and the case is remanded for further proceedings consistent with this opinion.

So ordered.

Note

To what factors did the Court look in order to determine whether the statute defined a strict liability offense? In the end, did the Court conclude the existence of a mens rea issue in the statute as a constitutional requirement or as a matter of statutory construction?

3. Due Process Concerns

Has the U.S. Supreme Court ever determined whether the imposition of a penalty in connection with a strict liability crime can offend the Due Process Clause? In reading *Stepniewski*, consider what limits the Due Process Clause places on the legislative enactments of strict liability offenses.

Stepniewski v. Gagnon, 732 F.2d 567 (7th Cir. 1984)

BAUER, Circuit Judge.

Petitioner-Appellee Richard Stepniewski filed a petition for a writ of habeas corpus in the district court claiming that his conviction without proof of criminal intent violates his constitutional right to due process of law. The district court agreed and granted the writ. We reverse.

I

On February 15, 1980, Stepniewski was convicted in Milwaukee County Circuit Court of twelve counts of home improvement trade practice violations, contrary to Wis.Stats. §§100.20(2) and 100.26(3) (1972). The court sentenced Stepniewski to one year incarceration plus six consecutive and five concurrent one year sentences, stayed by probation, for each of the twelve convictions. Upon a showing by the prosecution that Stepniewski was on probation for a felony theft by contractor conviction involving misappropriation of $24,000, the trial court imposed an additional six-month period of incarceration, to be served consecutively, under Wisconsin's Habitual Criminal Statute, Wis.Stats. §939.62 (1977). Both the Wisconsin Court of Appeals and the Wisconsin Supreme Court, affirmed the convictions.

The evidence at the state trial revealed that the petitioner on several occasions failed to specify in writing starting and completion dates for various projects. On other occasions, the petitioner did specify such dates, but the projects were never completed. In two cases when the work was left undone, the houses were severely damaged by winter weather. Many homeowners victimized by the petitioner were elderly and retired. . . .

Section 100.20(2) of the Trade Practices Act grants the Wisconsin Department of Agriculture authority to "issue general orders forbidding methods of competition in business or trade practices in business which are determined by the department to be unfair." Stepniewski was convicted under Section 100.26(3) of the Act for violating home improvement contractor regulations. Section 100.26(3) states in part:

> Any person . . . who intentionally refuses, neglects or fails to obey any regulation made under section . . . 100.20 shall, for each offense, be punished by a fine of not less than twenty-five nor more than five thousand dollars, or by imprisonment in the county jail for not more than one year, or by both such fine and imprisonment. . . .

> AG 110.02 Prohibited trade practices. No seller shall engage in the following unfair methods of competition or unfair trade practices: . . .

> (7) PERFORMANCE . . . .

> (b) Fail to begin or complete work on the dates or within the time period specified in the home improvement contract, or as otherwise represented, unless the delay is for reason of labor stoppage, unavailability of supplies or materials, unavoidable casualties, or any other case beyond the seller's control. Any changes in the dates or time periods stated in a written contract shall be agreed to in writing.

> AG 110.05 Home improvement contract requirements.

> . . .

> (2) Home improvement contracts and all changes in the terms and conditions thereof, required under this section to be in writing, shall be signed by all parties thereto, and shall clearly and accurately set forth in legible form all terms and conditions of the contract, and particularly the following: . . .

> (d) The dates or time period on or within which the work is to begin and to be completed by the seller.

The Wisconsin Supreme Court interpreted the word "intentionally" in section 100.26(3) as modifying only "refuses," and not "neglects" or "fails." The court thus concluded that mere failure to obey the regulation can result in conviction. This court is bound to accept the construction of the Act by the Wisconsin Supreme Court. Our task is to determine whether that construction violates the due process clause of the United States Constitution.

II

In his petition for a writ of habeas corpus, Stepniewski claimed that he could not constitutionally be convicted and sentenced under the Act without any finding of criminal intent. The district court agreed and held that, on the basis of *Morissette v. United States*, 342 U.S. 246 (1952), a strict liability crime can be valid under the due process clause of the fifth and fourteenth amendments only if "the 'nature and quality' of the crime [is] more heinous than the proscribed conduct in the case at bar." The district court read *Morissette* to establish, as a matter of constitutional law, three factors for determining whether the "nature and quality" of an offense precludes application of strict liability. The district court set those factors as: (1) whether the defendant is in a position to avoid transgressions by the exercise of reasonable care; (2) whether the penalty is relatively small; and (3) whether a conviction would result in no grave damage to the defendant's reputation.

The district court incorrectly interprets *Morissette*. Although the *Morissette* court enunciated various factors, including those used by the district court, for federal courts to consider when reviewing statutes that arguably impose strict liability, the Court did not establish those factors as principles of constitutional law. Rather, the Court discusses the factors as general policy concerns which in part explain the historical development of strict liability crimes. This discussion assisted the Court in ultimately concluding that when

> Congress borrows terms of art in which are accumulated the legal tradition and meaning of centuries of practice, it presumably knows and adopts the cluster of ideas that were attached to each borrowed word. . . . [Therefore] absence of contrary direction may be taken as satisfaction with widely accepted definitions, not as departure from them.

The Court thus held that Congress' mere omission of intent from a statute punishing conversion of United States property would not be interpreted as the removal of the intent element of the crime. Federal courts have applied these various factors when interpreting federal criminal statutes which the government sought to apply as strict liability offenses.

III

A

A state or the federal government does not violate due process protections each time it chooses not to include intent to violate a regulation as an element of the crime. "The power of the legislature to declare an offense, and to exclude the elements of knowledge and due diligence from any inquiry as to its commission, cannot, we think, be questioned." *Chicago, B. & Q. Ry. v. United States,* 220 U.S. 559, 578 (1911). Similarly, "[t]he objection that punishment of a person for an act as a crime when ignorant of the facts making it so, involves a denial of due process of law has more than once been overruled." *Williams v. North Carolina,* 325 U.S. 226, 238 (1945). Moreover, "public policy may require that in the prohibition or punishment of particular acts it may be provided that he who shall do them shall do them at his peril and will not be heard to plead in defense good faith or ignorance." *Shevlin-Carpenter Co. v. Minnesota,* 218 U.S. 57, 70 (1910).

The United States Supreme Court has not ruled specifically when, if ever, the imposition of strict liability in a criminal statute by itself violates the due process clause of the fourteenth amendment. The Supreme Court has recognized, however, that strict liability criminal offenses are not necessarily unconstitutional, and that the federal courts should interpret a law as one of strict liability only when Congress clearly so intends. In addition, the Court has stated that no single rule resolves whether a crime must require intent to be valid, "for the law on the subject is neither settled nor static."

The petitioner offers Supreme Court dicta to the effect that "[p]encils, dental floss, paper clips may also be regulated. But they may be the type of products which might raise substantial due process questions if Congress did not require . . . '*mens rea*' as to each ingredient of the offense." *United States v. International Minerals & Chemical Corp.,* 402 U.S. 558, 564–65 (1971). That analysis, although instructive, does not compel the result in the district court.

Traditional common law offenses, such as murder and assault, usually require some showing of intent before they are punished. Regulatory measures dealing with the possession or transportation of drugs, explosives, or dangerous chemicals, for example, often do not require any showing of intent to violate the regulation by the actor before a conviction can be obtained. A state's decisions regarding which actions or activities will give rise to strict criminal liability rest within that state's sound legislative discretion.

B

To determine the constitutionality of Section 100.26(3), we apply basically the same standards applicable to criminal statutes which do not impose strict liability. Due process prohibits such statutes from shifting burdens of proof onto the defendant, prohibits punishment of wholly passive conduct, protects against vague or overbroad statutes, and requires that statutes must give fair warning of prohibited conduct. The due process clause imposes little other restraint on the state's power to define criminal acts.

The regulation before us does not threaten the first due process consideration. A state cannot require a defendant to prove the absence of a fact necessary to constitute the crime. The government must prove each element of the charged crime beyond a reasonable doubt. The petitioner does not argue that the state failed to prove each element, save of course intent, beyond a reasonable doubt. The petitioner instead contends that the element of intent should have been part of the state's burden of proof. But, removing the element of intent for the offense does not amount to shifting the burden of proof; rather, the state has chosen to redefine what conduct violates the statute. The state still must prove each element of the strict liability crime beyond a reasonable doubt.

Nor does the crime here punish wholly passive conduct. The petitioner actively solicited the contracts at issue, and usually initiated the contacts between the petitioner and his victims. The petitioner's conduct thus is quite unlike the defendant's conduct in *Lambert v. California* 355 U.S. 225 (1957), where the defendant was convicted for mere failure to register upon arrival in Los Angeles as a convicted felon. The Supreme Court concluded that the wholly passive conduct there could not properly form the basis for criminal liability. The law here attacks wrongful active conduct. The conduct involved also is not a "status crime," such as drug addiction, for which the Supreme Court has proscribed punishment under the eighth amendment. *Robinson v. California,* 370 U.S. 660 (1962).

A longstanding principle of constitutional law is that a statute can be neither vague nor overbroad. . . . Section 100.26(3) raises no substantial question of vagueness. The regulations issued thereunder clearly enunciate that home improvement agreements require inclusion of starting and completion dates within the contract. Moreover, the regulations state in detail the performance requirements once a contract is entered. . . .

The due process clause also requires that, the state, when defining a crime, must "give a person of ordinary intelligence fair notice that his contemplated conduct is forbidden by the statute." . . .

The central inquiry here is whether Wisconsin gave the petitioner fair warning of the prohibited conduct so that it is not unreasonable to expect him to conform his conduct to those standards. We think that it did . . . .

The petitioner "held [himself] out to the public as [a] person[ ] having an expertise in home improvements. [He] sought out, by advertising and referrals," his clients. The home improvements industry in Wisconsin is regulated; the petitioner is deemed to have knowledge of the regulations and thus fair warning of the prohibited conduct. The statutory requirements imposed upon the petitioner are not so onerous that he cannot reasonably be expected to conform to them.

The Supreme Court has upheld similarly rigorous laws. In *United States v. Dotterweich*, 320 U.S. 277 (1943), for example, the Court recognized the reasonableness of imposing strict liability under the Federal Food, Drug, and Cosmetic Act, which restricts, among other things, sales of adulterated or misbranded drugs and punishes "persons whose failure to exercise the authority and supervisory responsibility reposed in them by the business organization resulted in the violation complained of." *United States v. Park,* 421 U.S. 658, 671 (1975). The Court also has sustained, on due process grounds, convictions under regulatory measures dealing with the possession or transportation of drugs, unregistered handguns, and sulphuric acid without proof of intent to violate the regulations. *United States v. Balint,* 258 U.S. 250 (1922); *United States v. Freed,* 401 U.S. 601 (1971); *United States v. International Minerals Corp.,* 402 U.S. 558

(1971). In these cases the regulations concerned conduct which the defendants could "reasonably understand to be proscribed."

Section 100.26(3) infringes none of the due process clause protections. Principally, Section 100.26(3) gives fair warning of the proscribed conduct largely because the petitioner reasonably could have expected his conduct, in that regulated business, to be illegal. Therefore, the grant of the writ of habeas corpus is reversed.

REVERSED.

4. Strict Liability and Punishment

Can a strict liability offense have imprisonment as a potential penalty? What does the court in *Koczwara* conclude?

Commonwealth v. Koczwara, 397 Pa. 575 (1959)

[The defendant, a licensed bar owner, was charged with violating Pennsylvania's Liquor Code by allowing unaccompanied minors into the bar and permitting the sale of alcohol to minors.]

COHEN, Justice.

This is an appeal from the judgment of the Court of Quarter Sessions of Lackawanna County sentencing the defendant to three months in the Lackawanna County Jail, a fine of five hundred dollars and the costs of prosecution, in a case involving violations of the Pennsylvania Liquor Code. . . .

Defendant raises two contentions, both of which, in effect, question whether the undisputed facts of this case support the judgment and sentence imposed by the Quarter Sessions Court. Judge Hoban found as fact that "in every instance the purchase [by minors] was made from a bartender, not identified by name, and service to the boys was made by the bartender. There was *no* evidence that the defendant was present on any one of the occasions testified to by these witnesses, nor that he had any personal knowledge of the sales to them or to other persons on the premises." We, therefore, must determine the criminal responsibility of a licensee of the Liquor Control Board for acts committed by his employees upon his premises, without his personal knowledge, participation, or presence, which acts violate a valid regulatory statute passed under the Commonwealth's police power.

While an employer in almost all cases is not criminally responsible for the unlawful acts of his employees, unless he consents to, approves, or participates in such acts, courts all over the nation have struggled for years in applying this rule within the framework of "controlling the sale of intoxicating liquor." At common law, any attempt to invoke the doctrine of *respondeat superior* in a criminal case would have run afoul of our deeply ingrained notions of criminal jurisprudence that guilt must be personal and individual. In recent decades, however, many states have enacted detailed regulatory provisions in fields which are essentially noncriminal, e.g., pure food and drug acts, speeding ordinances, building regulations, and child labor, minimum wage and maximum hour legislation. Such statutes are generally enforceable by light penalties, and although violations are labelled crimes, the considerations applicable to them are totally different from those applicable to true crimes, which involve moral delinquency and which are punishable by imprisonment or another serious penalty. Such so-called statutory crimes are in reality an attempt to utilize the machinery of criminal administration as an enforcing arm for social regulations of a purely civil nature, with the punishment totally unrelated to questions of moral wrongdoing or guilt. It is here that the social interest in the general well-being and security of the populace has been held to outweigh the individual interest of the particular defendant. The penalty is imposed despite the defendant's lack of a criminal intent or mens rea.

Not the least of the legitimate police power areas of the legislature is the control of intoxicating liquor. As Mr. Justice B. R. Jones recently stated in In re Tahiti Bar, Inc., 1959, 395 Pa. 355, 360, "There is perhaps no other area of permissible state action within which the exercise of the police power of a state is more plenary than in the regulation and control of the use and sale of alcoholic beverages." It is abundantly clear that the conduct of the liquor business is lawful only to the extent and manner permitted by statute. Individuals who embark on such an enterprise do so with knowledge of considerable peril, since their actions are rigidly circumscribed by the Liquor Code.

Because of the peculiar nature of this business, one who applies for and receives permission from the Commonwealth to carry on the liquor trade assumes the highest degree of responsibility to his fellow citizens. As the licensee of the Board, he is under a duty not only to regulate his own personal conduct in a manner consistent with the permit he has received, but also to control the acts and conduct of any employee to whom he entrusts the sale of liquor. Such fealty is the *quid pro quo* which the Commonwealth demands in return for the privilege of entering the highly restricted and, what is more important, the highly *dangerous* business of selling intoxicating liquor.

In the instant case, the defendant has sought to surround himself with all the safeguards provided to those within the pale of criminal sanctions. He has argued that a statute imposing criminal responsibility should be construed strictly, with all doubts resolved in his favor. While the defendant's position is entirely correct, we must remember that we are dealing with a statutory crime within the state's plenary police power. In the field of liquor regulation, the legislature has enacted a comprehensive Code aimed at regulating and controlling the use and sale of alcoholic beverages. The question here raised is whether the legislature *intended* to impose vicarious criminal liability on the licensee-principal for acts committed on his premises without his presence, participation or knowledge. . . .

In the Liquor Code, Section 493, the legislature has set forth twenty-five specific acts which are condemned as unlawful, and for which penalties are provided in Section 494. Subsections (1) and (14) of Section 493 contain the two offenses charged here. In neither of these subsections is there any language which would require the prohibited acts to have been done either knowingly, wilfully or intentionally, there being a significant absence of such words as "knowingly, wilfully, etc." That the legislature intended such a requirement in other related sections of the same Code is shown by examining Section 492(15), wherein it is made unlawful to *knowingly* sell any malt beverages to a person engaged in the business of illegally selling such beverages. The omission of any such word in the subsections of Section 494 is highly significant. It indicates a legislative intent to eliminate both knowledge and criminal intent as necessary ingredients of such offenses. To bolster this conclusion, we refer back to Section 491 wherein the Code states, "It shall be unlawful (1) For any person, by himself *or by an employe or agent*, to expose or keep for sale, or directly or *indirectly* . . . to sell or offer to sell any liquor within this Commonwealth, except in accordance with the provisions of this act and the regulations of the board." The Superior Court has long placed such an interpretation on the statute.

As the defendant has pointed out, there is a distinction between the requirement of a mens rea and the imposition of vicarious absolute liability for the acts of another. It may be that the courts below, in relying on prior authority, have failed to make such a distinction. In any case, we fully recognize it. Moreover, we find that the intent of the legislature in enacting this Code was not only to eliminate the common law requirement of a mens rea, but also to place a very high degree of responsibility upon the holder of a liquor license to make certain that neither he nor anyone in his employ commit any of the prohibited acts upon the licensed premises. Such a burden of care is imposed upon the licensee in order to protect the public from the potentially noxious effects of an inherently dangerous business. We, of course, express no opinion as to the *wisdom* of the legislature's imposing vicarious responsibility under certain sections of the Liquor Code. There may or may not be an economic-sociological justification for such liability on a theory of deterrence. Such determination is for the legislature to make, so long as the constitutional requirements are met.

Can the legislature, consistent with the requirements of due process, thus establish absolute criminal liability? Were this the defendant's first violation of the Code, and the penalty solely a minor fine of from $100–$300, we would have no hesitation in upholding such a judgment. Defendant, by accepting a liquor license, must bear this financial risk. Because of a prior conviction for violations of the Code, however, the trial judge felt compelled under the mandatory language of the statute, Section 494(a), to impose not only an increased fine of five hundred dollars, but also a three month sentence of imprisonment. Such sentence of imprisonment in a case where liability is imposed vicariously cannot be sanctioned by this Court consistently with the law of the land clause of Section 9, Article I of the Constitution of the Commonwealth of Pennsylvania., P.S.

The Courts of the Commonwealth have already strained to permit the legislature to carry over the civil doctrine of *respondeat superior* and to apply it as a means of enforcing the regulatory scheme that covers the liquor trade. We have done so on the theory that the Code established petty misdemeanors involving only light monetary fines. It would be unthinkable to impose vicarious criminal responsibility in cases involving true crimes. Although to hold a principal criminally liable might possibly be an effective means of enforcing law and order, it would do violence to our more sophisticated modern-day concepts of justice. Liability for all true crimes, wherein an offense carries with it a jail sentence, must be based exclusively upon personal causation. It can be readily imagined that even a licensee who is meticulously careful in the choice of his employees cannot supervise every single act of the subordinates. A man's liberty cannot rest on so frail a reed as whether his employee will commit a mistake in judgment.

This Court is ever mindful of its duty to maintain and establish the proper safeguards in a criminal trial. To sanction the imposition of imprisonment here would make a serious change in the substantive criminal law of the Commonwealth, one for which we find no justification. We have found *no* case in any jurisdiction which has permitted a *prison term* for a vicarious offense. . . .

In holding that the punishment of imprisonment deprives the defendant of due process of law under these facts, we are not declaring that Koczwara must be treated as a first offender under the Code. He has clearly violated the law for a second time and must be punished accordingly. Therefore, we are only holding that so much of the judgment as calls for imprisonment is invalid, and we are leaving intact the five hundred dollar fine imposed by Judge Hoban under the subsequent offense section. . . .

Judgment, as modified, is affirmed.

Note

How does the court classify the crimes to which strict liability can apply? Would the result have been different if Koczwara knew that his bartender had previously served alcohol to minors? Can a state legislature enact a strict liability offense that allows for some limited imprisonment without violating the Due Process Clause?

prove *Motive helps Mens rea*

D.   Transferred Intent

1.   Introduction

Assume *A* throws a rock at *B*. He misses *B* but hits *C*. Can *A* be charged with a battery as it concerns *C*? In other words, can *A*'s intent to commit a battery against *B* transfer to *C*, who is the unintended victim? The answer is "yes." Courts have sanctioned this theory of liability under a doctrine known as "transferred intent." Essentially, the defendant's intent to harm one person transfers over to the unintended victim.

However, again assume *A* throws a rock at *B*. He misses *B*, but breaks a storefront window and is charged with destruction of property. The intent to injure cannot be transferred to the offense related to the broken window. The general rule is that you cannot substitute the mens rea for one crime with the mens rea of another, notwithstanding the completion of the actus reus.[*]

Regina v. Faulkner, 13 Cox Cr.C. 550 (Ir. 1877)

Case reserved by Lawson, J.

[A]t the Cork Summer Assizes, 1876, the prisoner was indicted for setting fire to the ship *Zemindar*, on the high seas, on the 26th day of June, 1876. . . . It was proved that the *Zemindar* was on her voyage home with a cargo of rum, sugar, and cotton, worth £50,000. That the prisoner was a seaman on board, that he went into the bulk head, and forecastle hold, opened the sliding door in the bulk head, and so got into the hold where the rum was stored; he had no business there, and no authority to go there and went for the purpose of stealing some rum, that he bored hole in the cask with a gimlet, that the rum ran out, that when trying to put a spile in the hole out of which the rum was running, he had a lighted match in his hand; that the rum caught fire; that the prisoner himself was burned on the arms and neck; and that the ship caught fire and was completely destroyed. At the close of the case for the Crown, counsel for the prisoner asked for a direction of an acquittal on the ground that on the facts proved the indictment was not sustained, nor the allegation that the

---

[*] The Model Penal Code has a transferred intent provision.

§2.03(2)(a) provides in part:

> (2)   When purposely or knowingly causing a particular result is an element of an offense, the element is not established if the actual result is not within the purpose or the contemplation of the actor unless:
>
>> (a)   the actual result differs from that designed or contemplated, as the case may be, only in the respect that a different person or different property is injured or affected.

prisoner had unlawfully and maliciously set fire to the ship proved. The Crown contended that inasmuch as the prisoner was at the time engaged in the commission of a felony, the indictment was sustained, and the allegation of the intent was immaterial.

At the second hearing of the case before the Court for Crown Cases Reserved, the learned judge made the addition of the following paragraph to the case stated by him for the court.

"It was conceded that the prisoner had no actual intention of burning the vessel, and I was not asked to leave any question as to the jury as to the prisoner's knowing the probable consequences his act, or as to his reckless conduct."

The learned judge told the jury that although the prisoner had no actual intention of burning the vessel, still if they found he was engaged in stealing the rum, and that the fire took place in the manner above stated, they ought to find him guilty. The jury found the prisoner guilty on both counts, and he was sentenced to seven years penal servitude. The question for the court was whether the direction of the learned judge was right, if not, the conviction should be quashed. . . .

BARRY, J.

—A very broad proposition has been contended for by the Crown, namely, that if, while a person is engaged in mitting a felony, or, having committed it, is endeavouring to conceal his act, or prevent or spoil waste consequent on that act, he accidently does some collateral act which if done wilfully would be another felony either at common law or by statute, he is guilty of the latter felony. I am by no means anxious to throw any doubt upon, or limit in any way, the legal responsibility of those who engage in the commission of felony, or acts *mala in se*; but I am not prepared without more consideration to give my assent to so wide a proposition. No express authority either by way of decision or dictum from judge or text writer has been cited in support of it. . . . The jury were . . . directed to give a verdict of guilty upon the simple ground that the firing of the ship, though accidental, was caused by an act done in the course of, or immediately consequent upon, a felonious operation, and no question of the prisoner's malice, constructive or otherwise, was left to the jury. I am of opinion that, according to *Reg. v. Pembliton*, that direction was erroneous, and that the conviction should be quashed.

FITZGERALD, J.

—I concur in opinion with my brother Barry, and for the reasons he has given, that the direction of the learned judge cannot be sustained in law, and that therefore the conviction should be quashed. I am further of opinion that in order to establish the charge of felony under sect. 42, the intention of the accused forms an element in the crime to the extent that it should appear that the defendant intended to do the very act with which he is charged, or that it was the necessary consequence of some other felonious or criminal act in which he was engaged, or that having a probable result which the defendant foresaw, or ought to have foreseen, he, nevertheless, persevered in such other felonious or criminal act. The prisoner did not intend to set fire to the ship; the fire was not the necessary result of the felony he was attempting; and if it was a probable result, which he ought to have foreseen, of the felonious transaction on which he was engaged, and from which a malicious design to commit the injurious act with which he is charged might have been fairly imputed to him, that view of the case was not submitted to the jury. On the contrary, it was excluded from their consideration on the requisition of the counsel for the prosecution. Counsel for the prosecution in effect insisted that the defendant, being engaged in the commission of, or in an attempt to commit a felony, was criminally responsible for every result that was occasioned thereby, even though it was not a probable consequence of his act or such as he could have reasonably foreseen or intended. No authority has been cited for a proposition so extensive, and I am of opinion that it is not warranted by law. . . .

O'BRIEN, J.

—I am also opinion that the conviction should be quashed, and I was of that opinion before the case for our consideration was amended by my brother Lawson. I had inferred from the original case that his direction to the jury was to the effect now expressly stated by amendment, and that, at the trial, the Crown's counsel conceded that the prisoner had no intention of burning the vessel, or of igniting the rum; and raised no questions as to prisoner's imagining or having any ground for supposing that the fire would be the result or consequence of his act in stealing the rum. With respect to *Reg. v. Pembliton* (12 Cox C. C. 607), it appears to me there were much stronger grounds in that case for upholding the conviction than exist in the case before us. In that case the breaking of the window was the act of the prisoner. He threw the stone that broke it; he threw it with the unlawful intent of striking some one of the crowd about, and the breaking of the window, was the direct and immediate result of his act. And yet the Court unanimously quashed the conviction upon the ground that, although the prisoner threw the stone intending to strike some one or more persons, he did not intend to break the window. . . .

KEOGH, J.

—I have the misfortune to differ from the other members of the Court. . . . I am, therefore, of opinion, that the conviction should stand, as I consider all questions of intention and malice are closed by the finding of the jury, that the prisoner committed the act with which he was charged whilst engaged in the commission of a substantive felony. . . .

Conviction quashed.

2. Unintended Victim

The court in *Faulkner* held that the intent to commit larceny cannot be used to supply the intent to commit arson. What if the actor's mens rea is to kill one person, but he inadvertently injures another? Consider this issue in the following case and compare the result to the one reached in *Regina v. Faulkner*.

Regina v. Smith, 169 Eng. Rep. 845 (1855)

The following is the substance of a case stated by Crompton, J.

The prisoner was convicted, before him, at the Winchester summer assizes, 1855, on an indictment charging him with wounding one Taylor, with intent to murder him. The prisoner was posted as a sentry at one post, and Taylor as a sentry at an adjoining post. The prisoner, intending to murder one Maloney, and supposing Taylor to be Maloney, shot at and wounded Taylor. The jury found that the prisoner intended to murder Maloney, not knowing that the party he shot at was Taylor, but supposing him to be Maloney, and that he intended to murder the individual he shot at, supposing him to be Maloney. Sentence of death was recorded; and the question was reserved, whether the prisoner could properly be convicted on this state of facts of wounding Taylor with intent to murder him.

The case was not argued by counsel. . . .

Parke, B.

There is no doubt but the prisoner intended to hit Taylor, but he mistook the particular person.

Conviction affirmed.

E. Motive

"Motive" is defined as the reason why a person acts. It is not synonymous with intent and it is not an element of a crime (unless required by statute or the crime itself). Assume *A*'s business is failing and he decides to burn the building where his business is located in order to collect the insurance proceeds. *A*'s motive was to defraud the insurance company. It is not an element of arson, yet it helps to explain his behavior. Motive alone is not sufficient to convict someone, but it may be relevant as it relates to establishing the requisite intent. Thus, *A*'s motive in the above example helps to establish the mens rea for arson. For more information, see Joshua Dressler, *Understanding Criminal Law* §10.04[A][2] (6th ed. 2012).

Chapter 14
Mental Competency, Insanity, Guilty but Mentally Ill, and Diminished Capacity

A. Introduction

In this chapter, issues related to a defendant's competency to stand trial will be considered, as well as the defenses of insanity and diminished capacity. We will also review the guilty but mentally ill verdict choice. Although the procedures that explore these issues vary, they all involve the defendant's mental state (either in court or at the time of the commission of the crime).

A verdict of "guilty but mentally ill" is not a defense, but rather an alternative verdict generally favored by the prosecution inasmuch as the defendant is found "guilty" notwithstanding the existence of some mental illness falling short of insanity.

B. Mental Competency

The issue of competency may arise before trial and may be determinative of whether a defendant will proceed to trial. In *Dusky v. United States*, 362 U.S. 402 (1960), the Supreme Court held that "[w]e also agree with the suggestion of the Solicitor General that it is not enough for the district judge to find that 'the defendant [is] oriented to time and place and [has] some recollection of events,' but that the 'test must be whether he has sufficient present ability to consult with his lawyer with a reasonable degree of rational understanding—and whether he has a rational as well as factual understanding of the proceedings against him.' "

Are there minimal constitutional standards to which a state must adhere regarding whether a defendant is competent to stand trial? Consider this issue in the following case.

Cooper v. Oklahoma, 517 U.S. 348 (1996)

Justice STEVENS delivered the opinion of the Court.

In Oklahoma the defendant in a criminal prosecution is presumed to be competent to stand trial unless he proves his incompetence by clear and convincing evidence. Okla. Stat., Tit. 22, §1175.4(B) (1991). Under that standard a defendant may be put to trial even though it is more likely than not that he is incompetent. The question we address in this case is whether the application of that standard to petitioner violated his right to due process under the Fourteenth Amendment.

In 1989 petitioner was charged with the brutal killing of an 86-year-old man in the course of a burglary. After an Oklahoma jury found him guilty of first-degree murder and recommended punishment by death, the trial court imposed the death penalty. The Oklahoma Court of Criminal Appeals affirmed the conviction and sentence.

Petitioner's competence was the focus of significant attention both before and during his trial. On five separate occasions a judge considered whether petitioner had the ability to understand the charges against him and to assist defense counsel. On the first occasion, a pretrial judge relied on the opinion of a clinical psychologist employed by the State to find petitioner incompetent. Based on that determination, he committed petitioner to a state mental health facility for treatment.

Upon petitioner's release from the hospital some three months later, the trial judge heard testimony concerning petitioner's competence from two state-employed psychologists. These experts expressed conflicting opinions regarding petitioner's ability to participate in his defense. The judge resolved the dispute against petitioner, ordering him to proceed to trial.

At the close of a pretrial hearing held one week before the trial was scheduled to begin, the lead defense attorney raised the issue of petitioner's competence for a third time. Counsel advised the court that petitioner was behaving oddly and refusing to communicate with him. Defense counsel opined that it would be a serious matter "if he's not faking." After listening to counsel's concerns, however, the judge declined to revisit his earlier determination that petitioner was competent to stand trial.

Petitioner's competence was addressed a fourth time on the first day of trial, when petitioner's bizarre behavior prompted the court to conduct a further competency hearing at which the judge observed petitioner and heard testimony from several lay witnesses, a third psychologist, and petitioner himself. The expert concluded that petitioner was presently incompetent and unable to communicate effectively with counsel, but that he could probably achieve competence within six weeks if treated aggressively. While stating that he did not dispute the psychologist's diagnosis, the trial judge ruled against petitioner. In so holding, however, the court voiced uncertainty . . . .

Incidents that occurred during the trial, as well as the sordid history of petitioner's childhood that was recounted during the sentencing phase of the proceeding, were consistent with the conclusions expressed by the expert. In a final effort to protect his client's interests, defense counsel moved for a mistrial or a renewed investigation into petitioner's competence. After the court summarily denied these motions, petitioner was convicted and sentenced to death.

In the Court of Criminal Appeals, petitioner contended that Oklahoma's presumption of competence, combined with its statutory requirement that a criminal defendant establish incompetence by clear and convincing evidence, Okla. Stat., Tit. 22, §1175.4(B) (1991), placed such an onerous burden on him as to violate his right to due process of law. The appellate court rejected this argument. After noting that it can be difficult to determine whether a defendant is malingering, given "the inexactness and uncertainty attached to [competency] proceedings," the court held that the standard was justified because the "State has great interest in assuring its citizens a thorough and speedy judicial process," and because a "truly incompetent criminal defendant, through his attorneys and experts, can prove incompetency with relative ease." We granted certiorari to review the Court of Criminal Appeals' conclusion that application of the clear and convincing evidence standard does not violate due process.

No one questions the existence of the fundamental right that petitioner invokes. We have repeatedly and consistently recognized that "the criminal trial of an incompetent defendant violates due process." . . . The test for incompetence is also well settled. A defendant may not be put to trial unless he " 'has sufficient present ability to consult with his lawyer with a reasonable degree of rational understanding . . . [and] a rational as well as factual understanding of the proceedings against him.' "

Our recent decision in *Medina v. California*, 505 U.S. 437 (1992) establishes that a State may presume that the defendant is competent and require him to shoulder the burden of proving his incompetence by a preponderance of the evidence. In reaching that conclusion we held that the relevant inquiry was whether the presumption " 'offends some principle of justice so rooted in the traditions and conscience of our people as to be ranked as fundamental.' " *Id.*, at 445 (quoting *Patterson v. New York*, 432 U.S. 197, 202 (1977)). . . .

The question we address today is quite different from the question posed in *Medina*. Petitioner's claim requires us to consider whether a State may proceed with a criminal trial after the defendant has demonstrated that he is more likely than not incompetent. Oklahoma does not contend that it may require the defendant to prove incompetence beyond a reasonable doubt. The State maintains, however, that the clear and convincing standard provides a reasonable accommodation of the opposing interests of the State and the defendant. We are persuaded, by both traditional and modern practice and the importance of the constitutional interest at stake, that the State's argument must be rejected. . . .

A heightened standard does not decrease the risk of error, but simply reallocates that risk between the parties. In cases in which competence is at issue, we perceive no sound basis for allocating to the criminal defendant the large share of the risk which accompanies a clear and convincing evidence standard. We assume that questions of competence will arise in a range of cases including not only those in which one side will prevail with relative ease, but also those in which it is more likely than not that the defendant is incompetent but the evidence is insufficiently strong to satisfy a clear and convincing standard. While important state interests are unquestionably at stake, in these latter cases the defendant's fundamental right to be tried only while competent outweighs the State's interest in the efficient operation of its criminal justice system. . . .

For the foregoing reasons, the judgment is reversed, and the case is remanded to the Oklahoma Court of Criminal Appeals for further proceedings not inconsistent with this opinion.

It is so ordered.

Note

A defendant found incompetent to stand trial might be held until found competent. Ironically, this could result in a longer period of confinement than if the defendant had been found guilty of the charged offense. However, the Supreme Court has held that, under the Due Process Clause, a defendant cannot be incarcerated indefinitely. If it appears that the defendant is not likely to be deemed competent, the state must either release the defendant or look to civil commitment procedures. *See Jackson v. Indiana*, 406 U.S. 715, 733 (1972).

C. Insanity

Suppose a defendant commits murder in a particularly brutal and horrific manner. It would seem that such an individual must have been suffering from a severe mental illness to act in such an antisocial manner. Thus, one might assume, this defendant must have been insane. His severe mental illness, however, does not necessarily equate to being *legally* insane.

The defense of insanity has a long and controversial history. The courts, legislators, and medical experts have struggled to define legal insanity, which, if established, is a complete defense. The struggle has been to determine the types of mental abnormalities that society believes are sufficiently severe to absolve the defendant of criminal responsibility. In other words, when does mental illness eclipse criminal responsibility?

As will be discussed, there are several different tests for determining legal insanity. However, all must result from a mental disease or defect at the time the crime was committed. The legal definition of "mental disease or defect" will not necessarily be the same as definitions recognized by professional organizations, such as the American Psychiatric Association, or in other medical resources, such as the *Diagnostic and Statistical Manual of Mental Disorders*. Competing social policy concerns will influence the legal determination of a recognized disease or defect. This section will explore several tests for determining whether a defendant is legally insane. Even though insanity is a complete defense, a finding of insanity will, depending upon the jurisdiction, likely result in a period of civil confinement.

1. The *M'Naghten* Test

In *M'Naghten's Case*, [1843] 8 Eng. Rep. 718 (Cent. Crim. Ct.), Daniel M'Naghten killed Sir Robert Peel, apparently intending to kill the British Prime Minister. He was under the delusion that Peel was trying to kill him. At his trial, he claimed insanity. It was held that insanity is established if the defendant "was laboring under such a defect of reason, from disease of the mind, as not to know the nature and quality of the act he was doing; or, if he did know it, that he did not know that what he was doing was wrong."

Thereafter, the *M'Naghten* test became the standard for determining legal insanity in the United States. Because of the narrowness of this test, it is limited to cognitive illnesses; some jurisdictions have added a volitional prong to *M'Naghten*, referred to as "irresistible impulse." Thus, even if a defendant can differentiate right from wrong, he could be deemed insane if he is unable to control his conduct as a result of his mental disease or defect.

Does *M'Naghten* appear to be utilitarian in its application? If so, are the goals of a utilitarian model met under the *M'Naghten* test?

2. The *Durham* Test

As you read the *Durham* decision, consider how its test for insanity compares with *M'Naghten*. Specifically, consider the reach of each test as it concerns who may be able to better avail himself of an insanity defense.

Durham v. United States, 214 F.2d 862 (D.C. Cir. 1954)

BAZELON, Circuit Judge.

Monte Durham was convicted of housebreaking, by the District Court sitting without a jury. The only defense asserted at the trial was that Durham was of unsound mind at the time of the offense. We are now urged to reverse the conviction (1) because the trial court did not correctly apply existing rules governing the burden of proof on the defense of insanity, and (2) because existing tests of criminal responsibility are obsolete and should be superseded.

I. . . .

His conviction followed the trial court's rejection of the defense of insanity in these words:

> I don't think it has been established that the defendant was of unsound mind as of July 13, 1951, in the sense that he didn't know the difference between right and wrong or that even if he did, he was subject to an irresistible impulse by reason of the derangement of mind.
>
> While, of course, the burden of proof on the issue of mental capacity to commit a crime is upon the Government, just as it is on every other issue, nevertheless, the Court finds that there is not sufficient to contradict the usual presumption of [sic] the usual inference of sanity.
>
> *There is no testimony concerning the mental state of the defendant as of July 13, 1951, and therefore the usual presumption of sanity governs.*
>
> *While if there was some testimony as to his mental state as of that date, the burden of proof would be on the Government to overcome it. There has been no such testimony, and the usual presumption of sanity prevails. . . .*
>
> Mr. Ahern, I think you have done very well by your client and defended him very ably, but I think under the circumstances there is nothing that anybody could have done. [Emphasis supplied.]

We think this reflects error requiring reversal. . . .

II.

It has been ably argued by counsel for Durham that the existing tests in the District of Columbia for determining criminal responsibility, i.e., the so-called right-wrong test supplemented by the irresistible impulse test, are not satisfactory criteria for determining criminal responsibility. We are argued to adopt a different test to be applied on the retrial of this case. This contention has behind it nearly a century of agitation for reform.

A.

The right-wrong test, approved in this jurisdiction in 1882, was the exclusive test of criminal responsibility in the District of Columbia until 1929 when we approved the irresistible impulse test as a supplementary test in Smith v. United States. The right-wrong test has its roots in England. There, by the first quarter of the eighteenth century, an accused escaped punishment if he could not distinguish "good and evil," i.e., if he "doth not know what he is doing, no more than . . . a wild beast." Later in the same century, the "wild beast" test was abandoned and "right and wrong" was substituted for "good and evil." And toward the middle of the nineteenth century, the House of Lords in the famous M'Naghten case restated what had become the accepted "right-wrong" test in a form which has since been followed, not only in England but in most American jurisdictions as an exclusive test of criminal responsibility:

> . . . the jurors ought to be told in all cases that every man is to be presumed to be sane, and to possess a sufficient degree of reason to be responsible for his crimes, until the contrary be proved to their satisfaction; and that, to establish a defence on the ground of insanity, it must be clearly proved that, at the time of the committing of the act, the party accused was labouring under such a defect of reason, from disease of the mind, as not to know the nature and quality of the act he was doing, or, if he did know it, that he did not know he was doing what was wrong.

As early as 1838, Isaac Ray, one of the founders of the American Psychiatric Association, in his now classic Medical Jurisprudence of Insanity, called knowledge of right and wrong a "fallacious" test of criminal responsibility. This view has long since been substantiated by enormous developments in knowledge of mental life. In 1928 Mr. Justice Cardozo said to the New York Academy of Medicine: "Everyone concedes that the present [legal] definition of insanity has little relation to the truths of mental life." . . .

We find that as an exclusive criterion the right-wrong test is inadequate in that (a) it does not take sufficient amount of physic realities and scientific knowledge, and (b) it is based upon one symptom and so cannot validly be applied in all circumstances. We find that the "irresistible impulse" test is also inadequate in that it gives no recognition to mental illness characterized by brooding and reflection and so relegates acts caused by such illness to the application of the inadequate right-wrong test. We conclude that a broader test should be adopted.

B.

In the District of Columbia, the formulation of tests of criminal responsibility is entrusted to the courts and, in adopting a new test, we invoke our inherent power to make the change prospectively.

The rule we now hold must be applied on the retrial of this case and in future cases is not unlike that followed by the New Hampshire court since 1870. It is simply that an accused is not criminally responsible if his unlawful act was the product of mental disease or mental defect.

We use "disease" in the sense of a condition which is considered capable of either improving or deteriorating. We use "defect" in the sense of a condition which is not considered capable of either improving or deteriorating and which may be either congenital, or the result of injury, or the residual effect of a physical or mental disease.

Whenever there is "some evidence" that the accused suffered from a diseased or defective mental condition at the time the unlawful act was committed, the trial court must provide the jury with guides for determining whether the accused can be held criminally responsible. We do not, and indeed could not, formulate an instruction, which would be either appropriate or binding in all cases. But under the rule now announced, any instruction should in some way convey to the jury the sense and substance of the following: If you the jury believe beyond a reasonable doubt that the accused was not suffering from a diseased or defective mental condition at the time he committed the criminal act charged, you may find him guilty. If you believe he was suffering from a diseased or defective mental condition when he committed the act, but believe beyond a reasonable doubt that the act was not the product of such mental abnormality, you may find him guilty. Unless you believe beyond a reasonable doubt either that he was not suffering from a diseased or defective mental condition, or that the act was not the product of such abnormality, you must find the accused not guilty by reason of insanity. Thus your task would not be completed upon finding, if you did find, that the accused suffered from a mental disease or defect. He would still be responsible for his unlawful act if there was no causal connection between such mental abnormality and the act. These questions must be determined by you from the facts which you find to be fairly deducible from the testimony and the evidence in this case. . . .

The legal and moral traditions of the western world require that those who, of their own free will and with evil intent (sometimes called *mens rea*), commit acts which violate the law, shall be criminally responsible for those acts. Our traditions also require that where such acts stem from and are the product of a mental disease or defect as those terms are used herein, moral blame shall not attach, and hence there will not be criminal responsibility. The rule we state in this opinion is designed to meet these requirements.

Reversed and remanded for a new trial.

Note

Durham was an attempt to improve upon *M'Naghten.* Compare *M'Naghten,* even as supplemented by "irresistible impulse," with the "product" test adopted by the *Durham* court. Which test is broader? Why? The court eventually rejected the product test. *See United States v. Brawner*, 471 F.2d 969 (D.C. Cir. 1972). Today, the product test only applies in New Hampshire. *See* Joshua Dressler, *Understanding Criminal Law* §25.04[C][4][a] (6th ed. 2012).

3. Model Penal Code

The drafters of the MPC, in response to criticism that *M'Naghten* and irresistible impulse were very narrow in application, developed a new test for insanity. Rather than requiring total incapacity, the MPC queries whether the defendant lacked *substantial capacity*. In addition, the MPC includes both a cognitive and volitional prong. While broader than *M'Naghten* and irresistible impulse, the MPC test is not as broad as the product test, which would arguably include only slight impairments.

a. Model Penal Code Provisions

§4.01. Mental Disease or Defect Excluding Responsibility

> (1) A person is not responsible for criminal conduct if at the time of such conduct as a result of mental disease or defect he lacks substantial capacity either to appreciate the criminality [wrongfulness] of his conduct or to conform his conduct to the requirements of law.
>
> (2) As used in this Article, the terms "mental disease or defect" do not include an abnormality manifested only by repeated criminal or otherwise antisocial conduct.

§4.03. Mental Disease or Defect Excluding Responsibility Is Affirmative Defense; Requirement of Notice; Form of Verdict and Judgment When Finding of Irresponsibility Is Made

> (1) Mental disease or defect excluding responsibility is an affirmative defense.
>
> (2) Evidence of mental disease or defect excluding responsibility is not admissible unless the defendant, at the time of entering his plea of not guilty or within ten days thereafter or at such later time as the Court may for good cause permit, files a written notice of his purpose to rely on such defense.
>
> (3) When the defendant is acquitted on the ground of mental disease or defect excluding responsibility, the verdict and the judgment shall so state.

b.   **Cases**

People v. Drew, 22 Cal.3d 333 (1978)

TOBRINER, Justice.

For over a century California has followed the *M'Naghten* test to define the defenses of insanity and idiocy. The deficiencies of that test have long been apparent, and judicial attempts to reinterpret or evade the limitations of *M'Naghten* have proven inadequate. We shall explain why we have concluded that we should discard the *M'Naghten* language, and update the California test of mental incapacity as a criminal defense by adopting the test proposed by the American Law Institute and followed by the federal judiciary and the courts of 15 states.

Understandably, in view of our past adherence to *M'Naghten*, neither the psychiatrists who examined defendant nor the jury evaluated defendant's capacity in terms of the ALI test. Since the evidentiary record indicates that defendant, a former mental patient with a history of irrational assaultive behavior, lacked the capacity to conform his conduct to legal requirements, we conclude that the court's failure to instruct the jury under the ALI test was prejudicial, and therefore reverse the conviction.

Defendant Drew also contends that Evidence Code section 522, which requires a defendant to prove insanity by a preponderance of the evidence, is unconstitutional. Controlling precedent in the United States Supreme Court mandates the rejection of this contention. . . .

Statement of Facts.

Defendant Drew, a 22-year-old man, was drinking in a bar in Brawley during the early morning of October 26, 1975. He left $5 on the bar to pay for drinks and went to the men's room. When he returned, the money was missing. Drew accused one Truman Sylling, a customer at the bar, of taking the money. A heated argument ensued, and the bartender phoned for police assistance.

Officers Guerrero and Bonsell arrived at the bar. When Guerrero attempted to question Sylling, Drew interfered to continue the argument. Bonsell then asked Drew to step outside. Drew refused. Bonsell took Drew by the hand, and he and Officer Schulke, who had just arrived at the bar, attempted to escort Drew outside. Drew broke away from the officers and struck Bonsell in the face. Bonsell struck his head against the edge of the bar and fell to the floor. Drew fell on top of him and attempted to bite him, but was restrained by Guerrero and Schulke. Drew continued to resist violently until he was finally placed in a cell at the police station.

Charged with battery on a peace officer (Pen. Code, §243), obstructing an officer (Pen. Code, §148), and disturbing the peace (Pen. Code, §415), Drew pled not guilty and not guilty by reason of insanity. . . .

This court should adopt the American Law Institute test, as stated in section 4.01, subpart (1) of the Model Penal Code, to define the defense of insanity.

The trial court instructed the jury that "Legal insanity . . . means a diseased or deranged condition of the mind which makes a person incapable of knowing or understanding the nature and quality of his act, or makes a person incapable of knowing or understanding that his act was wrong." We explain that this instruction, based on the *M'Naghten* test, was erroneous, and on the record before us constitutes prejudicial error requiring reversal of the judgment.

The purpose of a legal test for insanity is to identify those persons who, owing to mental incapacity, should not be held criminally responsible for their conduct. The criminal law rests on a postulate of free will that all persons of sound mind are presumed capable of conforming their behavior to legal requirements and that when any such person freely chooses to violate the law, he may justly be held responsible. From the earliest days of the common law, however, the courts have recognized that a few persons lack the mental capacity to conform to the strictures of the law. . . .

The California Penal Code codifies the defense of mental incapacity. . . . [S]ection 26 specifies that "All persons are capable of committing crimes except those belonging to the following classes" and includes among those classes "Idiots" and "Lunatics and insane persons."

Although the Legislature has thus provided that "insanity" is a defense to a criminal charge, it has never attempted to define that term. The task of describing the circumstances under which mental incapacity will relieve a defendant of criminal responsibility has become the duty of the judiciary.

Since *People v. Coffman* (1864) 24 Cal. 230, 235, the California courts have followed the *M'Naghten* rule to define the defense of insanity. . . .

Despite its widespread acceptance, the deficiencies of *M'Naghten* have long been apparent. Principal among these is the test's exclusive focus upon the cognitive capacity of the defendant, an outgrowth of the then current psychological theory under which the mind was divided into separate independent compartments, one of which could be diseased without affecting the others. . . .

M'Naghten's exclusive emphasis on cognition would be of little consequence if all serious mental illness impaired the capacity of the affected person to know the nature and wrongfulness of his action. . . . An insane person may therefore often know the nature and quality of his act and that it is wrong and forbidden by law, and yet commit it as a result of the mental disease." . . .

. . . "*M'Naghten*'s single track emphasis on the cognitive aspect of the personality recognizes no degrees of incapacity. Either the defendant knows right from wrong or he does not . . . . But such a test is grossly unrealistic . . . . As the commentary to the American Law Institute's Model Penal Code observes, 'The law must recognize that when there is no black and white it must content itself with different shades of gray.' " (*United States v. Freeman*, 357 F.2d 606, 618–619, quoting ALI, Model Pen. Code, Tent. Drafts, Nos. 1, 2, 3, and 4, p. 158.)

In short, *M'Naghten* purports to channel psychiatric testimony into the narrow issue of cognitive capacity, an issue often unrelated to the defendant's illness or crime. The psychiatrist called as a witness faces a dilemma: either he can restrict his testimony to the confines of *M'Naghten*, depriving the trier of fact of a full presentation of the defendant's mental state, or he can testify that the defendant cannot tell "right" from "wrong" when that is not really his opinion because by so testifying he acquires the opportunity to put before the trier of fact the reality of defendant's mental condition. . . .

Even if the psychiatrist is able to place before the trier of fact a complete picture of the defendant's mental incapacity, that testimony reaches the trier of fact weakened by cross-examination . . . . As a result, conscientious juries have often returned verdicts of sanity despite plain evidence of serious mental illness and unanimous expert testimony that the defendant was insane. . . .

In our opinion the continuing inadequacy of *M'Naghten* as a test of criminal responsibility cannot be cured by further attempts to interpret language dating from a different era of psychological thought, nor by the creation of additional concepts designed to evade the limitations of *M'Naghten*. It is time to recast *M'Naghten* in modern language, taking account of advances in psychological knowledge and changes in legal thought.

The definition of mental incapacity appearing in section 4.01 of the American Law Institute's Model Penal Code represents the distillation of nine years of research, exploration, and debate by the leading legal and medical minds of the country. It specifies that "A person is not responsible for criminal conduct if at the time of such conduct as a result of mental disease or defect he lacks substantial capacity either to appreciate the criminality (wrongfulness) of his conduct or to conform his conduct to the requirements of law."

Adhering to the fundamental concepts of free will and criminal responsibility, the American Law Institute test restates *M'Naghten* in language consonant with the current legal and psychological thought. It has won widespread acceptance, having been adopted by every federal circuit except for the first circuit and by 15 states.

"In the opinion of most thoughtful observers this proposed test [the ALI test] is a significant improvement over *M'Naughton* [sic]." The advantages may be briefly summarized. First the ALI test adds a volitional element, the ability to conform to legal requirements, which is missing from the *M'Naghten* test. Second, it avoids the all-or-nothing language of *M'Naghten* and permits a verdict based on lack of substantial capacity. Third, the ALI test is broad enough to permit a psychiatrist to set before the trier of fact a full picture of the defendant's mental impairments and flexible enough to adapt to future changes in psychiatric theory and diagnosis. Fourth, by referring to the defendant's capacity to "appreciate" the wrongfulness of his conduct the test confirms our holding in *People v. Wolff*, 61 Cal.2d 795, that mere verbal knowledge of right and wrong does not prove sanity. . . .

The defendant retains the burden of proof on the issue of insanity.

Evidence Code section 522 provides explicitly that "The party claiming that any person, including himself, is or was insane has the burden of proof on that issue." The trial judge in the present case accordingly charged the jury that "the defendant has the burden of proving his legal insanity by a preponderance of the evidence." . . .

Disposition of this appeal. . . .

Finally, we recognize that in setting out a legal test to decide whether or not a person is insane we deal in a matter so delicate and obscure that it cannot be captured in a perfect definition. Yet because of the grave, and often life and death consequences that follow from a decision as to the sanity of an offender, we are surely enjoined to spare no effort to frame the best standard that is currently extant. We cannot justify the retention of a test based upon the single factor of cognition that has been abandoned by almost all the experts in the field and that has been rejected by all except one of the federal circuits and by an impressive number of state courts.

. . . We cannot continue to cast human beings in an ancient and discarded psychological mould. We must at least to the best of our limited ability accept the reality of the human psyche, as expert opinion depicts it, and bring the law as close as possible to an appraisal of the human being. We must recognize in certain cases his substantial incapacity either to appreciate the criminality of his conduct or to conform his conduct to the requirements of law. In judgment upon the sanity of the fragile and often inadequate human being we cannot be frozen into a stereotyped, rejected formula of the past.

The judgment is reversed and the cause remanded for a new trial on the issue raised by defendant's plea of not guilty by reason of insanity.

RICHARDSON, Justice, dissenting.

I respectfully dissent. My objection to the majority's approach may be briefly stated. I believe that a major change in the law of the type contemplated by the majority should be made by the Legislature. . . .

Note

In 1982, California adopted the traditional *M'Naghten* test. *See* Cal. Pen. Code §25(b)(1982).

4. *M'Naghten* Compared to the Model Penal Code and Other Tests

As you read *State v. White*, consider how it compares with *Drew*. Specifically, what concerns does the court in *White* have with the "irresistible impulse," as well as the MPC and "product" tests? Why does the court in *White* prefer *M'Naghten*?

State v. White, 60 Wash. 2d 551 (1962)

DONWORTH, Judge.

Appellant was charged, by Information, with committing two murders alleged to have been committed at different times and places on the same day (December 24, 1959). [Defendant raised the defense of insanity as to this charge.] . . .

Appellant contends that:

> The court erred in giving instruction No. 33 and further erred in failing to give the appellant's requested instructions on mental irresponsibility, which is the American Law Institute test for mental irresponsibility.

Instruction No. 33 told the jury that:

> You are instructed that the term 'mental irresponsibility', as used alternatively with the term 'insanity' in the further plea of the defendant and elsewhere in these instructions, means what is defined in law as criminal insanity. Therefore, if you find that the defendant was mentally irresponsible under the definition as contained herein, you must find the defendant not guilty by reason of mental irresponsibility.
>
> If the defendant is to be acquitted upon his plea of mental irresponsibility or insanity, he must convince you by a preponderance of the evidence that, at the time the crime is alleged to have been committed, his mind was diseased to such extent that he was unable to perceive the moral qualities of the act with which he is charged, and was unable to tell right from wrong with reference to the particular act charged. A person may be sick or diseased in body or mind and yet be able to distinguish right from wrong with respect to a particular act.

Proposed instruction No. 21 (if substituted in place of No. 33) would have stated the rule as follows:

> 'You are instructed that the term "mental irresponsibility", as used alternatively with the term "insanity" in the further plea of the defendant and elsewhere in these instructions, means what is defined in

law as criminal insanity. Therefore, if you find that the defendant was mentally irresponsible under the definition as contained herein, you must find the defendant not guilty by reason of mental irresponsibility.

'Mental irresponsibility means that the defendant is not responsible for the crimes charged herein if at the time of said crimes, as a result of mental disease or defect, he lacked substantial capacity either to appreciate the criminality of his act, or to conform his conduct to the requirements of law.

'The terms "mental disease" or "defect" do not include an abnormality manifested only by repeated criminal or otherwise anti-social conduct.'

The essential difference between the two instructions is that the instruction which was given to the jury did not allow for an acquittal based on insanity or mental irresponsibility, if the accused had cognition (the ability to understand the nature and quality of his acts) with regard to what he did, even though his volition (his capacity "to conform his conduct to the requirements of the law") may have been substantially impaired by mental disease or defect. In other words, under the given instruction, the defense of "not guilty by reason of mental irresponsibility" is not available to a person who has the ability to understand the nature and quality of his acts, but, because of mental disease or defect, is somehow unable to control his own behavior.

The proposed but rejected instruction was based upon §4.01 of the Model Penal Code, which test has since been adopted by the American Law Institute, on May 24, 1962. The concept that volitional control is an element of sanity for the purpose of criminal responsibility is accepted in several states. Some recognize "irresistible impulse" as a defense; others use language much like that found in the American Law Institute test.

The instruction which was assigned as error (No. 33) is based on the *M'Naghten* rule, which is the law in the majority of states.

The question whether the jury was correctly instructed is squarely presented by the facts of this case. There was substantial evidence from which the jury could have found that appellant could not control his own behavior, even though, at the time, he knew the difference between right and wrong. . . .

Before the two tests between which the trial court was compelled to make a choice are discussed, a third test should be mentioned. That third test is the "product" test, often called the Durham rule because of the widespread notoriety it received upon being adopted in the District of Columbia in Durham v. United States, 94 App. D.C. 228 (1954). In essence, this rule is that a defendant in a criminal case is not responsible if his unlawful act was the product of a mental disease or mental defect. The rule in New Hampshire has been stated in the same way for over ninety years. . . .

However, very recently the Court of Appeals in the District of Columbia has gone far beyond the original Durham rule as it was first adopted by that court in 1954.

In Campbell v. United States, D.C. Cir., 307 F.2d 597 (1962), the conviction of a defendant with an "emotionally unstable personality" (administratively classified by government psychiatrists as a mental disease since 1957) was reversed. It was held by the majority that the instructions of the trial court placed too much emphasis upon the defendant's capacity to control his own behavior, rather than simply instructing the jury that they must determine whether the criminal act was a product of a mental disease. They say that the test is whether he would have committed the act if he had not been the victim of a mental disease, to wit, an emotionally unstable personality. Thus, they hold that the defendant could be found innocent if his motivation was the result of such mental disease, regardless of whether or not the sanctions of the criminal law as a deterrent could have influenced him.

The fallacy in that view, as pointed out by Judge Burger in his very vigorous dissent, is that almost all criminals could come under such a definition of insanity. . . .

The implications of the Campbell decision are enormous. It is sufficient for our purposes to say that, in the State of Washington, we must rely on the statutory criminal law as an instrument of social control until the legislature decides otherwise. Until that time, the definition of criminal responsibility must remain a legal question.

> When we say that the standard of criminal responsibility is a legal rather than a medical or scientific problem, we are saying that in a larger sense it is a social question in that it is established to regulate the social order.
>
> . . .

The question before us is whether we, as the majority of jurisdictions, should refuse to extend absolute immunity from criminal responsibility to persons who, although capable of understanding the nature and quality of the acts (the ability to distinguish between right and wrong), are unable to control their own behavior as a result of mental disease or defect. . . .

What is meant by "criminal insanity" and "mental irresponsibility" in our statute? It has consistently been held that both terms mean the same thing for purposes of criminal responsibility. The test is M'Naghten. . . . Washington has rejected the volitional test as embodied in the so-called "irresistible impulse" rule. . . .

In order to foreclose any doubt as to the matter, we shall discuss the issue of the continued validity of M'Naghten in this state. . . .

One argument for such change is that we must take advantage of new developments in psychiatry. There is nothing new about the idea that some people who know what they are doing still cannot control their actions. In fact, acceptance by a court of law of the idea that such people should be relieved of criminal responsibility led to the adoption of the M'Naghten rule in England.

We reiterate that there is no reason why the legal definition of insanity should keep up with the medical definition of insanity. The term has a different meaning and a different purpose in each context. The only arguments that should be considered are those arguments which are relevant to the question of what kind, or degree, of mental disease or defect should relieve a person of criminal responsibility for his acts.

This brings us to the crucial argument for change. It is contended that if a man does not have control over his own behavior, he has no free will and cannot be blamed for his misbehavior. Therefore, the interests of both society and the individual defendant would best be served if such a defendant were not held criminally responsible for his actions. It is the latter part of this contention that we feel merits full consideration.

The answers to this crucial contention are several, and each is alone sufficient, in our opinion, to dispose of it. First, the legislature has established a policy in this state that only the most extreme degree of insanity will relieve a defendant of criminal liability. Any arguments for change in policy should, therefore, be addressed to the legislature. Second, the test proposed by appellant is extremely difficult to apply. Third, from the point of view of social utility and the purposes of the criminal law, the M'Naghten test is preferable to the American Law Institute test. . . .

Since insanity is available as a complete defense only because it has been held to be a constitutional right, we cannot extend that defense beyond the minimum which is constitutionally required. Therefore, the defense is available only to those persons who have lost contact with reality so completely that they are beyond any of the influences of the criminal law. . . .

The classic criticism of "irresistible impulse"—which applies also to any test which includes volition (such as the American Law Institute test)—is that such a test is extremely hard to apply with any hope of reasonable accuracy. . . .

With regard to capacity to control one's behavior, it would appear that there is no more psychiatric certainty today than there was when this court decided State v. Maish, 29 Wash.2d 52 (1947).

Finally, M'Naghten is preferable to the American Law Institute test in that the M'Naghten rule better serves the basic purpose of the criminal law—to minimize crime in society. . . .

In summary, then, not only would any other rule be difficult to apply, but the M'Naghten rule is, for good reason, the established rule in the State of Washington. There was no error in giving the jury the instruction (No. 33) based on that test, nor in refusing to instruct on the basis of any other test of mental responsibility as requested by appellant. . . .

We have carefully considered each of appellant's assignments of error in the light of the record and the law applicable thereto. We are of the opinion that appellant had a fair trial. Finding no reversible error in the record, the judgment and sentence of the trial court entered upon the several verdicts of the jury must be affirmed. . . .

The judgment and sentence is hereby affirmed.

5. Insanity Defense Reform Act

In response to the successful insanity defense raised by John Hinckley in his 1981 attempt to kill President Reagan, Congress enacted the Insanity Defense Reform Act. *See* 18 U.S.C. §17. Hinckley believed that killing the president would impress actress Jodi Foster. At the time, the federal courts followed the MPC test. Specifically, the jury was instructed on the second (or volitional) prong of the MPC test. After being found not guilty by reason of insanity, Hinckley was confined in a hospital (and as of 2014, he is still there).

The *Hinckley* verdict proved to be a watershed moment as it relates to the insanity defense. Many in the public, legal, and medical communities were outraged by the verdict.

As you read the following case, consider how the federal statute compares with the other tests for insanity previously discussed. The court considers whether it is constitutional to impose the burden on the defendant to establish the defense, as well as what evidentiary restrictions are placed upon expert witnesses as it concerns the defendant's claim of insanity.

United States v. Freeman, 804 F.2d 1574 (11th Cir. 1986)

HILL, Circuit Judge:

Appellant Dwayne Freeman challenges his conviction of bank robbery under 18 U.S.C. §2113(b), (d) (1982). At trial, the facts surrounding the robbery and the defendant's guilt were never at issue. Freeman merely contests the trial court's determination that the defendant was sane at the time of the offense. Freeman bases his appeal upon two grounds. First, he challenges the constitutionality of the Insanity Defense Reform Act of 1984, Pub.L. No. 98–473, §402, 98 Stat. 1837, 2057 (codified at 18 U.S.C.A. §20 (Supp.1986); Fed.R.Evid. 704(b)). Second, Freeman asserts that as a matter of law, he has established his insanity by clear and convincing evidence. We reject both of the defendant's arguments.

The Insanity Defense Reform Act produced three principal changes to the insanity defense in federal courts. First, the definition of insanity was restricted so that a valid defense only exists where the defendant was "unable to appreciate the nature and quality or the wrongfulness of his acts" at the time of the offense. The amendment thus eliminated the volitional prong of the defense; prior to the act, a defendant could assert a valid defense if he were unable to appreciate the nature of his act *or* unable to conform his conduct to the requirements of law. The second change produced by the Act resulted in a shifting of the burden of proof from the government to the defendant. Prior to the Act, the government was required to prove beyond a reasonable doubt that the defendant was sane at the time of the offense. Under the current act, the defendant must prove his insanity by clear and convincing evidence to escape criminal liability. The third change prohibits experts for either the government or defendant from testifying as to the ultimate issue of the accused's sanity. The act changes Federal Rules of Evidence 704 so as to provide:

> No expert witness testifying with respect to the mental state or condition of a defendant in a criminal case may state an opinion or inference as to whether the defendant did or did not have the mental state or condition constituting an element of the crime charged or of a defense thereto. Such ultimate issues are matters for the trier of fact alone.

Fed.R.Evid. 704(b).

The defendant's principal contention concerning the constitutionality of the act pertains to the burden of proof being placed upon the defendant. . . .

In *Leland v. Oregon*, 343 U.S. 790 (1952), the Supreme Court held that a state could constitutionally require a defendant to prove insanity beyond a reasonable doubt. . . .

. . . Therefore, *Leland* compels a holding that the aspect of the Insanity Reform Act of 1984 requiring a defendant to prove insanity by clear and convincing evidence is constitutional.

Additionally, we hold that the Act's restriction against opinion testimony as to the ultimate issue of insanity does not restrict the defendant in the preparation of his defense in violation of the fifth amendment [sic]. Federal Rule of Evidence 704 merely reserves for the jury the authority to determine the sanity of the accused under the statutory standards. The defendant is not prohibited from introducing evidence which would assist the jury in making this determination. Furthermore, the restriction on testimony going to the ultimate issue is applicable to the government, as well as the defendant. There is no constitutional violation.

The definitional change of insanity brought about by the Insanity Reform Act does not violate the defendant's constitutional rights. Admittedly, under the new statute, a defendant who is unable to conform his actions to the requirements of law may be convicted of a crime. Such a conviction, however, does not constitute cruel and unusual punishment. A primary reason that the definition of insanity was altered by the Insanity Reform Act is that psychiatrists themselves are unable to agree upon the meaning of "an irresistible impulse." In light of the uncertain nature of psychiatric theory in this area, we decline to alter Congress' decision that society must be protected from individuals who may be unable to conform their conduct to the law. When psychiatrists are unable to diagnose, much less treat, such individuals, it is not cruel and unusual punishment for Congress to restrict the defense of insanity to those persons who are capable of proving that they did not understand the nature and quality of the act committed.

Freeman additionally contends that he has established his insanity by clear and convincing evidence. Dwayne Freeman asserted that he was an enthusiastic volunteer for the "Save the Children" campaign to feed starving children in drought stricken Ethiopia. Freeman's evidence was that he degenerated to the point of obsession. He then became depressed about not raising enough money for the children. On February 26, 1985, Freeman robbed a bank, allegedly to obtain money for the Ethiopia fund. . . .

A psychiatric team from the federal institute at Springfield, Missouri did conclude that Freeman was suffering from severe mental illness and was manic depressive or possibly schizophrenic. Additionally, Freeman presented evidence showing that he had been hearing noises and was experiencing severe depression prior to the robbery. Ample evidence exists, however, indicating that Freeman knew his conduct was wrongful. The evidence shows Freeman changed his clothes after robbing the bank to avoid identification. Freeman employed a mask, handgun, and satchel to execute the robbery and avoid apprehension. He informed bank personnel that if the police were called, he would come back and kill everyone. When spotted by police, Freeman ran to avoid apprehension. Finally, Freeman's probation officer observed Freeman's demeanor as being entirely appropriate following his arrest. The district court's decision was not clearly erroneous.

We therefore AFFIRM the district court's decision.

D. Guilty but Mentally Ill

According to *People v. Ramsey,* the Michigan legislature enacted the guilty but mentally ill (GBMI) statute because "large numbers of persons found not guilty by reason of insanity, whom professionals had determined to be presently sane, were released from institutions, with tragic results. Two of the released persons soon committed violent crimes." "Amid public outcry," the legislature responded with the GBMI verdict. As will be seen in *Ramsey,* the apparent purpose was to limit the number of defendants who could successfully urge an insanity defense.

As you read *Ramsey,* consider how the verdict differentiates mental illness from insanity. Also, consider the consequences for a defendant found GBMI.

People v. Ramsey, 422 Mich. 500 (1985)

BRICKLEY, Justice.

These cases involve the constitutionality of M.C.L. §768.36; M.S.A. §28.1059, the statute which introduced the verdict of guilty but mentally ill to this state. In both cases, it is asserted that the guilty but mentally ill verdict violates principles of due process of law. We hold the statute to be constitutional.

I

Defendant Bruce Ramsey was charged with first-degree murder, M.C.L. §750.316; M.S.A. §28.548, as a result of the death of his wife. Ramsey had first choked her, and then stabbed her thirty-two times. At trial, he raised the defense of insanity, claiming he believed that he was exorcising a demon from his wife by stabbing her and that she would return to life once the demon was removed.

In the trial court, defendant moved that the verdict of guilty but mentally ill be held unconstitutional and that the jury not be instructed on that verdict. According to defendant, he opted for a bench trial because his motion was denied.

Several witnesses, including Ramsey himself, testified in support of his claim of insanity. Defendant was portrayed as the product of a Southern fundamentalist religious family who had strayed from the church by drinking alcohol, smoking marijuana, and having an extra-marital affair.

A few months before the killing, Ramsey visited his mother in Kentucky. She gave him a pamphlet entitled "Defeated Enemies," which concerned demons and demon-possessed people. Both Ramsey and a woman by the name of Cross testified that that weekend, Ramsey, while engaged in sexual intercourse with Cross, suffered a psychotic episode; Ramsey thought that Cross was a devil. Ramsey fled the room. When later found by Cross, Ramsey insisted that they return to their room to pray, which they did.

Ramsey testified regarding an episode the day before the killing. He found in the clogged choke of his truck a sign from God that he should stay with his wife. He also found messages from God in the lyrics of popular songs.

The day of the killing, Ramsey, after a full day of work, called his mother in Kentucky. He was excited; his mother described him as exuberant over his "return to God."

As for the killing itself, which was witnessed by Ramsey's children, who testified at trial, the victim and Ramsey had apparently argued. One of Ramsey's children testified that the victim came to the child's room crying. Ramsey entered the room and said, "Walk." The victim left the room and locked herself in the bathroom. Ramsey broke down the bathroom door.

Ramsey testified that he had attempted to choke, and then to stab, the demon out of his wife. Ramsey's son testified that he heard Ramsey say, "Die demon, die." When Ramsey realized that the victim was dead and was not returning to life, he placed her body in bed, crawled in next to her, and stabbed himself in the chest. Found in that position by the police (the children had fled to a neighbor's home), Ramsey was taken to a hospital. There, he made statements to family and friends to the effect that he was "screwed up" and that his wife "wasn't supposed to die." Hospital psychiatrists diagnosed Ramsey as acutely psychotic upon admission.

Psychiatrists called by the prosecution and the defense differed over whether Ramsey was mentally ill or insane at the time of the killing. . . .

II

. . . Ramsey . . . contend[s] that the guilty but mentally ill verdict denied [him] the due process of law guaranteed by the Fourteenth Amendment to the United States Constitution. . . . Ramsey argues that the danger of jury compromise due to the existence of the guilty but mentally ill verdict caused him to waive his right to a jury trial, and, therefore, he should be allowed to challenge the constitutionality of the verdict. [The other] argument is more straightforward. . . . He contends that the submission of the guilty but mentally ill verdict to the jury encouraged the jury to return that verdict as a compromise between the verdict of guilty and the verdict of not guilty by reason of insanity. . . .

. . . [O]ur task is to decide if the guilty but mentally ill verdict violates principles of fairness by, according to defendants, deflecting a jury's attention from the issues of guilt or innocence by adding an irrelevant verdict which brings the risk of impermissible jury compromise. We must stress, however, that we are not concerned with the wisdom of the verdict. Arguments that a statute is unwise or results in bad policy should be addressed to the Legislature. Our concern here is only whether the statute is invalid because it denies criminal defendants a fair trial.

M.C.L. §768.36(1); M.S.A. §28.1059(1) provides:

> If the defendant asserts a defense of insanity in compliance with section 20a [MCL 768.20a; MSA 28.1043(1)], the defendant may be found 'guilty but mentally ill' if, after trial, the trier of fact finds all of the following beyond a reasonable doubt:
>
> (a) That the defendant is guilty of an offense.
>
> (b) That the defendant was mentally ill at the time of the commission of that offense.
>
> (c) That the defendant was not legally insane at the time of the commission of that offense.

M.C.L. §768.21a; M.S.A. §28.1044(1) defines insanity:

> A person is legally insane if, as a result of mental illness . . . that person lacks substantial capacity either to appreciate the wrongfulness of his conduct or to conform his conduct to the requirements of the law."

Finally, mental illness is defined in M.C.L. §330.1400a; M.S.A. §14.800(400a) as:

> [A] substantial disorder of thought or mood which significantly impairs judgment, behavior, capacity to recognize reality, or ability to cope with the ordinary demands of life."

The history of the guilty but mentally ill verdict is well set forth in Smith & Hall, *Evaluating Michigan's guilty but mentally ill verdict: An empirical study*, 16 U. of Mich.J.L.Ref. 77 (1982). For our purposes here, it suffices to state that the statute was a reaction to this Court's decision in *People v. McQuillan*, 392 Mich. 511 (1974). Following that decision, a large number of persons found not guilty by reason of insanity, whom professionals had determined to be presently sane, were released from institutions, with tragic results. Two of the released persons soon committed violent crimes. . . . Amid public outcry, the Legislature responded with the guilty but mentally ill verdict.

The major purpose in creating the guilty but mentally ill verdict is obvious. It was to limit the number of persons who, in the eyes of the Legislature, were *improperly* being relieved of all criminal responsibility by way of the insanity verdict. . . .

It is claimed that the guilty but mentally ill verdict introduces a confusing irrelevancy into jury deliberations. Therefore, the first question we must face is whether the inclusion of the guilty but mentally ill verdict is so confusing to the jury that it denies a defendant a fair trial.

To a certain extent, we must agree that the inclusion of the verdict complicates a trial and creates a greater opportunity for confusion. Under prior law, the jury had only to decide whether the defendant was sane. Under present law, the jury must engage in a two-step inquiry. But the fact that an extra step is added to the inquiry hardly makes the inquiry beyond a jury's competence. . . .

We conclude that the Legislature has created a clear distinction between mental illness and insanity. Of course, in particular cases, this distinction may be very subtle and difficult for the jury to apply. But, it is no more subtle or difficult than the distinction between the intent to do great bodily harm and the intent to kill, a distinction we allow juries to make which often determines whether a defendant is guilty of first- or second-degree murder. In short, we cannot say that the legislative distinctions between mental illness and insanity deny the right to a fair trial.

. . . Ramsey . . . contend[s] that the inclusion of the guilty but mentally ill verdict infringed on [his] right to a fair trial by creating an unjustifiable risk of a compromise verdict. We find this claim to be wholly speculative, and must reject it. . . .

III

Ramsey raises two additional issues regarding the guilty but mentally ill verdict. First, he argues that as a matter of policy this Court should hold that a mentally ill defendant cannot entertain the malice necessary to support a murder conviction. Alternatively, he argues that we should find that a trial court must, in its findings of fact following a bench trial, affirmatively state that the mental illness did not negate the necessary intent for second-degree murder.

Malice aforethought, or stated otherwise, the mental state necessary for the crime of murder, requires the intent to kill, the intent to do great bodily harm, and the intentional creation of a great risk of death or great bodily harm with the knowledge that death is the probable result. A finding of mental illness, even when defined as a substantial disorder of thought or mood, does not inexorably lead to the conclusion that the defendant did not entertain the requisite malice aforethought for murder. . . .

Thus, while his mental illness may be a consideration in evaluating the requisite state of mind for the crime charged, we decline to accept Ramsey's invitation to hold that a finding of mental illness negates malice aforethought as a matter of law.

The trial court in this case found that *Ramsey* entertained the malice aforethought necessary to support a conviction of second-degree murder. Defendant would have us require that the trial judge affirmatively state that the mental illness did not affect the defendant's ability to form the requisite intent.

Had the trial judge indicated a refusal to consider the defendant's mental illness as a diminishing factor in his decision of whether defendant possessed the requisite malice aforethought, we would find it necessary to address the question of the extent to which mental illness could diminish the intent requirement for second-degree murder. But he did not. We therefore are faced with a statement by the judge that defendant possessed the requisite intent.

We are disinclined, under the circumstances of this case, to place a further burden on the fact-finding of a judge in a bench trial which would require, in addition to a finding of guilt on the elements of the crime, an affirmative statement that all potential mitigating factors have been considered and rejected.

. . . [O]ne matter . . . requires additional consideration. . . . He claims that error which requires reversal occurred when the trial court, over objection, instructed the jury on the disposition of a defendant found not guilty by reason of insanity and on the disposition of a defendant found guilty but mentally ill. The Court of Appeals rejected [that] claim on the strength of authorities now questionable in light of our recent decision in *People v. Goad*, 421 Mich. 20 (1984).

In *Goad,* we held that it was error to instruct the jury as to the disposition of a defendant found not guilty by reason of insanity. However, we expressly stated that our holding was prospective, which makes it inapplicable [here]. As to the propriety of giving instructions on the disposition of a defendant found guilty but mentally ill (CJI 7:8:01), *Goad, supra,* p. 37, strongly intimated that such instructions are also improper:

> We hold that in all jury instructions given more than 30 days after the filing of this opinion, the jurors shall not be given any information including, but not limited to, CJI 7:8:07 and 7:8:08 requiring the disposition of the defendant after their verdict.

We would now similarly hold jurors should not be instructed on the disposition of a defendant found guilty but mentally ill. Although error occurred in the instant case, it does not require reversal, for the reasons stated in *Goad*.

LEVIN, Justice (dissenting).

I would hold that the guilty but mentally ill verdict is unconstitutional because a jury cannot, consistent with the right of an accused in a criminal prosecution to a trial by jury, be called upon to provide a special finding explicating a guilty or not guilty verdict.

The form of the special finding called for by the statute establishing the guilty but mentally ill verdict, and the jury instructions contemplated by that statute—and those actually given in the instant case . . .—are also violative of the Due Process Clause because they focus the deliberations and the verdict on a finding that is not determinative of the central issue of guilt or innocence, thereby impermissibly impairing the accused's rights to a fair trial and to be presumed innocent. . . .

Note

GBMI is a verdict choice when the defendant raises an insanity defense. In order to find a defendant GBMI, the jury must make several findings: (1) the prosecutor has met the requisite mens rea and actus reus with respect to the offense(s) charged; (2) the defendant was mentally ill at the time the offense was committed (i.e., there existed a mental disease or defect); and (3) the defendant was not legally insane at the time of the commission of the offense (i.e., even with the mental illness, the insanity test was not satisfied). In Michigan, the insanity test is based on the MPC. *See* M.C.L. §768.21a.

Often a defendant found GBMI is sentenced consistent with a straight guilty verdict; however, the defendant may serve his time in a special correctional institution where he may receive treatment. This defendant ordinarily remains incarcerated for the full term of his sentence, even if found to have been cured. At present, a "substantial minority" of states recognize this verdict. *See* Joshua Dressler, *Understanding Criminal Law* §25.07 (6th ed. 2012).

E. Diminished Capacity

Unlike insanity, which if successful is a complete defense, diminished capacity merely reduces the defendant's degree of culpability. It operates more like a rule of evidence than a defense because it reduces the degree of the offense charged, rather than excuse its commission. Its most common application is to establish a lack of specific intent regarding the charged offense. For example, in a first degree murder case, because of the defendant's mental illness, the prosecution is unable to establish premeditation and, thus, cannot satisfy the mens rea requirements. Michigan and a few other states have rejected this defense. *See, e.g., People v. Carpenter*, 276 Mich. 283 (Mich. 2001).

State v. Smith, 136 Vt. 520 (1978)

BARNEY, Chief Judge.

This is a prosecution for the rape of a sixteen year old babysitter and the murder of her charge, her eight year old cousin. As is so frequent in cases involving serious criminal violence, sanity is a critical issue. It is the principal concern of the appeal.

The killing is conceded, both below and here, and no issues separately contesting the rape conviction are urged here. No extended recital of facts is required. The defendant was twenty-one years old at the time of these events. The evidence disclosed that the defendant, after finding out that the babysitter was alone with her charge, went to the apartment and was admitted by the little boy while the babysitter was on the telephone. He explained his presence by claiming he had permission to borrow some records from the little boy's mother. Shortly thereafter he assaulted the babysitter and the rape occurred. Afterwards the defendant attempted to strangle the boy with a cord, then finally killed him by stabbing him with a large knife he got from the kitchen. When that happened the babysitter grabbed for the knife, cutting her hand, succeeding in knocking the defendant down, and escaped. As she ran into the street he apparently threw the knife at her but missed. The babysitter fled to a neighbor's and when the police arrived the defendant was gone. When the identity of the defendant became known, the foster family with whom he was living was contacted. He was later brought by one of them to the police station.

Almost simultaneously with the issuance of the warrant and before arraignment, the State moved for a mental examination in anticipation of a plea of insanity. That motion asserted that the defendant had a history of treatment for personality disorders at Metropolitan State Hospital in Waltham, Massachusetts; New Hampshire Hospital in Concord, New Hampshire; and Waterbury State Hospital in Waterbury, Vermont. The motion was granted at the arraignment and the examination undertaken. . . .

There remains only the claim that the trial court should have charged on what is coming to be known as "diminished capacity." This issue was before the trial court and may occur on retrial, therefore it is appropriate for review on this appeal.

Contrary to the position taken by the State, our cases do not limit the application of the "diminished capacity" doctrine to the use of intoxicants. Rather, the matter of intoxication has been noted as one area of its application, where supported by appropriate facts.

The concept is directed at the evidentiary duty of the State to establish those elements of the crime charged requiring a conscious mental ingredient. There is no question that it may overlap the insanity defense in that insanity itself is concerned with mental conditions so incapacitating as to totally bar criminal responsibility. The distinction is that diminished capacity is legally applicable to disabilities not amounting to insanity, and its consequences, in homicide cases, operate to reduce the degree of the crime rather than to excuse its commission. Evidence offered under this rubric is relevant to prove the existence of a mental defect or obstacle to the presence of a state of mind which is an element of the crime, for example: premeditation or deliberation.

Since these states of mind are neither complex nor difficult to achieve, aside from special instances involving drugs, alcohol, injury or emotional frenzy, the issue frequently tends to reduce itself to situations involving lack of mental capacity itself.

For the purposes of the matter before us it is sufficient to say that where the evidence in any form supports it, a request to charge on the jury's duty to determine the existence of the states of mind required to establish the particular crime at issue in the light of any diminished capacity should be carefully reviewed by the trial court, and if appropriate, given.

Reversed and remanded.

F. Model Penal Code Provisions

§4.02. Evidence of Mental Disease or Defect Admissible When Relevant to Element of the Offense [; Mental Disease or Defect Impairing Capacity as Ground for Mitigation of Punishment in Capital Cases].

(1) Evidence that the defendant suffered from a mental disease or defect is admissible whenever it is relevant to prove that the defendant did or did not have a state of mind that is an element of the offense.

Note

Subsection (1) of §4.02 indicates that evidence about mental disease or defect may be introduced to show that a defendant did or did not have the state of mind required for *any* offense. Approximately 15 states follow the MPC approach. *See* Joshua Dressler, *Understanding Criminal Law* §26.02[B][2] (6th ed. 2012).

Recall from *State v. Dumlao*, 6 Haw. App. 173 (1986), discussed previously in the homicide chapter, that the MPC also recognizes a partial responsibility defense as it concerns homicide committed under the influence of extreme mental or emotional disturbance (EMED). *See* MPC §210.3(1)(b).[*] If the EMED is established, it reduces the homicide to manslaughter.

---

[*] §210.3. Manslaughter

   (1) Criminal homicide constitutes manslaughter when: . . .
   (b) a homicide which would otherwise be murder is committed under the influence of extreme mental or emotional disturbance for which there is reasonable explanation or excuse. The reasonableness of such explanation or excuse shall be determined from the viewpoint of a person in the actor's situation under the circumstances as he believes them to be. . . .

Chapter 15
Intoxication

A. Introduction

In terms of the so-called "intoxication defense," it is important to recognize that there are two vastly different approaches depending on whether the actor's intoxication was involuntary or voluntary. The former is treated much like the insanity defense and will be discussed briefly in this chapter. Voluntary intoxication on the other hand is more controversial. Courts today vary widely in recognizing voluntary intoxication as a defense. The growing trend is to refuse to accept voluntary intoxication as a defense to any crime. For example, Michigan and Montana have eliminated the defense by statute. *See* M.C.L. §768.37. *See also Montana v Egelhoff,* 518 U.S. 37 (1996). A minority of jurisdictions recognize the defense in any crime if it negates the mens rea. *See* Joshua Dressler, *Understanding Criminal Law* §24.03 (6th ed. 2012). A third approach is more common and consistent with the common law as of the 19th century: voluntary intoxication is only a defense to a specific intent crime and only when it is extreme enough to deprive the actor of the capacity to form the specific intent.

Because the voluntary intoxication defense is generally only available as a defense to specific intent crimes, it is critical to know which crimes are specific intent and which are general intent. One way to look at the distinction is that general intent crimes require the prosecution to prove only that the defendant intended to commit the actus reus of the offense. At common law, rape, battery, the malice crimes (e.g., arson, murder), and the negligence or reckless crimes (e.g., manslaughter) were considered general intent. Other common law crimes, such as larceny and burglary, were considered specific intent (generally defined as intent to accomplish something beyond the criminal act itself).

B.   Voluntary Intoxication

1.   What policy considerations are relied upon to support the use of the voluntary intoxication defense? What limitations are there?

Note that there are two issues discussed in *Langworthy*: (1) the history and applicability of the intoxication defense and (2) whether second degree murder and criminal sexual conduct are specific intent offenses.

People v. Langworthy and Lundy, 416 Mich. 630 (1982)

FITZGERALD, Chief Justice.

The common ground of these cases is that, at their trials, both defendants attempted to utilize voluntary intoxication as a defense to charges of crimes which Michigan appellate courts previously have held to be general-intent crimes. Both defendants request this Court to expand the category of specific-intent crimes to include the offenses they were convicted of, *i.e.*, first-degree criminal sexual conduct and second-degree murder, in order to make available to them the defense of voluntary intoxication.

FACTS

Defendant Lundy was found guilty but mentally ill of three counts of first-degree criminal sexual conduct, M.C.L. §750.520b; M.S.A. §28.788(2), and sentenced to three concurrent life terms. The convictions arose from the October 30, 1978, rape of his adult sister. The crime, carried out with the use of a knife as a threatening weapon, involved three penetrations.

At Lundy's bench trial, the major issue centered on defendant's mental state at the time of the commission of the crime. His defense was predicated upon expert testimony regarding his mental state as well as evidence that he had been sniffing glue and drinking alcohol immediately prior to the crime. The trial court rejected Lundy's insanity defense as well as his intoxication defense, ruling as to the latter that first-degree criminal sexual conduct is a general-intent crime.

The Court of Appeals affirmed in a memorandum opinion.

Defendant Langworthy was convicted of second-degree murder, M.C.L. §750.520b; M.S.A. §28.549, and was sentenced to 60 to 90 years in prison.

After a bench trial, the trial judge found that on the night of November 5, 1976, defendant, Roy Schipani, and Alan Parker were together indulging in alcohol and drugs in a house in Ypsilanti. Parker left sometime during the early morning hours to purchase cigarettes at a gas station. There he met the decedent, William Wedge, who returned to the house with Parker.

The trial judge further found that Wedge was intoxicated and offensive and that Wedge made certain comments which irritated defendant. Wedge then passed out and the three others discussed robbing Wedge. Defendant suggested that they "blow him away" and then he turned up the stereo, went to a closet where he got a rifle and shot Wedge in the mouth and in the chest.

The trial judge determined that the defendant was not mentally ill or legally insane at the time of the commission of the crime. He found that defendant had taken at least 400 milligrams of Valium and some codeine and Nembutal and had been drinking Southern Comfort and Coke at the time of the crime. The trial judge concluded:

> However, the Court finds that as a result of the drugs and alcohol his judgment and his appreciation of the consequence of his actions was grossly impaired.
>
> That he committed the act knowingly with malice but 'without a real concept of the consequence of the act.' That he had a conscious intent to commit the crime but that his judgment and appreciation of the consequence of his act was grossly impaired as the result of the drugs and alcohol.

The Court of Appeals affirmed in an unpublished opinion per curiam, ruling, *inter alia,* that second-degree murder is not a specific-intent crime and that, therefore, voluntary intoxication was not a defense.

THE VOLUNTARY INTOXICATION DEFENSE

Every jurisdiction in this country recognizes the general principle that voluntary intoxication is not any excuse for crime. This is in accord with the common-law rule dating back to the sixteenth century which allowed no concession to a defendant because of his intoxication. However, by the early nineteenth century, the English courts began to fashion a doctrine to mitigate the harshness and rigidity of the traditional rule. The doctrine, which has come to be known as the exculpatory rule, was stated by Judge Stephen as follows:

> [A]lthough you cannot take drunkenness as any excuse for crime, yet when the crime is such that the intention of the party committing it is one of its constituent elements, you may look at the fact that a man was in drink in considering whether he formed the intention necessary to constitute the crime.

It is said that the theory behind this exculpatory doctrine is that it does not hold that drunkenness will excuse crime; rather, it inquires whether the very crime which the law defines has in fact been committed. Almost every state, by statute or by common law, has adopted the exculpatory rule, and Michigan is no exception.

> While it is true that drunkenness cannot excuse crime, it is equally true that when a certain intent is a necessary element in a crime, the crime cannot have been committed when the intent did not exist.

The applicability of the exculpatory rule rests entirely on the determination whether the offense involved is categorized as a general- or specific-intent crime.

> It is important in this decision to emphasize that intoxication may only negative the existence of *specific intent*. Examination of the cases reveals that where the rule was applied, it was done so in cases where the crime charged also involved a specific intent.

Thus, if a crime is determined to require only a general intent, the defendant's voluntary intoxication during the commission of an offense may not be asserted as a defense to the existence of the mental element of that crime.

The general intent-specific intent dichotomy arose as a compromise between the perceived need to afford some relief to the intoxicated offender whose moral culpability was considered less than that of a sober person who committed the same offense and the view that a person who voluntarily becomes drunk and commits a crime should not escape the consequences. Although the rule seems logical on the surface, it has proven to be far from logical in application. While specific intent can easily be defined as "a particular criminal intent beyond the act done"[9] (whereas general intent is the intent simply to do the physical act), the ease of stating the definition belies the difficulty of applying it in practice. In order to appreciate the problem, one need only note the divergence of opinion among the jurisdictions as to which crimes require a specific intent and, therefore, to which crimes the exculpatory rule applies.

It has been noted that the law with respect to voluntary intoxication and criminal responsibility has shown little tendency to change or develop despite advances socially and medically in this area; and, we might add, despite strong criticism from treatise writers, law review commentators, case law, and the drafters of the Model Penal Code. My Brother Levin summarized the major criticisms of the exculpatory rule while on the Court of Appeals:

> It has also been maintained that the availability of the intoxication defense should not depend on whether a court chooses to characterize an element of the crime charged as separate from the element of general intent. It has been observed that neither common experience nor psychology knows of any such phenomenon as 'general intent' distinguishable from 'specific intent.' It does seem incongruous to make the admissibility of mitigating evidence depend on whether the statutory definition of a crime

---

[9] *People v. Depew*, 215 Mich. 317, 320 (1921). LaFave & Scott, Criminal Law, § 28, p. 202:
[T]he most common usage of 'specific intent' is to designate a special mental element which is required above and beyond any mental state required with respect to the *actus reus* of a crime.

includes a separately stated intent, and other methods of defining specific intent are highly manipulable.

The clumsiness of the exculpatory device has been criticized. A defendant who is charged with a specific intent crime may go free if he can prove he was intoxicated; this result contrasts sharply with the absolute denial of relief to the intoxicated offender charged with a crime of general intent.

If the function of the general/specific intent distinction is to eliminate the defense as to lesser included offenses, *e.g.,* assault and battery, but to retain it for the more serious offenses, *e.g.,* armed robbery, and in that manner mitigate the general rule that intoxication is not a defense, then manifestly this should be done on a consistent basis. The right to interpose this defense should depend on something more substantial than a technical distinction that was seized upon by a judge 130 years ago and adopted by other judges to reach results thought sound in the cases then before them.

While we recognize the illogic and incongruity of the general intent-specific intent dichotomy, the remedy is not clear-cut. One solution, of course, would be to join the ranks of those few states which do not allow the voluntary intoxication defense even where a specific intent is required. We agree, however, with Professors LaFave and Scott that this view is clearly wrong. It would require us to ignore basic concepts of criminal culpability as well as modern scientific views on alcoholism.

The alternative would be to allow the intoxication defense to be asserted against any charge of crime which traditionally has required general or specific intent. Although this Court has the power to so modify the common-law rule, we believe that it would be imprudent to take that step at this time. While abolishing the general intent-specific intent distinction may rid the courts of an illogical rule, it would do nothing to help solve the problem of the intoxicated offender, both from the standpoint of the offender and from the standpoint of society which suffers from the acts of the intoxicated offender. Moreover, because the parties before us did not specifically address the issue of abolishing the exculpatory rule, we do not have the benefit of an adversarial presentation of the pros and cons of such an action. This Court should be hesitant to abolish an established common-law rule without a fully developed presentation of both sides of the question.

The problem of alcoholism and crime is complex, requiring studies and policy considerations beyond the ability of any judicial body. Various solutions which have been proposed would require legislative action. We urge the Legislature to consider the intoxicated-offender problem and to modernize Michigan law on this subject. Until the Legislature takes action or until we are persuaded to modify the common-law rule in an appropriate case in the future, we shall continue to struggle with applying the rule case by case.

IS FIRST—DEGREE CRIMINAL SEXUAL CONDUCT A SPECIFIC INTENT CRIME?

Defendant Lundy asks this Court to find that first-degree criminal sexual conduct includes the element of specific intent. His only argument is that felonious assault is a specific-intent crime and, therefore, in those criminal sexual conduct situations where felonious assault is a lesser included offense logic dictates that specific intent is also an element of the criminal sexual conduct. Because Lundy possessed a weapon while committing the criminal sexual conduct herein, he argues that specific intent was an element of proof which the intoxication defense should have been allowed to negative.

This case requires us to decide whether first-degree criminal sexual conduct is a general- or specific-intent crime. We have previously held, under the predecessor to the criminal sexual conduct statute, that rape is not a specific-intent crime. . . . This comports with the overwhelming weight of authority which holds that rape is a general-intent crime.

An examination of the statute convinces us that the Legislature did not intend to include specific intent as an element of first-degree criminal sexual conduct. Neither the first-degree criminal sexual conduct statute nor the corresponding statutory definition of "sexual penetration" contains any language whatsoever regarding intent. The fact that the Legislature must have been cognizant, in enacting the first-degree criminal sexual conduct provision, of the established rule that rape does not require specific intent, combined with the absence of any provision regarding intent, considerably weakens defendant's argument that his crime is a specific-intent offense. If the Legislature wanted to add specific intent as an element, knowing that the predecessor statute had been consistently construed as a general-intent crime, it would have specifically done so. The fact that it did not leads us to conclude that the Legislature intended to maintain the general rule that "no intent is requisite other than that evidenced by the doing of the acts constituting the offense", *i.e.,* general intent.

Moreover, one of the purposes of the new act was to strengthen the laws against sexual violence by removing certain evidentiary obstacles to the prosecution of sexual assault. This further strengthens our conclusion that it is unlikely that a new element of proof would be added without specific mention.

Finally, we reject defendant's argument that if an applicable lesser included offense of a criminal sexual conduct offense requires specific intent, it necessarily follows that the greater offense also requires proof of specific intent. Other courts presented with this argument have rejected it, and we reject it also. . . .

Accordingly, we conclude that first-degree criminal sexual conduct is a general-intent crime for which the defense of voluntary intoxication is not available.

IS SECOND–DEGREE MURDER A GENERAL OR SPECIFIC INTENT CRIME?

Defendant Langworthy petitions this Court to extend to second-degree murder cases the rule in *People v. Garcia*, 398 Mich. 250 (1976), that non-felony first-degree murder is a specific-intent crime. Defendant urges this Court to adopt the California rule of diminished capacity.

In support of his position, defendant has cited for our consideration cases from other jurisdictions which allow murder to be reduced to manslaughter through the successful assertion of the voluntary intoxication defense. We have reviewed these cases and others, and we have concluded that they are not applicable to the situation existing in Michigan. An examination of the jurisdictions which defendant relies upon demonstrates why the cases are clearly distinguishable.

Unlike that of Michigan, the statutory schemes of some states do not divide murder into degrees. To further complicate comparison, these states may require, as an element of their single crime of murder, premeditation or some other specific mental element (such as intent to kill) not required for second-degree murder in Michigan. These states do no more than Michigan already does with respect to first-degree murder, *i.e.,* allow intoxication to negate the element of premeditation (or intent to kill) and reduce the degree of the offense. The difference is that in these states negation of premeditation, for example, means that murder has not been proven at all, whereas in Michigan it only means that first-degree murder has not been proven. This difference is due to the legislative classification of homicide, which we have no control over and, consequently, which makes these cases distinguishable.

Other states allow charges of second-degree murder to be reduced to manslaughter, but this result is mandated by the particular statutory definition of the required *mens rea*. In Colorado, for instance, under a prior statute, second-degree murder was not a specific-intent crime, and voluntary intoxication was not a defense. Under the revised statute, the inclusion of the term "intentionally" caused the Colorado Supreme Court to redefine second-degree murder as a specific-intent crime. Michigan has no statutory *mens rea* requirement for second-degree murder which would mandate similar treatment.

Some of the other states which defendant refers us to have case-law definitions of malice which require premeditation or intent to kill as necessary requirements. Michigan does not have either of these elements as a prerequisite to second-degree murder.[31] . . .

Thus, we find that all of the jurisdictions which defendant relies upon as persuasive authority for his position are not applicable to our circumstances in Michigan. In any event, despite the existence of cases which allow a proper

---

[31] As discussed below, in Michigan the intent to kill will satisfy the malice requirement, but it is not required.

voluntary intoxication defense to reduce murder or second-degree murder to manslaughter, the majority rule remains as follows:

> It is now generally held that intoxication may be considered where murder is divided into degrees, and in many states, may have the effect of reducing homicide from murder in the first degree to murder in the second degree. In fact, in most states the only consideration given to the fact of drunkenness or intoxication at the time of the commission of the homicide is to enable the court and jury to determine whether the prisoner may be guilty of murder in the second degree, rather than of murder in the first degree. The rule followed by most courts is that intoxication will not reduce a homicide from murder to manslaughter.

Defendant also contends that the distinction between first- and second-degree murder is not so great as to require the difference in treatment vis-a-vis the intoxication defense. He argues that because "the line drawn is a fine one", the emphasis should not be placed on the difference between first- and second-degree murder; rather, the emphasis should be placed on the difference between murder and manslaughter, the former distinction only being necessary for punishment purposes. At oral argument, defense counsel stressed that willfulness is the common thread of first- and second-degree murder and that the Criminal Jury Instructions use the term willfulness in conjunction with both crimes. Thus, defense counsel argued, voluntary intoxication should be allowed to negate the willfulness element of both degrees of murder.

Contrary to defense counsel's argument, our reading of the relevant jury instructions indicates no requirement of willfulness for second-degree murder. The requirement of a "wilful" killing is contained only in the language of the first-degree murder statute. Furthermore, while the distinction between first- and second-degree murder, on the facts of a particular case, may at times appear to be a "fine line", it nevertheless represents a policy decision of our Legislature to punish more severely certain types of murder which it considered to be more serious. We do not question the wisdom of that policy decision.

We find that there is more than a sufficient basis to distinguish between the degrees of murder to require that specific intent be demonstrated for first-degree murder only. In *People v. Garcia, supra,* we held that "wilful" killing means the "intent to accomplish the result of death". Moreover, specific intent to kill is a necessary constituent of the elements of premeditation and deliberation. It would be difficult, if not impossible, to premeditate and deliberate a killing without at the same time possessing the specific intent to kill. This logic, however, does not apply to second-degree murder.

The *mens rea* requirement for second-degree murder is supplied by the element of malice. While the intent to kill satisfies the malice requirement, it is not a necessary element of second-degree murder. An intent to inflict great bodily harm or a wanton and willful disregard of the likelihood that the natural tendency of a person's behavior is to cause death or great bodily harm may also satisfy the malice requirement. With respect to the element of malice encompassing wanton and willful disregard, we concur with the majority rule that voluntary intoxication is not a defense. We agree with the analysis of Professors LaFave and Scott:

> The person who unconsciously creates risk because he is voluntarily drunk is perhaps morally worse than one who does so because he is sober but mentally deficient. At all events, the cases generally hold that drunkenness does not negative a depraved heart by blotting out consciousness of risk, and the Model Penal Code, which generally requires awareness of the risk for depraved-heart murder (and for recklessness manslaughter), so provides.

Because second-degree murder does not require intent to kill, but rather, only wanton and willful disregard malice need be shown; and, because we have concluded that voluntary intoxication may not negate this latter category of malice, we believe that voluntary intoxication should not be a defense to a charge of second-degree murder. We are aware that there may be second-degree murder cases which involve only the intent to kill or the intent to do great bodily harm types of malice. We are further aware that these two categories of malice sound suspiciously akin to the traditional language of specific intent. However, we decline to extend the defense of voluntary intoxication to these cases on the grounds of public policy. . . .

We hold that second-degree murder is not a specific-intent crime for which the defense of voluntary intoxication may be asserted. . . .

CONCLUSION

Although we consider the general intent-specific intent dichotomy an unsatisfactory concept in the law, we believe it is more appropriate for the Legislature to fashion reform in this area, and we strongly recommend such reform. For the present, we hold that the defense of voluntary intoxication is not available to charges of the crimes of first-degree criminal sexual conduct and second-degree murder. Or, to use the traditional rubric, we hold that the above offenses are crimes of general intent. The Court of Appeals is affirmed in both cases.

Note

Exactly twenty years after the *Langworthy* decision, the Michigan Legislature accepted the invitation of the Supreme Court and enacted an intoxication defense statute. However, the Legislature did not heed the Court's words that eliminating voluntary intoxication as a defense to specific intent crimes would "ignore basic concepts of criminal culpability as well as modern scientific views on alcoholism." The statute, MCL §768.37, enacted in 2002, eliminates voluntary intoxication as a defense to any crime unless the defendant can show that "he or she voluntarily consumed a legally obtained and properly used medication or other substance and did not know and reasonably should not have known that he or she would become intoxicated or impaired."

2. **When is a trial judge required to give an instruction on the defense of voluntary intoxication?**

State v. Cameron, 104 N.J. 42 (1986)

CLIFFORD, J.

This appeal presents a narrow, but important, issue concerning the role that a defendant's voluntary intoxication plays in a criminal prosecution. The specific question is whether the evidence was sufficient to require the trial court to charge the jury on defendant's intoxication, as defendant requested. The Appellate Division reversed defendant's convictions, holding that it was error not to have given an intoxication charge. We granted the State's petition for certification and defendant's cross-petition and now reverse.

I

Defendant, Michele Cameron, age 22 at the time of trial, was indicted for second degree aggravated assault, possession of a weapon, a broken bottle, with a purpose to use it unlawfully, and fourth degree resisting arrest. A jury convicted defendant of all charges. After merging the possession count into the assault charge, the trial court imposed sentences aggregating seven years in the custody of the Commissioner of the Department of Corrections, with a three year period of parole ineligibility and certain monetary penalties.

The charges arose out of an incident of June 6, 1981, on a vacant lot in Trenton. The unreported opinion of the Appellate Division depicts the following tableau of significant events:

> The victim, Joseph McKinney, was playing cards with four other men. Defendant approached and disrupted the game with her conduct. The participants moved their card table to a new location within the lot. Defendant followed them, however, and overturned the table. The table was righted and the game resumed. Shortly thereafter, defendant attacked McKinney with a broken bottle. As a result of that attack he sustained an injury to his hand, which necessitated 36 stitches and caused permanent injury.
>
> Defendant reacted with violence to the arrival of the police. She threw a bottle at their vehicle, shouted obscenities, and tried to fight them off. She had to be restrained and handcuffed in the police wagon.

The heart of the Appellate Division's reversal of defendant's conviction is found in its determination that voluntary intoxication is a defense when it negates an essential element of the offense-here, purposeful conduct. We agree with that proposition. Likewise are we in accord with the determinations of the court below that all three of the charges of which this defendant convicted-aggravated assault, the possession offense, and resisting arrest-have purposeful conduct as an element of the offense; and that a person acts purposely "with respect to the nature of his conduct or a result thereof if it is his conscious object to engage in conduct of that nature or to cause such a result." We part company with the Appellate Division, however, in its conclusion that the circumstances disclosed by the evidence in this case required that the issue of defendant's intoxication be submitted to the jury.

The court below noted that every witness who testified gave some appraisal of defendant's condition. On the basis of that evidence the Appellate Division concluded that

> defendant's conduct was both bizarre and violent. She had been drinking and could not be reasoned with. The victim thought she was intoxicated and two police officers thought she was under the influence of something. Not one witness who testified thought that her conduct was normal. Therefore, it was for the jury to determine if she was intoxicated, and if so, whether the element of purposefulness was negated thereby.

The quoted passage reflects a misapprehension of the level of proof required to demonstrate intoxication for purposes of demonstrating an inability to engage in purposeful conduct.

II

Under the common law intoxication was not a defense to a criminal charge. Rather than being denominated a defense, intoxication was viewed as a "condition of fact," or, in a homicide case, as "a mere circumstance to be considered in determining whether premeditation was present or absent."

Notwithstanding the general proposition that voluntary intoxication is no defense, the early cases nevertheless held that in some circumstances intoxication could be resorted to for defensive purposes-specifically, to show the absence of a specific intent.

> The exceptional immunity extended to the drunkard is limited to those instances where the crime involves a specific, actual intent. When the degree of intoxication is such as to render the person incapable of entertaining such intent, it is an effective defence. If it falls short of this it is worthless.

The principle that developed from the foregoing approach—that intoxication formed the basis for a defense to a "specific intent" crime but not to one involving only "general" intent—persisted for about three-quarters of a century, or until this Court's decision in *State v. Maik*, 60 *N.J.* 203 (1972). . . . ("if defendant was so intoxicated or in such a condition of mind because he was getting over a debauch that his faculties were prostrated and rendered him incapable of forming a specific intent to kill with . . . willful, deliberate and premeditated character, then although it is no defence or justification, his offence would be murder in the second degree"); (proof that defendant had been intoxicated for five to six weeks preceding assault on his wife and expert testimony that that condition would cause "unsoundness of mind" does not excuse consequences of crime, but justifies jury charge directed to question of whether defendant acted with requisite mental state); (evidence of defendant's deliberate search for murder weapon sufficient to support jury's conclusion that defendant's faculties were not "so far prostrated by intoxication as to render him incapable of forming an intent to kill"); (no error in charge to jury that "intoxication is an affirmative defense," which defendant must establish by fair preponderance of evidence; intoxication so great as to prostrate defendant's faculties and render him incapable of forming specific intent to kill would make defendant not guilty of first degree murder).

Eventually the problems inherent in the application of the specific-general intent dichotomy surfaced. In State v. Maik, *supra*, this Court dwelt on the elusiveness of the distinction between "specific" and "general" intent crimes, particularly as that distinction determined what role voluntary intoxication played in a criminal prosecution. Chief Justice Weintraub's opinion for the Court restated the original proposition that "a defendant will not be relieved of criminal responsibility because he was under the influence of intoxicants or drugs voluntarily taken," and then set forth four exceptions to that rule: (1) the ingestion of drugs for medication, producing unexpected or bizarre results; (2) impairment of mental faculties negating only premeditation or deliberation, to preclude elevation to first degree murder; (3) reduction of felony homicide to second degree murder when the felonious intent is negated; and (4) when insanity results.

Maik, a murder prosecution, was not given a uniform reading. As later pointed out in State v. Stasio, 78 N.J. 467 (1979), the Appellate Division in State v. Del Vecchio, 142 N.J.Super. 359 (1976), limited *Maik*'s sweep to the proposition that voluntary intoxication is relevant only to the determination of whether a murder may be raised to first degree, whereas Judge Allcorn, dissenting in State v. Atkins, 151 N.J.Super. 555, 573 (App.Div. 1977) rev'd, 78 N.J. 454 (1979), read *Maik* to rule out voluntary intoxication as a defense to any criminal prosecution, irrespective of whether a specific or general intent was an element of the offense. It thus fell to the Court in *Stasio* to resolve the difference in interpretations that had been accorded *Maik*, an undertaking that we recognize met with but limited success.

A majority of the Court in *Stasio* found the difference between general and specific intent to be "not readily ascertainable," and concluded that honoring the distinction would give rise to "incongruous results by irrationally allowing intoxication to excuse some crimes but not others." On the one hand, therefore, the Court brought some stability to the area, with its holding that absent one or more of the exceptions stated in *Maik,* the principle that voluntary intoxication will not excuse criminal conduct was applicable to all crimes. But on the other hand, because of critically important legislation that was looming in the background at the time of the *Stasio* decision, the opinion may have posed more questions than it answered.

Specifically, the Court's result in *Stasio* was heavily influenced by its prognostication-mistaken, as it later developed-on what action the legislature might take in respect of its treatment of intoxication. Before *Stasio* was decided, the legislature enacted the New Jersey Code of Criminal Justice, N.J.S.A. 2C:1 1 to 98–4 (Code). The Code did not become effective, however, until September 1, 1979, almost a year after *Stasio* was argued and some nine months after it was decided. The Court correctly recited the pertinent Code provisions, suggested some possible incongruities and, in reliance on the Deputy Attorney General's implication that the legislature would be importuned to "modify the provisions dealing with intoxication" and that therefore the legislature might act to change the Code, determined to adhere to what it concluded was the *Maik* principle, namely, that absent one of the four exceptions, intoxication will not constitute a defense to any crime.

Justice Handler's concurrence in Stasio, 78 N.J. at 485, took a different approach. Although the concurrence agreed with the majority and with *Maik* that the "attempted differentiation between so-called specific intent and general intent crimes . . . is an unhelpful, misleading and often confusing distinction," and that the "availability of voluntary intoxication as a defense in terms of that distinction . . . has led to anomalous results," it did not accept the proposition that "if the separation between so-called specific and general intent crimes is rejected, voluntary intoxication as a defense must also be rejected." According to the concurrence,

> [t]he criminal laws need not be impotent or ineffective when dealing with an intoxicated criminal. The question should always be whether under particular circumstances a defendant ought to be considered responsible for his conduct.

The concurring opinion in *Stasio* took the position that when dealing with the issue of intoxication, the focus at trial should be on the mental state required for the commission of the particular crime charged. In particular, a defendant ought not be considered responsible when the effect of his intoxication

> reached such a level, operating upon the defendant's mind, . . . as to deprive him of his will to act. . . . I would accordingly require, in order to generate a reasonable doubt as to a defendant's responsibility for his acts, that it be shown he

was so intoxicated that he could not think, or that his mind
did not function with consciousness or volition.

Justice Pashman's concurrence and dissent likewise would have hinged the success of an intoxication defense on "a showing of such a great prostration of the faculties that the requisite mental state was totally lacking."

We have drawn at such length on the minority opinions in *Stasio* because, as will become apparent, they are much closer to the Code's view of intoxication, and thus to the law governing this appeal, than is the majority opinion in *Stasio*.

III

Which brings us to the Code.

As indicated, after *Stasio* had been decided, the Code became effective, on September 1, 1979. It in effect displaced the Court's opinion in *Stasio* and in large measure confirmed the approach of the concurring opinions in *Stasio* . . . .

As originally enacted (a 1983 amendment of section d. is of no relevance here) N.J.S.A. 2C:2–8 provided:

a. Except as provided in subsection d. of this section, intoxication of the actor is not a defense unless it negatives an element of the offense.

b. When recklessness establishes an element of the offense, if the actor, due to self-induced intoxication, is unaware of a risk of which he would have been aware had he been sober, such unawareness is immaterial.

c. Intoxication does not, in itself, constitute mental disease within the meaning of chapter 4.

d. Intoxication which (1) is not self-induced or (2) is pathological is an affirmative defense if by reason of such intoxication the actor at the time of his conduct lacks substantial and adequate capacity either to appreciate its wrongfulness or to conform his conduct to the requirement of law.

e. Definitions. In this section unless a different meaning plainly is required:

(1) "Intoxication" means a disturbance of mental or physical capacities resulting from the introduction of substances into the body;

(2) "self-induced intoxication" means intoxication caused by substances which the actor knowingly introduces into his body, the tendency of which to cause intoxication he knows or ought to know, unless he introduces them pursuant to medical advice or under such circumstances as would afford a defense to a charge of crime;

(3) "Pathological intoxication" means intoxication grossly excessive in degree, given the amount of the intoxicant, to which the actor does not know he is susceptible.

As is readily apparent, self-induced intoxication is not a defense unless it negatives an element of the offense. Under the common-law intoxication defense, as construed by the Commission, intoxication could either exculpate or mitigate guilt "if the defendant's intoxication, in fact, prevents his having formed a mental state which is an element of the offense and if the law will recognize the proof of the lack of that mental state." Thus, the Commission recognized that under pre-Code law, intoxication was admissible as a defense to a "specific" intent, but not a "general" intent, crime.

The original proposed Code rejected the specific/general intent distinction, choosing to rely instead on the reference to the four states of culpability for offenses under the Code: negligent, reckless, knowing, and purposeful conduct, N.J.S.A. 2C:2–2(b). Although the Code employs terminology that differs from that used to articulate the common-law principles referable to intoxication, the Commission concluded that the ultimately-enacted statutory intoxication defense would achieve the same result as that reached under the common law. In essence, "[t]hat which the cases now describe as a 'specific intent' can be equated, for this purpose, with that which the Code defines as 'purpose' and 'knowledge.' *See* §2C:2–2b. A 'general intent' can be equated with that which the Code defines as 'recklessness,' or criminal 'negligence.' " *Code Commentary* at 68. Therefore, according to the Commissioners, N.J.S.A. 2C:2–8(a) and (b) would serve much the same end as was achieved by the common-law approach. Specifically, N.J.S.A. 2C:2–8(a) permits evidence of intoxication as a defense to crimes requiring either "purposeful" or "knowing" mental states but it excludes evidence of intoxication as a defense to crimes requiring mental states of only recklessness or negligence.

N.J.S.A. 2C:2–8 was modeled after the Model Penal Code (MPC) §2.08. The drafters of the MPC, as did the New Jersey Commission, criticized the specific-general intent distinction, and adopted instead the same four states of culpability eventually enacted in the Code. In the commentary, the drafters of the MPC expressly stated their intention that intoxication be admissible to disprove the culpability factors of purpose or knowledge, but that for crimes requiring only recklessness or negligence, exculpation based on intoxication should be excluded as a matter of law.

The drafters explicitly determined that intoxication ought to be accorded a significance that is entirely co-extensive with its relevance to disprove purpose or knowledge, when they are the requisite mental elements of a specific crime. . . . [W]hen the definition of a crime or a degree thereof requires proof of such a state of mind, the legal policy involved will almost certainly obtain whether or not the absence of purpose or knowledge is due to the actor's self-induced intoxication or to some other cause.

The policy reasons for requiring purpose or knowledge as a requisite element of some crimes are that in the absence of those states of mind, the criminal conduct would not present a comparable danger, or the actor would not pose as significant a threat. Moreover, the ends of legal policy are better served by subjecting to graver sanctions those who consciously defy legal norms. It was those policy reasons that dictated the result that the intoxication defense should be available when it negatives purpose or knowledge. The drafters concluded: "If the mental state which is the basis of the law's concern does not exist, the reason for its non-existence is quite plainly immaterial."

Thus, when the requisite culpability for a crime is that the person act "purposely" or "knowingly," evidence of voluntary intoxication is admissible to disprove that requisite mental state. The language of N.J.S.A. 2C:2–8 and its legislative history make this unmistakably clear and lend support to *Stasio*'s . . . minority [opinion].

IV

The foregoing discussion establishes that proof of voluntary intoxication would negate the culpability elements in the offenses of which this defendant was convicted. The charges—aggravated assault, possession of a weapon with a purpose to use it unlawfully, and resisting arrest—all require purposeful conduct (aggravated assault uses "purposely" or "knowingly" in the alternative). The question is what level of intoxication must be demonstrated before a trial court is required to submit the issue to a jury. What quantum of proof is required?

The guiding principle is simple enough of articulation. We need not here repeat the citations to authorities already referred to in this opinion that use the language of "prostration of faculties such that defendant was rendered incapable of forming an intent." Justice Depue's instruction to a jury over a century ago, quoted with approval in State v. Treficanto, 106 N.J.L. 344 (1929) remains good law:

> You should carefully discriminate between that excitable condition of the mind produced by drink, which is not incapable of forming an intent, but determines to act on a slight provocation, and such prostration of the faculties by intoxication as puts the accused in such a state that he is incapable of forming an intention from which he shall act.

See also State v. Stasio, supra:

> [I]t is not the case that every defendant who has had a few drinks may successfully urge the defense. The mere intake of even large quantities of alcohol will not suffice. Moreover, the defense cannot be established solely by showing that the

defendant might not have committed the offense had he been sober. What is required is a showing of such a great prostration of the faculties that the requisite mental state was totally lacking. That is, to successfully invoke the defense, an accused must show that he was so intoxicated that he did not have the intent to commit an offense. Such a state of affairs will likely exist in very few cases. [78 N.J. at 495 (Pashman, J., concurring and dissenting).]

So firmly fixed in our case law is the requirement of "prostration of faculties" as the minimum requirement for an intoxication defense that we feel secure in our assumption that the legislature intended nothing different in its statutory definition of intoxication: "a disturbance of mental or physical capacities resulting from the introduction of substances into the body." N.J.S.A. 2C:2–8(e)(1). In order to satisfy the statutory condition that to qualify as a defense intoxication must negative an element of the offense, the intoxication must be of an extremely high level. Therefore, consistency between the definition of intoxication and the effect given it by the legislature require that the standard be "prostration of faculties." Less certain is how that standard is to be satisfied. . . .

From all of the above we conclude that some of the factors pertinent to the determination of intoxication sufficient to satisfy the test of "prostration of faculties"—a shorthand expression used here to indicate a condition of intoxication that renders the actor incapable of purposeful or knowing conduct—are the following: the quantity of intoxicant consumed, the period of time involved, the actor's conduct as perceived by others (what he said, how he said it, how he appeared, how he acted, how his coordination or lack thereof manifested itself), any odor of alcohol or other intoxicating substance, the results of any tests to determine blood-alcohol content, and the actor's ability to recall significant events.

V

Measured by the foregoing standard and evidence relevant thereto, it is apparent that the record in this case is insufficient to have required the trial court to grant defendant's request to charge intoxication. . . .

True, the victim testified that defendant was drunk, and defendant herself said she felt "pretty intoxicated," "pretty bad," and "very intoxicated." But these are no more than conclusory labels, of little assistance in determining whether any drinking produced a prostration of faculties.

More to the point is the fact that defendant carried a quart of wine, that she was drinking (we are not told over what period of time) with other people on the vacant lot, that about a pint of the wine was consumed, and that defendant did not drink this alone but rather "gave most of it out, gave some of it out." Defendant's conduct was violent, abusive, and threatening. But with it all there is not the slightest suggestion that she did not know what she was doing or that her faculties were so beclouded by the wine that she was incapable of engaging in purposeful conduct. That the purpose of the conduct may have been bizarre, even violent, is not the test. The critical question is whether defendant was capable of forming that bizarre or violent purpose, and we do not find sufficient evidence to permit a jury to say she was not.

Defendant's own testimony, if believed, would furnish a basis for her actions. She said she acted in self-defense, to ward off a sexual attack by McKinney and others. She recited the details of that attack and of her reaction to it with full recall and in explicit detail, explaining that her abuse of the police officers was sparked by her being upset by their unfairness in locking her up rather than apprehending McKinney.

Ordinarily, of course, the question of whether a defendant's asserted intoxication satisfies the standards enunciated in this opinion should be resolved by the jury. But here, viewing the evidence and the legitimate inferences to be drawn therefrom in the light most favorable to defendant, the best that can be made of the proof of intoxication is that defendant may have been extremely agitated and distraught. It may even be that a fact-finder could conclude that her powers of rational thought and deductive reasoning had been affected. But there is no suggestion in the evidence that defendant's faculties were so prostrated by her consumption of something less than a pint of wine as to render her incapable of purposeful or knowing conduct. The trial court correctly refused defendant's request.

To the extent that the basis for the trial court's ruling lay in its perception that an intoxication defense was inconsistent with self-defense and for that reason could not be allowed, the court was in error. A defendant may of course urge inconsistent defenses, and a trial court must charge the jury on both or all of them, despite any inconsistency, when there is sufficient evidence to warrant their submission to the jury. Because the evidence was insufficient to justify submission of the intoxication issue to the jury, the trial court's refusal to charge intoxication was correct.

VI

To recapitulate: (1) under the Code voluntary intoxication is a defense to a criminal charge that contains as an essential element proof that a defendant acted purposely or knowingly; (2) the Code definition of "intoxication" contemplates a condition by which the mental or physical capacities of the actor, because of the introduction of intoxicating substances into the body, are so prostrated as to render him incapable of purposeful or knowing conduct.

It is important to acknowledge as well what this opinion does *not* decide. Because the issues have not, at any point in the trial or appellate proceedings, been briefed or argued, we have not addressed the question of which party has the burden of producing evidence of intoxication when that evidence is relevant to the case, nor which party has the ultimate burden of persuasion and by what standard of proof. We say no more here in that regard than that of course the

State always has the burden of establishing all the essential elements of the charge beyond a reasonable doubt. This is, at bottom, a "sufficiency of the evidence" decision.

VII . . .

The judgment below is reversed and the cause is remanded to the Appellate Division for further proceedings consistent with this opinion.

3.   Can voluntary intoxication "cause" insanity?

Can an extremely intoxicated defendant raise an insanity defense on the basis that he was intoxicated?

State v. Cooper, 111 Ariz. 332 (1974)

HOLOHAN, Justice.

The appellant, Eugene Raymond Cooper, was convicted of kidnapping and assault with a deadly weapon for which he was sentenced to confinement for concurrent terms of 30 years to life for each offense. He appeals, raising the single issue of whether it was error for the trial court to refuse to submit the issue of insanity to the jury.

The appellant had been reported to the police as driving recklessly on the street and around a shopping center parking lot. A patrolman pursued appellant at high speed through rush-hour traffic. The appellant shot at and wounded the pursuing police officer. Shortly thereafter appellant kidnapped a man from a parking lot at gunpoint. The kidnap victim eventually wrestled the gun away from appellant, and the auto crashed into the divider on a freeway. Appellant fled on foot and was soon apprehended.

Pursuant to the request of the defense, an examination of the defendant's mental condition was ordered by the trial court. The court-appointed psychiatrists reported that the defendant was competent to assist his counsel and that the defendant understood the nature of the proceedings. A hearing was held, and the trial court found that the defendant was competent to stand trial.

The defendant gave timely notice of his intention to raise the defense of insanity at the trial.

During the trial the defense offered testimony by a psychiatrist and a psychologist as to the defendant's mental condition at the time of the offense. After hearing the evidence the trial court ruled that the evidence presented did not raise an issue as to the defendant's sanity, and the trial court refused all instructions submitted by the defense on the issue of sanity. The trial court did instruct the jury on the effect of voluntary intoxication in terms substantially the same as stated in the statute. A.R.S. §13–132.

There is a presumption of sanity in every criminal case. To rebut that presumption and cause sanity to become an issue in the case, the defendant must introduce sufficient evidence to generate a doubt as to his sanity. If the evidence generates a reasonable doubt as to sanity, the burden falls upon the state to prove sanity beyond a reasonable doubt. Arizona has long adhered to the rule that the test of insanity is the M'Naghten rule.

The defense argues that not only did the evidence presented generate a reasonable doubt of the defendant's sanity but it would fully support a finding that the defendant was insane at the time of the commission of the criminal acts charged. The defense points out that both the psychiatrist and psychologist testified that the defendant was insane under the M'Naghten standard.

The state concedes that each of the defense experts testified that the defendant did not know the nature and quality of his acts and that he did not know he was doing wrong at the time of the acts charged, but the state points out that the condition of the defendant's mind was caused by his use of drugs and this does not constitute the defense of insanity. We agree.

The record shows that both of the defense experts testified that without the use of the drugs during the time in question the defendant would have been sane. They agreed that it was the use of drugs which induced his mental incapacity. The psychiatrist described the condition of the defendant as toxic psychosis, and the psychologist labeled it as "acute drug induced psychotic episode."

The authorities have distinguished between an existing state of mental illness and a temporary episode of mental incapacity caused by the voluntary use of liquor or drugs. In the first instance the defense of insanity is available even though the state of mental illness may have been brought about by excessive or prolonged use of liquor or drugs, but in the latter instance the defense is not available. While the cases usually deal with excessive use of liquor, the same principles are applicable to drugs. Voluntary intoxication, whether by alcohol or drugs, is not a defense to crime, but evidence of such intoxication is admissible to show lack of specific intent.

It is not contested that the defendant had been voluntarily taking amphetamines for several days prior to the conduct at issue. Prior to that time the experts for the defense state that the defendant was sane. His subsequent condition, leading to his bizarre actions, was a result of an artificially produced state of mind brought on by his own hand at his own choice. The voluntary actions of the defendant do not provide an excuse in law for his subsequent, irrational conduct.

The defendant's burden to overcome the presumption of sanity was not met; therefore, the refusal of the trial court to instruct on insanity was correct.

Affirmed.

4. Statutory Abolition of the Voluntary Intoxication Defense

Montana v. Egelhoff, 518 U.S. 37 (1996)

Justice SCALIA announced the judgment of the Court and delivered an opinion, in which THE CHIEF JUSTICE, Justice KENNEDY, and Justice THOMAS join.

We consider in this case whether the Due Process Clause is violated by Montana Code Annotated §45–2–203, which provides, in relevant part, that voluntary intoxication "may not be taken into consideration in determining the existence of a mental state which is an element of [a criminal] offense."

I

In July 1992, while camping out in the Yaak region of northwestern Montana to pick mushrooms, respondent made friends with Roberta Pavola and John Christenson, who were doing the same. On Sunday, July 12, the three sold the mushrooms they had collected and spent the rest of the day and evening drinking, in bars and at a private party in Troy, Montana. Some time after 9 p.m., they left the party in Christenson's 1974 Ford Galaxy station wagon. The drinking binge apparently continued, as respondent was seen buying beer at 9:20 p.m. and recalled "sitting on a hill or a bank passing a bottle of Black Velvet back and forth" with Christenson.

At about midnight that night, officers of the Lincoln County, Montana, sheriff's department, responding to reports of a possible drunk driver, discovered Christenson's station wagon stuck in a ditch along U.S. Highway 2. In the front seat were Pavola and Christenson, each dead from a single gunshot to the head. In the rear of the car lay respondent, alive and yelling obscenities. His blood-alcohol content measured .36 percent over one hour later. On the floor of the car, near the brake pedal, lay respondent's .38-caliber handgun, with four loaded rounds and two empty casings; respondent had gunshot residue on his hands.

Respondent was charged with two counts of deliberate homicide, a crime defined by Montana law as "purposely" or "knowingly" causing the death of another human being. Mont. Code Ann. §45–5–102 (1995). A portion of the jury charge, uncontested here, instructed that "[a] person acts purposely when it is his conscious object to engage in conduct of that nature or to cause such a result," and that "[a] person acts knowingly when he is aware of his conduct or when he is aware under the circumstances his conduct constitutes a crime; or, when he is aware there exists the high probability that his conduct will cause a specific result." Respondent's defense at trial was that an unidentified fourth person must have committed the murders; his own extreme intoxication, he claimed, had rendered him physically incapable of committing the murders, and accounted for his inability to recall the events of the night of July 12. Although respondent was allowed to make this use of the evidence that he was intoxicated, the jury was instructed, pursuant to Mont. Code Ann. §45–2–203 (1995), that it could not consider respondent's "intoxicated condition . . . in determining the existence of a mental state which is an element of the offense." The jury found respondent guilty on both counts, and the court sentenced him to 84 years' imprisonment.

The Supreme Court of Montana reversed. It reasoned (1) that respondent "had a due process right to present and have considered by the jury all relevant evidence to rebut the State's evidence on all elements of the offense charged," and (2) that evidence of respondent's voluntary intoxication was "clear[ly] . . . relevant to the issue of whether [respondent] acted knowingly and purposely." Because §45–2–203 prevented the jury from considering that evidence with regard to that issue, the court concluded that the State had been "relieved of part of its burden to prove beyond a reasonable doubt every fact necessary to constitute the crime charged," and that respondent had therefore been denied due process. We granted certiorari.

II

The cornerstone of the Montana Supreme Court's judgment was the proposition that the Due Process Clause guarantees a defendant the right to present and have considered by the jury *"all relevant evidence* to rebut the State's evidence on all elements of the offense charged." (emphasis added). Respondent does not defend this categorical rule; he acknowledges that the right to present relevant evidence "has not been viewed as absolute." That is a wise concession, since the proposition that the Due Process Clause guarantees the right to introduce all relevant evidence is simply indefensible. As we have said: "The accused does not have an unfettered right to offer [evidence] that is incompetent, privileged, or otherwise inadmissible under standard rules of evidence." Relevant evidence may, for example, be excluded on account of a defendant's failure to comply with procedural requirements. And any number of familiar and unquestionably constitutional evidentiary rules also authorize the exclusion of relevant evidence. For example, Federal (and Montana) Rule of Evidence 403 provides: *"Although relevant,* evidence may be excluded if its probative value is substantially outweighed by the danger of unfair prejudice, confusion of the issues, or misleading the jury, or by considerations of undue delay, waste of time, or needless presentation of cumulative evidence." (Emphasis added.) Hearsay rules similarly prohibit the introduction of testimony which, though unquestionably relevant, is deemed insufficiently reliable. Of course, to say that the right to introduce relevant evidence is not absolute is not to say that the Due Process Clause places *no* limits upon restriction of that right. But it is to say that the defendant asserting such a limit must sustain the usual heavy burden that a due process claim entails:

> [P]reventing and dealing with crime is much more the
> business of the States than it is of the Federal Government,
> and . . . we should not lightly construe the Constitution so as

to intrude upon the administration of justice by the individual States. Among other things, it is normally 'within the power of the State to regulate procedures under which its laws are carried out,' . . . and its decision in this regard is not subject to proscription under the Due Process Clause unless 'it offends some principle of justice so rooted in the traditions and conscience of our people as to be ranked as fundamental.' Patterson v. New York, 432 U.S. 197, 201–202 (1977). . . .

Our primary guide in determining whether the principle in question is fundamental is, of course, historical practice. Here that gives respondent little support. By the laws of England, wrote Hale, the intoxicated defendant "shall have no privilege by this voluntary contracted madness, but shall have the same judgment as if he were in his right senses." 1 M. Hale, Pleas of the Crown 32–33. According to Blackstone and Coke, the law's condemnation of those suffering from *dementia affectata* was harsher still: Blackstone, citing Coke, explained that the law viewed intoxication "as an aggravation of the offence, rather than as an excuse for any criminal misbehaviour." 4 W. Blackstone, Commentaries 25–26. This stern rejection of inebriation as a defense became a fixture of early American law as well. The American editors of the 1847 edition of Hale wrote:

> Drunkenness, it was said in an early case, can never be received as a ground to excuse or palliate an offence: this is not merely the opinion of a speculative philosopher, the argument of counsel, or the *obiter dictum* of a single judge, but it is a sound and long established maxim of judicial policy, from which perhaps a single dissenting voice cannot be found. But if no other authority could be adduced, the uniform decisions of our own Courts from the first establishment of the government, would constitute it now a part of the common law of the land. 1 Hale, *supra*, at 32, n. 3.

In an opinion citing the foregoing passages from Blackstone and Hale, Justice Story rejected an objection to the exclusion of evidence of intoxication as follows:

> This is the first time, that I ever remember it to have been contended, that the commission of one crime was an excuse for another. Drunkenness is a gross vice, and in the contemplation of some of our laws is a crime; and I learned in my earlier studies, that so far from its being in law an excuse for murder, it is rather an aggravation of its malignity." United States v. Cornell, 25 F. Cas. 650, 657–658 (No. 14,868) (CC R.I. 1820).

The historical record does not leave room for the view that the common law's rejection of intoxication as an "excuse" or "justification" for crime would nonetheless permit the defendant to show that intoxication prevented the requisite *mens rea*. Hale, Coke, and Blackstone were familiar, to say the least, with the concept of *mens rea*, and acknowledged that drunkenness "deprive[s] men of the use of reason," 1 Hale, *supra*, at 32; see also Blackstone, *supra*, at 25. It is inconceivable that they did not realize that an offender's drunkenness might impair his ability to form the requisite intent; and inconceivable that their failure to note this massive exception from the general rule of disregard of intoxication was an oversight. Hale's statement that a drunken offender shall have the same judgment "as if he were in his right senses" must be understood as precluding a defendant from arguing that, because of his intoxication, he could not have possessed the *mens rea* required to commit the crime. . . .

Against this extensive evidence of a lengthy common-law tradition decidedly against him, the best argument available to respondent is the one made by his *amicus* and conceded by the State: Over the course of the 19th century, courts carved out an exception to the common law's traditional across-the-board condemnation of the drunken offender, allowing a jury to consider a defendant's intoxication when assessing whether he possessed the mental state needed to commit the crime charged, where the crime was one requiring a "specific intent." The emergence of this new rule is often traced to an 1819 English case, in which Justice Holroyd is reported to have held that "though voluntary drunkenness cannot excuse from the commission of crime, yet where, as on a charge of murder, the material question is, whether an act was premeditated or done only with sudden heat and impulse, the fact of the party being intoxicated [is] a circumstance proper to be taken into consideration." 1 W. Russell, Crimes and Misdemeanors 8. This exception was "slow to take root," however, even in England. Indeed, in the 1835 case of *King v. Carroll,* 173 Eng. Rep. 64, 65 (N. P.), Justice Park claimed that Holroyd had "retracted his opinion" in *Grindley,* and said "there is no doubt that that case is not law." In this country, as late as 1858 the Missouri Supreme Court could speak as categorically as this:

> To look for deliberation and forethought in a man maddened
> by intoxication is vain, for drunkenness has deprived him of
> the deliberating faculties to a greater or less extent; and if
> this deprivation is to relieve him of all responsibility or to
> diminish it, the great majority of crimes committed will go
> unpunished. This however is not the doctrine of the common
> law; and to its maxims, based as they obviously are upon
> true wisdom and sound policy, we must adhere. State v.
> Cross, 27 Mo. 332, 338 (1858).

And as late as 1878, the Vermont Supreme Court upheld the giving of the following instruction at a murder trial:

> The voluntary intoxication of one who without provocation
> commits a homicide, although amounting to a frenzy, that is,
> although the intoxication amounts to a frenzy, does not

excuse him from the same construction of his conduct, and
the same legal inferences upon the question of
premeditation and intent, as affecting the grade of his crime,
which are applicable to a person entirely sober. State v.
Tatro, 50 Vt. 483, 487 (1878).

Eventually, however, the new view won out, and by the end of the 19th century, in most American jurisdictions, intoxication could be considered in determining whether a defendant was capable of forming the specific intent necessary to commit the crime charged.

On the basis of this historical record, respondent's *amicus* argues that "[t]he old common-law rule . . . was no longer deeply rooted at the time the Fourteenth Amendment was ratified." That conclusion is questionable, but we need not pursue the point, since the argument of *amicus* mistakes the nature of our inquiry. It is not the State which bears the burden of demonstrating that its rule is "deeply rooted," but rather respondent who must show that the principle of procedure *violated* by the rule (and allegedly required by due process) is " 'so rooted in the traditions and conscience of our people as to be ranked as fundamental.' " Patterson v. New York, 432 U.S., at 202. Thus, even assuming that when the Fourteenth Amendment was adopted the rule Montana now defends was no longer generally applied, this only cuts off what might be called an *a fortiori* argument in favor of the State. The burden remains upon respondent to show that the "new common-law" rule—that intoxication may be considered on the question of intent—was so deeply rooted at the time of the Fourteenth Amendment (or perhaps has become so deeply rooted since) as to be a fundamental principle which that Amendment enshrined.

That showing has not been made. Instead of the uniform and continuing acceptance we would expect for a rule that enjoys "fundamental principle" status, we find that fully one-fifth of the States either never adopted the "new common-law" rule at issue here or have recently abandoned it.

It is not surprising that many States have held fast to or resurrected the common-law rule prohibiting consideration of voluntary intoxication in the determination of *mens rea,* because that rule has considerable justification—which alone casts doubt upon the proposition that the opposite rule is a "fundamental principle." A large number of crimes, especially violent crimes, are committed by intoxicated offenders; modern studies put the numbers as high as half of all homicides, for example. Disallowing consideration of voluntary intoxication has the effect of increasing the punishment for all unlawful acts committed in that state, and thereby deters drunkenness or irresponsible behavior while drunk. The rule also serves as a specific deterrent, ensuring that those who prove incapable of controlling violent impulses while voluntarily intoxicated go to prison. And finally, the rule comports with and implements society's moral perception that one who has voluntarily impaired his own faculties should be responsible for the consequences. . . .

In sum, not every widespread experiment with a procedural rule favorable to criminal defendants establishes a fundamental principle of justice. Although the rule allowing a jury to consider evidence of a defendant's voluntary intoxication where relevant to *mens rea* has gained considerable acceptance, it is of too recent vintage, and has not received sufficiently uniform and permanent allegiance, to qualify as fundamental, especially since it displaces a lengthy common-law tradition which remains supported by valid justifications today.

III . . .

"The doctrines of *actus reus, mens rea,* insanity, mistake, justification, and duress have historically provided the tools for a constantly shifting adjustment of the tension between the evolving aims of the criminal law and changing religious, moral, philosophical, and medical views of the nature of man. This process of adjustment has always been thought to be the province of the States." The people of Montana have decided to resurrect the rule of an earlier era, disallowing consideration of voluntary intoxication when a defendant's state of mind is at issue. Nothing in the Due Process Clause prevents them from doing so, and the judgment of the Supreme Court of Montana to the contrary must be reversed.

It is so ordered.

Justice O'CONNOR, with whom Justice STEVENS, Justice SOUTER, and Justice BREYER join, dissenting.

The Montana Supreme Court unanimously held that Mont.Code Ann. §45–2–203 (1995) violates due process. I agree. Our cases establish that due process sets an outer limit on the restrictions that may be placed on a defendant's ability to raise an effective defense to the State's accusations. Here, to impede the defendant's ability to throw doubt on the State's case, Montana has removed from the jury's consideration a category of evidence relevant to determination of mental state where that mental state is an essential element of the offense that must be proved beyond a reasonable doubt. Because this disallowance eliminates evidence with which the defense might negate an essential element, the State's burden to prove its case is made correspondingly easier. The justification for this disallowance is the State's desire to increase the likelihood of conviction of a certain class of defendants who might otherwise be able to prove that they did not satisfy a requisite element of the offense. In my view, the statute's effect on the criminal proceeding violates due process. . . .

C.   Involuntary Intoxication

Involuntary intoxication is still viewed as a valid defense in most jurisdictions. If a defendant becomes extremely intoxicated and is without fault in doing so, the law treats it in a similar way as an insanity defense: it is a complete defense to both general and specific intent crimes. Although rare, the defense is designed for those cases where (1) a defendant has an unexpected and extreme reaction to medication, (2) the defendant is coerced into consuming intoxicants, or (3) the defendant unknowingly consumes a substance that causes him or her to become intoxicated. *See* Joshua Dressler, *Understanding Criminal Law* §24.06 (6th ed. 2012).

D. Michigan's Voluntary Intoxication Defense Statute

M.C.L. §768.37. Defenses; voluntary consumption of alcoholic liquor, drug, or other substance or compound

(1) Except as provided in subsection (2), it is not a defense to any crime that the defendant was, at that time, under the influence of or impaired by a voluntarily and knowingly consumed alcoholic liquor, drug, including a controlled substance, other substance or compound, or combination of alcoholic liquor, drug, or other substance or compound.

(2) It is an affirmative defense to a specific intent crime, for which the defendant has the burden of proof by a preponderance of the evidence, that he or she voluntarily consumed a legally obtained and properly used medication or other substance and did not know and reasonably should not have known that he or she would become intoxicated or impaired.

(3) As used in this section:

(a) "Alcoholic liquor" means that term as defined in section 105 of the Michigan liquor control code of 1998, 1998 PA 58, MCL 436. 1105.

(b) "Consumed" means to have eaten, drunk, ingested, inhaled, injected, or topically applied, or to have performed any combination of those actions, or otherwise introduced into the body.

(c) "Controlled substance" means that term as defined in section 7104 of the public health code, 1978 PA 368, MCL 333.7104.

E. Practice Problems on Intoxication

Defendant was accused of robbing a convenience store. Because Defendant threatened the store employee with a large meat fork, the prosecutor charged him with armed robbery. According to the employee,

Defendant came in late at night while no other customers were in the store and demanded all the money in the cash register, two packs of Camel cigarettes, and two bottles of expensive whiskey. The employee identified Defendant as the robber and told police he was a regular customer who usually just bought cheap alcohol and cigarettes. The employee also told police that because he knew Defendant, he had tried to talk Defendant out of committing the robbery. But Defendant did not listen and seemed to be "pretty drunk."

When the police found Defendant the next morning and arrested him, Defendant said he had no memory of the night before. He said he had been drinking heavily for two days and was "really sorry" if he hurt anyone.

Defendant plans to raise an intoxication defense to the armed robbery charge. What should the defense attorney argue in support of the defense? What should the prosecutor argue in opposition? What verdict should the jury return if they accept Defendant's defense?

F. Model Penal Code Provisions

§2.08. Intoxication

(1) Except as provided in Subsection (4) of this Section, intoxication of the actor is not a defense unless it negatives an element of the offense.

(2) When recklessness establishes an element of the offense, if the actor, due to self-induced intoxication, is unaware of a risk of which he would have been aware had he been sober, such unawareness is immaterial.

(3) Intoxication does not, in itself, constitute mental disease within the meaning of Section 4.01.

(4) Intoxication that (a) is not self-induced or (b) is pathological is an affirmative defense if by reason of such intoxication the actor at the time of his conduct lacks substantial capacity either to appreciate its criminality [wrongfulness] or to conform his conduct to the requirements of law.

(5) Definitions. In this Section unless a different meaning plainly is required:

(a) "intoxication" means a disturbance of mental or physical capacities resulting from the introduction of substances into the body;

(b) "self-induced intoxication" means intoxication caused by substances that the actor knowingly introduces into his body, the tendency of which to cause intoxication he knows or ought to know, unless he introduces them pursuant to medical advice or under such circumstances as would afford a defense to a charge of crime;

(c) "pathological intoxication" means intoxication grossly excessive in degree, given the amount of the intoxicant, to which the actor does not know he is susceptible.

Chapter 16
Mistake

A. Introduction

Mistake defenses are divided into two categories: (1) mistake of law and (2) mistake of fact. Although the analysis of the two defenses is somewhat different, the end result is the same. Generally speaking, a defendant can claim a valid mistake defense if the mistake (of law or fact) negates the requisite mens rea.

Basing a defense on mistake of law is more complicated because there is a general rule—ignorance of the law is no defense—that must be overcome. If the defendant misinterprets the criminal law (*Marrero*), he generally cannot raise that as a defense. However, if he misinterprets a non-penal law (*Weiss*) and his mistake negates the required mens rea, he likely does have a defense. Finally, there are rare occasions when ignorance of the criminal law can provide a defense where the criminal statute itself requires that the defendant willfully or knowingly violate the law.

Mistake or ignorance of fact cases are typically easier to resolve. The questions are, simply, (1) did the defendant make a mistake about a factual situation, and, if so, (2) did that mistake negate her mens rea for the crime. As you will soon see, the availability of the defense often depends on whether the mistake was honest (and, in some instances, also reasonable). *See generally* Joshua Dressler, *Understanding Criminal Law* §§12.01–12.04, 13.01–13.03 (6th ed. 2012).

B.   Mistake of Law

1.   Reasonable Reliance Doctrine: Can a defense be based on an actor's own interpretation of the penal law?

Marrero explores whether mistake of law is a viable defense when the defendant misinterprets—arguably reasonably—the criminal law. It also reaffirms the general rule that ignorance of the criminal law is no defense.

People v. Marrero, 69 N.Y.2d 382 (1987)

BELLACOSA, Judge.

The defense of mistake of law is not available to a Federal corrections officer arrested in a Manhattan social club for possession of a loaded .38 caliber automatic pistol who claimed he mistakenly believed he was entitled, pursuant to the interplay of CPL 2.10, 1.20 and Penal Law §265.20, to carry a handgun without a permit as a peace officer. . . .

On the trial of the case, the court rejected the defendant's argument that his personal misunderstanding of the statutory definition of a peace officer is enough to excuse him from criminal liability under New York's mistake of law statute. The court refused to charge the jury on this issue and defendant was convicted of criminal possession of a weapon in the third degree. We affirm the Appellate Division order upholding the conviction.

Defendant was a Federal corrections officer in Danbury, Connecticut, and asserted that status at the time of his arrest in 1977. He claimed at trial that there were various interpretations of fellow officers and teachers, as well as the peace officer statute itself, upon which he relied for his mistaken belief that he could carry a weapon with legal impunity.

The starting point for our analysis is the New York mistake statute as an outgrowth of the dogmatic common-law maxim that ignorance of the law is no excuse. The central issue is whether defendant's personal misreading or misunderstanding of a statute may excuse criminal conduct in the circumstances of this case.

The common-law rule on mistake of law was clearly articulated in Gardner v. People, (62 N.Y. 299). In *Gardner,* the defendants misread a statute and mistakenly believed that their conduct was legal. The court insisted, however, that the "mistake of law" did not relieve the defendants of criminal liability. The statute at issue, relating to the removal of election officers, required that prior to removal, written notice must be given to the officer sought to be removed. The statute provided one exception to the notice requirement: "removal . . . shall only be made after notice in writing . . . unless made while the inspector is actually on duty on a day of registration, revision of registration, or election, and for improper conduct." The defendants construed the statute to mean that an election officer could be removed without notice for improper conduct at any time. The court ruled that removal without notice could only occur for improper conduct on a day of registration, revision of registration or election.

In ruling that the defendant's misinterpretation of the statute was no defense, the court said: "The defendants made a mistake of law. Such mistakes do not excuse the commission of prohibited acts. 'The rule on the subject appears to be, that in acts *mala in se,* the intent governs, but in those *mala prohibita,* the only inquiry is, has the law been violated?' The act prohibited must be intentionally done. A mistake as to the fact of doing the act will excuse the party, but if the act is intentionally done, the statute declares it a misdemeanor, irrespective of the motive or intent . . . The evidence offered [showed] that the defendants were of [the] opinion that the statute did not require notice to be given before removal. This opinion, if entertained in good faith, mitigated the character of the act, but was not a defence *[sic]."* . . .

The desirability of the *Gardner*-type outcome, which was to encourage the societal benefit of individuals' knowledge of and respect for the law, is underscored by Justice Holmes' statement: "It is no doubt true that there are many cases in which the criminal could not have known that he was breaking the law, but to admit the excuse at all would be to encourage ignorance where the law-maker has determined to make men know and obey, and justice to the individual is rightly outweighed by the larger interests on the other side of the scales" (Holmes, The Common Law, at 48 [1881]).

The revisors of New York's Penal Law intended no fundamental departure from this common-law rule in Penal Law §15.20, which provides in pertinent part:

§15.20. *Effect of ignorance or mistake upon liability.* . . .

2. A person is not relieved of criminal liability for conduct because he engages in such conduct under a mistaken belief that it does not, as a matter of law, constitute an offense, unless such mistaken belief is founded upon an official statement of the law contained in (a) a statute or other enactment . . . (d) an interpretation of the statute or law relating to the offense, officially made or issued by a public servant, agency, or body legally charged or empowered with the responsibility or privilege of administering, enforcing or interpreting such statute or law.

This section was added to the Penal Law as part of the wholesale revision of the Penal Law in 1965. When this provision was first proposed, commentators viewed the new language as codifying "the established common law maxim on mistake of law, while at the same time recognizing a defense when the erroneous belief is founded upon an 'official statement of the law' " (Note, Proposed Penal Law of New York, 64 Colum L Rev 1469, 1486 [1964]).

The defendant claims as a first prong of his defense that he is entitled to raise the defense of mistake of law under section 15.20(2)(a) because his mistaken belief that his conduct was legal was founded upon an official statement of the law contained in the statute itself. Defendant argues that his mistaken interpretation of the statute was reasonable in view of the alleged ambiguous wording of the peace officer exemption statute, and that his "reasonable" interpretation of an "official statement" is enough to satisfy the requirements of subdivision (2)(a). However, the whole thrust of this exceptional exculpatory concept, in derogation of the traditional and common-law principle, was intended to be a very narrow escape valve. Application in this case would invert that thrust and make mistake of law a generally applied or available defense instead of an unusual exception which the very opening words of the mistake statute make so clear, i.e., "A person is not relieved of criminal liability for conduct . . . unless." The momentarily enticing argument by defendant that his view of the statute would only allow a defendant to get the issue generally before a jury further supports the contrary view because that consequence is precisely what would give the defense the unintended broad practical application.

The prosecution further counters defendant's argument by asserting that one cannot claim the protection of mistake of law under section 15.20(2)(a) simply by misconstruing the meaning of a statute but must instead establish that the statute relied on actually permitted the conduct in question and was only later found to be erroneous. To buttress that argument, the People analogize New York's official statement defense to the approach taken by the Model Penal Code (MPC). Section 2.04 of the MPC provides:

Section 2.04. *Ignorance or Mistake.*

(3) A belief that conduct does not legally constitute an offense is a defense to a prosecution for that offense based upon such conduct when . . . (b) he acts in reasonable reliance upon an official statement of the law, *afterward determined to be invalid or erroneous,* contained in (i) a statute or other enactment" (emphasis added).

Although the drafters of the New York statute did not adopt the precise language of the Model Penal Code provision with the emphasized clause, it is evident and has long been believed that the Legislature intended the New York statute to be similarly construed. In fact, the legislative history of section 15.20 is replete with references to the influence of the Model Penal Code provision. The proposition that New York adopted the MPC general approach finds additional support in the comments to section 2.04. It is not without significance that no one for over 20 years of this statute's existence has made a point of arguing or noting or holding that the difference in wording has the broad and dramatically sweeping interpretation which is now proposed. Such a turnabout would surely not have been accidentally produced or allowed. . . .

It was early recognized that the "official statement" mistake of law defense was a statutory protection against prosecution based on reliance of a statute that did *in fact* authorize certain conduct. "It seems obvious that society must rely on some statement of the law, and that conduct which *is in fact* 'authorized' . . . should not be subsequently condemned. The threat of punishment under these circumstances can have no deterrent effect unless the actor doubts the validity of the official pronouncement—*a questioning of authority that is itself undesirable* " (Note, Proposed Penal Law of New York, 64 Colum.L.Rev. 1469, 1486 [emphasis added]). While providing a narrow escape hatch, the idea was simultaneously to encourage the public to read and rely on official statements of the law, not to have individuals conveniently and personally question the validity and interpretation of the law and act on that basis. If later the statute was invalidated, one who mistakenly acted in reliance on the authorizing statute would be relieved of criminal liability. That makes sense and is fair. To go further does not make sense and would create a legal chaos based on individual selectivity.

In the case before us, the underlying statute never *in fact authorized* the defendant's conduct; the defendant only thought that the statutory exemptions permitted his conduct when, in fact, the primary statute clearly forbade his conduct. Moreover, by adjudication of the final court to speak on the subject in this very case, it turned out that even the exemption statute did not permit this defendant to possess the weapon. It would be ironic at best and an odd perversion at worst for this court now to declare that the same defendant is nevertheless free of criminal responsibility.

The "official statement" component in the mistake of law defense in both paragraphs (a) and (d) adds yet another element of support for our interpretation and holding. Defendant tried to establish a defense under Penal Law §15.20(2)(d) as a second prong. But the interpretation of the statute relied upon must be "officially made or issued by a public servant, agency or body legally charged or empowered with the responsibility or privilege of administering, enforcing or interpreting such statute or law." We agree with the People that the trial court also properly rejected the defense under Penal Law §15.20(2)(d) since none of the interpretations which defendant proffered meets the requirements of the statute. The fact that there are various complementing exceptions to section 15.20, none of which defendant could bring himself under, further emphasizes the correctness of our view which decides this case under particular statutes with appropriate precedential awareness.

It must also be emphasized that, while our construction of Penal Law §15.20 provides for narrow application of the mistake of law defense, it does not, as the dissenters contend, "rule out *any* defense based on mistake of law." To the contrary, mistake of law is a viable exemption in those instances where an individual demonstrates an effort to learn what the law is, relies on the validity of that law and, later, it is determined that there was a *mistake in the law itself.*

The modern availability of this defense is based on the theory that where the government has affirmatively, albeit unintentionally, misled an individual as to what may or may not be legally permissible conduct, the individual should not be punished as a result. This is salutary and enlightened and should be firmly supported in appropriate cases. However, it also follows that where, as here, the government is not responsible for the error (for there is none except in the defendant's own mind), mistake of law should not be available as an excuse. . . .

We recognize that some legal scholars urge that the mistake of law defense should be available more broadly where a defendant misinterprets a potentially ambiguous statute not previously clarified by judicial decision and reasonably believes in good faith that the acts were legal. Professor Perkins, a leading supporter of this view, has said: "[i]f the meaning of a statute is not clear, and has not been judicially determined, one who has acted 'in good faith' should not be held guilty of crime if his conduct would have been proper had the statute meant what he 'reasonably believed' it to mean, even if the court should decide later that the proper construction is otherwise." . . . In this case, the forbidden act of possessing a weapon is clear and unambiguous, and only by the interplay of a double exemption does defendant seek to escape criminal responsibility, i.e., the peace officer statute and the mistake statute.

We conclude that the better and correctly construed view is that the defense should not be recognized, except where specific intent is an element of the offense or where the misrelied-upon law has later been properly adjudicated as wrong. Any broader view fosters lawlessness. It has been said in support of our preferred view in relation to other available procedural protections: "A statute . . . which is so indefinite that it 'either forbids or requires the doing of an act in terms so vague that men of common intelligence must necessarily guess at its meaning and differ as to its application, violates the first essential of due process of law' and is unconstitutional. If the court feels that a statute is sufficiently definite to meet this test, it is hard to see why a defense of mistake of law is needed. Such a statute could hardly mislead the defendant into believing that his acts were not criminal, if they do in fact come under its ban . . . [I]f the defense of mistake of law based on indefiniteness is raised, the court is . . . going to require proof . . . that the act was sufficiently definite to guide the conduct of reasonable men. Thus, the need for such a defense is largely supplied by the constitutional guarantee."

Strong public policy reasons underlie the legislative mandate and intent which we perceive in rejecting defendant's construction of New York's mistake of law defense statute. If defendant's argument were accepted, the exception would swallow the rule. Mistakes about the law would be encouraged, rather than respect for and adherence to law. There would be an infinite number of mistake of law defenses which could be devised from a good-faith, perhaps reasonable but mistaken, interpretation of criminal statutes, many of which are concededly complex. Even more troublesome are the opportunities for wrongminded individuals to contrive in bad faith solely to get an exculpatory notion before the jury. These are not *in terrorem* arguments disrespectful of appropriate adjudicative procedures; rather, they are the realistic and practical consequences were the dissenters' views to prevail. Our holding comports with a statutory scheme which was not designed to allow false and diversionary stratagems to be provided for many more cases than the statutes contemplated. This would not serve the ends of justice but rather would serve game playing and evasion from properly imposed criminal responsibility.

Accordingly, the order of the Appellate Division should be affirmed.

2. When can the actor's misinterpretation of a non-penal law provide a defense?

Like *Marrero*, *People v. Weiss* involves an argument based on the defendant's misinterpretation of the law, but it is not the penal law that the defendant misinterpreted. In reading *Weiss*, focus on the law he wrongly interpreted. Notice that he did not argue that he did not know kidnapping was against the law.

People v. Weiss, 276 N.Y. 384 (1938)

O'BRIEN, Judge.

These appellants, without authority of law, seized and confined Paul H. Wendel, who was suspected or whom some pretended to suspect of the commission of a murder in New Jersey which had attracted attention throughout the country. They have been convicted of the crime of kidnapping as defined by section 1250 of the Penal Law, which provides: "A person who wilfully: 1. Seizes, confines, inveigles, or kidnaps another, with intent to cause him, without authority of law, to be secretly confined or imprisoned within this state, or to be sent out of the state or to be sold as a slave, or in any way held to service or kept or detained, against his will . . . is guilty of kidnapping."

. . . In order to make out the crime of kidnapping, proof beyond a reasonable doubt must be produced that the defendant willfully intended, without authority of law, to confine or imprison another. To illustrate the difference: A reputable citizen is approached by a man, clothed in a police uniform and wearing a police shield, who requests him to assist in the arrest of one whom he describes as a murderer. The law-abiding citizen, in good faith and in the belief that he is performing his duty, assists the uniformed stranger and participates in the arrest of one who is entirely innocent. While the citizen may be answerable in damages in a civil action, he is not guilty of the crime of kidnapping, even though proof is later adduced that the uniformed stranger is an imposter and a kidnapper. In such a case, far from intending to seize or confine the prisoner without authority of law, he believed that his act was with such authority. In prosecutions for kidnapping, therefore, willful intent to seize a person without authority of law is the essential issue. Inferences of fact as to intent depend upon the degree of credibility accorded to witnesses by the jury and may be drawn from the defendant's disbelief or belief in the legality of his act. For the purpose of enabling the jury to draw its inference of fact, a defendant is entitled to the right of informing the jury in respect to his belief. His testimony may be of such a character as to fail to convince a jury, yet, nevertheless, he is entitled as a legal right to produce it for what it may be worth and to have it considered by the jury.

Appellant Schlossman testified that, prior to the seizure of Wendel, he had a conversation with appellant Weiss and with Ellis Parker, Jr., at a hotel in New York. His counsel attempted to introduce testimony in relation to statements by Parker, for the purpose of showing Schlossman's belief in his authority to act, but the offer was excluded and an exception taken. The following statement by Schlossman to Parker was, however, admitted: "I have got to have something to show that I am doing something within the law, helping you out this way, so he took out a badge, Secret Service of the State of New Jersey, and gave it to me and said he is hereby appointing me a special deputy to help him in the Lindbergh case." The questions, "Did you desire to help a detective solve any part of the Lindbergh mystery at that time?" and "Did you think at that time that you were taking part in some noble work?" were excluded and exceptions taken. The court stated: "That does not affect the question of his innocence or guilt, what he thought about those matters." Exception was taken to the exclusion of testimony by which appellant Weiss attempted to show that Parker had informed him of his official position and also to the exclusion of testimony by Weiss that he believed that the arrest of Wendel was made with authority of law. The following testimony in relation to a conversation between Weiss and Parker was stricken out and an exception noted: "I said, 'Now, listen. Suppose I arrest this man and we use these badges and he raises an outcry, and it proves to be an arrest illegally and there is police all over the street and the neighborhood and they should happen to come over. What happens then?' He [Parker] said: 'Well, that is what I am here for.' He says, 'You have the proper authority and if they question you I am there to prove who I am and whatever you done is the proper thing. Q. Did you believe that—what he told you? A. Yes." Exception was taken also to the ruling which sustained objection to this question directed to Weiss: "Did you believe that you were doing your Police work?"

Counsel for defendants requested: "That if the defendants, or either of them, acted in the honest belief that his act in seizing and confining Wendel was done with authority of law, even if they were mistaken in such belief, that they cannot be convicted of seizing, confining or kidnapping Wendel, with intent, to cause him without authority of law to be confined or imprisoned within the State, and the jury must acquit such defendants or defendant." To this request the court replied: "I not only decline to charge that but I repeat that the question of good faith is no defense." The jury was also instructed that "even if they [defendants] did believe it, it is no defense in this case." If such interpretation is to prevail, then it must follow that in every instance where a defendant admits the fact that he intended to make the arrest and the courts later declare the arrest to have been made without authority of law, he must necessarily be convicted as a kidnapper, irrespective of his belief or his intentions to conform with the law. A peace officer, in the mistaken belief that he is acting with authority of law, makes an illegal arrest and later, in an effort to extort a confession, puts his prisoner through the third degree. He is guilty of the crime of assault or of official oppression, but he is certainly not a kidnapper. The question of assault is not in this case. So the trial judge charged.

The intent of defendants to seize and confine Wendel cannot be doubted, but their intent to perform these acts without authority of law depends upon the state of mind of the actors. If in good faith they believed that they were acting within the law, there could have been no intent to act "without authority of law." Their belief or disbelief indicates intent or lack of it, and they were entitled to testify in respect to their intent based upon their belief.

No matter how doubtful the credibility of these defendants may be or how suspicious the circumstances may appear, we cannot say as matter of law that, even in so strong a case as this for the prosecution, the jury was not entitled to consider the question whether defendants in good faith believed that they were acting with authority of law. We are, therefore, constrained to reverse the judgment of conviction and order a new trial for the purpose of submitting that question of fact to the jury.

The judgments should be reversed and a new trial ordered.

3. Importance of Statutory Language

Can the penal statute itself sometimes give the defendant a potential mistake of law defense? Why are adverbs important in statutory construction?

Ratzlaf v. United States, 510 U.S. 135 (1994)

Justice GINSBURG delivered the opinion of the Court.

Federal law requires banks and other financial institutions to file reports with the Secretary of the Treasury whenever they are involved in a cash transaction that exceeds $10,000. It is illegal to "structure" transactions—*i.e.,* to break up a single transaction above the reporting threshold into two or more separate transactions—for the purpose of evading a financial institution's reporting requirement. "A person willfully violating" this antistructuring provision is subject to criminal penalties. This case presents a question on which Courts of Appeals have divided: Does a defendant's purpose to circumvent a bank's reporting obligation suffice to sustain a conviction for "willfully violating" the antistructuring provision? We hold that the "willfulness" requirement mandates something more. To establish that a defendant "willfully violat[ed]" the antistructuring law, the Government must prove that the defendant acted with knowledge that his conduct was unlawful.

I

On the evening of October 20, 1988, defendant-petitioner Waldemar Ratzlaf ran up a debt of $160,000 playing blackjack at the High Sierra Casino in Reno, Nevada. The casino gave him one week to pay. On the due date, Ratzlaf returned to the casino with cash of $100,000 in hand. A casino official informed Ratzlaf that all transactions involving more than $10,000 in cash had to be reported to state and federal authorities. The official added that the casino could accept a cashier's check for the full amount due without triggering any reporting requirement. The casino helpfully placed a limousine at Ratzlaf's disposal, and assigned an employee to accompany him to banks in the vicinity. Informed that banks, too, are required to report cash transactions in excess of $10,000, Ratzlaf purchased cashier's checks, each for less than $10,000 and each from a different bank. He delivered these checks to the High Sierra Casino.

Based on this endeavor, Ratzlaf was charged with "structuring transactions" to evade the banks' obligation to report cash transactions exceeding $10,000; this conduct, the indictment alleged, violated 31 U.S.C. §§5322(a) and 5324(3). The trial judge instructed the jury that the Government had to prove defendant's knowledge of the banks' reporting obligation and his attempt to evade that obligation, but did not have to prove defendant knew the structuring was unlawful. Ratzlaf was convicted, fined, and sentenced to prison.

Ratzlaf maintained on appeal that he could not be convicted of "willfully violating" the antistructuring law solely on the basis of his knowledge that a financial institution must report currency transactions in excess of $10,000 and his intention to avoid such reporting. To gain a conviction for "willful" conduct, he asserted, the Government must prove he was aware of the illegality of the "structuring" in which he engaged. . . . We . . . now conclude that, to give effect to the statutory "willfulness" specification, the Government had to prove Ratzlaf knew the structuring he undertook was unlawful. We therefore reverse the judgment of the Court of Appeals.

II

A

Congress enacted the Currency and Foreign Transactions Reporting Act in 1970 in response to increasing use of banks and other institutions as financial intermediaries by persons engaged in criminal activity. The Act imposes a variety of reporting requirements on individuals and institutions regarding foreign and domestic financial transactions. The reporting requirement relevant here, §5313(a), applies to domestic financial transactions. Section 5313(a) reads:

> When a domestic financial institution is involved in a transaction for the payment, receipt, or transfer of United States coins or currency (or other monetary instruments the Secretary of the Treasury prescribes), in an amount, denomination, or amount and denomination, or under

circumstances the Secretary prescribes by regulation, the institution and any other participant in the transaction the Secretary may prescribe shall file a report on the transaction at the time and in the way the Secretary prescribes. . . .

To deter circumvention of this reporting requirement, Congress enacted an antistructuring provision, 31 U.S.C. §5324, as part of the Money Laundering Control Act of 1986, which Ratzlaf is charged with "willfully violating," reads:

No person shall for the purpose of evading the reporting requirements of section 5313(a) with respect to such transaction—. . .

(3) structure or assist in structuring, or attempt to structure or assist in structuring, any transaction with one or more domestic financial institutions.

The criminal enforcement provision at issue, 31 U.S.C. §5322(a), sets out penalties for "[a] person willfully violating," *inter alia,* the antistructuring provision. Section 5322(a) reads:

A person willfully violating this subchapter or a regulation prescribed under this subchapter shall be fined not more than $250,000, or [imprisoned] for not more than five years, or both.

B

Section 5324 forbids structuring transactions with a "purpose of evading the reporting requirements of section 5313(a)." Ratzlaf admits that he structured cash transactions, and that he did so with knowledge of, and a purpose to avoid, the banks' duty to report currency transactions in excess of $10,000. The statutory formulation under which Ratzlaf was prosecuted, however, calls for proof of "willful[ness]" on the actor's part. The trial judge in Ratzlaf's case, with the Ninth Circuit's approbation, treated §5322(a)'s "willfulness" requirement essentially as surplusage—as words of no consequence. Judges should hesitate so to treat statutory terms in any setting, and resistance should be heightened when the words describe an element of a criminal offense.

"Willful," this Court has recognized, is a "word of many meanings," and "its construction [is] often . . . influenced by its context." Spies v. United States, 317 U.S. 492, 497 (1943). Accordingly, we view §§5322(a) and 5324(3) mindful of the complex of provisions in which they are embedded. In this light, we count it significant that §5322(a)'s omnibus "willfulness" requirement, when applied to other provisions in the same subchapter, consistently has been read by the Courts of Appeals to require both "knowledge of the reporting requirement" *and* a "specific intent to commit the crime," *i.e.,* "a purpose to disobey the law."

Notable in this regard are 31 U.S.C. §5314 [concerning records and reports on monetary transactions with foreign financial agencies] and §5316 [concerning declaration of the transportation of more than $10,000 into, or out of, the United States]. Decisions involving these provisions describe a "willful" actor as one who violates "a known legal duty." . . .

A term appearing in several places in a statutory text is generally read the same way each time it appears. We have even stronger cause to construe a *single* formulation, here §5322(a), the same way each time it is called into play.

The United States urges, however, that §5324 violators, by their very conduct, exhibit a purpose to do wrong, which suffices to show "willfulness":

> On occasion, criminal statutes—including some requiring proof of 'willfulness'—have been understood to require proof of an intentional violation of a known legal duty, *i.e.*, specific knowledge by the defendant that his conduct is unlawful. But where that construction has been adopted, it has been invoked only to ensure that the defendant acted with a wrongful purpose. . . .

> The anti-structuring statute, 31 U.S.C. §5324, satisfies the 'bad purpose' component of willfulness by explicitly defining the wrongful purpose necessary to violate the law: it requires proof that the defendant acted with the purpose to evade the reporting requirement of Section 5313(a). Brief for United States 23–25.

" '[S]tructuring is not the kind of activity that an ordinary person would engage in innocently,' " the United States asserts. It is therefore "reasonable," the Government concludes, "to hold a structurer responsible for evading the reporting requirements without the need to prove specific knowledge that such evasion is unlawful." Brief for United States 29.

Undoubtedly there are bad men who attempt to elude official reporting requirements in order to hide from Government inspectors such criminal activity as laundering drug money or tax evasion. But currency structuring is not inevitably nefarious. Consider, for example, the small business operator who knows that reports filed under 31 U.S.C. §5313(a) are available to the Internal Revenue Service. To reduce the risk of an IRS audit, she brings $9,500 in cash to the bank twice each week, in lieu of transporting over $10,000 once each week. That person, if the United States is right, has committed a criminal offense, because she structured cash transactions "for the specific purpose of depriving the Government of the information that Section 5313(a) is designed to obtain." Nor is a person who structures a currency transaction invariably motivated by a desire to keep the Government in the dark. But under the Government's construction an individual would commit a felony against the United States by making cash deposits in small doses, fearful that the bank's reports would increase the likelihood of burglary, or in an endeavor to keep a former spouse unaware of his wealth.

Courts have noted "many occasions" on which persons, without violating any law, may structure transactions "in order to avoid the impact of some regulation or tax." This Court, over a century ago, supplied an illustration:

> The Stamp Act of 1862 imposed a duty of two cents upon a bank-check, when drawn for an amount not less than twenty dollars. A careful individual, having the amount of twenty dollars to pay, pays the same by handing to his creditor two checks of ten dollars each. He thus draws checks in payment of his debt to the amount of twenty dollars, and yet pays no stamp duty. . . . While his operations deprive the government of the duties it might reasonably expect to receive, it is not perceived that the practice is open to the charge of fraud. He resorts to devices to avoid the payment of duties, but they are not illegal. He has the legal right to split up his evidences of payment, and thus to avoid the tax. United States v. Isham, 84 U.S. (17 Wall.) 496, 506, (1873).

In current days, as an *amicus* noted, countless taxpayers each year give a gift of $10,000 on December 31 and an identical gift the next day, thereby legitimately avoiding the taxable gifts reporting required by 26 U.S.C. §2503(b).

In light of these examples, we are unpersuaded by the argument that structuring is so obviously "evil" or inherently "bad" that the "willfulness" requirement is satisfied irrespective of the defendant's knowledge of the illegality of structuring. Had Congress wished to dispense with the requirement, it could have furnished the appropriate instruction.

In §5322, Congress subjected to criminal penalties only those "willfully violating" §5324, signaling its intent to require for conviction proof that the defendant knew not only of the bank's duty to report cash transactions in excess of $10,000, but also of his duty not to avoid triggering such a report. There are, we recognize, contrary indications in the statute's legislative history. But we do not resort to legislative history to cloud a statutory text that is clear. Moreover, were we to find §5322(a)'s "willfulness" requirement ambiguous as applied to §5324, we would resolve any doubt in favor of the defendant. Hughey v. United States, 495 U.S. 411, 422 (1990) (lenity principles "demand resolution of ambiguities in criminal statutes in favor of the defendant"); Crandon v. United States, 494 U.S. 152, 160 (1990) ("Because construction of a criminal statute must be guided by the need for fair warning, it is rare that legislative history or statutory policies will support a construction of a statute broader than that clearly warranted by the text."); United States v. Bass, 404 U.S. 336, 347–350 (1971) (rule of lenity premised on concepts that " 'fair warning should be given to the world in language that the common world will understand, of what the law intends to do if a certain line is passed' " and that "legislatures and not courts should define criminal activity") (quoting McBoyle v. United States, 283 U.S. 25, 27 (1931) (Holmes, J.)).

We do not dishonor the venerable principle that ignorance of the law generally is no defense to a criminal charge. In particular contexts, however, Congress may decree otherwise. That, we hold, is what Congress has done with respect to 31 U.S.C. §5322(a) and the provisions it controls. To convict Ratzlaf of the crime with which he was charged, violation of 31 U.S.C. §§5322(a) and 5324(3), the jury had to find he knew the structuring in which he engaged was unlawful. Because the jury was not properly instructed in this regard, we reverse the judgment of the Ninth Circuit and remand this case for further proceedings consistent with this opinion.

It is so ordered.

Note

In 1996, two short years after the *Ratzlaff* decision, Congress amended 31 U.S.C. §5322 to eliminate the willfulness requirement.

Cheek v. United States, 498 U.S. 192 (1991)

Justice WHITE delivered the opinion of the Court.

Title 26, §7201 of the United States Code provides that any person "who willfully attempts in any manner to evade or defeat any tax imposed by this title or the payment thereof" shall be guilty of a felony. Under 26 U.S.C. §7203, "[a]ny person required under this title . . . or by regulations made under authority thereof to make a return . . . who willfully fails to . . . make such return" shall be guilty of a misdemeanor. This case turns on the meaning of the word "willfully" as used in §§7201 and 7203.

I

Petitioner John L. Cheek has been a pilot for American Airlines since 1973. He filed federal income tax returns through 1979 but thereafter ceased to file returns. He also claimed an increasing number of withholding allowances— eventually claiming 60 allowances by mid-1980—and for the years 1981 to 1984 indicated on his W-4 forms that he was exempt from federal income taxes. In 1983, petitioner unsuccessfully sought a refund of all tax withheld by his employer in 1982. Petitioner's income during this period at all times far exceeded the minimum necessary to trigger the statutory filing requirement.

As a result of his activities, petitioner was indicted for 10 violations of federal law. He was charged with six counts of willfully failing to file a federal income tax return for the years 1980, 1981, and 1983 through 1986, in violation of §7203. He was further charged with three counts of willfully attempting to evade his income taxes for the years 1980, 1981, and 1983 in violation of 26 U.S.C. §7201. In those years, American Airlines withheld substantially less than the amount of tax petitioner owed because of the numerous allowances and exempt status he claimed on his W-4 forms. The tax offenses with which petitioner was charged are specific intent crimes that require the defendant to have acted willfully.

At trial, the evidence established that between 1982 and 1986, petitioner was involved in at least four civil cases that challenged various aspects of the federal income tax system. In all four of those cases, the plaintiffs were informed by the courts that many of their arguments, including that they were not taxpayers within the meaning of the tax laws, that wages are not income, that the Sixteenth Amendment does not authorize the imposition of an income tax on individuals, and that the Sixteenth Amendment is unenforceable, were frivolous or had been repeatedly rejected by the courts. During this time period, petitioner also attended at least two criminal trials of persons charged with tax offenses. In addition, there was evidence that in 1980 or 1981 an attorney had advised Cheek that the courts had rejected as frivolous the claim that wages are not income.

Cheek represented himself at trial and testified in his defense. He admitted that he had not filed personal income tax returns during the years in question. He testified that as early as 1978, he had begun attending seminars sponsored by, and following the advice of, a group that believes, among other things, that the federal tax system is unconstitutional. Some of the speakers at these meetings were lawyers who purported to give professional opinions about the invalidity of the federal income tax laws. Cheek produced a letter from an attorney stating that the Sixteenth Amendment did not authorize a tax on wages and salaries but only on gain or profit. Petitioner's defense was that, based on the indoctrination he received from this group and from his own study, he sincerely believed that the tax laws were being unconstitutionally enforced and that his actions during the 1980-1986 period were lawful. He therefore argued that he had acted without the willfulness required for conviction of the various offenses with which he was charged.

In the course of its instructions, the trial court advised the jury that to prove "willfulness" the Government must prove the voluntary and intentional violation of a known legal duty, a burden that could not be proved by showing mistake, ignorance, or negligence. The court further advised the jury that an objectively reasonable good-faith misunderstanding of the law would negate willfulness, but mere disagreement with the law would not. The court described Cheek's beliefs about the income tax system and instructed the jury that if it found that Cheek "honestly and reasonably believed that he was not required to pay income taxes or to file tax returns," a not guilty verdict should be returned.

After several hours of deliberation, the jury sent a note to the judge that stated in part:

> We have a basic disagreement between some of us as
> to if Mr. Cheek honestly & reasonably believed that he was
> not required to pay income taxes. . . .

> Page 32 [the relevant jury instruction] discusses good faith misunderstanding & disagreement. Is there any additional clarification you can give us on this point?

The District Judge responded with a supplemental instruction containing the following statements:

> [A] person's opinion that the tax laws violate his constitutional rights does not constitute a good faith misunderstanding of the law. Furthermore, a person's disagreement with the government's tax collection systems and policies does not constitute a good faith misunderstanding of the law.

At the end of the first day of deliberation, the jury sent out another note saying that it still could not reach a verdict because " '[w]e are divided on the issue as to if Mr. Cheek honestly & reasonably believed that he was not required to pay income tax.' " When the jury resumed its deliberations, the District Judge gave the jury an additional instruction. This instruction stated in part that "[a]n honest but unreasonable belief is not a defense and does not negate willfulness," and that "[a]dvice or research resulting in the conclusion that wages of a privately employed person are not income or that the tax laws are unconstitutional is not objectively reasonable and cannot serve as the basis for a good faith misunderstanding of the law defense." The court also instructed the jury that "[p]ersistent refusal to acknowledge the law does not constitute a good faith misunderstanding of the law." Approximately two hours later, the jury returned a verdict finding petitioner guilty on all counts.

Petitioner appealed his convictions, arguing that the District Court erred by instructing the jury that only an objectively reasonable misunderstanding of the law negates the statutory willfulness requirement. The United States Court of Appeals for the Seventh Circuit rejected that contention and affirmed the convictions. In prior cases, the Seventh Circuit had made clear that good-faith misunderstanding of the law negates willfulness only if the defendant's beliefs are objectively reasonable; in the Seventh Circuit, even actual ignorance is not a defense unless the defendant's ignorance was itself objectively reasonable. In its opinion in this case, the court noted that several specified beliefs, including the beliefs that the tax laws are unconstitutional and that wages are not income, would not be objectively reasonable. Because the Seventh Circuit's interpretation of "willfully" as used in these statutes conflicts with the decisions of several other Courts of Appeals, we granted certiorari.

II

The general rule that ignorance of the law or a mistake of law is no defense to criminal prosecution is deeply rooted in the American legal system. Based on the notion that the law is definite and knowable, the common law presumed that every person knew the law. This common-law rule has been applied by the Court in numerous cases construing criminal statutes.

The proliferation of statutes and regulations has sometimes made it difficult for the average citizen to know and comprehend the extent of the duties and obligations imposed by the tax laws. Congress has accordingly softened the impact of the common-law presumption by making specific intent to violate the law an element of certain federal criminal tax offenses. Thus, the Court almost 60 years ago interpreted the statutory term "willfully" as used in the federal criminal tax statutes as carving out an exception to the traditional rule. This special treatment of criminal tax offenses is largely due to the complexity of the tax laws. In *United States v. Murdock,* 290 U.S. 389 (1933), the Court recognized that:

> Congress did not intend that a person, by reason of a bona
> fide misunderstanding as to his liability for the tax, as to his
> duty to make a return, or as to the adequacy of the records
> he maintained, should become a criminal by his mere failure
> to measure up to the prescribed standard of conduct.

The Court held that the defendant was entitled to an instruction with respect to whether he acted in good faith based on his actual belief. In *Murdock,* the Court interpreted the term "willfully" as used in the criminal tax statutes generally to mean "an act done with a bad purpose," or with "an evil motive."

Subsequent decisions have refined this proposition. In *United States v. Bishop,* 412 U.S. 346 (1973), we described the term "willfully" as connoting "a voluntary, intentional violation of a known legal duty," and did so with specific reference to the "bad faith or evil intent" language employed in *Murdock.* Still later, *United States v. Pomponio,* 429 U.S. 10 (1976) (*per curiam*), addressed a situation in which several defendants had been charged with willfully filing false tax returns. The jury was given an instruction on willfulness similar to the standard set forth in *Bishop.* In addition, it was instructed that " '[g]ood motive alone is never a defense where the act done or omitted is a crime.' " The defendants were convicted but the Court of Appeals reversed, concluding that the latter instruction was improper because the statute required a finding of bad purpose or evil motive.

We reversed the Court of Appeals, stating that "the Court of Appeals incorrectly assumed that the reference to an 'evil motive' in *United States v. Bishop, supra,* and prior cases, "requires proof of any motive other than an intentional violation of a known legal duty." As "the other Courts of Appeals that have considered the question have recognized, willfulness in this context simply means a voluntary, intentional violation of a known legal duty." We concluded that after instructing the jury on willfulness, "[a]n additional instruction on good faith was unnecessary." Taken together, *Bishop* and *Pomponio* conclusively establish that the standard for the statutory willfulness requirement is the "voluntary, intentional violation of a known legal duty."

III

Cheek accepts the *Pomponio* definition of willfulness, but asserts that the District Court's instructions and the Court of Appeals' opinion departed from that definition. In particular, he challenges the ruling that a good-faith misunderstanding of the law or a good-faith belief that one is not violating the law, if it is to negate willfulness, must be objectively reasonable. We agree that the Court of Appeals and the District Court erred in this respect.

A

Willfulness, as construed by our prior decisions in criminal tax cases, requires the Government to prove that the law imposed a duty on the defendant, that the defendant knew of this duty, and that he voluntarily and intentionally violated that duty. We deal first with the case where the issue is whether the defendant knew of the duty purportedly imposed by the provision of the statute or regulation he is accused of violating, a case in which there is no claim that the provision at issue is invalid. In such a case, if the Government proves actual knowledge of the pertinent legal duty, the prosecution, without more, has satisfied the knowledge component of the willfulness requirement. But carrying this burden requires negating a defendant's claim of ignorance of the law or a claim that because of a misunderstanding of the law, he had a good-faith belief that he was not violating any of the provisions of the tax laws. This is so because one cannot be aware that the law imposes a duty upon him and yet be ignorant of it, misunderstand the law, or believe that the duty does not exist. In the end, the issue is whether, based on all the evidence, the Government has proved that the defendant was aware of the duty at issue, which cannot be true if the jury credits a good-faith misunderstanding and belief submission, whether or not the claimed belief or misunderstanding is objectively reasonable.

In this case, if Cheek asserted that he truly believed that the Internal Revenue Code did not purport to treat wages as income, and the jury believed him, the Government would not have carried its burden to prove willfulness, however unreasonable a court might deem such a belief. Of course, in deciding whether to credit Cheek's good-faith belief claim, the jury would be free to consider any admissible evidence from any source showing that Cheek was aware of his duty to file a return and to treat wages as income, including evidence showing his awareness of the relevant provisions of the Code or regulations, of court decisions rejecting his interpretation of the tax law, of authoritative rulings of the Internal Revenue Service, or of any contents of the personal income tax return forms and accompanying instructions that made it plain that wages should be returned as income.

We thus disagree with the Court of Appeals' requirement that a claimed good-faith belief must be objectively reasonable if it is to be considered as possibly negating the Government's evidence purporting to show a defendant's awareness of the legal duty at issue. Knowledge and belief are characteristically questions for the factfinder, in this case the jury. Characterizing a particular belief as not objectively reasonable transforms the inquiry into a legal one and would prevent the jury from considering it. It would of course be proper to exclude evidence having no relevance or probative value with respect to willfulness; but it is not contrary to common sense, let alone impossible, for a defendant to be ignorant of his duty based on an irrational belief that he has no duty, and forbidding the jury to consider evidence that might negate willfulness would raise a serious question under the Sixth Amendment's jury trial provision.

. . .

It was therefore error to instruct the jury to disregard evidence of Cheek's understanding that, within the meaning of the tax laws, he was not a person required to file a return or to pay income taxes and that wages are not taxable income, as incredible as such misunderstandings of and beliefs about the law might be. Of course, the more unreasonable the asserted beliefs or misunderstandings are, the more likely the jury will consider them to be nothing more than simple disagreement with known legal duties imposed by the tax laws and will find that the Government has carried its burden of proving knowledge.

B

Cheek asserted in the trial court that he should be acquitted because he believed in good faith that the income tax law is unconstitutional as applied to him and thus could not legally impose any duty upon him of which he should have been aware. Such a submission is unsound, not because Cheek's constitutional arguments are not objectively reasonable or frivolous, which they surely are, but because the *Murdock-Pomponio* line of cases does not support such a position. Those cases construed the willfulness requirement in the criminal provisions of the Internal Revenue Code to require proof of knowledge of the law. This was because in "our complex tax system, uncertainty often arises even among taxpayers who earnestly wish to follow the law," and " '[i]t is not the purpose of the law to penalize frank difference of opinion or innocent errors made despite the exercise of reasonable care.' "

Claims that some of the provisions of the tax code are unconstitutional are submissions of a different order. They do not arise from innocent mistakes caused by the complexity of the Internal Revenue Code. Rather, they reveal full knowledge of the provisions at issue and a studied conclusion, however wrong, that those provisions are invalid and unenforceable. Thus in this case, Cheek paid his taxes for years, but after attending various seminars and based on his own study, he concluded that the income tax laws could not constitutionally require him to pay a tax.

We do not believe that Congress contemplated that such a taxpayer, without risking criminal prosecution, could ignore the duties imposed upon him by the Internal Revenue Code and refuse to utilize the mechanisms provided by Congress to present his claims of invalidity to the courts and to abide by their decisions. There is no doubt that Cheek, from year to year, was free to pay the tax that the law purported to require, file for a refund and, if denied, present his claims of invalidity, constitutional or otherwise, to the courts. See 26 U.S.C. §7422. Also, without paying the tax, he could have challenged claims of tax deficiencies in the Tax Court, §6213, with the right to appeal to a higher court if unsuccessful. §7482(a)(1). Cheek took neither course in some years, and when he did was unwilling to accept the outcome. As we see it, he is in no position to claim that his good-faith belief about the validity of the Internal Revenue Code negates willfulness or provides a defense to criminal prosecution under §§7201 and 7203. Of course, Cheek was free in this very case to present his claims of invalidity and have them adjudicated, but like defendants in criminal cases in other contexts, who "willfully" refuse to comply with the duties placed upon them by the law, he must take the risk of being wrong.

We thus hold that in a case like this, a defendant's views about the validity of the tax statutes are irrelevant to the issue of willfulness and need not be heard by the jury, and, if they are, an instruction to disregard them would be proper. For this purpose, it makes no difference whether the claims of invalidity are frivolous or have substance. It was therefore not error in this case for the District Judge to instruct the jury not to consider Cheek's claims that the tax laws were unconstitutional. However, it was error for the court to instruct the jury that petitioner's asserted beliefs that wages are not income and that he was not a taxpayer within the meaning of the Internal Revenue Code should not be considered by the jury in determining whether Cheek had acted willfully.

IV

For the reasons set forth in the opinion above, the judgment of the Court of Appeals is vacated, and the case is remanded for further proceedings consistent with this opinion.

It is so ordered.

4. Due Process Requirement of Fair Notice

Related to the ignorance of law defense is the due process right to notice. Although everyone is presumed to know the dictates of the criminal law, occasionally a case arises in which a reasonable person would not be aware that certain conduct was illegal. Consider this possibility as you read *Lambert*.

Lambert v. California, 355 U.S. 225 (1957)

Mr. Justice DOUGLAS delivered the opinion of the Court.

Section 52.38(a) of the Los Angeles Municipal Code defines "convicted person" as follows:

Any person who, subsequent to January 1, 1921, has been or hereafter is convicted of an offense punishable as a felony in the State of California, or who has been or who is hereafter convicted of any offense in any place other than the State of California, which offense, if committed in the State of California, would have been punishable as a felony.

Section 52.39 provides that it shall be unlawful for "any convicted person" to be or remain in Los Angeles for a period of more than five days without registering; it requires any person having a place of abode outside the city to register if he comes into the city on five occasions or more during a 30-day period; and it prescribes the information to be furnished the Chief of Police on registering.

Section 52.43(b) makes the failure to register a continuing offense, each day's failure constituting a separate offense.

Appellant, arrested on suspicion of another offense, was charged with a violation of this registration law. The evidence showed that she had been at the time of her arrest a resident of Los Angeles for over seven years. Within that period she had been convicted in Los Angeles of the crime of forgery, an offense which California punishes as a felony. Though convicted of a crime punishable as a felony, she had not at the time of her arrest registered under the Municipal Code. At the trial, appellant asserted that §52.39 of the Code denies her due process of law and other rights under the Federal Constitution, unnecessary to enumerate. The trial court denied this objection. The case was tried to a jury which found appellant guilty. The court fined her $250 and placed her on probation for three years. Appellant, renewing her constitutional objection, moved for arrest of judgment and a new trial. This motion was denied. On appeal the constitutionality of the Code was again challenged. The Appellate Department of the Superior Court affirmed the judgment, holding there was no merit to the claim that the ordinance was unconstitutional. The case is here on appeal. . . . The case having been argued and reargued, we now hold that the registration provisions of the Code as sought to be applied here violate the Due Process requirement of the Fourteenth Amendment.

The registration provision, carrying criminal penalties, applies if a person has been convicted "of an offense punishable as a felony in the State of California" or, in case he has been convicted in another State, if the offense "would have been punishable as a felony" had it been committed in California. No element of willfulness is by terms included in the ordinance nor read into it by the California court as a condition necessary for a conviction.

We must assume that appellant had no actual knowledge of the requirement that she register under this ordinance, as she offered proof of this defense which was refused. The question is whether a registration act of this character violates due process where it is applied to a person who has no actual knowledge of his duty to register, and where no showing is made of the probability of such knowledge. . . .

We do not go with Blackstone in saying that "a vicious will" is necessary to constitute a crime, for conduct alone without regard to the intent of the doer is often sufficient. There is wide latitude in the lawmakers to declare an offense and to exclude elements of knowledge and diligence from its definition. But we deal here with conduct that is wholly passive—mere failure to register. It is unlike the commission of acts, or the failure to act under circumstances that should alert the doer to the consequences of his deed. The rule that "ignorance of the law will not excuse" is deep in our law, as is the principle that of all the powers of local government, the police power is "one of the least limitable." On the other hand, due process places some limits on its exercise. Engrained in our concept of due process is the requirement of notice. Notice is sometimes essential so that the citizen has the chance to defend charges. Notice is required before property interests are disturbed, before assessments are made, before penalties are assessed. Notice is required in a myriad of situations where a penalty or forfeiture might be suffered for mere failure to act. . . .

Registration laws are common and their range is wide. Many such laws are akin to licensing statutes in that they pertain to the regulation of business activities. But the present ordinance is entirely different. Violation of its provisions is unaccompanied by any activity whatever, mere presence in the city being the test. Moreover, circumstances which might move one to inquire as to the necessity of registration are completely lacking. At most the ordinance is but a law enforcement technique designed for the convenience of law enforcement agencies through which a list of the names and addresses of felons then residing in a given community is compiled. The disclosure is merely a compilation of former convictions already publicly recorded in the jurisdiction where obtained. Nevertheless, this appellant on first becoming aware of her duty to register was given no opportunity to comply with the law and avoid its penalty, even though her default was entirely innocent. She could but suffer the consequences of the ordinance, namely, conviction with the imposition of heavy criminal penalties thereunder. We believe that actual knowledge of the duty to register or proof of the probability of such knowledge and subsequent failure to comply are necessary before a conviction under the ordinance can stand. As Holmes wrote in The Common Law, "A law which punished conduct which would not be blameworthy in the average member of the community would be too severe for that community to bear." Its severity lies in the absence of an opportunity either to avoid the consequences of the law or to defend any prosecution brought under it. Where a person did not know of the duty to register and where there was no proof of the probability of such knowledge, he may not be convicted consistently with due process. Were it otherwise, the evil would be as great as it is when the law is written in print too fine to read or in a language foreign to the community.

Reversed.

C. Mistake of Fact

A mistake of fact defense requires that the mistake be one that negates the mens rea. In all cases, the defendant's mistake must be bona fide (i.e., honest or in good faith)—that is, the mistake was made because of a belief the defendant actually held.

For a specific intent offense like larceny, a bona fide but mistaken and unreasonable belief by the defendant that the property he was taking actually belonged to him is sufficient. If the defendant actually believed that he was taking his own coat rather than someone else's, he cannot be guilty of larceny as he did not intend to permanently deprive another of his property. If the defendant, however, is charged with a general intent crime, his mistake must be both bona fide and reasonable. Finally, a mistake of fact—even if honest and reasonable—does not negate criminal responsibility for a strict liability offense. *See* Joshua Dressler, *Understanding Criminal Law* §12.03 (6th ed. 2012).

People v. Vogel, 46 Cal.2d 798 (1956)

TRAYNOR, Justice.

Defendant appeals from a judgment of conviction entered on a jury verdict finding him guilty of bigamy and from an order denying his motion for a new trial.

On September 17, 1944, defendant married Peggy Lambert in a civil ceremony in New Orleans, Louisiana. He was in the Coast Guard and was sent overseas six days after the marriage. Upon his discharge in December, 1945, he returned to Peggy. In 1947 they were remarried in a religious ceremony in New Orleans. They had two children. Peggy testified that they separated several times, and defendant also testified that the marriage was an unhappy one.

In September, 1950, defendant was called to active duty for the Korean War. Peggy received an allotment as his wife until November 13, 1951, when he was released from active duty. Upon his release he did not return to Peggy.

In December, 1951, Peggy and the children moved to St. Louis, Missouri. On April 15, 1952, she was seriously injured in an automobile accident. Defendant learned of her injury on May 19, 1952, went to St. Louis, and took her and the children to New Orleans, where he remained until August, 1952.

On March 6, 1953, defendant married Stelma Roberts, the prosecuting witness, in San Diego County, California. Stelma was granted a final decree of divorce on July 1, 1954.

At the trial Peggy testified that she had never divorced defendant. She admitted that she had obtained a driver's license in her maiden name in 1951. Defendant admitted that he had not divorced Peggy and conceded that he could not prove by record or other direct evidence that she had divorced him. He sought to testify that in 1950, before his call to active duty, Peggy told him that she was going to divorce him in a jurisdiction unknown to him so that he could not contest the custody of their children. The court rejected such testimony as immaterial. He offered other evidence tending to show that during his absence Peggy had married an Earl Heck, namely, testimony of Mr. and Mrs. Lucas, owners of an apartment in St. Louis, Missouri, that Peggy and the children lived in one of their apartments with Heck during the first four months of 1952, that she received mail, telephone calls, and visitors as Mrs. Earl Heck, and that when she was injured in the automobile accident she was identified as Mrs. Heck. The court rejected the evidence on the ground that it would show merely a "barnyard romance" and that under People v. Kelly, 32 Cal.App.2d 624, defendant's good faith belief that she had divorced him and married Heck was immaterial.

We have concluded that defendant is not guilty of bigamy, if he had a bona fide and reasonable belief that facts existed that left him free to remarry. As in other crimes, there must be a union of act and wrongful intent. So basic is this requirement that it is an invariable element of every crime unless excluded expressly or by necessary implication. Sections 281 and 282 do not expressly exclude it nor can its exclusion therefrom be reasonably implied.

Certainly its exclusion cannot be implied from the mere omission of any reference to intent in the definition of bigamy, for the commissioners' annotation to section 20 makes it clear that such an omission was not meant to exclude intent as an element of the crime but to shift to defendant the burden of proving that he did not have the requisite intent. The commissioners' quote at length from People v. Harris, 29 Cal. 678, 681–682. That case involved a conviction for twice voting at the same election. The defendant sought to defend upon the ground that he was so drunk at the time he voted the second time that he did not know what he was doing and that he therefore had no criminal intent. The court held that the trial court erred in excluding from the jury any consideration of the mental state of the defendant by reason of his intoxicated condition, stating: "It is laid down in the books on the subject, that it is a universal doctrine that to constitute what the law deems a crime there must concur both an evil act and an evil intent. . . . Therefore the intent with which the unlawful act was done must be proved as well as the other material facts stated in the indictment; which may be by evidence either direct or indirect, tending to establish the fact, or by inference of law from other facts proved. When the act is proved to have been done by the accused, if it be an act in itself unlawful, the law in the first instance presumes it to have been intended, and the proof of justification or excuse lies on the defendant to overcome this legal and natural presumption. Now, when the statute declares the act of voting more than once at the same election by the same person to be a felony, it must be understood as implying that the interdicted act must be done with a criminal intention, or under circumstances from which such intention may be inferred. The defendant's counsel, at the trial, seems to have apprehended the true rule of law on the subject, and to have regarded the burden as on the defendant to

show by evidence that the act of his voting the second time was not criminal."
. . .

The "correct and authoritative exposition of Sec. 20" as applied in People v. Harris to the crime of twice voting in the same election applies with even greater force to the crime of bigamy and compels the conclusion that guilty knowledge, which was formerly a part of the definition of bigamy was omitted from section 281 to reallocate the burden of proof on that issue in a bigamy trial. Thus, the prosecution makes a prima facie case upon proof that the second marriage was entered into while the first spouse was still living and his bona fide and reasonable belief that facts existed that left the defendant free to remarry is a defense to be proved by the defendant.

Nor must the exclusion of wrongful intent be implied from the two exceptions set forth in section 282. Obviously they are not all inclusive, for it cannot be seriously contended that an insane person or a person who married for the second time while unconscious, could be convicted of bigamy. Moreover, the mere enumeration of specific defenses appropriate to particular crimes does not exclude general defenses based on sections 20 and 26. . . .

It is also significant that under section 61, subd. 2, of the Civil Code a subsequent marriage contracted by a person when the former husband or wife of such person "is generally reputed or believed by such person to be dead . . . is valid until its nullity is adjudged by a competent tribunal", even if the former husband or wife has not been absent for five years and the general repute or belief proves to be erroneous. It would be anomalous to hold that although in the Civil Code the Legislature sanctions such a marriage and makes it valid until it is annulled (it may never be annulled and may therefore always be valid), in the Penal Code the Legislature makes such a person guilty of bigamy. Nor would it be reasonable to hold that a person is guilty of bigamy who remarries in good faith in reliance on a judgment of divorce or annulment that is subsequently found not to be the "judgment of a competent Court" Pen. Code, §282, particularly when such a judgment is obtained by the former husband or wife of such person in any one of the numerous jurisdictions in which such judgments can be obtained. Since it is often difficult for laymen to know when a judgment is not that of a competent court, we cannot reasonably expect them always to have such knowledge and make them criminals if their bona fide belief proves to be erroneous.

The foregoing construction of sections 281 and 282 is consistent with good sense and justice. The severe penalty imposed for bigamy, the serious loss of reputation conviction entails, the infrequency of the offense, and the fact that it has been regarded for centuries as a crime involving moral turpitude, make it extremely unlikely that the Legislature meant to include the morally innocent to make sure the guilty did not escape. . . .

In a prosecution for bigamy evidence that a person is generally reputed to be married is admissible as tending to show actual marriage. The same evidence that would tend to prove an actual marriage, if offered by the People, could

490 Criminal Law: Cases, Statutes, and Problems

reasonably form the basis for an honest belief by a defendant that there was such marriage, that it was legally entered into, and that he was, therefore, free to remarry. The evidence offered to show that Peggy had married Earl Heck should therefore have been admitted. The statement allegedly made by Peggy that she was going to divorce defendant was admissible on the issue of his belief that she had done so and it was also admissible to impeach her testimony that she did not tell him that she was going to divorce him. The exclusion of this evidence was clearly prejudicial, for it deprived defendant of the defense of a bona fide and reasonable belief that facts existed that left him free to remarry. Defendant did not waive this defense by offering the evidence on the issue of Peggy's actually getting a divorce rather than on the issue of good faith, for the trial court expressly stated that it would exclude all such evidence on the basis of People v. Kelly, supra, 32 Cal.App.2d 624. . . .

The judgment and order are reversed.

SHENK, Justice.
I dissent.
The defendant was charged by information with the violation of section 281 of the Panel Code, a felony, in that on March 6, 1953, in San Diego County, he married Stelma G. Roberts, having a lawful wife, Peggy Vogel, then living. He was found guilty as charged. Imposition of sentence was suspended and probation was granted on condition that he spend four months in the adult detention facility in San Diego; that he support his children in accordance with a support agreement; that he should not leave the State of California; that within one year he 'absolve' a marriage contract made by him with a Mrs. Harrington on February 15, 1954, in Tiajuana, Mexico.

The prosecution proved the successive marriages of the defendant, to Peggy in 1944 and to Stelma in 1953. Peggy testified that she had not obtained a divorce from the defendant and that she had not received any notice indicating that he was seeking a divorce from her. In the absence of conflicting evidence this would be a showing sufficient to support a conviction for bigamy. The defendant conceded that he had not obtained a divorce from Peggy.

Bigamy is a statutory crime, defined in section 281 of the Penal Code, as follows: "Every person having a husband or wife living, who marries any other person, except in the cases specified in the next section, is guilty of bigamy." The exceptions contained in section 282 are as follows:

The last section does not extend—
1. To any person by reason of any former marriage, whose husband or wife by such marriage has been absent for five successive years without being known to such person within that time to be living; nor
2. To any person by reason of any former marriage which has been pronounced void, annulled, or dissolved by the judgment of a competent Court.

While the legislature has provided a condition and a term of years after which a person may in good faith reasonably conclude that an absent spouse is dead, it has provided no such condition or term for concluding that an absent spouse has procured a divorce. The legislature has not, either expressly or by reasonable implication, made a mere belief in the existence of a prior divorce a defense to a bigamy prosecution.

The defendant's contention that he had married Stelma honestly believing that Peggy had theretofore divorced him was properly rejected. "It is a familiar rule that, to constitute crime, there must be a union of act and intent; but our Code provides that 'the word "willfully," when applied to the intent with which an act is done or omitted, implies simply a purpose or willingness to commit the act, or make the omission referred to. It does not require any intent to violate law, or to injure another, or to acquire any advantage.'' People v. O'Brien, 96 Cal. 171, 176; People v. Hartman, 130 Cal. 487, 490. It was said in Matter of Ahart, 172 Cal. 762, at page 764: "[S]ome acts [are] made crimes by the very terms of the law where the fraudulent or wicked intent is conclusively presumed from the commission of the act itself, or where the act is denounced as criminal without regard to the facinorous intent." The act of bigamy involves moral turpitude on the part of the bigamist. It also creates a serious mischief to society which the law seeks to prevent by penal sanctions.

The opinion refers to the comment of the Code Commissioners that the opinion in People v. Harris, 29 Cal. 678, 679, is a correct and authoritative exposition of section 20 of the Penal Code. It was there held that a defendant may introduce evidence to show that he was intoxicated at the time he committed the act complained of (voting twice at the same election), not as an excuse for the crime but to enable the jury to determine whether he was incapable of knowing what he was doing by reason of intoxication. That rule has no application to a charge of bigamy where the defendant voluntarily and consciously has entered into a second marriage knowing that his first spouse is alive. A specific intent to commit the crime of bigamy is not required by statute expressly nor by reasonable interpretation. The validity of marriages is of sufficient social importance to uphold the legislature's purpose to provide that where the specific statutory exceptions do not apply a person remarries at his peril. Any change in this regard should be made by the legislature.

This court holds that the evidence rejected by the trial court was admissible on the issue whether facts existed which left the defendant free to remarry. I cannot agree with this conclusion. The defendant conceded that he could offer no direct evidence of a divorce. As circumstantial evidence he offered the following: a purported declaration by Peggy in 1950 that she was going to divorce him in a jurisdiction unknown to him; a driver's license issued to Peggy in her maiden name in 1951 in Louisiana, and testimony or a Mr. and Mrs. Lucas tending to show cohabitation between Peggy and Earl Heck in 1952.

Defendant offered to prove Peggy's 1950 declaration on the theory that it was admissible under the Hillmon doctrine as evidence that she had later obtained a divorce. Declarations of intent have generally been held admissible to prove a completed act only where the declarant is dead or otherwise unavailable, or where they fall within other exceptions to the hearsay rule. This declaration is not within those exceptions.

In those jurisdictions where an honest but erroneous belief, reasonably entertained, that a valid divorce has been granted as to a prior marriage constitutes a defense to a prosecution for bigamy, it is required that a bona fide attempt be made to ascertain the facts. A mere belief, without a further showing of diligent inquiry and investigation is clearly insufficient.

The fact that a driver's license was issued to Peggy under her maiden name would not have furnished proof of divorce. This license was obtained during the time when she was receiving allotment checks as the defendant's wife. In order to obtain a default divorce during the time he was in military service she was required by law, Soldiers' and Sailors' Civil Relief Act of 1940, 54 Stats. 1180, ch. 888, §200, to execute an affidavit that her husband was in military service. The presumption is that she obeyed the law.

Nor was the testimony of Mr. and Mrs. Lucas admissible as proof of a divorce. The defendant contends that their evidence would have established a marriage by cohabitation and repute from which a presumption of validity would arise. The presumption in favor of the legality of a marriage does not arise in favor of a marriage proved solely by cohabitation and repute. In view of the statutory requirement of solemnization it arises only in favor of a marriage regularly solemnized. Moreover the presumption of validity of a ceremonial marriage is applied only in civil cases. The authorities are in general agreement that it may not be relied upon by a defendant in a bigamy prosecution.

Section 4½ of Article VI of the Constitution of this state enjoins upon the court the duty not to reverse a judgment of on order denying a motion for a new trial on account of an improper "rejection of evidence . . . unless, after an examination of the entire cause, including the evidence, . . . the error complained of has resulted in a miscarriage of justice."

The rejected evidence was not competent to prove that Peggy had obtained a divorce. Even if the rejection of that evidence was error no prejudice resulted. The defendant received a fair trial. The jury was fully and fairly instructed and the proof of guilt of violation of the statute was without substantial conflict.

I would affirm the judgment and order.

D. Mistake of Age in Statutory Rape

One area in which mistake of fact generally does not provide a defense is statutory rape where the defendant honestly and reasonably believes the victim is old enough to consent. The general rule is that such a mistake does not provide a defense. As such, statutory rape is strict-liability with regard to the element of the age of the victim. *See* Joshua Dressler, *Understanding Criminal Law* §12.03[B] (6th ed. 2012).

This rule is not universal, as the next two cases illustrate.[*] Which decision is more supportive of the goals of the criminal law? Which is more realistic?

People v. Hernandez, 61 Cal.2d 529 (1964) (In Bank)

PEEK, Justice.

By information defendant was charged with statutory rape. Following his plea of not guilty he was convicted as charged by the court sitting without a jury and the offense determined to be a misdemeanor.

Section 261 of the Penal Code provides in part as follows: "Rape is an act of sexual intercourse, accomplished with a female not the wife of the perpetrator, under either of the following circumstances: 1. Where the female is under the age of 18 years; . . . ."

The sole contention raised on appeal is that the trial court erred in refusing to permit defendant to present evidence going to his guilt for the purpose of showing that he had in good faith a reasonable belief that the prosecutrix was 18 years or more of age.

The undisputed facts show that the defendant and the prosecuting witness were not married and had been companions for several months prior to January 3, 1961—the date of the commission of the alleged offense. Upon that date the prosecutrix was 17 years and 9 months of age and voluntarily engaged in an act of sexual intercourse with defendant.

In support of his contention defendant relies upon Penal Code, §20, which provides that "there must exist a union, or joint operation of act and intent, or criminal negligence" to constitute the commission of a crime. He further relies upon section 26 of that code which provides that one is not capable of committing a crime who commits an act under an ignorance or mistake of fact which disapproves any criminal intent.

---

[*] In a 2000 decision, the California Court of Appeal recognized the limited reach of the *Hernandez* ruling: "The Supreme Court's 1964 decision in *Hernandez* was the first in the country to hold a defendant's mistaken belief as to the age of a victim was a defense to a charge of statutory rape or sex crimes involving minors. (Annot., Mistake or Lack of Information as to Victim's Age as Defense to Statutory Rape (1997) 46 A.L.R.5th 499.) Most jurisdictions that have considered the issue have declined to follow *Hernandez*; however, the Model Penal Code section 213.6(1) allows a defense of reasonable mistake as to age and various states have some version of the defense by statute. (46 A.L.R.5th at p. 509.) The majority rule in the United States remains that a defendant's knowledge of the age of a victim is not an essential element of statutory rape. (46 A.L.R.5th at p. 508.)" *People v. Scott*, 83 Cal. App. 4th 784, 798 n. 9 (2000).

Thus the sole issue relates to the question of intent and knowledge entertained by the defendant at the time of the commission of the crime charged.

Consent of the female is often an unrealistic and unfortunate standard for branding sexual intercourse a crime as serious as forcible rape. Yet the consent standard has been deemed to be required by important policy goals. We are dealing here, of course, with statutory rape where, in one sense, the lack of consent of the female is not an element of the offense. In a broader sense, however, the lack of consent is deemed to remain an element but the law makes a conclusive presumption of the lack thereof because she is presumed too innocent and naive to understand the implications and nature of her act. The law's concern with her capacity or lack thereof to so understand is explained in part by a popular conception of the social, moral and personal values which are preserved by the abstinence from sexual indulgence on the part of a young woman. An unwise disposition of her sexual favor is deemed to do harm both to herself and the social mores by which the community's conduct patterns are established. Hence the law of statutory rape intervenes in an effort to avoid such a disposition. This goal, moreover, is not accomplished by penalizing the naive female but by imposing criminal sanctions against the male, who is conclusively presumed to be responsible for the occurrence.

The assumption that age alone will bring an understanding of the sexual act to a young woman is of doubtful validity. Both learning from the cultural group to which she is a member and her actual sexual experiences will determine her level of comprehension. The sexually experienced 15-year old may be far more acutely aware of the implications of sexual intercourse than her sheltered cousin who is beyond the age of consent. A girl who belongs to a group whose members indulge in sexual intercourse at an early age is likely to rapidly acquire an insight into the rewards and penalties of sexual indulgence. Nevertheless, even in circumstances where a girl's actual comprehension contradicts the law's presumption, the male is deemed criminally responsible for the act, although himself young and naive and responding to advances which may have been made to him.

The law as presently constituted does not concern itself with the relative culpability of the male and female participants in the prohibited sexual act. Even where the young woman is knowledgeable it does not impose sanctions upon her. The knowledgeable young man, on the other hand, is penalized and there are none who would claim that under any construction of the law this should be otherwise. However, the issue raised by the rejected offer of proof in the instant case goes to the culpability of the young man who acts without knowledge that an essential factual element exists and has, on the other hand, a positive, reasonable belief that it does not exist.

The primordial concept of mens rea, the guilty mind, expresses the principle that it is not conduct alone but conduct accompanied by certain specific mental states which concerns, or should concern the law. In a broad sense the concept may be said to relate to such important doctrines as justification, excuse, mistake, necessity and mental capacity, but in the final analysis it means simply that there must be a "joint operation of act and intent," as expressed in section 20 of the Penal Code, to constitute the commission of a criminal offense. The statutory law, however, furnishes no assistance to the courts beyond that, and the casebooks are filled to overflowing with the courts' struggles to determine just what state of mind should be considered relevant in particular contexts. . . .

Statutory rape has long furnished a fertile battleground upon which to argue that the lack of knowledgeable conduct is a proper defense. The law in this state now rests, as it did in 1896, with this court's decision in People v. Ratz, 115 Cal. 132, at pages 134 and 135, where it is stated: "The claim here made is not a new one. It has frequently been pressed upon the attention of courts, but in no case, so far as our examination goes, has it met with favor. The object and purpose of the law are too plain to need comment, the crime too infamous to bear discussion. The protection of society, of the family, and of the infant, demand that one who has carnal intercourse under such circumstances shall do so in peril of the fact, and he will not be heard against the evidence to urge his belief that the victim of his outrage had passed the period which would make his act a crime." The age of consent at the time of the Ratz decision was 14 years, and it is noteworthy that the purpose of the rule, as there announced, was to afford protection to young females therein described as "infants." The decision on which the court in Ratz relied was The Queen v. Prince, L.R. 2 Crown Cas. 154. However England has now, by statute, departed from the strict rule, and excludes as a crime an act of sexual intercourse with a female between the ages of 13 and 16 years if the perpetrator is under the age of 24 years, has not previously been charged with a like offense, and believes the female "to be of the age of sixteen or over and has reasonable cause for the belief."

The rationale of the Ratz decision, rather than purporting to eliminate intent as an element of the crime, holds that the wrongdoer must assume the risk; that, subjectively, when the act is committed, he consciously intends to proceed regardless of the age of the female and the consequences of his act, and that the circumstances involving the female, whether she be a day or a decade less than the statutory age, are irrelevant. There can be no dispute that a criminal intent exists when the perpetrator proceeds with utter disregard of, or in the lack of grounds for, a belief that the female has reached the age of consent. But if he participates in a mutual act of sexual intercourse, believing his partner to be beyond the age of consent, with reasonable grounds for such belief, where is his criminal intent? In such circumstances he has not consciously taken any risk. Instead he has subjectively eliminated the risk by satisfying himself on reasonable evidence that the crime cannot be committed. If it occurs that he has been misled, we cannot realistically conclude that for such reason alone the intent with which he undertook the act suddenly becomes more heinous.

While the specific contentions herein made have been dealt with and rejected both within and without this state, the courts have uniformly failed to satisfactorily explain the nature of the criminal intent present in the mind of one who in good faith believes he has obtained a lawful consent before engaging in the prohibited act. As in the Ratz case the courts often justify convictions on policy reasons which, in effect, eliminate the element of intent. The Legislature, of course, by making intent an element of the crime, has established the prevailing policy from which it alone can properly advise us to depart. . . .

We are persuaded that the reluctance to accord to a charge of statutory rape the defense of a lack of criminal intent has no greater justification than in the case of other statutory crimes, where the Legislature has made identical provision with respect to intent. " 'At common law an honest and reasonable belief in the existence of circumstances, which, if true, would make the act for which the person is indicted an innocent act, has always been held to be a good defense. . . . So far as I am aware it has never been suggested that these exceptions do not equally apply to the case of statutory offenses unless they are excluded expressly or by necessary implication.' " Our departure from the views expressed in Ratz is in no manner indicative of a withdrawal from the sound policy that it is in the public interest to protect the sexually naive female from exploitation. No responsible person would hesitate to condemn as untenable a claimed good faith belief in the age of consent of an "infant" female whose obviously tender years preclude the existence of reasonable grounds for that belief. However, the prosecutrix in the instant case was but three months short of 18 years of age and there is nothing in the record to indicate that the purposes of the law as stated in Ratz can be better served by foreclosing the defense of a lack of intent. This is not to say that the granting to consent by even a sexually sophisticated girl known to be less than the statutory age is a defense. We hold only that in the absence of a legislative direction otherwise, a charge of statutory rape is defensible wherein a criminal intent is lacking. . . .

Some question has been raised that the offer of proof of defendant's reasonable belief in the age of the prosecutrix was insufficient to justify the pleading of such belief as a defense to the act. It is not our purpose here to make a determination that the defendant entertained a reasonable belief. Suffice to state that the offer demonstrated a sufficient basis upon which, when fully developed, the trier of fact might have found in defendant's favor. We conclude that it was reversible error to reject the offer.

The judgment is reversed.

People v. Cash, 419 Mich. 230 (1984)

WILLIAMS, Chief Justice.

The main issue presented in this case requires us to reconsider whether a reasonable mistake of fact as to a complainant's age is a defense to a statutory rape charge. Over 61 years ago, this Court enunciated a rule rejecting such a defense in *People v. Gengels,* 218 Mich. 632 (1922), which involved a similar charge under the former statutory rape statute. We reaffirm the *Gengels* rule and likewise reject this defense in cases brought under §520d(1)(a) of the third-degree criminal sexual conduct statute. . . .

I.   FACTS

On the evening of September 23, 1979, the complainant, who was one month shy of her 16th birthday, met the defendant at a Greyhound bus station in Detroit. The complainant was running away from home at the time. After talking with complainant for a couple of hours and gaining her trust, defendant persuaded complainant to accompany him on a drive in his car. They drove to a motel in Marshall, Michigan, where two separate acts of sexual intercourse took place. The complainant managed to leave the motel room undetected after defendant fell asleep, and awakened the person in charge of the motel, who in turn called the police. The defendant was charged with two counts of third-degree criminal sexual conduct, namely, engaging in sexual penetration with a person between the ages of 13 and 16 years. Documents found in the court file indicate that at the time of the offense, the defendant was 30 years old.

At the preliminary examination, complainant admitted that she told defendant that she was 17 years old. The defendant had also indicated to the police at the time of his arrest that the complainant told him she was 17. The complainant was described by defendant as being 5' 8" tall and weighing about 165 pounds.

Prior to trial, defendant brought a motion requesting that the jury be instructed that a reasonable mistake as to the complainant's age is a defense, or, in the alternative, that the charges be dismissed on the ground that the complainant is collaterally estopped from asserting that she was 16 since at the time of the offense she stated that she was 17. Following a hearing, the trial court denied defendant's motion and entered its opinion and order to that effect.

During the course of jury voir dire, defendant asserted his right to represent himself. The trial court permitted defendant to proceed in his own defense with his attorney remaining present to assist defendant. At trial, the complainant testified that she had voluntarily, though reluctantly, engaged in sexual intercourse with defendant out of fear that defendant would otherwise harm her. Defendant tried to impeach the complainant with questions about her lifestyle to show that she was "street-wise", but the trial court prohibited this cross-examination. Defendant was also prohibited from questioning complainant's mother as to her daughter's lifestyle. . . .

The trial court instructed the jury that the defense theory was one of mistake of fact and that defendant reasonably believed that complainant had reached the age of consent. Over defendant's objection, the court later instructed the jury that "[i]t is no defense that the defendant believed that [the complainant] was 16 years old or older at the time of the alleged act".

The defendant was found guilty by the jury of third-degree criminal sexual conduct, M.C.L. §750.520d(1)(a); M.S.A. §28.788(4)(1)(a), and was sentenced to a term of from 5 to 15 years in prison. The Court of Appeals affirmed defendant's conviction in an unpublished per curiam opinion. We granted leave to appeal on August 10, 1982.

II.   REASONABLE–MISTAKE–OF–AGE DEFENSE
A.   *The Gengels Decision*

This Court first stated that a good-faith or reasonable mistake as to the complainant's age is not a defense to a statutory rape charge in *People v. Gengels,* 218 Mich. 632 (1922), nearly 61 years ago. In that case, the defendant was convicted under the predecessor to the current criminal sexual conduct statute of carnally knowing a female child under 16 years of age. The defendant testified that the complainant told him that she was 18 years old. This Court reversed the defendant's conviction and granted a new trial on the ground that the prosecutor had impermissibly impeached the defendant by collateral evidence of similar acts. While recognizing that such evidence may be admissible where guilt of a particular crime depends on intent, the Court noted:

> But in the crime charged here proof of the intent goes with proof of the act of sexual intercourse with a girl under the age of consent. It is not necessary for the prosecution to prove want of consent. Proof of consent is no defense, for a female child under the statutory age is legally incapable of consenting. Neither is it any defense that the accused believed from the statement of his victim or others that she had reached the age of consent. 33 Cyc, p 1438, and cases cited." *Gengels, supra,* p. 641.

The *Gengels* decision has only been cited once in this state's courts for the proposition that mistake of age is not a defense to a statutory rape charge. *People v. Doyle,* 16 Mich. App. 242 (1969), *lv. den.* 382 Mich. 753 (1969). In *Doyle,* the defendant was charged with taking indecent liberties with a female under 16 years of age. The Court of Appeals observed that "[c]urrent social and moral values make more realistic the California view that a reasonable and honest mistake of age is a valid defense to a charge of statutory rape, *People v. Hernandez,* 61 Cal.2d 529 (1964)". The Court, however, concluded that it was bound to follow the *Gengels* rule and therefore refused to adopt the mistake-of-age defense in indecent liberties cases. Neither in *Gengels* nor in *Doyle* was the constitutionality of the rule prohibiting the defense of a reasonable mistake of age to a statutory rape charge squarely presented.

B.   *Is Gengels Still Viable?*

This Court for the first time has the opportunity to review the rule announced in *Gengels* and determine whether it is still viable under the successor provision of the third-degree criminal sexual conduct statute and, if so, whether it comports with a defendant's right to due process. . . .

In the present case, defendant directly attacks the constitutionality of the [CSC] statute on due process grounds for imposing criminal liability without requiring proof of specific criminal intent, *i.e.*, that the accused know that the victim is below the statutory age of consent. In particular, he argues that the crime of statutory rape is rooted in the common law and, as with other common-law offenses, the element of intent must be implied within the statutory definition of a crime, absent clear legislative language to the contrary. We are urged by defendant to construe the statute's silence with respect to the element of intent as not negating the defense of a reasonable mistake of fact as to the complainant's age.

In support of his argument, defendant relies primarily on two out-of-state cases which represent the minority view that, in a statutory rape prosecution, an accused's reasonable, though mistaken, belief that the complainant was of the age of consent is a valid defense. *People v. Hernandez,* 61 Cal.2d 529 (1964); *State v. Guest,* 583 P.2d 836 (Alas., 1978). In both these cases, the Court engrafted a *mens rea* element onto the statutes in question where they were otherwise silent as to any requisite criminal intent.

The vast majority of states, as well as the federal courts, which have considered this identical issue have rejected defendant's arguments and do not recognize the defense of a reasonable mistake of age to a statutory rape charge. For the reasons discussed below, we agree with the majority's position.

After careful examination of the statute in the instant case and its legislative history, we are persuaded that the Legislature, in enacting the new criminal sexual conduct code, 1974 P.A. 266, intended to omit the defense of a reasonable mistake of age from its definition of third-degree criminal sexual conduct involving a 13- to 16-year-old, and we follow the legislative intention.

First, a general rule of statutory construction is that the Legislature is "presumed to know of and legislate in harmony with existing laws". *People v. Harrison,* 194 Mich. 363, 369 (1916). The Legislature must have been aware of our earlier decision rejecting the reasonable-mistake-of-age defense under the old statutory rape statute. Had the Legislature desired to revise the existing law by allowing for a reasonable-mistake-of-age defense, it could have done so, but it did not do so. This is further supported by the fact that under another provision of the same section of the statute, concerning the mentally ill or physically helpless rape victim, the Legislature specifically provided for the defense of a reasonable mistake of fact by adding the language that the actor "knows or has reason to know" of the victim's condition where the prior statute contained no requirement of intent. The Legislature's failure to include similar language under the section of the statute in question indicates to us the Legislature's intent to adhere to the *Gengels* rule that the actual, and not the apparent, age of the complainant governs in statutory rape offenses.

Second, while the crime of statutory rape has its origins in the English common law, Michigan's new criminal sexual conduct statute represents a major attempt by the Legislature to redefine the law of sexually assaultive crimes, including that of statutory rape. It is well established that the Legislature may, pursuant to its police powers, define criminal offenses without requiring proof of a specific criminal intent and so provide that the perpetrator proceed at his own peril regardless of his defense of ignorance or an honest mistake of fact. In the case of statutory rape, such legislation, in the nature of "strict liability" offenses, has been upheld as a matter of public policy because of the need to protect children below a specified age from sexual intercourse on the presumption that their immaturity and innocence prevents them from appreciating the full magnitude and consequences of their conduct.

Analysis of the statutory scheme adopted by the Legislature to define criminal sexual conduct further reveals that the Legislature cannot reasonably be said to have intended that a defense based on reasonable mistake of fact concerning the victim's age be available to persons charged under the act.

We are dealing with a statute, passed by the Legislature just nine years ago, which shows, on its face, that the age of the victim was carefully considered in defining and establishing the severity of the criminal conduct. The age of the victim is balanced against the nature of the sexual conduct to establish a graduated system of punishment.

Under the prior rape or carnal knowledge statute, sexual penetration of a female under the age of 16 was defined as rape, punishable by life imprisonment or any term of years. In 1974, when the Legislature revised the law of criminal sexual conduct, it could have retained this definition of "statutory rape" and could have continued to punish it as criminal sexual conduct in the first degree, *i.e.*, by life imprisonment or any term of years. The Legislature chose not to do so. The Legislature, alternatively, could have completely decriminalized consensual sexual activity with a person between the ages of 13 and 16, or, for that matter, it could have made age irrelevant. But it chose not to do so. What the Legislature did choose to do was to create a system of definitions and punishments which considers the age of the victim, the type of sexual contact, and several limited situations in which the relationship of authority between victim and defendant warrant, in the legislative judgment, an increase in punishment.

Thus, the Legislature has determined that sexual penetration of a victim under 13 years of age is first-degree criminal sexual conduct which is punishable by life imprisonment or any term of years. M.C.L. §§750.520b(1)(a), 750.520b(2); M.S.A. §§28.788(2)(1)(a), 28.788(2)(2). But sexual penetration of a victim 13 or older, but under 16 years of age, is third-degree criminal sexual conduct, with a maximum punishment of 15 years in prison. M.C.L. §§750.520d(1)(a), 750.520d(2); M.S.A. §§28.788(4)(1)(a), 28.788(4)(2). However, if the victim is at least 13, but less than 16 years of age, and is a member of the defendant's household or related to the defendant, a person who engages in sexual penetration of that victim is guilty of first-degree criminal sexual conduct and may receive a maximum sentence of life imprisonment. M.C.L. §§750.520b(1)(b), 750.520b(2); M.S.A. §§28.788(2)(1)(b), 28.788(2)(2).

These discrete choices made by the Legislature evidence careful consideration of age and a deliberate determination to retain the law of statutory rape where the prohibited conduct occurred and the victim was within the protected age group.

One critic has argued that the exclusion of a reasonable-mistake-of-age defense in statutory rape cases is no longer justified given the increased age of consent, the realities of modern society that young teens are more sexually mature, and the seriousness of the penalty as compared with other strict liability offenses. We are not convinced that the policy behind the statutory rape laws of protecting children from sexual exploitation and possible physical or psychological harm from engaging in sexual intercourse is outmoded. Indeed, the United States Supreme Court recently acknowledged the state's authority to regulate the sexual behavior of minors in order to promote their physical and mental well-being, even under a gender-based statutory rape law.

C.   *Is the Defense of a Reasonable Mistake of Age Constitutionally Mandated?*

Contrary to defendant's contention, the mistake-of-age defense, at least with regard to statutory rape crimes, is not constitutionally mandated. We quote with approval the following language from *Nelson v. Moriarty*, 484 F.2d 1034, 1035-1036 (CA 1, 1973):

> Petitioner claims that his honest belief that the prosecutrix of the statutory rape charge was over sixteen years of age should constitute a defense, of constitutional dimensions, to statutory rape. The effect of *mens rea* and mistake on state criminal law has generally been left to the discretion of the states. . . . The Supreme Court has never held that an honest mistake as to the age of the prosecutrix is a constitutional defense to statutory rape, . . . and nothing in the Court's recent decisions clarifying the scope of procreative privacy, . . . suggests that a state may no longer place the risk of mistake as to the prosecutrix's age on the person engaging in sexual intercourse with a partner who may be young enough to fall within the protection of the statute. Petitioner's argument is without merit.

Moreover, given the already highly emotional setting of a statutory rape trial, the allowance of a mistake-of-age defense would only cause additional undue focus on the complainant by the jury's scrutinizing her appearance and any other visible signs of maturity. The obvious problem is that because early adolescents tend to grow at a rapid rate, by the time of trial a relatively undeveloped young girl or boy may have transformed into a young woman or man. A better procedure would be to permit any mitigating and ameliorating evidence in support of a defendant's mistaken belief as to the complainant's age to be considered by the trial judge at the time of sentencing.

We again note that our decision is in line with the preponderant majority of jurisdictions, both state and federal, which do not recognize the reasonable-mistake-of-age defense for statutory rape offenses and have likewise upheld against due process challenges their respective statutes' imposition of criminal liability without the necessity of proving the defendant's knowledge that the victim was below the designated age. Accordingly, we reaffirm our earlier opinion in *Gengels* and reject the reasonable-mistake-of-age defense for cases brought under §520d(1)(a) of the third-degree criminal sexual conduct statute. . . .

V.   CONCLUSION

We find that the Legislature intentionally omitted the defense of a reasonable mistake of age from its statutory definition of third-degree criminal sexual conduct involving a 13- to 16-year-old. Moreover, we hold that this defense is not constitutionally compelled. . . .

Accordingly, we affirm defendant's conviction.

E.   Practice Problems on Mistake

Defendant decided to go deer hunting one week before the start of deer hunting season. He took his gun into the woods and, within minutes, spotted a large deer standing perfectly still. Defendant shot a bullet into the deer but it did not move. Defendant then went closer, only to discover that the deer was stuffed. As he stood next to the fake deer, conservation officers emerged from the bushes and arrested him for attempting to kill a deer out of season.

Defendant has been charged with attempt to violate the following statute:

§420.14

> No wild life shall be pursued, taken, killed, possessed or disposed of, except in the manner, to the extent, and at the time or times permitted by such rules and regulations; and any pursuit, taking, killing, possession, or disposition thereof, except as permitted by such rules and regulations, are hereby prohibited. Any person violating this section shall be guilty of a misdemeanor.

Defendant has retained you as his attorney and has asked if he has a defense to this charge. What advice would you give him?

F.   Model Penal Code Provisions

§2.04. Ignorance or Mistake

(1)   Ignorance or mistake as to a matter of fact or law is a defense if:
> (a)   the ignorance or mistake negatives the purpose, knowledge, belief, recklessness or negligence required to establish a material element of the offense; or
> (b)   the law provides that the state of mind established by such ignorance or mistake constitutes a defense.

(2)   Although ignorance or mistake would otherwise afford a defense to the offense charged, the defense is not available if the defendant would be guilty of another offense had the situation been as he supposed. In such case, however, the ignorance or mistake of the defendant shall reduce the grade and degree of the offense of which he may be convicted to those of the offense of which he would be guilty had the situation been as he supposed.

(3)   A belief that conduct does not legally constitute an offense is a defense to a prosecution for that offense based upon such conduct when:
> (a)   the statute or other enactment defining the offense is not known to the actor and has not been published or otherwise reasonably made available prior to the conduct alleged; or
> (b)   he acts in reasonable reliance upon an official statement of the law, afterward determined to be invalid or erroneous, contained in (i) a statute or other enactment; (ii) a judicial decision, opinion or judgment; (iii) an administrative order or grant of permission; or (iv) an official interpretation of the public officer or body charged by law with responsibility for the interpretation, administration or enforcement of the law defining the offense.

(4)   The defendant must prove a defense arising under Subsection (3) of this Section by a preponderance of evidence.

Chapter 17
Duress, Necessity, Consent, and Condonation

A. Introduction

The complete defenses of duress and necessity operate in much the same manner with one primary difference. The duress defense is appropriate when the defendant is threatened by another person with death or serious injury to commit the crime. A necessity defense, on the other hand, is appropriate where the pressure to commit the offense comes from a non-human source, a so-called "act of God," or physical forces beyond the defendant's control. If the defendant burns another's dwelling because someone has threatened the defendant with imminent death or bodily harm unless he commits the arson, the defendant could claim a duress defense. However, if the defendant burns the dwelling in order to create a firebreak to stop a wildfire and, thereby, save many more houses, he could claim necessity.

A generally accepted limitation on duress and necessity is that neither are a complete defense to murder. This rule makes sense when you consider that both defenses generally require the actor to choose the "lesser of two evils."[*] Since there is no evil less than murder, duress or necessity will only reduce an intentional murder to manslaughter. *See* Joshua Dressler, *Understanding Criminal Law* §23.04 (6th ed. 2012).

Consent is a defense only when the charged offense includes lack of consent as an element. *See* 1 Wharton, Crim. Law §46 (15th ed. 2013). At common law, these crimes were rape, larceny, kidnapping, burglary, and minor batteries. Otherwise, the general rule is that consent of the victim is not a defense. This general rule applies in all cases in which the victim condones or forgives the actor after the fact. This makes sense when you consider that a crime is an offense against the state and the condonation of the victim does not

---

[*] Duress can sometimes apply even when the defendant perpetrates a greater evil. *See* Joshua Dressler, *Understanding Criminal Law* §23.03 (6th ed. 2012).

control the prosecutor's decision to file criminal charges, except in extremely rare cases where there is a specific statute to the contrary. *See* Wayne LaFave, *Criminal Law* §6.5(d) (5th ed. 2010).

B. Duress

1. Imminent Threat against a Third Party

Haney clearly explains the requirements for a duress defense, but also looks at a unique situation: Can a defendant claim a duress defense if he or she was not the person threatened, but was merely assisting the threatened person?

Duress is often raised as a defense in prison escape cases. As a result, some states have enacted specific statutes to cover this situation. The relevant Michigan statute, M.C.L. §768.21b, is reproduced at the end of this case.

United States v. Haney, 287 F.3d 1266 (10th Cir. 2002)

HENRY, Circuit Judge.

Robert M. Haney appeals his conviction and sentence for violation of 18 U.S.C. §1791(a)(2) (possession of escape paraphernalia in prison). Mr. Haney asserts that the district court erred in (1) not permitting him to raise a defense of duress—a defense the jury accepted, on a related count, as to Mr. Haney's co-defendant . . . . Exercising jurisdiction under 28 U.S.C. §1291, we vacate Mr. Haney's conviction for possession of escape paraphernalia. . . .

I. BACKGROUND

Following his escape from prison, the television show "America's Most Wanted" incorrectly described Tony S. Francis, friend and co-defendant of Mr. Haney, as a leader of the Aryan Brotherhood, a prison gang preaching white supremacy. Once recaptured, Mr. Francis found himself housed in the federal penitentiary in Florence, Colorado; Mr. Francis developed anxiety about his incarceration in this facility for at least two reasons. First, Mr. Francis feared the reaction of African-American prisoners because at least some of those prisoners had, in all likelihood, heard the claim of Aryan Brotherhood membership made by "America's Most Wanted." Second, Mr. Francis feared the reaction of members of the Aryan Brotherhood because, in reality, Mr. Francis was not a member of that prison gang.

In 1997, prison authorities became concerned about growing racial tension in the Florence penitentiary; beginning on September 3, 1997, prison authorities "locked down" the penitentiary for ten days. Immediately after prison authorities lifted the lock-down, three African American inmates threatened Mr. Francis. The inmates approached Mr. Francis, told him that they had seen him on "America's Most Wanted," and offered a warning to the effect that: "When the shit jumps off, you know what time it is"—i.e., a race war was brewing and Mr. Francis was a target.

Mr. Francis concluded that his only option was to attempt a prison escape. In their respective testimonies, Mr. Francis and Mr. Haney each explained this implicit decision not to seek the aid of the prison authorities as resting on the alleged fact that seeking such aid did not constitute a reasonable alternative. Mr. Francis and Mr. Haney testified that, had Mr. Francis sought such assistance, Mr. Francis and Mr. Haney's fellow inmates would have labeled Mr. Francis a snitch, thereby placing Mr. Francis in further danger. Additionally, according to the testimony of Mr. Francis and Mr. Haney, because the special housing units were far from free from violence, placing Mr. Francis in protective custody would also have proven of limited benefit.

Mr. Haney agreed to help Mr. Francis in Mr. Francis' attempted escape. Mr. Haney used his position as an employee in the prison laundry to collect a variety of escape paraphernalia. On September 26, 1997—approximately two weeks after the initial threat—Mr. Francis was shown a "kite" (a note) in which an inmate commented that Mr. Francis was still considered a target. This threat provided renewed impetus for the escape attempt.

On the night of October 3, 1997, Mr. Francis and Mr. Haney gathered the collected escape paraphernalia and hid in the prison yard. As they hid, however, Mr. Haney endeavored to convince Mr. Francis that an escape attempt was, in fact, imprudent; Mr. Haney argued, in effect: "[T]he best possible solution would be to get caught trying to escape, thereby getting placed into disciplinary segregation without having to report the death threats to prison officials." Mr. Francis ultimately agreed. After two hours of strewing the yard with the escape paraphernalia, the two inmates were finally caught.

The United States charged both Mr. Francis and Mr. Haney with 1) violation of 18 U.S.C. §1791(a)(2) (possession of escape paraphernalia in prison) and 2) violation of 18 U.S.C. §751(a) (attempted escape). As to Mr. Francis, the district court instructed the jury on the duress defense in regard to both counts; as to Mr. Haney, however, the court refused to give a duress instruction on either count. The jury convicted both Mr. Francis and Mr. Haney of possessing escape paraphernalia but acquitted both Mr. Francis and Mr. Haney of attempting to escape. In acquitting Mr. Francis of the attempted escape, the jury expressly invoked the duress defense.

II.   DISCUSSION: Applicability of the Duress Defense

Mr. Haney argues that he was entitled to present a duress defense to the jury. In order to have a theory of defense submitted to the jury, a defendant must present sufficient evidence, on each element of the defense, by which the jury could find in the defendant's favor. Indeed, a "defendant is entitled to jury instructions on any theory of defense finding support in the evidence and the law. Failure to so instruct is reversible error." *United States v. Scafe,* 822 F.2d

928, 932 (10th Cir.1987). The district court concluded that Mr. Haney failed to present sufficient evidence as to the elements of the duress defense and thus that the duress defense was, as a matter of law, inapplicable to Mr. Haney.

As defined in the recent caselaw of our circuit, the duress defense typically consists of three elements:

1) The threat of immediate infliction, upon the defendant, of death or bodily harm;

2) The defendant's well-grounded fear that the threat will be carried out; AND

3) The defendant's lack of a reasonable opportunity to otherwise avert the threatened harm.

By his own admission, Mr. Haney cannot meet the elements of the duress defense, as described above. Quite basically, Mr. Haney makes no allegation that he ever feared for his own safety. Mr. Haney seeks to overcome this obstacle by proposing an extension of the duress defense; Mr. Haney argues that the duress defense should encompass defendants who correctly recognize that another individual's safety is at risk. Thus, Mr. Haney would describe the elements of the duress defense as requiring:

1) The threat of immediate infliction, upon the defendant *or a third person,* of death or bodily harm;

2) The defendant's well-grounded fear that the threat will be carried out; AND

3) The defendant's, *and third person's,* lack of a reasonable opportunity to otherwise avert the threatened harm.

The government presents no argument that the duress defense should not extend, in at least certain circumstances, to third parties, thereby essentially conceding the point. Rather, the government presses two grounds on which we might nevertheless conclude, as a matter of law, that the duress defense is here unavailable to Mr. Haney. The government first suggests that the duress defense should be extended to third parties only where the defendant enjoys a familial relationship with the threatened individual. Second, the government suggests that Mr. Haney produced inadequate evidence to create a jury question as to either the first or third element of the duress defense. We address these arguments in turn.

A.   Third Party Duress

1.   Whether the duress defense should ever extend to third parties

Despite the fact that the government essentially abandons this position (presenting no argument and citing no cases or other legal authority), we begin our discussion of third party duress by considering whether the duress defense should ever be available when a third party (a party other than the defendant) is threatened with death or bodily harm. Logic and overwhelming legal authority conjoin in establishing that the duress defense should, indeed, extend to third parties.

The principle underlying the duress defense is one of hard-nosed practicality: sometimes social welfare is maximized by forgiving a relatively minor offense in order to avoid a greater social harm. Where A, with apparent credibility, threatens to shoot B unless B jaywalks (and where B, in fear of the threat, possesses no reasonable opportunity to otherwise avert the shooting), the law excuses B's relatively minor offense in order to avoid the greater social harm threatened by A. The same logic dictates that so, too, where A, again with apparent credibility, threatens to shoot B unless C jaywalks, the defense of third party duress should excuse C's relatively minor offense (at least so long as (1) C actually feared that A would execute the shooting and (2) neither B nor C possessed a reasonable alternative to otherwise avert the shooting).

Commentators and the caselaw agree that the duress defense should extend to the defense of third parties. Leading criminal law scholars Wayne R. LaFave and Austin W. Scott, Jr. have noted, first, that "[t]he overwhelming majority of [state duress statutes] extend to threats of harm to third parties" and, second, that "as a matter of principle, the threatened harm need not be directed at the defendant himself." The scholar-drafters of the Model Penal Code concur. Section 2.09(1) of the Code provides: "It is an affirmative defense that the actor engaged in the conduct . . . because he was coerced to do so by the use of, or a threat to use, unlawful force against his person *or the person of another*." (Emphasis added).

The federal case law is apparently uniform in extending the duress defense to threats against third parties. We know of no federal case categorically declining to apply the duress defense in the third party context.

2.   Whether the duress defense, once extended to third parties, should be limited to third parties with a familial relationship to the defendant

It is true that, as the government observes, most cases of third-party duress involve familial relationships between the defendant and the threatened individual; however, neither logic nor practicality supports such a 'family relationship' limitation. Returning to our basic illustration of the duress defense above, why should it matter whether C (who jaywalks in order to prevent A from shooting B) enjoys a family relationship with B; in either case, permitting C to jaywalk avoids the greater social harm. . . .

In sum, we see no principled justification for limiting the duress defense to defendants whose own safety is threatened. Nor do we see any justification for limiting the duress defense to defendants in a familial relationship with the threatened individual. Such distinctions would be arbitrary and unjust. As Mr. Haney correctly observes, the duress defense is appropriately defined not by "the nature of the relationship between the alleged law-breaker and the beneficiary third party" but by the "nature of the crime committed and the benefit conferred upon the third party."

B. Sufficiency of the Evidence

Nor can we accept the government's argument that Mr. Haney failed to produce adequate evidence to create a jury issue on either the first or third element of the duress defense. Here, of course, the government's position is weakened (though not logically foreclosed) by the fact that the jury explicitly invoked the duress defense to acquit Mr. Francis of the charged attempted escape. The fact that the jury, hearing much of the same evidence that Mr. Haney would have applied toward his own duress defense, accepted the duress defense in a related context suggests that Mr. Haney did, indeed, offer sufficient evidence. . . .

Because a jury could have concluded (1) that the threat against Mr. Francis was immediate in nature, (2) that Mr. Haney actually possessed a well-grounded fear that the threat would be executed, and (3) that neither Mr. Haney nor Mr. Francis, in order to avert the threatened harm, maintained any reasonable alternative to possessing escape paraphernalia, the district court should have granted Mr. Haney's request for jury instructions on the duress defense.

III. CONCLUSION

For the reasons set forth above, we decline to limit the duress defense to defendants related by familial ties to a threatened individual and we further conclude that Mr. Haney presented adequate evidence to create a jury issue as to the applicability of that defense to his alleged possession of escape paraphernalia. Obviously we express no further opinion as to the likely merits of Mr. Haney's duress defense. Should the government choose to retry this case, the government, with the duress issue now in play, may well produce overwhelming evidence as to either the non-immediacy of the threat against Mr. Francis or the existence of reasonable alternatives to the possession of escape paraphernalia. These, however, are considerations for a jury: we VACATE Mr. Haney's conviction and sentence and REMAND for further proceedings consistent with this opinion.

Note

On rehearing *en banc,* the 10th Circuit vacated the *Haney* decision, holding that Haney waived his claim to a duress instruction at trial. *United States v. Haney,* 318 F.3d 1161 (10th Cir. 2003) (en banc).

2. Pattern Jury Instructions

6.05 COERCION; DURESS

(1) One of the questions in this case is whether the defendant was coerced, or forced, to commit the crime. Here,

unlike the other matters I have discussed with you, the defendant has the burden of proof.

(2)   Coercion can excuse a crime, but only if the following five factors are met:

(A) First, that the defendant reasonably believed there was a present, imminent, and impending threat of death or serious bodily injury *[to himself] [to another]*;

(B) Second, that the defendant had not recklessly or negligently placed himself *[another]* in a situation in which it was probable that he would be forced to choose the criminal conduct;

(C) Third, that the defendant had no reasonable, legal alternative to violating the law;

(D) Fourth, that the defendant reasonably believed his criminal conduct would avoid the threatened harm; and

(E) Fifth, that the defendant did not maintain the illegal conduct any longer than absolutely necessary.

(3)   If the defendant proves by a preponderance of the evidence the five elements listed above, then you must find the defendant not guilty.

(4)   Preponderance of the evidence is defined as "more likely than not." In other words, the defendant must convince you that the five factors are more likely true than not true.

3.   Michigan's Duress Statute

M.C.L. §768.21b. Defense of duress in breaking prison

(1)   If a defendant charged with breaking prison proposes to offer in his or her defense testimony to establish the defense of duress at the time of the alleged offense, the defendant at the time of arraignment on the information or within 15 days after that arraignment, but not less than 10 days before the trial of the case, or at such other time as the court directs, shall file and serve upon the prosecuting attorney a notice in writing of the intention to claim that defense. The notice shall contain, as particularly as is known to the defendant or the defendant's attorney, the names of witnesses to be called in behalf of the defendant to establish that defense. The defendant's notice shall include specific information relative to the defense.

(2)   Within 10 days after the receipt of the defendant's notice but not later than 5 days before the trial of the case, or at such other time as the court may direct, the prosecuting attorney shall file and serve upon the defendant a notice of rebuttal which shall contain, as particularly as is known to the prosecuting attorney, the names of the

witnesses whom the prosecuting attorney proposes to call in rebuttal to controvert the defendant's defense at the trial of the case.

(3)   Both the defendant and the prosecuting attorney shall be under a continuing duty to promptly disclose the names of additional witnesses which come to the attention of either party after filing the respective notices as provided in this section. Upon motion with notice to the other party and upon a showing by the moving party that the name of an additional witness was not available when the notice required by subsection (1) or (2) was filed, and could not have been available by the exercise of due diligence, the additional witness may be called by the moving party to testify as a witness for the purpose of establishing or rebutting the defense of duress or necessity.

(4)   In determining whether or not the defendant broke prison while under duress the jury or court may consider the following conditions if supported by competent evidence:

   (a)   Whether the defendant was faced with a specific threat of death, forcible sexual attack or substantial bodily injury in the immediate future.

   (b)   Whether there was insufficient time for a complaint to the authorities.

   (c)   Whether there was a history of complaints by the defendant which failed to provide relief.

   (d)   Whether there was insufficient time or opportunity to resort to the courts.

   (e)   Whether force or violence was not used towards innocent persons in the prison break.

   (f)   Whether the defendant immediately reported to the proper authorities upon reaching a position of safety from the immediate threat.

4.   Model Penal Code Provisions

§2.09. Duress

(1)   It is an affirmative defense that the actor engaged in the conduct charged to constitute an offense because he was coerced to do so by the use of, or a threat to use, unlawful force against his person or the person of another, that a person of reasonable firmness in his situation would have been unable to resist.

(2)   The defense provided by this Section is unavailable if the actor recklessly placed himself in a situation in which it was probable that he would be subjected to duress. The defense is also unavailable if he was negligent in placing himself in such a situation, whenever negligence suffices to establish culpability for the offense charged.

(3) It is not a defense that a woman acted on the command of her husband, unless she acted under such coercion as would establish a defense under this Section. [The presumption that a woman acting in the presence of her husband is coerced is abolished.]

(4) When the conduct of the actor would otherwise be justifiable under Section 3.02, this Section does not preclude such defense.

C. Necessity

1. "Choice of Evils"

It is always helpful in these cases to ask yourself if the defendant did the right thing. What would you have done under the circumstances in *Toops*?

Toops v. State, 643 N.E.2d 387 (Ind. App. 5 Dist. 1994)

RUCKER, Judge.

The driver of the car in which Terry Toops was a passenger panicked at the sight of police and dove into the back seat. When the car began to career out of control, Toops grabbed the steering wheel and drove for some distance even though he was intoxicated at the time. Toops was ultimately convicted of Count I—Operating A Vehicle While Intoxicated, Count II—Operating A Vehicle With 10% Or More Of Alcohol In Blood, Count III—Operating A Vehicle While Intoxicated With A Prior Offense Of Operating While Intoxicated, and Count IV—Operating A Vehicle With 10% Or More Alcohol In Blood With A Prior Offense Of Operating A Vehicle While Intoxicated. Toops now appeals raising four issues for our review. However, because one issue is dispositive we address it only: whether the trial court erred in refusing Toops's proposed jury instruction regarding the defense of necessity.

We reverse.

In the late evening hours of October 30, 1992, Terry Toops, Warren Cripe and Ed Raisor were present at Toops's home in Logansport, Indiana drinking beer. Around 3:00 a.m. the following morning the trio decided to drive to a store in town. Because he was intoxicated, Toops agreed to allow Cripe to drive Toops's car. Toops sat in the front passenger seat and Raisor sat in the rear. Toops began to feel ill during the drive and stuck his head out the window for fresh air. In the meantime, Sheriff's Deputy Michael Day and Town Marshall Gary Layer were on routine patrol when they observed a person later identified as Toops hanging out the car window. The officers decided to investigate and made a u-turn to follow the car. Cripe saw the patrol car turn around and panicked because he was a minor and had been drinking. He let go of the steering wheel and jumped into the back seat of the car. The car began to career out of control, leaving its lane, veering into the northbound lane of traffic then veering back into the southbound lane. Toops finally slid into the driver's seat and brought the car under control.

The officers overtook the car and noted that Toops, whom they had originally seen hanging out of the car window, was now seated behind the steering wheel. The officers also noted that Cripe and Raisor were seated in the back seat of the car. At the officers' request, Toops submitted to a breath test which revealed a BAC of .21%. As a result Toops was arrested and charged with various alcohol related traffic offenses. He was also charged with Criminal Recklessness, Operating a Vehicle Without a Seat Belt, and Driving Left of Center, all of which the State dismissed prior to trial. After a trial by jury Toops was convicted on all remaining counts. This appeal ensued in due course.

At the close of evidence Toops tendered the proposed jury instruction:

> The Defendant in this case has raised the defense of "Necessity" to excuse his assuming the controls of the vehicle at a time when he was intoxicated. "Necessity" involves a choice between two admitted evils where other options are unavailable. "Necessity" justifies illegal conduct if that conduct was the sole reasonable alternative available to Defendant given the circumstances of the case.
>
> In this case, the Defendant, Terry Toops, has admitted that he assumed control of the vehicle at a time when he was intoxicated. If you find that the Defendant's illegal conduct was justified by the circumstances, then you should find the Defendant "Not Guilty."

The trial court refused to give the instruction indicating "I cannot find that necessity is a recognized defense in the State of Indiana."

The origins of the necessity defense are lost in antiquity. At least one writer advances the notion that it may be traced to the Bible itself, the analogy being the destruction of property to save human lives: "Then the mariners were afraid, and cried every man unto his god, and cast forth the wares that were in the ship into the sea, to lighten it of them." Charles E. Torcia, *Wharton's Criminal Law* §90 (15th ed. 1993) quoting Jonah, c. 1, v. 5. In the criminal context the defense of necessity arose in the common law to excuse criminal conduct when a defendant was confronted with two evils and chose to engage in the prohibited conduct because it represented the lesser of the two evils. The underlying rationale is that to impose punishment upon a person who acted reasonably to avoid the greater harm serves neither to rehabilitate that person nor to deter others presented with a similar situation. It has also been observed that "[n]o action . . . can be criminal if it is not possible for a man to do otherwise. An unavoidable crime is a contradiction; whatever is unavoidable is no crime; and whatever is a crime is not unavoidable." John H. Gillett, *Gillett On Criminal Law* §7 (2d Ed. 1895) quoting Rutherforth's Inst. c. 18, sec. 9.

One of the leading decisions in this country recognizing the defense of necessity in a criminal law context is found in the landmark case of *United States v. Holmes,* 26 Fed. Cas. 360 (No. 15,383) (C.C.E.D.Pa. 1842). In that case a ship sank at sea forcing the survivors to crowd into a leaking lifeboat. The crew decided to throw sixteen passengers overboard to prevent the boat from sinking. Holmes, a crew member who participated in tossing passengers into the sea, was convicted of manslaughter and sentenced to six months' imprisonment. On appeal Holmes argued that his conduct was justified given the choices confronting him. Although rejecting Holmes's argument because the method of determining who was to live or die was not fair, the court nonetheless accepted the principle that committing a harm, even the taking of human life, could sometimes be justified because it avoided the loss of even more lives, which was a greater harm. *Id.*

The common law defense of necessity has evolved over the years and is often referred to as the "choice of evils" defense. In some jurisdictions the elements of the defense have been given statutory recognition, and in other jurisdictions the elements have been set forth in the case law. Although the confines of the necessity defense vary from jurisdiction to jurisdiction, the central element involves the emergency nature of the situation. That is, under the force of extreme circumstances, conduct that would otherwise constitute a crime is justifiable and not criminal because of the greater harm which the illegal act seeks to prevent.

Neither this court nor our supreme court has had occasion to discuss the parameters or the applicability of the common law necessity defense in a criminal context. However, our supreme court has recognized the existence of the defense. In any event, contrary to the State's argument, to say that the common law defense of necessity is not a recognized defense in the State of Indiana is incorrect. True, it has not been addressed in any substantive way by a court of review in this State. However, while there are no common law crimes in this State, the same is not true for common law defenses. The law in this jurisdiction is well settled that a defendant in a criminal case is entitled to have the jury instructed on any theory or defense which has some foundation in the evidence. And this is so even if the evidence is weak or inconsistent. There is no question that the evidence presented in this case raised a jury question as to whether Toops's control of the car while intoxicated, an illegal act, was necessary to prevent a greater harm, namely: an automobile collision potentially resulting in personal injury or property damage. Because the trial judge has a statutory duty to state to the jury "all matters of law which are necessary for their information in giving their verdict" Ind. Code §35–37–22(5), the failure to give any instruction on the necessity defense in this case was error.

We recognize that the test for reviewing the propriety of the trial court's decision to refuse a tendered instruction is: (1) whether the instruction correctly states the law; (2) whether there was evidence in the record to support the giving of the instruction; and (3) whether the substance of the instruction is covered by other instructions given by the court. In this case the record is clear that the second and third prongs of the test were met. The State contends, however, that the first prong is missing here, namely: Toops's tendered instruction is an incorrect statement of the law. Thus, the argument continues, the trial court did not err in refusing to give the instruction. We disagree. By covering the general confines of the necessity defense, Toops's instruction was correct but incomplete. However, to be upheld an instruction need not be a full statement of the law as long as it is a correct statement of the law. Here, the trial court not only refused to give Toops's tendered instruction, the court refused to give any instruction, reasoning the defense of necessity was not recognized in this State. This was error.

However, having determined error does not mean that we endorse the wording of Toops's proposed instruction. As we have indicated, the instruction represents an incomplete statement of the law. That incompleteness is understandable however because no Indiana case has specifically set forth the elements of the necessity defense. In that regard we agree with the California court's holding in *People v. Pena* (1983), 197 Cal. Rptr. 264, 271, that the following requirements have traditionally been held to be prerequisites in establishing a necessity defense: (1) the act charged as criminal must have been done to prevent a significant evil; (2) there must have been no adequate alternative to the commission of the act; (3) the harm caused by the act must not be disproportionate to the harm avoided; (4) the accused must entertain a good-faith belief that his act was necessary to prevent greater harm; (5) such belief must be objectively reasonable under all the circumstances; and (6) the accused must not have substantially contributed to the creation of the emergency. In the event of retrial on remand the foregoing elements should be incorporated into any tendered instruction on the defense of necessity.

For the reasons set forth herein, the judgment of the trial court is reversed and this cause is remanded.

Reversed and remanded.

2. Revisiting *Dudley and Stephens*

We now revisit the case of the men marooned at sea. Again, ask yourself what you would have done in this situation. Also, notice how *Dudley and Stephens* is a stark example of why duress and necessity are not complete defenses to murder. Should these defendants have been convicted of something less than murder?

The Queen v. Dudley and Stephens, 14 Q.B.D. 273 (1884)

LORD COLERIDGE, C.J.

The two prisoners, Thomas Dudley and Edwin Stephens, were indicted for the murder of Richard Parker on the high seas on the 25th of July in the present year. They were tried before my Brother Huddleston at Exeter on the 6th of

November, and, under the direction of my learned Brother, the jury returned a special verdict, the legal effect of which has been argued before us, and on which we are now to pronounce judgment.

The special verdict as, after certain objections by Mr. Collins to which the Attorney General yielded, it is finally settled before us is as follows. [His Lordship read the special verdict as above set out.] From these facts, stated with the cold precision of a special verdict, it appears sufficiently that the prisoners were subject to terrible temptation, to sufferings which might break down the bodily power of the strongest man, and try the conscience of the best. Other details yet more harrowing, facts still more loathsome and appalling, were presented to the jury, and are to be found recorded in my learned Brother's notes. But nevertheless this is clear, that the prisoners put to death a weak and unoffending boy upon the chance of preserving their own lives by feeding upon his flesh and blood after he was killed, and with the certainty of depriving him, of any possible chance of survival. The verdict finds in terms that "if the men had not fed upon the body of the boy they would *probably* not have survived," and that "the boy being in a much weaker condition was *likely* to have died before them." They might possibly have been picked up next day by a passing ship; they might possibly not have been picked up at all; in either case it is obvious that the killing of the boy would have been an unnecessary and profitless act. It is found by the verdict that the boy was incapable of resistance, and, in fact, made none; and it is not even suggested that his death was due to any violence on his part attempted against, or even so much as feared by, those who killed him. Under these circumstances the jury say that they are ignorant whether those who killed him were guilty of murder, and have referred it to this Court to determine what is the legal consequence which follows from the facts which they have found. . . .

There remains to be considered the real question in the case whether killing under the circumstances set forth in the verdict be or be not murder. . . . First it is said that it follows from various definitions of murder in books of authority, which definitions imply, if they do not state, the doctrine, that in order to save your own life you may lawfully take away the life of another, when that other is neither attempting nor threatening yours, nor is guilty of any illegal act whatever towards you or any one else. But if these definitions be looked at they will not be found to sustain this contention. . . .

Is there, then, any authority for the proposition which has been presented to us? Decided cases there are none. The case of the seven English sailors referred to by the commentator on Grotius and by Puffendorf has been discovered by a gentleman of the Bar, who communicated with my Brother Huddleston, to convey the authority (if it conveys so much) of a single judge of the island of St. Kitts, when that island was possessed partly by France and partly by this country, somewhere about the year 1641. It is mentioned in a medical treatise published at Amsterdam, and is altogether, as authority in an English court, as unsatisfactory as possible. The American case cited by Brother

Stephen in his Digest, from Wharton on Homicide, in which it was decided, correctly indeed, that sailors had no right to throw passengers overboard to save themselves, but on the somewhat strange ground that the proper mode of determining who was to be sacrificed was to vote upon the subject by ballot, can hardly, as my Brother Stephen says, be an authority satisfactory to a court in this country. The observations of Lord Mansfield in the case of *Rex v. Stratton and Others*, striking and excellent as they are, were delivered in a political trial, where the question was whether a political necessity had arisen for deposing a Governor of Madras. But they have little application to the case before us which must be decided on very different considerations.

The one real authority of former time is Lord Bacon, who, in his commentary on the maxim, "necessitas inducit privilegium quoad jura privata," lays down the law as follows: "Necessity carrieth a privilege in itself. Necessity is of three sorts—necessity of conservation of life, necessity of obedience, and necessity of the act of God or of a stranger. First of conservation of life; if a man steal viands to satisfy his present hunger, this is no felony nor larceny. So if divers be in danger of drowning by the casting away of some boat or barge, and one of them get to some plank, or on the boat's side to keep himself above water, and another to save his life thrust him from it, whereby he is drowned, this is neither se defendendo nor by misadventure, but justifiable." On this it is to be observed that Lord Bacon's proposition that stealing to satisfy hunger is no larceny is hardly supported by Staundforde, whom he cites for it, and is expressly contradicted by Lord Hale in the passage already cited. And for the proposition as to the plank or boat, it is said to be derived from the canonists. At any rate he cites no authority for it, and it must stand upon his own. Lord Bacon was great even as a lawyer; but it is permissible to much smaller men, relying upon principle and on the authority of others, the equals and even the superiors of Lord Bacon as lawyers, to question the soundness of his dictum. There are many conceivable states of things in which it might possibly be true, but if Lord Bacon meant to lay down the broad proposition that a man may save his life by killing, if necessary, an innocent and unoffending neighbour, it certainly is not law at the present day.

There remains the authority of my Brother Stephen, who, both in his Digest and in his History of the Criminal Law, uses language perhaps wide enough to cover this case. The language is somewhat vague in both places, but it does not in either place cover this case of necessity, and we have the best authority for saying that it was not meant to cover it. If it had been necessary, we must with true deference have differed from him, but it is satisfactory [to] know that we have, probably at least, arrived at no conclusion in which if he had been a member of the Court he would have been unable to agree. Neither are we in conflict with any opinion expressed upon the subject by the learned persons who formed the commission for preparing the Criminal Code. They say on this subject:

We are certainly not prepared to suggest that necessity should in every case be a justification. We are equally unprepared to, suggest that necessity should in no case be a defence; we judge it better to leave such questions to be dealt with when, if ever, they arise in practice by applying the principles of law to the circumstances of the particular case.

It would have been satisfactory to us if these eminent persons could have told us whether the received definitions of legal necessity were in their judgment correct and exhaustive, and if not, in what way they should be amended but as it is we have, as they say, "to apply the principles of law to the circumstances of this particular case."

Now, except for the purpose of testing how far the conservation of a man's own life is in all cases and under all circumstances, an absolute, unqualified, and paramount duty, we exclude from our consideration all the incidents of war. We are dealing with a case of private homicide, not one imposed upon men in the service of their Sovereign and in the defence of their country. Now it is admitted that the deliberate killing of this unoffending and unresisting boy was clearly murder, unless the killing can be justified by some well-recognised excuse admitted by the law. It is further admitted that there was in this case no such excuse, unless the killing was justified by what has been called "necessity." But the temptation to the act which existed here was not what the law has ever called necessity. Nor is this to be regretted. Though law and morality are not the same, and many things may be immoral which are not necessarily illegal, yet the absolute divorce of law from morality would be of fatal consequence; and such divorce would follow if the temptation to murder in this case were to be held by law an absolute defence of it. It is not so. To preserve one's life is generally speaking a duty, but it may be the plainest and the highest duty to sacrifice it. War is full of instances in which it is a man's duty not to live, but to die. The duty, in case of shipwreck, of a captain to his crew, of the crew to the passengers, of soldiers to women and children, as in the noble case of the *Birkenhead*; these duties impose on men the moral necessity, not of the preservation, but of the sacrifice of their lives for others from which in no country, least of all, it is to be hoped, in England, will men ever shrink, as indeed, they have not shrunk. . . .

It is not suggested that in this particular case the deeds were "devilish," but it is quite plain that such a principle once admitted might be made the legal cloak for unbridled passion and atrocious crime. There is no safe path for judges to tread but to ascertain the law to the best of their ability and to declare it according to their judgment; and if in any case the law appears to be too severe on individuals, to leave it to the Sovereign to exercise that prerogative of mercy which the Constitution has intrusted to the hands fittest to dispense it.

It must not be supposed that in refusing to admit temptation to be an excuse for crime it is forgotten how terrible the temptation was; how awful the suffering; how hard in such trials to keep the judgment straight and the conduct pure. We are often compelled to set up standards we cannot reach ourselves, and to lay down rules which we could not ourselves satisfy. But a man has no right to declare temptation to be an excuse, though he might himself have yielded to it, nor allow compassion for the criminal to change or weaken in any manner the legal definition of the crime. It is therefore our duty to declare that the prisoners' act in this case was wilful murder, that the facts as stated in the verdict are no legal justification of the homicide; and to say that in our unanimous opinion the prisoners are upon this special verdict guilty of murder.

[The COURT then proceeded to pass sentence of death upon the prisoners. This sentence was afterwards commuted by the Crown to six months imprisonment.]

3. Practice Problems on Necessity

A self-employed limousine driver agrees to drive a man and woman to the airport. After the couple get into the limo, they signal to the driver to put down the window separating the driver from the passengers. As the driver does so, the woman in the back puts a gun into the back of the driver's neck. The male passenger then tells the driver to park in front of a nearby bank so that the man can go in and rob the bank. He also says that when he returns, he expects the driver to take the two of them to a specific location to avoid the police. If the driver fails to comply, the female passenger will kill him. Defendant does as he is ordered and the robbery is successful.

If the driver is charged with bank robbery as an accomplice, what should his defense be? Will it be successful? Why?

What if the driver is ordered under the same circumstances to run over a pedestrian and kill him? If he does so, does he have a defense to murder? If not, of what crime should he be convicted?

4. Model Penal Code Provisions

§3.02. Justification Generally: Choice of Evils

> (1) Conduct that the actor believes to be necessary to avoid a harm or evil to himself or to another is justifiable, provided that:
> > (a) the harm or evil sought to be avoided by such conduct is greater than that sought to be prevented by the law defining the offense charged; and
> > (b) neither the Code nor other law defining the offense provides exceptions or defenses dealing with the specific situation involved; and

(c) a legislative purpose to exclude the justification claimed does not otherwise plainly appear.

(2) When the actor was reckless or negligent in bringing about the situation requiring a choice of harms or evils or in appraising the necessity for his conduct, the justification afforded by this Section is unavailable in a prosecution for any offense for which recklessness or negligence, as the case may be, suffices to establish culpability.

D. Condonation

Why is forgiveness by the victim of a crime not a defense? What problems would this cause?

People v. Zito, 2001 WL 1263340 (New Rochelle City Ct. Oct. 2, 2001)

RIPPA, J.

The Defendant in this case was charged with Criminal Contempt in the Second Degree, in violation of Penal Law §215.50(3). The charges arose out of the Defendant's alleged violation of an order of protection issued in favor of the Defendant's ex-wife Katherine Zito, on May 2, 2001 by Judge Linda Jamieson of the Westchester County Family Court.

Said order, which had been duly served on the Defendant, directed him, inter alia, to

> [s]tay away from . . . Katherine Zito and/or from the home of Katherine Zito; . . . [r]efrain from communication . . . with Katherine Zito; . . . [r]efrain from assault, harassment, menacing, reckless endangerment, disorderly conduct, intimidation, threats or any criminal offense against . . . Katherine Zito.

A bench trial of the action took place on August 7, 2001. The Complainant, Katherine Zito, testified that on April 20, 2001 at approximately 7:00 a.m., she was coming out of her home to take out the trash when she heard a motorcycle and subsequently observed the Defendant drive by her home on his motorcycle without stopping. She stated that she next saw the Defendant proceed to the next intersection, make a turn and come back. He then stopped in the street in front of her home, where he revved his engine but did not alight from his bike. The Complainant then went inside her house.

Ms. Zito added that a couple of minutes later she heard the Defendant's motorcycle again, and when she opened the door she saw that the Defendant had returned. She then started screaming at him because one of her windows, which had been broken in the recent past, was broken again that week and she felt that Defendant had been the culprit. At that point, the Defendant yelled back at her "Did you have a good time f___ing your boyfriend last night?", "You're a piece of shit and a whore", "Was it all worth it?". The Complainant stated that she then went inside and called the police because she has known the Defendant to get very angry and lose control in the past, and she was worried.

On cross-examination, the Complainant testified that she and the Defendant had been married for one year in 1978 and then divorced. She explained that after the divorce, they continued living as husband and wife on and off for many years, had travelled as such, and had sent out invitations to her daughter's wedding as husband and wife. Even though the Complainant denied having lived with the Defendant after the issuance of the order of protection, she admitted that they had cohabitated overnight on a few occasions.

During her cross-examination, Ms. Zito admitted that there is a pending civil proceeding between her and the Defendant regarding ownership of the marital home. However, she denied that she is using the criminal charges as a way to force the Defendant into a favorable settlement in that case.

The Defendant, testifying on his own behalf, claimed that on the date in question, he was not in the City of New Rochelle but was instead in Bayonne, New Jersey, working on a television program of which he is a cast member. He stated that he must usually be on the set at 6:30 a.m. and, therefore, he could not have been in New Rochelle at 7:00 a.m. When asked if anyone could confirm his whereabouts, the Defendant explained that he had no witnesses in court who could place him at work on the date in question, because he was embarrassed to ask anyone to testify.

The Defendant related that he and the Complainant had lived together as husband and wife from the time of their divorce until 1999. He stated that even though the parties had reciprocal orders of protection, even after the issuance of the orders he and the Complainant had lived together for a month in an effort to reconcile. He stated that on other occasions he had also been back to the marital home; the most recent being a few days before April 20, 2001. He explained that for four months, even though he was living in a rented apartment in New Rochelle, he would spend some nights with the Complainant in the marital home and they would sleep in the same bed. The Complainant would either pick him up at his apartment or he would drive to her place himself; but he would not park in front of the house because of the order of protection.

On cross-examination the Defendant admitted to having accused the Complainant of having affairs and to having called her names sometimes, but he denied having done so on the date in question. The Defendant also admitted that he and the Complainant are in the midst of civil litigation over ownership of the marital home. He explained that even though the house had originally belonged to the Complainant, he had spent $400,000 renovating it while they were together and, therefore, he felt that the home also belonged to him.

DISCUSSION

In order to reach a decision regarding Defendant's guilt of criminal contempt or lack thereof, the Court must examine several issues. The first of such issues is whether the order of protection issued by the Family Court on May 2, 2000 was still in force on April 20, 2001 or whether the parties' conduct, and especially that of the Complainant, rendered the order of protection a nullity.

The Court is unaware of any statutory or case law which holds that condonation by a party in whose favor an order of protection is issued can vitiate a duly issued order of the court. Under our system of justice, an order of protection can only be modified or lifted by the court which originally issued it or by a court of superior jurisdiction. As such, no action on the part of the parties in whose favor or against whom the order was issued can act to nullify such order. Thus, the order of protection at issue herein was still valid and in force at the time of the alleged incident, despite the parties' tacit consent to disregard it. . . .

Commonwealth v. Rotonda, 434 Mass. 211 (2001)

CORDY, J.

The Commonwealth challenges the lawfulness of the terms and conditions imposed by a District Court judge in a continuance without a finding disposition made pursuant to G.L. c. 278, §18. It contends that such a continuance must include a condition of supervised probation, which this disposition did not, and also contends that it cannot be conditioned on the defendant's payment of money to the complaining victim, where restitution was neither an issue nor documented. The Commonwealth urges this court to vacate the disposition of the District Court and remand the case for trial. For the reasons set forth below, we find that the imposition of a condition of supervised probation is not a requirement of a continuance without a finding disposition made pursuant to G.L. c. 278, §18, but that the condition that a $5,000 payment be made to the complaining witness, in the circumstances of this case, is contrary to law and public policy. We therefore remand the case for further proceedings. . . .

. . . On December 22, 1998, the defendant, Gerard Rotonda, III, threatened and verbally accosted a traffic enforcement officer who had written him a parking ticket. After finding the ticket on his windshield, the defendant drove around the corner and confronted the officer, screaming invectives and racial slurs at her. Because the officer believed the defendant was going to hit her, she held down the transmit button on her radio so that others on the system could hear the altercation. The defendant eventually fled. The officer filed a complaint and the defendant was charged with violating the civil rights of another, without bodily injury, . . . and threatening to commit a crime . . . .

On December 6, 1999, the scheduled trial date, the defendant asked the District Court judge to continue the case in order to investigate late night threatening telephone calls that the defendant had been receiving, some of which had been traced to the victim's place of employment. Defense counsel also claimed that he was prepared to present evidence that, during the pendency of the case, the defendant's automobile had been vandalized several times and the front door of his apartment had been kicked down twice. The judge advised the parties that he was prepared to grant the continuance based on those representations. The victim, through the Commonwealth, objected to the continuance and requested that the case proceed to trial. The judge then asked the parties to confer and attempt to resolve the case without a trial.

Following the conference, the parties reported to the judge that they were unable to agree on a disposition—the defendant seeking a continuance without a finding for one year, and the prosecution insisting on a finding of guilty with one year's probation.

At this point, defense counsel provided the court with information regarding the defendant's background, including his lack of a criminal record, bachelor's and master's degrees in business administration, employment in the financial services industry in Boston, and his receipt while in high school of a commendation for having initiated CPR on an Army lieutenant who suffered a heart attack on a public street. In addition, defense counsel informed the judge that the acts alleged "were not indicative of the [d]efendant's character," and that he recently had married a member of a minority group.

After further discussion regarding how the judge might rule on the pending motion for a continuance, the defendant admitted to sufficient facts and tendered pleas of guilty, . . . together with a request that guilty findings not be entered and that the case be continued without a finding for one year. The Commonwealth recommended the entry of a guilty finding and a probationary sentence including community service. Following this exchange, the judge held a hearing during which the Commonwealth recited a summary of the facts underlying the charges, including the police report of the incident, and the victim made a statement about how the incident had affected her.

The judge found that the Commonwealth's recitation of facts was a sufficient basis to find the defendant guilty, and accepted the defendant's request, made over the Commonwealth's objection, to continue the case for one year without a finding, subject to certain conditions to be discussed below. In support of his decision to accept the defendant's terms, the judge found that the defendant readily admitted guilt and expressed contrition for his action; was a stranger to the victim and had not initiated further contact with her; had no prior involvement with the criminal justice system; held a responsible job in the financial services industry and the imposition of a guilty finding could affect his employment status and future employment; and did not present a danger to the victim. The judge also found that the incident was a single event lasting less than five minutes; that the Commonwealth was not seeking to have the defendant incarcerated; and that the interests of justice and the interest of the victim were protected by continuing the matter without a finding with the imposition of a "serious fine and conditions."

. . . [T]he judge then imposed a number of specific terms and conditions. The judge ordered that the defendant be placed on "unsupervised probation" for one year, on the condition that the defendant not have any contact with the victim, that he publicly apologize to her in front of her fellow employees and members of her union, and that he make a payment of $5,000 as "restitution" to her.

In overruling the Commonwealth's objection to this disposition, the judge ruled that it conformed to the requirements of G.L. c. 278, §18, and, because both charges were misdemeanors and did not implicate a mandatory minimum sentence, a continuance without a finding was not "otherwise prohibited by law." The judge further ruled that the defendant's request for probation without the requirement of reporting to a probation officer (unsupervised probation) was reasonable because of the defendant's lack of prior involvement with the criminal justice system, and further contact between the defendant and the victim was unlikely. The requirement to report in person or by telephone to a probation officer was thus not in the interests of justice. The judge, however, imposed all the other standard conditions of probation on the defendant including the requirement that he maintain gainful employment; notify the probation officer of any change in status including employment or housing; and refrain from committing any local, State, or Federal crimes. . . .

We now turn to one of the specific conditions imposed.

"Any act which is made punishable by law as a crime is an offence against the public, and, especially in this country, where all prosecutions are subject to the control of official prosecutors, and not of the individuals immediately injured, cannot lawfully be made the subject of private compromise, except so far as expressly authorized by statute. And this view is supported by the great weight of American authority." *Partridge v. Hood,* 120 Mass. 403, 407, 1876 WL 14291 (1876).

This bedrock principle of American justice is important for several reasons. Private payments exchanged for releases from criminal responsibility erode, if not completely erase, the demarcation between the criminal and civil systems of justice and "benefit the individual at the expense of defeating the course of public justice." Moreover, such payments create the perception that a class-based criminal justice system exists and that those with resources may buy their way out of criminal liability. Our law does not countenance payments directed to private parties for the purpose of or in connection with the termination of criminal proceedings absent clear statutory authority for such payments, and we are not disposed to construe such statutory provisions beyond their expressed purposes and specific requirements. Although G.L. c. 278, §18, does not enumerate, define, or limit the scope of the terms and conditions that the District Court may impose, the judge's imposition of the condition of a payment to the complaining witness is contrary to the public policy embodied in this

526 | Criminal Law: Cases, Statutes, and Problems

principle, and, in the circumstances of this case, is without support in any statutory provision.

If it was the judge's intention to impose a financial penalty on the defendant, he could have accomplished that legitimate objective by requiring the defendant to pay the "reasonable and actual expenses of the prosecution," pursuant to G.L. c. 280, §6. These expenses could have been significant, but would have been paid to the Commonwealth rather than to the complaining witness.

To the extent that the judge wanted to ensure that the victim of the defendant's conduct was made whole and was reimbursed for any economic loss caused by the defendant's actions and by the consequent prosecution of the case, he could have directed that restitution be calculated and made a requirement of the final disposition, for restitution is an appropriate consideration in sentencing. Victims are entitled to request restitution and judges are empowered to impose it pursuant to G.L. c. 258B, §3 (o). The purpose of restitution, however, is to compensate the injured party for losses incurred as a result of the defendant's criminal conduct. It is not to reward or create an incentive for the dismissal of criminal charges. The payment of restitution is limited to the economic losses caused by the conduct of the defendant and documented by the victim.

While such items as medical expenses, court-related travel expenses, property loss and damage, lost pay, or even lost paid vacation days required to be used to attend court proceedings might all be included in an appropriately documented restitution order, this was not the case here. A dollar amount was selected without regard to any fact other than whether it might "satisfy" the victim in this case.

For these reasons we find that the imposition of a financial payment to be made to a complaining witness as a condition of the continuance without a finding and dismissal, in the circumstances of this case, was contrary to law and public policy and not authorized by the court's power to impose terms and conditions on a continuance without a finding disposition as provided in G.L. c. 278, §18. . . .

So ordered.

Chapter 18
Preventing Escape, Defense of Property, and Defense of Habitation

A. Introduction

The defenses covered in this chapter are related in that the basic issue of each is determining when a person can use deadly force against someone committing, or fleeing from committing, a crime against that person or others. Very often these defenses overlap with each other, as well as with self-defense and defense of others. The general rule in this country has been that deadly force may not be used to defend or regain possession of personal property unless a person is also in danger. However, the right to use deadly force in such cases has been broadened by statute or case law in many states.

There are competing policy concerns in these cases. The courts and legislatures must weigh the goals of preventing crime, apprehending lawbreakers, and protecting the security of the home, against the goal of protecting the lives of innocent persons and felons alike.

B. Preventing Escape

1. Stopping the Fleeing Criminal

Many Americans possess firearms as a way to protect themselves from crime. Although the next section of this chapter discusses protecting against crime, these first cases deal with stopping a criminal who is fleeing from the crime to avoid capture.

What limitations are placed on the police in apprehending a criminal who is fleeing from his crime? Do the same limits apply to private citizens?

Tennessee v. Garner, 471 U.S. 1 (1985)

Justice WHITE delivered the opinion of the Court.

This case requires us to determine the constitutionality of the use of deadly force to prevent the escape of an apparently unarmed suspected felon. We conclude that such force may not be used unless it is necessary to prevent the escape and the officer has probable cause to believe that the suspect poses a significant threat of death or serious physical injury to the officer or others.

I

At about 10:45 p.m. on October 3, 1974, Memphis Police Officers Elton Hymon and Leslie Wright were dispatched to answer a "prowler inside call." Upon arriving at the scene they saw a woman standing on her porch and gesturing toward the adjacent house. She told them she had heard glass breaking and that "they" or "someone" was breaking in next door. While Wright radioed the dispatcher to say that they were on the scene, Hymon went behind the house. He heard a door slam and saw someone run across the backyard. The fleeing suspect, who was appellee-respondent's decedent, Edward Garner, stopped at a 6-feet-high chain link fence at the edge of the yard. With the aid of a flashlight, Hymon was able to see Garner's face and hands. He saw no sign of a weapon, and, though not certain, was "reasonably sure" and "figured" that Garner was unarmed. He thought Garner was 17 or 18 years old and about 5'5" or 5'7" tall. While Garner was crouched at the base of the fence, Hymon called out "police, halt" and took a few steps toward him. Garner then began to climb over the fence. Convinced that if Garner made it over the fence he would elude capture, Hymon shot him. The bullet hit Garner in the back of the head. Garner was taken by ambulance to a hospital, where he died on the operating table. Ten dollars and a purse taken from the house were found on his body.

In using deadly force to prevent the escape, Hymon was acting under the authority of a Tennessee statute and pursuant to Police Department policy. The statute provides that "[i]f, after notice of the intention to arrest the defendant, he either flee or forcibly resist, the officer may use all the necessary means to effect the arrest." Tenn.Code Ann. §40–7–108 (1982). The Department policy was slightly more restrictive than the statute, but still allowed the use of deadly force in cases of burglary. App. 140–144. The incident was reviewed by the Memphis Police Firearm's Review Board and presented to a grand jury. Neither took any action.

Garner's father then brought this action in the Federal District Court for the Western District of Tennessee, seeking damages under 42 U.S.C. §1983 for asserted violations of Garner's constitutional rights. The complaint alleged that the shooting violated the Fourth, Fifth, Sixth, Eighth, and Fourteenth Amendments of the United States Constitution. It named as defendants Officer Hymon, the Police Department, its Director, and the Mayor and city of Memphis. After a 3-day bench trial, the District Court entered judgment for all defendants. It dismissed the claims against the Mayor and the Director for lack of evidence. It then concluded that Hymon's actions were authorized by the Tennessee statute, which in turn was constitutional. Hymon had employed the only reasonable and practicable means of preventing Garner's escape. Garner had "recklessly and heedlessly attempted to vault over the fence to escape, thereby assuming the risk of being fired upon."

The Court of Appeals for the Sixth Circuit affirmed with regard to Hymon, finding that he had acted in good-faith reliance on the Tennessee statute and was therefore within the scope of his qualified immunity. It remanded for reconsideration of the possible liability of the city, however, in light of *Monell v. New York City Dept. of Social Services,* 436 U.S. 658 (1978), which had come down after the District Court's decision. The District Court was directed to consider whether a city enjoyed a qualified immunity, whether the use of deadly force and hollow point bullets in these circumstances was constitutional, and whether any unconstitutional municipal conduct flowed from a "policy or custom" as required for liability under *Monell.*

The District Court concluded that *Monell* did not affect its decision. While acknowledging some doubt as to the possible immunity of the city, it found that the statute, and Hymon's actions, were constitutional. Given this conclusion, it declined to consider the "policy or custom" question.

The Court of Appeals reversed and remanded. It reasoned that the killing of a fleeing suspect is a "seizure" under the Fourth Amendment, and is therefore constitutional only if "reasonable." The Tennessee statute failed as applied to this case because it did not adequately limit the use of deadly force by distinguishing between felonies of different magnitudes — "the facts, as found, did not justify the use of deadly force under the Fourth Amendment." Officers cannot resort to deadly force unless they "have probable cause . . . to believe that the suspect [has committed a felony and] poses a threat to the safety of the officers or a danger to the community if left at large." . . .

II

Whenever an officer restrains the freedom of a person to walk away, he has seized that person. While it is not always clear just when minimal police interference becomes a seizure, there can be no question that apprehension by the use of deadly force is a seizure subject to the reasonableness requirement of the Fourth Amendment.

A

A police officer may arrest a person if he has probable cause to believe that person committed a crime. Petitioners and appellant argue that if this requirement is satisfied the Fourth Amendment has nothing to say about *how* that seizure is made. This submission ignores the many cases in which this Court, by balancing the extent of the intrusion against the need for it, has examined the reasonableness of the manner in which a search or seizure is conducted. To determine the constitutionality of a seizure "[w]e must balance the nature and quality of the intrusion on the individual's Fourth Amendment interests against the importance of the governmental interests alleged to justify the intrusion." We have described "the balancing of competing interests" as "the key principle of the Fourth Amendment." Because one of the factors is the extent of the intrusion, it is plain that reasonableness depends on not only when a seizure is made, but also how it is carried out. . . .

B

The same balancing process . . . demonstrates that, notwithstanding probable cause to seize a suspect, an officer may not always do so by killing him. The intrusiveness of a seizure by means of deadly force is unmatched. The suspect's fundamental interest in his own life need not be elaborated upon. The use of deadly force also frustrates the interest of the individual, and of society, in judicial determination of guilt and punishment. Against these interests are ranged governmental interests in effective law enforcement. It is argued that overall violence will be reduced by encouraging the peaceful submission of suspects who know that they may be shot if they flee. Effectiveness in making arrests requires the resort to deadly force, or at least the meaningful threat thereof. . . .

Without in any way disparaging the importance of these goals, we are not convinced that the use of deadly force is a sufficiently productive means of accomplishing them to justify the killing of nonviolent suspects. The use of deadly force is a self-defeating way of apprehending a suspect and so setting the criminal justice mechanism in motion. If successful, it guarantees that that mechanism will not be set in motion. And while the meaningful threat of deadly force might be thought to lead to the arrest of more live suspects by discouraging escape attempts, the presently available evidence does not support this thesis. The fact is that a majority of police departments in this country have forbidden the use of deadly force against nonviolent suspects. If those charged with the enforcement of the criminal law have abjured the use of deadly force in arresting nondangerous felons, there is a substantial basis for doubting that the use of such force is an essential attribute of the arrest power in all felony cases. Petitioners and appellant have not persuaded us that shooting nondangerous fleeing suspects is so vital as to outweigh the suspect's interest in his own life.

The use of deadly force to prevent the escape of all felony suspects, whatever the circumstances, is constitutionally unreasonable. It is not better that all felony suspects die than that they escape. Where the suspect poses no immediate threat to the officer and no threat to others, the harm resulting from failing to apprehend him does not justify the use of deadly force to do so. It is no doubt unfortunate when a suspect who is in sight escapes, but the fact that the police arrive a little late or are a little slower afoot does not always justify killing the suspect. A police officer may not seize an unarmed, nondangerous suspect by shooting him dead. The Tennessee statute is unconstitutional insofar as it authorizes the use of deadly force against such fleeing suspects.

It is not, however, unconstitutional on its face. Where the officer has probable cause to believe that the suspect poses a threat of serious physical harm, either to the officer or to others, it is not constitutionally unreasonable to prevent escape by using deadly force. Thus, if the suspect threatens the officer with a weapon or there is probable cause to believe that he has committed a crime involving the infliction or threatened infliction of serious physical harm, deadly force may be used if necessary to prevent escape, and if, where feasible, some warning has been given. As applied in such circumstances, the Tennessee statute would pass constitutional muster.

III
A

It is insisted that the Fourth Amendment must be construed in light of the common-law rule, which allowed the use of whatever force was necessary to effect the arrest of a fleeing felon, though not a misdemeanant. . . .

The State and city argue that because this was the prevailing rule at the time of the adoption of the Fourth Amendment and for some time thereafter, and is still in force in some States, use of deadly force against a fleeing felon must be "reasonable." It is true that this Court has often looked to the common law in evaluating the reasonableness, for Fourth Amendment purposes, of police activity. On the other hand, it "has not simply frozen into constitutional law those law enforcement practices that existed at the time of the Fourth Amendment's passage." Because of sweeping change in the legal and technological context, reliance on the common-law rule in this case would be a mistaken literalism that ignores the purposes of a historical inquiry.

B

It has been pointed out many times that the common-law rule is best understood in light of the fact that it arose at a time when virtually all felonies were punishable by death. "Though effected without the protections and formalities of an orderly trial and conviction, the killing of a resisting or fleeing felon resulted in no greater consequences than those authorized for punishment of the felony of which the individual was charged or suspected." American Law Institute, Model Penal Code §3.07, Comment 3, p. 56 (Tentative Draft No. 8, 1958) (hereinafter Model Penal Code Comment). Courts have also justified the common-law rule by emphasizing the relative dangerousness of felons.

Neither of these justifications makes sense today. Almost all crimes formerly punishable by death no longer are or can be. And while in earlier times "the gulf between the felonies and the minor offences was broad and deep," today the distinction is minor and often arbitrary. Many crimes classified as misdemeanors, or nonexistent, at common law are now felonies. These changes have undermined the concept, which was questionable to begin with, that use of deadly force against a fleeing felon is merely a speedier execution of someone who has already forfeited his life. They have also made the assumption that a "felon" is more dangerous than a misdemeanant untenable. Indeed, numerous misdemeanors involve conduct more dangerous than many felonies.

There is an additional reason why the common-law rule cannot be directly translated to the present day. The common-law rule developed at a time when weapons were rudimentary. Deadly force could be inflicted almost solely in a hand-to-hand struggle during which, necessarily, the safety of the arresting officer was at risk. Handguns were not carried by police officers until the latter half of the last century. Only then did it become possible to use deadly force from a distance as a means of apprehension. As a practical matter, the use of deadly force under the standard articulation of the common-law rule has an altogether different meaning—and harsher consequences—now than in past centuries.

One other aspect of the common-law rule bears emphasis. It forbids the use of deadly force to apprehend a misdemeanant, condemning such action as disproportionately severe. In short, though the common-law pedigree of Tennessee's rule is pure on its face, changes in the legal and technological context mean the rule is distorted almost beyond recognition when literally applied.

C

In evaluating the reasonableness of police procedures under the Fourth Amendment, we have also looked to prevailing rules in individual jurisdictions. The rules in the States are varied. Some 19 States have codified the common-law rule, though in two of these the courts have significantly limited the statute. Four States, though without a relevant statute, apparently retain the common-law rule. Two States have adopted the Model Penal Code's provision verbatim. Eighteen others allow, in slightly varying language, the use of deadly force only if the suspect has committed a felony involving the use or threat of physical or deadly force, or is escaping with a deadly weapon, or is likely to endanger life or inflict serious physical injury if not arrested. Louisiana and Vermont, though without statutes or case law on point, do forbid the use of deadly force to prevent any but violent felonies. The remaining States either have no relevant statute or case law, or have positions that are unclear.

It cannot be said that there is a constant or overwhelming trend away from the common-law rule. In recent years, some States have reviewed their laws and expressly rejected abandonment of the common-law rule. Nonetheless, the long-term movement has been away from the rule that deadly force may be used against any fleeing felon, and that remains the rule in less than half the States.

This trend is more evident and impressive when viewed in light of the policies adopted by the police departments themselves. Overwhelmingly, these are more restrictive than the common-law rule. The Federal Bureau of Investigation and the New York City Police Department, for example, both forbid the use of firearms except when necessary to prevent death or grievous bodily harm. For accreditation by the Commission on Accreditation for Law Enforcement Agencies, a department must restrict the use of deadly force to situations where "the officer reasonably believes that the action is in defense of human life . . . or in defense of any person in immediate danger of serious physical injury." . . . In light of the rules adopted by those who must actually administer them, the older and fading common-law view is a dubious indicium of the constitutionality of the Tennessee statute now before us.

D

Actual departmental policies are important for an additional reason. We would hesitate to declare a police practice of long standing "unreasonable" if doing so would severely hamper effective law enforcement. But the indications are to the contrary. There has been no suggestion that crime has worsened in any way in jurisdictions that have adopted, by legislation or departmental policy, rules similar to that announced today. . . .

IV

The District Court concluded that Hymon was justified in shooting Garner because state law allows, and the Federal Constitution does not forbid, the use of deadly force to prevent the escape of a fleeing felony suspect if no alternative means of apprehension is available. This conclusion made a determination of Garner's apparent dangerousness unnecessary. The court did find, however, that Garner appeared to be unarmed, though Hymon could not be certain that was the case. Restated in Fourth Amendment terms, this means Hymon had no articulable basis to think Garner was armed.

In reversing, the Court of Appeals accepted the District Court's factual conclusions and held that "the facts, as found, did not justify the use of deadly force." We agree. Officer Hymon could not reasonably have believed that Garner—young, slight, and unarmed—posed any threat. Indeed, Hymon never attempted to justify his actions on any basis other than the need to prevent an escape. The District Court stated in passing that "[t]he facts of this case did not indicate to Officer Hymon that Garner was 'non-dangerous.' " This conclusion is not explained, and seems to be based solely on the fact that Garner had broken into a house at night. However, the fact that Garner was a suspected burglar could not, without regard to the other circumstances, automatically justify the use of deadly force. Hymon did not have probable cause to believe that Garner, whom he correctly believed to be unarmed, posed any physical danger to himself or others. . . .

V

We wish to make clear what our holding means in the context of this case. The complaint has been dismissed as to all the individual defendants. The State is a party only by virtue of 28 U.S.C. §2403(b) and is not subject to liability. The possible liability of the remaining defendants—the Police Department and the city of Memphis—hinges on *Monell v. New York City Dept. of Social Services,* 436 U.S. 658 (1978), and is left for remand. We hold that the statute is invalid insofar as it purported to give Hymon the authority to act as he did. As for the policy of the Police Department, the absence of any discussion of this issue by the courts below, and the uncertain state of the record, preclude any consideration of its validity.

The judgment of the Court of Appeals is affirmed, and the case is remanded for further proceedings consistent with this opinion.

So ordered.

Note

In *Plumhoff v. Rickard,* ___ US ___, 2014 WL 2178335 (May 27, 2014), the Court found that police did not violate a fleeing suspect's Fourth Amendment rights when they fired 15 rounds into his car, killing the suspect and his passenger. The suspect led the police in a five-minute car chase with speeds exceeding 100 miles per hour. They passed at least a dozen other motorists who were forced to get out of the way. Although the police eventually succeeded in stopping the suspect by blocking him with their cars, he kept spinning his wheels and rocking his car back and forth in an attempt to escape. After an officer fired three shots into the suspect's car, the suspect managed to put his car in reverse and drive down another street. At that point, other officers fired into the car causing it to crash, killing both persons in the car.

2. When can private citizens use deadly force to apprehend a fleeing felon?

A minority of states permit private citizens to use deadly force to apprehend a fleeing felon. *See* Joshua Dressler, *Understanding Criminal Law* §21.03 (6th ed. 2012). Michigan, as seen below, is one of those states. Note how the Michigan court limits the holding of *Garner.*

People v. Couch, 436 Mich. 414 (1990)

BOYLE, Justice.

We agree . . . that the decision of the United States Supreme Court in *Tennessee v. Garner,* 471 U.S. 1 (1985), did not "automatically" modify this state's criminal law with respect to the use of deadly force to apprehend a fleeing felon.

. . . *Garner's* pronouncements regarding the constitutionality of the use of such force are inapplicable to private citizens such as the defendant. Regardless of the defendant's status as a private citizen, however, the prosecution's argument that *Garner* applies directly to change this state's fleeing-felon rule fails because it is premised upon the notion that the United States Supreme Court can require a state to criminalize certain conduct. Clearly, the power to define conduct as a *state* criminal offense lies with the individual states, not with the federal government or even the United States Supreme Court. While the failure to proscribe or prevent certain conduct could possibly subject the state to *civil* liability for its failure to act, or for an individual's actions, if that state, for whatever reason, chooses not to criminalize such conduct, it cannot be compelled to do so.

Moreover, we fail to see how *Garner* can be applied "directly" in any event, since the Court in that case concluded only that the use of deadly force to apprehend a fleeing felon who posed no harm to the officer or others was "unreasonable" for purposes of the *Fourth Amendment.* In other words, *Garner* was a *civil* case which made no mention of the officer's criminal responsibility for his "unreasonable" actions. Thus, not only is the United States Supreme Court without authority to require this state to make shooting a nondangerous fleeing felon a *crime,* it has never even expressed an intent to do so.

. . . [W]e decline the opportunity to change the common-law fleeing-felon rule with respect to criminal liability to conform with *Garner.* Not only does this Court (and therefore the Court of Appeals) arguably lack the authority to do so, even prospectively, given the Legislature's adoption of and acquiescence in that rule, we must resist the temptation to do so. The question whether the common law, which allows the use of deadly force by a citizen only to apprehend a felon who is *in fact* guilty, has outlived its "utility" is a matter of compelling public interest, demanding a balancing of legitimate interests which this Court (and therefore the Court of Appeals) is institutionally unsuited to perform. In short, it is a question for the Legislature.

I

Justice Campbell observed long ago in *In re Lamphere,* 61 Mich. 105, 108 (1886), that

> [w]hile we have kept in our statute-books a general statute resorting to the common law for non-enumerated crimes, there has always been a purpose in our legislation to have the whole ground of criminal law defined, as far as possible, by statute. There is no crime whatever punishable by our laws except by virtue of a statutory provision. (Emphasis added).

Criminal homicide, or more precisely murder and manslaughter, has been a statutory offense in Michigan since 1846, when the state's first Penal Code was enacted. 1846 Mich. Rev. Stat., title xxx, "Of Crimes and the Punishment Thereof," ch. 153, §1, defined first-degree murder:

> All murder which shall be perpetrated by means of poison or lying in wait, or any other kind of wilful, deliberate, and premeditated killing, or which shall be committed in the perpetration, or attempt to perpetrate any arson, rape, robbery or burglary, shall be deemed murder of the first degree, and shall be punished by solitary confinement at hard labor in the state prison for life.

Section 2 defined second-degree murder:

> All other kinds of murder shall be deemed murder of the second degree, and shall be punished by imprisonment in the state prison for life, or any term of years, in the discretion of the court trying the same.

Section 10 referred to the crime of manslaughter:

> Every person who shall commit the crime of manslaughter, shall be punished by imprisonment in the state prison, not more than fifteen years, or by fine not exceeding one thousand dollars, or both, at the discretion of the court.

Obviously, the crimes of murder and manslaughter are not defined in these statutes in the sense that the elements of those offenses, along with any recognized defenses, are included in the language of the statutes. That does not mean, however, that they are left wholly undefined. As Justice Jackson stated in *Morissette v. United States,* 342 U.S. 246, 263 (1952):

> [W]here [a legislature] borrows terms of art in which are accumulated the legal tradition and meaning of centuries of practice, it presumably knows and adopts the cluster of ideas that were attached to each borrowed word in the body of learning from which it was taken and the meaning its use will convey to the judicial mind unless otherwise instructed. In such case, absence of contrary direction may be taken as satisfaction with widely accepted definitions, not as a departure from them.

Similarly, in *People v. Schmitt,* 275 Mich. 575, 577 (1936), this Court stated that "[i]n construing a statute wherein a public offense has been declared in the general terms of the common law, without more particular definition, the courts generally refer to the common law for the particular acts constituting the offense." Where the Legislature "has shown no disposition to depart from the common-law definition, *therefore it remains.*" *Id.* (Emphasis added.)

To the extent that the Legislature intended to convey "satisfaction with" the existing common-law definitions of murder and manslaughter and to adopt and embrace those definitions, *Morissette, supra,* 342 U.S. p. 263, it is debatable whether this Court still has the authority to change those definitions. The Legislature is presumed to have accepted the then-existing common-law rule that "[a]ny private person (and *a fortiori* a peace-officer) [may arrest a fleeing felon] . . . and if *they kill him,* provided he cannot otherwise be taken, it is justifiable. . . ." 4 Blackstone, Commentaries, p. 293 (emphasis in original). Thus, murder and manslaughter, arguably, are no longer common-law crimes in this state, but rather became statutory crimes as early as 1846, and we are no longer free to redefine what is not justifiable homicide by holding that a citizen is "not privileged to use deadly force to prevent a fleeing felon's escape unless the arresting citizen reasonably believes that the felon poses a threat of serious physical harm to that citizen or to others." Post, p. 695.

We need not resolve our authority to modify the common-law rule, however, because we find in any event that the presumption of legislative adoption is in this case affirmed by fifty years of legislative acquiescence in this Court's decision in *People v. Gonsler,* 251 Mich. 443, 446–447 (1930), in which we approved the trial court's instruction that

> [b]oth officers and private persons seeking to prevent a felon's escape must exercise reasonable care to prevent the escape of the felon without doing personal violence, *and it is only where killing him is necessary to prevent this escape, that the killing is justified. . . . If a killing is not justifiable, it is either murder or manslaughter.* (Emphasis added.)

II

Regardless of whether this Court has the authority to change the law of homicide, and make criminal something that has never before been a crime in this state, we nonetheless decline to do so in this case. "To declare what shall constitute a crime, and how it shall be punished, is an exercise of the sovereign power of a state, and is inherent in the legislative department of the government." *People v. Hanrahan,* 75 Mich. 611, 619 (1889). This is particularly true here.

The definitions of a "nondangerous" felony, or who is a nondangerous felon, and how such a felon may be apprehended are quintessentially matters of policy. They involve the delicate weighing and balancing of the particular nature and quality of the felonious intrusion on a citizen's interests, on the one hand, and the protection of the felon's interest in longevity on the other. There is an obvious difference, for example, in the citizen's interest in the sanctity of his home and his interest in his automobile or power boat, just as there is a clear distinction between setting fire to a dwelling and stealing a $200 bicycle, although all are felony/property offenses. Presumably for this reason, the penal codes of some states grant the authority to apprehend a fleeing felon through the use of deadly force if the arrest is for a "forcible" felony, and at least one state has defined forcible felony to include, among others, arson and burglary.

Since the Legislature has evidenced no general intent to reduce the penalties for "mere" property offenses, or, for that matter, major drug offenses, it may well be that the Legislature would not refine such distinctions with respect to the fleeing-felon rule, and would draw the line by saying that a person *who is in fact guilty* and chooses to flee from the scene of a felony assumes a risk to life and limb. For example, the Legislature may decide that the civil penalties for an improper exercise of the right to use deadly force, as well as the fact that the private citizen acts at his peril and is criminally responsible if he is wrong, are enough of a deterrent to the misuse of such authority.

The point is not that another rule may be wiser, or that there are not situations in which the loss of a felon's life is tragic, but rather that it is the Legislature that must determine whether the common-law rule has outlived its "utility." Stated otherwise, it is hard to conceive of an issue more demanding of public debate and the give-and-take of the legislative process than whether the citizens of Michigan are willing to assume the risk that certain criminals should remain at large rather than be subjected to the risk of harm at the hands of their victims. The clear question of policy, whether police officers or citizens should be subject to *criminal* liability for the killing of a nondangerous fleeing felon, is one for the Legislature, not this Court.

CONCLUSION

We affirm in part the decision of the Court of Appeals insofar as it holds that *Garner* did not change this state's criminal law with respect to the use of deadly force to apprehend a fleeing felon. . . . However, we reverse the decision of the Court of Appeals to "adopt[ ] a new standard," *People v. Couch,* 176 Mich. App. 254, 260, 439 N.W.2d 354 (1989), with respect to that rule.

Note

The Massachusetts Supreme Court took a different approach than Michigan. The *Klein* case below seems to represent the majority view. *See* Joshua Dressler, *Understanding Criminal Law* §21.03 (6th ed. 2012).

Commonwealth v. Klein, 372 Mass. 823 (1977)

HENNESSEY, Chief Justice.

The defendant, a dentist residing in Springfield, was found guilty by a jury of charges in two indictments. One indictment charged him with assault and battery by means of a dangerous weapon (a firearm) on Napoleon J. LaDue; the other indictment charged the same offense against John Savageau. Both offenses were alleged to have occurred on August 1, 1973. It is undisputed that the defendant shot and wounded the two men after they had in the nighttime broken into a drug store located across the street from the defendant's home. The defendant telephoned the police, and after a time went outside his home, armed with a pistol, and the confrontation occurred which gave rise to these indictments.

We hold that the judge charged the jury correctly in this case, as judged in light of principles of law which we in this case adopt governing the right of citizens to use deadly force in attempting to effect the arrest of felons. Further, we conclude that the jury were warranted in returning guilty verdicts on the evidence as considered in light of the judge's instructions to them. Nevertheless, since we are now expounding these rules of law for the first time in this Commonwealth, we also hold that the rules should not be applied retroactively against this defendant. Consequently, we are ordering that judgments of not guilty be entered as to both indictments. . .

[According to the testimony as summarized by the court, defendant took his handgun, went across the street to the store, and attempted to make a citizen's arrest of the two burglars as they left the store. When the two men refused to comply, defendant shot at them, striking one. He then shot at them again as they were running from the building, striking the other one.]

The central question in this case is whether the defendant was justified in using deadly force. We define deadly force as force intended or likely to cause death or great bodily harm. This tracks with our long-standing definition of a "dangerous weapon," viz.: an instrument that is likely to produce death or serious bodily injury. Clearly the defendant in this case used deadly force in firing shots from a handgun. . . .

We turn now to consideration of the defendant's claim that he was justified in using deadly force to prevent the escape of the two men from his attempt to make a citizen's arrest.

The defendant's arguments as to citizen's arrest are three in number. First, he contends that he was entitled on this ground to directed verdicts of not guilty. Second, he says that he is entitled at least to a new trial because the judge's charge to the jury was in error as too restrictive in its definition of the defendant's rights in the circumstances of this case. The third contention is that the law applicable to the citizen's right to use deadly force in arresting a felon has never been expounded in this Commonwealth. Therefore, the defendant says that, if he acted excessively in light of the applicable law as decided in this case, that law cannot fairly be applied retroactively to his detriment.

In a few instances, this court has considered the broad issue of the use of excessive force in effecting an arrest. However, it is true, as the defendant contends, that we have never clearly set the limits of the arresting citizen's right to use deadly force.

Thus, we must consider in this context what rules of law will best serve the public interest in this Commonwealth. Our common law has long recognized a private citizen's right to arrest. Nevertheless, limits must be set, as to the use of deadly force, against the dangers of uncontrolled vigilantism and anarchistic actions and particularly against the danger of death or injury of innocent persons at the hands of untrained volunteers using firearms. In our view, for example, there would be no wisdom in approving the unqualified right of a private citizen to use deadly force to prevent the escape of one who has committed a crime against property only.

Some jurisdictions have adopted such limiting rules. See 32 A.L.R.3d 1072–1077, Annot., 1078–1119 (1970). In *Commonwealth v. Chermansky*, 430 Pa. 170 (1968), for example, it was held that the prerequisites to justify the use of deadly force by a private person in order to effect the arrest or prevent the escape of a felon are that the person must be in fresh pursuit of the felon and that he must give notice of his purpose to make the arrest for the felony if the attendant circumstances are themselves insufficient to warn the felon of the intention of the pursuing party to arrest him; that such felony must actually have been committed by the person against whom the force is used; And the felony must be one which normally causes or threatens death or great bodily harm.

We have examined comparable law elsewhere, and we think the relevant provisions of the Model Penal Code will best serve this Commonwealth. These provisions were adopted after extensive debate among knowledgeable and distinguished contributors. In the past we have relied on portions of the code to clarify vague areas of our criminal law. Accordingly, we establish as the law of Massachusetts the rules (in so far as they are material to the instant case) as found in §3.07 of the Model Penal Code (Proposed Official Draft 1962). They are as follows:

Section 3.07. Use of Force in Law Enforcement.

(1) *Use of Force Justifiable to Effect an Arrest.* Subject to the provisions of this Section and of Section 3.09, the use of force upon or toward the person of another is justifiable when the actor is making or assisting in making an arrest and the actor believes that such force is immediately necessary to effect a lawful arrest.

(2) *Limitations on the Use of Force.*

(a) The use of force is not justifiable under this Section unless:

(i) the actor makes known the purpose of the arrest or believes that it is otherwise known by or cannot reasonably be made known to the person to be arrested; and

(ii) when the arrest is made under a warrant, the warrant is valid or believed by the actor to be valid.

(b) The use of *deadly force* [emphasis supplied] is not justifiable under this Section unless:

(1) the arrest is for a felony; and

(ii) the person effecting the arrest is authorized to act as a peace officer or is assisting a person whom he believes to be authorized to act as a peace officer; and

(iii) the actor believes that the force employed creates no substantial risk of injury to innocent persons; and

(iv) the actor believes that:

(1) the crime for which the arrest is made involved conduct including the use or threatened use of deadly force; or

(2) there is a substantial risk that the person to be arrested will cause death or serious bodily harm if his apprehension is delayed.

We further hold that, since the right of the defendant to arrest and prevent the escape of the victims was raised in the evidence, the burden of disproving this defense beyond a reasonable doubt rested on the Commonwealth.

The judge's instructions to the jury in this case were, in most important respects, consistent with the rules of the Model Penal Code quoted above. He charged in substance that deadly force could not be used to effect the arrest or prevent the escape of one who had committed a felony concerned with property only.

As measured by the principles which we have now established and the judge's charge, it is clear that the Commonwealth met its burden of proving beyond a reasonable doubt that the shootings were not justified. There was evidence which tended to show that, even though the victims had been engaged in a serious crime, it was a crime concerned with property only and entailed no threat of death or great bodily harm. Thus, under the rules of law that we have established here, the guilty verdicts were clearly warranted over the defendant's claim of justification.

We now consider the defendant's argument that the state of the law at the time of the occurrence of this incident in 1973 was such that a reasonable man, with knowledge of the law, would be led to believe that a private person would have the right to use such force as was necessary, including deadly force, to effect the arrest or prevent the escape of a person who committed a felony in his presence. . . .

We conclude that, in the circumstances of this case, the standards we have now established should not be applied retroactively. We reach this conclusion through considerations of fairness; it cannot fairly be said that the defendant was on notice of the possible criminality of his conduct. We need not consider whether, additionally, a retroactive application of the law to the defendant might be violative of his constitutional right to due process of law.

The defendant was aware that he had a citizen's right of arrest; the felony was committed in his presence; it could fairly be said that there was evidence that he gave notice to the two men that he intended their arrest and that he was assisting the police (whom the defendant had called) by attempting to prevent the escape of the men. He met the standards for justification of his use of the firearm (as we now for the first time establish them) in all respects except that the felons were not themselves engaged in a crime which threatened death or great bodily harm.

In these circumstances the defendant should not be held to have had knowledge of the "possible criminality" of his conduct (see *Mullaney v. Wilbur*, 421 U.S. 684 (1975)), and the law should not be applied retroactively against him. His judgment was undoubtedly poor; his conduct could justly be called rash. Nevertheless his intent was to assist the cause of law enforcement; on the evidence, no lawless motive or malicious spirit can be attributed to him.

In the interest of curbing the promiscuous use of firearms, and the unnecessary and dangerous use of deadly force in the community, we have now set limits applicable to arrests by private persons. The defendant can be held to have used excessive force only in light of the fact that the felons here were not themselves engaged in the use of threatened use of deadly force in their crimes directed against the drug store. Public knowledge of this somewhat subtle requirement of the law, a requirement which we shall apply in the future, should not be charged against the defendant retroactively.

Since the Commonwealth had the burden of disproving, by proof beyond a reasonable doubt, the defendant's assertion of justification, and, since we have concluded that he is not to be charged retroactively with the rules we have established in this opinion, it follows that in the circumstances of this case, as matter of law, the Commonwealth has not met its burden. The judgments are reversed and the verdicts set aside. Judgments of not guilty shall be entered as to both indictments.

So ordered.

C. Defense of Property

1. Cases

Is a car worth more than a human life? What interest was Ms. Emmons protecting when she used deadly force? Does it make any difference that the victim was not committing a crime?

Commonwealth v. Emmons, 157 Pa. Super. 495 (1945)

ARNOLD, Judge.

The defendant, Mildred E. Emmons, on September 21, 1943, shot one Edward Gray with a rifle and seriously injured him. She was indicted in three counts—assault and battery with intent to murder, aggravated assault and battery and simple assault and battery. The jury found her guilty of aggravated assault and battery. The Court overruled defendant's motion for new trial and sentence, and this appeal followed.

The defendant lived in a second floor apartment of a house in Secane, Upper Darby, Delaware County, Pa. The apartment house fronted on a forty foot wide improved street known as Broadway Avenue. On the side of the house was an unopened street known as Beechwood Avenue, which was a cul-de-sac ending at the rear of the apartment house premises, and was used by the defendant as a way to a garage on the premises.

The defendant had purchased under a bailment lease a Chevrolet Sedan automobile, and on September 21, 1943, was in default thereunder in the amount of $115.66, being two monthly installments. The bailment lease gave the bailor the right to repossess upon default. The lease had been assigned by the seller-bailor to a finance company, which determined to repossess. Its representative came to defendant's second floor apartment on September 21, 1943 at about 11 o'clock a. m., knocked on the door and also rang the doorbell. There was no response, the defendant later claiming she was asleep.

Defendant's automobile was at this time parked on the unopened cul-de-sac street called Beechwood Avenue. With the aid of Gray (an employe of a commercial garage) defendant's automobile was pushed backwards onto Broadway Avenue and parked near the curb, and the hood of the automobile was raised in order to check the serial numbers. Two shots were fired and the left femur bone in the leg of Edward Gray was badly shattered.

Circumstances led the police officers to interview the defendant who stated that she had fired with a .22 rifle, but did not recall how many shots. She said that she believed the men were stealing her automobile, and that she fired at a point near the intersection of the unopened street and Broadway Avenue, and did not aim at, or intend to shoot, anyone. There was, however, evidence on the part of the Commonwealth upon which the jury may well have found that the defendant intentionally shot Gray.

The various assignments of error raise but one question, viz:

Where in good faith and upon reasonable grounds, one believes her automobile is being stolen from where it was parked in broad daylight on an unopen street (or private way)—may one shoot the person believed to be the thief in order to prevent the supposed larceny? The learned Court below answered this question in the negative, and so do we.

While it has been asserted that some rule of law exists which justifies killing in order to prevent the commission of a felony, we are convinced that no such broadly stated rule exists. There is no right to kill in order to prevent *any* felony. To justify the killing it must be to prevent the commission of a felony which is either an atrocious crime or one attempted to be committed by force (or surprise) such as murder, arson, burglary, rape, kidnapping, sodomy or the like.

While we are unable to discover any Pennsylvania cases on the subject, all writers seem to be in accord, both where the death of the supposed felon results, and where some form of assault and battery is committed. . . .

In the present case the defendant was not defending her person, or her home or "castle". There was no felony by force, nor any atrocious crime, to be prevented. There was no danger to her, or her habitation. There was no force by an intruder for her to repel. There was no justification in law for her infliction of grievous bodily harm.

The assignments of error are overruled, the judgment of the Court below is affirmed, and defendant is directed to appear in the Court below at such time as she may be there called, and that she be by that Court committed until she has complied with her sentence or any part of it that had not been performed at the time the appeal was made a supersedeas.

2. Arizona's Justification Statute

A.R.S. 13–411. Justification; use of force in crime prevention; applicability

> (A) A person is justified in threatening or using both physical force and deadly physical force against another if and to the extent the person reasonably believes that physical force or deadly physical force is immediately necessary to prevent the other's commission of arson of an occupied structure under §13–1704, burglary in the second or first degree under §13-1507 or 13–1508, kidnapping under §13–1304, manslaughter under §13–1103, second or first degree murder under §13–1104 or 13–1105, sexual conduct with a minor under §13–1405, sexual assault under §13–1406, child molestation under §13–1410, armed robbery under §13–1904 or aggravated assault under §13–1204, subsection A, paragraphs 1 and 2.
>
> (B) There is no duty to retreat before threatening or using physical force or deadly physical force justified by subsection A of this section.
>
> (C) A person is presumed to be acting reasonably for the purposes of this section if the person is acting to prevent what the person reasonably believes is the imminent or actual commission of any of the offenses listed in subsection A of this section.
>
> (D) This section includes the use or threatened use of physical force or deadly physical force in a person's home, residence, place of business, land the person owns or leases, conveyance of any kind, or any other place in this state where a person has a right to be.

D. Defense of Habitation

1. Cases

Most jurisdictions provide a broader defense when protecting your own home. The Arizona statute cited above extends that right to other forceful and violent crimes. While reading the next two cases, note that both the California and Utah Supreme Courts base their decisions on statutes. Another example is the Oklahoma statute reproduced at the end of this section.

People v. Ceballos, 12 Cal.3d 470 (1974)

BURKE, Justice.

Don Ceballos was found guilty by a jury of assault with a deadly weapon (Pen. Code, §245). Imposition of sentence was suspended and he was placed on probation. He appeals from the judgment, contending primarily that his conduct was not unlawful because the alleged victim was attempting to commit burglary when hit by a trap gun mounted in the garage of defendant's dwelling and that the court erred in instructing the jury. We have concluded that the former argument lacks merit, that the court did not commit prejudicial error in instructing the jury, and that the judgment should be affirmed.

Defendant lived alone in a home in San Anselmo. The regular living quarters were above the garage, but defendant sometimes slept in the garage and had about $2,000 worth of property there.

In March 1970 some tools were stolen from defendant's home. On May 12, 1970, he noticed the lock on his garage doors was bent and pry marks were on one of the doors. The next day he mounted a loaded .22 caliber pistol in the garage. The pistol was aimed at the center of the garage doors and was connected by a wire to one of the doors so that the pistol would discharge if the door was opened several inches.

The damage to defendant's lock had been done by a 16-year-old boy named Stephen and a 15-year-old boy named Robert. On the afternoon of May 15, 1970, the boys returned to defendant's house while he was away. Neither boy was armed with a gun or knife. After looking in the windows and seeing no one, Stephen succeeded in removing the lock on the garage doors with a crowbar, and, as he pulled the door outward, he was hit in the face with a bullet from the pistol.

Stephen testified: He intended to go into the garage "(f)or musical equipment" because he had a debt to pay to a friend. His "way of paying that debt would be to take [defendant's] property and sell it" and use the proceeds to pay the debt. He "wasn't going to do it [i.e., steal] for sure, necessarily." He was there "to look around," and "getting in, I don't know if I would have actually stolen."

Defendant, testifying in his own behalf, admitted having set up the trap gun. He stated that after noticing the pry marks on his garage door on May 12, he felt he should "set up some kind of a trap, something to keep the burglar out of my home." When asked why he was trying to keep the burglar out, he replied, ". . . Because somebody was trying to steal my property . . . and I don't want to come home some night and have the thief in there . . . usually a thief is pretty desperate . . . and . . . they just pick up a weapon . . . if they don't have one . . . and do the best they can."

When asked by the police shortly after the shooting why he assembled the trap gun, defendant stated that "he didn't have much and he wanted to protect what he did have."

As heretofore appears, the jury found defendant guilty of assault with a deadly weapon. An assault is "an unlawful attempt, coupled with a present ability, to commit a violent injury on the person of another."

Defendant contends that had he been present he would have been justified in shooting Stephen since Stephen was attempting to commit burglary, that defendant had a right to do indirectly what he could have done directly, and that therefore any attempt by him to commit a violent injury upon Stephen was not "unlawful" and hence not an assault. The People argue that the rule in Gilliam is unsound, that as a matter of law a trap gun constitutes excessive force, and that in any event the circumstances were not in fact such as to warrant the use of deadly force.

The issue of criminal liability under statutes such as **Penal Code section 245** where the instrument employed is a trap gun or other deadly mechanical device appears to be one of first impression in this state, but in other jurisdictions courts have considered the question of criminal and civil liability for death or injuries inflicted by such a device.

At common law in England it was held that a trespasser, having knowledge that there are spring guns in a wood, cannot maintain an action for an injury received in consequence of his accidentally stepping on the wire of such gun. That case aroused such a protest in England that it was abrogated seven years later by a statute, which made it a misdemeanor to set spring guns with intent to inflict grievous bodily injury but excluded from its operation a spring gun set between sunset and sunrise in a dwelling house for the protection thereof.

In the United States, courts have concluded that a person may be held criminally liable under statutes proscribing homicides and shooting with intent to injure, or civilly liable, if he sets upon his premises a deadly mechanical device and that device kills or injures another. However, an exception to the rule that there may be criminal and civil liability for death or injuries caused by such a device has been recognized where the intrusion is, in fact, such that the person, were he present, would be justified in taking the life or inflicting the bodily harm with his own hands. The phrase "were he present" does not hypothesize the actual presence of the person, but is used in setting forth in an indirect manner the principle that a person may do indirectly that which he is privileged to do directly.

Allowing persons, at their own risk, to employ deadly mechanical devices imperils the lives of children, firemen and policemen acting within the scope of their employment, and others. Where the actor is present, there is always the possibility he will realize that deadly force is not necessary, but deadly mechanical devices are without mercy or discretion. Such devices "are silent instrumentalities of death. They deal death and destruction to the innocent as well as the criminal intruder without the slightest warning. The taking of human life [or infliction of great bodily injury] by such means is brutally savage and inhuman."

It seems clear that the use of such devices should not be encouraged. Moreover, whatever may be thought in torts, the foregoing rule setting forth an exception to liability for death or injuries inflicted by such devices "is inappropriate in penal law for it is obvious that it does not prescribe a workable standard of conduct; liability depends upon fortuitous results." We therefore decline to adopt that rule in criminal cases.

Furthermore, even if that rule were applied here, as we shall see, defendant was not justified in shooting Stephen. Penal Code section 197 provides: "Homicide is . . . justifiable . . . 1. When resisting any attempt to murder any person, or to commit a felony, or to do some great bodily injury upon any person; or, 2. When committed in defense of habitation, property, or person, against one who manifestly intends or endeavors, by violence or surprise, to commit a felony . . . ." (See also Pen. Code, §198.) Since a homicide is justifiable under the circumstances specified in section 197, *a fortiori* an attempt to commit a violent injury upon another under those circumstances is justifiable.

By its terms subdivision 1 of Penal Code section 197 appears to permit killing to prevent any "felony," but in view of the large number of felonies today and the inclusion of many that do not involve a danger of serious bodily harm, a literal reading of the section is undesirable. ". . . We must look further into the character of the crime, and the manner of its perpetration. *When these do not reasonably create a fear of great bodily harm*, as they could not if defendant apprehended only a misdemeanor assault, *there is no cause for the exaction of a human life.*"

. . . [S]ubdivision 2 of that section is likewise so limited. The term "violence of surprise" in subdivision 2 is found in common law authorities, and, whatever may have been the very early common law, the rule developed at common law that killing or use of deadly force to prevent a felony was justified only if the offense was a forcible and atrocious crime. "Surprise" means an unexpected attack—which includes force and violence and the word thus appears redundant.

Examples of forcible and atrocious crimes are murder, mayhem, rape and robbery. In such crimes "from their atrocity and violence human life [or personal safety from great harm] either is, or is presumed to be, in peril."

Burglary has been included in the list of such crimes. However, in view of the wide scope of burglary under Penal Code section 459, as compared with the common law definition of that offense, in our opinion it cannot be said that under all circumstances burglary under section 459 constitutes a forcible and atrocious crime.

Where the character and manner of the burglary do not reasonably create a fear of great bodily harm, there is no cause for exaction of human life or for the use of deadly force. The character and manner of the burglary could not reasonably create such a fear unless the burglary threatened, or was reasonably believed to threaten, death or serious bodily harm.

In the instant case the asserted burglary did not threaten death or serious bodily harm, since no one but Stephen and Robert was then on the premises. A defendant is not protected from liability merely by the fact that the intruder's conduct is such as would justify the defendant, were he present, in believing that the intrusion threatened death or serious bodily injury. There is ordinarily the possibility that the defendant, were he present, would realize the true state of affairs and recognize the intruder as one whom he would not be justified in killing or wounding.

We thus conclude that defendant was not justified under Penal Code section 197, subdivisions 1 or 2, in shooting Stephen to prevent him from committing burglary. Our conclusion is in accord with dictum indicating that there may be no privilege to use a deadly mechanical device to prevent a burglary of a dwelling house in which no one is present. . . .

We conclude that as a matter of law the exception to the rule of liability for injuries inflicted by a deadly mechanical device does not apply under the circumstances here appearing. . . .

The judgment is affirmed.

State v. Mitcheson, 560 P.2d 1120 (Utah 1977)

CROCKETT, Justice:

The defendant, Gary Alfred Mitcheson, was convicted of murder in the second degree for shooting Richard Herrera in the front yard of 432 South Fourth East, Price, Utah, at about 3:30 a.m. on February 7, 1976. He was sentenced to a term of five years to life in the state prison.

On his appeal the point of critical concern is his charge that the trial court erred in refusing his request to instruct the jury on the defense of using force in the protection of one's habitation.

The deceased, Richard Herrera, sold his car (a 1967 Chevrolet van) to Alfred Mitcheson, defendant's father, on December 15, 1975. The original wheels and tires had been changed for what are called "Mag Wheels" and tires, which have a wider tread. Some time after the father had taken possession of the van, a dispute arose between the parties over those wheels. The father, supported by the defendant, claimed that they had been included in the sale, but the deceased and his brother, Ernie Herrera, claimed they only agreed to loan the "Mag Wheels" and tires temporarily.

On several occasions in January, 1976, the two brothers requested that the wheels and tires be returned, but the defendant and his father did not comply. On one of those occasions the Herrera brothers and some friends went to the father's home to remove the wheels. The father protested and called the police. When they arrived they told the Herreras, the deceased and his brother, to leave the wheels alone and that any disagreement should be settled by going to court.

A few days thereafter, on February 6, 1976, the defendant was parked in the van at a drive-in restaurant when the deceased came up to the van, opened the door and hit the defendant on the jaw and eye; and made threats to the defendant to the effect that I will "put you under." A couple of hours later the defendant and some of his friends went to the home of Jerry Giraud, where they saw the deceased's car parked. There was a conversation in which the defendant offered to fight the deceased, which was then refused. But, they agreed to meet in the town park and fight at 2:00 o'clock the next afternoon.

Defendant and his friend, Wendell Johnson, drove to his father's house, where the defendant obtained a rifle. He and Johnson then arranged for a poker game to be held at the home of defendant's sister, Debbie, and went there in the van where they proceeded to play cards. Still later that night, at about 3:30 a.m., the deceased, Richard Herrera, and some of his friends drove up to this house for the stated purpose of removing the wheels from the van. When they entered upon her premises Debbie told them to leave. They did not comply. A considerable commotion ensued, including her screaming at them to get off her premises. Defendant came to the doorway of the house with the rifle. He fired a shot and Richard Herrera fell with a bullet wound in his neck from which he shortly expired.

The essence of the defense, and the basis for the requested instructions, was that the defendant was using the rifle as a backup resource in protection of the peace and security of his habitation and that its discharge and the striking of the deceased was an accident. The argument that the defendant was not entitled to that instruction is: (1) that the sister's home was not his habitation; and (2) that it was inconsistent with his own testimony and theory of defense that the shooting was an accident.

Defense of Habitation

The pertinent statute is 76–2–405, U.C.A. 1953, which provides in part:

> A person is justified in using force against another when and to the extent that he reasonably believes . . . necessary to prevent . . . other's unlawful entry into or attack upon his habitation; however, he is justified in the use of force which is intended to cause death or serious bodily injury only if:
>
> (1) The entry is made or attempted in a violent and tumultuous manner and he reasonably believes that the entry is attempted or made for the purpose of assaulting or offering personal violence to any person, dwelling or being therein . . . .

That statute has its roots in the ancient and honored doctrine of the common law that a man's home is his castle, and that even the peasant in his cottage may peaceably abide within the protective cloak of the law, and no one, not even the king nor all his armies can enter to disturb him.

In view of the salutary purpose of that statute, of preserving the peace and good order of society, it should be interpreted and applied in the broad sense to accomplish that purpose. Thus it would include not only a person's actual residence, but also whatever place he may be occupying peacefully as a substitute home or habitation, such as a hotel, motel, or even where he is a guest in the home of another; and so would apply to the defendant in his sister's home.

Issue of the Inconsistent Defenses

It is our judgment that the position of the defendant: that he was defending what he regarded as his habitation, is not necessarily inconsistent with his assertion that the discharge of the gun and the striking of the deceased in the neck was an accident. Furthermore, even if they were inconsistent, that should not deprive the defendant of either defense.

In a criminal case the defendant need not specially plead his defenses. The entry of a plea of not guilty places upon the State the burden of proving every element of the offense beyond a reasonable doubt. This gives the defendant the benefit of every defense thereto which may cause a reasonable doubt to exist as to his guilt, arising either from the evidence, or lack of evidence, in the case; and this is true whether his defenses are consistent or not.

On the basis of what has been said herein, it is our opinion that if the requested instruction had been given and the jury had so considered the evidence, there is a reasonable likelihood that it may have had some effect upon the verdict rendered. Therefore the defendant's request should have been granted. Accordingly, it is necessary that the judgment be reversed and that the case be remanded for a new trial. No costs awarded.

2. Oklahoma's Defense of Habitation Statute

O.S. 21–1289.25. Physical or deadly force against intruder

> (A)   The Legislature hereby recognizes that the citizens of the State of Oklahoma have a right to expect absolute safety within their own homes.
>
> (B)   Any occupant of a dwelling is justified in using any degree of physical force, including and not limited to deadly force, against another person who has made an unlawful entry into that dwelling, and when the occupant has a reasonable belief that such another person might use any physical force, no matter how slight, against any occupant of the dwelling.
>
> (C)   Any occupant of a dwelling using physical force, including but not limited to deadly force, pursuant to the provisions of subsection B of

this section, shall have an affirmative defense in any criminal prosecution for an offense arising from the reasonable use of such force and shall be immune from any civil liability for injuries or death resulting from the reasonable use of such force.

(D) The provisions of this section and the provisions of the Oklahoma Self-Defense Act, Sections 1 through 25 of this act, shall not be construed to require any person using a pistol pursuant to the provisions of this section to be licensed in any manner.

3. Practice Problems on Defense of Habitation

A homeowner was awakened at 3:30 am by a loud pounding on his front door. He grabbed his rifle and went to the front door. Looking out of the small window on the door, the homeowner saw an unfamiliar woman on his front porch. He did not see anyone else in front of his house or any unfamiliar cars parked nearby. The woman seemed disoriented and was screaming, "Let me in!" The homeowner shouted through the closed door for her to go away.

The woman then started kicking and pulling at the door, still shouting "Let me in!" The homeowner told her to go away or he would shoot her. She did not relent so the homeowner shouted for her to back away from the door. He waited for about 30 seconds and fired two shots through his door. One of the shots struck the woman and killed her. Subsequent investigation revealed that the woman was unarmed and had been in a car accident less than a mile from the homeowner's house. She also had alcohol and marijuana in her system and likely suffered a head injury in the car accident.

Under the principles enunciated in *Ceballos*, and using the Defense of Habitation statute provided in *Mitcheson*, can the homeowner successfully defend against a charge of murder by arguing that he was defending his home? Why or why not?

E. Model Penal Code Provisions

§3.07. Use of Force in Law Enforcement

(1) Use of Force Justifiable to Effect an Arrest. Subject to the provisions of this Section and of Section 3.09, the use of force upon or toward the person of another is justifiable when the actor is making or assisting in making an arrest and the actor believes that such force is immediately necessary to effect a lawful arrest.

(2) Limitations on the Use of Force.

(a) The use of force is not justifiable under this Section unless:

(i) the actor makes known the purpose of the arrest or believes that it is otherwise known by or cannot reasonably be made known to the person to be arrested; and

(ii) when the arrest is made under a warrant, the warrant is valid or believed by the actor to be valid.

(b) The use of deadly force is not justifiable under this Section unless:

(i) the arrest is for a felony; and

(ii) the person effecting the arrest is authorized to act as a peace officer or is assisting a person whom he believes to be authorized to act as a peace officer; and

(iii) the actor believes that the force employed creates no substantial risk of injury to innocent persons; and

(iv) the actor believes that:

(A) the crime for which the arrest is made involved conduct including the use or threatened use of deadly force; or

(B) there is a substantial risk that the person to be arrested will cause death or serious bodily injury if his apprehension is delayed.

(3) Use of Force to Prevent Escape from Custody. The use of force to prevent the escape of an arrested person from custody is justifiable when the force could justifiably have been employed to effect the arrest under which the person is in custody, except that a guard or other person authorized to act as a peace officer is justified in using any force, including deadly force, that he believes to be immediately necessary to prevent the escape of a person from a jail, prison, or other institution for the detention of persons charged with or convicted of a crime.

(4) Use of Force by Private Person Assisting an Unlawful Arrest.

(a) A private person who is summoned by a peace officer to assist in effecting an unlawful arrest, is justified in using any force that he would be justified in using if the arrest were lawful, provided that he does not believe the arrest is unlawful.

(b) A private person who assists another private person in effecting an unlawful arrest, or who, not being summoned, assists a peace officer in effecting an unlawful arrest, is justified in using any force that he would be justified in using if the arrest were lawful, provided that (i) he believes the arrest is lawful, and (ii) the arrest would be lawful if the facts were as he believes them to be.

(5) Use of Force to Prevent Suicide or the Commission of a Crime.

(a) The use of force upon or toward the person of another is justifiable when the actor believes that such force is immediately necessary to prevent such other person from committing suicide, inflicting serious bodily injury upon himself, committing or consummating the commission of a crime involving or threatening bodily injury, damage to or loss of property or a breach of the peace, except that:

(i)   any limitations imposed by the other provisions of this Article on the justifiable use of force in self-protection, for the protection of others, the protection of property, the effectuation of an arrest or the prevention of an escape from custody shall apply notwithstanding the criminality of the conduct against which such force is used; and

(ii) the use of deadly force is not in any event justifiable under this Subsection unless:

(A) the actor believes that there is a substantial risk that the person whom he seeks to prevent from committing a crime will cause death or serious bodily injury to another unless the commission or the consummation of the crime is prevented and that the use of such force presents no substantial risk of injury to innocent persons; or

(B) the actor believes that the use of such force is necessary to suppress a riot or mutiny after the rioters or mutineers have been ordered to disperse and warned, in any particular manner that the law may require, that such force will be used if they do not obey.

(b) The justification afforded by this Subsection extends to the use of confinement as preventive force only if the actor takes all reasonable measures to terminate the confinement as soon as he knows that he safely can, unless the person confined has been arrested on a charge of crime.

Chapter 19
Self-Defense, Defense of Others, and Imperfect Privilege

A. Introduction

Self-defense and defense of others are considered justification defenses. If the defendant is successful in raising one of these defenses, then he did not commit a wrongful act under the law; in fact, he did the right thing under the circumstances and should not be punished for it. The law gives the actor a privilege to use deadly force in situations where he (or another) is under the imminent threat of deadly force from someone else. The primary difference between the two defenses is that to raise self-defense, the defendant cannot have been the initial aggressor. With defense of others, however, most jurisdictions permit the defense even if the person the defendant is protecting was the initial aggressor, so long as the defendant was unaware of who started the affray. This is referred to as the "reasonable appearances" doctrine: the defendant is allowed to use deadly force to protect another if it *reasonably appears* to the defendant that the other person is in imminent danger of deadly force. A minority of jurisdictions still maintain the "alter ego" or "act at your peril" rule, which permits the defense only when the person in danger could have claimed self-defense himself. *See* Joshua Dressler, *Understanding Criminal Law* §19.01 (6th ed. 2012).

Imperfect privilege is exactly what it sounds like: the defendant's claim of self-defense is incomplete or imperfect. This was not a common law rule, yet it has been adopted by many states and, if successful, it typically results in a conviction for voluntary manslaughter. Other states, including Michigan, do not recognize the concept of imperfect self-defense. *See People v. Reese*, 491 Mich. 127 (2012).

B. Self-Defense

1. What are the specific requirements a defendant must meet to establish a self-defense claim?

What is the policy behind these requirements? Why are they so demanding? *Warrington* demonstrates a problem that arises in some self-defense cases. A defendant who would have had the right to claim self-defense can lose that right if he waits too long.

Warrington v. State, 840 A.2d 590 (Del. 2003)

BERGER, Justice:

At issue in this criminal appeal is the scope of the self-defense within a dwelling defense. Defendants below argue for reversal of their first degree murder convictions on the basis that the defense, once triggered, endures even after the intruder no longer poses a threat. We disagree. The relevant statute requires that the defendant have a reasonable belief that the intruder will injure someone within the dwelling. That reasonable belief must exist at the time a defendant acts in self-defense. Thus, after an intruder has been subdued, a jury could properly find that a killing is not justified as an act of self-defense.

Factual and Procedural Background
A. The Death of Jesse Pecco

Robert Wesley Warrington ("Wes"), then 22, and Andrew Warrington ("Drew"), then 18, are brothers who lived with their father at 100 Port Lewes in Sussex County. Wes owed an acquaintance, Jesse Pecco, approximately $800 for drugs that Wes had consumed instead of selling. In order to partially repay the debt, Wes forged a check from his father's bank account, making it out to himself in the amount of $700. Wes gave the check to Pecco on Friday, August 11, 2000, and the two men agreed to meet on Monday to cash the check.

Pecco did not go to the meeting place. Instead, he drove to 100 Port Lewes, and parked his car directly behind Wes's car so as to immobilize it. Pecco then entered the dwelling through its unlocked front door. Drew, who was upstairs watching television, heard shouts coming from the first floor. When he went downstairs to see what was happening, he found Pecco involved in a physical struggle with Wes. Drew soon realized that the two were fighting over control of a knife that Pecco was holding. Drew struck Pecco from behind, causing him to release the knife. According to Wes, Pecco then had the opportunity to leave the house, but instead chased Drew, who fled up the stairs. Both brothers maintain that Pecco was the aggressor in the fight, and that they believed he posed a threat.

The two brothers testified that they gained the upper hand as Wes stabbed Pecco repeatedly with the knife and Drew struck him repeatedly with a fireplace poker. Ultimately it was determined that Pecco sustained 13 stab wounds, including one that penetrated his left lung, and one that penetrated his heart. Expert testimony at trial revealed that he also suffered eight blunt-force blows to the head, causing a fractured skull and subdural hemorrhaging. Among Pecco's injuries were deep incise stabs to his hands, characteristic of defensive wounds.

During the altercation, a 911 call was made from the Warrington residence. DNA from blood marks found on the telephone used to make the call matched Pecco's DNA. One of these marks was located next to the "one" button on the telephone, indicating that it was Pecco who dialed the emergency number. Drew gave a conflicting account, saying that it was he who dialed the number, only to have Pecco knock the phone from his hands. The jury listened to the sounds of the fight, as recorded on the 911 tape, before reaching its conclusion regarding self-defense. The tape revealed that, towards the end of the fight, Pecco was pleading with the brothers to stop attacking him. He asked, "Why are you guys trying to kill me?" to which one of the brothers responded, "Good reasons." As he died, Pecco said, "Wes, show me some love. Give me a hug before I die. Give me a hug." Testimony demonstrated that Drew responded by kicking him in the face and telling him to shut up.

B.   Jury Instructions Below

Wes and Drew's (collectively "defendants") defense to the Pecco murder charges was self-defense within a dwelling. Accordingly, the trial judge instructed the jury:

> A defense raised in this case is justification. . . . The defense stems from the defendants' assertion that, at the time in question, their actions were justified. The elements of the defense of justification, in this case, are as follows: (1) That the defendants were in their own dwelling at the time of the incident. (2) That Mr. Pecco was [an] intruder unlawfully in defendants' dwelling at the time of the incident. . . . (3(b)) That the defendants reasonably believed that Mr. Pecco would inflict [personal] injury upon them. . . .
>
> In considering the [defendants'] reasonable belief . . . you may consider whether a reasonable man in the defendants' circumstances would have reasonably believed that the intruder would inflict personal injury upon them. You should, however keep in mind, that it is the defendants' state of mind which is at issue here and that it is only required that they, in fact, believed the intruder would inflict personal injury upon them. If, after considering all the evidence to support the defense of justification, you find that such evidence raises a reasonable doubt in your minds

as to the defendants' guilt, you should find the [defendants] not guilty of the crime charged.

At another point in the instruction, the judge clarified,

> As to the justification defense of a person unlawfully in a dwelling, if you find Mr. Pecco an intruder unlawfully in the defendants' dwelling and if the defendant overcame Jesse Pecco so that the defendant no longer believed he was in danger of physical injury or personal injury, and therefore, the defendant knew the use of deadly force was no longer necessary, then the continued use of deadly force was not justified. In other words, *if a person is initially justified in defending himself, but then knows that the danger to him has passed then the subsequent use of deadly force is not justified.* (Emphasis added.)

The jury found both Drew and Wes guilty of murder in the first degree, possession of a deadly weapon during the commission of a felony, and conspiracy in the first degree.

Discussion

Delaware's statute defining self-defense within a dwelling provides:

> In the prosecution of an occupant of a dwelling charged with killing or injuring an intruder who was unlawfully in said dwelling, it shall be a defense that the occupant was in the occupant's own dwelling at the time of the offense, and:
>
> (1)   The encounter between the occupant and intruder was sudden and unexpected, compelling the occupant to act instantly; or
>
> (2)   The occupant reasonably believed that the intruder would inflict personal injury upon the occupant or others in the dwelling; or
>
> (3)   The occupant demanded that the intruder disarm or surrender, and the intruder refused to do so.

The question presented in this case is whether the reasonable belief that the intruder would inflict injury must be contemporaneous with the forceful actions taken against the intruder. Defendants contend that, once both intrusion and reasonable belief of danger have occurred, the rightful occupant of the dwelling has "license to slay the intruder" without considering whether the intruder has been disabled so as to no longer pose a threat.

The doctrine of self-defense within a dwelling differs from self-defense in other contexts. A defendant attacked outside her home must retreat rather than use deadly force, but inside her own dwelling she has no duty to retreat, even if she could do so with "complete safety." An early phrasing of this doctrine can be found in *State v. Talley*, 33 A. 181 (Del. 1886): "As every man's dwelling house is also his castle of defense, in the eye of the law, he need not retreat at all (he being, in contemplation of law, in the same situation as one attacked elsewhere than in his own house who has retreated until he can do so no further, by reason of a wall or other obstruction that prevents him), but may slay his adversary thus attacking him."

In Delaware, the added protection granted to the occupant of a dwelling is not absolute. The statute provides a defense only in three circumstances: when the occupant 1) encounters the intruder suddenly and must act "instantly;" 2) reasonably believes that the intruder will inflict injury; or 3) demands that the intruder disarm or surrender and the intruder refuses. These three circumstances share a common element—the occupant is being placed in immediate peril. The plain meaning of this immediacy requirement is that the statute only affords protection if the occupant is confronted with one of the three circumstances *at the time* the occupant uses deadly force on the intruder.

Nothing in the statutory language or Delaware case law supports defendants' contention that what begins as self-defense can be turned into a license to kill. Defendants rely on several extremely broad self-defense within a dwelling statutes from other jurisdictions in arguing their position. For example, the California statute provides: "[a]ny person using force intended or likely to cause death . . . within his or her residence shall be presumed to have held a reasonable fear of imminent peril of death or great bodily injury . . . when that force is used. . . ." Colorado's so-called "make my day" statute provides the occupant of a dwelling immunity from prosecution:

> [A]ny occupant of a dwelling is justified in using . . . deadly force[ ] against another person when that other person has made an unlawful entry into the dwelling and when the occupant has a reasonable belief that such other person has committed a crime in the dwelling in addition to the uninvited entry, or is committing or intends to commit a crime against a person or property in addition to the uninvited entry and when the occupant reasonably believes that such other person might use any physical force, no matter how slight, against any occupant.

Delaware's statute, however, is not comparable to either of these statutes. Moreover, defendants have failed to identify any jurisdiction, including California and Colorado, where an occupant of a dwelling is justified in using deadly force after the intruder has been totally subdued.

Conclusion

Based on the foregoing, we conclude that the "added" jury instruction explaining the limitation on the defense of self-defense within a dwelling correctly stated the law. Accordingly, the judgments of the Superior Court are hereby AFFIRMED.

2. Duty to Retreat and the Castle Doctrine

Jurisdictions are divided on whether a person must retreat, rather than use force, if retreat can be done safely. A majority of jurisdictions, many adopting "Stand Your Ground" laws, do not require retreat. As you will see in the cases that follow, even "duty to retreat" states do not require retreat in certain locations like a home. This so-called "Castle Doctrine" becomes problematic when both the defendant and the attacker are members of the same household. *See* Joshua Dressler, *Understanding Criminal Law* §18.02[C] (6th ed. 2012).

Cooper v. United States, 512 A.2d 1002 (D.C. App 1986)

BELSON, Associate Judge:

A jury convicted Leon D. Cooper of voluntary manslaughter while armed, D.C. Code §§22–2405 and –3202, and carrying a pistol without a license, *id.* – 3204. On appeal, Cooper asserts that the trial judge erred when he refused to instruct the jury that the appellant had an unqualified right to stand his ground in the face of an attack in his home, but instead instructed the jury in the language of Instruction 5.16B, Criminal Jury Instructions for the District of Columbia (3d ed. 1978), the standard instruction on the use of deadly force in self-defense. Finding no error, we affirm.

Leon Cooper and his brother Robert Parker lived with their mother, Alice Cooper. In the early part of August 1981, Parker unexpectedly left home for 10 days. Early on the morning of August 12th, he returned. He did not tell his mother or brother where he had been.

Parker stayed home for much of the day. Mrs. Cooper returned from work in the evening, and Cooper returned from his job shortly afterward. Cooper was carrying a pistol when he returned. The three were sitting in Mrs. Cooper's small living room when the two brothers began to quarrel after Cooper asked Parker where he had been during the past 10 days.

Suddenly, the quarrel escalated, and the two brothers found themselves standing in the middle of the living room, shouting at each other. Parker hit Cooper in the head with a small radio; Mrs. Cooper ran upstairs to call for help. She then heard a "pop." She went downstairs and saw Parker lying on the floor. Cooper said "I have shot my brother" and "Mama, I am so sorry. I mean—." Cooper later told the police that he had just shot his brother, that his brother was hitting him with the radio and "I couldn't take it anymore and I just shot him."

At trial, Cooper's counsel objected to instruction 5.16B, the standard instruction given when the defendant raises a claim of self-defense. The court instructed the jury, in pertinent part:

> Now, if the defendant—If the defendant could have safely
> retreated but did not do so, his failure to retreat is a

circumstance which you may consider together with all the other circumstances in determining whether he went further in repelling the danger, real or apparent, than he was justified in doing so under the circumstances.

Before a person can avail himself [of] the plea of self-defense against a charge of homicide, he must do everything in his power, consistent with his own safety, to avoid the danger and avoid the necessity of taking life. However, if the defendant actually believed that he was in imminent danger of death or serious bodily harm, and that deadly force was necessary to repel such danger, he was not required to retreat or consider whether he could safely retreat. He was entitled to stand his ground and use such force as was reasonably necessary under the circumstances to save his life or protect himself from serious bodily harm.

This instruction virtually tracks the language of Instruction 5.16B.

Appellant took the position that the second sentence of the instruction which begins, "Before a person can avail himself [of] the plea of self-defense," inappropriately imposed a duty to retreat in the face of an attack. The trial court overruled counsel's objections. Defense counsel then asked the trial court for a "castle doctrine" instruction, *i.e.*, that a person has no duty whatsoever to retreat when attacked in his own home. The trial judge denied the request, stating that, in his opinion, the castle doctrine applies when a person in his home is attacked by a stranger or one who comes onto the premises without permission, but not when a fight occurs between two co-occupants. The jury found Cooper guilty of voluntary manslaughter while armed and carrying a pistol without a license, and the trial court sentenced him to a jail term of 8 to 24 years for the armed manslaughter conviction, and a consecutive term of 1 year for carrying a pistol without a license. This appeal followed.

We consider first whether, under the law of this jurisdiction, a person generally has the duty to retreat in the face of an assault by another, when retreat is a feasible alternative.

In *Gillis v. United States,* 400 A.2d 311 (D.C. 1979), this court considered whether a person threatened with death or serious bodily harm has a duty to retreat, if it can be done safely, before using deadly force in defense. Gillis claimed that he had acted in self-defense when a man named Smith approached him on a deserted street late at night and accused him of being with Smith's girlfriend. Gillis claimed that Smith reached in Smith's pocket, and pulled out a shiny object. Gillis then pulled out a pistol, shot, and mortally wounded Smith. Gillis was convicted of second-degree murder while armed. . . .

Faced with these apparently conflicting precedents, the *Gillis* court reconciled them in what it termed a "middle ground" approach to self-defense. The middle ground approach imposes no duty to retreat, but it "permit[s] the jury to consider whether a defendant, if he safely could have avoided further encounter by stepping back or walking away, was actually or apparently in imminent danger of bodily harm. In short, this rule permits the jury to determine if the defendant acted too hastily, was too quick to pull the trigger." We affirmed in *Gillis*, holding that the instruction given did not impose a duty to retreat, but allowed a failure to retreat, together with all the other circumstances, to be considered by the jury in determining whether the case was truly one of self-defense.

The unique question presented in this appeal is whether, when one is assaulted in one's home by a co-occupant, the availability of a means of retreat is as much a consideration as it otherwise is under the middle ground approach. No cases in this jurisdiction have been called to our attention which address the question regarding an occupant's duty or ability to retreat in the face of an assault by a co-occupant, nor have we been able to identify any. We look, then, to see how other courts have addressed this issue.

We begin by noting that the question whether an occupant has a duty to retreat when assaulted by a co-occupant will not arise in those jurisdictions which follow the American rule, for in those jurisdictions one can stand one's ground regardless of where one is assaulted, or by whom. Therefore, whatever guidance is available is provided by the courts of those jurisdictions which follow the common law, "retreat to the wall," rule.

Those jurisdictions following the common law rule have almost universally adopted the "castle doctrine" that one who through no fault of his own is attacked in one's own home is under no duty to retreat. While the status of the castle doctrine in the District of Columbia has never been squarely decided, we will assume for purposes of this discussion that appellant is correct in maintaining that the doctrine is applicable here.

Courts following the common law rule have split, however, regarding whether a defendant is entitled to a castle doctrine instruction when the defendant is assaulted by a co-occupant. An early case addressing this question was *People v. Tomlins*, 107 N.E. 496 (N.Y. 1914). In *Tomlins*, a father shot and killed his son in their cottage. The New York Court of Appeals held that an instruction which informed the jury that the father had a duty to retreat was erroneous. The court first noted that if a man is assaulted in his home, "he may stand his ground and resist the attack. He is under no duty to take to the fields and the highways, a fugitive from his own home." *Id.* The court then held that the rule is the same whether the attack is initiated by an intruder or a co-occupant; "why . . . should one retreat from his own house, when assailed by a partner or co-tenant, any more than when assailed by a stranger who is lawfully on the premises? Whither shall he flee, and how far, and when may he be permitted to return?" *Id.* at 498.

As other courts grappled with this question, they often returned to the questions posed by the *Tomlins* court, although frequently reaching a different result. A majority of courts favors giving a castle doctrine instruction when a defendant claims self-defense when attacked in his home by a co-occupant, while a substantial minority holds that the castle doctrine does not apply in this special circumstance. Those decisions which favor giving a castle doctrine instruction stress the occupant's interest in remaining in the home, while those that oppose giving the instruction focus on the entitlement of both combatants to occupy the house and the fact that they usually are related, and reason that the parties have some obligation to attempt to defuse the situation.

Having examined these authorities, we are convinced that the reasoning of those jurisdictions holding that a castle doctrine instruction should *not* be given in instances of co-occupant attacks is the more compelling. As the Florida Supreme Court noted in *Bobbitt,* 415 So.2d 724 (1982), both the decedent husband and accused wife in the case before it "had equal rights to be in the 'castle' and neither had the legal right to eject the other." *Id.* The court further observed:

> We see no reason why a mother should not retreat from her own son, even in her own kitchen. Such a view does not render her defenseless against a member of her family gone berserk, because . . . a person placed in the position of imminent danger of death or great bodily harm to himself by the wrongful attack of another has no duty to retreat if to do so would increase his own danger of death or great bodily harm.

Although in *Bobbitt,* the Florida Supreme Court used the analogy of a mother attacked by her son, that court's reasoning is also applicable to situations where a daughter attacks her father, a husband attacks his wife, or as here, a brother attacks his brother. Indeed, all co-occupants, even those unrelated by blood or marriage, have a heightened obligation to treat each other with a degree of tolerance and respect. That obligation does not evaporate when one co-occupant disregards it and attacks another. We are satisfied, moreover, that an instruction that embraces the middle ground approach appropriately permits the jury to consider the truly relevant question, *i.e.*, whether a defendant, "if he safely could have avoided further encounter by stepping back or walking away, was actually or apparently in imminent danger of bodily harm." *Gillis, supra,* 400 A.2d at 313. We hold that evidence that the defendant was attacked in his home by a co-occupant did not entitle him to an instruction that he had no duty whatsoever to retreat. The trial court did not err in refusing to give a castle doctrine instruction under the circumstances of this case. . . .

In view of the foregoing, we affirm Cooper's convictions.
Affirmed.

3. Reasonableness of Belief in Imminent Danger

The *LaVoie* case involved an appeal by the prosecutor after the trial judge granted a directed verdict of acquittal in favor of Mr. LaVoie. Principles of double jeopardy prohibit the prosecutor from seeking, and the appellate court from granting, a new trial. LaVoie was found not guilty and cannot be tried again for this offense. As the court below points out, the prosecutor is requesting the state supreme court to merely, "express . . . its disapproval of the action of the trial court." Not every state permits this type of prosecutorial appeal.

People v. LaVoie, 155 Colo. 551 (1986)

MOORE, Justice.

The defendant in error, to whom we will refer as defendant, was accused of the crime of murder in an information filed in the district court of Jefferson county. He entered a plea of not guilty and a jury was selected to try the case. At the conclusion of the evidence, the trial court, on motion of counsel for defendant, directed the jury to return a verdict of not guilty. It was the opinion of the trial court that the evidence was insufficient to warrant submission of any issue to the jury in that the sum total thereof established a clear case of justifiable homicide. The district attorney objected, and the case is here on writ of error requesting this court to render an opinion expressing its disapproval of the action of the trial court in directing the verdict of not guilty.

Eighteen witnesses testified during the trial; thirteen were called as witnesses for the prosecution and five for the defense, including the defendant himself. We have read the record and have found nothing therein which would warrant the submission of any issue to the jury for determination.

For purposes of focus and clarity we will summarize the pertinent facts leading up to the homicide. The defendant was employed as a pharmacist at the Kincaid Pharmacy, 7024 West Colfax Avenue, Lakewood, Colorado. His day's work ended at about 12:30 A.M. After leaving his place of employment, he obtained something to eat at a nearby restaurant and started on his way home. He was driving east on West Colfax Avenue, toward the city of Denver, at about 1:30 A.M. An automobile approached his car from the rear. The driver of this auto made contact with the rear bumper of defendant's car and thereupon forcibly, unlawfully, and deliberately accelerated his motor, precipitating the defendant forward for a substantial distance and through a red traffic light. There were four men in the automobile who were under the influence of intoxicating liquor in varying degrees. Prior to ramming the car of the defendant they had agreed to shove him along just for "kicks." The defendant applied his brakes to the full; but the continuing force from behind precipitated him forward, causing all four wheels to leave a trail of skid marks. When defendant's car ultimately came to a stop the auto containing the four men backed away a few feet. The defendant got out of his car and as he did so he placed a revolver beneath his belt. He had a permit to carry the gun. The four men got out of their auto and advanced toward the defendant threatening to "make you eat that damn gun," to "mop up the street with you," and also directed vile, profane and obscene language at him. The man who was in advance of his three companions kept moving toward defendant in a menacing manner. At this point the defendant shot him. As a result, he died at the scene of the affray.

In upholding the action of the trial court we think it sufficient to direct attention to the opinion of this court in People v. Urso, 129 Colo. 292, where we find, inter alia, the following pertinent language:

> . . . It is our opinion, and we so state, that if it is within the power of a trial court to set aside a verdict, not supported by competent legal evidence, then it is equally within the province and power of the court to prevent such a verdict ever coming into existence. In either position, before or after the verdict, the trial court is compelled to survey and analyze the evidence, and from the same evidence, his analysis would undoubtedly be the same before or after a verdict. If it is to the end that the evidence is insufficient or incompetent, and no part of it is convincing beyond a reasonable doubt, then he should be courageous enough to prevent a miscarriage of justice by a jury. . . .

The law of justifiable homicide is well set forth by this court in the case of Young v. People, 47 Colo. 352:

> . . . When a person has reasonable grounds for believing, and does in fact actually believe, that danger of his being killed, or of receiving great bodily harm, is imminent, he may act on such appearances and defend himself, even to the extent of taking human life when necessary, although it may turn out that the appearances were false, or although he may have been mistaken as to the extent of the real or actual danger. . . .

The defendant was a stranger to all four occupants of the auto. He was peaceably on his way home from work, which terminated after midnight. Under the law and the circumstances disclosed by the record, defendant had the right to defend himself against the threatened assault of those whose lawlessness and utter disregard of his rights resulted in the justifiable killing of one of their number.

The judgment is affirmed.

4. Is a defendant only required to have a subjective, honest belief or must it also be objectively reasonable?

Bernhard Goetz shot and seriously wounded four young men in a New York City subway after they asked him for money. The young men did not threaten Goetz with weapons, but one of them said, "Give me five dollars." Goetz responded by shooting them. The situation received a great deal of publicity and caused a national debate over whether Goetz was a hero for defending himself or a dangerous vigilante. The case also raised a significant issue pretrial that resolved the definition of self-defense in New York.

After the decision of the New York Court of Appeals below, Goetz was tried on charges of attempted murder, assault, reckless endangerment, and various firearms offenses. The jury found him guilty of only one offense: carrying an unlicensed firearm.

People v. Goetz, 68 N.Y.2d 96 (1986)

Chief Judge WACHTLER.

A Grand Jury has indicted defendant on attempted murder, assault, and other charges for having shot and wounded four youths on a New York City subway train after one or two of the youths approached him and asked for $5. The lower courts, concluding that the prosecutor's charge to the Grand Jury on the defense of justification was erroneous, have dismissed the attempted murder, assault and weapons possession charges. We now reverse and reinstate all counts of the indictment.

I.

The precise circumstances of the incident giving rise to the charges against defendant are disputed, and ultimately it will be for a trial jury to determine what occurred. We feel it necessary, however, to provide some factual background to properly frame the legal issues before us. Accordingly, we have summarized the facts as they appear from the evidence before the Grand Jury. We stress, however, that we do not purport to reach any conclusions or holding as to exactly what transpired or whether defendant is blameworthy. The credibility of witnesses and the reasonableness of defendant's conduct are to be resolved by the trial jury.

On Saturday afternoon, December 22, 1984, Troy Canty, Darryl Cabey, James Ramseur, and Barry Allen boarded an IRT express subway train in The Bronx and headed south toward lower Manhattan. The four youths rode together in the rear portion of the seventh car of the train. Two of the four, Ramseur and Cabey, had screwdrivers inside their coats, which they said were to be used to break into the coin boxes of video machines.

Defendant Bernhard Goetz boarded this subway train at 14th Street in Manhattan and sat down on a bench towards the rear section of the same car occupied by the four youths. Goetz was carrying an unlicensed .38 caliber pistol loaded with five rounds of ammunition in a waistband holster. The train left the 14th Street station and headed towards Chambers Street.

It appears from the evidence before the Grand Jury that Canty approached Goetz, possibly with Allen beside him, and stated "give me five dollars". Neither Canty nor any of the other youths displayed a weapon. Goetz responded by standing up, pulling out his handgun and firing four shots in rapid succession. The first shot hit Canty in the chest; the second struck Allen in the back; the third went through Ramseur's arm and into his left side; the fourth was fired at Cabey, who apparently was then standing in the corner of the car, but missed, deflecting instead off of a wall of the conductor's cab. After Goetz briefly surveyed the scene around him, he fired another shot at Cabey, who then was sitting on the end bench of the car. The bullet entered the rear of Cabey's side and severed his spinal cord.

All but two of the other passengers fled the car when, or immediately after, the shots were fired. The conductor, who had been in the next car, heard the shots and instructed the motorman to radio for emergency assistance. The conductor then went into the car where the shooting occurred and saw Goetz sitting on a bench, the injured youths lying on the floor or slumped against a seat, and two women who had apparently taken cover, also lying on the floor. Goetz told the conductor that the four youths had tried to rob him.

While the conductor was aiding the youths, Goetz headed towards the front of the car. The train had stopped just before the Chambers Street station and Goetz went between two of the cars, jumped onto the tracks and fled. Police and ambulance crews arrived at the scene shortly thereafter. Ramseur and Canty, initially listed in critical condition, have fully recovered. Cabey remains paralyzed, and has suffered some degree of brain damage.

On December 31, 1984, Goetz surrendered to police in Concord, New Hampshire, identifying himself as the gunman being sought for the subway shootings in New York nine days earlier. Later that day, after receiving *Miranda* warnings, he made two lengthy statements, both of which were tape recorded with his permission. In the statements, which are substantially similar, Goetz admitted that he had been illegally carrying a handgun in New York City for three years. He stated that he had first purchased a gun in 1981 after he had been injured in a mugging. Goetz also revealed that twice between 1981 and 1984 he had successfully warded off assailants simply by displaying the pistol.

According to Goetz's statement, the first contact he had with the four youths came when Canty, sitting or lying on the bench across from him, asked "how are you," to which he replied "fine". Shortly thereafter, Canty, followed by one of the other youths, walked over to the defendant and stood to his left, while the other two youths remained to his right, in the corner of the subway car. Canty then said "give me five dollars". Goetz stated that he knew from the smile on Canty's face that they wanted to "play with me". Although he was certain that none of the youths had a gun, he had a fear, based on prior experiences, of being "maimed".

Goetz then established "a pattern of fire," deciding specifically to fire from left to right. His stated intention at that point was to "murder [the four youths], to hurt them, to make them suffer as much as possible". When Canty again requested money, Goetz stood up, drew his weapon, and began firing, aiming for the center of the body of each of the four. Goetz recalled that the first two he shot "tried to run through the crowd [but] they had nowhere to run". Goetz then turned to his right to "go after the other two". One of these two "tried to run through the wall of the train, but . . . he had nowhere to go". The other youth (Cabey) "tried pretending that he wasn't with [the others]" by standing still, holding on to one of the subway hand straps, and not looking at Goetz. Goetz nonetheless fired his fourth shot at him. He then ran back to the first two youths to make sure they had been "taken care of". Seeing that they had both been shot, he spun back to check on the latter two. Goetz noticed that the youth who had been standing still was now sitting on a bench and seemed unhurt. As Goetz told the police, "I said '[y]ou seem to be all right, here's another' ", and he then fired the shot which severed Cabey's spinal cord. Goetz added that "if I was a little more under self-control . . . I would have put the barrel against his forehead and fired." He also admitted that "if I had had more [bullets], I would have shot them again, and again, and again."

II. . . .

On March 27, 1985, the second Grand Jury filed a 10-count indictment, containing four charges of attempted murder (Penal Law §§110.00, 125.25 [1]), four charges of assault in the first degree (Penal Law §120.10[1]), one charge of reckless endangerment in the first degree (Penal Law §120.25), and one charge of criminal possession of a weapon in the second degree (Penal Law §265.03 [possession of loaded firearm with intent to use it unlawfully against another]). Goetz was arraigned on this indictment on March 28, 1985, and it was consolidated with the earlier three-count indictment.

On October 14, 1985, Goetz moved to dismiss the charges contained in the second indictment alleging, among other things, that the evidence before the second Grand Jury was not legally sufficient to establish the offenses charged (see, CPL 210.20[1][b]), and that the prosecutor's instructions to that Grand Jury on the defense of justification were erroneous and prejudicial to the defendant so as to render its proceedings defective (see, CPL 210.20[1][c]; 210.35[5]). . . .

In an order dated January 21, 1986, Criminal Term 131 Misc. 2d 1, 502 N.Y.S.2d 577, granted Goetz's motion to the extent that it dismissed all counts of the second indictment, other than the reckless endangerment charge, with leave to resubmit these charges to a third Grand Jury. The court, after inspection of the Grand Jury minutes, first rejected Goetz's contention that there was not legally sufficient evidence to support the charges. It held, however, that the prosecutor, in a supplemental charge elaborating upon the justification defense, had erroneously introduced an objective element into this defense by instructing the grand jurors to consider whether Goetz's conduct was that of a "reasonable man in [Goetz's] situation". The court, citing prior decisions from both the First and Second Departments, concluded that the statutory test for whether the use of deadly force is justified to protect a person should be wholly subjective, focusing entirely on the defendant's state of mind when he used such force. It concluded that dismissal was required for this error because the justification issue was at the heart of the case. . . .

On appeal by the People, a divided Appellate Division affirmed Criminal Term's dismissal of the charges. The plurality opinion by Justice Kassal, concurred in by Justice Carro, agreed with Criminal Term's reasoning on the justification issue, stating that the grand jurors should have been instructed to consider only the defendant's subjective beliefs as to the need to use deadly force. Justice Kupferman concurred in the result reached by the plurality on the ground that the prosecutor's charge did not adequately apprise the grand jurors of the need to consider Goetz's own background and learning. . . .

Justice Asch, in a dissenting opinion in which Justice Wallach concurred, disagreed with both bases for dismissal relied upon by Criminal Term. On the justification question, he opined that the statute requires consideration of both the defendant's subjective beliefs and whether a reasonable person in defendant's situation would have had such beliefs. Accordingly, he found no error in the prosecutor's introduction of an objective element into the justification defense. . . . In a separate dissenting opinion, Justice Wallach stressed that the plurality's adoption of a purely subjective test effectively eliminated any reasonableness requirement contained in the statute.

Justice Asch granted the People leave to appeal to this court. We agree with the dissenters that . . . the prosecutor's charge to the Grand Jury on justification . . . [did not require] dismissal of any of the charges in the second indictment.

III.

Penal Law article 35 recognizes the defense of justification, which "permits the use of force under certain circumstances." One such set of circumstances pertains to the use of force in defense of a person, encompassing both self-defense and defense of a third person. Penal Law §35.15(1) sets forth the general principles governing all such uses of force: "[a] person may . . . use physical force upon another person when and to the extent he *reasonably believes* such to be necessary to defend himself or a third person from what he *reasonably believes* to be the use or imminent use of unlawful physical force by such other person" (emphasis added).

Section 35.15(2) sets forth further limitations on these general principles with respect to the use of "deadly physical force": "A person may not use deadly physical force upon another person under circumstances specified in subdivision one unless (a) He *reasonably believes* that such other person is using or about to use deadly physical force or (b) He *reasonably believes* that such other person is committing or attempting to commit a kidnapping, forcible rape, forcible sodomy or robbery" (emphasis added).

Thus, consistent with most justification provisions, Penal Law §35.15 permits the use of deadly physical force only where requirements as to triggering conditions and the necessity of a particular response are met. As to the triggering conditions, the statute requires that the actor "reasonably believes" that another person either is using or about to use deadly physical force or is committing or attempting to commit one of certain enumerated felonies, including robbery. As to the need for the use of deadly physical force as a response, the statute requires that the actor "reasonably believes" that such force is necessary to avert the perceived threat.

Because the evidence before the second Grand Jury included statements by Goetz that he acted to protect himself from being maimed or to avert a robbery, the prosecutor correctly chose to charge the justification defense in section 35.15 to the Grand Jury. The prosecutor properly instructed the grand jurors to consider whether the use of deadly physical force was justified to prevent either serious physical injury or a robbery, and, in doing so, to separately analyze the defense with respect to each of the charges. He elaborated upon the prerequisites for the use of deadly physical force essentially by reading or paraphrasing the language in Penal Law §35.15. The defense does not contend that he committed any error in this portion of the charge.

When the prosecutor had completed his charge, one of the grand jurors asked for clarification of the term "reasonably believes". The prosecutor responded by instructing the grand jurors that they were to consider the circumstances of the incident and determine "whether the defendant's conduct was that of a reasonable man in the defendant's situation". It is this response by the prosecutor—and specifically his use of "a reasonable man"—which is the basis for the dismissal of the charges by the lower courts. As expressed repeatedly in the Appellate Division's plurality opinion, because section 35.15 uses the term "*he* reasonably believes", the appropriate test, according to that court, is whether a defendant's beliefs and reactions were "reasonable *to him*". Under that reading of the statute, a jury which believed a defendant's testimony that he felt that his own actions were warranted and were reasonable would have to acquit him, regardless of what anyone else in defendant's situation might have concluded. Such an interpretation defies the ordinary meaning and significance of the term "reasonably" in a statute, and misconstrues the clear intent of the Legislature, in enacting section 35.15, to retain an objective element as part of any provision authorizing the use of deadly physical force.

Penal statutes in New York have long codified the right recognized at common law to use deadly physical force, under appropriate circumstances, in self-defense. These provisions have never required that an actor's belief as to the intention of another person to inflict serious injury be correct in order for the use of deadly force to be justified, but they have uniformly required that the belief comport with an objective notion of reasonableness. The 1829 statute, using language which was followed almost in its entirety until the 1965 recodification of the Penal Law, provided that the use of deadly force was justified in self-defense or in the defense of specified third persons "when there shall be a reasonable ground to apprehend a design to commit a felony, or to do some great personal injury, and there shall be imminent danger of such design being accomplished".

In *Shorter v. People,* 2 N.Y. 193, we emphasized that deadly force could be justified under the statute even if the actor's beliefs as to the intentions of another turned out to be wrong, but noted there had to be a reasonable basis, viewed objectively, for the beliefs. We explicitly rejected the position that the defendant's own belief that the use of deadly force was necessary sufficed to justify such force regardless of the reasonableness of the beliefs (*id.* at pp. 200-201).

In 1881, New York reexamined the many criminal provisions set forth in the revised statutes and enacted, for the first time, a separate Penal Code. The provision in the 1881 Penal Code for the use of deadly force in self-defense or to defend a third person was virtually a reenactment of the language in the 1829 statutes, and the "reasonble [sic] ground" requirement was maintained.

The 1909 Penal Law replaced the 1881 Penal Code. The language of section 205 of the 1881 code pertaining to the use of deadly force in self-defense or in defense of a third person was reenacted, verbatim, as part of section 1055 of the new Penal Law. Several cases from this court interpreting the 1909 provision demonstrate unmistakably that an objective element of reasonableness was a vital part of any claim of self-defense. . . .

Accordingly, the Law Revision Commission, in a 1937 Report to the Legislature on the Law of Homicide in New York, summarized the self-defense statute as requiring a "reasonable belief in the imminence of danger", and stated that the standard to be followed by a jury in determining whether a belief was reasonable "is that of a man of ordinary courage in the circumstances surrounding the defendant at the time of the killing." The Report added that New York did not follow the view, adopted in a few States, that "the jury is required to adopt the subjective view and judge from the standpoint of the very defendant concerned."

In 1961 the Legislature established a Commission to undertake a complete revision of the Penal Law and the Criminal Code. The impetus for the decision to update the Penal Law came in part from the drafting of the Model Penal Code by the American Law Institute, as well as from the fact that the existing law was poorly organized and in many aspects antiquated. Following the submission by the Commission of several reports and proposals, the Legislature approved the present Penal Law in 1965, and it became effective on September 1, 1967. The drafting of the general provisions of the new Penal Law . . . was particularly influenced by the Model Penal Code. While using the Model Penal Code provisions on justification as general guidelines, however, the drafters of the new Penal Law did not simply adopt them verbatim.

The provisions of the Model Penal Code with respect to the use of deadly force in self-defense reflect the position of its drafters that any culpability which arises from a mistaken belief in the need to use such force should be no greater than the culpability such a mistake would give rise to if it were made with respect to an element of a crime (Robinson, Criminal Law Defenses, *op. cit.*, at 410). Accordingly, under Model Penal Code §3.04(2)(b), a defendant charged with murder (or attempted murder) need only show that he *"believe[d]* that [the use of deadly force] was necessary to protect himself against death, serious bodily injury, kidnapping or [forcible] sexual intercourse" to prevail on a self-defense claim (emphasis added). If the defendant's belief was wrong, and was recklessly or negligently formed, however, he may be convicted of the type of homicide charge requiring only a reckless or negligent, as the case may be, criminal intent.

The drafters of the Model Penal Code recognized that the wholly subjective test set forth in section 3.04 differed from the existing law in most States by its omission of any requirement of reasonableness. The drafters were also keenly aware that requiring that the actor have a "reasonable belief" rather than just a "belief" would alter the wholly subjective test. This basic distinction was recognized years earlier by the New York Law Revision Commission and continues to be noted by the commentators.

New York did not follow the Model Penal Code's equation of a mistake as to the need to use deadly force with a mistake negating an element of a crime, choosing instead to use a single statutory section which would provide either a complete defense or no defense at all to a defendant charged with any crime involving the use of deadly force. The drafters of the new Penal Law adopted in large part the structure and content of Model Penal Code §3.04, but, crucially, inserted the word "reasonably" before "believes".

The plurality below agreed with defendant's argument that the change in the statutory language from "reasonable ground," used prior to 1965, to "he reasonably believes" in Penal Law §35.15 evinced a legislative intent to conform to the subjective standard contained in Model Penal Code §3.04. This argument, however, ignores the plain significance of the insertion of "reasonably". Had the drafters of section 35.15_wanted to adopt a subjective standard, they could have simply used the language of section 3.04. "Believes" by itself requires an honest or genuine belief by a defendant as to the need to use deadly force. Interpreting the statute to require only that the defendant's belief was "reasonable to *him,*" as done by the plurality below, would hardly be different from requiring only a genuine belief; in either case, the defendant's own perceptions could completely exonerate him from any criminal liability.

We cannot lightly impute to the Legislature an intent to fundamentally alter the principles of justification to allow the perpetrator of a serious crime to go free simply because that person believed his actions were reasonable and necessary to prevent some perceived harm. To completely exonerate such an individual, no matter how aberrational or bizarre his thought patterns, would allow citizens to set their own standards for the permissible use of force. It would also allow a legally competent defendant suffering from delusions to kill or perform acts of violence with impunity, contrary to fundamental principles of justice and criminal law.

We can only conclude that the Legislature retained a reasonableness requirement to avoid giving a license for such actions. The plurality's interpretation, as the dissenters below recognized, excises the impact of the word "reasonably". . . .

The conclusion that section 35.15 retains an objective element to justify the use of deadly force is buttressed by the statements of its drafters. The executive director and counsel to the Commission which revised the Penal Law have stated that the provisions of the statute with respect to the use of deadly physical force largely conformed with the prior law, with the only changes they noted not being relevant here (Denzer & McQuillan, Practice Commentary, McKinney's Cons. Laws of N.Y., Book 39, Penal Law §35.15, p. 63 [1967]). Nowhere in the legislative history is there any indication that "reasonably believes" was designed to change the law on the use of deadly force or establish a subjective standard. To the contrary, the Commission, in the staff comment governing arrests by police officers, specifically equated "[he] reasonably believes" with having a reasonable ground for believing (Penal Law §35.30; Fourth Interim Report of the Temporary State Commission on Revision of the Penal Law and Criminal Code at 17–18, 1965 NY Legis Doc No. 25). . . .

Goetz also argues that the introduction of an objective element will preclude a jury from considering factors such as the prior experiences of a given actor and thus, require it to make a determination of "reasonableness" without regard to the actual circumstances of a particular incident. This argument, however, falsely presupposes that an objective standard means that the background and other relevant characteristics of a particular actor must be ignored. To the contrary, we have frequently noted that a determination of reasonableness must be based on the "circumstances" facing a defendant or his "situation." Such terms encompass more than the physical movements of the potential assailant. As just discussed, these terms include any relevant knowledge the defendant had about that person. They also necessarily bring in the physical attributes of all persons involved, including the defendant. Furthermore, the defendant's circumstances encompass any prior experiences he had which could provide a reasonable basis for a belief that another person's intentions were to injure or rob him or that the use of deadly force was necessary under the circumstances.

Accordingly, a jury should be instructed to consider this type of evidence in weighing the defendant's actions. The jury must first determine whether the defendant had the requisite beliefs under section 35.15, that is, whether he believed deadly force was necessary to avert the imminent use of deadly force or the commission of one of the felonies enumerated therein. If the People do not prove beyond a reasonable doubt that he did not have such beliefs, then the jury must also consider whether these beliefs were reasonable. The jury would have to determine, in light of all the "circumstances", as explicated above, if a reasonable person could have had these beliefs. . . .

In *People v. Calbud, Inc.*, 426 N.Y.S.2d 238, 394–395, we stated that the prosecutor simply had to "provid[e] the Grand Jury with enough information to enable it intelligently to decide whether a crime has been committed and to determine whether there exists legally sufficient evidence to establish the material elements of the crime". Of course, as noted above, where the evidence suggests that a complete defense such as justification may be present, the prosecutor must charge the grand jurors on that defense, providing enough information to enable them to determine whether the defense, in light of the evidence, should preclude the criminal prosecution. The prosecutor more than adequately fulfilled this obligation here. His instructions were not as complete as the court's charge on justification should be, but they sufficiently apprised the Grand Jury of the existence and requirements of that defense to allow it to intelligently decide that there is sufficient evidence tending to disprove justification and necessitating a trial. The Grand Jury has indicted Goetz. It will now be for the petit jury to decide whether the prosecutor can prove beyond a reasonable doubt that Goetz's reactions were unreasonable and therefore excessive.

IV. . . .

Accordingly, the order of the Appellate Division should be reversed, and the dismissed counts of the indictment reinstated.

5. When does the defendant have a duty to retreat?

In a "duty to retreat state," are there places where a person does not have to retreat? Is the availability of a safe avenue of retreat still relevant in the "stand your ground" states?

State v. Davis, 214 S.C. 34 (1948)

OXNER, Justice.

Appellant, Mack Davis, was indicted and tried for the murder of Norman Gordon, Jr. He sought to excuse the homicide on the ground of self-defense. The trial resulted in a verdict of guilty with recommendation to the mercy of the Court and he was sentenced to imprisonment for life. The only question to be determined on this appeal is whether in establishing his plea of self-defense, appellant had the right to claim immunity from the law of retreat.

About 11 o'clock on Saturday night, August 2, 1947, appellant shot the deceased in a cornfield near a filling station and store operated by W. H. Hinds in a rural section of Florence County. Sometime late that afternoon these two Negroes had an argument at a tobacco barn where the deceased was working, as a result of which the deceased, apparently without much, if any, provocation, slapped or struck appellant and knocked him down. Appellant immediately left the scene. That night about 9 o'clock he came to the store of Mr. Hinds. About an hour and a half later the deceased arrived and asked Hinds to lend him a gun, stating, according to Hinds, "I believe Mack (appellant) is going to shoot me." Hinds refused to do so and told the deceased that he didn't "want any shooting around here." The deceased replied that he had a gun at the tobacco barn which he could get and then left. About the same time or shortly thereafter, appellant went across the road in the direction of his home. Approximately a half hour later Hinds and several of those in the store heard the sound of a shotgun. They made an investigation and found the deceased lying fatally wounded in the cornfield at a point about 25 or 30 yards from the store and about 15 feet from the road, with a rifle near his body. He died shortly thereafter while being carried to the office of a physician.

Appellant testified that after hearing the conversation between the deceased and Hinds, he became alarmed and went home for the purpose of securing his shotgun, intending to return to the store where he had several matters to attend to. He said that he planned to approach the store from the rear through the cornfield because the deceased might see him first if he entered through the front. According to his testimony, while in the cornfield he saw the deceased approaching and squatted to escape observation but that the deceased when within close range recognized him and raised his rifle, whereupon he (appellant) shot in defense of his life. The theory of the State was that appellant concealed himself in the cornfield for the purpose of shooting the deceased as the latter returned to the store.

Appellant lived at the home of his sister and brother-in-law, a distance of about four-tenths of a mile from the scene of the homicide. The field in question was owned by Hinds and cultivated by appellant's brother-in-law as a sharecropper. Appellant worked for him and had assisted in cultivating this corn, which had been laid by at the time of the homicide, but the record does not disclose whether his compensation was in the form of wages or a share in the crop. The deceased also worked on some farm in the same community.

Counsel for appellant requested the Court "to charge the jury that the defendant was on the premises on which he was working and the law of retreat would not apply to him." The request was refused and the jury was instructed that it was incumbent upon appellant to establish all of the elements of self-defense, including that of retreating, which the Court then qualified as follows: "I charge you as a matter of law that if a person is threatened with a gun, any kind of firearms, within shooting range, why, obviously there is no duty to retreat; and it is only in cases where a person can with safety avoid a difficulty that he is required to retreat under the law to avoid committing murder."

Before entering into a discussion of the general question of whether appellant is entitled to claim immunity from the law of retreat, we digress by saying that it may be argued with some reason that appellant was not prejudiced by the refusal of his request. If the jury accepted his version of the occurrence, he was assaulted within close range with a rifle and under these circumstances the jury was charged that he did not have to retreat. However, we do not rest our decision on this ground, preferring to leave undecided the question of whether appellant was prejudiced by the refusal of his request.

It is now well established in this State that if a person is assaulted while on his own premises and is without fault in bringing on the difficulty, he is not bound to retreat in order to invoke the benefit of the doctrine of self-defense, but may stand his ground and repel the attack with as much force as is reasonably necessary. This is true whether the attack occurs in defendant's home, place of business, or elsewhere on property owned or lawfully occupied by him. It was also held in State v. Marlowe, 112 S.E. 921, 922, that a member of a club, wrongfully attacked by another in the club rooms, was under no duty to retreat, the Court observing: "A man is no more bound to allow himself to be run out of his rest room than his workshop." In some jurisdictions the rule has been extended so as to relieve the defendant from the necessity of retreating if attacked in any place where he has a right to be, as when he is lawfully on a public street or highway. We have not gone that far. In State v. McGee, 193 S.E. 303, 306, the Court stated that "The fact that the defendant was on a public highway, where all men have equal rights, and in his automobile, did not constitute any one of those special privileges obviating the necessity of retreating before killing." It was held in State v. Gordon, 128 S.C. 422, that where a foreman on a farm was assaulted by one of the employees under him at the place where they were working, he was not required to retreat. The Court concluded that the place of work "was the defendant's place of business within the meaning of that term as employed in the law of retreat."

In the case at bar, we do not think under the circumstances that appellant is entitled to claim immunity from the law of retreat. The homicide did not occur at or within the curtilage of the home in which he resided. This house was located across the public road and at some distance from the scene of the shooting. Nor was appellant attacked while working at his "place of business". It is true that he had assisted during the year in cultivating the corn in this field but his presence there on the night in question was wholly unrelated to his employment. There is no showing that he even had any interest in the corn crop. Whether his brother-in-law, the sharecropper, would have been required to retreat if attacked in this cornfield under similar circumstances is a question that is not before us.

All exceptions are overruled and judgment affirmed.

Brown v. United States, 256 U.S. 335 (1921)

Mr. Justice HOLMES delivered the opinion of the Court.

The petitioner was convicted of murder in the second degree committed upon one Hermis at a place in Texas within the exclusive jurisdiction of the United States, and the judgment was affirmed by the Circuit Court of Appeals. . . .

The . . . question concerns the instructions at the trial. There had been trouble between Hermis and the defendant for a long time. There was evidence that Hermis had twice assaulted the defendant with a knife and had made threats communicated to the defendant that the next time, one of them would go off in a black box. On the day in question the defendant was at the place above mentioned superintending excavation work for a post office. In view of Hermis's threats he had taken a pistol with him and had laid it in his coat upon a dump. Hermis was driven up by a witness, in a cart to be loaded, and the defendant said that certain earth was not to be removed, whereupon Hermis came toward him, the defendant says, with a knife. The defendant retreated some twenty or twenty-five feet to where his coat was and got his pistol. Hermis was striking at him and the defendant fired four shots and killed him. The judge instructed the jury among other things that "it is necessary to remember, in considering the question of self defence, that the party assaulted is always under the obligation to retreat so long as retreat is open to him, provided that he can do so without subjecting himself to the danger of death or great bodily harm." The instruction was reinforced by the further intimation that unless "retreat would have appeared to a man of reasonable prudence, in the position of the defendant, as involving danger of death or serious bodily harm" the defendant was not entitled to stand his ground. An instruction to the effect that if the defendant had reasonable grounds of apprehension that he was in danger of losing his life or of suffering serious bodily harm from Hermis he was not bound to retreat was refused. So the question is brought out with sufficient clearness whether the formula laid down by the Court and often repeated by the ancient law is adequate to the protection of the defendant's rights.

It is useless to go into the developments of the law from the time when a man who had killed another no matter how innocently had to get his pardon, whether of grace or of course. Concrete cases or illustrations stated in the early law in conditions very different from the present, like the reference to retreat in Coke, Third Inst. 55, and elsewhere, have had a tendency to ossify into specific rules without much regard for reason. Other examples may be found in the law as to trespass ab initio, and as to fresh complaint after rape. Rationally the failure to retreat is a circumstance to be considered with all the others in order to determine whether the defendant went farther than he was justified in doing; not a categorical proof of guilt. The law has grown, and even if historical mistakes have contributed to its growth it has tended in the direction of rules consistent with human nature. Many respectable writers agree that if a man reasonably believes that he is in immediate danger of death or grievous bodily harm from his assailant he may stand his ground and that if he kills him he has not succeeded the bounds of lawful self defence. Detached reflection cannot be demanded in the presence of an uplifted knife. Therefore in this Court, at least, it is not a condition of immunity that one in that situation should pause to consider whether a reasonable man might not think it possible to fly with safety or to disable his assailant rather than to kill him. Rowe v. United States, 164 U.S. 546, 558. The law of Texas very strongly adopts these views as is shown by many cases . . . .

It is true that in the case of Beard he was upon his own land (not in his house,) and in that of Rowe he was in the room of a hotel, but those facts, although mentioned by the Court, would not have bettered the defence by the old common law and were not appreciably more favorable than that the defendant here was at a place where he was called to be, in the discharge of his duty. There was evidence that the last shot was fired after Hermis was down. The jury might not believe the defendant's testimony that it was an accidental discharge, but the suggestion of the Government that this Court may disregard the considerable body of evidence that the shooting was in self defence is based upon a misunderstanding of what was meant by some language in Battle v. United States, 209 U.S. 36, 38. Moreover if the last shot was intentional and may seem to have been unnecessary when considered in cold blood, the defendant would not necessarily lose his immunity if it followed close upon the others while the heat of the conflict was on, and if the defendant believed that he was fighting for his life.

The Government presents a different case. It denies that Hermis had a knife and even that Brown was acting in self defence. Not-withstanding the repeated threats of Hermis and intimations that one of the two would die at the next encounter, which seem hardly to be denied, of course it was possible for the jury to find that Brown had not sufficient reason to think that his life was in danger at that time, that he exceeded the limits of reasonable self defence or even that he was the attacking party. But upon the hypothesis to which the evidence gave much color, that Hermis began the attack, the instruction that we have stated was wrong.

Judgment reversed.

C. Self-Defense and Battered Woman Syndrome

If a woman kills her abuser based in part on the past abuse, does that expand her right to claim self-defense? What relevance is the past history of abuse to the self-defense claim? The next two cases concern exactly the situation described: the defendants killed their husbands after suffering years of abuse. The law certainly does not permit the defendant to wait until the abuser is sleeping (as Mrs. Stewart did). As the court points out, that is not self-defense; it is an execution.

Importantly, both cases created some flexibility in the strict self-defense test for women who can prove that they were suffering from "battered woman syndrome" at the time of the killing; however, the two courts describe that flexibility in very different ways. Note also that *Stewart* is a prosecutor's appeal following an acquittal much like *LaVoie*. Therefore, the court's decision cannot affect Mrs. Stewart's fate.

State v. Stewart, 243 Kan. 639 (1988)

LOCKETT, Justice.

A direct appeal by the prosecution upon a question reserved asks whether the statutory justification for the use of deadly force in self-defense provided by K.S.A. 21–3211 excuses a homicide committed by a battered wife where there is no evidence of a deadly threat or imminent danger contemporaneous with the killing. An *amicus curiae* brief has been filed by the Kansas County and District Attorney Association.

Peggy Stewart fatally shot her husband, Mike Stewart, while he was sleeping. She was charged with murder in the first degree, K.S.A. 21–3401. Defendant pled not guilty, contending that she shot her husband in self-defense. Expert evidence showed that Peggy Stewart suffered from the battered woman syndrome. Based upon the battered woman syndrome, the trial judge instructed the jury on self-defense. The jury found Peggy Stewart not guilty.

The State stipulates that Stewart "suffered considerable abuse at the hands of her husband," but contends that the trial court erred in giving a self-defense instruction since Peggy Stewart was in no imminent danger when she shot her sleeping husband. We agree that under the facts of this case the giving of the self-defense instruction was erroneous. We further hold that the trial judge's self-defense instruction improperly allowed the jury to determine the reasonableness of defendant's belief that she was in imminent danger from her individual subjective viewpoint rather than the viewpoint of a reasonable person in her circumstances.

Following an annulment from her first husband and two subsequent divorces in which she was the petitioner, Peggy Stewart married Mike Stewart in 1974. Evidence at trial disclosed a long history of abuse by Mike against Peggy and her two daughters from one of her prior marriages. Laura, one of Peggy's daughters, testified that early in the marriage Mike hit and kicked Peggy, and that after the first year of the marriage Peggy exhibited signs of severe psychological problems. Subsequently, Peggy was hospitalized and diagnosed as having symptoms of paranoid schizophrenia; she responded to treatment and was soon released. It appeared to Laura, however, that Mike was encouraging Peggy to take more than her prescribed dosage of medication.

In 1977, two social workers informed Peggy that they had received reports that Mike was taking indecent liberties with her daughters. Because the social workers did not want Mike to be left alone with the girls, Peggy quit her job. In 1978, Mike began to taunt Peggy by stating that Carla, her 12-year-old daughter, was "more of a wife" to him than Peggy.

Later, Carla was placed in a detention center, and Mike forbade Peggy and Laura to visit her. When Mike finally allowed Carla to return home in the middle of summer, he forced her to sleep in an un-air conditioned room with the windows nailed shut, to wear a heavy flannel nightgown, and to cover herself with heavy blankets. Mike would then wake Carla at 5:30 a.m. and force her to do all the housework. Peggy and Laura were not allowed to help Carla or speak to her.

When Peggy confronted Mike and demanded that the situation cease, Mike responded by holding a shotgun to Peggy's head and threatening to kill her. Mike once kicked Peggy so violently in the chest and ribs that she required hospitalization. Finally, when Mike ordered Peggy to kill and bury Carla, she filed for divorce. Peggy's attorney in the divorce action testified in the murder trial that Peggy was afraid for both her and her children's lives.

One night, in a fit of anger, Mike threw Carla out of the house. Carla, who was not yet in her teens, was forced out of the home with no money, no coat, and no place to go. When the family heard that Carla was in Colorado, Mike refused to allow Peggy to contact or even talk about Carla.

Mike's intimidation of Peggy continued to escalate. One morning, Laura found her mother hiding on the school bus, terrified and begging the driver to take her to a neighbor's home. That Christmas, Mike threw the turkey dinner to the floor, chased Peggy outside, grabbed her by the hair, rubbed her face in the dirt, and then kicked and beat her.

After Laura moved away, Peggy's life became even more isolated. Once, when Peggy was working at a cafe, Mike came in and ran all the customers off with a gun because he wanted Peggy to go home and have sex with him right that minute. He abused both drugs and alcohol, and amused himself by terrifying Peggy, once waking her from a sound sleep by beating her with a baseball bat. He shot one of Peggy's pet cats, and then held the gun against her head and threatened to pull the trigger. Peggy told friends that Mike would hold a shotgun to her head and threaten to blow it off, and indicated that one day he would probably do it.

In May 1986, Peggy left Mike and ran away to Laura's home in Oklahoma. It was the first time Peggy had left Mike without telling him. Because Peggy was suicidal, Laura had her admitted to a hospital. There, she was diagnosed as having toxic psychosis as a result of an overdose of her medication. On May 30, 1986, Mike called to say he was coming to get her. Peggy agreed to return to Kansas. Peggy told a nurse she felt like she wanted to shoot her husband. At trial, she testified that she decided to return with Mike because she was not able to get the medical help she needed in Oklahoma.

When Mike arrived at the hospital, he told the staff that he "needed his housekeeper." The hospital released Peggy to Mike's care, and he immediately drove her back to Kansas. Mike told Peggy that all her problems were in her head and he would be the one to tell her what was good for her, not the doctors. Peggy testified that Mike threatened to kill her if she ever ran away again. As soon as they arrived at the house, Mike forced Peggy into the house and forced her to have oral sex several times.

The next morning, Peggy discovered a loaded .357 magnum. She testified she was afraid of the gun. She hid the gun under the mattress of the bed in a spare room. Later that morning, as she cleaned house, Mike kept making remarks that she should not bother because she would not be there long, or that she should not bother with her things because she could not take them with her. She testified she was afraid Mike was going to kill her.

Mike's parents visited Mike and Peggy that afternoon. Mike's father testified that Peggy and Mike were affectionate with each other during the visit. Later, after Mike's parents had left, Mike forced Peggy to perform oral sex. After watching television, Mike and Peggy went to bed at 8:00 p.m. As Mike slept, Peggy thought about suicide and heard voices in her head repeating over and over, "kill or be killed." At this time, there were two vehicles in the driveway and Peggy had access to the car keys. About 10:00 p.m., Peggy went to the spare bedroom and removed the gun from under the mattress, walked back to the bedroom, and killed her husband while he slept. She then ran to the home of a neighbor, who called the police.

When the police questioned Peggy regarding the events leading up to the shooting, Peggy stated that things had not gone quite right that day, and that when she got the chance she hid the gun under the mattress. She stated that she shot Mike to "get this over with, this misery and this torment." When asked why she got the gun out, Peggy stated to the police:

> I'm not sure exactly what . . . led up to it . . . and my head started playing games with me and I got to thinking about things and I said I didn't want to be by myself again. . . . I got the gun out because there had been remarks made about me being out there alone. It was as if Mike was going to do something again like had been done before. He had gotten me down here from McPherson one time and he went and told them that I had done something and he had me put out of the house and was taking everything I had. And it was like he was going to pull the same thing over again.

Two expert witnesses testified during the trial. The expert for the defense, psychologist Marilyn Hutchinson, diagnosed Peggy as suffering from "battered woman syndrome," or post-traumatic stress syndrome. Dr. Hutchinson testified that Mike was preparing to escalate the violence in retaliation for Peggy's running away. She testified that loaded guns, veiled threats, and increased sexual demands are indicators of the escalation of the cycle. Dr. Hutchinson believed Peggy had a repressed knowledge that she was in a "really grave lethal situation."

The State's expert, psychiatrist Herbert Modlin, neither subscribed to a belief in the battered woman syndrome nor to a theory of learned helplessness as an explanation for why women do not leave an abusive relationship. Dr. Modlin testified that abuse such as repeated forced oral sex would not be trauma sufficient to trigger a post-traumatic stress disorder. He also believed Peggy was erroneously diagnosed as suffering from toxic psychosis. He stated that Peggy was unable to escape the abuse because she suffered from schizophrenia, rather than the battered woman syndrome.

At defense counsel's request, the trial judge gave an instruction on self-defense to the jury. The jury found Peggy not guilty.

The first issue is whether we have jurisdiction to hear this appeal. K.S.A. 1987 Supp. 22–3602(b) provides:

> Appeals to the supreme court may be taken by the prosecution from cases before a district judge as a matter of right in the following cases, and no others:
>
> (1) From an order dismissing a complaint, information or indictment;
>
> (2) from an order arresting judgment;
>
> (3) upon a question reserved by the prosecution; or
>
> (4) upon an order granting a new trial in any case involving a class A or B felony.

Although the State may not appeal an acquittal, it may reserve questions for appeal. *State v. Martin,* 232 Kan. 778, 779 (1983). We will not entertain an appeal by the prosecution merely to determine whether the trial court committed error. *State v. Lamkin,* 229 Kan. 104 (1981). The appeal by the prosecution must raise a question of statewide interest, the answer to which is essential to the just administration of criminal law. *State v. Martin,* 232 Kan. at 780.

The question reserved is whether the trial judge erred in instructing on self-defense when there was no imminent threat to the defendant and no evidence of any argument or altercation between the defendant and the victim contemporaneous with the killing. We find this question and the related question of the extent to which evidence of the battered woman syndrome will be allowed to expand the statutory justification for the use of deadly force in self-defense are questions of statewide importance.

The State claims that under the facts the instruction should not have been given because there was no lethal threat to defendant contemporaneous with the killing. The State points out that Peggy's annulment and divorces from former husbands, and her filing for divorce after leaving Mike, proved that Peggy knew there were non-lethal methods by which she could extricate herself from the abusive relationship.

Under the common law, the excuse for killing in self-defense is founded upon necessity, be it real or apparent. Early Kansas cases held that killing in self-defense was justifiable when the defendant had reasonable grounds to believe that an aggressor (1) had a design to take the defendant's life, (2) attempted to execute the design or was in an apparent situation to do so, and (3) induced in the defendant a reasonable belief that he intended to do so immediately. *State v. Horne,* 9 Kan. 119, 129 (1872), *overruled on other grounds* 15 Kan. 547, 554 (1875).

In *State v. Rose,* 30 Kan. 501 (1883), we approved an instruction on self-defense which stated in part: "[B]efore a person can take the life of another, it must reasonably appear that his own life must have been in imminent danger, or that he was in imminent danger of some great bodily injury from the hands of the person killed. No one can attack and kill another because he may fear injury at some future time." 30 Kan. at 503. The perceived imminent danger had to occur in the present time, specifically during the time in which the defendant and the deceased were engaged in their final conflict. 30 Kan. at 506.

These common-law principles were codified in K.S.A. 21–3211, which provides:

> A person is justified in the use of force against an aggressor when and to the extent it appears to him and he reasonably believes that such conduct is necessary to defend himself or another against such aggressor's imminent use of unlawful force.

The traditional concept of self-defense has posited one-time conflicts between persons of somewhat equal size and strength. When the defendant claiming self-defense is a victim of long-term domestic violence, such as a battered spouse, such traditional concepts may not apply. Because of the prior history of abuse, and the difference in strength and size between the abused and the abuser, the accused in such cases may choose to defend during a momentary lull in the abuse, rather than during a conflict. See Comment, *Criminal Law: The Kansas Approach to the Battered Woman's Use of Self-Defense* [*State v. Hundley,* 236 Kan. 461 (1985)], 25 Washburn L.J. 174 (1985). However, in order to warrant the giving of a self-defense instruction, the facts of the case must still show that the spouse was in imminent danger close to the time of the killing.

A person is justified in using force against an aggressor when it appears to that person and he or she reasonably believes such force to be necessary. A reasonable belief implies both an honest belief and the existence of facts which would persuade a reasonable person to that belief. K.S.A. 21–3211. A self-defense instruction must be given if there is any evidence to support a claim of self-defense, even if that evidence consists solely of the defendant's testimony. *State v. Hill,* 242 Kan. 68, 78 (1987).

Where self-defense is asserted, evidence of the deceased's long-term cruelty and violence towards the defendant is admissible. *State v. Hundley,* 236 Kan. 461, 464 (1985); *State v. Gray,* 179 Kan. 133 (1956). In cases involving battered spouses, expert evidence of the battered woman syndrome is relevant to a determination of the reasonableness of the defendant's perception of danger. *State v. Hodges,* 239 Kan. 63 (1986). Other courts which have allowed such evidence to be introduced include those in Florida, Georgia, Illinois, Maine,

New Jersey, New York, Pennsylvania, Washington, and Wisconsin. However, no jurisdictions have held that the existence of the battered woman syndrome in and of itself operates as a defense to murder.

In order to instruct a jury on self-defense, there must be some showing of an imminent threat or a confrontational circumstance involving an overt act by an aggressor. There is no exception to this requirement where the defendant has suffered long-term domestic abuse and the victim is the abuser. In such cases, the issue is not whether the defendant believes homicide is the solution to past or future problems with the batterer, but rather whether circumstances surrounding the killing were sufficient to create a reasonable belief in the defendant that the use of deadly force was necessary.

In three recent Kansas cases where battered women shot their husbands, the women were clearly threatened in the moments prior to the shootings. *State v. Hundley,* 236 Kan. 461, involved a severely abused wife, Betty Hundley, who shot her husband, Carl, when he threatened her and reached for a beer bottle. Several weeks prior to the shooting, Betty had moved to a motel. Carl continued to harass her and threaten her life. On the day of the shooting, Carl threatened to kill her. That night he forcibly broke into Betty's motel room, beat and choked her, painfully shaved her pubic hair, and forced her to have intercourse with him. Thereafter, he pounded a beer bottle on the night stand and demanded that Betty get him some cigarettes. Betty testified that he had attacked her with beer bottles before. She pulled a gun from her purse and demanded that Carl leave. When Carl saw the gun he stated: "You are dead, bitch, now." Betty fired the gun and killed Carl.

In *State v. Osbey,* 238 Kan. 280 (1985), Osbey was convicted of first-degree murder of her husband. On the day of the shooting, the husband had a gun and had communicated threats to kill Osbey both to her and others. He had shown the gun to a friend of Osbey's who warned Osbey. After an argument, when the husband was moving out, Osbey threw his chair towards his van. Osbey's husband said, "I'm sick of this shit," picked up some record albums from inside the van, and started towards the house. Osbey ran inside, loaded a gun, and told her husband to stay back because she did not want to hurt him. Her husband said he did not want to hurt her, either, and reached behind the albums he was carrying. Fearing he was reaching for his gun, Osbey shot him.

In *State v. Hodges,* 239 Kan. 63 (1986), on the night of the shooting, the husband attacked Hodges and beat her head against a doorjamb twenty times. He then said he was going to kill her. Hodges was then kicked and beaten before making her way into another room. When her husband said, "God damn you. Get in here now!" she grabbed a gun, ran to the doorway, and shot him.

On appeal, none of these cases raised the issue of the propriety of the self-defense instruction. Each case involved a threat of death to the wife and a violent confrontation between husband and wife, contemporaneous with the shooting. Here, however, there is an absence of imminent danger to defendant: Peggy told a nurse at the Oklahoma hospital of her desire to kill Mike. She later voluntarily agreed to return home with Mike when he telephoned her. She stated that after leaving the hospital Mike threatened to kill her if she left him again. Peggy showed no inclination to leave. In fact, immediately after the shooting, Peggy told the police that she was upset because she thought Mike would leave her. Prior to the shooting, Peggy hid the loaded gun. The cars were in the driveway and Peggy had access to the car keys. After being abused, Peggy went to bed with Mike at 8 p.m. Peggy lay there for two hours, then retrieved the gun from where she had hidden it and shot Mike while he slept.

Under these facts, the giving of the self-defense instruction was erroneous. Under such circumstances, a battered woman cannot reasonably fear imminent life-threatening danger from her sleeping spouse. We note that other courts have held that the sole fact that the victim was asleep does not preclude a self-defense instruction. In *State v. Norman,* 89 N.C. App. 384 (1988), cited by defendant, the defendant's evidence disclosed a long history of abuse. Each time defendant attempted to escape, her husband found and beat her. On the day of the shooting, the husband beat defendant continually throughout the day, and threatened either to cut her throat, kill her, or cut off her breast. In the afternoon, defendant shot her husband while he napped. The North Carolina Court of Appeals held it was reversible error to fail to instruct on self-defense. The court found that, although decedent was napping at the time defendant shot him, defendant's unlawful act was closely related in time to an assault and threat of death by decedent against defendant and that the decedent's nap was "but a momentary hiatus in a continuous reign of terror." 89 N.C. App. at 394.

There is no doubt that the North Carolina court determined that the sleeping husband was an evil man who deserved the justice he received from his battered wife. Here, similar comparable and compelling facts exist. But, as one court has stated: "To permit capital punishment to be imposed upon the subjective conclusion of the [abused] individual that prior acts and conduct of the deceased justified the killing would amount to a leap into the abyss of anarchy." *Jahnke v. State,* 682 P.2d 991, 997 (Wyo. 1984). Finally, our legislature has not provided for capital punishment for even the most heinous crimes. We must, therefore, hold that when a battered woman kills her sleeping spouse when there is no imminent danger, the killing is not reasonably necessary and a self-defense instruction may not be given. To hold otherwise in this case would in effect allow the execution of the abuser for past or future acts and conduct.

One additional issue must be addressed. In its *amicus curiae* brief, the Kansas County and District Attorney Association contends the instruction given by the trial court improperly modified the law of self-defense to be more generous to one suffering from the battered woman syndrome than to any other defendant relying on self-defense. We agree and believe it is necessary to clarify certain portions of our opinion in *State v. Hodges,* 239 Kan. 63.

Here, the trial judge gave the instruction approved in *State v. Simon,* 231 Kan. 572, 575 (1982), stating:

> The defendant has claimed her conduct was justified as self-defense.
>
> A person is justified in the use of force against an aggressor when and to the extent it appears to him and he reasonably believes that such conduct is necessary to defend himself or another against such aggressor's imminent use of unlawful force. Such justification requires both a belief on the part of the defendant and the existence of facts that would persuade a reasonable person to that belief.

The trial judge then added the following:

> You must determine, from the viewpoint of the defendant's mental state, whether the defendant's belief in the need to defend herself was reasonable in light of her subjective impressions and the facts and circumstances known to her.

This addition was apparently encouraged by the following language in *State v. Hodges,* 239 Kan. 63:

> Where the battered woman syndrome is an issue in the case, the standard for reasonableness concerning an accused's belief in asserting self-defense is not an objective, but a subjective standard. The jury must determine, from the viewpoint of defendant's mental state, whether defendant's belief in the need to defend herself was reasonable.

The statement that the reasonableness of defendant's belief in asserting self-defense should be measured from the defendant's own individual subjective viewpoint conflicts with prior law. Our test for self-defense is a two-pronged one. We first use a subjective standard to determine whether the defendant sincerely and honestly believed it necessary to kill in order to defend. We then use an objective standard to determine whether defendant's belief was reasonable—specifically, whether a reasonable person in defendant's circumstances would have perceived self-defense as necessary. In *State v. Hundley,* 236 Kan. at 467, we stated that, in cases involving battered spouses, "[t]he objective test is how a reasonably prudent battered wife would perceive [the aggressor's] demeanor."

Hundley makes clear that it was error for the trial court to instruct the jury to employ solely a subjective test in determining the reasonableness of defendant's actions. Insofar as the above-quoted language in *State v. Hodges* can be read to sanction a subjective test, this language is disapproved.

The appeal is sustained.

People v. Humphrey, 13 Cal.4th 1073 (1996)

CHIN, Justice.

The Legislature has decreed that, when relevant, expert testimony regarding "battered woman's syndrome" is generally admissible in a criminal action. (Evid. Code, §1107.) We must determine the purposes for which a jury may consider this evidence when offered to support a claim of self-defense to a murder charge.

The trial court instructed that the jury could consider the evidence in deciding whether the defendant actually believed it was necessary to kill in self-defense, but not in deciding whether that belief was reasonable. The instruction was erroneous. Because evidence of battered woman's syndrome may help the jury understand the circumstances in which the defendant found herself at the time of the killing, it is relevant to the reasonableness of her belief. Moreover, because defendant testified, the evidence was relevant to her credibility. The trial court should have allowed the jury to consider this testimony in deciding the reasonableness as well as the existence of defendant's belief that killing was necessary.

Finding the error prejudicial, we reverse the judgment of the Court of Appeal.

I.   THE FACTS
A.   Prosecution Evidence

During the evening of March 28, 1992, defendant shot and killed Albert Hampton in their Fresno home. Officer Reagan was the first on the scene. A neighbor told Reagan that the couple in the house had been arguing all day. Defendant soon came outside appearing upset and with her hands raised as if surrendering. She told Officer Reagan, "I shot him. That's right, I shot him. I just couldn't take him beating on me no more." She led the officer into the house, showed him a .357 magnum revolver on a table, and said, "There's the gun." Hampton was on the kitchen floor, wounded but alive.

A short time later, defendant told Officer Reagan, "He deserved it. I just couldn't take it anymore. I told him to stop beating on me." "He was beating on me, so I shot him. I told him I'd shoot him if he ever beat on me again." A paramedic heard her say that she wanted to teach Hampton "a lesson." Defendant told another officer at the scene, Officer Terry, "I'm fed up. Yeah, I shot him. I'm just tired of him hitting me. He said, 'You're not going to do nothing about it.' I showed him, didn't I? I shot him good. He won't hit anybody else again. Hit me again; I shoot him again. I don't care if I go to jail. Push come to shove, I guess people gave it to him, and, kept hitting me. I warned him. I warned him not to hit me. He wouldn't listen."

Officer Terry took defendant to the police station, where she told the following story. The day before the shooting, Hampton had been drinking. He hit defendant while they were driving home in their truck and continued hitting her when they arrived. He told her, "I'll kill you," and shot at her. The bullet went through a bedroom window and struck a tree outside. The day of the shooting, Hampton "got drunk," swore at her, and started hitting her again. He walked into the kitchen. Defendant saw the gun in the living room and picked it up. Her jaw hurt, and she was in pain. She pointed the gun at Hampton and said, "You're not going to hit me anymore." Hampton said, "What are you doing?" Believing that Hampton was about to pick something up to hit her with, she shot him. She then put the gun down and went outside to wait for the police.

Hampton later died of a gunshot wound to his chest. The neighbor who spoke with Officer Reagan testified that shortly before the shooting, she heard defendant, but not Hampton, shouting. The evening before, the neighbor had heard a gunshot. Defendant's blood contained no drugs but had a blood-alcohol level of .17 percent. Hampton's blood contained no drugs or alcohol.

B. Defense Evidence

Defendant claimed she shot Hampton in self-defense. To support the claim, the defense presented first expert testimony and then nonexpert testimony, including that of defendant herself.

1. *Expert Testimony*

Dr. Lee Bowker testified as an expert on battered woman's syndrome. The syndrome, he testified, "is not just a psychological construction, but it's a term for a wide variety of controlling mechanisms that the man or it can be a woman, but in general for this syndrome it's a man, uses against the woman, and for the effect that those control mechanisms have."

Dr. Bowker had studied about 1,000 battered women and found them often inaccurately portrayed "as cardboard figures, paper-thin punching bags who merely absorb the violence but didn't do anything about it." He found that battered women often employ strategies to stop the beatings, including hiding, running away, counter-violence, seeking the help of friends and family, going to a shelter, and contacting police. Nevertheless, many battered women remain in the relationship because of lack of money, social isolation, lack of self-confidence, inadequate police response, and a fear (often justified) of reprisals by the batterer. "The battering man will make the battered woman depend on him and generally succeed at least for a time." A battered woman often feels responsible for the abusive relationship, and "she just can't figure out a way to please him better so he'll stop beating her." In sum, "It really is the physical control of the woman through economics and through relative social isolation combined with the psychological techniques that make her so dependent."

Many battered women go from one abusive relationship to another and seek a strong man to protect them from the previous abuser. "[W]ith each successful victimization, the person becomes less able to avoid the next one." The violence can gradually escalate, as the batterer keeps control using ever more severe actions, including rape, torture, violence against the woman's loved ones or pets, and death threats. Battered women sense this escalation. In Dr. Bowker's "experience with battered women who kill in self-defense their abusers, it's always related to their perceived change of what's going on in a relationship. They become very sensitive to what sets off batterers. They watch for this stuff very carefully. . . . Anybody who is abused over a period of time becomes sensitive to the abuser's behavior and when she sees a change acceleration begin in that behavior, it tells them something is going to happen. . . ."

Dr. Bowker interviewed defendant for a full day. He believed she suffered not only from battered woman's syndrome, but also from being the child of an alcoholic and an incest victim. He testified that all three of defendant's partners before Hampton were abusive and significantly older than she.

Dr. Bowker described defendant's relationship with Hampton. Hampton was a 49-year-old man who weighed almost twice as much as defendant. The two had a battering relationship that Dr. Bowker characterized as a "traditional cycle of violence." The cycle included phases of tension building, violence, and then forgiveness-seeking in which Hampton would promise not to batter defendant anymore and she would believe him. During this period, there would be occasional good times. For example, defendant told Dr. Bowker that Hampton would give her a rose. "That's one of the things that hooks people in. Intermittent reinforcement is the key." But after a while, the violence would begin again. The violence would recur because "basically . . . the woman doesn't perfectly obey. That's the bottom line." For example, defendant would talk to another man, or fail to clean house "just so."

The situation worsened over time, especially when Hampton got off parole shortly before his death. He became more physically and emotionally abusive, repeatedly threatened defendant's life, and even shot at her the night before his death. Hampton often allowed defendant to go out, but she was afraid to flee because she felt he would find her as he had in the past. "He enforced her belief that she can never escape him." Dr. Bowker testified that unless her injuries were so severe that "something absolutely had to be treated," he would not expect her to seek medical treatment. "That's the pattern of her life. . . ."

Dr. Bowker believed defendant's description of her experiences. In his opinion, she suffered from battered woman's syndrome in "about as extreme a pattern as you could find."

2. Nonexpert Testimony

Defendant confirmed many of the details of her life and relationship with Hampton underlying Dr. Bowker's opinion. She testified that her father forcefully molested her from the time she was seven years old until she was fifteen. She described her relationship with another abusive man as being like "Nightmare on Elm Street." Regarding Hampton, she testified that they often argued and that he beat her regularly. Both were heavy drinkers. Hampton once threw a can of beer at her face, breaking her nose. Her dental plates hurt because Hampton hit her so often. He often kicked her, but usually hit her in the back of the head because, he told her, it "won't leave bruises." Hampton sometimes threatened to kill her, and often said she "would live to regret it." Matters got worse towards the end.

The evening before the shooting, March 27, 1992, Hampton arrived home "very drunk." He yelled at her and called her names. At one point when she was standing by the bedroom window, he fired his .357 Magnum revolver at her. She testified, "He didn't miss me by much either." She was "real scared."

The next day, the two drove into the mountains. They argued, and Hampton continually hit her. While returning, he said that their location would be a good place to kill her because "they wouldn't find [her] for a while." She took it as a joke, although she feared him. When they returned, the arguing continued. He hit her again, then entered the kitchen. He threatened, "This time, bitch, when I shoot at you, I won't miss." He came from the kitchen and reached for the gun on the living room table. She grabbed it first, pointed it at him, and told him "that he wasn't going to hit [her]." She backed Hampton into the kitchen. He was saying something, but she did not know what. He reached for her hand and she shot him. She believed he was reaching for the gun and was going to shoot her.

Several other witnesses testified about defendant's relationship with Hampton, his abusive conduct in general, and his physical abuse of, and threats to, defendant in particular. This testimony generally corroborated defendant's. A neighbor testified that the night before the shooting, she heard a gunshot. The next morning, defendant told the neighbor that Hampton had shot at her, and that she was afraid of him. After the shooting, investigators found a bullet hole through the frame of the bedroom window and a bullet embedded in a tree in line with the window. Another neighbor testified that shortly before hearing the shot that killed Hampton, she heard defendant say, "Stop it, Albert. Stop it."

C.   Procedural History

Defendant was charged with murder with personal use of a firearm. At the end of the prosecution's case-in-chief, the court granted defendant's motion under Penal Code section 1118.1 for acquittal of first degree murder.

The court instructed the jury on second degree murder and both voluntary and involuntary manslaughter. It also instructed on self-defense, explaining that an actual and reasonable belief that the killing was necessary was a complete defense; an actual but unreasonable belief was a defense to murder, but not to voluntary manslaughter. In determining reasonableness, the jury was to consider what "would appear to be necessary to a reasonable person in a similar situation and with similar knowledge."

The court also instructed: "Evidence regarding Battered Woman's Syndrome has been introduced in this case. Such evidence, if believed, may be considered by you only for the purpose of determining whether or not the defendant held the necessary subjective honest [belief] which is a requirement for both perfect and imperfect self-defense. However, that same evidence regarding Battered Woman's Syndrome may not be considered or used by you in evaluating the objective reasonableness requirement for perfect self-defense." . . .

"Battered Woman's Syndrome seeks to describe and explain common reactions of women to that experience. Thus, you may consider the evidence concerning the syndrome and its effects only for the limited purpose of showing, if it does show, that the defendant's reactions, as demonstrated by the evidence, are not inconsistent with her having been physically abused or the beliefs, perceptions, or behavior of victims of domestic violence."

During deliberations, the jury asked for and received clarification of the terms "subjectively honest and objectively unreasonable." It found defendant guilty of voluntary manslaughter with personal use of a firearm. The court sentenced defendant to prison for eight years, consisting of the lower term of three years for manslaughter, plus the upper term of five years for firearm use. The Court of Appeal remanded for resentencing on the use enhancement, but otherwise affirmed the judgment.

We granted defendant's petition for review.

II.   DISCUSSION
A.   Background

With an exception not relevant here, Evidence Code section 1107, subdivision (a), makes admissible in a criminal action expert testimony regarding "battered woman's syndrome, including the physical, emotional, or mental effects upon the beliefs, perceptions, or behavior of victims of domestic violence. . . ." Under subdivision (b) of that section, the foundation for admission is sufficient "if the proponent of the evidence establishes its relevancy and the proper qualifications of the expert witness." Defendant presented the evidence to support her claim of self-defense. It is undisputed that she established the proper qualifications of the expert witness. The only issue is to what extent defendant established its "relevancy." To resolve this question we must examine California law regarding self-defense.

For killing to be in self-defense, the defendant must actually and reasonably believe in the need to defend. If the belief subjectively exists but is objectively unreasonable, there is "imperfect self-defense," i.e., "the defendant is deemed to have acted without malice and cannot be convicted of murder," but can be convicted of manslaughter. To constitute "perfect self-defense," i.e., to exonerate the person completely, the belief must also be objectively reasonable. As the Legislature has stated, "[T]he circumstances must be sufficient to excite the fears of a reasonable person. . . ." (Pen. Code, §198; see also §197, subds. 2, 3.) Moreover, for either perfect or imperfect self-defense, the fear must be of imminent harm. "Fear of future harm—no matter how great the fear and no matter how great the likelihood of the harm—will not suffice.

The defendant's fear must be of *imminent* danger to life or great bodily injury." (*In re Christian S.*, (1994) 7 Cal. 4th 768, 783, italics in original.)

Although the belief in the need to defend must be objectively reasonable, a jury must consider what "would appear to be necessary to a reasonable person in a similar situation and with similar knowledge. . . ." (CALJIC No. 5.50.) It judges reasonableness "from the point of view of a reasonable person in the position of defendant. . . ." (*People v. McGee* (1947) 31 Cal. 2d 229, 238.) To do this, it must consider all the " 'facts and circumstances . . . in determining whether the defendant acted in a manner in which *a reasonable man* would act in protecting his own life or bodily safety.' " (*People v. Moore* (1954) 43 Cal. 2d 517, 528, italics in original.) As we stated long ago, ". . . a defendant is entitled to have a jury take into consideration all the elements in the case which might be expected to operate on his mind. . . ." (*People v. Smith* (1907) 151 Cal. 619, 628.)

We recently discussed this question in a different context. In *People v. Ochoa* (1993) 6 Cal. 4th 1199, the defendant was convicted of gross vehicular manslaughter while intoxicated. The offense requires "gross negligence," the test for which is "objective: whether a reasonable person in the defendant's position would have been aware of the risk involved." The defendant argued that, "because the test of gross negligence is an objective one . . ., evidence of his own subjective state of mind was irrelevant and unduly prejudicial." We disagreed. "In determining whether a reasonable person *in defendant's position* would have been aware of the risks, the jury should be given relevant facts as to what defendant knew, including his actual awareness of those risks." "[A]lthough the test for gross negligence was an objective one, '[t]he jury should therefore consider all relevant circumstances. . . .'" (*Ibid.*, quoting *People v. Bennett* (1991) 54 Cal. 3d 1032, 1038.)

What we said in *Ochoa* about the defendant's actual awareness applies to this case. Although the ultimate test of reasonableness is objective, in determining whether a reasonable person in defendant's position would have believed in the need to defend, the jury must consider all of the relevant circumstances in which defendant found herself.

With these principles in mind, we now consider the relevance of evidence of battered woman's syndrome to the elements of self-defense.

B. Battered Woman's Syndrome

Battered woman's syndrome "has been defined as 'a series of common characteristics that appear in women who are abused physically and psychologically over an extended period of time by the dominant male figure in their lives.' (*State v. Kelly* (1984) 97 N.J. 178, 193; ["a pattern of psychological symptoms that develop after somebody has lived in a battering relationship"]; Note, *Battered Women Who Kill Their Abusers* (1993) 106 Harv. L. Rev. 1574, 1578.) . . .

The trial court allowed the jury to consider the battered woman's syndrome evidence in deciding whether defendant actually believed she needed to kill in self-defense. The question here is whether the evidence was also relevant on the reasonableness of that belief. Two Court of Appeal decisions have considered the relevance of battered woman's syndrome evidence to a claim of self-defense.

People v. Aris (1989) 215 Cal. App. 3d 1178, 1185, applied "the law of self-defense in the context of a battered woman killing the batterer while he slept after he had beaten the killer and threatened serious bodily injury and death when he awoke." There, unlike here, the trial court refused to instruct the jury on perfect self-defense, but it did instruct on imperfect self-defense. The appellate court upheld the refusal, finding that "defendant presented no substantial evidence that a reasonable person under the same circumstances would have perceived imminent danger and a need to kill in self-defense." The trial court admitted some evidence of battered woman's syndrome, but the defendant argued that it erred "by excluding expert testimony (1) that defendant was a battered woman based on the expert's psychological evaluation of the defendant and (2) 'explaining how the psychological impact of being a battered woman affected her perception of danger at the time she shot her husband.' "

Although the trial court did not instruct on perfect self-defense, the appellate court first concluded that battered woman's syndrome evidence is not relevant to the reasonableness element. "[T]he questions of the reasonableness of a defendant's belief that self-defense is necessary and of the reasonableness of the actions taken in self-defense do not call for an evaluation of the defendant's subjective *state of mind,* but for an objective evaluation of the defendant's assertedly defensive *acts.* California law expresses the criterion for this evaluation in the objective terms of whether *a reasonable person,* as opposed to the *defendant,* would have believed and acted as the defendant did. We hold that expert testimony about a defendant's state of mind is not relevant to the reasonableness of the defendant's self-defense."

The court then found the evidence "highly relevant to the first element of self-defense—defendant's actual, subjective perception that she was in danger and that she had to kill her husband to avoid that danger. . . ." The relevance to the defendant's actual perception lies in the opinion's explanation of how such a perception would reasonably follow from the defendant's experience as a battered woman. This relates to the prosecution's argument that such a perception of imminent danger makes no sense when the victim is asleep and a way of escape open and, therefore, she did not actually have that perception." The trial court thus erred in not admitting the testimony to show "how the defendant's particular experiences as a battered woman affected her perceptions of danger, its imminence, and what actions were necessary to protect herself."

Concerned "that the jury in a particular case may misuse such evidence to establish the reasonableness requirement for perfect self-defense, for which purpose it is irrelevant," the *Aris* court stated that, "upon request whenever the jury is instructed on perfect self-defense, trial courts should instruct that such testimony is relevant only to prove the honest belief requirement for both perfect and imperfect self-defense, not to prove the reasonableness requirement for perfect self-defense." The trial court gave such an instruction here, thus creating the issue before us.

In *People v. Day* (1992) 2 Cal. App. 4th 405, the defendant moved for a new trial following her conviction of involuntary manslaughter. Supported by an affidavit by Dr. Bowker, she argued that her attorney should have presented evidence of battered woman's syndrome to aid her claim of self-defense. Relying on *Aris,* the appellate court first found that the evidence would not have been relevant to show the objective reasonableness of the defendant's actions. It also found, however, that the evidence would have been admissible to rehabilitate the defendant's credibility as a witness. Finding that counsel's failure to present the evidence was prejudicial, the court reversed the judgment.

The Attorney General argues that *People v. Aris, supra,* 215 Cal. App. 3d 1178, and *People v. Day, supra,* 2 Cal. App. 4th 405, were correct that evidence of battered woman's syndrome is irrelevant to reasonableness. We disagree. Those cases too narrowly interpreted the reasonableness element. *Aris* and *Day* failed to consider that the jury, in determining objective reasonableness, must view the situation from the *defendant's perspective.* Here, for example, Dr. Bowker testified that the violence can escalate and that a battered woman can become increasingly sensitive to the abuser's behavior, testimony relevant to determining whether defendant reasonably believed when she fired the gun that this time the threat to her life was imminent. Indeed, the prosecutor argued that, "from an objective, reasonable man's standard, there was no reason for her to go get that gun. This threat that she says he made was like so many threats before. There was no reason for her to react that way." Dr. Bowker's testimony supplied a response that the jury might not otherwise receive. As violence increases over time, and threats gain credibility, a battered person might become sensitized and thus able reasonably to discern when danger is real and when it is not. "[T]he expert's testimony might also enable the jury to find that the battered [woman] . . . is particularly able to predict accurately the likely extent of violence in any attack on her. That conclusion could significantly affect the jury's evaluation of the *reasonableness* of defendant's fear for her life." (*State v. Kelly* (1984) 97 N.J. 178, italics added.)

The Attorney General concedes that Hampton's behavior towards defendant, including prior threats and violence, was relevant to reasonableness but distinguishes between evidence of this *behavior*—which the trial court fully admitted—and *expert testimony* about its effects on defendant. The distinction is untenable. "To effectively present the situation as perceived by the defendant, and the reasonableness of her fear, the defense has the option to explain her feelings to enable the jury to overcome stereotyped impressions about women who remain in abusive relationships. It is appropriate that the jury be given a professional explanation of the battering syndrome and its effects on the woman through the use of expert testimony."

The Attorney General also argues that allowing consideration of this testimony would result in an undesirable "battle of the experts" and raises the specter of other battles of experts regarding other syndromes. The Legislature, however, has decided that, if relevant, expert evidence on battered woman's syndrome is admissible. We have found it relevant; it is therefore admissible. We express no opinion on the admissibility of expert testimony regarding other possible syndromes in support of a claim of self-defense, but we rest today's holding on Evidence Code section 1107.

Contrary to the Attorney General's argument, we are not changing the standard from objective to subjective, or replacing the reasonable "person" standard with a reasonable "battered woman" standard. Our decision would not, in another context, compel adoption of a "'reasonable gang member' standard." Evidence Code section 1107 states "a rule of evidence only" and makes "no substantive change." The jury must consider defendant's situation and knowledge, which makes the evidence relevant, but the ultimate question is whether a reasonable person, not a reasonable battered woman, would believe in the need to kill to prevent imminent harm. Moreover, it is the jury, not the expert that determines whether defendant's belief and, ultimately, her actions, were objectively reasonable.

Battered woman's syndrome evidence was also relevant to defendant's credibility. It "would have assisted the jury in objectively analyzing [defendant's] claim of self-defense by dispelling many of the commonly held misconceptions about battered women." For example, in urging the jury not to believe defendant's testimony that Hampton shot at her the night before the killing, the prosecutor argued that "if this defendant truly believed that [Hampton] had shot at her, on that night, I mean she would have left. . . . If she really believed that he had tried to shoot her, she would not have stayed." Dr. Bowker's testimony " 'would help dispel the ordinary lay person's perception that a woman in a battering relationship is free to leave at any time. The expert evidence would counter any "common sense" conclusions by the jury that if the beatings were really that bad the woman would have left her husband much earlier. Popular misconceptions about battered women would be put to rest. . . .' " (*People v. Day, supra,* 2 Cal. App. 4th at p. 417, quoting *State v. Hodges* (1986) 716 P.2d 563, 567.) "[I]f the jury had understood [defendant's] conduct in light of [battered woman's syndrome] evidence, then the jury may well have concluded her version of the events was sufficiently credible to warrant an acquittal on the facts as she related them." (*People v. Day, supra,* 2 Cal. App. 4th at p. 415.)

As *Day* recognizes, *People v. McAlpin* (1991) 53 Cal. 3d 1289 supports this conclusion. There we held that expert testimony regarding parental reluctance to report child molestation was admissible to bolster a witness's credibility: "Most jurors, fortunately, have been spared the experience of being the parent of a sexually molested child. Lacking that experience, jurors can rely only on their intuition or on relevant evidence introduced at trial. . . . [Evidence that parents often do not report child molestation] would therefore 'assist the trier of fact' (Evid. Code, §801, subd. (a)) by giving the jurors information they needed to objectively evaluate [the witness's] credibility." (*Id.* at p. 1302.) As in *McAlpin,* the expert testimony in this case was " 'needed to disabuse jurors of commonly held misconceptions. . . .' " It was relevant "to explain a behavior pattern that might otherwise appear unreasonable to the average person. Evidence of [battered woman's syndrome] not only explains how a battered woman might think, react, or behave, it places the behavior in an understandable light." Thus, it was admissible under Evidence Code sections 801 and 1107.

We do not hold that Dr. Bowker's entire testimony was relevant to both prongs of perfect self-defense. Just as many types of evidence may be relevant to some disputed issues but not all, some of the expert evidence was no doubt relevant only to the subjective existence of defendant's belief. Evidence merely showing that a person's use of deadly force is scientifically explainable or empirically common does not, in itself, show it was objectively reasonable. To dispel any possible confusion, it might be appropriate for the court, on request, to clarify that, in assessing reasonableness, the question is whether a reasonable person in the defendant's circumstances would have perceived a threat of imminent injury or death, and not whether killing the abuser was reasonable in the sense of being an understandable response to ongoing abuse; and that, therefore, in making that assessment, the jury may not consider evidence merely showing that an abused person's use of force against the abuser is understandable.

We also emphasize that, as with any evidence, the jury may give this testimony whatever weight it deems appropriate in light of the evidence as a whole. The ultimate judgment of reasonableness is solely for the jury. We simply hold that evidence of battered woman's syndrome is generally *relevant* to the reasonableness, as well as the subjective existence, of defendant's belief in the need to defend, and, to the extent it is relevant, the jury may *consider* it in deciding both questions. The court's contrary instruction was erroneous. We disapprove of *People v. Aris, supra,* 215 Cal. App. 3d 1178, and *People v. Day, supra,* 2 Cal. App. 4th 405, to the extent they are inconsistent with this conclusion. . . .

Although we do not know what weight the jury would have given the expert testimony in determining reasonableness, the testimony "was not only relevant, but critical in permitting the jury to evaluate [defendant's] testimony free of the misperceptions regarding battered women." (*People v. Day, supra,* 2

Cal. App. 4th at p. 419.) Overall, the evidence, including defendant's corroborated testimony about the shooting the night before, presented a plausible case for perfect self-defense. The actual verdict was reasonable, but so too would have been a different one. Under all of these circumstances, it is reasonably probable the error affected the verdict adversely to defendant.

III. DISPOSITION

The judgment of the Court of Appeal is reversed.

D. Defense of Others

1. Why is the reasonable appearances doctrine more widely used than the "act at your peril" rule? How does it satisfy the goals of the criminal law?

State v. Bernardy, 25 Wash. App. 146 (1980)

ANDERSEN, Judge.

FACTS OF CASE

Kenneth Bernardy (defendant) appeals from a jury conviction of second-degree assault and judgment and sentence entered thereon.

On September 4, 1977, Steven Wilson became involved in a fight with Larry Curtis Harrison, a friend of the defendant. Testimony introduced at trial indicated that Wilson started the altercation and then was knocked to the ground by Harrison. While lying on the ground, Wilson was kicked in the head several times by the defendant.

The defendant testified that he kicked Wilson in order to protect his friend, Harrison, because Wilson was trying to get up and another participant, one Greg Gowens, was coming to Wilson's assistance. He also testified that he was wearing tennis shoes at the time. Wilson sustained serious head injuries as a result of the fight.

The defendant argues that he was not afforded effective representation of counsel and that his conviction was not supported by sufficient evidence. Our review of the entire record, including the defendant's personal restraint petition and his pro se brief, reveals that these contentions are without merit.

The defendant also assigns as error on this appeal that the trial court refused his proposed instruction concerning the legal privilege of defending another.

One issue is determinative.

ISSUE

Should the trial court have instructed the jury regarding the legal privilege of defending another?

DECISION

CONCLUSION. Evidence was presented which, if believed, would have allowed the jury to conclude that the defendant acted reasonably in defense of another. The trial court therefore erred in not instructing the jury on the legal privilege of defending another.

An individual who acts in defense of another person, reasonably believing him to be the innocent party and in danger, is justified in using force necessary to protect that person even if, in fact, the party whom he is defending was the aggressor. If properly requested by the defense, a "defense of others" instruction must be given whenever there is evidence from which the jury could conclude that, under the circumstances, the actor's apprehension of danger and use of force were reasonable.

As to the apprehension of danger in this case, the defendant testified that he believed Gowens was coming to the assistance of Wilson, that Wilson was trying to get up and that together they were a danger to Harrison. With regard to the force used, the defendant testified that he was wearing tennis shoes, used the sides of his feet and did not believe the kicks would cause Wilson any serious damage. Although we are satisfied that the evidence clearly supports the verdict, a trial court is bound to give an instruction on a party's theory of the case when, as in this situation, there is evidence to support it. The failure to do so constitutes reversible error.

Reversed and remanded for a new trial.

2. **How has the law of defense of others changed from the common law rule? Why were these changes made? Is it good policy?**

Alexander v. State, 52 Md. App. 171 (1982)

LOWE, Judge.

In the decade that commenced with the assassination of President Kennedy, climaxed with the creation of this Court, and concluded with the marriage of Tiny Tim, violence proliferated, partly because police were constitutionally hobbled in controlling a rebellious reaction and partly because citizens were reluctant—or afraid—to become "involved" in deterring that violence. This reticence seemed to emanate less from fear of physical harm than from the potential consequences of a legal aftermath. Representative was the 1964 New York homicide of Catherine "Kitty" Genovese, who was viciously ravaged and repeatedly stabbed while onlookers turned their backs to avoid witnessing the butchery, and neighbors closed their doors and windows to shut out her screams of anguish until her suffering was finally ended by the murderer. Witnesses who were interviewed excused their indifference by noting that the law did not protect a protector from criminal assault charges if the one he aids was initially in the wrong, however misleading appearances may have been. The onlookers hesitated to become involved in the fracas at their legal peril. Even if their hearts had been stout enough to enter the fray in defense of a stranger being violently assaulted, the fear of legal consequences chilled their better instincts.

At common law, the privilege of using force for crime prevention did not include authority for intervenors to protect third persons who were strangers to the intervenor. The privilege, even now in some jurisdictions, was limited to the protection of those closely related to, or associated with, the intervenor. That restriction to family or close associates was imposed because the right evolved not from the right of self-defense, as most cases imply, but from the right to protect one's property. R. Perkins, *Criminal Law* (2nd ed. 1969) at 1018–1019. III W. Blackstone, *Commentaries on the Law of England* 3 (facsimile ed. 1979), described the right as only Blackstone could:

> In these cases, if the party himself, or any of these his
> relations, be forceably attacked on his person or property, it
> is lawful for him to repel force by force; and the breach of
> the peace which happens is chargeable upon him only who
> began the affray.

Although it was merely a defense, an excuse for breach of the peace (or even homicide), Blackstone put great emphasis upon the natural source of this legal right. He felt that it

> is justly called the primary law of nature, so it is not, neither
> can it be in fact, taken away by the law of society.

Perhaps because the right to protect one's "property" (*i.e.,* his household, which included wife, children, servants, etc.) carried the same limitations upon the degree of force employed as did self-defense, many, if not most, of the courts in this country addressed the issue from the view that no force could be justifiably employed unless the protected person may have justifiably defended himself. That generally was the law espoused by the leading New York case of *People v. Young,* 11 N.Y. 2d 274 (1962), where the court affirmed the conviction for assault of a defendant who, in good faith, intervened in a struggle between a plain clothes police officer and a person whose arrest the police officer was attempting to effect.

The Maryland Court of Appeals has never directly addressed the issue, but inclined with the majority by strong dicta in 1957. In *Guerriero v. State,* 213 Md. 545, 549 (1957), the Court acknowledged, if somewhat grudgingly, that:

> A third person, closely related to or associated with one
> attacked in such a manner that he could properly have
> defended himself by the use of force, has a right to go to the
> defense of the person attacked and to use the same degree

and character of force that the one attacked could have used.

The care with which the Court chose to refrain from espousing any law beyond the narrow confines of the facts of that case is emphasized by the next sentence, in which the court hesitated to concede that a brother was a sufficiently close relative to warrant a right to that defense.

> The cases differ as to whether, and under what circumstances, one may so defend a brother in danger but we assume, without deciding, that he may, since the State concedes the point.

Early in this Court's judicial life, it carefully adhered to that narrow and restricted espousal of the right to aid third persons, limiting the beneficiaries of such right to relatives or close associates of the intervenor, but more significantly for our present purposes, by restricting the right to

> such a manner that he [the victim] could properly have defended himself by the use of force . . . . *Tipton v. State*, 1 Md. App. 556, 560 (1967).

Although the reciprocal right limitation was not clearly or definitively expressed in either *Guerriero* or *Tipton*, both cases showed Maryland leaning toward the New York view that one goes to the aid of another at his peril, and his protection from criminal charges depends not on what appears to him when he intervenes, but rather upon the rights of the person whom he has succored. As Perkins, *supra*, points out,

> It has been common but quite unfortunate to say that the defender 'stands in the shoes' of the one defended with exactly the same privilege or lack of privilege as possessed by the latter.

Perkins finds fault with that theory because it forces a Good Samaritan to gamble not only his health but his freedom and reputation, and overlooks the likelihood that the intervenor might have acted entirely without mens rea, and perhaps even with the highest sense of duty. It deals with such a defender as the willing participant in a brawl; whereas, from his standpoint (with the facts as they reasonably appear to him), he may be seeking to defend an innocent victim from a felonious assault.

Perkins' preferred position better fulfills our contemporary social needs by merging the encouragement of crime prevention with the privilege of defending others. It was approved instinctively by this Court in *Gray v. State*, 6 Md. App. 677, 685—686, (1969), without mentioning *Guerriero*, *Tipton* or even *Young*. *Gray*'s failure to address those older cases or the common law cases might have been justified because Maryland abrogated its common law status in that regard in 1965 by broadly extending the right to intervene to aid an apparent victim of a violent assault. Md. Ann. Code (1982 Repl. Vol.), Art. 27, §12A, provided that:

> *"Any person witnessing a violent assault* upon the person of another *may lawfully aid the person being assaulted* by assisting in that person's defense. The force exerted upon the attacker or attackers by the person witnessing the assault may be that degree of force which the assaulted person is allowed to assert in defending himself." (Emphasis added).

But in *Gray* we didn't mention the statute either. . . Judge Morton said for this Court that:

> Under the circumstances, we are of the opinion that the jury was fairly apprised of the law relating to a homicide committed in defense of a close relative and, accordingly, find no prejudicial error by the trial court in refusing to grant the instruction as submitted. . . .

Maryland thus appears to have been in the forefront in safeguarding the right which Blackstone recognized as a legal adjunct of natural instincts, and in adopting what Perkins recommends as the more "enlightened view."

> Subject to the familiar limitations as to the degree of force permitted, one who is himself free from fault may intervene and use force to protect an innocent victim of intended crime. And under the sound view he is protected by the usual mistake-of-fact doctrine and may act upon the situation as it reasonably seems to be.

The clear and unambiguous language of the statute is that the *witnessing* of the violent assault is that which affords protection for the intervenor. There is no reference at all in the Act indicating as a prerequisite to legal absolution that the apparent *victim* be faultless. To interpret the statute as limited by the common law restrictions would eliminate any purpose for its enactment.

The appellant, Ralph Alexander, a prisoner in the Maryland Penitentiary, was convicted by a jury in the Criminal Court of Baltimore (along with Bruce Shreeves, a fellow prisoner), of an assault on a correctional officer, Dale Tscheulin. As might be expected, the witnesses for the State and those for the defense saw the same scene from divergent points of view. The State's witnesses contended that Officer Tscheulin was attacked by Shreeves, who was subsequently assisted in assaulting the officer by appellant Alexander. Appellant Alexander and his witnesses alleged that another officer, Samuel Stokes, Jr., had apparently grabbed prisoner Shreeves from behind, without provocation, and then Officer Tscheulin came to the scene and started hitting Shreeves. Although Shreeves implicitly acknowledged his initial aggression, he contended that Alexander had seen only the violent overreactions by the guards, and that Alexander's actions were therefore appropriate according to his limited view of the situation.

When Alexander approached Tscheulin to state that he didn't have to "beat on" Shreeves as he was doing (according to Alexander), Tscheulin turned around and struck him. Alexander stated that he then simply grabbed the bars and pinned Tscheulin between himself and the bars, but did not strike him; whereupon, he returned to his cell. The State's version did not vary substantially except as to the degree of force used by Alexander. Tscheulin and Stokes agreed that they were subduing Shreeves, who had approached them with a fighting pose on the catwalk of the third tier when the prisoners were ordered to "lock in" after exercise period. Alexander rushed upon the scene, leapt on Tscheulin, who was preoccupied with Shreeves, and struck the officer in the chest and head.

The issue here is not which version to believe, for that, of course, is the role of the factfinder. The issue is whether the trial court erred when it instructed the jury in regard to the law applicable to the defense theory that appellant intervened to aid the apparent victim of an assault. The judge instructed the jurors on defendant Shreeves' right of self-defense as well as appellant's right of self-defense, if they chose to believe that right was raised by the facts or inferences available from the evidence. He then added:

> Now, as to the defendant Alexander there is an additional factor you have to consider. He has a right to go to the defense of Mr. Shreeves to the same extent that Mr. Shreeves has a right to defend himself. The defendant Alexander's right of self-defense is the same as that of the defendant Shreeves but no more, no less. In other words, if Shreeves had the right to defend himself, then Alexander had the right to go help him defend himself; if Shreeves did not have the right to defend himself, then Alexander didn't have the right to go help Shreeves defend himself. He stands in the same shoes as Shreeves when he elects to come to his assistance. . . .

The appellant objected timely, arguing that Alexander's right to intervene was not tied to the actual propriety of Shreeves' conduct, but rather depended upon what the jury believed Alexander's conduct was intended to do. . . .

But as is apparent from our prologue, appellee has relied upon the common law as it *may* have existed in 1957. The statute enacted by the Legislature in 1965 dealing with unrelated third persons aiding those under assault was not considered by the parties or the court below, or the parties on appeal. Under the facts of this case, however, the statute is particularly apposite if peculiarly not noted by anyone; yet the failure to discover the statute is easily explained, if not justified. The index of the Maryland Code, to speak charitably, leaves something to be desired.

Contextually we doubt that the Legislature gave any thought to the application of §12A in a circumstance behind prison walls. But laws in this "nation of laws" must apply to all persons equally. The facts and circumstances, and even the "prison atmosphere" may, however, give rise to inferences which change or even nullify the applicability or the effect of laws. A factfinder here, for instance, may, in light of the structured setting, consider whether Alexander was witnessing two guards properly subduing a recalcitrant prisoner in a segregation area when he leapt at an opportunity to release his pent-up frustrations on a guard, as was argued by the State at trial—

> You've got officers, you've got something going on down here, some people say it was a fight, but you've got another situation going on down there, an excellent opportunity to give a little bit and maybe get away without anybody seeing you. The frustration factor—

or whether Alexander saw two overzealous guards violently assaulting a fellow prisoner, and intervened, as he contended, to prevent injury to his fellow inmate and avoid the type of explosive incident so likely to arise in that volatile punitive segregation section of the penitentiary. That was the theory that appellant tried to convey and that which his codefendant sought to put across in proper person on his behalf. . . .

In light of appellant's singular defense and his counsel's pointed objection to the instructions, we believe the court erred in not correcting its instruction, which linked Alexander's fate to Shreeve's culpability. An intervenor's right to react is not strictly coterminous with a participant's right to self-defense. Under the court's instruction, Shreeves' admissions sealed Alexander's fate regardless of Alexander's view of the situation.

Under the statute, however, Alexander must be judged on his own conduct, based upon his own observation of the circumstances as they reasonably appeared to him. The reasonableness of his perceptions and the bona fides of his reactions are key elements of consideration by the factfinder, who must review the totality of the circumstances in their setting. Whether it is reasonable for a fellow prisoner to have perceived that two guards subduing a prisoner on a catwalk of a maximum security prison are violently assaulting him, may be contrasted, for example, with the reasonableness of a priest's perceptions of two men similarly "subduing" a nun in an isolated area of a darkened cemetery. Even assuming that both priest and prisoner "reasonably" perceived a violent assault, still it must be decided whether the reaction to intervene was a *bona fide* attempt to aid the person being assaulted. Even an intent to punish the offender or to avenge his victim will not suffice. The purpose of the intervention must have been "to aid" the victim, or the statutory absolution is lost.

Whatever the law may have been in Maryland prior to 1965, it is clear that the Legislature, motivated by increasing violence in society and the reluctance of citizens to "get involved," sought to afford protection to a defender who acts while injury may still be prevented, rather than awaiting judicial reprisals which are geared to provide punishment after the damage has been done. The probability of that having been appellant's motivation in this prison setting, however, remains a jury question under the proper instructions. . . .

JUDGMENT REVERSED; CASE REMANDED FOR RETRIAL. . . .

3. The Narrow View

What if the defendant's brother in *Saunders* had started the altercation with the victim? Under West Virginia law, would Saunders be able to claim a defense of others?

State v. Saunders, 175 W.Va. 16 (1985)

NEELY, Chief Justice:

"The Hill" in downtown Beckley, West Virginia is a rough part of town. Its bars, poolrooms, speakeasies, and disco joints cater to an evening sub-culture that emerges at night to the dismay of the ordinary, law-abiding citizen. It was outside of one of "The Hill's" establishments, the Nite Flite, that on 29 November 1981 the appellant, Robert Saunders, fatally shot Phillip Kincannon in the left buttocks, a wound from which Mr. Kincannon later bled to death on a pool table. Our appellant insists that by shooting Mr. Kincannon he was defending his brother, James Saunders. He argues that his conviction of first-degree murder and sentence of life imprisonment with a recommendation of mercy should be reversed because, *inter alia*, the circuit court refused an instruction on defense of another as an extension of the affirmative defense of self-defense.

I.

Confusion and conflicting testimony surround the death of Mr. Kincannon. It appears, however, that the appellant's brother, James Saunders, was involved in a series of fights with the Kincannon brothers, Phillip and Brian. During one of these altercations, Brian Kincannon, assisted by his brother, wrestled James Saunders to the ground and pinned him in a full nelson.

Our appellant, while not directly involved in the melee between his brother and the Kincannons, had participated in much of the verbal foreplay that led to the fracas. That night, when Robert Saunders went to the Nite Flite his brother James and Phillip Kincannon were exchanging angry words. (James' lady companion, who accompanied him, had that evening adorned herself in a silken scarf presented to her by Phillip Kincannon—a former beau of hers; this infuriated Mr. Kincannon). Robert Saunders testified that when he intervened on his brother's behalf, Phillip Kincannon retreated to recruit his brother Brian to his aid. Fearing a brawl, the Nite Flite's owner escorted the Saunders brothers outside.

When the Saunders emerged from the bar the Kincannons confronted them. James was attacked and overwhelmed. Robert—a slight young man weighing under 130 pounds stood nervously aside. But when James was on the ground, tightly held by Phillip Kincannon, and being "frisked" for a weapon that he did not have, Robert Saunders panicked. The appellant and two other witnesses subsequently testified that Brian Kincannon was exclaiming that he would kill James with James' own (non-existent) weapon.

The appellant at this time insists that he was afraid for his brother's life. He knew that one of the witnesses to the fight, Mr. Ronnie Campbell kept a gun in his automobile. Suddenly he darted over to Mr. Campbell's vehicle to extract the .357-calibre Magnum revolver. Mr. Campbell testified that although he snatched the gun from Mr. Saunders immediately and placed it under his belt, the appellant suddenly grabbed it from him and fired a shot over the heads of the combatants. The appellant testified that he then lowered the revolver, aimed at the deceased's leg and fired. He claims he did not realize that he hit the deceased but rather became frightened, dropped the revolver and fled. A few hours later that same night he voluntarily turned himself into the police.

The appellant presents this Court with five assignments of error. . . . This Court reverses on the basis of the fourth assignment of error, that which deals with the refusal of the court to give any of the appellants instructions on the issue of defense of another.

II.

Over one hundred years ago this Court held that the right of self-defense may be exercised in behalf of a brother, or of a stranger. In 1883, this Court stated:

> What one may lawfully do in defence of himself—when threatened with death or great bodily harm, he may do in behalf of a brother; but if the brother was in fault in provoking an assault, that brother must retreat as far as he safely can, before his brother would be justified in taking the life of his assailant in his defence of the brother. But if the brother was so drunk as not to be mentally able to know his duty to retreat, or was physically unable to retreat, a brother is not bound to stand by and see him killed or suffer great bodily harm, because he does not under such circumstances retreat. It is only the faultless, who are exempt from the necessity of retreating while acting in self-defence. Those in fault must retreat, if able to do so; if from the fierceness of the attack or for other reasons they are unable to retreat, they will be excused by the law for not doing so. *State of W.Va. v. Greer,* 22 W.Va. 800, at 819 (1883).

In the case before us the lower court refused any instructions on defense of another and apparently proceeded under the erroneous assumption that defense of another is not law in West Virginia. The court accordingly excluded the following defense instruction: "The court instructs you that if you believe from the evidence that Robert Saunders believed that his brother was about to be killed or in danger of great bodily harm, he had a right to use force to prevent his brother from being killed or injured."

The State counters that the court's refusal to give instructions in regard to the defense of another was harmless error. It notes that an unnumbered defendant's instruction, that was given, informed the jury that if the defendant's use of a dangerous and deadly weapon resulted from sudden passion brought about by his brother's being beaten, assaulted, and struck by the deceased and his brother without fault on the part of the defendant, then malice cannot be presumed. The State maintains that had the jury believed that the appellant was acting in defense of himself or his brother, a verdict of voluntary manslaughter would have been returned. Because the jury did not believe that contention, obviously the jury found that the appellant unlawfully, feloniously and maliciously, etc. murdered the deceased and thus the conviction of first-degree murder ought be affirmed by this Court.

The defense instruction to which the State refers is not improper but it is insufficient to explain to the jury the affirmative defense of defense of another, a defense available in this State and in many other jurisdictions. As such the instruction on which the State relies as an adequate statement of the right to defend another was misleading, confusing, and hence inadequate *on the issue of defense of another*." Instructions in a criminal case which are confusing, misleading or incorrectly state the law should not be given." *State v. Bolling,* 162 W.Va. 103 (1978).

Although this Court has not dealt directly in recent years with the defense of another defense, we are not bereft totally of collateral precedent. In *State v. Collins,* 154 W.Va. 771 (1971), this Court was presented with a situation in which a tavern owner fatally shot two patrons who were involved in a barroom brawl with a third customer. The Court failed to address directly the question of defense of another because it determined there was no necessity for the tavern owner to fire any shots other than his first two warning shots to end the disturbance. Although the tavern owner pleaded that he shot the patrons to protect, in addition to himself, the third party from injury or death, the evidence indicated that when he shot the fatal rounds the fight was over and "there was no necessity for him to act as he did to protect Marcum from danger of death or serious injury." *State v. Collins,* 154 W.Va. at 781.

The Court's holding in *Collins* prompted a lengthy dissent by Judge Browning. The judge would have reversed the tavern owner's conviction because of the trial court's failure to include an instruction on defense of another. He noted that defense of another was still good law in West Virginia, 154 W.Va. at 802–03. The Court, however, held that since the fight had already ended, an instruction on defense of another would have misled the jury. The Court added, somewhat gratuitously, that:

> . . . it is unnecessary to consider or determine whether
> the [excluded] instruction correctly states the law as to the

right of a person to intervene to protect another person whose life is in danger and as to the degree of force he may use to repel the attack of the assailant; and those questions are not discussed, considered or determined." *State v. Collins,* 154 W.Va. at 782.

In discussing the use of deadly force by the occupant of a dwelling on an unlawful intruder who threatens imminent physical violence or the commission of a felony, this Court has stated that "[t]he taking of life to prevent the commission of a felony, however, is not limited to self-defense in the home, but is part of a more general rule relating to crime prevention." *State v. W.J.B.* 276 S.E.2d 550, 555 (1981). In *W.J.B.*, this Court opined that: "[w]e have recognized the accepted rule that the defendant may interpose the defense of self-defense in protecting a member of his family as well as in protecting himself." 276 S.E.2d at 557.

Other jurisdictions grant that one has the right to intervene on behalf of another in certain situations. The right to defense of another usually falls under the rubric of self-defense. One simply steps into the shoes of the victim and is able to do only as much as the victim himself would lawfully be permitted to do. *See State v. Barnes,* 675 S.W.2d 195 (Tenn.Crim.App. 1984); *State v. Matthews,* 459 So.2d 40 (La.App. 1 Cir.1984), *cause remanded by State v. Matthews,* 464 So.2d 298 (1985); *Commonwealth v. Gray,* 271 A.2d 486, 488 (1970); *People v. Young,* 210 N.Y.S.2d 358 (1961).

In the recent *Barnes* case, the Tennessee Court of Criminal Appeals dismissed a conviction for involuntary manslaughter where the appellant's defense was that he struck the deceased in defense of a lady who was being assaulted. The court stated: "A person can do whatever the person for whom he intervenes could have done in his own self-defense." *State v. Barnes,* 675 S.W.2d at 196.

The validity of a claim of defense of another, like the question of self-defense, is properly a matter for the jury's determination. This Court has frequently stated, in cases of self-defense, that the prosecution must prove beyond a reasonable doubt that the defendant did not act in self-defense in order successfully to overcome the defendant's affirmative defense. In this case, the jury ought to have been provided with the proffered instruction on defense of another because the defense exists in West Virginia and because, in this case, there is sufficient evidence to allow the jury to consider whether the appellant believed the Kincannons were going to injure seriously or even kill his brother.

Accordingly we reverse the circuit court and remand this case for a new trial consistent with this opinion. Because the appellant will receive a new trial, it's unnecessary to address the appellant's other assignments of error.

Reversed and Remanded.

Note

In 1999, the West Virginia Supreme Court abandoned the view espoused in *Saunders* and adopted a reasonable appearances standard for defense of others: "the reasonable belief standard 'shifts the emphasis to [the] defendant's reliance on reasonable appearances rather than exposing him to the peril of liability for defending another where appearances were deceiving and there was no actual imminent danger.' " *State v. Cook*, 204 W.Va. 591 (1999) (quoting *Morris v. State*, 405 So.2d 81, 83 (Ala. Crim. App.1981)).

E. Imperfect Privilege

Self-defense and defense of others, if established by the defendant, provide a privilege to use deadly force and will result in a not guilty verdict. Imperfect privilege, which includes both imperfect self-defense and defense of others, is not a complete defense but a mitigator or partial defense.

While reading the following cases, ask yourself these questions: (1) did the defendant have the right to use self-defense at any time during his confrontation with the victim; if so, (2) why was his use of deadly force not justified; and (3) why is his defense imperfect?

State v. Jones, 27 Kan. App. 2d 910 (2000)

RICHARD M. SMITH, District Judge, assigned:

Clarence Jones appeals his conviction of unintentional second-degree murder. We reverse and remand for a new trial.

On February 4, 1998, Clarence Jones, age 15, shot and killed Justin Stanley, age 16. The events that led up to this tragic event began that morning in a music class attended by both young men. A disruption occurred where Stanley threatened other members of the class. He was sent to the office for his behavior. Apparently Jones had laughed at Stanley sometime during the incident. Before leaving school, Stanley and some other individuals confronted Jones, trying to pick a fight. Stanley threatened Jones, but Jones walked away. Jones reported the incident to a school security officer and a school administrator. He told the school administrator that he would like to leave school early because he was afraid of Stanley. Jones was granted a pass to go home. Jones took a circuitous route home out of fear that Stanley might be waiting for him.

Jones made it home without event and was playing video games when Stanley and his friends arrived at Jones' home. Jones' sister answered the door and told them Jones was not there. Upon hearing Stanley argue with his sister, Jones went to the door and asked Stanley why they were fighting. Stanley threatened Jones. Jones told Stanley he did not have time for fighting and shut the door. Stanley tried to force his way in and threatened to kill Jones and "spray-up" his house. Stanley then left.

Jones believed Stanley's threats. He went to his grandmother's home a half block away and called his mother. His mother said she would leave work and come directly home. In the meantime, a friend arrived and told Jones that Stanley and his friends were in a car looking for him and they had a gun.

Jones' mother arrived and took the children to Nations Bank to get a key from a relative who worked there. She planned to take Jones and his sisters to a relative's house where they would be safe. As Jones headed into the bank to be with his mother, a neighbor, Marcus Tillman, appeared. Tillman gave Jones a gun as he was heading into the bank. Jones later testified that he was unfamiliar with guns and their use.

While Jones, his mother, and his sisters were at the bank, Stanley arrived. Jones' mother, Stanley, and other individuals began to argue. Jones shot the gun once into the air. Stanley then said, "You f—k up. You pulled this rooty tooty ass gun on me. I got something for you," and went to the trunk of his car. Jones told Stanley to back away from the car, which he did. Jones did not believe at this time that Stanley had retrieved a gun, so Jones put his gun away in his mother's car.

The verbal altercations continued. Jones repeatedly asked Stanley what they were fighting about and Jones' mother asked Stanley why he was bothering her son. She told Jones to go inside the bank and he did. Stanley's brother arrived in another automobile, jumped out, made some comments, and then swung and hit Jones' sister, knocking her to the ground. Seeing this, Jones came out of the bank. The individuals with Stanley began closing in on Jones. Jones testified he asked them to leave him alone and they responded, "f—k that." Jones went to his mother's car, got the gun, and began shooting. Jones testified he fired several shots because they seemed to keep coming at him and he thought he saw Stanley reach for a gun. As Jones shot the gun, the individuals turned and ran away. Stanley was shot once in the back of the head and later died at a hospital. No gun was found on Stanley.

At trial considerable effort was spent by the defense placing Jones' character in issue. The evidence indicated Jones had no prior record for arrests or convictions. He was not involved in gangs and did not use illegal drugs. He attended church every Sunday, liked music, and played various musical instruments. The music teacher in charge of the class where the dispute began testified that Jones was not the type to cause trouble or fight and described Jones as well-mannered, soft-spoken, friendly, and likable. A police officer testified that Jones was respectful, honest, and nonviolent. The vice-president of the Wyandotte High School junior class testified that Jones had a reputation for being honest and nonviolent, and for not being involved in gangs, drugs, and fights. Another police officer testified that Jones was a good kid with a good demeanor and was always smiling. One character witness testified that Jones was a very respectful person, very intelligent, well-mannered, never got in trouble, stayed in school, and was the type of person that a mother would want her son to be.

Jones asserted self-defense. He testified he was afraid of Stanley because Stanley was bigger and weighed approximately 100 pounds more than Jones. Jones testified he was afraid of Stanley because, prior to the shooting, Stanley had robbed the occupants of a house at gunpoint and Jones was among the individuals who had been robbed of some minor personal property. Jones also presented evidence indicating that Stanley was a violent person who sold drugs.

Further specific facts in evidence will be reviewed as necessary to consider the pertinent issues on appeal. . . .

Jones . . . argues he was entitled to an instruction on the doctrine of imperfect self-defense. . . .

Imperfect self-defense is an intentional killing committed with an unreasonable but honest belief that circumstances justified deadly force. This lesser degree of homicide is codified in K.S.A. 21–3403(b), which provides that voluntary manslaughter is the intentional killing of a human being committed "upon an unreasonable but honest belief that circumstances existed that justified deadly force under K.S.A. 21–3211, 21–3212, or 21–3213 and amendments thereto."

The Kansas Supreme Court explained the history behind this statutory provision in *State v. Ordway,* 261 Kan. 776, 787–88 (1997):

> Legislative history of K.S.A. 21-3403 shows that the definition of voluntary manslaughter was expanded by the addition of subsection (b) in 1992. L. 1992, ch. 298, §5. Until then, the statute defined voluntary manslaughter as an intentional killing upon a sudden quarrel or in the heat of passion. Notes on proposed criminal code revisions were attached to the minutes of the Senate Judiciary Committee from March 22, 1992, which contained the following comments about subsection (b) of 21–3403:
>
> > (b) "Imperfect right to self-defense" manslaughter.
> >
> > This new subsection covers intentional killings that result from an unreasonable but honest belief that deadly force was justified in self-defense. In essence, the defendant meets the subjective, but not the objective, test for self-defense. This so-called "imperfect right to self-defense" is recognized in various forms. Kansas apparently recognizes it for unintentional killings under involuntary manslaughter. The Model Penal Code also follows this approach. Some states, e.g. Illinois, recognize this partial defense for intentional killings. *See,* LaFave, Criminal Law pp. 665–666. (1986).
> >
> > Applying this partial defense to intentional killings is simply a recognition of the practical realities of plea

bargaining and jury verdicts. Often it is unjust to prosecute and convict such killers of murder and it is equally unjust to acquit them. This new subsection provides a middle category that is theoretically sound and legitimizes the realities of plea bargaining and jury verdicts.

In this case, the jury was instructed on intentional second-degree murder, unintentional second-degree murder, voluntary manslaughter, and involuntary manslaughter. The trial court instructed the jury on voluntary manslaughter as a lesser included offense of second-degree murder as follows:

In considering whether the defendant is guilty of murder in the second-degree you should also consider the lesser offense of voluntary manslaughter. If there is a reasonable doubt as to which of these two offenses the defendant is guilty, the defendant may be convicted of voluntary manslaughter only.

To establish this charge each of the following claims must be proved:

1. The defendant intentionally killed Justin Stanley,

2. *That it was done upon sudden quarrel or in the heat of passion;*

3. That this act occurred on or about the 4th day of February, 1998, in Wyandotte County, Kansas. [Emphasis added].

The court's instructions defined heat of passions as follows:

As used in these instructions, the following terms have the following definitions: . . .

(b) Heat of Passion

Heat of Passion means any intense or vehement emotional excitement which was spontaneously provoked from circumstances. Such emotional state of mind must be of such degree as would cause an ordinary person to act on impulse without reflection.

There was no evidence of a spontaneously provoked intense or vehement emotional excitement. The instruction on that form of voluntary manslaughter was error. The court failed to instruct upon the applicable form of voluntary manslaughter based upon imperfect self-defense. Where evidence is admitted that a killing is done under the mitigating circumstances of an unreasonable but honest belief that deadly force is necessary, it is error to fail to so instruct. The question is whether instructing on the wrong form of voluntary manslaughter and failing to instruct on imperfect self-defense constituted clear error.

The entire theory of the State's case supported by the evidence was that Jones intentionally killed Stanley without premeditation. This was based upon how and when Jones went to the car and got the gun, how he kept shooting even though Stanley's group ran away, and the fact that Stanley's wound was to the back of his head. The defense was one of pure self-defense supported by substantial evidence. The jury was instructed on intentional second-degree murder, unintentional second-degree murder, voluntary manslaughter based upon sudden quarrel/heat of passion, and involuntary manslaughter. The jury was never properly instructed, that if it believed the killing was intentional, done under the honest but unreasonable belief that deadly force was justified, then Jones could only be convicted of voluntary manslaughter.

This court is firmly convinced that if the jury had been properly instructed, there is a real possibility it would have rendered a different verdict. Evidence was admitted which would have supported a verdict of intentional second-degree murder. Jones presented evidence in support of self-defense. Obviously, the jury chose a middle ground between the positions of the State and Jones. Had the jury been provided the specific option which the legislature intended and best fit the facts as proved, there is a real possibility of a different verdict. Failure to instruct on voluntary manslaughter based upon imperfect self-defense was clear error in this case. . . .

Reversed and remanded for new trial.

State v. Sety, 121 Ariz. 354 (1979)

SCHROEDER, Judge.

In the morning hours of March 19, 1976, D.C. died as the result of injuries inflicted by the appellant, David Sety, during a bizarre series of confrontations at an isolated campground. Appellant was tried on an open charge of murder. During trial the court granted a directed verdict of acquittal as to first degree murder, and the jury convicted the appellant of second degree murder. On post-trial motions, the trial court reduced the charge to voluntary manslaughter and sentenced Sety to serve not less than nine nor more than ten years in the Arizona State Prison.

Appellant Sety appeals from the judgment and sentence, and the State appeals from the trial court's reduction of the conviction from second degree murder to voluntary manslaughter. We affirm the conviction and modify the sentence.

SUFFICIENCY OF THE EVIDENCE SUPPORTING
VOLUNTARY MANSLAUGHTER AND SECOND DEGREE MURDER

Sety initially contends that the court should have directed a verdict of acquittal with respect to all charges. In its appeal the State urges that the trial court abused its discretion when, following the trial, it reduced the conviction from second degree murder to voluntary manslaughter. Resolution of both issues turns upon the unusual facts developed at trial.

On the day in question, the appellant was camping alone in an area below Bartlett Lake Dam in Maricopa County, Arizona. Sety testified that at approximately 6:00 a. m., the obviously intoxicated victim, D.C., awakened him and engaged him in a rambling discussion, primarily about weapons. D.C. admired the appellant's hunting knife, asked Sety to sharpen D.C.'s own knife and then boasted of having killed eight people with that knife. Sety testified that he was shaken by this talk and that he crawled into his camper to get a pistol. Sety stated that as he emerged from the camper D.C. was pointing a gun directly at his head and laughing in a threatening manner.

D.C. continued to talk about weapons, pulled a number of them from his car, and then began firing a large caliber rifle across the river. Thereafter, D.C. loaded his weapon, repeatedly pointed it at Sety and joked about how afraid Sety was of him. Finally, Sety grabbed his own pistol and told D.C. to "freeze." The armed D.C. continued to approach, prompting Sety to fire two warning shots and to take D.C.'s rifle from him. Sety testified that D.C. then reached into his jacket as if to take a gun from his belt. The appellant fired, striking D.C. in the side, told D.C. he was making a citizen's arrest and ordered him to begin walking toward the dam keeper's house. The two men then left the site near the camper, referred to at trial as site A, and proceeded toward the house. The physical evidence and Sety's testimony up to that point are not in dispute. The State does not contend that Sety was guilty of any culpable conduct prior to the time that the men left site A.

The two men then headed in the direction of the dam keeper's house, with Sety constantly prodding the resistant D.C. According to Sety's testimony, when D.C. attempted to flee back toward the arsenal of weapons at site A, Sety fired first one or more warning shots and then two shots which struck D.C. in the back. The victim fell on his back and lay motionless, apparently dead. As Sety approached him, however, D.C. grabbed him and pulled him to the ground. Sety stated that he choked the victim into unconsciousness, went back to the camper to reload his pistol and then returned to where D.C. was lying, designated during trial as site B. Sety then cut off part of the victim's clothing explaining at various times that he did so in order to make it harder for D.C. to flee, to search for weapons or to determine the extent of the victim's wounds. Physical evidence found at site B, including the outer shirt worn by D.C., shell casings and evidence of a struggle corroborated Sety's version of the events.

At this point, however, the physical evidence and Sety's version of the incident diverge somewhat. Sety testified that as he again began prodding D.C. in the direction of the dam keeper's house, D.C. knocked the rifle from Sety's grasp and ran. Sety fired several pistol shots from what he claimed was a distance of roughly 75 feet. D.C. fell and, by Sety's account, pretended to be dead. Sety testified, however, that as he looked more closely D.C. reached up suddenly to grab him. As he jerked away, Sety claimed that his gun discharged striking D.C. in the head. Certain at last that D.C. was dead Sety continued to the dam keeper's house and reported the homicide to the Sheriff's Department.

Thus, according to Sety, the wounds which he inflicted upon D.C. after they left site B were all either in self-defense or in justified furtherance of a citizen's arrest. He argues that, based upon his testimony, he should have been acquitted of all charges.

The physical evidence, however, does not fully support Sety's version of what transpired after D.C. and Sety left site B. Although Sety testified that D.C. had bolted from scene B and had been shot at a distance of approximately 75 feet, D.C.'s undershirt, which he was wearing at the time the final shots were fired, showed evidence of powder burns indicating shots fired at a very close range. Shell casings were found fairly close to the corpse rather than at the greater distance indicated by Sety's testimony. The State also presented evidence of the trajectory of the bullets which could be interpreted as rebutting Sety's claim that he fired these shots from a distance at the fleeing D.C. The State's evidence suggests that Sety fired at least two final shots, in addition to the shot which struck D.C. in the head, at very close range, and not, as he asserted, while D.C. was in flight. The State thus presented evidence from which the jury could have concluded that the victim was shot repeatedly in circumstances which no longer justified deadly force. This evidence contradicted Sety's proffered defenses. We conclude that the evidence presented was sufficient to find criminal culpability.

Having rejected the appellant's argument that he was entitled to a judgment of acquittal of all charges we now consider the State's contention that the trial court erred in reducing the conviction to voluntary manslaughter from second degree murder.

The presence of malice distinguishes murder from manslaughter under the statutes in effect at the time of this incident. A.R.S. §13–451(A) provided that "murder is the unlawful killing of a human being with malice aforethought." A.R.S. §13–455 defined manslaughter as "the unlawful killing of a human being without malice." Malice has been defined as the absence of justification, excuse or mitigation. *State v. Maloney*, 101 Ariz. 111 (1966); *Viliborghi v. State of Arizona*, 45 Ariz. 275 (1935). The trial court properly reduced the conviction to manslaughter only if the evidence was not sufficient to show an absence of justification, excuse or mitigation.

The State's principal argument in its appeal is that Sety's use of a deadly weapon supplies the element of malice. This is, however, only a presumption and may be rebutted by evidence of mitigation, justification or excuse sufficient to raise a reasonable doubt as to the existence of malice. See *State v. Maloney, supra*, and authorities cited therein. We find it difficult to conceive of a case in which this presumption is rebutted by stronger evidence of mitigation. In its briefs and at trial the State has conceded that Sety's initial use of force was fully justified and not culpable. There is no doubt that the provocation and terror which precipitated this killing were instigated by the intrusion of the seemingly crazed D.C. into the pre-dawn solitude of the appellant's campground. In our view, this is a classic illustration of manslaughter resulting from mitigating circumstances.

> . . . As a matter of juridical science, any circumstance of substantial mitigation should be sufficient to reduce to manslaughter a killing that would otherwise be murder. Suppose, for example, the defendant thought he was in imminent danger of death and must kill to save himself from being murdered, and that he did kill for that reason. Suppose, also, there was no actual danger to his life at the moment, and the facts fell a little short of reasonable grounds for a belief in such danger. His homicide is not excused; but if the circumstances came rather close to such as would constitute an excuse his guilt is of manslaughter rather than murder, . . . Perkins, Criminal Law (1st ed. 1957), at 40.

The real factual issue presented in this case was whether the amount of force used by Sety was excessive under the circumstances. We believe that there was sufficient evidence for the jury to reject Sety's defenses and to convict him of manslaughter, but that the evidence did not support a murder conviction. At most, appellant was guilty of excessive retaliation constituting manslaughter rather than murder. See *People v. Robinson*, 14 Ill. App. 3d 135 (1973), holding that the person acting in unreasonable fear of bodily harm is guilty of manslaughter; in accord, *People v. Chapman*, 49 Ill. App. 3d 553 (1977); *Commonwealth v. Walley*, 466 Pa. 363 (1976).

Accordingly, we conclude that the trial court's reduction of the conviction from second degree murder to voluntary manslaughter was mandated by the evidence. . . .

Conviction affirmed and sentence modified.

F.   Florida's Self-Defense Statute—"Stand Your Ground"

More than half the states have self-defense statutes that permit the defendant to stand his or her ground, i.e., there is no duty to retreat from an imminent deadly threat no matter where it occurs. Florida is one example.

F.S. 776.012. Use of force in defense of person

> A person is justified in using force, except deadly force, against another when and to the extent that the person reasonably believes that such conduct is necessary to defend himself or herself or another against the other's imminent use of unlawful force. However, a person is justified in the use of deadly force and does not have a duty to retreat if:
> (1)   He or she reasonably believes that such force is necessary to prevent imminent death or great bodily harm to himself or herself or

another or to prevent the imminent commission of a forcible felony; or

(2)   Under those circumstances permitted pursuant to §776.013.

F.S. 776.013. Home protection; use of deadly force; presumption of fear of death or great bodily harm

(1)   A person is presumed to have held a reasonable fear of imminent peril of death or great bodily harm to himself or herself or another when using defensive force that is intended or likely to cause death or great bodily harm to another if:

(a)   The person against whom the defensive force was used was in the process of unlawfully and forcefully entering, or had unlawfully and forcibly entered, a dwelling, residence, or occupied vehicle, or if that person had removed or was attempting to remove another against that person's will from the dwelling, residence, or occupied vehicle; and

(b)   The person who uses defensive force knew or had reason to believe that an unlawful and forcible entry or unlawful and forcible act was occurring or had occurred.

(2)   The presumption set forth in subsection (1) does not apply if:

(a)   The person against whom the defensive force is used has the right to be in or is a lawful resident of the dwelling, residence, or vehicle, such as an owner, lessee, or titleholder, and there is not an injunction for protection from domestic violence or a written pretrial supervision order of no contact against that person; or

(b)   The person or persons sought to be removed is a child or grandchild, or is otherwise in the lawful custody or under the lawful guardianship of, the person against whom the defensive force is used; or

(c)   The person who uses defensive force is engaged in an unlawful activity or is using the dwelling, residence, or occupied vehicle to further an unlawful activity; or

(d)   The person against whom the defensive force is used is a law enforcement officer, as defined in §943.10(14), who enters or attempts to enter a dwelling, residence, or vehicle in the performance of his or her official duties and the officer identified himself or herself in accordance with any applicable law or the person using force knew or reasonably should have known that the person entering or attempting to enter was a law enforcement officer.

(3)   A person who is not engaged in an unlawful activity and who is attacked in any other place where he or she has a right to be has no duty to retreat and has the right to stand his or her ground and meet

force with force, including deadly force if he or she reasonably believes it is necessary to do so to prevent death or great bodily harm to himself or herself or another or to prevent the commission of a forcible felony.

(4) A person who unlawfully and by force enters or attempts to enter a person's dwelling, residence, or occupied vehicle is presumed to be doing so with the intent to commit an unlawful act involving force or violence.

G. Practice Problems on Self-Defense

One beautiful Sunday afternoon, Defendant, while visiting his mother, was out in front of her house washing his car. Victim was walking his dogs with his girlfriend. Girlfriend had been dating Defendant, but they broke up a few months earlier. When Victim saw Defendant, he walked over to him and began accusing Defendant of treating Girlfriend badly. This led to a loud argument. According to Defendant, he saw Victim reaching into his pocket and thought Victim was getting a gun and was going to kill him. Defendant told police he had heard from others that Victim often carried a handgun. Defendant quickly grabbed a baseball bat from the open trunk of his car and hit Victim in the head, killing him.

Girlfriend told police that as soon as the argument started, she took the dog from Victim and kept walking. She did not see anything, but heard the two men arguing followed by a loud cracking noise. When she turned around to look, she saw Defendant get into his car and drive away. Girlfriend then called the police. According to Girlfriend, the police, and the EMT who first treated Victim, there was no gun found on or near Victim.

Assume Defendant is charged with murder of Victim. Can he successfully raise a self-defense claim? Why or why not? Does he have any alternative defense theories?

H. Model Penal Code Provisions

§3.04. Use of Force in Self-Protection

(1) Use of Force Justifiable for Protection of the Person. Subject to the provisions of this Section and of Section 3.09, the use of force upon or toward another person is justifiable when the actor believes that such force is immediately necessary for the purpose of protecting himself against the use of unlawful force by such other person on the present occasion.

(2) Limitations on Justifying Necessity for Use of Force.

(a) The use of force is not justifiable under this Section:

(i) to resist an arrest that the actor knows is being made by a peace officer, although the arrest is unlawful; or

(ii) to resist force used by the occupier or possessor of property or by another person on his behalf, where the actor knows that the person using the force is doing so under a claim of right to protect the property, except that this limitation shall not apply if:

(A) the actor is a public officer acting in the performance of his duties or a person lawfully assisting him therein or a person making or assisting in a lawful arrest; or

(B) the actor has been unlawfully dispossessed of the property and is making a re-entry or recaption justified by Section 3.06; or

(C) the actor believes that such force is necessary to protect himself against death or serious bodily injury.

(b) The use of deadly force is not justifiable under this Section unless the actor believes that such force is necessary to protect himself against death, serious bodily injury, kidnapping or sexual intercourse compelled by force or threat; nor is it justifiable if:

(i) the actor, with the purpose of causing death or serious bodily injury, provoked the use of force against himself in the same encounter; or

(ii) the actor knows that he can avoid the necessity of using such force with complete safety by retreating or by surrendering possession of a thing to a person asserting a claim of right thereto or by complying with a demand that he abstain from any action that he has no duty to take, except that:

(A) the actor is not obliged to retreat from his dwelling or place of work, unless he was the initial aggressor or is assailed in his place of work by another person whose place of work the actor knows it to be; and

(B) a public officer justified in using force in the performance of his duties or a person justified in using force in his assistance or a person justified in using force in making an arrest or preventing an escape is not obliged to desist from efforts to perform such duty, effect such arrest or prevent such escape because of resistance or threatened resistance by or on behalf of the person against whom such action is directed.

(c) Except as required by paragraphs (a) and (b) of this Subsection, a person employing protective force may estimate the necessity thereof under the circumstances as he believes them to be when the force is used, without retreating, surrendering possession, doing any other act that he has no legal duty to do or abstaining from any lawful action.

(3)   Use of Confinement as Protective Force. The justification afforded by this Section extends to the use of confinement as protective force only if the actor takes all reasonable measures to terminate the confinement as soon as he knows that he safely can, unless the person confined has been arrested on a charge of crime.

§3.05. Use of Force for the Protection of Other Persons

(1)   Subject to the provisions of this Section and of Section 3.09, the use of force upon or toward the person of another is justifiable to protect a third person when:

(a)   the actor would be justified under Section 3.04 in using such force to protect himself against the injury he believes to be threatened to the person whom he seeks to protect; and

(b)   under the circumstances as the actor believes them to be, the person whom he seeks to protect would be justified in using such protective force; and

(c)   the actor believes that his intervention is necessary for the protection of such other person.

(2)   Notwithstanding Subsection (1) of this Section:

(a)   when the actor would be obliged under Section 3.04 to retreat, to surrender the possession of a thing or to comply with a demand before using force in self-protection, he is not obliged to do so before using force for the protection of another person, unless he knows that he can thereby secure the complete safety of such other person; and

(b)   when the person whom the actor seeks to protect would be obliged under Section 3.04 to retreat, to surrender the possession of a thing or to comply with a demand if he knew that he could obtain complete safety by so doing, the actor is obliged to try to cause him to do so before using force in his protection if the actor knows that he can obtain complete safety in that way; and

(c)   neither the actor nor the person whom he seeks to protect is obliged to retreat when in the other's dwelling or place of work to any greater extent than in his own.

§3.06. Use of Force for Protection of Property

(1)   Use of Force Justifiable for Protection of Property. Subject to the provisions of this Section and of Section 3.09, the use of force upon or

toward the person of another is justifiable when the actor believes that such force is immediately necessary:

(a) to prevent or terminate an unlawful entry or other trespass upon land or a trespass against or the unlawful carrying away of tangible, movable property, provided that such land or movable property is, or is believed by the actor to be, in his possession or in the possession of another person for whose protection he acts; or

(b) to effect an entry or re-entry upon land or to retake tangible movable property, provided that the actor believes that he or the person by whose authority he acts or a person from whom he or such other person derives title was unlawfully dispossessed of such land or movable property and is entitled to possession, and provided, further, that:

(i) the force is used immediately or on fresh pursuit after such dispossession; or

(ii) the actor believes that the person against whom he uses force has no claim of right to the possession of the property and, in the case of land, the circumstances, as the actor believes them to be, are of such urgency that it would be an exceptional hardship to postpone the entry or re-entry until a court order is obtained.

(2) Meaning of Possession. For the purposes of Subsection (1) of this Section:

(a) a person who has parted with the custody of property to another who refuses to restore it to him is no longer in possession, unless the property is movable and was and still is located on land in his possession;

(b) a person who has been dispossessed of land does not regain possession thereof merely by setting foot thereon;

(c) a person who has a license to use or occupy real property is deemed to be in possession thereof except against the licensor acting under claim of right.

(3) Limitations on Justifiable Use of Force.

(a) Request to Desist. The use of force is justifiable under this Section only if the actor first requests the person against whom such force is used to desist from his interference with the property, unless the actor believes that:

(i) such request would be useless; or

(ii) it would be dangerous to himself or another person to make the request; or

(iii) substantial harm will be done to the physical condition of the property that is sought to be protected before the request can effectively be made.

(b)   Exclusion of Trespasser. The use of force to prevent or terminate a trespass is not justifiable under this Section if the actor knows that the exclusion of the trespasser will expose him to substantial danger of serious bodily injury.

(c)   Resistance of Lawful Re-entry or Recaption. The use of force to prevent an entry or re-entry upon land or the recaption of movable property is not justifiable under this Section, although the actor believes that such re-entry or recaption is unlawful, if:

>   (i)   the re-entry or recaption is made by or on behalf of a person who was actually dispossessed of the property; and

>   (ii)   it is otherwise justifiable under Subsection (1)(b) of this Section.

(d)   Use of Deadly Force. The use of deadly force is not justifiable under this Section unless the actor believes that:

>   (i)   the person against whom the force is used is attempting to dispossess him of his dwelling otherwise than under a claim of right to its possession; or

>   (ii)   the person against whom the force is used is attempting to commit or consummate arson, burglary, robbery or other felonious theft or property destruction and either:

>   >   (A)   has employed or threatened deadly force against or in the presence of the actor; or

>   >   (B)   the use of force other than deadly force to prevent the commission or the consummation of the crime would expose the actor or another in his presence to substantial danger of serious bodily injury.

(4)   Use of Confinement as Protective Force. The justification afforded by this Section extends to the use of confinement as protective force only if the actor takes all reasonable measures to terminate the confinement as soon as he knows that he can do so with safety to the property, unless the person confined has been arrested on a charge of crime.

(5)   Use of Device to Protect Property. The justification afforded by this Section extends to the use of a device for the purpose of protecting property only if:

(a)   the device is not designed to cause or known to create a substantial risk of causing death or serious bodily injury; and

(b)   the use of the particular device to protect the property from entry or trespass is reasonable under the circumstances, as the actor believes them to be; and

(c)   the device is one customarily used for such a purpose or reasonable care is taken to make known to probable intruders the fact that it is used.

(6) Use of Force to Pass Wrongful Obstructor. The use of force to pass a person whom the actor believes to be purposely or knowingly and unjustifiably obstructing the actor from going to a place to which he may lawfully go is justifiable, provided that:

(a) the actor believes that the person against whom he uses force has no claim of right to obstruct the actor; and

(b) the actor is not being obstructed from entry or movement on land that he knows to be in the possession or custody of the person obstructing him, or in the possession or custody of another person by whose authority the obstructor acts, unless the circumstances, as the actor believes them to be, are of such urgency that it would not be reasonable to postpone the entry or movement on such land until a court order is obtained; and

(c) the force used is not greater than would be justifiable if the person obstructing the actor were using force against him to prevent his passage.

§3.09. Mistake of Law as to Unlawfulness of Force or Legality of Arrest; Reckless or Negligent Use of Otherwise Justifiable Force; Reckless or Negligent Injury or Risk of Injury to Innocent Persons

(1) The justification afforded by Sections 3.04 to 3.07, inclusive, is unavailable when:

(a) the actor's belief in the unlawfulness of the force or conduct against which he employs protective force or his belief in the lawfulness of an arrest that he endeavors to effect by force is erroneous; and

(b) his error is due to ignorance or mistake as to the provisions of the Code, any other provision of the criminal law or the law governing the legality of an arrest or search.

(2) When the actor believes that the use of force upon or toward the person of another is necessary for any of the purposes for which such belief would establish a justification under Sections 3.03 to 3.08 but the actor is reckless or negligent in having such belief or in acquiring or failing to acquire any knowledge or belief that is material to the justifiability of his use of force, the justification afforded by those Sections is unavailable in a prosecution for an offense for which recklessness or negligence, as the case may be, suffices to establish culpability.

(3) When the actor is justified under Sections 3.03 to 3.08 in using force upon or toward the person of another but he recklessly or negligently injures or creates a risk of injury to innocent persons, the justification afforded by those Sections is unavailable in a prosecution for such recklessness or negligence towards innocent persons.

Chapter 20
Entrapment

A. Introduction

Entrapment is not a defense in the traditional sense; it is neither an excuse nor a justification. A successful entrapment claim relieves a defendant of criminal liability on the basis that the police overreached and induced the criminal behavior. In terms of the basic entrapment defense, there are two different versions depending on the jurisdiction. The federal government and many states use the "subjective" test of entrapment while other states use the "objective" test. Both tests focus initially on whether the government induced the defendant to commit the crime. But, if the answer to that question is "yes," the court must go on to determine whether the defendant was predisposed to commit the crime under the subjective test. If so, the defendant cannot successfully claim entrapment, even if the government induced the criminal behavior. The policy behind this version of the defense is that it is not fair to punish someone who would not have committed the offense but for government provocation.

The objective test is perhaps easier for the defendant to establish because it only focuses on the behavior of the police. Was the police behavior extreme enough that it would cause a "normally law-abiding person" to commit the crime? The policy here is to punish the government for overreaching.

Finally, as the Supreme Court has noted (*see United States v. Russell* below), even if a classic entrapment defense cannot work (e.g., the defendant was predisposed), the charges can still be dismissed if the government overreaching is "repugnant to the American criminal justice system." This is often referred to as a due process violation.

B. The Subjective Test

Why does the Supreme Court impose the subjective test? Does it promote the purposes of criminal law? What are the Court's policy considerations?

United States v. Poehlman, 217 F.3d 692 (CA 9 Cal. 2000)

KOZINSKI, Circuit Judge.

Mark Poehlman, a cross-dresser and foot-fetishist, sought the company of like-minded adults on the Internet. What he found, instead, were federal agents looking to catch child molesters. We consider whether the government's actions amount to entrapment.

I

After graduating from high school, Mark Poehlman joined the Air Force, where he remained for nearly 17 years. Eventually, he got married and had two children. When Poehlman admitted to his wife that he couldn't control his compulsion to cross-dress, she divorced him. So did the Air Force, which forced him into early retirement, albeit with an honorable discharge.

These events left Poehlman lonely and depressed. He began trawling Internet "alternative lifestyle" discussion groups in an effort to find a suitable companion. Unfortunately, the women who frequented these groups were less accepting than he had hoped. After they learned of Poehlman's proclivities, several retorted with strong rebukes. One even recommended that Poehlman kill himself. Evidently, life in the HOV lane of the information superhighway is not as fast as one might have suspected.

Eventually, Poehlman got a positive reaction from a woman named Sharon. Poehlman started his correspondence with Sharon when he responded to an ad in which she indicated that she was looking for someone who understood her family's "unique needs" and preferred servicemen. Poehlman answered the ad and indicated that he "was looking for a long-term relationship leading to marriage," "didn't mind children," and "had unique needs too."

Sharon responded positively to Poehlman's e-mail. She said she had three children and was "looking for someone who understands us and does not let society's views stand in the way." She confessed that there were "some things I'm just not equipped to teach [the children]" and indicated that she wanted "someone to help with their special education." . . .

In his next e-mail, . . . Poehlman disclosed the specifics of his "unique needs." He also explained that he has strong family values and would treat Sharon's children as his own. Sharon's next e-mail focused on the children, explaining to Poehlman that she was looking for a "special man teacher" for them but not for herself. She closed her e-mail with the valediction, "If you understand and are interested, please write back. If you don't share my views I understand. Thanks again for your last letter."

Poehlman replied by expressing uncertainty as to what Sharon meant by special man teacher. He noted that he would teach the children "proper morals and give support to them where it is needed," and he reiterated his interest in Sharon.

Sharon again rebuffed Poehlman's interest in her: "One thing I should make really clear though, is that there can't be anything between me and my sweethearts special teacher." She then asked Poehlman for a description of what he would teach her children as a first lesson, promising "not to get mad or upset at anything written. If I disagree with something I'll just say so. I do like to watch, though. I hope you don't think I'm too weird."

Poehlman finally got the hint and expressed his willingness to play sex instructor to Sharon's children. In later e-mails, Poehlman graphically detailed his ideas to Sharon, usually at her prompting. Among these ideas were oral sex, anal sex and various acts too tasteless to mention. The correspondence blossomed to include a phone call from Sharon and hand written notes from one of her children. Poehlman made decorative belts for all the girls and shipped the gifts to them for Christmas.

Poehlman and Sharon eventually made plans for him to travel to California from his Florida home. After arriving in California, Poehlman proceeded to a hotel room where he met Sharon in person. She offered him some pornographic magazines featuring children, which he accepted and examined. He commented that he had always looked at little girls. Sharon also showed Poehlman photos of her children: Karen, aged 7, Bonnie, aged 10, and Abby, aged 12. She then directed Poehlman to the adjoining room, where he was to meet the children, presumably to give them their first lesson under their mother's protective supervision. Upon entering the room however, Poehlman was greeted by Naval Criminal Investigation Special Agents, FBI agents and Los Angeles County Sheriff's Deputies.

Poehlman was arrested and charged with attempted lewd acts with a minor in violation of California law. He was tried, convicted and sentenced to a year in state prison. Two years after his release, Poehlman was again arrested and charged with federal crimes arising from the same incident. A jury convicted him of crossing state lines for the purpose of engaging in sex acts with a minor in violation of 18 U.S.C. §2423(b). He was sentenced to 121 months. Poehlman challenges the conviction on the grounds that it violates double jeopardy and that he was entrapped. Because we find there was entrapment, we need not address double jeopardy.

II

"In their zeal to enforce the law . . . Government agents may not originate a criminal design, implant in an innocent person's mind the disposition to commit a criminal act, and then induce commission of the crime so that the Government may prosecute." *Jacobson v. United States,* 503 U.S. 540, 548 (1992). On the other hand, "the fact that officers or employees of the Government merely afford opportunity or facilities for the commission of the offense does not defeat the prosecution. Artifice and stratagem may be employed to catch those engaged in criminal enterprises." *Sorrells v. United States,* 287 U.S. 435, 441

(1932). The defense of entrapment seeks to reconcile these two, somewhat contradictory, principles.

When entrapment is properly raised, the trier of fact must answer two related questions: First, did government agents induce the defendant to commit the crime? And, second, was the defendant predisposed? We discuss inducement at greater length below, . . . but at bottom the government induces a crime when it creates a special incentive for the defendant to commit the crime. This incentive can consist of anything that materially alters the balance of risks and rewards bearing on defendant's decision whether to commit the offense, so as to increase the likelihood that he will engage in the particular criminal conduct. Even if the government induces the crime, however, defendant can still be convicted if the trier of fact determines that he was predisposed to commit the offense. Predisposition, which we also discuss at length below, is the defendant's willingness to commit the offense *prior* to being contacted by government agents, coupled with the wherewithal to do so. While our cases treat inducement and predisposition as separate inquiries, the two are obviously related: If a defendant is predisposed to commit the offense, he will require little or no inducement to do so; conversely, if the government must work hard to induce a defendant to commit the offense, it is far less likely that he was predisposed.

To raise entrapment, defendant need only point to evidence from which a rational jury could find that he was induced to commit the crime but was not otherwise predisposed to do so. Defendant need not present the evidence himself; he can point to such evidence in the government's case-in-chief, or extract it from cross-examination of the government's witnesses. The burden then shifts to the government to prove beyond a reasonable doubt that defendant was *not* entrapped.

The district court properly determined that the government was required to prove that Poehlman was not entrapped and gave an appropriate instruction. The jury nonetheless convicted Poehlman, which means that either it did not find that the government induced him, or did find that Poehlman was predisposed to commit the crime. Poehlman argues that he was entrapped as a matter of law. To succeed, he must persuade us that, viewing the evidence in the light most favorable to the government, no reasonable jury could have found in favor of the government as to inducement or lack of predisposition.

Inducement

"Inducement can be any government conduct creating a substantial risk that an otherwise law-abiding citizen would commit an offense, including persuasion, fraudulent representations, threats, coercive tactics, harassment, promises of reward, or pleas based on need, sympathy or friendship." *United States v. Davis,* 36 F.3d 1424, 1430 (9th Cir. 1994). Poehlman argues that he was induced by government agents who used friendship, sympathy and psychological pressure to "beguile[ ] him into committing crimes which he otherwise would not have attempted." *Sherman v. United States,* 356 U.S. 369, 376 (1958).

According to Poehlman, before he started corresponding with Sharon, he was harmlessly cruising the Internet looking for an adult relationship; the idea of sex with children had not entered his mind. . . .

It was Sharon who first suggested that Poehlman develop a relationship with her daughters: "I've had to be both mother and father to my sweethearts, but there are some things I'm just not equipped to teach them. I'm looking for someone to help with their special education.". . .

In the same e-mail, Poehlman expressed a continued interest in an adult relationship with Sharon: "I have to be honest and tell you I would hope you would support and enjoy me sexually as well as in company and hopefully love and the sexual relations that go with it." It was only after Sharon made it clear that agreeing to serve as sexual mentor to her daughters was a condition to any further communications between her and Poehlman that he agreed to play the role Sharon had in mind for him.

The government argues that it did not induce Poehlman because Sharon did not, in so many words, suggest he have sex with her daughters. But this is far too narrow a view of the matter. The clear implication of Sharon's messages is that this is precisely what she had in mind. Contributing to this impression is repeated use of the phrases "special teacher" and "man teacher," and her categorical rejection of Poehlman's suggestion that he would treat her daughters as his own children and teach them proper morals with a curt, "I don't think you understand."

In case the references to a special man teacher were insufficient to convey the idea that she was looking for a sexual mentor for her daughters, Sharon also salted her correspondence with details that clearly carried sexual innuendo. In her second e-mail to Poehlman, she explained that she had "discussed finding a special man teacher with my sweethearts and you should see the look of joy and excitement on their faces. They are very excited about the prospect of finding such a teacher." To round out the point, Sharon further explained that "I want my sweethearts to have the same special memories I have . . . . I've told them about my special teacher and the memories I have. I still get goosebumps thinking about it." From Sharon's account, one does not get the impression that her own special teacher had given her lessons in basket weaving or croquet. Finally, Sharon's third e-mail to Poehlman clearly adds to the suggestion of a sexual encounter between him and her daughters when she states: "I do like to watch, though. I hope you don't think I'm too weird." In light of Sharon's earlier statements, it's hard to escape the voyeuristic implications of this statement. After all, there would be nothing weird about having Sharon watch Poehlman engaged in normal father-daughter activities.

Sharon did not merely invite Poehlman to have a sexual relationship with her minor daughters, she made it a condition of her own continued interest in him. Sharon, moreover, pressured Poehlman to be explicit about his plans for teaching the girls: "Tell me more about how their first lesson will go. This will help me make my decision as to who their teacher will be." The implication is that unless Poehlman came up with lesson plans that were sufficiently creative, Sharon would discard Poehlman and select a different mentor for her daughters.

Sharon eventually drew Poehlman into a protracted e-mail exchange which became increasingly intimate and sexually explicit. Approximately three weeks into the correspondence, Poehlman started signing off as Nancy, the name he adopts when dressing in women's clothes. Sharon promptly started using that name, offering an important symbol of acceptance and friendship. In the same e-mail, Sharon complained that Poehlman had neglected to discuss the education of her two younger girls. "I thought it curious that you did not mention Bonnie or Karen. Are they too young to start their educations? I don't want them to feel left out, but at the same time If you aren't comfortable with them please say so."

Sharon also pushed Poehlman to be more explicit about his plans for the oldest daughter: "Abby is very curious (but excited) about what you expect her to do and I haven't been able to answer all her questions. Hope to hear from you soon." Poehlman responded to Sharon's goading: "Bonnie and Karen being younger need to learn how to please, before they can be taught how to be pleased. they will start be exploring each others body together as well as mine and yours, they will learn how to please both men and women and they will be pleasein Abby as well."

Over six months and scores of e-mails, Sharon persistently urged Poehlman to articulate his fantasies concerning the girls. Meanwhile Poehlman continued his efforts to establish a relationship with Sharon. . . .

As Justice Frankfurter noted in his concurrence in *Sherman,*

> Of course in every case of this kind the intention that the particular crime be committed originates with the police, and without their inducement the crime would not have occurred. But it is perfectly clear [that] . . . where the police in effect simply furnished the opportunity for the commission of the crime, that this is not enough to enable the defendant to escape conviction.

Sherman v. United States, 356 U.S. 369, 382 (1958) (Frankfurter, J., concurring). Whether the police did more than provide an opportunity—whether they actually induced the crime, as that term is used in our entrapment jurisprudence—depends on whether they employed some form of suasion that materially affected what Justice Frankfurter called the "self-struggle [to] resist ordinary temptations." *Id.* at 384 (Frankfurter, J., concurring).

Where government agents merely make themselves available to participate in a criminal transaction, such as standing ready to buy or sell illegal drugs, they do not induce commission of the crime. "An improper 'inducement' . . . goes beyond providing an ordinary 'opportunity to commit a crime.' An 'inducement' consists of an 'opportunity' *plus* something else— typically, excessive pressure by the government upon the defendant or the government's taking advantage of an alternative, non-criminal type of motive." *United States v. Gendron,* 18 F.3d 955, 961 (1st Cir. 1994) (quoting *Jacobson,* 503 U.S. at 550, 112 S. Ct. 1535).

In *Jacobson,* the government conceded inducement based on the fact that the defendant there committed the offense after numerous contacts from the government spanning over two years, during the course of which government agents "wav[ed] the banner of individual rights and disparag[ed] the legitimacy and constitutionality of efforts to restrict the availability of sexually explicit materials." *Jacobson,* 503 U.S. at 552. In doing so, "the Government not only excited petitioner's interest in sexually explicit materials banned by law but also exerted substantial pressure on petitioner to obtain and read such material as part of a fight against censorship and infringement of individual rights." *Id. Jacobson* is consistent with prior cases such as *Sherman,* where the government played upon defendant's weakness as a drug user, and *Sorrells,* where the government agent called upon defendant's loyalty to a fellow war veteran to induce him to commit the offense.

Cases like *Jacobson, Sherman* and *Sorrells* demonstrate that even very subtle governmental pressure, if skillfully applied, can amount to inducement. In *Jacobson,* for example, the government merely advanced the view that the law in question was illegitimate and that, by ordering the prohibited materials, defendant would be joining in "a fight against censorship and the infringement of individual rights." *Id.* at 552. In *Sorrells,* the inducement consisted of repeated requests, made in an atmosphere of comradery among veterans. *See Sorrells,* 287 U.S. at 439–41. In *Sherman,* the inducement consisted of establishing a friendly relationship with the defendant, and then playing on his sympathy for the supposed suffering of a fellow drug user. *See Sherman,* 356 U.S. at 371. In *Hollingsworth,* the inducement was nothing more than giving the defendant the idea of committing the crime, coupled with the means to do it. *See Hollingsworth,* 27 F.3d at 1200–02.

Measured against these precedents, there is no doubt that the government induced Poehlman to commit the crime here. Had Sharon merely responded enthusiastically to a hint from Poehlman that he wanted to serve as her daughters' sexual mentor, there certainly would have been no inducement. But Sharon did much more. Throughout the correspondence with Poehlman, Sharon made it clear that she had made a firm decision about her children's sexual education, and that she believed that having Poehlman serve as their sexual mentor would be in their best interest. She made repeated references to her own sexual mentor, explaining that he could have mentored her daughters, had he not died in a car crash in 1985. While parental consent is not a defense to statutory rape, it nevertheless can have an effect on the "self-struggle [to] resist ordinary temptations." *Sherman,* 356 U.S. at 384 (Frankfurter, J., concurring). This is particularly so where the parent does not merely consent but casts the activity as an act of parental responsibility and the selection of a sexual mentor as an expression of friendship and confidence. Not only did this diminish the risk of detection, it also allayed fears defendant might have had that the activities would be harmful, distasteful or inappropriate, particularly since Sharon claimed to have herself benefitted from such experiences.

It is clear, moreover, that Poehlman continued to long for an adult relationship with Sharon, as well as a father-like relationship with the girls. He offered marriage; talked about quitting his job and moving to California; discussed traveling with Sharon and the girls; even offered his military health insurance benefits as an inducement. While refusing to give Poehlman hope of a sexual relationship with her, Sharon encouraged these fantasies; she went so far as to check out Poehlman's job prospects in California. The government thus played on Poehlman's obvious need for an adult relationship, for acceptance of his sexual proclivities and for a family, to draw him ever deeper into a sexual fantasy world involving these imaginary girls.

. . . Through its aggressive intervention, the government materially affected the normal balance between risks and rewards from the commission of the crime, and thereby induced Poehlman to commit the offense.

Predisposition

The jury could, nevertheless, have found Poehlman guilty if it found that he was predisposed to commit the offense. Quite obviously, by the time a defendant actually commits the crime, he will have become disposed to do so. However, the relevant time frame for assessing a defendant's disposition comes before he has any contact with government agents, which is doubtless why it's called *pre*disposition. In our case, the question is whether there is evidence to support a finding that Poehlman was disposed to have sex with minors prior to opening his correspondence with Sharon. . . .

. . . [T]he fact that Poehlman willingly crossed state lines to have sex with minors after his prolonged and steamy correspondence with Sharon cannot, alone, support a finding of predisposition. It is possible, after all, that it was the government's inducement that brought Poehlman to the point where he became willing to break the law. . . . [W]e must consider what evidence there is as to Poehlman's state of mind *prior* to his contact with Sharon.

On this score, the record is sparse indeed; it is easier to say what the record does not contain than what it does. The government produced no e-mails or chat room postings where Poehlman expressed an interest in sex with children, or even the view that sex with children should be legalized. Nor did the government produce any notes, tapes, magazines, photographs, letters or similar items which disclosed an interest in sex with children, despite a thorough search of Poehlman's home. There was no testimony from the playmates of Poehlman's children, his ex-wife or anyone else indicating that Poehlman had behaved inappropriately toward children or otherwise manifested a sexual interest in them. Sharon's ad, to which Poehlman responded, does not clearly suggest that sex with children was to be the object of the relationship . . . . While one might presume that one or more of the children are minors, the phrase "unique needs" could, just as easily, connote children with physical disabilities, or merely the plight of a single mother of three.

Poehlman does not appear to have responded to her ad because it mentions children or their special needs. During the crucial first few exchanges, when Sharon focused Poehlman's attention on those special needs, he expressed confusion as to what she had in mind. Instead of exploiting the ambiguity in Sharon's messages to suggest the possibility of sex with her daughters, Poehlman pushed the conversation in the opposite direction, offering to act as a father figure to the girls and teach them "proper morals." While Poehlman's reluctance might have been borne of caution—the way a drug dealer might demur when he is unsure whether a prospective buyer is a government agent—the fact remains that Poehlman's earliest messages (which would be most indicative of his pre-existing state of mind) provide no support for the government's case on predisposition. To the contrary, Poehlman's reluctance forced Sharon to become more aggressive in her suggestions, augmenting the defendant's case for inducement.

Poehlman's enthusiastic, protracted and extreme descriptions of the sexual acts he would perform with Sharon's daughters are, according to the government, its strongest evidence of Poehlman's predisposition. Indeed, once he got the idea of what Sharon had in mind, Poehlman expressed few concerns about the morality, legality or appropriateness of serving as the girls' sexual mentor. But Poehlman was not convicted of writing smutty e-mails; he was convicted of crossing state lines, some six months later, to have sex with minors. The problem with using Poehlman's e-mails as evidence of predisposition is that they were all in response to specific, pointed suggestions by Sharon. The e-mails thus tell us what Poehlman's disposition was once the government had implanted in his mind the idea of sex with Sharon's children, but not whether Poehlman would have engaged in such conduct had he not been pushed in that direction by the government. In short, Poehlman's erotic e-mails cannot provide proof of predisposition because nothing he says in them helps differentiate his state of mind prior to the government's intervention from that afterwards.

It is entirely plausible to infer that . . . it was the government's graduated response—including e-mail correspondence, handwritten letters from the girls and Sharon, the use of intimate names, a photograph of Poehlman sent to Sharon, Poehlman handcrafting gifts for the girls and Sharon's willingness to help Poehlman look for a job in Southern California— that brought Poehlman to the point where he was willing to cross state lines for the purpose of having sex with the three young girls. Since the government has the burden of proof as to predisposition, materials like these e-mails, which do not demonstrate any preexisting propensity to engage in the criminal conduct at issue, simply cannot carry that burden.

This is not to say that statements made after the government's inducement can never be evidence of predisposition. If, after the government begins inducing a defendant, he makes it clear that he would have committed the offense even without the inducement, that would be evidence of predisposition. But only those statements that indicate a state of mind untainted by the inducement are relevant to show predisposition. Poehlman's protracted correspondence with Sharon, in fact, undermines the view that he was predisposed to commit the offense. Even as his e-mails became more intimate and explicit—usually in response to Sharon's constant hectoring for more details about Poehlman's lesson plans—he never gave any indication that being a sexual mentor to the girls in any way fulfilled his preexisting fantasies. To the contrary, Poehlman repeatedly tried to integrate Sharon's expectations of him into his own fantasies by insisting that the girls (and Sharon) parade around the house in nylons and high-heeled pumps ("as high of a heel as they can handle,")—as Poehlman himself apparently does.

The only indication in the record of any preexisting interest in children is Poehlman's statement in the hotel room that he has "always looked at little girls." But this is hardly an indication that he was prone to engage in sexual relations with minors. Having carefully combed the record for any evidence that Poehlman was predisposed to commit the offense of which he was convicted, we find none. To the extent the jury might have found that Poehlman was predisposed to commit the offense, that finding cannot be sustained.

Conclusion

"When the Government's quest for convictions leads to the apprehension of an otherwise law-abiding citizen who, if left to his own devices, likely would have never run afoul of the law, the courts should intervene." *Jacobson,* 503 U.S. at 553–54. So far as this record discloses, Poehlman is such a citizen. Prior to his unfortunate encounter with Sharon, he was on a quest for an adult relationship with a woman who would understand and accept his proclivities, which did not include sex with children. There is surely enough real crime in our society that it is unnecessary for our law enforcement officials to spend months luring an obviously lonely and confused individual to cross the line between fantasy and criminality. The judgment of conviction is REVERSED on grounds of insufficiency of the evidence and the case is REMANDED with instructions that defendant be released forthwith.

The mandate shall issue at once.

United States v. Russell, 411 U.S. 423 (1973)

Mr. Justice REHNQUIST delivered the opinion of the Court.

Respondent Richard Russell was charged in three counts of a five-count indictment returned against him and codefendants John and Patrick Connolly. After a jury trial in the District Court, in which his sole defense was entrapment, respondent was convicted on all three counts of having unlawfully manufactured and processed methamphetamine ("speed") and of having unlawfully sold and delivered that drug. . . . He was sentenced to concurrent terms of two years in prison for each offense, the terms to be suspended on the condition that he spend six months in prison and be placed on probation for the following three years. On appeal, the United States Court of Appeals for the Ninth Circuit, one judge dissenting reversed the conviction solely for the reason that an undercover agent supplied an essential chemical for manufacturing the methamphetamine which formed the basis of respondent's conviction. The court concluded that as a matter of law "a defense to a criminal charge may be founded upon an intolerable degree of governmental participation in the criminal enterprise." We granted certiorari and now reverse that judgment.

There is little dispute concerning the essential facts in this case. On December 7, 1969, Joe Shapiro, an undercover agent for the Federal Bureau of Narcotics and Dangerous Drugs, went to respondent's home on Whidbey Island in the State of Washington where he met with respondent and his two codefendants, John and Patrick Connolly. Shapiro's assignment was to locate a laboratory where it was believed that methamphetamine was being manufactured illicitly. He told the respondent and the Connollys that he represented an organization in the Pacific Northwest that was interested in controlling the manufacture and distribution of methamphetamine. He then made an offer to supply the defendants with the chemical phenyl-2-propanone, an essential ingredient in the manufacture of methamphetamine, in return for one-half of the drug produced. This offer was made on the condition that Agent Shapiro be shown a sample of the drug which they were making and the laboratory where it was being produced.

During the conversation, Patrick Connolly revealed that he had been making the drug since May 1969 and since then had produced three pounds of it. John Connolly gave the agent a bag containing a quantity of methamphetamine that he represented as being from "the last batch that we made." Shortly thereafter, Shapiro and Patrick Connolly left respondent's house to view the laboratory which was located in the Connolly house on Whidbey Island. At the house, Shapiro observed an empty bottle bearing the chemical label phenyl-2-propanone.

By prearrangement, Shapiro returned to the Connolly house on December 9, 1969, to supply 100 grams of propanone and observe the manufacturing process. When he arrived he observed Patrick Connolly and the respondent cutting up pieces of aluminum foil and placing them in a large flask. There was testimony that some of the foil pieces accidentally fell on the floor and were picked up by the respondent and Shapiro and put into the flask. Thereafter, Patrick Connolly added all of the necessary chemicals, including the propanone brought by Shapiro, to make two batches of methamphetamine. The manufacturing process having been completed the following morning, Shapiro was given one-half of the drug and respondent kept the remainder. Shapiro offered to buy, and the respondent agreed to sell, part of the remainder for $60.

About a month later, Shapiro returned to the Connolly house and met with Patrick Connolly to ask if he was still interested in their 'business arrangement.' Connolly replied that he was interested but that he had recently obtained two additional bottles of phenyl-2-propanone and would not be finished with them for a couple of days. He provided some additional methamphetamine to Shapiro at that time. Three days later Shapiro returned to the Connolly house with a search warrant and, among other items, seized an empty 500-gram bottle of propanone and a 100-gram bottle, not the one he had provided, that was partially filled with the chemical.

There was testimony at the trial of respondent and Patrick Connolly that phenyl-2-propanone was generally difficult to obtain. At the request of the Bureau of Narcotics and Dangerous Drugs, some chemical supply firms had voluntarily ceased selling the chemical.

At the close of the evidence, and after receiving the District Judge's standard entrapment instruction, the jury found the respondent guilty on all counts charged. On appeal, the respondent conceded that the jury could have found him predisposed to commit the offenses, but argued that on the facts presented there was entrapment as a matter of law. The Court of Appeals agreed, although it did not find the District Court had misconstrued or misapplied the traditional standards governing the entrapment defense. Rather, the court in effect expanded the traditional notion of entrapment, which focuses on the predisposition of the defendant, to mandate dismissal of a criminal prosecution whenever the court determines that there has been "an intolerable degree of governmental participation in the criminal enterprise." In this case the court decided that the conduct of the agent in supplying a scarce ingredient essential for the manufacture of a controlled substance established that defense.

This new defense was held to rest on either of two alternative theories. One theory is based on two lower court decisions which have found entrapment, regardless of predisposition, whenever the government supplies contraband to the defendants. The second theory, a nonentrapment rationale, is based on a recent Ninth Circuit decision that reversed a conviction because a government investigator was so enmeshed in the criminal activity that the prosecution of the defendants was held to be repugnant to the American criminal justice system. The court below held that these two rationales constitute the same defense, and that only the label distinguishes them. In any event, it held that "[b]oth theories are premised on fundamental concepts of due process and evince the reluctance of the judiciary to countenance 'overzealous law enforcement.' "

This Court first recognized and applied the entrapment defense in *Sorrells v. United States*, 287 U.S. 435 (1932). In *Sorrells*, a federal prohibition agent visited the defendant while posing as a tourist and engaged him in conversation about their common war experiences. After gaining the defendant's confidence, the agent asked for some liquor, was twice refused, but upon asking a third time the defendant finally capitulated, and was subsequently prosecuted for violating the National Prohibition Act.

Mr. Chief Justice Hughes, speaking for the Court, held that as a matter of statutory construction the defense of entrapment should have been available to the defendant. Under the theory propounded by the Chief Justice, the entrapment defense prohibits law enforcement officers from instigating a criminal act by persons "otherwise innocent in order to lure them to its commission and to punish them." Thus, the thrust of the entrapment defense was held to focus on the intent or predisposition of the defendant to commit the crime. "[I]f the defendant seeks acquittal by reason of entrapment he cannot complain of an appropriate and searching inquiry into his own conduct and predisposition as bearing upon that issue."

Mr. Justice Roberts concurred but was of the view "that courts must be closed to the trial of a crime instigated by the government's own agents." The difference in the view of the majority and the concurring opinions is that in the former the inquiry focuses on the predisposition of the defendant, whereas in the latter the inquiry focuses on whether the government "instigated the crime."

In 1958 the Court again considered the theory underlying the entrapment defense and expressly reaffirmed the view expressed by the *Sorrells* majority. In *Sherman* the defendant was convicted of selling narcotics to a Government informer. As in *Sorrells*, it appears that the Government agent gained the confidence of the defendant and, despite initial reluctance, the defendant finally acceded to the repeated importunings of the agent to commit the criminal act. On the basis of *Sorrels*, this Court reversed the affirmance of the defendant's conviction.

In affirming the theory underlying *Sorrells*, Mr. Chief Justice Warren for the Court, held that "[t]o determine whether entrapment has been established, a line must be drawn between the trap for the unwary innocent and the trap for the unwary criminal." Justice Frankfurter stated in an opinion concurring in the result that he believed Mr. Justice Roberts had the better view in *Sorrells* and would have framed the question to be asked in an entrapment defense in terms of "whether the police conduct revealed in the particular case falls below standards . . . for the proper use of governmental power."

In the instant case, respondent asks us to reconsider the theory of the entrapment defense as it is set forth in the majority opinions in *Sorrells* and *Sherman*. His principal contention is that the defense should rest on constitutional grounds. He argues that the level of Shapiro's involvement in the manufacture of the methamphetamine was so high that a criminal prosecution for the drug's manufacture violates the fundamental principles of due process. The respondent contends that the same factors that led this Court to apply the exclusionary rule to illegal searches and seizures and confessions should be considered here. But he would have the Court go further in deterring undesirable official conduct by requiring that any prosecution be barred absolutely because of the police involvement in criminal activity. The analogy is imperfect in any event, for the principal reason behind the adoption of the exclusionary rule was the Government's "failure to observe its own laws." Unlike the situations giving rise to [these] holdings . . . , the Government's conduct here violated no independent constitutional right of the respondent. Nor did Shapiro violate any federal statute or rule or commit any crime in infiltrating the respondent's drug enterprise.

Respondent would overcome this basic weakness in his analogy to the exclusionary rule cases by having the Court adopt a rigid constitutional rule that would preclude any prosecution when it is shown that the criminal conduct would not have been possible had not an undercover agent "supplied an indispensable means to the commission of the crime that could not have been obtained otherwise, through legal or illegal channels." Even if we were to surmount the difficulties attending the notion that due process of law can be embodied in fixed rules, and those attending respondent's particular formulation, the rule he proposes would not appear to be of significant benefit to him. For, on the record presented, it appears that he cannot fit within the terms of the very rule he proposes.

The record discloses that although the propanone was difficult to obtain, it was by no means impossible. The defendants admitted making the drug both before and after those batches made with the propanone supplied by Shapiro. . . . Thus, the facts in the record amply demonstrate that the propanone used in the illicit manufacture of methamphetamine not only *could* have been obtained without the intervention of Shapiro but was in fact obtained by these defendants.

While we may someday be presented with a situation in which the conduct of law enforcement agents is so outrageous that due process principles would absolutely bar the government from invoking judicial processes to obtain a conviction, the instant case is distinctly not of that breed. Shapiro's contribution of propanone to the criminal enterprise already in process was scarcely objectionable. The chemical is by itself a harmless substance and its possession is legal. While the Government may have been seeking to make it more difficult for drug rings, such as that of which respondent was a member, to obtain the chemical, the evidence described above shows that it nonetheless was obtainable. The law enforcement conduct here stops far short of violating that "fundamental fairness, shocking to the universal sense of justice," mandated by the Due Process Clause of the Fifth Amendment.

The illicit manufacture of drugs is not a sporadic, isolated criminal incident, but a continuing, though illegal, business enterprise. In order to obtain convictions for illegally manufacturing drugs, the gathering of evidence of past unlawful conduct frequently proves to be an all but impossible task. Thus in drug-related offenses law enforcement personnel have turned to one of the only practicable means of detection: the infiltration of drug rings and a limited participation in their unlawful present practices. Such infiltration is a recognized and permissible means of investigation; if that be so, then the supply of some item of value that the drug ring requires must, as a general rule, also be permissible. For an agent will not be taken into the confidence of the illegal entrepreneurs unless he has something of value to offer them. Law enforcement tactics such as this can hardly be said to violate "fundamental fairness" or "shocking to the universal sense of justice."

Respondent also urges, as an alternative to his constitutional argument, that we broaden the nonconstitutional defense of entrapment in order to sustain the judgment of the Court of Appeals. This Court's opinions in *Sorrells v. United States*, and *Sherman v. United States*, held that the principal element in the defense of entrapment was the defendant's predisposition to commit the crime. Respondent conceded in the Court of Appeals, as well he might, "that he may have harbored a predisposition to commit the charged offenses." Yet he argues that the jury's refusal to find entrapment under the charge submitted to it by the trial court should be overturned and the views of Justices Roberts and Frankfurter, in *Sorrells* and *Sherman*, respectively, which make the essential element of the defense turn on the type and degree of governmental conduct, be adopted as the law.

We decline to overrule these cases. *Sorrells* is a precedent of long standing that has already been once reexamined in *Sherman* and implicitly there reaffirmed. Since the defense is not of a constitutional dimension, Congress may address itself to the question and adopt any substantive definition of the defense that it may find desirable.

Critics of the rule laid down in *Sorrells* and *Sherman* have suggested that its basis in the implied intent of Congress is largely fictitious, and have pointed to what they conceive to be the anomalous difference between the treatment of a defendant who is solicited by a private individual and one who is entrapped by a government agent. Questions have been likewise raised as to whether "predisposition" can be factually established with the requisite degree of certainty. Arguments such as these, while not devoid of appeal, have been twice previously made to this Court, and twice rejected by it, first in *Sorrells* and then in *Sherman*.

We believe that at least equally cogent criticism has been made of the concurring views in these cases. Commenting in *Sherman* on Mr. Justice Roberts' position in *Sorrells* that "although the defendant could claim that the Government had induced him to commit the crime, the Government could not reply by showing that the defendant's criminal conduct was due to his own readiness and not to the persuasion of government agents," Mr. Chief Justice Warren quoted the observation of Judge Learned Hand in an earlier stage of that proceeding:

> Indeed, it would seem probable that, if there were no reply [to the claim of inducement], it would be impossible ever to secure

> convictions of any offences which consist of transactions that are carried on in secret. *United States v. Sherman*, 2 Cir., 200 F.2d 880, 882. *Sherman v. United States*, 356 U.S., at 377 n. 7.

Nor does it seem particularly desirable for the law to grant complete immunity from prosecution to one who himself planned to commit a crime, and then committed it, simply because government undercover agents subjected him to inducements which might have seduced a hypothetical individual who was not so predisposed. . . .

Several decisions of the United States district courts and courts of appeals have undoubtedly gone beyond this Court's opinions in *Sorrells* and *Sherman* in order to bar prosecutions because of what they thought to be, for want of a better term, "overzealous law enforcement." But the defense of entrapment enunciated in those opinions was not intended to give the federal judiciary a "chancellor's foot" veto over law enforcement practices of which it did not approve. The execution of the federal laws under our Constitution is confided primarily to the Executive Branch of the Government, subject to applicable constitutional and statutory limitations and to judicially fashioned rules to enforce those limitations. We think that the decision of the Court of Appeals in this case quite unnecessarily introduces an unmanageably subjective standard which is contrary to the holdings of this Court in *Sorrells* and *Sherman*.

Those cases establish that entrapment is a relatively limited defense. It is rooted, not in any authority of the Judicial Branch to dismiss prosecutions for what it feels to have been "overzealous law enforcement," but instead in the notion that Congress could not have intended criminal punishment for a defendant who has committed all the elements of a proscribed offense but was induced to commit them by the Government.

Sorrells and *Sherman* both recognize "that the fact that officers or employees of the Government merely afford opportunities or facilities for the commission of the offense does not defeat the prosecution." Nor will the mere fact of deceit defeat a prosecution, for there are circumstances when the use of deceit is the only practicable law enforcement technique available. It is only when the Government's deception actually implants the criminal design in the mind of the defendant that the defense of entrapment comes into play.

Respondent's concession in the Court of Appeals that the jury finding as to predisposition was supported by the evidence is, therefore, fatal to his claim of entrapment. He was an active participant in an illegal drug manufacturing enterprise which began before the Government agent appeared on the scene, and continued after the Government agent had left the scene. He was, in the words of *Sherman, supra*, not an "unwary innocent" but an "unwary criminal." The Court of Appeals was wrong, we believe, when it sought to broaden the principle laid down in *Sorrells* and *Sherman*. Its judgment is therefore reversed.

Reversed.

Mr. Justice DOUGLAS, with whom Mr. Justice BRENNAN concurs, dissenting.

A federal agent supplied the accused with one chemical ingredient of the drug known as methamphetamine ("speed") which the accused manufactured and for which act he was sentenced to prison. His defense was entrapment, which the Court of Appeals sustained and which the Court today disallows. Since I have an opposed view of entrapment, I dissent. . . .

In my view, the fact that the chemical ingredient supplied by the federal agent might have been obtained from other sources is quite irrelevant. Supplying the chemical ingredient used in the manufacture of this batch of "speed" made the United States an active participant in the unlawful activity. As stated by Mr. Justice Brandeis, dissenting in *Casey v. United States, supra*, 276 U.S., at 423:

> I am aware that courts—mistaking relative social values and forgetting that a desirable end cannot justify foul means— have, in their zeal to punish, sanctioned the use of evidence obtained through criminal violation of property and personal rights or by other practices of detectives even more revolting. But the objection here is of a different nature. It does not rest merely upon the character of the evidence or upon the fact that the evidence was illegally obtained. The obstacle to the prosecution lies in the fact that the alleged crime was instigated by officers of the government; that the act for which the government seeks to punish the defendant is the fruit of their criminal conspiracy to induce its commission. The government may set decoys to entrap criminals. But it may not provoke or create a crime and then punish the criminal, its creature. . . .

Federal agents play a debased role when they become the instigators of the crime, or partners in its commission, or the creative brain behind the illegal scheme. That is what the federal agent did here when he furnished the accused with one of the chemical ingredients needed to manufacture the unlawful drug.

Mr. Justice STEWART, with whom Mr. Justice BRENNAN and Mr. Justice MARSHALL join, dissenting. . . .

I

In *Sorrells v. United States, supra*, and *Sherman v. United States, supra*, the Court took what might be called a "subjective" approach to the defense of entrapment. In that view, the defense is predicated on an unexpressed intent of Congress to exclude from its criminal statutes the prosecution and conviction of persons, "otherwise innocent," who have been lured to the commission of the prohibited act through the Government's instigation. The key phrase in this formulation is "otherwise innocent," for the entrapment defense is available under this approach only to those who would not have committed the crime but for the Government's inducements. Thus, the subjective approach focuses on the conduct and propensities of the particular defendant in each individual case: if he is "otherwise innocent," he may avail himself of the defense; but if he had the "predisposition" to commit the crime, or if the "criminal design" originated with him, then—regardless of the nature and extent of the Government's participation—there has been no entrapment. And, in the absence of a conclusive showing one way or the other, the question of the defendant's "predisposition" to the crime is a question of fact for the jury. The Court today adheres to this approach.

The concurring opinion of Mr. Justice Roberts, joined by Justices Brandeis and Stone, in the *Sorrells* case, and that of Mr. Justice Frankfurter, joined by Justices Douglas, Harlan, and Brennan, in the *Sherman* case, took a different view of the entrapment defense. In their concept, the defense is not grounded on some unexpressed intent of Congress to exclude from punishment under its statutes those otherwise innocent persons tempted into crime by the Government, but rather on the belief that "the methods employed on behalf of the Government to bring about conviction cannot be countenanced." Thus, the focus of this approach is not on the propensities and predisposition of a specific defendant, but on "whether the police conduct revealed in the particular case falls below standards, to which common feelings respond, for the proper use of governmental power." Phrased another way, the question is whether—regardless of the predisposition to crime of the particular defendant involved—the governmental agents have acted in such a way as is likely to instigate or create a criminal offense. Under this approach, the determination of the lawfulness of the Government's conduct must be made—as it is on all questions involving the legality of law enforcement methods—by the trial judge, not the jury.

In my view, this objective approach to entrapment advanced by the Roberts opinion in *Sorrells* and the Frankfurter opinion in *Sherman* is the only one truly consistent with the underlying rationale of the defense. Indeed, the very basis of the entrapment defense itself demands adherence to an approach that focuses on the conduct of the governmental agents, rather than on whether the defendant was "predisposed" or "otherwise innocent." I find it impossible to believe that the purpose of the defense is to effectuate some unexpressed congressional intent to exclude from its criminal statutes persons who committed a prohibited act, but would not have done so except for the Government's inducements. For, as Mr. Justice Frankfurter put it, "the only legislative intention that can with any show of reason be extracted from the statute is the intention to make criminal precisely the conduct in which the defendant has engaged." Since, by definition, the entrapment defense cannot arise unless the defendant actually committed the proscribed act, that defendant is manifestly covered by the terms of the criminal statute involved.

Furthermore, to say that such a defendant is "otherwise innocent" or not "predisposed" to commit the crime is misleading, at best. The very fact that he has committed an act that Congress has determined to be illegal demonstrates conclusively that he is not innocent of the offense. He may not have originated the precise plan or the precise details, but he was "predisposed" in the sense that he has proved to be quite capable of committing the crime. That he was induced, provoked, or tempted to do so by government agents does not make him any more innocent or any less predisposed than he would be if he had been induced, provoked, or tempted by a private person—which, of course, would not entitle him to cry "entrapment." Since the only difference between these situations is the identity of the tempter, it follows that the significant focus must be on the conduct of the government agents, and not on the predisposition of the defendant.

The purpose of the entrapment defense, then, cannot be to protect persons who are "otherwise innocent." Rather, it must be to prohibit unlawful governmental activity in instigating crime. . . .

II

In the case before us, I think that the District Court erred in submitting the issue of entrapment to the jury, with instructions to acquit only if it had a reasonable doubt as to the respondent's predisposition to committing the crime. Since, under the objective test of entrapment, predisposition is irrelevant and the issue is to be decided by the trial judge, the Court of Appeals, I believe, would have been justified in reversing the conviction on this basis alone. But since the appellate court did not remand for consideration of the issue by the District Judge under an objective standard, but rather found entrapment as a matter of law and directed that the indictment be dismissed, we must reach the merits of the respondent's entrapment defense.

Since, in my view, it does not matter whether the respondent was predisposed to commit the offense of which he was convicted, the focus must be, rather, on the conduct of the undercover government agent. What the agent did here was to meet with a group of suspected producers of methamphetamine, including the respondent; to request the drug; to offer to supply the chemical phenyl-2-propanone in exchange for one-half of the methamphetamine to be manufactured therewith; and, when that offer was accepted, to provide the needed chemical ingredient, and to purchase some of the drug from the respondent. . . .

In this case, the chemical ingredient was available only to licensed persons, and the Government itself had requested suppliers not to sell that ingredient even to people with a license. Yet the Government agent readily offered, and supplied, that ingredient to an unlicensed person and asked him to make a certain illegal drug with it. The Government then prosecuted that person for making the drug produced with the very ingredient which its agent had so helpfully supplied. This strikes me as the very pattern of conduct that should be held to constitute entrapment as a matter of law.

It is the Government's duty to prevent crime, not to promote it. Here, the Government's agent asked that the illegal drug be produced for him, solved his quarry's practical problems with the assurance that he could provide the one essential ingredient that was difficult to obtain, furnished that element as he had promised, and bought the finished product from the respondent — all so that the respondent could be prosecuted for producing and selling the very drug for which the agent had asked and for which he had provided the necessary component. Under the objective approach that I would follow, this respondent was entrapped, regardless of his predisposition or "innocence." . . .

Note

The defendant in *Russell* argued that he could not have committed the crime without the assistance of the government. Why was this not entrapment? Is there a difference between inducement and opportunity? Compare Justice Douglas' and Justice Stewart's dissents with the majority opinion. Which opinion strikes you as better policy?

Jacobson v. United States, 503 U.S. 540 (1992)

Justice WHITE delivered the opinion of the Court.

On September 24, 1987, petitioner Keith Jacobson was indicted for violating a provision of the Child Protection Act of 1984 (Act), which criminalizes the knowing receipt through the mails of a "visual depiction [that] involves the use of a minor engaging in sexually explicit conduct. . . ." Petitioner defended on the ground that the Government entrapped him into committing the crime through a series of communications from undercover agents that spanned the 26 months preceding his arrest. Petitioner was found guilty after a jury trial. The Court of Appeals affirmed his conviction, holding that the Government had carried its burden of proving beyond reasonable doubt that petitioner was predisposed to break the law and hence was not entrapped.

Because the Government overstepped the line between setting a trap for the "unwary innocent" and the "unwary criminal," and as a matter of law failed to establish that petitioner was independently predisposed to commit the crime for which he was arrested, we reverse the Court of Appeals' judgment affirming his conviction.

I

In February 1984, petitioner, a 56-year-old veteran-turned-farmer who supported his elderly father in Nebraska, ordered two magazines and a brochure from a California adult bookstore. The magazines, entitled Bare Boys I and Bare Boys II, contained photographs of nude preteen and teenage boys. The contents of the magazines startled petitioner, who testified that he had expected to receive photographs of "young men 18 years or older." On cross-examination, he explained his response to the magazines:

> [PROSECUTOR]: [Y]ou were shocked and surprised that there were pictures of very young boys without clothes on, is that correct?
>
> [JACOBSON]: Yes, I was.
>
> [PROSECUTOR]: Were you offended? . . .
>
> [JACOBSON]: I was not offended because I thought these were a nudist type publication. Many of the pictures were out in a rural or outdoor setting. There was—I didn't draw any sexual connotation or connection with that.

The young men depicted in the magazines were not engaged in sexual activity, and petitioner's receipt of the magazines was legal under both federal and Nebraska law. Within three months, the law with respect to child pornography changed; Congress passed the Act illegalizing the receipt through the mails of sexually explicit depictions of children. In the very month that the new provision became law, postal inspectors found petitioner's name on the mailing list of the California bookstore that had mailed him Bare Boys I and II. There followed over the next 2½ years repeated efforts by two Government agencies, through five fictitious organizations and a bogus pen pal, to explore petitioner's willingness to break the new law by ordering sexually explicit photographs of children through the mail.

The Government began its efforts in January 1985 when a postal inspector sent petitioner a letter supposedly from the American Hedonist Society, which in fact was a fictitious organization. The letter included a membership application and stated the Society's doctrine: that members had the "right to read what we desire, the right to discuss similar interests with those who share our philosophy, and finally that we have the right to seek pleasure without restrictions being placed on us by outdated puritan morality." Petitioner enrolled in the organization and returned a sexual attitude questionnaire that asked him to rank on a scale of one to four his enjoyment of various sexual materials, with one being "really enjoy," two being "enjoy," three being "somewhat enjoy," and four being "do not enjoy." Petitioner ranked the entry "[p]re-teen sex" as a two, but indicated that he was opposed to pedophilia.

For a time, the Government left petitioner alone. But then a new "prohibited mailing specialist" in the Postal Service found petitioner's name in a file, and in May 1986, petitioner received a solicitation from a second fictitious consumer research company, "Midlands Data Research," seeking a response from those who "believe in the joys of sex and the complete awareness of those lusty and youthful lads and lasses of the neophite [sic] age." The letter never explained whether "neophite" referred to minors or young adults. Petitioner responded: "Please feel free to send me more information, I am interested in teenage sexuality. Please keep my name confidential."

Petitioner then heard from yet another Government creation, "Heartland Institute for a New Tomorrow" (HINT), which proclaimed that it was "an organization founded to protect and promote sexual freedom and freedom of choice. We believe that arbitrarily imposed legislative sanctions restricting *your* sexual freedom should be rescinded through the legislative process." The letter also enclosed a second survey. Petitioner indicated that his interest in "[p]reteen sex-homosexual" material was above average, but not high. In response to another question, petitioner wrote: "Not only sexual expression but freedom of the press is under attack. We must be ever vigilant to counter attack right wing fundamentalists who are determined to curtail our freedoms."

HINT replied, portraying itself as a lobbying organization seeking to repeal "all statutes which regulate sexual activities, except those laws which deal with violent behavior, such as rape. HINT is also lobbying to eliminate any legal definition of 'the age of consent.'" These lobbying efforts were to be funded by sales from a catalog to be published in the future "offering the sale of various items which we believe you will find to be both interesting and stimulating." HINT also provided computer matching of group members with similar survey responses; and, although petitioner was supplied with a list of potential "pen pals," he did not initiate any correspondence.

Nevertheless, the Government's "prohibited mailing specialist" began writing to petitioner, using the pseudonym "Carl Long." The letters employed a tactic known as "mirroring," which the inspector described as "reflect[ing] whatever the interests are of the person we are writing to." Petitioner responded at first, indicating that his interest was primarily in "male-male items." Inspector "Long" wrote back:

> My interests too are primarily male-male items. Are you satisfied with the type of VCR tapes available? Personally, I like the amateur stuff better if its [*sic*] well produced as it can get more kinky and also seems more real. I think the actors enjoy it more.

Petitioner responded:

> As far as my likes are concerned, I like good looking young guys (in their late teens and early 20's) doing their thing together.

Petitioner's letters to "Long" made no reference to child pornography. After writing two letters, petitioner discontinued the correspondence.

By March 1987, 34 months had passed since the Government obtained petitioner's name from the mailing list of the California bookstore, and 26 months had passed since the Postal Service had commenced its mailings to petitioner. Although petitioner had responded to surveys and letters, the Government had no evidence that petitioner had ever intentionally possessed or been exposed to child pornography. The Postal Service had not checked petitioner's mail to determine whether he was receiving questionable mailings from persons—other than the Government—involved in the child pornography industry.

At this point, a second Government agency, the Customs Service, included petitioner in its own child pornography sting, "Operation Borderline," after receiving his name on lists submitted by the Postal Service. Using the name of a fictitious Canadian company called "Produit Outaouais," the Customs Service mailed petitioner a brochure advertising photographs of young boys engaging in sex. Petitioner placed an order that was never filled.

The Postal Service also continued its efforts in the Jacobson case, writing to petitioner as the "Far Eastern Trading Company Ltd." The letter began:

> As many of you know, much hysterical nonsense has appeared in the American media concerning 'pornography' and what must be done to stop it from coming across your borders. This brief letter does not allow us to give much comments; however, why is your government spending millions of dollars to exercise international censorship while tons of drugs, which makes yours the world's most crime ridden country are passed through easily.

The letter went on to say:

> [W]e have devised a method of getting these to you without prying eyes of U.S. Customs seizing your mail. . . . After consultations with American solicitors, we have been advised that once we have posted our material through your system, it cannot be opened for any inspection without authorization of a judge.

The letter invited petitioner to send for more information. It also asked petitioner to sign an affirmation that he was "not a law enforcement officer or agent of the U.S. Government acting in an undercover capacity for the purpose of entrapping Far Eastern Trading Company, its agents or customers." Petitioner responded. A catalog was sent and petitioner ordered Boys Who Love Boys, a pornographic magazine depicting young boys engaged in various sexual activities. Petitioner was arrested after a controlled delivery of a photocopy of the magazine.

When petitioner was asked at trial why he placed such an order, he explained that the Government had succeeded in piquing his curiosity:

> Well, the statement was made of all the trouble and the hysteria over pornography and I wanted to see what the material was. It didn't describe the—I didn't know for sure what kind of sexual action they were referring to in the Canadian letter.

In petitioner's home, the Government found the Bare Boys magazines and materials that the Government had sent to him in the course of its protracted investigation, but no other materials that would indicate that petitioner collected, or was actively interested in, child pornography.

Petitioner was indicted for violating 18 U.S.C. §2252(a)(2)(A). The trial court instructed the jury on the petitioner's entrapment defense, petitioner was convicted, and a divided Court of Appeals for the Eighth Circuit, sitting en banc, affirmed, concluding that "Jacobson was not entrapped as a matter of law." We granted certiorari.

II

There can be no dispute about the evils of child pornography or the difficulties that laws and law enforcement have encountered in eliminating it. Likewise, there can be no dispute that the Government may use undercover agents to enforce the law. "It is well settled that the fact that officers or employees of the Government merely afford opportunities or facilities for the commission of the offense does not defeat the prosecution. Artifice and stratagem may be employed to catch those engaged in criminal enterprises." *Sorrells v. United States,* 287 U.S. 435, 441 (1932); *Sherman,* 356 U.S., at 372; *United States v. Russell,* 411 U.S. 423, 435–436 (1973).

In their zeal to enforce the law, however, Government agents may not originate a criminal design, implant in an innocent person's mind the disposition to commit a criminal act, and then induce commission of the crime so that the Government may prosecute. Where the Government has induced an individual to break the law and the defense of entrapment is at issue, as it was in this case, the prosecution must prove beyond reasonable doubt that the defendant was disposed to commit the criminal act prior to first being approached by Government agents.

Thus, an agent deployed to stop the traffic in illegal drugs may offer the opportunity to buy or sell drugs and, if the offer is accepted, make an arrest on the spot or later. In such a typical case, or in a more elaborate "sting" operation involving government-sponsored fencing where the defendant is simply provided with the opportunity to commit a crime, the entrapment defense is of little use because the ready commission of the criminal act amply demonstrates the defendant's predisposition. Had the agents in this case simply offered petitioner the opportunity to order child pornography through the mails, and petitioner—who must be presumed to know the law—had promptly availed himself of this criminal opportunity, it is unlikely that his entrapment defense would have warranted a jury instruction.

But that is not what happened here. By the time petitioner finally placed his order, he had already been the target of 26 months of repeated mailings and communications from Government agents and fictitious organizations. Therefore, although he had become predisposed to break the law by May 1987, it is our view that the Government did not prove that this predisposition was independent and not the product of the attention that the Government had directed at petitioner since January 1985.

The prosecution's evidence of predisposition falls into two categories: evidence developed prior to the Postal Service's mail campaign, and that developed during the course of the investigation. The sole piece of preinvestigation evidence is petitioner's 1984 order and receipt of the Bare Boys magazines. But this is scant if any proof of petitioner's predisposition to commit an illegal act, the criminal character of which a defendant is presumed to know. It may indicate a predisposition to view sexually oriented photographs that are responsive to his sexual tastes; but evidence that merely indicates a generic inclination to act within a broad range, not all of which is criminal, is of little probative value in establishing predisposition.

Furthermore, petitioner was acting within the law at the time he received these magazines. Receipt through the mails of sexually explicit depictions of children for noncommercial use did not become illegal under federal law until May 1984, and Nebraska had no law that forbade petitioner's possession of such material until 1988. Evidence of predisposition to do what once was lawful is not, by itself, sufficient to show predisposition to do what is now illegal, for there is a common understanding that most people obey the law even when they disapprove of it. This obedience may reflect a generalized respect for legality or the fear of prosecution, but for whatever reason, the law's prohibitions are matters of consequence. Hence, the fact that petitioner legally ordered and received the Bare Boys magazines does little to further the Government's burden of proving that petitioner was predisposed to commit a criminal act. This is particularly true given petitioner's unchallenged testimony that he did not know until they arrived that the magazines would depict minors.

The prosecution's evidence gathered during the investigation also fails to carry the Government's burden. Petitioner's responses to the many communications prior to the ultimate criminal act were at most indicative of certain personal inclinations, including a predisposition to view photographs of preteen sex and a willingness to promote a given agenda by supporting lobbying organizations. Even so, petitioner's responses hardly support an inference that he would commit the crime of receiving child pornography through the mails. Furthermore, a person's inclinations and "fantasies . . . are his own and beyond the reach of government. . . ." *Paris Adult Theatre I v. Slaton,* 413 U.S. 49, 67 (1973); *Stanley v. Georgia,* 394 U.S. 557, 565–566 (1969).

On the other hand, the strong arguable inference is that, by waving the banner of individual rights and disparaging the legitimacy and constitutionality of efforts to restrict the availability of sexually explicit materials, the Government not only excited petitioner's interest in sexually explicit materials banned by law but also exerted substantial pressure on petitioner to obtain and read such material as part of a fight against censorship and the infringement of individual rights. For instance, HINT described itself as "an organization founded to protect and promote sexual freedom and freedom of choice" and stated that "the most appropriate means to accomplish [its] objectives is to promote honest dialogue among concerned individuals and to continue its lobbying efforts with State Legislators." These lobbying efforts were to be financed through catalog sales. Mailings from the equally fictitious American Hedonist

Society, and the correspondence from the nonexistent Carl Long, endorsed these themes.

Similarly, the two solicitations in the spring of 1987 raised the spectre of censorship while suggesting that petitioner ought to be allowed to do what he had been solicited to do. The mailing from the Customs Service referred to "the worldwide ban and intense enforcement on this type of material," observed that "what was legal and commonplace is now an 'underground' and secretive service," and emphasized that "[t]his environment forces us to take extreme measures" to ensure delivery. The Postal Service solicitation described the concern about child pornography as "hysterical nonsense," decried "international censorship," and assured petitioner, based on consultation with "American solicitors," that an order that had been posted could not be opened for inspection without authorization of a judge. It further asked petitioner to affirm that he was not a Government agent attempting to entrap the mail order company or its customers. In these particulars, both Government solicitations suggested that receiving this material was something that petitioner ought to be allowed to do.

Petitioner's ready response to these solicitations cannot be enough to establish beyond reasonable doubt that he was predisposed, prior to the Government acts intended to create predisposition, to commit the crime of receiving child pornography through the mails. The evidence that petitioner was ready and willing to commit the offense came only after the Government had devoted 2½ years to convincing him that he had or should have the right to engage in the very behavior proscribed by law. Rational jurors could not say beyond a reasonable doubt that petitioner possessed the requisite predisposition prior to the Government's investigation and that it existed independent of the Government's many and varied approaches to petitioner. As was explained in *Sherman,* where entrapment was found as a matter of law, "the Government [may not] pla[y] on the weaknesses of an innocent party and beguil[e] him into committing crimes which he otherwise would not have attempted."

Law enforcement officials go too far when they "implant in the mind of an innocent person the *disposition* to commit the alleged offense and induce its commission in order that they may prosecute." Like the *Sorrells* Court, we are "unable to conclude that it was the intention of the Congress in enacting this statute that its processes of detection and enforcement should be abused by the instigation by government officials of an act on the part of persons otherwise innocent in order to lure them to its commission and to punish them." When the Government's quest for convictions leads to the apprehension of an otherwise law-abiding citizen who, if left to his own devices, likely would have never run afoul of the law, the courts should intervene.

Because we conclude that this is such a case and that the prosecution failed, as a matter of law, to adduce evidence to support the jury verdict that petitioner was predisposed, independent of the Government's acts and beyond a reasonable doubt, to violate the law by receiving child pornography through the mails, we reverse the Court of Appeals' judgment affirming the conviction of Keith Jacobson.

It is so ordered.

C. The Objective Test

Why does California adopt the objective test? What policy considerations does the court rely on?

People v. Barraza, 23 Cal.3d 675 (1979) (In Bank)

MOSK, Justice.

We confront in this criminal appeal . . . the proper test to be applied to the defense of entrapment.

Defendant appeals from his conviction on two counts of selling heroin. The first count charged defendant with selling heroin to an undercover narcotics agent of the Los Angeles County Sheriff's Department on August 25, 1975. At trial, the agent testified that defendant sold her a yellow balloon containing heroin for $25 of county-advanced funds. Defendant, testifying in his own behalf, gave a different account of his interaction with the narcotics agent on that date, contradicting her testimony that a sale of heroin had occurred.

Count II charged a second sale of heroin on September 11, 1975; both the female agent and the defendant testified that the agent tried to contact defendant by telephoning the Golden State Mental Health Detoxification Center, where he worked as a patient care technician, several times during the three weeks between the dates of the two alleged heroin sale transactions. On September 11, the agent finally succeeded in speaking to defendant and asked him if he had "anything"; defendant asked her to come to the detoxification center. The two then met at the center and talked for some time—a few minutes according to the agent, more than an hour by the defendant's account.

The agent's version of this encounter described defendant as hesitant to deal because "he had done a lot of time in jail and he couldn't afford to go back to jail and . . . he had to be careful about what he was doing." She further testified that after she convinced defendant she "wasn't a cop," he gave her a note, to present to a woman named Stella, which read: "Saw Cheryl [the agent]. Give her a pair of pants [argot for heroin]. [signed] Cal." The agent concluded her testimony by stating that she then left defendant, used the note to introduce herself to the dealer Stella, and purchased an orange balloon containing heroin.

Defendant described a somewhat different pattern of interaction with the agent at their September 11th meeting. He related that he had asked her to come and see him because he was "fed up with her" and wanted her to quit calling him at the hospital where he worked because he was afraid she would cause him to lose his job. He insisted he told her during their conversation that he did not have anything; that he had spent more than 23 years in prison but now he had held a job at the detoxification center for four years, was on methadone and was clean, and wanted the agent to stop "bugging" him. He testified that the agent persisted in her efforts to enlist his aid in purchasing heroin, and that finally after more than an hour of conversation when the agent asked for a note to introduce her to a source of heroin he agreed to give her a note to "get her off . . . [his] back." According to the defendant, he told the agent that he did not know if Stella had anything, and gave her a note which read: "Saw Cheryl. If you have a pair of pants, let her have them." . . .

Defendant urges that his conviction on the second count must be reversed because the trial court erred in failing to instruct the jury sua sponte on the defense of entrapment. His contention requires that we reexamine the entrapment doctrine to determine the manner in which the defense must be raised.

Though long recognized by the courts of almost every United States jurisdiction, the defense of entrapment has produced a deep schism concerning its proper theoretical basis and mode of application. The opposing views have been delineated in a series of United States Supreme Court decisions. The court first considered the entrapment defense in *Sorrells v. United States* (1932) 287 U.S. 435. The majority held that entrapment tended to establish innocence, reasoning that Congress in enacting the criminal statute there at issue could not have intended to punish persons otherwise innocent who were lured into committing the proscribed conduct by governmental instigation. This focus on whether persons were "otherwise innocent" led the majority to adopt what has become known as the subjective or origin-of-intent test under which entrapment is established only if (1) governmental instigation and inducement overstep the bounds of permissibility, and (2) the defendant did not harbor a preexisting criminal intent. Under the subjective test a finding that the defendant was predisposed to commit the offense would negate innocence and therefore defeat the defense. Finally, because entrapment was viewed as bearing on the guilt or innocence of the accused, the issue was deemed proper for submission to the jury.

Justice Roberts wrote an eloquent concurring opinion, joined by Justices Brandeis and Stone, in which he argued that the purpose of the entrapment defense is to deter police misconduct. He emphatically rejected the notion that the defendant's conduct or predisposition had any relevance: "The applicable principle is that courts must be closed to the trial of a crime instigated by the government's own agents. No other issue, no comparison of equities as between the guilty official and the guilty defendant, has any place in the enforcement of this overruling principle of public policy." Because he viewed deterrence of impermissible law enforcement activity as the proper rationale for the entrapment defense, Justice Roberts concluded that the defense was inappropriate for jury consideration: "It is the province of the court and of the court alone to protect itself and the government from such prostitution of the criminal law."

In *Sherman v. United States* (1958) 356 U.S. 369, the majority refused to adopt the "objective" theory of entrapment urged by Justice Roberts, choosing rather to continue recognizing as relevant the defendant's own conduct and predisposition. The court held that "a line must be drawn between the trap for the unwary innocent and the trap for the unwary criminal." Justice Frankfurter, writing for four members of the court in a concurring opinion, argued forcefully for Justice Roberts' objective theory: "The courts refuse to convict an entrapped defendant, not because his conduct falls outside the proscription of the statute, but because, even if his guilt be admitted, the methods employed on behalf of the Government to bring about conviction cannot be countenanced." He reasoned that "a test that looks to the character and predisposition of the defendant rather than the conduct of the police loses sight of the underlying reason for the defense of entrapment. No matter what the defendant's past record and present inclinations to criminality, or the depths to which he has sunk in the estimation of society, certain police conduct to ensnare him into further crime is not to be tolerated by an advanced society. . . . Permissible police activity does not vary according to the particular defendant concerned . . . ." "Human nature is weak enough," he wrote, "and sufficiently beset by temptations without government adding to them and generating crime." Justice Frankfurter concluded that guidance as to appropriate official conduct could only be provided if the court reviewed police conduct and decided the entrapment issue.

The United States Supreme Court recently reviewed the theoretical basis of the entrapment defense in *United States v. Russell* (1973) 411 U.S. 423, and once again the court split five votes to four in declining to overrule the subjective theory adopted in *Sorrells*.

The principle currently applied in California represents a hybrid position, fusing elements of both the subjective and objective theories of entrapment. In *People v. Benford* (1959) 53 Cal. 2d 1, 9, this court unanimously embraced the public policy/deterrence rationale that Justices Roberts and Frankfurter had so persuasively urged. In doing so, we ruled inadmissible on the issue of entrapment the most prejudicial inquiries that are allowed under the subjective theory, i. e., evidence that the defendant "had previously committed similar crimes or had the reputation of being engaged in the commission of such crimes or was suspected by the police of criminal activities . . . ." . . .

For all the foregoing reasons we hold that the proper test of entrapment in California is the following: was the conduct of the law enforcement agent likely to induce a normally law-abiding person to commit the offense? For the purposes of this test, we presume that such a person would normally resist the temptation to commit a crime presented by the simple opportunity to act unlawfully. Official conduct that does no more than offer that opportunity to the suspect for example, a decoy program is therefore permissible; but it is impermissible for the police or their agents to pressure the suspect by overbearing conduct such as badgering, cajoling, importuning, or other affirmative acts likely to induce a normally law-abiding person to commit the crime.

Although the determination of what police conduct is impermissible must to some extent proceed on an ad hoc basis, guidance will generally be found in the application of one or both of two principles. First, if the actions of the law enforcement agent would generate in a normally law-abiding person a motive for the crime other than ordinary criminal intent, entrapment will be established. An example of such conduct would be an appeal by the police that would induce such a person to commit the act because of friendship or sympathy, instead of a desire for personal gain or other typical criminal purpose. Second, affirmative police conduct that would make commission of the crime unusually attractive to a normally law-abiding person will likewise constitute entrapment. Such conduct would include, for example, a guarantee that the act is not illegal or the offense will go undetected, an offer of exorbitant consideration, or any similar enticement.

Finally, while the inquiry must focus primarily on the conduct of the law enforcement agent, that conduct is not to be viewed in a vacuum; it should also be judged by the effect it would have on a normally law-abiding person situated in the circumstances of the case at hand. Among the circumstances that may be relevant for this purpose, for example, are the transactions preceding the offense, the suspect's response to the inducements of the officer, the gravity of the crime, and the difficulty of detecting instances of its commission. We reiterate, however, that under this test such matters as the character of the suspect, his predisposition to commit the offense, and his subjective intent are irrelevant. . . .

Though controverted by the People, there is substantial evidence herein supportive of an entrapment defense, even under the subjective test previously followed. Defendant's testimony, if believed, tends to establish that he was a man who, after a long history of drug addiction and criminal behavior, was making a sincere effort to gain control of his life and to function responsibly in his community. He had held a steady job for some four years, during which time he managed to become completely free of heroin use by participating in a methadone maintenance program. His characterization of the course of conduct between himself and the undercover narcotics agent is consistent with his contention that he was a past offender trying desperately to reform himself but was prevented from doing so by an overzealous law enforcement agent who importuned him relentlessly until his resistance was worn down and overcome.

Further, such a defense is not inconsistent with the defendant's theory on the second count. His defense of denial did not extend to the inculpatory *act* alleged—providing the agent with a note to facilitate her heroin purchase transaction with another—but only to the *intent* with which such act was committed. He claimed only that he did not intend to participate in a heroin sale when he provided the agent with the note. He does not subvert his position in arguing, "and irrespective of my intent, the overzealous law enforcement conduct directed at me constitutes entrapment." Chief Justice Traynor made it clear for this court, without dissent in *People v. Perez* (1965) 62 Cal. 2d 769, 775, that a defendant need not admit his guilt, or even commission of the act, to raise a defense of entrapment.

In the circumstances of this case the issue of entrapment was not submitted to the jury under any other instructions. Accordingly, the court's error in failing to instruct sua sponte on this defense was prejudicial, and the conviction on count II must be set aside.

The judgment is reversed.

D. Pattern Jury Instructions

6.03 ENTRAPMENT

(1) One of the questions in this case is whether the defendant was entrapped.

(2) Entrapment has two related elements. One is that the defendant was not already willing to commit the crime. The other is that the government, or someone acting for the government, induced or persuaded the defendant to commit it.

(3) If the defendant was not already willing to commit the crime prior to first being approached by government agents or other persons acting for the government, and the government persuaded him to commit it, that would be entrapment. But if the defendant was already willing to commit the crime prior to first being approached by government agents or other persons acting for the government, it would not be entrapment, even if the government provided him with a favorable opportunity to commit the crime, or made the crime easier, or participated in the crime in some way.

(4) It is sometimes necessary during an investigation for a government agent to pretend to be a criminal, and to offer to take part in a crime. This may be done directly, or the agent may have to work through an informant or a decoy. This is permissible, and without more is not entrapment. The crucial question in entrapment cases is whether the government persuaded a defendant who was not already willing to commit a crime to go ahead and commit it.

(5) The government has the burden of proving beyond a reasonable doubt that the defendant was already willing to commit the crime prior to first being approached by government agents or other persons

acting for the government. Let me suggest some things that you may consider in deciding whether the government has proved this:

(A)   Ask yourself what the evidence shows about the defendant's character and reputation.

(B)   Ask yourself if the idea for committing the crime originated with or came from the government.

(C)   Ask yourself if the defendant took part in the crime for profit.

(D)   Ask yourself if the defendant took part in any similar criminal activity with anyone else before or afterwards.

(E)   Ask yourself if the defendant showed any reluctance to commit the crime and, if he did, whether he was overcome by government persuasion.

(F)   And ask yourself what kind of persuasion and how much persuasion the government used.

(6)   Consider all the evidence, and decide if the government has proved that the defendant was already willing to commit the crime. Unless the government proves this beyond a reasonable doubt, you must find the defendant not guilty.

Committee Commentary 6.03 (current through April 1, 2013)

A valid entrapment defense has two related elements: government inducement of the crime, and a lack of predisposition on the part of the defendant to engage in the criminal conduct. *Mathews v. United States*, 485 U.S. 58, 62–63 (1988). See also *United States v. Nelson*, 922 F.2d 311, 317 (6th Cir. 1990).

In defining predisposition, the Sixth Circuit relies on the five factors identified in *United States v. Nelson*, 922 F.2d 311, 317 (6th Cir. 1990). See, e.g., *United States v. Harris*, 1995 WL 6220, 2–3 (6th Cir. 1995) (unpublished) (quoting *United States v. McLernon*, 746 F.2d 1098, 1112 (6th Cir. 1984)). Those five factors are: (1) the character or reputation of the defendant; (2) whether the suggestion of the criminal activity was originally made by the government; (3) whether the defendant was engaged in criminal activity for profit; (4) whether the defendant evidenced reluctance to commit the offense but was overcome by government persuasion; and (5) the nature of the inducement or persuasion offered by the government. Nelson, supra at 317. These five factors appear in plain English terms in parts (A), (B), (C), (E), and (F) of paragraph 5.

The pattern instruction adds a sixth factor, paragraph (D) ("Ask yourself if the defendant took part in any similar criminal activity with anyone else before or afterwards."). This addition has been specifically approved by a panel of the Sixth Circuit. *United States v. Stokes*, 1993 WL 312009, 3 (6th Cir. 1993) (unpublished). In *Stokes*, the panel explained that paragraph (D) concerns the evidence that may be considered when answering whether predisposition existed, and that "a jury may look at evidence of the defendant's character both before and after his arrest. Ex post facto evidence is relevant because it may shed light on whether defendant is the type of person who could commit the crime in question." *Id.*

In *Jacobson v. United States*, 503 U.S. 540 (1992), the Court refined the predisposition element, holding that to be convicted, a defendant must be predisposed to commit the criminal act prior to first being approached by government agents. *Jacobson*, 503 U.S. at 549. The words in paragraphs (3) and (5), "prior to first being approached by government agents or other persons acting for the government," are drawn from the *Jacobson* decision and from the modified instruction approved in *United States v. Smith*, 1994 WL 162584, 4 (6th Cir. 1994) (unpublished).

In paragraphs (2), (3) and (5), the instruction refers to the question of whether the defendant was "already willing" to commit the crime before being approached by government agents. In *Jacobson*, the Court used the term "predisposed" as opposed to "already willing." 503 U.S. at 549. The Committee decided to use the term "already willing" rather than "predisposed" because the Sixth Circuit has approved the use of "already willing," see *United States v. Sherrod*, 33 F.3d 723, 726 (6th Cir. 1994), and because it is consistent with a plain English approach.

In *Mathews v. United States*, 485 U.S. 58 (1988), the Supreme Court held that even if a defendant denies one or more elements of the crime for which he is charged, he is entitled to an entrapment instruction whenever there is sufficient evidence from which a reasonable jury could find that the government entrapped him.

As long as the defendant shows a predisposition to commit an offense, governmental participation in the commission of an offense by itself cannot be the basis of an entrapment defense. *United States v. Tucker*, 28 F.3d 1420 (6th Cir. 1994); *United States v. Leja*, 563 F.2d 244 (6th Cir. 1977).

No instruction on entrapment need be given unless there is some evidence of both government inducement and lack of predisposition. *United States v. Nelson, supra*, 922 F.2d at 317. It is the duty of the trial judge to determine whether there is sufficient evidence of entrapment to allow the issue to go before the jury. If there is, then the burden shifts to the government to prove predisposition. *United States v. Meyer*, 803 F.2d 246, 249 (6th Cir. 1986). The government must prove beyond a reasonable doubt that the defendant was predisposed to commit the crime. See, e.g., *United States v. Jones*, 575 F.2d 81, 83–84 (6th Cir. 1978).

E.   Model Penal Code Provisions

§2.13. Entrapment

(1) A public law enforcement official or a person acting in cooperation with such an official perpetrates an entrapment if for the purpose of obtaining evidence of the commission of an offense, he induces or encourages another person to engage in conduct constituting such offense by either:

    (a)   making knowingly false representations designed to induce the belief that such conduct is not prohibited; or

    (b)   employing methods of persuasion or inducement that create a substantial risk that such an offense will be committed by persons other than those who are ready to commit it.

(2) Except as provided in Subsection (3) of this Section, a person prosecuted for an offense shall be acquitted if he proves by a preponderance of evidence that his conduct occurred in response to an entrapment. The issue of entrapment shall be tried by the Court in the absence of the jury.

(3) The defense afforded by this Section is unavailable when causing or threatening bodily injury is an element of the offense charged and the prosecution is based on conduct causing or threatening such injury to a person other than the person perpetrating the entrapment.

Table of Cases

Table of Statutes

Table of Model Penal Code Provisions

Table of Pattern Jury Instructions

Index

A